Advance Praise for *Head First C*

"*Head First C* could quite possibly turn out to be the best C book of all time. I don't say that lightly. I could easily see this become the standard C textbook for every college C course. Most books on programming follow a fairly predictable course through keywords, control-flow constructs, syntax, operators, data types, subroutines, etc. These can serve as a useful reference, as well as a fairly academic introduction to the language. This book, on the other hand, takes a totally different approach. It teaches you how to be a real C programmer. I wish I had had this book 15 years ago!"

— Dave Kitabjian, Director of Software Development, NetCarrier Telecom

"*Head First C* is an accessible, light-hearted introduction to C programming, in the classic Head First style. Pictures, jokes, exercises, and labs take the reader gently but steadily through the fundamentals of C—including arrays, pointers, structs, and functions—before moving into more advanced topics in Posix and Linux system programming, such as processes and threads."

— Vince Milner, software developer

T0256445

Praise for other *Head First* books

"Kathy and Bert's *Head First Java* transforms the printed page into the closest thing to a GUI you've ever seen. In a wry, hip manner, the authors make learning Java an engaging 'what're they gonna do next?' experience."

—Warren Keuffel, *Software Development Magazine*

"Beyond the engaging style that drags you forward from know-nothing into exalted Java warrior status, *Head First Java* covers a huge amount of practical matters that other texts leave as the dreaded 'exercise for the reader...' It's clever, wry, hip, and practical—there aren't a lot of textbooks that can make that claim and live up to it while also teaching you about object serialization and network launch protocols. "

— Dr. Dan Russell, Director of User Sciences and Experience Research, IBM Almaden Research Center; artificial intelligence instructor, Stanford University

"It's fast, irreverent, fun, and engaging. Be careful—you might actually learn something!"

— Ken Arnold, former Senior Engineer at Sun Microsystems; coauthor (with James Gosling, creator of Java), *The Java Programming Language*

"I feel like a thousand pounds of books have just been lifted off of my head."

— Ward Cunningham, inventor of the Wiki and founder of the Hillside Group

"Just the right tone for the geeked-out, casual-cool guru coder in all of us. The right reference for practical development strategies—gets my brain going without having to slog through a bunch of tired, stale professor-speak."

— Travis Kalanick, founder of Scour and Red Swoosh; member of the MIT TR100

"There are books you buy, books you keep, books you keep on your desk, and thanks to O'Reilly and the Head First crew, there is the penultimate category, Head First books. They're the ones that are dog-eared, mangled, and carried everywhere. *Head First SQL* is at the top of my stack. Heck, even the PDF I have for review is tattered and torn."

— Bill Sawyer, ATG Curriculum Manager, Oracle

"This book's admirable clarity, humor, and substantial doses of clever make it the sort of book that helps even nonprogrammers think well about problem solving."

— Cory Doctorow, coeditor of Boing Boing; author, *Down and Out in the Magic Kingdom* and *Someone Comes to Town, Someone Leaves Town*

Praise for other *Head First* books

"I received the book yesterday and started to read it…and I couldn't stop. This is definitely très 'cool.' It is fun, but they cover a lot of ground, and they are right to the point. I'm really impressed."

— Erich Gamma, IBM Distinguished Engineer and coauthor of *Design Patterns*

"One of the funniest and smartest books on software design I've ever read."

— Aaron LaBerge, VP Technology, ESPN.com

"What used to be a long trial-and-error learning process has now been reduced neatly into an engaging paperback."

— Mike Davidson, CEO, Newsvine, Inc.

"Elegant design is at the core of every chapter here, each concept conveyed with equal doses of pragmatism and wit."

— Ken Goldstein, Executive Vice President, Disney Online

"I ♥ *Head First HTML with CSS & XHTML*—it teaches you everything you need to learn in a 'fun coated' format."

— Sally Applin, UI designer and artist

"Usually when reading through a book or article on design patterns, I'd have to occasionally stick myself in the eye with something just to make sure I was paying attention. Not with this book. Odd as it may sound, this book makes learning about design patterns fun.

"While other books on design patterns are saying 'Bueller…Bueller…Bueller…,' this book is on the float belting out 'Shake it up, baby!'"

— Eric Wuehler

"I literally love this book. In fact, I kissed this book in front of my wife."

— Satish Kumar

Other related books from O'Reilly

C in a Nutshell

Practical C Programming

C Pocket Reference

Algorithms with C

Secure Programming Cookbook for C and C++

Other books in O'Reilly's *Head First* series

Head First Programming

Head First Rails

Head First Java™

Head First Object-Oriented Analysis and Design (OOA&D)

Head First HTML5 Programming

Head First HTML with CSS and XHTML

Head First Design Patterns

Head First Servlets and JSP

Head First EJB

Head First PMP

Head First SQL

Head First Software Development

Head First JavaScript

Head First Ajax

Head First Statistics

Head First 2D Geometry

Head First Algebra

Head First PHP & MySQL

Head First Mobile Web

Head First Web Design

Head First C

Wouldn't it be dreamy if there were a book on C that was easier to understand than the space shuttle flight manual? I guess it's just a fantasy...

David Griffiths
Dawn Griffiths

O'REILLY®

Beijing • Boston • Farnham • Sebastopol • Tokyo

Head First C

by David Griffiths and Dawn Griffiths

Published by O'Reilly Media, Inc., 1005 Gravenstein Highway North, Sebastopol, CA 95472.

O'Reilly Media books may be purchased for educational, business, or sales promotional use. Online editions are also available for most titles (*http://my.safaribooksonline.com*). For more information, contact our corporate/institutional sales department: (800) 998-9938 or *corporate@oreilly.com*.

Series Creators: Kathy Sierra, Bert Bates
Editor: Brian Sawyer
Cover Designer: Karen Montgomery
Production Editor: Teresa Elsey
Production Services: Rachel Monaghan
Indexer: Ellen Troutman Zaig
Brain Image on Spine: Eric Freeman
Page Viewers: Mum and Dad, Carl

Printing History:

April 2012: First Edition.

Mum and Dad →

← Carl

No kittens were harmed in the making of this book. Really.

ISBN: 978-1-449-39991-7
[LSI] [2013-07-26]

To Dennis Ritchie (1941–2011), the father of C.

Authors of Head First C

David Griffiths

Dawn Griffiths

David Griffiths began programming at age 12, when he saw a documentary on the work of Seymour Papert. At age 15, he wrote an implementation of Papert's computer language LOGO. After studying pure mathematics at university, he began writing code for computers and magazine articles for humans. He's worked as an agile coach, a developer, and a garage attendant, but not in that order. He can write code in over 10 languages and prose in just one, and when not writing, coding, or coaching, he spends much of his spare time traveling with his lovely wife—and coauthor—Dawn.

Before writing *Head First C*, David wrote two other Head First books: *Head First Rails* and *Head First Programming.*

You can follow David on Twitter at *http://twitter.com/dogriffiths.*

Dawn Griffiths started life as a mathematician at a top UK university, where she was awarded a first-class honors degree in mathematics. She went on to pursue a career in software development and has over 15 years experience working in the IT industry.

Before joining forces with David on *Head First C*, Dawn wrote two other Head First books (*Head First Statistics* and *Head First 2D Geometry*) and has also worked on a host of other books in the series.

When Dawn's not working on Head First books, you'll find her honing her Tai Chi skills, running, making bobbin lace, or cooking. She also enjoys traveling and spending time with her husband, David.

Table of Contents (Summary)

	Intro	xxvii
1	Getting Started with C: *Diving in*	1
2	Memory and Pointers: *What are you pointing at?*	41
2.5	Strings: *String theory*	83
3	Creating Small Tools: *Do one thing and do it well*	103
4	Using Multiple Source Files: *Break it down, build it up*	157
	C Lab 1: *Arduino*	207
5	Structs, Unions, and Bitfields: *Rolling your own structures*	217
6	Data Structures and Dynamic Memory: *Building bridges*	267
7	Advanced Functions: *Turn your functions up to 11*	311
8	Static and Dynamic Libraries: *Hot-swappable code*	351
	C Lab 2: *OpenCV*	389
9	Processes and System Calls: *Breaking boundaries*	397
10	Interprocess Communication: *It's good to talk*	429
11	Sockets and Networking: *There's no place like 127.0.0.1*	467
12	Threads: *It's a parallel world*	501
	C Lab 3: *Blasteroids*	523
i	Leftovers: *The top ten things (we didn't cover)*	539
ii	C Topics: *Revision roundup*	553

Table of Contents (the real thing)

Intro

Your brain on C. Here *you* are trying to *learn* something, while here your *brain* is, doing you a favor by making sure the learning doesn't *stick*. Your brain's thinking, "Better leave room for more important things, like which wild animals to avoid and whether naked snowboarding is a bad idea." So how *do* you trick your brain into thinking that your life depends on knowing C?

Who is this book for?	xxviii
We know what you're thinking	xxix
Metacognition	xxxi
Bend your brain into submission	xxxiii
Read me	xxxiv
The technical review team	xxxvi
Acknowledgments	xxxvii

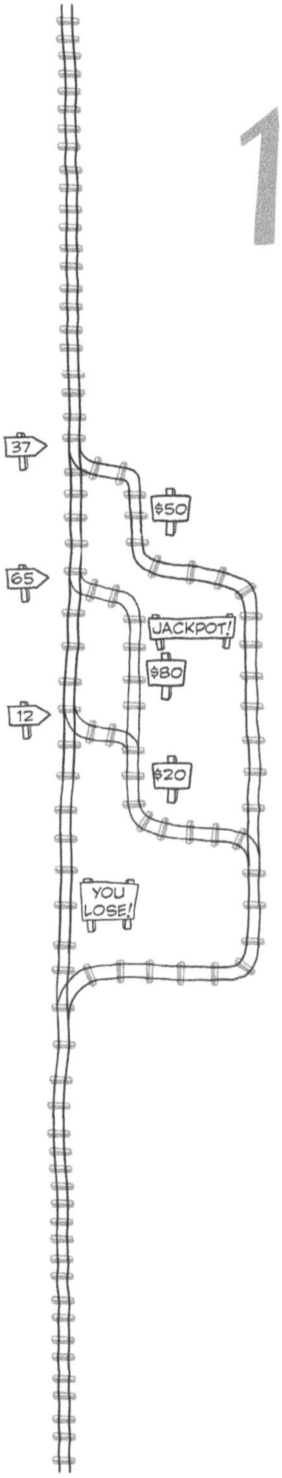
37
65
12
$50
JACKPOT!
$80
$20
YOU LOSE!

1

getting started with C

Diving in

Want to get inside the computer's head?

Need to write **high-performance code** for a new game? Program an **Arduino**? Or use that advanced **third-party library** in your iPhone app? If so, then C's here to help. C works at a **much lower level** than most other languages, so understanding C gives you a much better idea of **what's really going on**. C can even help you better understand other languages as well. So dive in and grab your compiler, and you'll soon get started in no time.

C is a language for small, fast programs 2
But what does a complete C program look like? 5
But how do you run the program? 9
Two types of command 14
Here's the code so far 15
Card counting? In C? 17
There's more to booleans than equals... 18
What's the code like now? 25
Pulling the ol' switcheroo 26
Sometimes once is not enough... 29
Loops often follow the same structure... 30
You use break to break out... 31
Your C Toolbox 40

2 memory and pointers

What are you pointing at?

If you really want to kick butt with C, you need to understand how C handles memory.

The C language gives you a lot more *control* over how your program uses the **computer's memory**. In this chapter, you'll strip back the covers and see exactly what happens when you **read and write variables**. You'll learn **how arrays work**, how to avoid some **nasty memory SNAFUs,** and most of all, you'll see how **mastering pointers and memory addressing** is key to becoming a kick-ass C programmer.

STACK
HEAP
GLOBALS
CONSTANTS
CODE
LINK A6, #VARSIZE
MOVEM.L D0-D7/A1-A5,-(SP)
MOVE.L SP, SAVESTK(A6)
MOVE.L SP, SAVEAS(A6)
MOVE.L GRAFGLOBALS(A5),A0
...

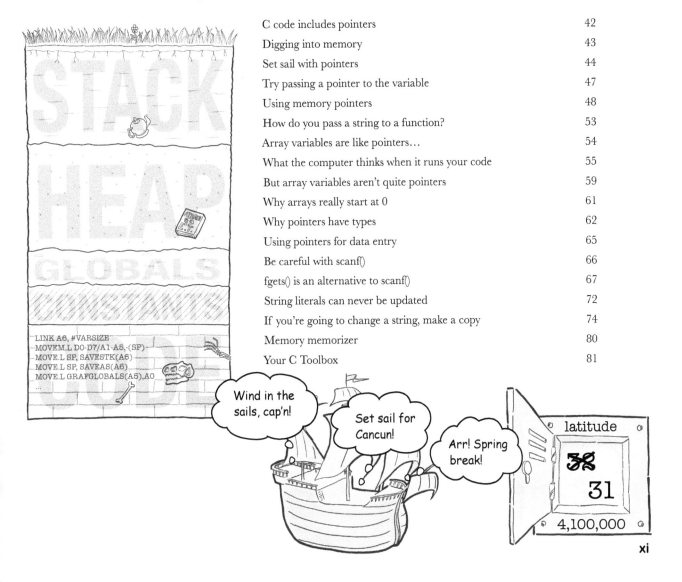

C code includes pointers	42
Digging into memory	43
Set sail with pointers	44
Try passing a pointer to the variable	47
Using memory pointers	48
How do you pass a string to a function?	53
Array variables are like pointers…	54
What the computer thinks when it runs your code	55
But array variables aren't quite pointers	59
Why arrays really start at 0	61
Why pointers have types	62
Using pointers for data entry	65
Be careful with scanf()	66
fgets() is an alternative to scanf()	67
String literals can never be updated	72
If you're going to change a string, make a copy	74
Memory memorizer	80
Your C Toolbox	81

Wind in the sails, cap'n!
Set sail for Cancun!
Arr! Spring break!
latitude
38
31
4,100,000

2.5

strings

String theory

There's more to strings than reading them.

You've seen how strings in C are actually `char` *arrays* but what does C allow you to *do* with them? That's where ***string.h*** comes in. *string.h* is part of the C Standard Library that's dedicated to **string manipulation**. If you want to ***concatenate*** strings together, ***copy*** one string to another, or ***compare*** two strings, the functions in *string.h* are there to help. In this chapter, you'll see how to create an **array of strings**, and then take a close look at how to ***search within strings*** using the **`strstr()`** function.

Desperately seeking Frank	84
Create an array of arrays	85
Find strings containing the search text	86
Using the strstr() function	89
It's time for a code review	94
Array of arrays vs. array of pointers	98
Your C Toolbox	101

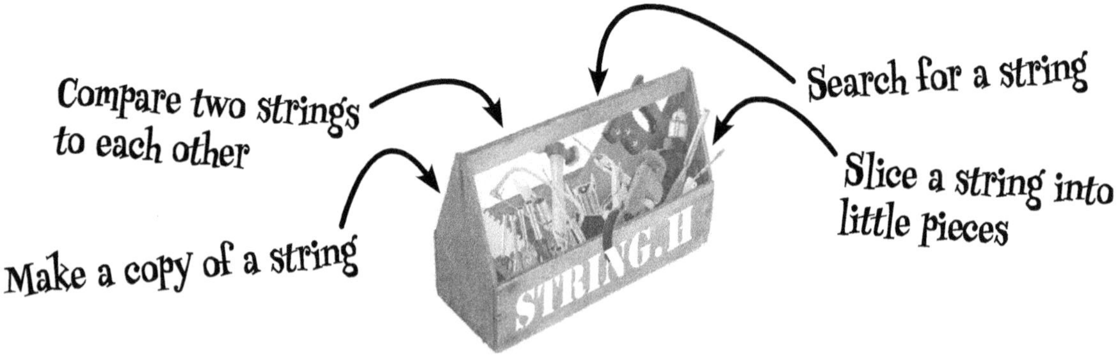

Compare two strings to each other
Search for a string
Slice a string into little pieces
Make a copy of a string
STRING.H

3

creating small tools

Do one thing and do it well

Every operating system includes small tools.

Small tools written in C perform **specialized small tasks**, such as reading and writing files, or filtering data. If you want to perform more complex tasks, you can even *link several tools together*. But how are these small tools built? In this chapter, you'll look at the building blocks of creating small tools. You'll learn how to control **command-line options**, how to manage **streams of information**, and **redirection**, getting tooled up in no time.

Small tools can solve big problems	104
Here's how the program should work	108
But you're not using files...	109
You can use redirection	110
Introducing the Standard Error	120
By default, the Standard Error is sent to the display	121
fprintf() prints to a data stream	122
Let's update the code to use fprintf()	123
Small tools are flexible	128
Don't change the geo2json tool	129
A different task needs a different tool	130
Connect your input and output with a pipe	131
The bermuda tool	132
But what if you want to output to more than one file?	137
Roll your own data streams	138
There's more to main()	141
Let the library do the work for you	149
Your C Toolbox	156

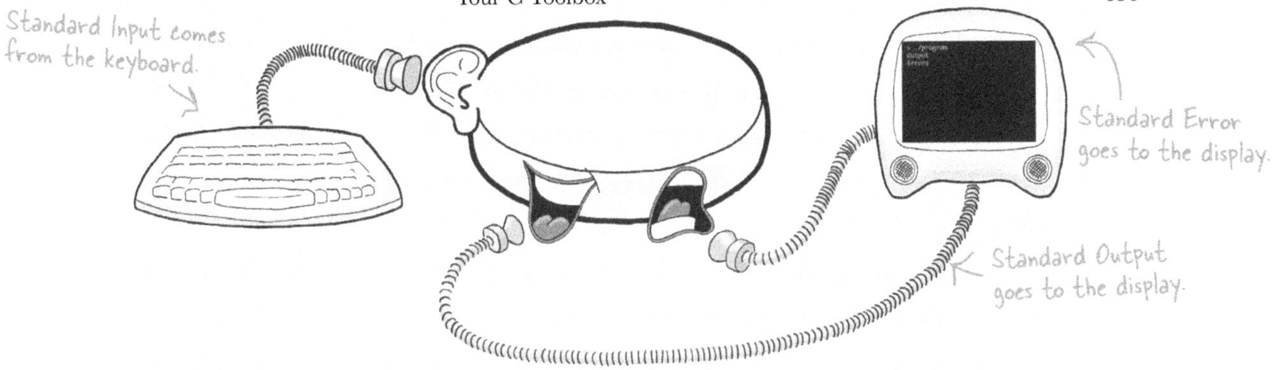

Standard Input comes from the keyboard.
Standard Error goes to the display.
Standard Output goes to the display.

4 using multiple source files

Break it down, build it up

If you create a big program, you don't want a big source file.

Can you imagine how difficult and time-consuming a single source file for an enterprise-level program would be to maintain? In this chapter, you'll learn how C allows you to break your source code into **small, manageable chunks** and then rebuild them into **one huge program**. Along the way, you'll learn a bit more about **data type subtleties** and get to meet your new best friend: **`make`**.

gcc -c
gcc -o

Your quick guide to data types	162
Don't put something big into something small	163
Use casting to put floats into whole numbers	164
Oh no…it's the out-of-work actors…	168
Let's see what's happened to the code	169
Compilers don't like surprises	171
Split the declaration from the definition	173
Creating your first header file	174
If you have common features…	182
You can split the code into separate files	183
Compilation behind the scenes	184
The shared code needs its own header file	186
It's not rocket science…or is it?	189
Don't recompile every file	190
First, compile the source into object files	191
It's hard to keep track of the files	196
Automate your builds with the make tool	198
How make works	199
Tell make about your code with a makefile	200
Liftoff!	205
Your C Toolbox	206

C Lab 1

Arduino

Ever wished your plants could tell you when they need watering? Well, with an Arduino, they can! In this lab, you'll build an Arduino-powered plant monitor, all coded in C.

5 structs, unions, and bitfields

Rolling your own structures

Most things in life are more complex than a simple number.

So far, you've looked at the basic data types of the C language, but what if you want to go beyond numbers and pieces of text, and **model things in the real world**? `structs` allow you to model **real-world complexities** by writing your own structures. In this chapter, you'll learn how to **combine the basic data types** into `struct`s, and even **handle life's uncertainties** with `unions`. And if you're after a simple yes or no, ***bitfields*** may be just what you need.

Sometimes you need to hand around a lot of data	218
Cubicle conversation	219
Create your own structured data types with a struct	220
Just give them the fish	221
Read a struct's fields with the "." operator	222
Can you put one struct inside another?	227
How do you update a struct?	236
The code is cloning the turtle	238
You need a pointer to the struct	239
(*t).age vs. *t.age	240
Sometimes the same type of thing needs different types of data	246
A union lets you reuse memory space	247
How do you use a union?	248
An enum variable stores a symbol	255
Sometimes you want control at the bit level	261
Bitfields store a custom number of bits	262
Your C Toolbox	266

This is Myrtle...
...but her clone is sent to the function.
Turtle "t"

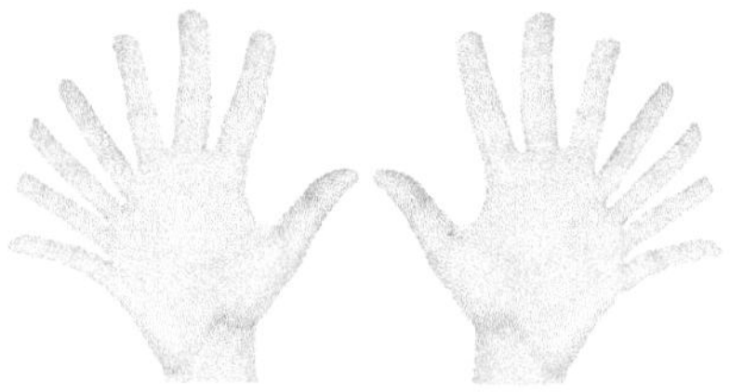

6

data structures and dynamic memory

Building bridges

Sometimes, a single struct is simply not enough.

To model complex data requirements, you often need to **link `structs` together**. In this chapter, you'll see how to use **`struct` pointers** to connect custom data types into **large, complex data structures**. You'll explore *key principles* by creating **linked lists**. You'll also see how to make your data structures cope with flexible amounts of data by **dynamically allocating memory on the heap**, and freeing it up when you're done. And if good housekeeping becomes tricky, you'll also learn how `valgrind` can help.

Do you need flexible storage?	268
Linked lists are like chains of data	269
Linked lists allow inserts	270
Create a recursive structure	271
Create islands in C…	272
Inserting values into the list	273
Use the heap for dynamic storage	278
Give the memory back when you're done	279
Ask for memory with malloc()…	280
Let's fix the code using the strdup() function	286
Free the memory when you're done	290
An overview of the SPIES system	300
Software forensics: using valgrind	302
Use valgrind repeatedly to gather more evidence	303
Look at the evidence	304
The fix on trial	307
Your C Toolbox	309

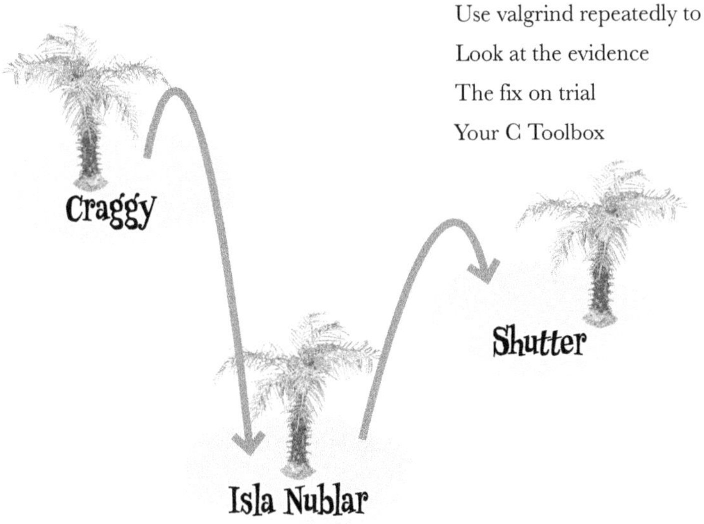
Craggy
Isla Nublar
Shutter

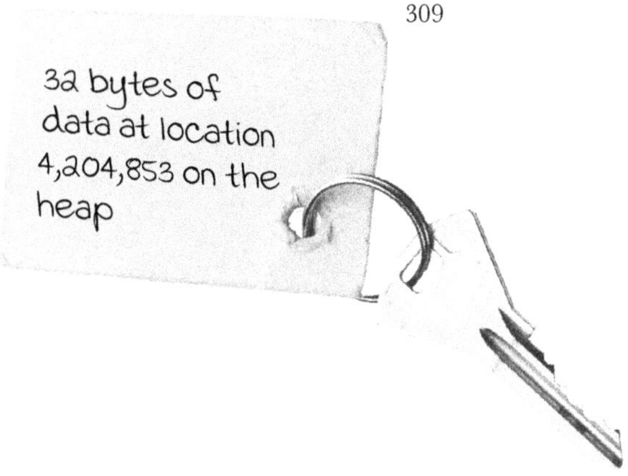
32 bytes of data at location 4,204,853 on the heap

advanced functions

7 Turn your functions up to 11

Basic functions are great, but sometimes you need more.

So far, you've focused on the basics, but what if you need even more *power* and *flexibility* to achieve what you want? In this chapter, you'll see how to **up your code's IQ** by **passing functions as parameters**. You'll find out how to **get things sorted with comparator functions**. And finally, you'll discover how to make your code *super stretchy* with **variadic functions**.

Looking for Mr. Right...	312
Pass code to a function	316
You need to tell find() the name of a function	317
Every function name is a pointer to the function...	318
...but there's no function data type	319
How to create function pointers	320
Get it sorted with the C Standard Library	325
Use function pointers to set the order	326
Automating the Dear John letters	334
Create an array of function pointers	338
Make your functions streeeeeetchy	343
Your C Toolbox	350

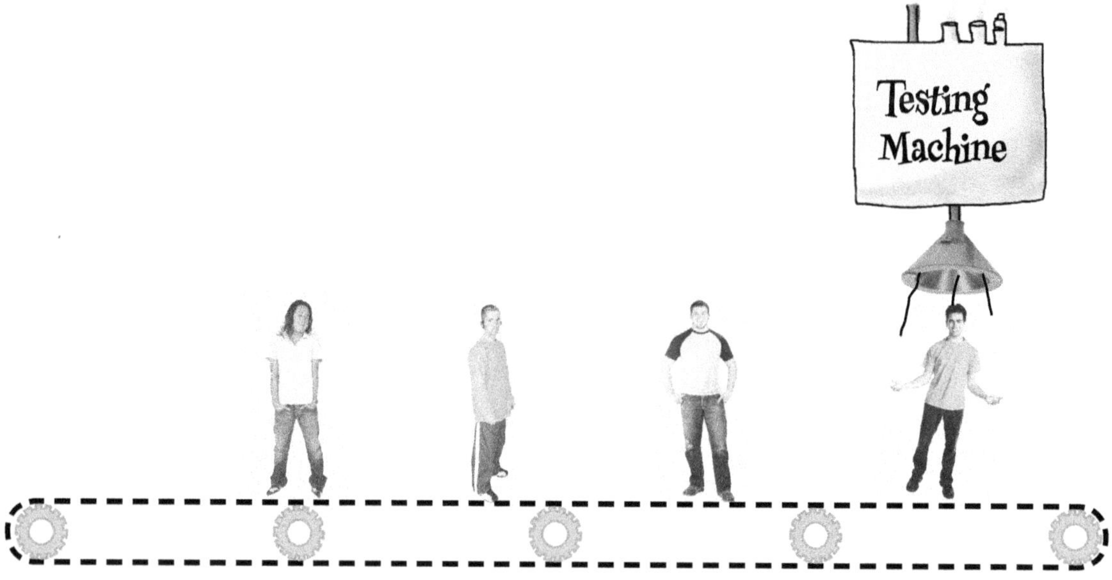

Testing Machine

8 static and dynamic libraries

Hot-swappable code

You've already seen the power of standard libraries.

Now it's time to use that power for your *own* code. In this chapter, you'll see how to create your **own libraries** and **reuse the same code across several programs**. What's more, you'll learn how to share code at runtime with **dynamic libraries**. You'll learn the secrets of the *coding gurus*. And by the end of the chapter, you'll be able to write code that you can scale and manage simply and efficiently.

Code you can take to the bank	352
Angle brackets are for standard headers	354
But what if you want to share code?	355
Sharing .h header files	356
Share .o object files by using the full pathname	357
An archive contains .o files	358
Create an archive with the ar command...	359
Finally, compile your other programs	360
The Head First Gym is going global	365
Calculating calories	366
But things are a bit more complex...	369
Programs are made out of lots of pieces...	370
Dynamic linking happens at runtime	372
Can you link .a at runtime?	373
First, create an object file	374
What you call your dynamic library depends on your platform	375
Your C Toolbox	387

Raisins, flour, butter, anchovies...

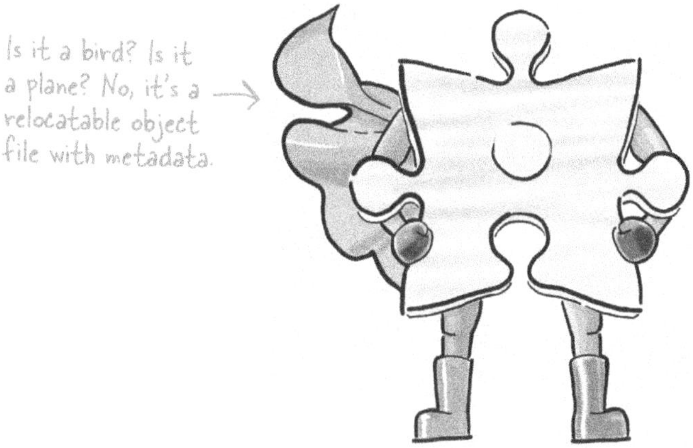
Is it a bird? Is it a plane? No, it's a relocatable object file with metadata.

C Lab 2

OpenCV

Imagine if your computer could keep an eye on your house while you're out, and tell you who's been prowling around. In this lab, you'll build a C-powered intruder detector using the cleverness of OpenCV.

OpenCV

9 processes and system calls

Breaking boundaries

It's time to think outside the box.

You've already seen that you can build complex applications by connecting small tools together on the command line. But what if you want to *use other programs* from inside your own code? In this chapter, you'll learn how to use **system services** to create and control ***processes***. That will give your programs access to *email*, the *Web,* and *any other tool you've got installed*. By the end of the chapter, you'll have the power to go ***beyond C.***

System calls are your hotline to the OS	398
Then someone busted into the system…	402
Security's not the only problem	403
The exec() functions give you more control	404
There are many exec() functions	405
The array functions: execv(), execvp(), execve()	406
Passing environment variables	407
Most system calls go wrong in the same way	408
Read the news with RSS	416
exec() is the end of the line for your program	420
Running a child process with fork() + exec()	421
Your C Toolbox	427

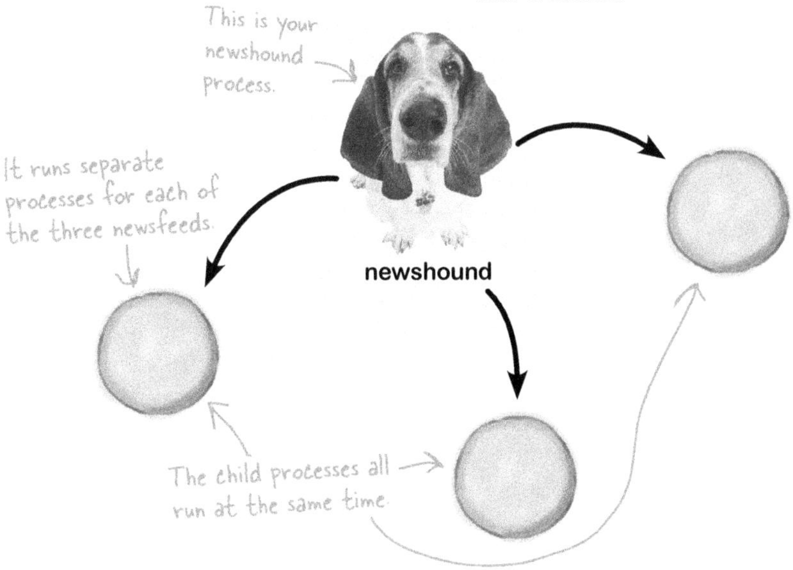
This is your newshound process.
It runs separate processes for each of the three newsfeeds.
newshound
The child processes all run at the same time.

10 interprocess communication

It's good to talk

Creating processes is just half the story.

What if you want to *control* the process once it's running? What if you want to *send it data*? Or *read its output*? **Interprocess communication** lets processes work together to *get the job done*. We'll show you how to multiply the **power** of your code by letting it ***talk*** to other programs on your system.

Redirecting input and output	430
A look inside a typical process	431
Redirection just replaces data streams	432
fileno() tells you the descriptor	433
Sometimes you need to wait…	438
Stay in touch with your child	442
Connect your processes with pipes	443
Case study: opening stories in a browser	444
In the child	445
In the parent	445
Opening a web page in a browser	446
The death of a process	451
Catching signals and running your own code	452
sigactions are registered with sigaction()	453
Rewriting the code to use a signal handler	454
Use kill to send signals	457
Sending your code a wake-up call	458
Your C Toolbox	466

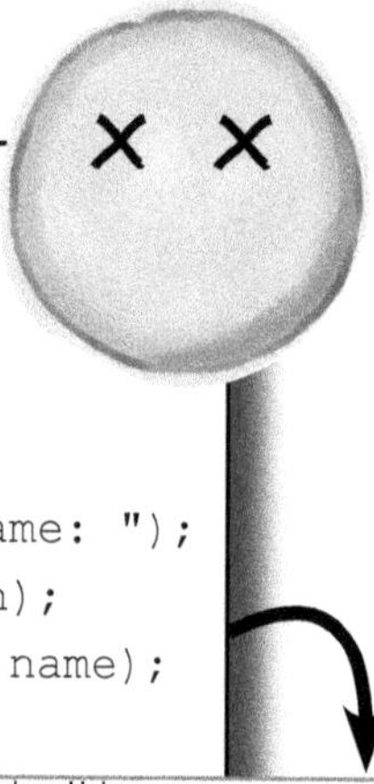

```
#include <stdio.h>

int main()
{
  char name[30];
  printf("Enter your name: ");
  fgets(name, 30, stdin);
  printf("Hello %s\n", name);
  return 0;
}
```

```
File Edit Window Help
> ./greetings
Enter your name: ^C
>
```

If you press Ctrl-C, the program stops running. But why?

11 sockets and networking

There's no place like 127.0.0.1

Programs on different machines need to talk to each other.

You've learned how to use I/O to communicate with files and how processes on the same machine can communicate with each other. Now you're going to *reach out to the rest of the world*, and learn how to write C programs that can talk to other programs **across the network** and **across the *world***. By the end of this chapter, you'll be able to create **programs that behave as servers** and **programs that behave as clients**.

The Internet knock-knock server	468
Knock-knock server overview	469
BLAB: how servers talk to the Internet	470
A socket's not your typical data stream	472
Sometimes the server doesn't start properly	476
Why your mom always told you to check for errors	477
Reading from the client	478
The server can only talk to one person at a time	485
You can fork() a process for each client	486
Writing a web client	490
Clients are in charge	491
Create a socket for an IP address	492
getaddrinfo() gets addresses for domains	493
Your C Toolbox	500

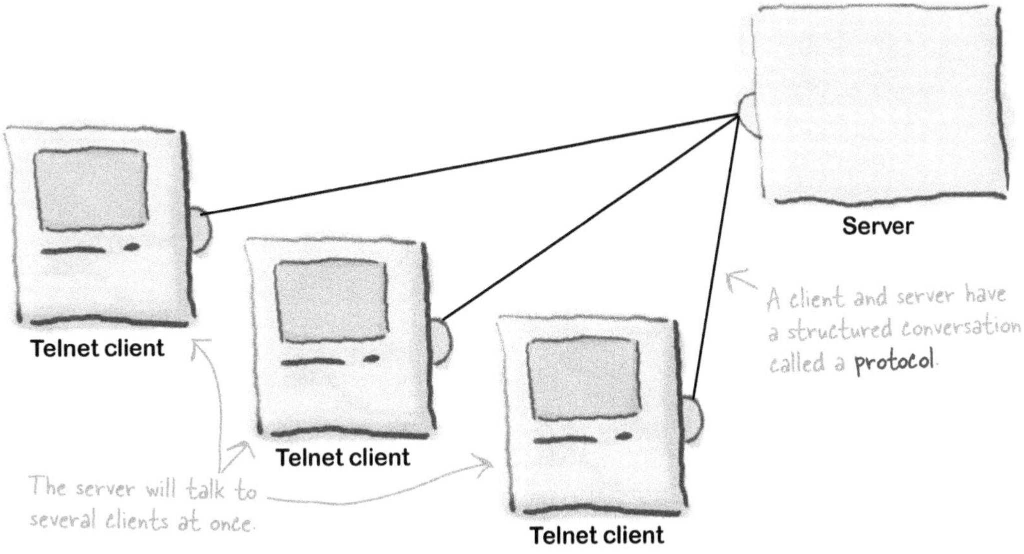

Server
Telnet client
Telnet client
Telnet client
A client and server have a structured conversation called a protocol.
The server will talk to several clients at once.

12

threads

It's a parallel world

Programs often need to do several things at the same time.

POSIX threads can make your code more responsive by **spinning off several pieces of code to run in parallel**. But be careful! Threads are powerful tools, but you don't want them crashing into each other. In this chapter, you'll learn how to put up **traffic signs** and **lane markers** that will ***prevent a code pileup***. By the end, you will know how to **create POSIX threads** and how to use **synchronization mechanisms** to ***protect the integrity of sensitive data***.

Tasks are sequential…or not…	502
…and processes are not always the answer	503
Simple processes do one thing at a time	504
Employ extra staff: use threads	505
How do you create threads?	506
Create threads with pthread_create	507
The code is not thread-safe	512
You need to add traffic signals	513
Use a mutex as a traffic signal	514
Your C Toolbox	521

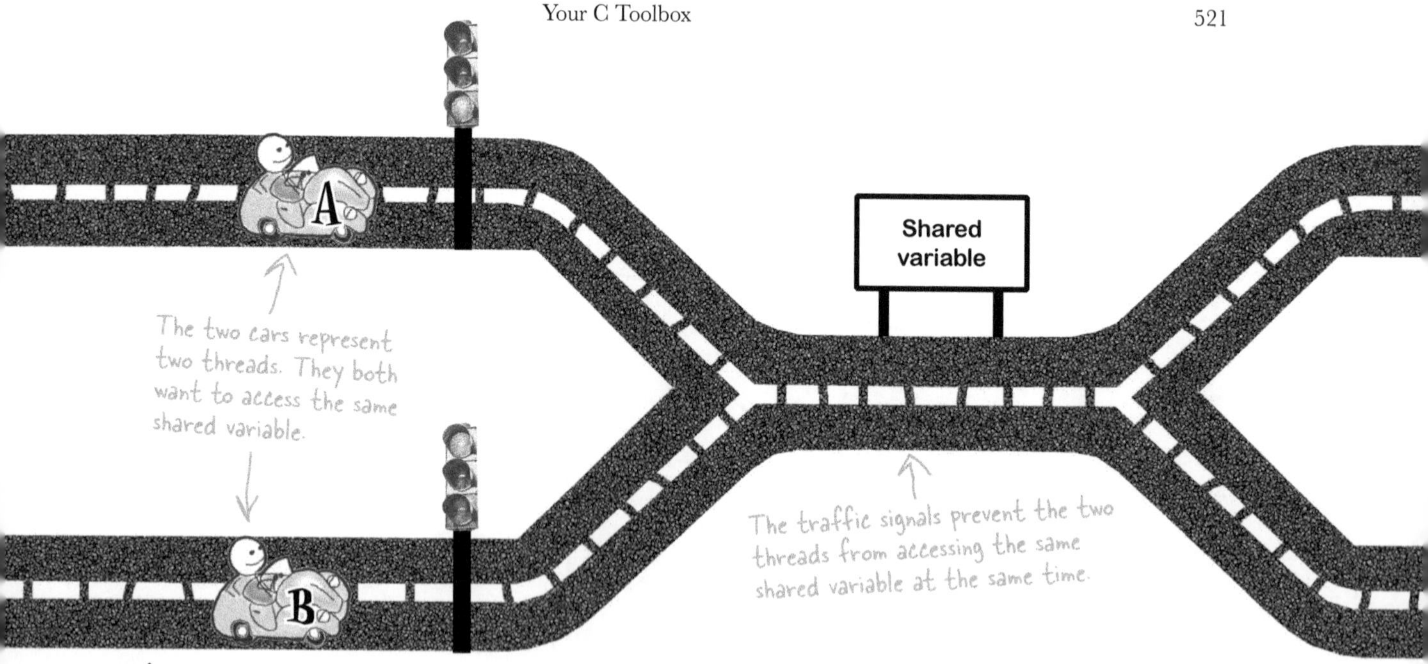

A
B
Shared variable
The two cars represent two threads. They both want to access the same shared variable.
The traffic signals prevent the two threads from accessing the same shared variable at the same time.

C Lab 3

Blasteroids

In this lab, you're going to pay tribute to one of the most popular and long-lived video games of them all. It's time to write Blasteroids!

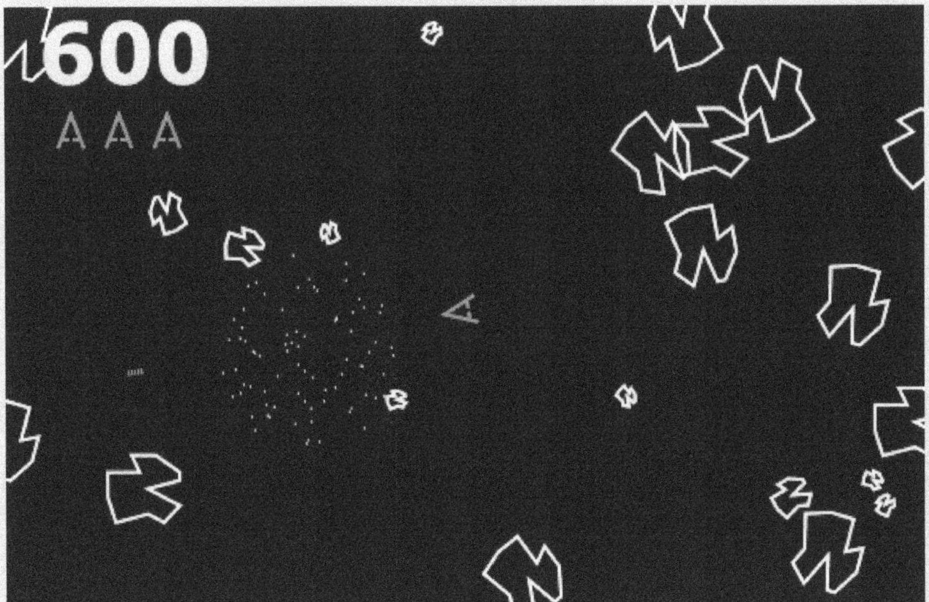
600

leftovers

The top ten things (we didn't cover)

Even after all that, there's still a bit more.

There are just a few more things we think you need to know. We wouldn't feel right about ignoring them, even though they need only a brief mention, and we really wanted to give you a book you'd be able to lift without extensive training at the local gym. So before you put the book down, **read through these tidbits**.

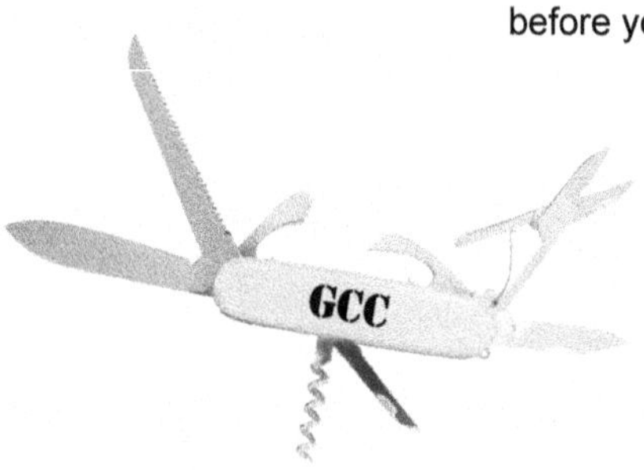
GCC

#1. Operators	540
#2. Preprocessor directives	542
#3. The static keyword	543
#4. How big stuff is	544
#5. Automated testing	545
#6. More on gcc	546
#7. More on make	548
#8. Development tools	550
#9. Creating GUIs	551
#10. Reference material	552

c topics

Revision roundup

Ever wished all those great C facts were in one place?

This is a roundup of all the C topics and principles we've covered in the book. Take a look at them, and see if you can remember them all. Each fact has the chapter it came from alongside it, so it's easy for you to refer back if you need a reminder. You might even want to cut these pages out and tape them to your wall.

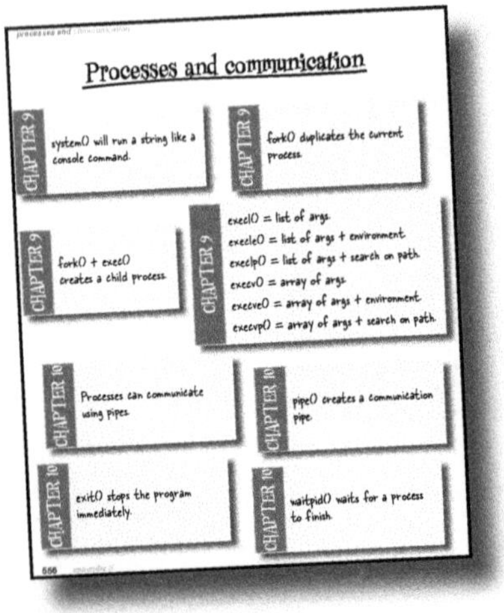
Processes and communication
CHAPTER 9
system() will run a string like a console command.
CHAPTER 9
fork() duplicates the current process.
CHAPTER 9
fork() + exec() creates a child process.
CHAPTER 9
execl() = list of args.
execle() = list of args + environment.
execlp() = list of args + search on path.
execv() = array of args.
execve() = array of args + environment.
execvp() = array of args + search on path.
CHAPTER 10
Processes can communicate using pipes.
CHAPTER 10
pipe() creates a communication pipe.
CHAPTER 10
exit() stops the program immediately.
CHAPTER 10
waitpid() waits for a process to finish.

how to use this book

Intro

I can't believe they put ***that*** in a C book.
Is this book for you?
This book is for anyone with the money to pay for it. And it makes a great gift for that special someone.
Head First
C

In this section, we answer the burning question:
"So why DID they put that in a C book?"

Who is this book for?

If you can answer "yes" to all of these:

1. Do you already know how to program in another programming language?

2. Do you want to master C, create the next big thing in software, make a small fortune, and retire to your own private island?

3. Do you prefer actually doing things and applying the stuff you learn over listening to someone in a lecture rattle on for hours on end?

OK, maybe that one's a little far-fetched. But, you gotta start somewhere, right?

this book is for you.

Who should probably back away from this book?

If you can answer "yes" to any of these:

1. Are you looking for a quick introduction or reference book to C?

2. Would you rather have your toenails pulled out by 15 screaming monkeys than learn something new? Do you believe a C book should cover *everything* and if it bores the reader to tears in the process, then so much the better?

this book is ***not*** for you.

[Note from Marketing: this book is for anyone with a credit card... we'll accept a check, too.]

We know what you're thinking

"How can *this* be a serious C book?"

"What's with all the graphics?"

"Can I actually *learn* it this way?"

We know what your *brain* is thinking

Your brain thinks THIS is important.

Your brain craves novelty. It's always searching, scanning, *waiting* for something unusual. It was built that way, and it helps you stay alive.

So what does your brain do with all the routine, ordinary, normal things you encounter? Everything it *can* to stop them from interfering with the brain's *real* job—recording things that *matter*. It doesn't bother saving the boring things; they never make it past the "this is obviously not important" filter.

How does your brain *know* what's important? Suppose you're out for a day hike and a tiger jumps in front of you—what happens inside your head and body?

Neurons fire. Emotions crank up. *Chemicals surge.*

And that's how your brain knows…

This must be important! Don't forget it!

But imagine you're at home or in a library. It's a safe, warm, tiger-free zone. You're studying. Getting ready for an exam. Or trying to learn some tough technical topic your boss thinks will take a week, ten days at the most.

Just one problem. Your brain's trying to do you a big favor. It's trying to make sure that this *obviously* unimportant content doesn't clutter up scarce resources. Resources that are better spent storing the really *big* things. Like tigers. Like the danger of fire. Like how you should never have posted those party photos on your Facebook page. And there's no simple way to tell your brain, "Hey brain, thank you very much, but no matter how dull this book is, and how little I'm registering on the emotional Richter scale right now, I really *do* want you to keep this stuff around."

Great. Only 600 more dull, dry, boring pages.
Your brain thinks THIS isn't worth saving.

We *think* of a "Head First" reader as a learner.

So what does it take to *learn* something? First, you have to *get* it, then make sure you don't *forget* it. It's not about pushing facts into your head. Based on the latest research in cognitive science, neurobiology, and educational psychology, *learning* takes a lot more than text on a page. We know what turns your brain on.

Some of the Head First learning principles:

Make it visual. Images are far more memorable than words alone, and make learning much more effective (up to 89% improvement in recall and transfer studies). It also makes things more understandable. **Put the words within or near the graphics** they relate to, rather than on the bottom or on another page, and learners will be up to *twice* as likely to solve problems related to the content.

Use a conversational and personalized style. In recent studies, students performed up to 40% better on post-learning tests if the content spoke directly to the reader, using a first-person, conversational style rather than taking a formal tone. Tell stories instead of lecturing. Use casual language. Don't take yourself too seriously. Which would *you* pay more attention to: a stimulating dinner-party companion, or a lecture?

Get the learner to think more deeply. In other words, unless you actively flex your neurons, nothing much happens in your head. A reader has to be motivated, engaged, curious, and inspired to solve problems, draw conclusions, and generate new knowledge. And for that, you need challenges, exercises, and thought-provoking questions, and activities that involve both sides of the brain and multiple senses.

Get—and keep—the reader's attention. We've all had the "I really want to learn this, but I can't stay awake past page one" experience. Your brain pays attention to things that are out of the ordinary, interesting, strange, eye-catching, unexpected. Learning a new, tough, technical topic doesn't have to be boring. Your brain will learn much more quickly if it's not.

Touch their emotions. We now know that your ability to remember something is largely dependent on its emotional content. You remember what you care about. You remember when you *feel* something. No, we're not talking heart-wrenching stories about a boy and his dog. We're talking emotions like surprise, curiosity, fun, "what the…?" , and the feeling of "I rule!" that comes when you solve a puzzle, learn something everybody else thinks is hard, or realize you know something that "I'm more technical than thou" Bob from Engineering *doesn't*.

Metacognition: thinking about thinking

If you really want to learn, and you want to learn more quickly and more deeply, pay attention to how you pay attention. Think about how you think. Learn how you learn.

I wonder how I can trick my brain into remembering this stuff...

Most of us did not take courses on metacognition or learning theory when we were growing up. We were *expected* to learn, but rarely *taught* to learn.

But we assume that if you're holding this book, you really want to learn how to program in C. And you probably don't want to spend a lot of time. If you want to use what you read in this book, you need to *remember* what you read. And for that, you've got to *understand* it. To get the most from this book, or *any* book or learning experience, take responsibility for your brain. Your brain on *this* content.

The trick is to get your brain to see the new material you're learning as Really Important. Crucial to your well-being. As important as a tiger. Otherwise, you're in for a constant battle, with your brain doing its best to keep the new content from sticking.

So just how *DO* you get your brain to treat programming like it was a hungry tiger?

There's the slow, tedious way, or the faster, more effective way. The slow way is about sheer repetition. You obviously know that you *are* able to learn and remember even the dullest of topics if you keep pounding the same thing into your brain. With enough repetition, your brain says, "This doesn't *feel* important to him, but he keeps looking at the same thing *over* and *over* and *over*, so I suppose it must be."

The faster way is to do ***anything that increases brain activity,*** especially different *types* of brain activity. The things on the previous page are a big part of the solution, and they're all things that have been proven to help your brain work in your favor. For example, studies show that putting words *within* the pictures they describe (as opposed to somewhere else in the page, like a caption or in the body text) causes your brain to try to makes sense of how the words and picture relate, and this causes more neurons to fire. More neurons firing = more chances for your brain to *get* that this is something worth paying attention to, and possibly recording.

A conversational style helps because people tend to pay more attention when they perceive that they're in a conversation, since they're expected to follow along and hold up their end. The amazing thing is, your brain doesn't necessarily *care* that the "conversation" is between you and a book! On the other hand, if the writing style is formal and dry, your brain perceives it the same way you experience being lectured to while sitting in a roomful of passive attendees. No need to stay awake.

But pictures and conversational style are just the beginning…

Here's what WE did:

We used ***pictures***, because your brain is tuned for visuals, not text. As far as your brain's concerned, a picture really *is* worth a thousand words. And when text and pictures work together, we embedded the text *in* the pictures because your brain works more effectively when the text is *within* the thing it refers to, as opposed to in a caption or buried in the body text somewhere.

We used ***redundancy***, saying the same thing in *different* ways and with different media types, and *multiple senses*, to increase the chance that the content gets coded into more than one area of your brain.

We used concepts and pictures in ***unexpected*** ways because your brain is tuned for novelty, and we used pictures and ideas with at least *some* ***emotional*** *content*, because your brain is tuned to pay attention to the biochemistry of emotions. That which causes you to *feel* something is more likely to be remembered, even if that feeling is nothing more than a little ***humor***, ***surprise***, or ***interest.***

We used a personalized, ***conversational style***, because your brain is tuned to pay more attention when it believes you're in a conversation than if it thinks you're passively listening to a presentation. Your brain does this even when you're *reading*.

We included more than 80 ***activities***, because your brain is tuned to learn and remember more when you ***do*** things than when you *read* about things. And we made the exercises challenging-yet-doable, because that's what most people prefer.

We used ***multiple learning styles***, because *you* might prefer step-by-step procedures, while someone else wants to understand the big picture first, and someone else just wants to see an example. But regardless of your own learning preference, *everyone* benefits from seeing the same content represented in multiple ways.

We include content for ***both sides of your brain***, because the more of your brain you engage, the more likely you are to learn and remember, and the longer you can stay focused. Since working one side of the brain often means giving the other side a chance to rest, you can be more productive at learning for a longer period of time.

And we included ***stories*** and exercises that present ***more than one point of view,*** because your brain is tuned to learn more deeply when it's forced to make evaluations and judgments.

We included ***challenges***, with exercises, and by asking ***questions*** that don't always have a straight answer, because your brain is tuned to learn and remember when it has to *work* at something. Think about it—you can't get your *body* in shape just by *watching* people at the gym. But we did our best to make sure that when you're working hard, it's on the *right* things. That ***you're not spending one extra dendrite*** processing a hard-to-understand example, or parsing difficult, jargon-laden, or overly terse text.

We used ***people***. In stories, examples, pictures, etc., because, well, *you're* a person. And your brain pays more attention to *people* than it does to *things*.

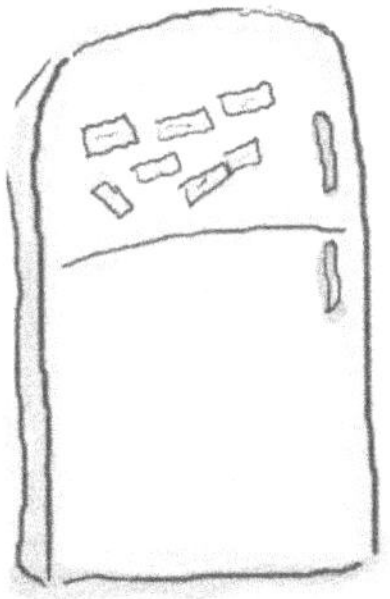

Here's what YOU can do to bend your brain into submission

So, we did our part. The rest is up to you. These tips are a starting point; listen to your brain and figure out what works for you and what doesn't. Try new things.

Cut this out and stick it on your refrigerator.

1. **Slow down. The more you understand, the less you have to memorize.**

   Don't just *read*. Stop and think. When the book asks you a question, don't just skip to the answer. Imagine that someone really *is* asking the question. The more deeply you force your brain to think, the better chance you have of learning and remembering.

2. **Do the exercises. Write your own notes.**

   We put them in, but if we did them for you, that would be like having someone else do your workouts for you. And don't just *look* at the exercises. **Use a pencil.** There's plenty of evidence that physical activity *while* learning can increase the learning.

3. **Read "There Are No Dumb Questions."**

   That means all of them. They're not optional sidebars, ***they're part of the core content!*** Don't skip them.

4. **Make this the last thing you read before bed. Or at least the last challenging thing.**

   Part of the learning (especially the transfer to long-term memory) happens *after* you put the book down. Your brain needs time on its own, to do more processing. If you put in something new during that processing time, some of what you just learned will be lost.

5. **Talk about it. Out loud.**

   Speaking activates a different part of the brain. If you're trying to understand something, or increase your chance of remembering it later, say it out loud. Better still, try to explain it out loud to someone else. You'll learn more quickly, and you might uncover ideas you hadn't known were there when you were reading about it.

6. **Drink water. Lots of it.**

   Your brain works best in a nice bath of fluid. Dehydration (which can happen before you ever feel thirsty) decreases cognitive function.

7. **Listen to your brain.**

   Pay attention to whether your brain is getting overloaded. If you find yourself starting to skim the surface or forget what you just read, it's time for a break. Once you go past a certain point, you won't learn faster by trying to shove more in, and you might even hurt the process.

8. **Feel something.**

   Your brain needs to know that this *matters*. Get involved with the stories. Make up your own captions for the photos. Groaning over a bad joke is *still* better than feeling nothing at all.

9. **Write a lot of code!**

   There's only one way to learn to program in C: **write a lot of code**. And that's what you're going to do throughout this book. Coding is a skill, and the only way to get good at it is to practice. We're going to give you a lot of practice: every chapter has exercises that pose a problem for you to solve. Don't just skip over them—a lot of the learning happens when you solve the exercises. We included a solution to each exercise—don't be afraid to **peek at the solution** if you get stuck! (It's easy to get snagged on something small.) But try to solve the problem before you look at the solution. And definitely get it working before you move on to the next part of the book.

Read me

This is a learning experience, not a reference book. We deliberately stripped out everything that might get in the way of learning whatever it is we're working on at that point in the book. And the first time through, you need to begin at the beginning, because the book makes assumptions about what you've already seen and learned.

We assume you're new to C, but not to programming.

We assume that you've already done some programming. Not a lot, but we'll assume you've already seen things like loops and variables in some other language, like JavaScript. C is actually a pretty advanced language, so if you've never done any programming *at all,* then you might want to read some other book before you start on this one. We'd suggest starting with *Head First Programming.*

You need to install a C compiler on your computer.

Throughout the book, we'll be using the *Gnu Compiler Collection* (`gcc`) because it's free and, well, we think it's just a pretty darned good compiler. You'll need to make sure you have `gcc` installed on your machine. The good news is, if you have a *Linux* computer, then you should already have `gcc`. If you're using a Mac, you'll need to install the Xcode/Developer tools. You can either download these from the Apple *App Store* or by downloading them from Apple. If you're on a Windows machine, you have a couple options. *Cygwin* (*http://www.cygwin.com*) gives you a complete simulation of a *UNIX* environment, including `gcc`. But if you want to create programs that will work on Windows plain-and-simple, then you might want to install the *Minimalist GNU for Windows* (MingW) from *http://www.mingw.org.*

All the code in this book is intended to run across *all* these operating systems, and we've tried hard not to write anything that will only work on one type of computer. Occasionally, there will be some differences, but we'll make sure to point those out to you.

We begin by teaching some basic C concepts, and then we start putting C to work for you right away.

We cover the fundamentals of C in Chapter 1. That way, by the time you make it all the way to Chapter 2, you are creating programs that actually do something real, useful, and—gulp!—fun. The rest of the book then builds on your C skills, turning you from *C newbie* to *coding ninja master* in no time.

The activities are NOT optional.

The exercises and activities are not add-ons; they're part of the core content of the book. Some of them are to help with memory, some are for understanding, and some will help you apply what you've learned. ***Don't skip the exercises.***

The redundancy is intentional and important.

One distinct difference in a Head First book is that we want you to *really* get it. And we want you to finish the book remembering what you've learned. Most reference books don't have retention and recall as a goal, but this book is about *learning*, so you'll see some of the same concepts come up more than once.

The examples are as lean as possible.

Our readers tell us that it's frustrating to wade through 200 lines of an example looking for the two lines they need to understand. Most examples in this book are shown within the smallest possible context, so that the part you're trying to learn is clear and simple. Don't expect all of the examples to be robust, or even complete—they are written specifically for learning, and aren't always fully functional.

The Brain Power exercises don't have answers.

For some of them, there is no right answer, and for others, part of the learning experience of the Brain Power activities is for you to decide if and when your answers are right. In some of the Brain Power exercises, you will find hints to point you in the right direction.

The technical review team

Dave Kitabjian

Vince Milner

Technical reviewers:

Dave Kitabjian has two degrees in electrical and computer engineering and about 20 years of experience consulting, integrating, architecting, and building information system solutions for clients from Fortune 500 firms to high-tech startups. Outside of work, Dave likes to play guitar and piano and spend time with his wife and three kids.

Vince Milner has been developing in C (and many other languages) on a wide variety of platforms for over 20 years. When not studying for his master's degree in mathematics, he can be found being beaten at board games by six-year-olds and failing to move house.

Acknowledgments

Our editor:

Many thanks to **Brian Sawyer** for asking us to write this book in the first place. Brian believed in us every step of the way, gave us the freedom to try out new ideas, and didn't panic too much when deadlines loomed.

Brian Sawyer

The O'Reilly team:

A big thank you goes to the following people who helped us out along the way: **Karen Shaner** for her expert image-hunting skills and for generally keeping the wheels oiled; **Laurie Petrycki** for keeping us well fed and well motivated while in Boston; **Brian Jepson** for introducing us to the wonderful world of the Arduino; and the **early release team** for making early versions of the book available for download. Finally, thanks go to **Rachel Monaghan** and the production team for expertly steering the book through the production process and for working so hard behind the scenes. You guys are awesome.

Family, friends, and colleagues:

We've made a lot of friends on our Head First journey. A special thanks goes to **Lou Barr**, **Brett McLaughlin**, and **Sanders Kleinfeld** for teaching us so much.

David: My thanks to **Andy Parker**, **Joe Broughton**, **Carl Jacques**, and **Simon Jones** and the many other friends who have heard so little from me whilst I was busy scribbling away.

Dawn: Work on this book would have been a lot harder without my amazing support network of family and friends. Special thanks go to **Mum and Dad**, **Carl**, **Steve**, **Gill**, **Jacqui**, **Joyce**, and **Paul**. I've truly appreciated all your support and encouragement.

The without-whom list:

Our technical review team did a truly excellent job of keeping us straight and making sure what we covered was spot on. We're also incredibly grateful to all the people who gave us feedback on early releases of the book. We think the book's much, much better as a result.

Finally, our thanks to **Kathy Sierra** and **Bert Bates** for creating this extraordinary series of books.

Safari® Books Online

Safari Books Online (*www.safaribooksonline.com*) is an on-demand digital library that delivers expert content in both book and video form from the world's leading authors in technology and business. Technology professionals, software developers, web designers, and business and creative professionals use Safari Books Online as their primary resource for research, problem solving, learning, and certification training.

Safari Books Online offers a range of product mixes and pricing programs for organizations, government agencies, and individuals. Subscribers have access to thousands of books, training videos, and prepublication manuscripts in one fully searchable database from publishers like O'Reilly Media, Prentice Hall Professional, Addison-Wesley Professional, Microsoft Press, Sams, Que, Peachpit Press, Focal Press, Cisco Press, John Wiley & Sons, Syngress, Morgan Kaufmann, IBM Redbooks, Packt, Adobe Press, FT Press, Apress, Manning, New Riders, McGraw-Hill, Jones & Bartlett, Course Technology, and dozens more. For more information about Safari Books Online, please visit us online.

1 getting started with c

Diving in

Don't you just love the deep blue C? Come on in—the water's lovely!

Want to get inside the computer's head?

Need to write **high-performance code** for a new game? Program an **Arduino**? Or use that advanced **third-party library** in your iPhone app? If so, then C's here to help. C works at a **much lower level** than most other languages, so understanding C gives you a much better idea of **what's really going on**. C can even help you better understand other languages as well. So dive in and grab your compiler, and you'll soon get started in no time.

C is a language for small, fast programs

The C language is designed to create small, fast programs. It's lower-level than most other languages; that means *it creates code that's a lot closer to what machines really understand.*

The way C works

Computers really only understand one language: machine code, a binary stream of 1s and 0s. You convert your C code into machine code with the aid of a **compiler**.

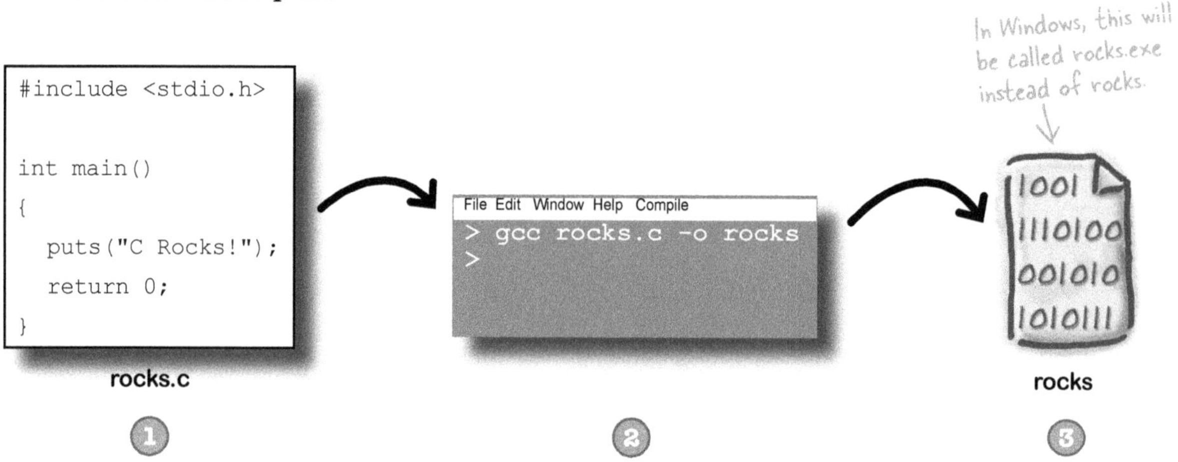

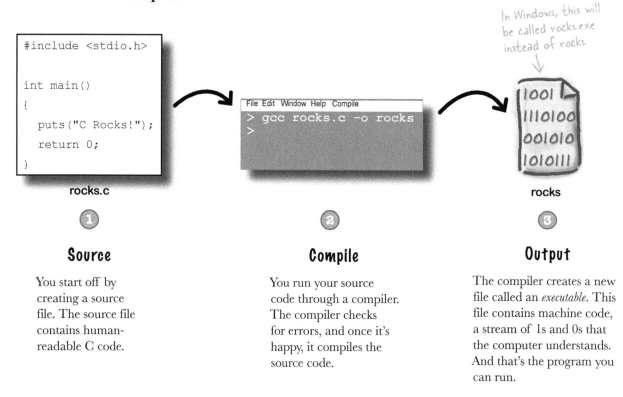

#include <stdio.h>
int main()
{
puts("C Rocks!");
return 0;
}
rocks.c
File Edit Window Help Compile
> gcc rocks.c -o rocks
>
In Windows, this will be called rocks.exe instead of rocks.
1001
1110100
001010
1010111
rocks
1
2
3

Source

You start off by creating a source file. The source file contains human-readable C code.

Compile

You run your source code through a compiler. The compiler checks for errors, and once it's happy, it compiles the source code.

Output

The compiler creates a new file called an *executable*. This file contains machine code, a stream of 1s and 0s that the computer understands. And that's the program you can run.

C is used where speed, space, and portability are important. Most operating systems are written in C. Most other computer languages are also written in C. And most game software is written in C.

There are three C standards that you may stumble across. ANSI C is from the late 1980s and is used for the oldest code. A lot of things were fixed up in the C99 standard from 1999. And some cool new language features were added in the current standard, C11, released in 2011. The differences between the different versions aren't huge, and we'll point them out along the way.

Sharpen your pencil

Try to guess what each of these code fragments does.

Describe what you think the code does.

```
int card_count = 11;
if (card_count > 10)
    puts("The deck is hot. Increase bet.");
```

```
int c = 10;
while (c > 0) {
    puts("I must not write code in class");
    c = c - 1;
}
```

```
/* Assume name shorter than 20 chars. */
char ex[20];
puts("Enter boyfriend's name: ");
scanf("%19s", ex);
printf("Dear %s.\n\n\tYou're history.\n", ex);
```

```
char suit = 'H';
switch(suit) {
case 'C':
    puts("Clubs");
    break;
case 'D':
    puts("Diamonds");
    break;
case 'H':
    puts("Hearts");
    break;
default:
    puts("Spades");
}
```

Sharpen your pencil Solution

Don't worry if you don't understand all of this yet. Everything is explained in greater detail later in the book.

`int card_count = 11;`	Create an integer variable and set it to 11.
`if (card_count > 10)`	Is the count more than 10?
`    puts("The deck is hot. Increase bet.");`	If so, display a message on the command prompt.

An integer is a whole number.

This displays a string on the command prompt or terminal.

`int c = 10;`	Create an integer variable and set it to 10.
`while (c > 0) {`	As long as the value is positive...
`    puts("I must not write code in class");`	...display a message...
`    c = c - 1;`	...and decrease the count.
`}`	This is the end of the code that should be repeated.

The braces define a **block statement**.

`/* Assume name shorter than 20 chars. */`	This is a comment.
`char ex[20];`	Create an array of 20 characters.
`puts("Enter boyfriend's name: ");`	Display a message on the screen.
`scanf("%19s", ex);`	Store what the user enters into the array.
`printf("Dear %s.\n\n\tYou're history.\n", ex);`	Display a message including the text entered.

This means "store everything the user types into the ex array."

This will insert this string of characters here in place of the %s.

`char suit = 'H';`	Create a character variable; store the letter H.
`switch(suit) {`	Look at the value of the variable.
`case 'C':`	Is it 'C'?
`    puts("Clubs");`	If so, display the word "Clubs."
`    break;`	Then skip past the other checks.
`case 'D':`	Is it 'D'?
`    puts("Diamonds");`	If so, display the word "Diamonds."
`    break;`	Then skip past the other checks.
`case 'H':`	Is it 'H'?
`    puts("Hearts");`	If so, display the word "Hearts."
`    break;`	Then skip past the other checks.
`default:`	Otherwise...
`    puts("Spades");`	Display the word "Spades."
`}`	This is the end of the tests.

A **switch** statement checks a single variable for different values.

But what does a complete C program look like?

To create a full program, you need to enter your code into a *C source file*. C source files can be created by any text editor, and their filenames usually end with *.c*. ← This is just a convention, but you should follow it.

Let's have a look at a typical C source file.

1 C programs normally begin with a comment.
The comment describes the purpose of the code in the file, and might include some license or copyright information. There's no absolute need to include a comment here—or anywhere else in the file—but it's good practice and what most C programmers will expect to find.

The comment starts with /*.

These *s are optional. They're only there to make it look pretty.

The comment ends with */.

```
/*
 * Program to calculate the number of cards in the shoe.
 * This code is released under the Vegas Public License.
 * (c)2014, The College Blackjack Team.
 */
#include <stdio.h>

int main()
{
    int decks;
    puts("Enter a number of decks");
    scanf("%i", &decks);
    if (decks < 1) {
        puts("That is not a valid number of decks");
        return 1;
    }
    printf("There are %i cards\n", (decks * 52));
    return 0;
}
```

2 Next comes the include section.
C is a very, very small language and it can do almost nothing without the use of *external libraries*. You will need to tell the compiler what external code to use by including header files for the relevant libraries. The header you will see more than any other is *stdio.h*. The `stdio` library contains code that allows you to read and write data from and to the terminal.

3 The last thing you find in a source file are the functions.
All C code runs inside functions. The most important function you will find in any C program is called the **`main()` function**. The `main()` function is the starting point for all of the code in your program.

So let's look at the main() function in a little more detail.

The main() Function Up Close

The computer will start running your program from the `main()` function. The name is important: if you don't have a function called `main()`, your program won't be able to start.

The `main()` function has a **return type** of `int`. So what does this mean? Well, when the computer runs your program, it will need to have some way of deciding if the program ran successfully or not. It does this by checking the *return value* of the `main()` function. If you tell your `main()` function to return 0, this means that the program was successful. If you tell it to return any other value, this means that there was a problem.

This is the return type. It should always be **int** for the main() function.

Because the function is called "main," the program will start here.

If we had any parameters, they'd be mentioned here.

The body of the function is always surrounded by **braces**.

```
int main()
{
    int decks;
    puts("Enter a number of decks");
    scanf("%i", &decks);
    if (decks < 1) {
        puts("That is not a valid number of decks");
        return 1;
    }
    printf("There are %i cards\n", (decks * 52));
    return 0;
}
```

The function name comes after the return type. That's followed by the function parameters if there are any. Finally, we have the *function body*. The function body **must** be surrounded by *braces*.

Geek Bits

The `printf()` function is used to display **formatted output**. It replaces format characters with the values of variables, like this:

The first parameter will be inserted here as a string.

First parameter

```
printf("%s says the count is %i", "Ben", 21);
```

The second parameter will be inserted here as an integer.

Second parameter

You can include as many parameters as you like when you call the `printf()` function, but make sure you have a matching % format character for each one.

If you want to check the exit status of a program, type:

```
echo %ErrorLevel%
```

in Windows, or:

```
echo $?
```

in Linux or on the Mac.

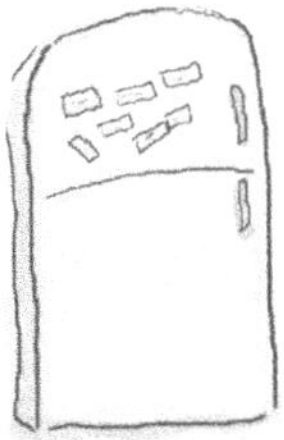

Code Magnets

The College Blackjack Team was working on some code on the dorm fridge, but someone mixed up the magnets! Can you reassemble the code from the magnets?

```
/*
 * Program to evaluate face values.
 * Released under the Vegas Public License.
 * (c)2014 The College Blackjack Team.
 */

......................................................................

......................................................................

................ main()
{
    char card_name[3];
    puts("Enter the card_name: ");
    scanf("%2s", card_name);
    int val = 0;
    if (card_name[0] == 'K') {
        val = 10;
    } else if (card_name[0] == 'Q') {

        ............................................................

    } else if (card_name[0] == ................) {
        val = 10;

    }...................... (card_name[0] == ........) {

        ............................................................
    } else {
        val = atoi(card_name);
    }
    printf("The card value is: %i\n", val);

    .................... 0;
}
```

Enter two characters for the card name. → `scanf("%2s", card_name);`

This converts the text into a number. → `atoi(card_name)`

Magnets: `<stdlib.h>` `;` `;` `val = 11` `int` `'J'` `#include` `'A'` `return` `else` `#include` `if` `val = 10` `<stdio.h>`

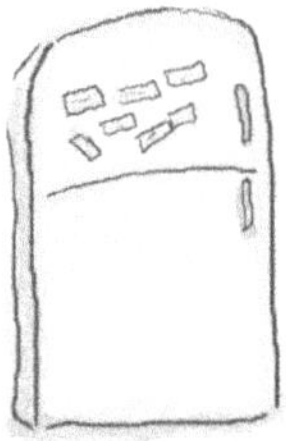

Code Magnets Solution

The College Blackjack Team was working on some code on the dorm fridge, but someone mixed up the magnets! You were to reassemble the code from the magnets.

```
/*
 * Program to evaluate face values.
 * Released under the Vegas Public License.
 * (c)2014 The College Blackjack Team.
 */
#include <stdio.h>
#include <stdlib.h>
int main()
{
    char card_name[3];
    puts("Enter the card_name: ");
    scanf("%2s", card_name);
    int val = 0;
    if (card_name[0] == 'K') {
        val = 10;
    } else if (card_name[0] == 'Q') {
        val = 10;
    } else if (card_name[0] == 'J') {
        val = 10;
    } else if (card_name[0] == 'A') {
        val = 11;
    } else {
        val = atoi(card_name);
    }
    printf("The card value is: %i\n", val);
    return 0;
}
```

there are no Dumb Questions

Q: What does `card_name[0]` mean?

A: It's the first character that the user typed. So if he types 10, `card_name[0]` would be 1.

Q: Do you always write comments using /* and */?

A: If your compiler supports the C99 standard, then you can begin a comment with //. The compiler treats the rest of that line as a comment.

Q: How do I know which standard my compiler supports?

A: Check the documentation for your compiler. `gcc` supports all three standards: ANSI C, C99, and C11.

But how do you run the program?

C is a *compiled language*. That means the computer will not interpret the code directly. Instead, you will need to convert—or *compile*—the human-readable source code into machine-readable *machine code*.

To compile the code, you need a program called a **compiler**. One of the most popular C compilers is the *GNU Compiler Collection* or **gcc**. `gcc` is available on a lot of operating systems, and it can compile lots of languages other than C. Best of all, it's completely free.

Here's how you can compile and run the program using `gcc`.

1. **Save the code from the Code Magnets exercise on the opposite page in a file called cards.c.**

cards.c
C source files usually end .c.

2. **Compile with `gcc cards.c -o cards` at a command prompt or terminal.**

```
File Edit Window Help Compile
> gcc cards.c -o cards
>
```

Compile cards.c to a file called cards.

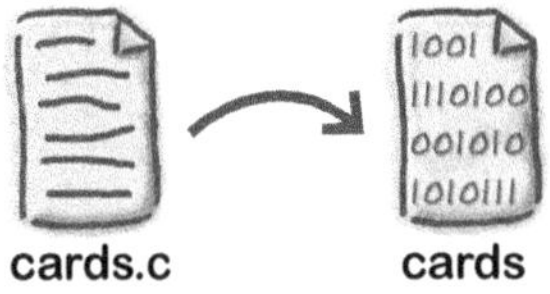
cards.c
cards
This will be cards.exe if you're on Windows.

3. **Run by typing `cards` on Windows, or `./cards` on Mac, Linux, and Cygwin.**

```
File Edit Window Help Compile
> ./cards
Enter the card_name:
```

Geek Bits

You can compile and run your code on most machines using this trick:

&& here means "and then if it's successful, do this..."

```
gcc zork.c -o zork && ./zork
```

You should put "zork" instead of "./zork" on a Windows machine.

This command will run the new program only if it compiles successfully. If there's a problem with the compile, it will skip running the program and simply display the errors on the screen.

Do this!

You should create the *cards.c* file and compile it now. We'll be working on it more and more as the chapter progresses.

Test Drive

Let's see if the program compiles and runs. Open up a command prompt or terminal on your machine and try it out.

This line compiles the code and creates the cards program.

This line runs the program. If you're on Windows, don't type the ./

Running the program again

The user enters the name from a card...

...and the program displays the corresponding value.

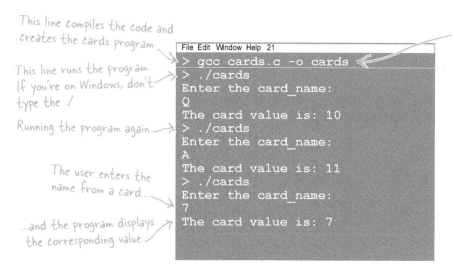

```
File Edit Window Help 21
> gcc cards.c -o cards
> ./cards
Enter the card_name:
Q
The card value is: 10
> ./cards
Enter the card_name:
A
The card value is: 11
> ./cards
Enter the card_name:
7
The card value is: 7
```

Remember: you can combine the compile and run steps together (turn back a page to see how).

The program works!

Congratulations! You have compiled and run a C program. The `gcc` compiler took the human-readable source code from *cards.c* and converted it into computer-readable *machine code* in the `cards` program. If you are using a Mac or Linux machine, the compiler will have created the machine code in a file called ***cards***. But on Windows, all programs need to have a *.exe* extension, so the file will be called ***cards.exe***.

there are no Dumb Questions

Q: Why do I have to prefix the program with ./ when I run it on Linux and the Mac?

A: On Unix-style operating systems, programs are run only if you specify the directory where they live or if their directory is listed in the PATH environment variable.

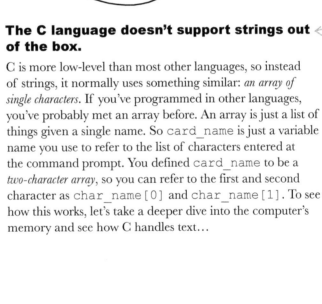

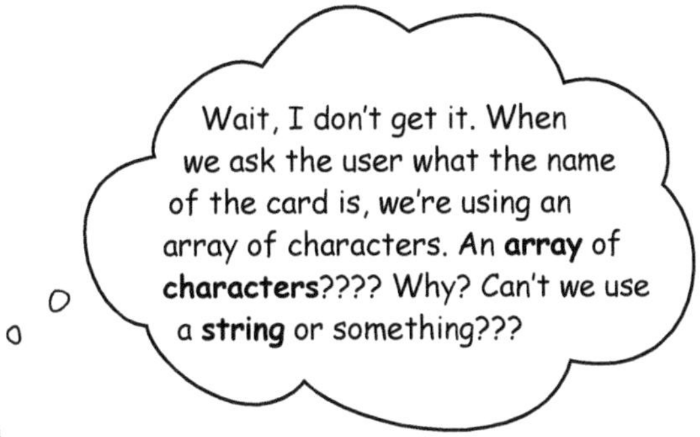
Wait, I don't get it. When we ask the user what the name of the card is, we're using an array of characters. An **array** of **characters**???? Why? Can't we use a **string** or something???

The C language doesn't support strings out of the box.

But there are a number of C extension libraries that **do** give you strings.

C is more low-level than most other languages, so instead of strings, it normally uses something similar: *an array of single characters*. If you've programmed in other languages, you've probably met an array before. An array is just a list of things given a single name. So `card_name` is just a variable name you use to refer to the list of characters entered at the command prompt. You defined `card_name` to be a *two-character array*, so you can refer to the first and second character as `char_name[0]` and `char_name[1]`. To see how this works, let's take a deeper dive into the computer's memory and see how C handles text…

Strings Way Up Close

Strings are just character arrays. When C sees a string like this:

```
s = "Shatner"
```

it reads it like it was just an array of separate characters:

This is how you define an array in C.

```
s = {'S', 'h', 'a', 't', 'n', 'e', 'r'}
```

Each of the characters in the string is just an element in an array, which is why you can refer to the individual characters in the string by using an index, like `s[0]` and `s[1]`.

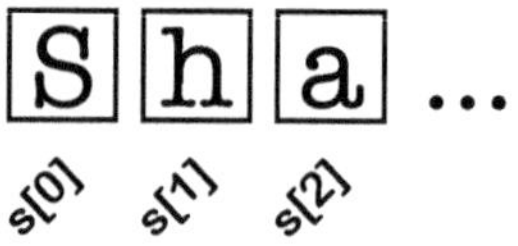

S
h
a
...
s[0]
s[1]
s[2]

Don't fall off the end of the string

But what happens when C wants to read the contents of the string? Say it wants to print it out. Now, in a lot of languages, the computer keeps pretty close track of the size of an array, but C is more low-level than most languages and can't always work out exactly *how long* an array is. If C is going to display a string on the screen, it needs to know when it gets to the end of the character array. And it does this by adding a **sentinel character**.

'\0'

C knows to stop when it sees \0.

The sentinel character is an additional character at the end of the string that has the value `\0`. Whenever the computer needs to read the contents of the string, it goes through the elements of the character array one at a time, until it reaches `\0`. That means that when the computer sees this:

```
s = "Shatner"
```

it actually stores it in memory like this:

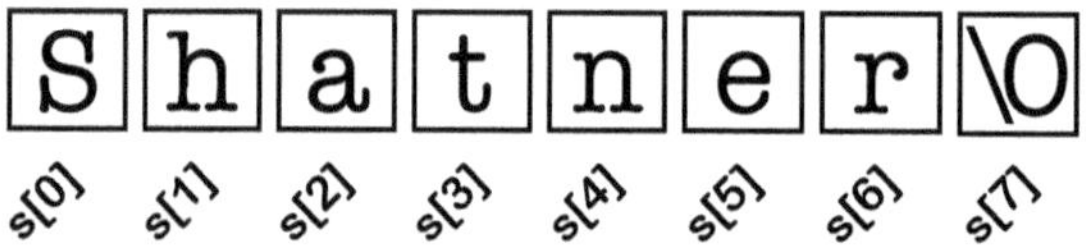

S
h
a
t
n
e
r
\0
s[0]
s[1]
s[2]
s[3]
s[4]
s[5]
s[6]
s[7]

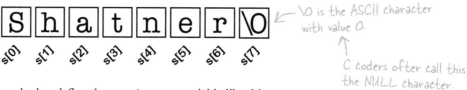

\0 is the ASCII character with value 0.

C coders often call this the NULL character.

That's why in our code we had to define the `card_name` variable like this:

```
char card_name[3];
```

The `card_name` string is only ever going to record one or two characters, but because strings end in a *sentinel character* we have to allow for an extra character in the array.

there are no Dumb Questions

Q: Why are the characters numbered from 0? Why not 1?

A: The index is an offset: it's a measure of how far the character is from the first character.

Q: Why?

A: The computer will store the characters in consecutive bytes of memory. It can use the index to calculate the location of the character. If it knows that `c[0]` is at memory location 1,000,000, then it can quickly calculate that `c[96]` is at 1,000,000 + 96.

Q: Why does it need a sentinel character? Doesn't it know how long the string is?

A: Usually, it doesn't. C is not very good at keeping track of how long arrays are, and a string is just an array.

Q: It doesn't know how long arrays are???

A: No. Sometimes the compiler can work out the length of an array by analyzing the code, but usually C relies on you to keep track of your arrays.

Q: Does it matter if I use single quotes or double quotes?

A: Yes. Single quotes are used for individual characters, but double quotes are always used for strings.

Q: So should I define my strings using quotes (") or as explicit arrays of characters?

A: Usually you will define strings using quotes. They are called **string literals**, and they are easier to type.

Q: Are there any differences between string literals and character arrays?

A: Only one: string literals are constant.

Q: What does that mean?

A: It means that you can't change the individual characters once they are created.

Q: What will happen if I try?

A: It depends on the compiler, but `gcc` will usually display a bus error.

Q: A bus error? What the heck's a bus error?

A: C will store string literals in memory in a different way. A bus error just means that your program can't update that piece of memory.

Painless Operations

Not all equals signs are equal.

In C, the equals sign (=) is used for **assignment**. But a double equals sign (==) is used for **testing equality**.

```
teeth = 4;
```
Set teeth to the value 4.

```
teeth == 4;
```
Test if teeth has the value 4.

If you want to increase or decrease a variable, then you can save space with the += and -= assignments.

```
teeth += 2;
```
Adds 2 to teeth.

```
teeth -= 2;
```
Takes away 2 teeth.

Finally, if you want to increase or decrease a variable by 1, use ++ and --.

```
teeth++;
```
Increase by 1.

```
teeth--;
```
Decrease by 1.

Two types of command

So far, every command you've seen has fallen into one of the following two categories.

Do something

Most of the commands in C are statements. Simple statements are *actions*; they *do* things and they *tell us* things. You've met statements that define variables, read input from the keyboard, or display data to the screen.

```
split_hand();   <- This is a simple statement.
```

Sometimes you group statements together to create *block statements*. Block statements are groups of commands surrounded by braces.

```
{
    deal_first_card();
    deal_second_card();
    cards_in_hand = 2;
}
```

These commands form a **block statement** because they are surrounded by braces.

Do something only if something is true

Control statements such as `if` check a condition before running the code:

```
if (value_of_hand <= 16)   <- This is the condition.
    hit();                 <- Run this statement if the condition is true.
else
    stand();               <- Run this statement if the condition is false.
```

`if` statements typically need to do more than one thing when a condition is true, so they are often used with block statements:

```
if (dealer_card == 6) {
    double_down();
    hit();
}
```

BOTH of these commands will run if the condition is true. The commands are grouped inside a single block statement.

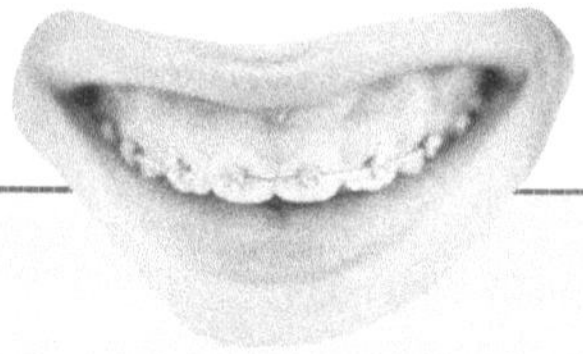

Do you need braces?

Block statements allow you to treat a *whole set of statements* as if they were a *single statement*. In C, the `if` condition works like this:

```
if (countdown == 0)
  do_this_thing();
```

The `if` condition runs a **single statement**. So what if you want to run several statements in an `if`? If you wrap a list of statements in braces, C will treat them as though they were just one statement:

```
if (x == 2) {
  call_whitehouse();
  sell_oil();
  x = 0;
}
```

C coders like to keep their code short and snappy, so most will omit braces on `if` conditions and `while` loops. So instead of writing:

```
if (x == 2) {
    puts("Do something");
}
```

most C programmers write:

```
if (x == 2)
    puts("Do something");
```

Here's the code so far

```
/*
 * Program to evaluate face values.
 * Released under the Vegas Public License.
 * (c)2014 The College Blackjack Team.
 */
#include <stdio.h>
#include <stdlib.h>
int main()
{
    char card_name[3];
    puts("Enter the card_name: ");
    scanf("%2s", card_name);
    int val = 0;
    if (card_name[0] == 'K') {
        val = 10;
    } else if (card_name[0] == 'Q') {
        val = 10;
    } else if (card_name[0] == 'J') {
        val = 10;
    } else if (card_name[0] == 'A') {
        val = 11;
    } else {
        val = atoi(card_name);
    }
    printf("The card value is: %i\n", val);
    return 0;
}
```

I've had a thought. Could this check if a card value is in a particular range? That might be handy...

liding
uthwash

Advertising Feature

I CAN MAKE YOU RICH JUST LIKE ME!

The Eddie Rich blackjack correspondence school

Hey, how's it going? You look to me like a smart guy. And I know, 'cause I'm a smart guy too! Listen, I'm onto a sure thing here, and I'm a nice guy, so I'm going to let you in on it. See, I'm an expert in card counting. The Capo di tutti capi. What's card counting, you say? Well, to me, it's a career!

Seriously, card counting is a way of improving the odds when you play blackjack. In blackjack, if there are plenty of high-value cards left in the shoe, then the odds are slanted in favor of the player. That's you!

Card counting helps you keep track of the number of high-value cards left. Say you start with a count of 0.

Then the dealer leads with a Queen—that's a high card. That's one less available in the deck, so you reduce the count by one:

It's a queen → count – 1

But if it's a low card, like a 4, the count goes up by one:

It's a four → count + 1

High cards are 10s and the face cards (Jack, Queen, King). Low cards are 3s, 4s, 5s, and 6s.

You keep doing this for every low card and every high card until the count gets real high, then you lay on cash in your next bet and ba-da-bing! Soon you'll have more money than my third wife!

If you'd like to learn more, then enroll today in my Blackjack Correspondence School. Learn more about card counting as well as:

* How to use the Kelly Criterion to maximize the value of your bet
* How to avoid getting whacked by a pit boss
* How to get cannoli stains off a silk suit
* Things to wear with plaid

For more information, contact Cousin Vinny c/o the Blackjack Correspondence School.

Wig Straps
For MEN

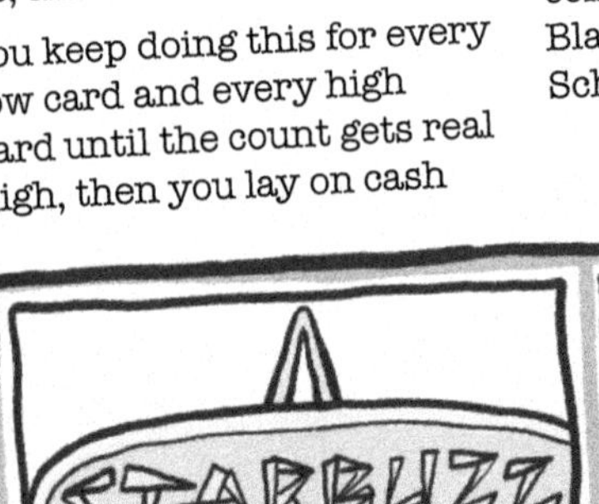
STARBUZZ
HOTEL

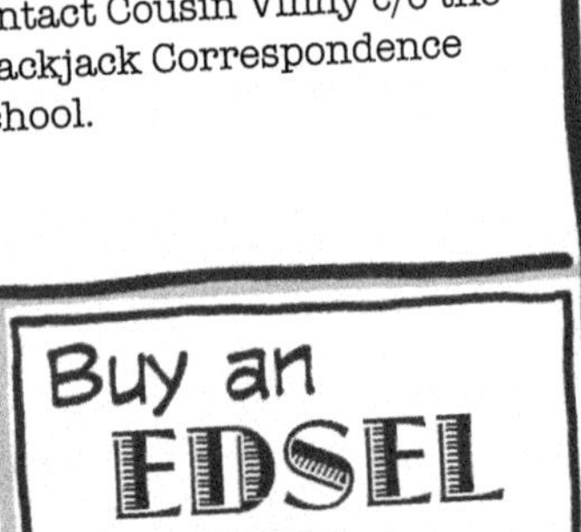
Buy an
EDSEL

Card counting? In C?

Card counting is a way to increase your chances of winning at blackjack. By keeping a running count as the cards are dealt, a player can work out the best time to place large bets and the best time to place small bets. Even though it's a powerful technique, it's really quite simple.

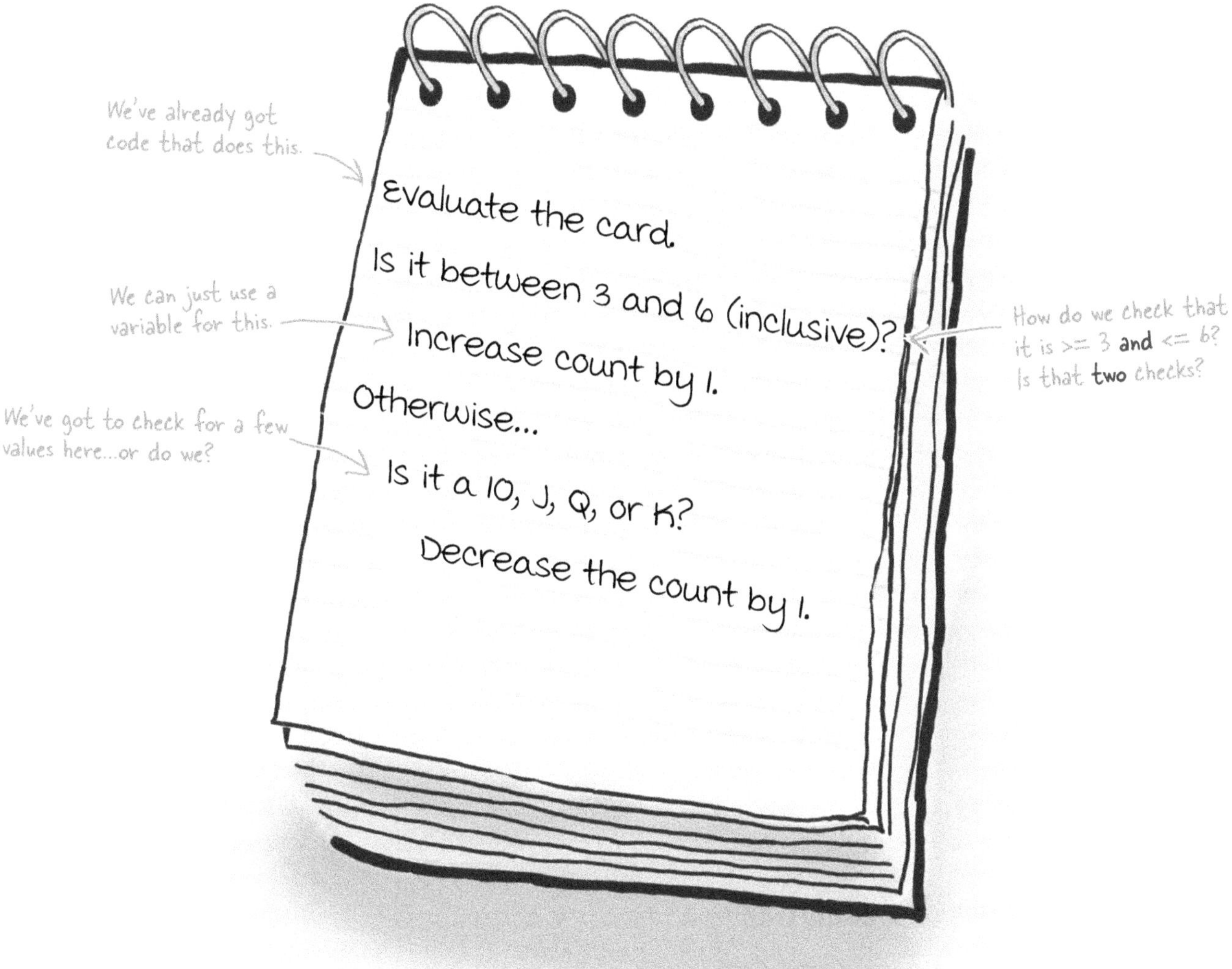
We've already got code that does this.
Evaluate the card.
Is it between 3 and 6 (inclusive)?
We can just use a variable for this.
Increase count by 1.
How do we check that it is >= 3 **and** <= 6? Is that **two** checks?
Otherwise...
We've got to check for a few values here...or do we?
Is it a 10, J, Q, or K?
Decrease the count by 1.

How difficult would this be to write in C? You've looked at how to make a single test, but the card-counting algorithm needs to check multiple conditions: you need to check that a number is >= 3 as well as checking that it's <= 6.

You need a set of operations that will allow you to combine conditions together.

There's more to booleans than equals...

So far, you've looked at `if` statements that check if a single condition is true, but what if you want to check several conditions? Or check if a single condition is *not* true?

&& checks if two conditions are true

The *and* operator (`&&`) evaluates to true, only if **both** conditions given to it are true.

```
if ((dealer_up_card == 6) && (hand == 11))
    double_down();
```

Both of these conditions need to be true for this piece of code to run.

The *and* operator is efficient: if the first condition is false, then the computer won't bother evaluating the second condition. It knows that if the first condition is false, then the whole condition must be false.

|| checks if one of two conditions is true

The *or* operator (`||`) evaluates to true, if **either** condition given to it is true.

```
if (cupcakes_in_fridge || chips_on_table)
    eat_food();
```

Either can be true.

If the first condition is true, the computer won't bother evaluating the second condition. It knows that if the first condition is true, the *whole condition* must be true.

! flips the value of a condition

! is the *not* operator. It reverses the value of a condition.

```
if (!brad_on_phone)
    answer_phone();
```

! means "not"

Geek Bits

In C, boolean values are represented by numbers. To C, the number 0 is the value for false. But what's the value for true? Anything that is not equal to 0 is treated as true. So there is nothing wrong in writing C code like this:

```
int people_moshing = 34;
if (people_moshing)
    take_off_glasses();
```

In fact, C programs often use this as a shorthand way of checking if something is not 0.

Exercise

You are going to modify the program so that it can be used for card counting. It will need to display one message if the value of the card is from 3 to 6. It will need to display a different message if the card is a 10, Jack, Queen, or King.

```
int main()
{
    char card_name[3];
    puts("Enter the card_name: ");
    scanf("%2s", card_name);
    int val = 0;
    if (card_name[0] == 'K') {
        val = 10;
    } else if (card_name[0] == 'Q') {
        val = 10;
    } else if (card_name[0] == 'J') {
        val = 10;
    } else if (card_name[0] == 'A') {
        val = 11;
    } else {
        val = atoi(card_name);
    }
    /* Check if the value is 3 to 6 */
    if ..................................................................................
        puts("Count has gone up");
    /* Otherwise check if the card was 10, J, Q, or K */
    else if ..........................................................................
        puts("Count has gone down");
    return 0;
}
```

The Polite Guide to Standards

The ANSI C standard has no value for true and false. C programs treat the value 0 as false, and any other value as true. The C99 standard does allow you to use the words *true* and *false* in your programs—but the compiler treats them as the values 1 and 0 anyway.

Exercise Solution

You were to modify the program so that it can be used for card counting. It needed to display one message if the value of the card is from 3 to 6. It needed to display a different message if the card is a 10, Jack, Queen, or King.

```
int main()
{
    char card_name[3];
    puts("Enter the card_name: ");
    scanf("%2s", card_name);
    int val = 0;
    if (card_name[0] == 'K') {
        val = 10;
    } else if (card_name[0] == 'Q') {
        val = 10;
    } else if (card_name[0] == 'J') {
        val = 10;
    } else if (card_name[0] == 'A') {
        val = 11;
    } else {
        val = atoi(card_name);
    }
    /* Check if the value is 3 to 6 */
    if ((val > 2) && (val < 7))
        puts("Count has gone up");
    /* Otherwise check if the card was 10, J, Q, or K */
    else if (val == 10)
        puts("Count has gone down");
    return 0;
}
```

There are a few ways of writing this condition.

Did you spot that you just needed a single condition for this?

there are no Dumb Questions

Q: Why not just | and &?

A: You can use & and | if you want. The & and | operators will **always evaluate both conditions**, but && and || can often skip the second condition.

Q: So why do the & and | operators exist?

A: Because they do more than simply evaluate logical conditions. They perform bitwise operations on the individual bits of a number.

Q: Huh? What do you mean?

A: Well, 6 & 4 is equal to 4, because if you checked which binary digits are common to 6 (110 in binary) and 4 (100 in binary), you get 4 (100).

Test Drive

Let's see what happens when you compile and run the program now:

This line compiles and runs the code.

We run it a few times to check that the different value ranges work.

```
File Edit Window Help FiveOfSpades
> gcc cards.c -o cards && ./cards
Enter the card_name:
Q
Count has gone down

> ./cards
Enter the card_name:
8

> ./cards
Enter the card_name:
3
Count has gone up

>
```

The code works. By combining multiple conditions with a boolean operator, you check for a range of values rather than a single value. You now have the basic structure in place for a card counter.

The computer says the card was low. The count went up! Raise the bet! Raise the bet!
Stealthy communication device
NO-LIMIT TEXAS HOLD'EM

The Compiler Exposed

This week's interview:
What Has gcc Ever Done for Us?

Head First: May I begin by thanking you, `gcc`, for finding time in your very busy schedule to speak to us.

gcc: That's not a problem, my friend. A pleasure to help.

Head First: `gcc`, you can speak many languages, is that true?

gcc: I am fluent in over six million forms of communication…

Head First: Really?

gcc: Just teasing. But I do speak many languages. C, obviously, but also C++ and Objective-C. I can get by in Pascal, Fortran, PL/I, and so forth. Oh, and I have a smattering of Go…

Head First: And on the hardware side, you can produce machine code for many, many platforms?

gcc: Virtually any processor. Generally, when a hardware engineer creates a new type of processor, one of the first things she wants to do is get some form of me running on it.

Head First: How have you achieved such incredible flexibility?

gcc: My secret, I suppose, is that there are two sides to my personality. I have a frontend, a part of me that understands some type of source code.

Head First: Written in a language such as C?

gcc: Exactly. My frontend can convert that language into an intermediate code. All of my language frontends produce the same sort of code.

Head First: You say there are two sides to your personality?

gcc: I also have a backend: a system for converting that intermediate code into machine code that is understandable on many platforms. Add to that my knowledge of the particular executable file formats for just about every operating system you've ever heard of…

Head First: And yet, you are often described as a mere translator. Do you think that's fair? Surely that's not all you are.

gcc: Well, of course I do a little more than simple translation. For example, I can often spot errors in code.

Head First: Such as?

gcc: Well, I can check obvious things such as misspelled variable names. But I also look for subtler things, such as the redefinition of variables. Or I can warn the programmer if he chooses to name variables after existing functions and so on.

Head First: So you check code quality as well, then?

gcc: Oh, yes. And not just quality, but also performance. If I discover a section of code inside a loop that could work equally well outside a loop, I can very quietly move it.

Head First: You do rather a lot!

gcc: I like to think I do. But in a quiet way.

Head First: `gcc`, thank you.

BE the Compiler

Each of the C files on this page represents a complete source file. Your job is to play compiler and determine whether each of these files will compile, and if not, why not. For extra bonus points, say what you think the output of each compiled file will be when run, and whether you think the code is working as intended.

A

```
#include <stdio.h>

int main()
{
    int card = 1;
    if (card > 1)
        card = card - 1;
        if (card < 7)
            puts("Small card");
    else {
      puts("Ace!");
    }
    return 0;
}
```

B

```
#include <stdio.h>

int main()
{
    int card = 1;
    if (card > 1) {
        card = card - 1;
        if (card < 7)
            puts("Small card");
    else
      puts("Ace!");
    }
    return 0;
}
```

C

```
#include <stdio.h>

int main()
{
    int card = 1;
    if (card > 1) {
        card = card - 1;
        if (card < 7)
            puts("Small card");
    } else
      puts("Ace!");

    return 0;
}
```

D

```
#include <stdio.h>

int main()
{
    int card = 1;
    if (card > 1) {
        card = card - 1;
        if (card < 7)
            puts("Small card");
    else
      puts("Ace!");

    return 0;
}
```

BE the Compiler Solution

Each of the C files on this page represents a complete source file. Your job is to play compiler and determine whether each of these files will compile, and if not, why not. For extra bonus points, say what you think the output of each compiled file will be when run, and whether you think the code is working as intended.

A

```
#include <stdio.h>

int main()
{
    int card = 1;
    if (card > 1)
        card = card - 1;
        if (card < 7)
            puts("Small card");
    else {
      puts("Ace!");
    }
    return 0;
}
```

The code compiles. The program displays "Small card." But it doesn't work properly because the else is attached to the wrong if.

B

```
#include <stdio.h>

int main()
{
    int card = 1;
    if (card > 1) {
        card = card - 1;
        if (card < 7)
            puts("Small card");
    else
      puts("Ace!");
    }
    return 0;
}
```

The code compiles. The program displays nothing and is not really working properly because the else is matched to the wrong if.

C

```
#include <stdio.h>

int main()
{
    int card = 1;
    if (card > 1) {
        card = card - 1;
        if (card < 7)
            puts("Small card");
    } else
      puts("Ace!");

    return 0;
}
```

The code compiles. The program displays "Ace!" and is properly written.

D

```
#include <stdio.h>

int main()
{
    int card = 1;
    if (card > 1) {
        card = card - 1;
        if (card < 7)
            puts("Small card");
    else
      puts("Ace!");

    return 0;
}
```

The code won't compile because the braces are not matched.

What's the code like now?

```
int main()
{
    char card_name[3];
    puts("Enter the card_name: ");
    scanf("%2s", card_name);
    int val = 0;
    if (card_name[0] == 'K') {
        val = 10;
    } else if (card_name[0] == 'Q') {
        val = 10;
    } else if (card_name[0] == 'J') {
        val = 10;
    } else if (card_name[0] == 'A') {
        val = 11;
    } else {
        val = atoi(card_name);
    }
    /* Check if the value is 3 to 6 */
    if ((val > 2) && (val < 7))
        puts("Count has gone up");
    /* Otherwise check if the card was 10, J, Q, or K */
    else if (val == 10)
        puts("Count has gone down");
    return 0;
}
```

Hmmm...is there something we can do with that sequence of if statements? They're all checking the same value, card_name[0], and most of them are setting the val variable to 10. I wonder if there's a more efficient way of saying that in C.

C programs often need to check the same value several times and then perform very similar pieces of code for each case.

Now, you can just use a sequence of `if` statements, and that will probably be just fine. But C gives you an alternative way of writing this kind of logic.

C can perform logical tests with the switch statement.

Pulling the ol' switcheroo

Sometimes when you're writing conditional logic, you need to check the value of the same variable over and over again. To prevent you from having to write lots and lots of `if` statements, the C language gives you another option: the **`switch`** statement.

The `switch` statement is kind of like an `if` statement, except it can test for multiple values of a *single variable*:

```
switch(train) {
case 37:
  winnings = winnings + 50;
  break;
case 65:
  puts("Jackpot!");
  winnings = winnings + 80;
case 12:
  winnings = winnings + 20;
  break;
default:
  winnings = 0;
}
```

If the train == 37, add 50 to the winnings and then skip to the end.

If the train == 65, add 80 to the winnings AND THEN also add 20 to the winnings; then, skip to the end.

If the train == 12, just add 20 to the winnings.

For any other value of train, set the winnings back to ZERO.

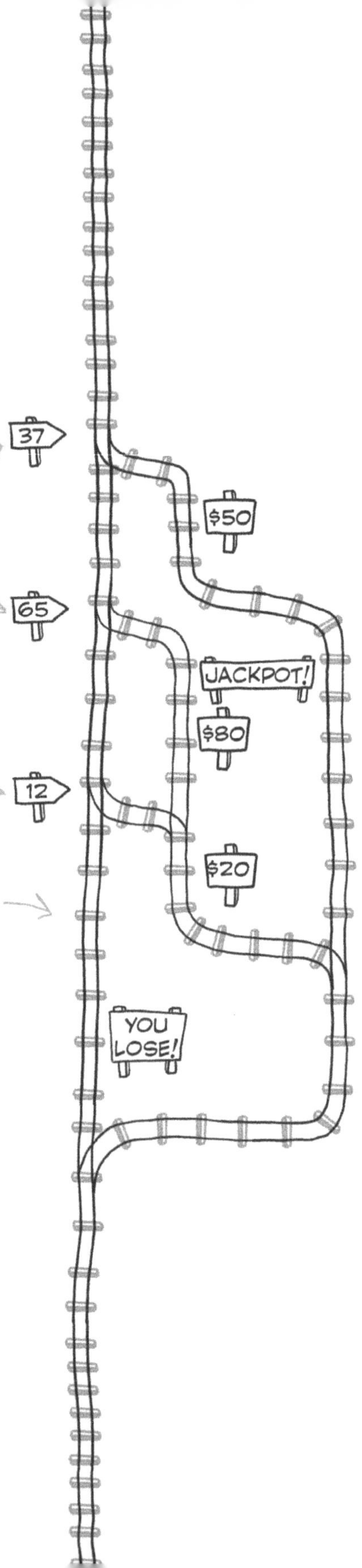
37
$50
65
JACKPOT!
$80
12
$20
YOU LOSE!

When the computer hits a `switch` statement, it checks the value it was given, and then looks for a matching `case`. When it finds one, it runs *all* of the code that follows it until it reaches a `break` statement. **The computer keeps going until it is told to break out of the `switch` statement.**

> **Watch it!**
>
> **Missing breaks can make your code buggy.**
>
> *Most C programs have a `break` at the end of each `case` section to make the code easier to understand, even at the cost of some efficiency.*

Sharpen your pencil

Let's look at that section of your `cards` program again:

```
int val = 0;
if (card_name[0] == 'K') {
    val = 10;
} else if (card_name[0] == 'Q') {
    val = 10;
} else if (card_name[0] == 'J') {
    val = 10;
} else if (card_name[0] == 'A') {
    val = 11;
} else {
    val = atoi(card_name);
}
```

Do you think you can rewrite this code using a `switch` statement? Write your answer below:

Sharpen your pencil Solution

You were to rewrite the code using a `switch` statement.

```
int val = 0;
if (card_name[0] == 'K') {
    val = 10;
} else if (card_name[0] == 'Q') {
    val = 10;
} else if (card_name[0] == 'J') {
    val = 10;
} else if (card_name[0] == 'A') {
    val = 11;
} else {
    val = atoi(card_name);
}
```

```
int val = 0;
switch(card_name[0]) {
case 'K':
case 'Q':
case 'J':
    val = 10;
    break;
case 'A':
    val = 11;
    break;
default:
    val = atoi(card_name);
}
```

BULLET POINTS

- `switch` statements can replace a sequence of `if` statements.
- `switch` statements check a single value.
- The computer will start to run the code at the first matching `case` statement.
- It will continue to run until it reaches a `break` or gets to the end of the `switch` statement.
- Check that you've included `break`s in the right places; otherwise, your `switch`es will be buggy.

there are no Dumb Questions

Q: Why would I use a `switch` statement instead of an `if`?

A: If you are performing multiple checks on the same variable, you might want to use a `switch` statement.

Q: What are the advantages of using a `switch` statement?

A: There are several. First: clarity. It is clear that an entire block of code is processing a single variable. That's not so obvious if you just have a sequence of `if` statements. Secondly, you can use fall-through logic to reuse sections of code for different cases.

Q: Does the `switch` statement have to check a variable? Can't it check a value?

A: Yes, it can. The `switch` statement will simply check that two values are equal.

Q: Can I check strings in a `switch` statement?

A: No, you can't use a `switch` statement to check a string of characters or any kind of array. The `switch` statement will only check a single value.

Sometimes once is not enough...

Two cards???
Oh crap...

You've learned a lot about the C language, but there are still some important things to learn. You've seen how to write programs for many different situations, but there is one fundamental thing that we haven't really looked at yet. What if you want your program to do something *again and again and again*?

Using while loops in C

Loops are a special type of control statement. A control statement decides *if* a section of code will be run, but a loop statement decides *how many times* a piece of code will be run.

The most basic kind of loop in C is the `while` loop. A `while` loop runs code *over and over and over* as long as some condition remains true.

This checks the condition before running the body.

```
while (<some condition>) {
    ... /* Do something here */
}
```

The **body** is between the braces.

If you have only one line in the body, you don't need the braces.

When it gets to the end of the body, the computer checks if the loop condition is still true. If it is, the body code runs again.

```
while (more_balls)
    keep_juggling();
```

Do you do while?

There's another form of the `while` loop that checks the loop condition *after* the loop body is run. That means the loop always executes **at least once**. It's called the `do...while` **loop**:

```
do {
  /* Buy lottery ticket */
} while(have_not_won);
```

Loops often follow the same structure...

You can use the `while` loop anytime you need to repeat a piece of code, but a lot of the time your loops will have the same kind of structure:

- Do something simple before the loop, like set a counter.
- Have a simple test condition on the loop.
- Do something at the end of a loop, like update a counter.

For example, this is a `while` loop that counts from 1 to 10:

```
int counter = 1;
while (counter < 11) {
  printf("%i green bottles, hanging on a wall\n", counter);
  counter++;
}
```

This is the loop startup code.

This is the loop condition.

This is the loop update code that runs at the end of the loop body to update a counter.

Remember: counter++ means "increase the counter variable by one."

Loops like this have code that prepares variables for the loop, some sort of condition that is checked each time the loop runs, and finally some sort of code at the end of the loop that updates a counter or something similar.

...and the for loop makes this easy

Because this pattern is so common, the designers of C created the **`for`** loop to make it a little more concise. Here is that same piece of code written with a `for` loop:

```
int counter;
for (counter = 1; counter < 11; counter++) {
  printf("%i green bottles, hanging on a wall\n", counter);
}
```

This is the text condition checked **before** the loop runs each time.

This is the code that will run **after** each loop.

This initializes the loop variable.

Because there's only one line in the loop body, you could actually have skipped these braces.

`for` loops are actually used a *lot* in C—as much, if not more than, `while` loops. Not only do they make the code slightly shorter, but they're also easier for other C programmers to read, because all of the code that controls the loop—the stuff that controls the value of the `counter` variable—is now contained in the `for` statement and is taken out of the loop body.

Every for loop needs to have something in the body.

You use break to break out...

You can create loops that check a condition at the beginning or end of the loop body. But what if you want to escape from the loop from somewhere in the middle? You could always restructure your code, but sometimes it's just simpler skip out of the loop immediately using the **break** statement:

```
while(feeling_hungry) {
    eat_cake();
    if (feeling_queasy) {
        /* Break out of the while loop */
        break;
    }
    drink_coffee();
}
```

"break" skips out of the loop immediately.

A break statement will break you straight out of the current loop, skipping whatever follows it in the loop body. breaks can be useful because they're sometimes the simplest and best way to end a loop. But you might want to avoid using too many, because they can also make the code a little harder to read.

...and continue to continue

If you want to skip the rest of the loop body and go back to the start of the loop, then the continue statement is your friend:

```
while(feeling_hungry) {
    if (not_lunch_yet) {
        /* Go back to the loop condition */
        continue;
    }
    eat_cake();
}
```

"continue" takes you back to the start of the loop.

Watch it!

The break statement is used to break out of loops and also switch statements.

Make sure that you know what you're breaking out of when you break.

Tales from the Crypt

breaks don't break if statements.

On January 15, 1990, AT&T's long-distance telephone system crashed, and 60,000 people lost their phone service. The cause? A developer working on the C code used in the exchanges tried to use a break to break out of an if statement. But breaks don't break out of ifs. Instead, the program skipped an entire section of code and introduced a bug that interrupted 70 million phone calls over nine hours.

Writing Functions Up Close

Before you try out your new loop mojo, let's go on a detour and take a quick look at functions.

So far, you've had to create one function in every program you've written, the `main()` function:

```
int main()
{
  puts("Too young to die; too beautiful to live");
  return 0;
}
```

This function returns an **int** value. → `int`

This is the name of the function. → `main`

Nothing between these parentheses. → `()`

The body of the function is surrounded by braces.

The body of the function—the part that does stuff. → `puts(...)`

When you're done, you return a value. → `return 0;`

Pretty much all functions in C follow the same format. For example, this is a program with a custom function that gets called by `main()`:

```
#include <stdio.h>

int larger(int a, int b)
{
  if (a > b)
    return a;
  return b;
}

int main()
{
  int greatest = larger(100, 1000);
  printf("%i is the greatest!\n", greatest);
  return 0;
}
```

Returns an int value → `int larger(...)`

This function takes two **arguments**: a and b. Both arguments are ints.

Calling the function here → `larger(100, 1000)`

The `larger()` function is slightly different from `main()` because it takes ***arguments*** or ***parameters***. An **argument** is just a local variable that gets its value from the code that calls the function. The `larger()` function takes two arguments—a and b—and then it returns the value of whichever one is larger.

The Polite Guide to Standards

The `main()` function has an `int` return type, so you should include a `return` statement when you get to the end. But if you leave the `return` statement out, the code will still compile—though you may get a warning from the compiler. A **C99** compiler will insert a `return` statement for you if you forget. Use **`-std=c99`** to compile to the C99 standard.

Void Functions Up Close

Most functions in C have a return value, but sometimes you might want to create a function that has nothing useful to return. It might just *do* stuff rather than *calculate* stuff. Normally, functions always have to contain a `return` statement, but not if you give your function the return type **`void`**:

The void return type means the function won't return anything.

```
void complain()
{
  puts("I'm really not happy");
}
```

There's no need for a return statement because it's a void function.

In C, the keyword `void` means *it doesn't matter*. As soon as you tell the C compiler that you don't care about returning a value from the function, you don't need to have a `return` statement in your function.

there are no Dumb Questions

Q: If I create a `void` function, does that mean it can't contain a `return` statement?

A: You can still include a `return` statement, but the compiler will most likely generate a warning. Also, there's no point to including a `return` statement in a `void` function.

Q: Really? Why not?

A: Because if you try to read the value of your `void` function, the compiler will refuse to compile your code.

Chaining Assignments

Almost everything in C has a return value, and not just function calls. In fact, even things like assignments have return values. For example, if you look at this statement:

```
x = 4;
```

It assigns the number 4 to a variable. The interesting thing is that the expression "`x = 4`" *itself* has the value that was assigned: 4. So why does that matter? Because it means you can do cool tricks, like chaining assignments together:

The assignment "x = 4" has the value 4.

So now y is also set to 4.

```
y = (x = 4);
```

That line of code will set both `x` **and** `y` to the value 4. In fact, you can shorten the code slightly by removing the parentheses:

```
y = x = 4;
```

You'll often see chained assignments in code that needs to set several variables to the same value.

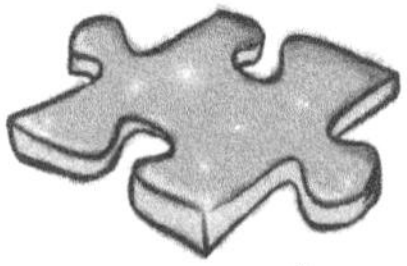

Mixed Messages

A short C program is listed below. One block of the program is missing. Your challenge is to **match the candidate block of code** (on the left) **with the output** that you'd see if the block were inserted. Not all of the lines of output will be used, and some of the lines of output might be used more than once. Draw lines connecting the candidate blocks of code with their matching command-line output.

```
#include <stdio.h>

int main()
{
    int x = 0;
    int y = 0;
    while (x < 5) {
        [                ]
        printf("%i%i ", x, y);
        x = x + 1;
    }
    return 0;
}
```

Candidate code goes here.

Candidates:

Match each candidate with one of the possible outputs.

```
y = x - y;
```

```
y = y + x;
```

```
y = y + 2;
if (y > 4)
    y = y - 1;
```

```
x = x + 1;
y = y + x;
```

```
if (y < 5) {
    x = x + 1;
    if (y < 3)
        x = x - 1;
}
y = y + 2;
```

Possible output:

```
22 46
```

```
11 34 59
```

```
02 14 26 38
```

```
02 14 36 48
```

```
00 11 21 32 42
```

```
11 21 32 42 53
```

```
00 11 23 36 410
```

```
02 14 25 36 47
```

Exercise

Now that you know how to create `while` loops, modify the program to keep a running count of the card game. Display the count after each card and end the program if the player types X. Display an error message if the player types a bad card value like 11 or 24.

```
#include <stdio.h>
#include <stdlib.h>
int main()
{
    char card_name[3];
    int count = 0;
    do {
        puts("Enter the card_name: ");
        scanf("%2s", card_name);
        int val = 0;
        switch(card_name[0]) {
        case 'K':
        case 'Q':
        case 'J':
            val = 10;
            break;
        case 'A':
            val = 11;
            break;
        case 'X':          <- What will you do here?
            ..............................................
        default:
            val = atoi(card_name);
            ..............................................
            ..............................................
            ..............................................
            ..............................................
            ..............................................
        }
        if ((val > 2) && (val < 7)) {
            count++;
        } else if (val == 10) {
            count--;
        }
        printf("Current count: %i\n", count);
    } while (..............................................)
    return 0;
}
```

You need to display an error if the val is not in the range 1 to 10. You should also skip the rest of the loop body and try again.

Add 1 to count. → `count++;`

Subtract 1 from count. → `count--;`

You need to stop if she enters X.

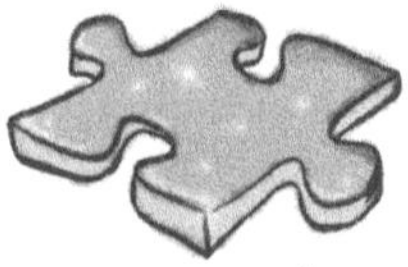

Mixed Messages Solution

A short C program is listed below. One block of the program is missing. Your challenge was to **match the candidate block of code** (on the left) **with the output** that you'd see if the block were inserted. Not all of the lines of output were used. You were to draw lines connecting the candidate blocks of code with their matching command-line output.

```
#include <stdio.h>

int main()
{
    int x = 0;
    int y = 0;
    while (x < 5) {
        [                    ]   <- Candidate code goes here.

        printf("%i%i ", x, y);
        x = x + 1;
    }
    return 0;
}
```

Candidates:

```
y = x - y;
```

```
y = y + x;
```

```
y = y + 2;
if (y > 4)
    y = y - 1;
```

```
x = x + 1;
y = y + x;
```

```
if (y < 5) {
    x = x + 1;
    if (y < 3)
        x = x - 1;
}
y = y + 2;
```

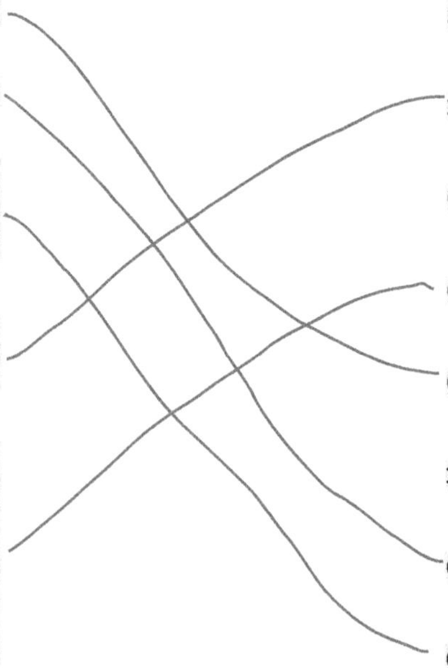

Possible output:

```
22 46
11 34 59
02 14 26 38
02 14 36 48
00 11 21 32 42
11 21 32 42 53
00 11 23 36 410
02 14 25 36 47
```

Exercise Solution

Now that you know how to create `while` loops, you were to modify the program to keep a running count of the card game. Display the count after each card and end the program if the player types X. Display an error message if the player types a bad card value like 11 or 24.

```
#include <stdio.h>
#include <stdlib.h>
int main()
{
    char card_name[3];
    int count = 0;
    do {
        puts("Enter the card_name: ");
        scanf("%2s", card_name);
        int val = 0;
        switch(card_name[0]) {
        case 'K':
        case 'Q':
        case 'J':
            val = 10;
            break;
        case 'A':
            val = 11;
            break;
        case 'X':
            continue;
        default:
            val = atoi(card_name);
            if ((val < 1) || (val > 10)) {
                puts("I don't understand that value!");
                continue;
            }
        }
        if ((val > 2) && (val < 7)) {
            count++;
        } else if (val == 10) {
            count--;
        }
        printf("Current count: %i\n", count);
    } while (card_name[0] != 'X');
    return 0;
}
```

break wouldn't break us out of the loop, because we're inside a switch statement. We need a **continue** to go back and check the loop condition again.

This is just one way of writing this condition.

You need another **continue** here because you want to keep looping.

You need to check if the first character was an X.

Test Drive

Now that the card-counting program is finished, it's time to take it for a spin. What do you think? Will it work?

Remember: you don't need "./" if you're on Windows.

This will compile and run the program.

We now check if it looks like a correct card value.

The count is increasing!

```
File Edit Window Help GoneLoopy
> gcc card_counter.c -o card_counter && ./card_counter
Enter the card_name:
4
Current count: 1
Enter the card_name:
K
Current count: 0
Enter the card_name:
3
Current count: 1
Enter the card_name:
5
Current count: 2
Enter the card_name:
23
I don't understand that value!
Enter the card_name:
6
Current count: 3
Enter the card_name:
5
Current count: 4
Enter the card_name:
3
Current count: 5
Enter the card_name:
X
```

By betting big when the count was high, I made a fortune!
NO-LIMIT TEXAS HOLD'EM

The card counting program works!

You've completed your first C program. By using the power of C statements, loops, and conditions, you've created a fully functioning card counter.

Great job!

Disclaimer: Using a computer for card counting is illegal in many states, and those casino guys can get kinda gnarly. So don't do it, OK?

there are no Dumb Questions

Q: Why do I need to compile C? Other languages like JavaScript aren't compiled, are they?

A: C is compiled to make the code fast. Even though there are languages that aren't compiled, some of those—like JavaScript and Python—often use some sort of hidden compilation to improve their speed.

Q: Is C++ just another version of C?

A: No. C++ was originally designed as an extension of C, but now it's a little more than that. C++ and Objective-C were both created to use object orientation with C.

Q: What's object orientation? Will we learn it in this book?

A: Object orientation is a technique to deal with complexity. We won't specifically look at it in this book.

Q: C looks a lot like JavaScript, Java, C#, etc.

A: C has a very compact syntax and it's influenced many other languages.

Q: What does `gcc` stand for?

A: The Gnu Compiler Collection.

Q: Why "collection"? Is there more than one?

A: The Gnu Compiler Collection can be used to compile many languages, though C is probably still the language with which it's used most frequently.

Q: Can I create a loop that runs forever?

A: Yes. If the condition on a loop is the value 1, then the loop will run forever.

Q: Is it a good idea to create a loop that runs forever?

A: Sometimes. An infinite loop (a loop that runs forever) is often used in programs like network servers that perform one thing repeatedly until they are stopped. But most coders design loops so that they will stop sometime.

BULLET POINTS

- A `while` loop runs code as long as its condition is true.
- A `do-while` loop is similar, but runs the code at least once.
- The `for` loop is a more compact way of writing certain kinds of loops.
- You can exit a loop at any time with `break`.
- You can skip to the loop condition at any time with `continue`.
- The `return` statement returns a value from a function.
- `void` functions don't need `return` statements.
- Most expressions in C have values.
- Assignments have values so you can chain them together (`x = y = 0`).

Your C Toolbox

You've got Chapter 1 under your belt, and now you've added C basics to your toolbox. For a complete list of tooltips in the book, see Appendix ii.

switch statements efficiently check for multiple values of a variable.

Simple statements are commands.

Block statements are surrounded by { and } (braces).

Every program needs a main() function.

You need to compile your C program before you run it.

#include includes external code for things like input and output.

if statements run code if something is true.

You can use the && operator on the command line to run your program only if it compiles.

-o specifies the output file.

You can use && and || to combine conditions together.

gcc is the most popular C compiler.

Your source files should have a name ending in .c.

while repeats code as long as a condition is true.

do-while loops run code at least once.

count++ means add 1 to count.

count-- means subtract 1 from count.

for loops are a more compact way of writing loops.

2 memory and pointers

What are you pointing at?

...and of course, Mommy never lets me stay out after 6 p.m.
Thank heavens my boyfriend variable isn't in read-only memory.

If you really want to kick butt with C, you need to understand how C handles memory.

The C language gives you a lot more *control* over how your program uses the **computer's memory**. In this chapter, you'll strip back the covers and see exactly what happens when you **read and write variables**. You'll learn **how arrays work**, how to avoid some **nasty memory SNAFUs,** and most of all, you'll see how **mastering pointers and memory addressing** is key to becoming a kick-ass C programmer.

C code includes pointers

Pointers are one of the most fundamental things to understand in the C programming language. So what's a pointer? A **pointer** is just the address of a piece of data in memory.

Pointers are used in C for a couple of reasons.

To best understand pointers, go slowly.

1. **Instead of passing around a whole copy of the data, you can just pass a pointer.**

I've got the answer you need; it's right here in the Encyclopedia Britannica.
This is a copy of the information you need.
Or you could just look at page 241.
This is a pointer: the location of the information.

2. **You might want two pieces of code to work on the same piece of data rather than a separate copy.**

You were supposed to sign the birthday card we left in the lunch room.
But I prefer this one—it's got kittens!

Pointers help you do both these things: avoid copies and share data. But if pointers are just addresses, why do some people find them confusing? Because they're a **form of indirection**. If you're not careful, you can quickly get lost chasing pointers through memory. The trick to learning how to use C pointers is to *go slowly*.

Relax

Don't try to rush this chapter.

Pointers are a simple idea, but you need to take your time and understand everything. Take frequent breaks, drink plenty of water, and if you really get stuck, take a nice long bath.

Digging into memory

To understand what pointers are, you'll need to dig into the memory of the computer.

Every time you declare a variable, the computer creates space for it somewhere in memory. If you declare a variable *inside* a function like `main()`, the computer will store it in a section of memory called the **stack**. If a variable is declared *outside any function*, it will be stored in the **globals** section of memory.

```
int y = 1;

int main()
{
  int x = 4;
  return 0;
}
```

Variable y will live in the **globals** section. Memory address 1,000,000. Value 1.

Variable x will live in the **stack**. Memory address 4,100,000. Value 4.

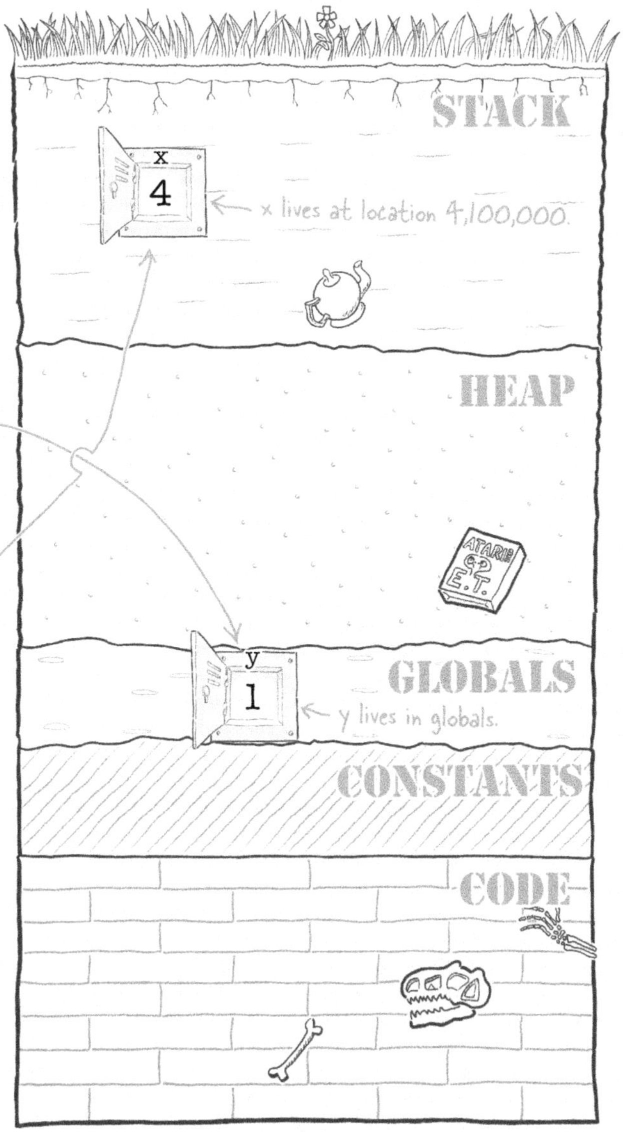

STACK
x
4
x lives at location 4,100,000.
HEAP
ATARI
E.T.
y
1
GLOBALS
y lives in globals.
CONSTANTS
CODE

The computer might allocate, say, memory location 4,100,000 in the stack for the x variable. If you assign the number 4 to the variable, the computer will store 4 at location 4,100,000.

If you want to find out the memory address of the variable, you can use the **&** operator:

&x is the **address** of x.

```
printf("x is stored at %p\n", &x);
```

%p is used to format addresses.

This is what the code will print.

```
x is stored at 0x3E8FA0
```

This is 4,100,000 in **hex** (base 16) format.

You'll probably get a different address on your machine.

The address of the variable tells you where to find the variable in memory. That's why an address is also called a ***pointer***, because it ***points*** to the variable in memory.

A variable declared inside a function is usually stored in the stack.
A variable declared outside a function is stored in globals.

Set sail with pointers

Imagine you're writing a game in which players have to navigate their way around the…

BERMUDA RECTANGLE

The game will need to keep control of lots of things, like scores and lives and the current location of the players. You won't want to write the game as one large piece of code; instead, you'll create lots of smaller functions that will each do something useful in the game:

`go_south_east()`

`go_north_west()`

`speaks_in_present_tense()`

`go_south()`

`acquire_facial_hair()`

`eat_rat()`

`die_of_scurvy()`

`make_one_sequel_too_many()`

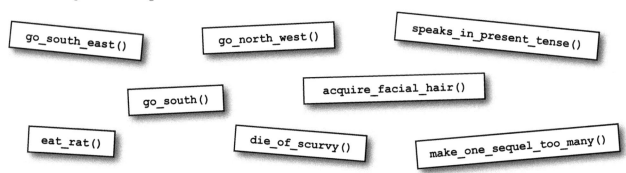

What does any of this have to do with pointers? Let's begin coding without worrying about pointers at all. You'll just use variables as you always have. A major part of the game is going to be navigating your ship around the Bermuda Rectangle, so let's dive deeper into what the code will need to do in one of the navigation functions.

Set sail sou'east, Cap'n

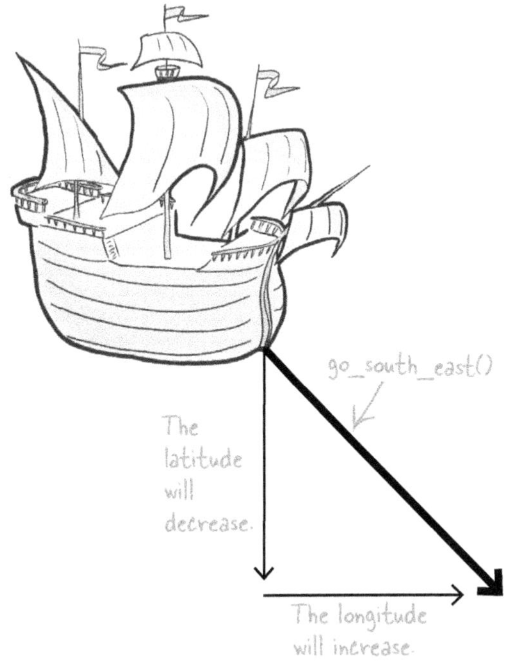
go_south_east()
The latitude will decrease.
The longitude will increase.

The game will track the location of players using *latitudes* and *longitudes*. The latitude is how far north or south the player is, and the longitude is her position east or west. If a player wants to travel southeast, that means her latitude will go *down*, and her longitude will go *up*:

So you could write a `go_south_east()` function that takes arguments for the latitude and longitude, which it will then increase and decrease:

```
#include <stdio.h>

void go_south_east(int lat, int lon)
{
  lat = lat - 1;
  lon = lon + 1;
}

int main()
{
  int latitude = 32;
  int longitude = -64;
  go_south_east(latitude, longitude);
  printf("Avast! Now at: [%i, %i]\n", latitude, longitude);
  return 0;
}
```

Pass in the latitude and longitude.

Decrease the latitude.

Increase the longitude.

The program starts a ship at location [32, –64], so if it heads southeast, the ship's new position will be [31, –63]. At least it will be *if the code works…*

BRAIN POWER

Look at the code carefully. Do you think it will work? Why? Why not?

Test Drive

We be becalmed, cap'n!
Arr! We be writin' a bad Amazon review!

The code should move the ship southeast from [32, –64] to the new location at [31, –63]. But if you compile and run the program, this happens:

WTF? The ship is still in the same place.

Where's The Fightin'?

```
File Edit Window Help Savvy?
> gcc southeast.c -o southeast
> ./southeast
Avast! Now at: [32, -64]
>
```

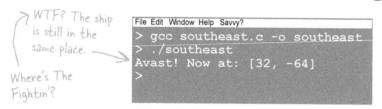

The ship's location stays *exactly* the same as before.

C sends arguments as values

The code broke because of the way that C calls functions.

1. Initially, the `main()` function has a local variable called `latitude` that had value 32.

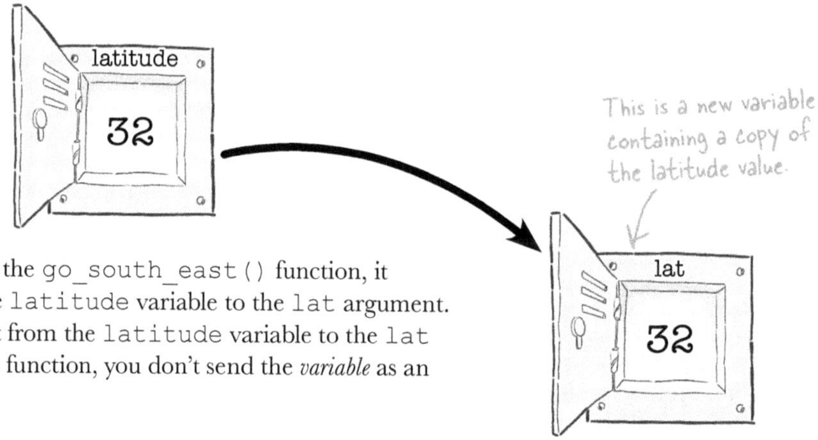
latitude
32
This is a new variable containing a copy of the latitude value.
lat
32

2. When the computer calls the `go_south_east()` function, it **copies the value** of the `latitude` variable to the `lat` argument. This is just an assignment from the `latitude` variable to the `lat` variable. When you call a function, you don't send the *variable* as an argument, just its *value.*

3. When the `go_south_east()` function changes the value of `lat`, the function is just changing its local copy. That means when the computer returns to the `main()` function, the `latitude` variable still has its original value of 32.

Only the local copy gets changed.
The original variable keeps its original value.
lat
32
31
latitude
32

But if that's how C calls functions, how can you ever write a function that updates a variable?

It's easy if you use pointers...

Try passing a pointer to the variable

Instead of passing the *value* of the `latitude` and `longitude` variables, what happens if you pass their *addresses*? If the `longitude` variable lives in the stack memory at location 4,100,000, what happens if you pass the location number 4,100,000 as a parameter to the `go_south_east()` function?

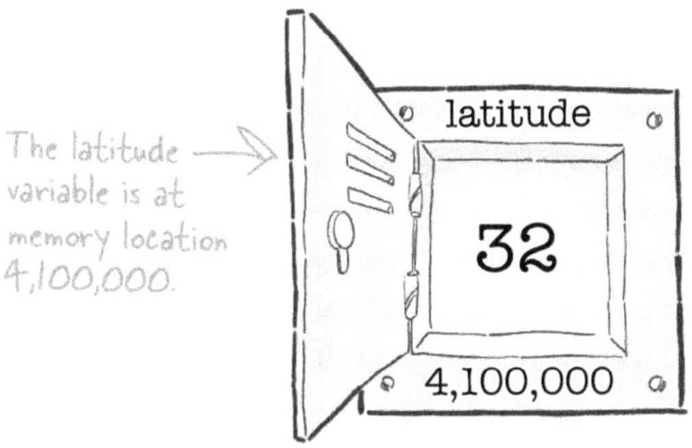
The latitude variable is at memory location 4,100,000.
latitude
32
4,100,000

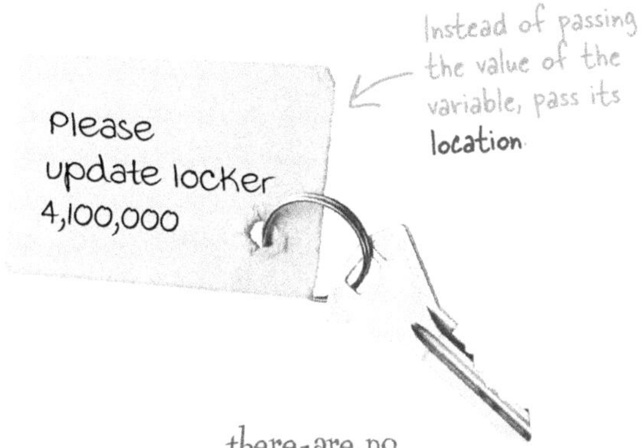
Please update locker 4,100,000
Instead of passing the value of the variable, pass its location.

If the `go_south_east()` function is told that the `latitude` value lives at location 4,100,000, then it will not only be able to find the current `latitude` value, but it will also be able to change the contents of the original `latitude` variable. All the function needs to do is read and update the contents of memory location 4,100,000.

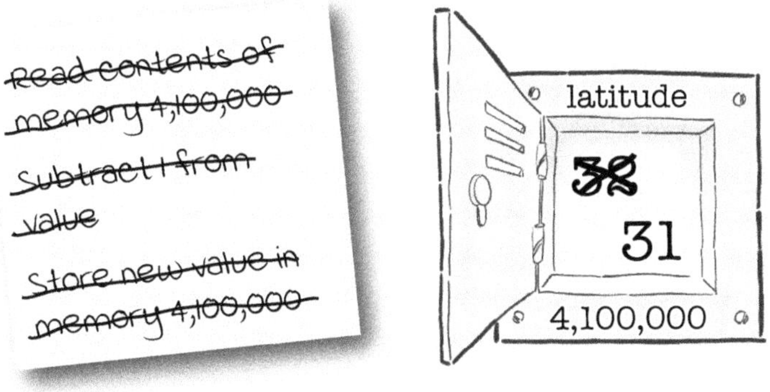
~~Read contents of memory 4,100,000~~
~~Subtract 1 from value~~
~~Store new value in memory 4,100,000~~
latitude
~~32~~
31
4,100,000

Because the `go_south_east()` function is updating the original `latitude` variable, the computer will be able to print out the updated location when it returns to the `main()` function.

Pointers make it easier to share memory

This is one of the main reasons for using pointers—to let functions *share* memory. The data created by one function can be modified by another function, so long as it knows where to find it in memory.

Now that you know the theory of using pointers to fix the `go_south_east()` function, it's time to look at the details of how you do it.

there are no Dumb Questions

Q: I printed the location of the variable on my machine and it wasn't 4,100,000. Did I do something wrong?

A: You did nothing wrong. The memory location your program uses for the variables will be different from machine to machine.

Q: Why are local variables stored in the stack and globals stored somewhere else?

A: Local and global variables are used differently. You will only ever get one copy of a global variable, but if you write a function that calls itself, you might get very many instances of the same local variable.

Q: What are the other areas of the memory used for?

A: You'll see what the other areas are for as you go through the rest of the book.

Using memory pointers

There are **three** things you need to know in order to use pointers to read and write data.

1 **Get the address of a variable.**

You've already seen that you can find where a variable is stored in memory using the **&** operator:

The %p format will print out the location in **hex** (base 16) format.

```
int x = 4;
printf("x lives at %p\n", &x);
```

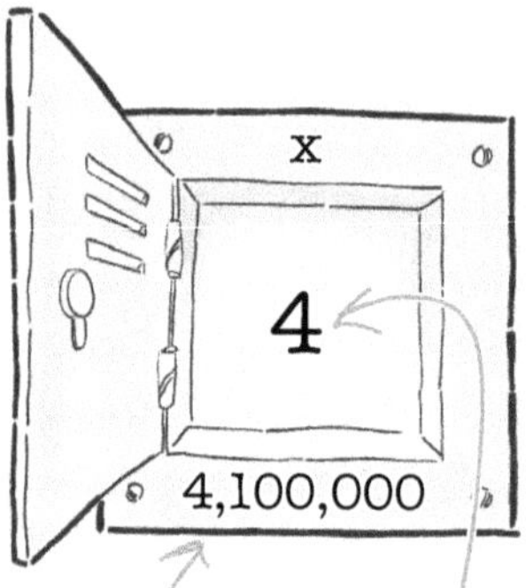
x
4
4,100,000

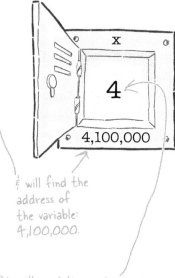

& will find the address of the variable: 4,100,000.

But once you've got the address of a variable, you may want to store it somewhere. To do that, you will need a **pointer variable**. A pointer variable is just a variable that stores a memory address. When you declare a pointer variable, you need to say what kind of data is stored at the address it will point to:

This is a pointer variable for an address that stores an int.

```
int *address_of_x = &x;
```

2 **Read the contents of an address.**

When you have a memory address, you will want to read the data that's stored there. You do that with the ***** operator:

```
int value_stored = *address_of_x;
```

This will read the contents at the memory address given by address_of_x. This will be set to 4: the value originally stored in the x variable.

The * and & operators are opposites. The & operator takes a piece of data and tells you where it's stored. The * operator takes an address and tells you what's stored there. Because pointers are sometimes called *references*, the * operator is said to **dereference** a pointer.

3 **Change the contents of an address.**

If you have a pointer variable and you want to change the data at the address where the variable's pointing, you can just use the * operator again. But this time you need to use it on the **left side** of an assignment:

```
*address_of_x = 99;
```

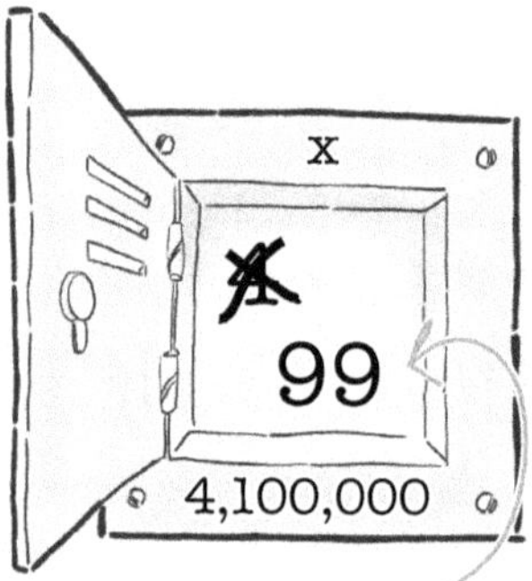
x
4
99
4,100,000

This will change the contents of the original x variable to 99.

OK, now that you know how to read and write the contents of a memory location, it's time for you to fix the go_south_east() function.

N
W
E
S

Compass Magnets

Now you need to fix the `go_south_east()` function so that it uses pointers to update the correct data. Think carefully about what type of data you want to pass to the function, and what operators you'll need to use to update the location of the ship.

```
#include <stdio.h>


void go_south_east(.............. lat, .............. lon)
{

  .............. = .............. - 1;

  .............. = .............. + 1;
}

int main()
{
  int latitude = 32;
  int longitude = -64;

  go_south_east(.............., ..............);
  printf("Avast! Now at: [%i, %i]\n", latitude, longitude);
  return 0;
}
```

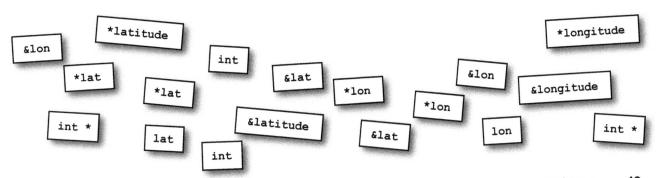

What kinds of arguments will store memory addresses for ints?

*Remember: you're going to pass the **addresses** of variables.*

`&lon` `*latitude` `*lat` `int *` `*lat` `lat` `int` `int` `&latitude` `&lat` `*lon` `&lat` `*lon` `&lon` `lon` `*longitude` `&longitude` `int *`

Compass Magnets Solution

You needed to fix the `go_south_east()` function so that it uses pointers to update the correct data. You were to think carefully about what type of data you want to pass to the function, and what operators you'll need to use to update the location of the ship.

```
#include <stdio.h>

void go_south_east(int * lat, int * lon)
{
  *lat = *lat - 1;
  *lon = *lon + 1;
}

int main()
{
  int latitude = 32;
  int longitude = -64;

  go_south_east(&latitude, &longitude);
  printf("Avast! Now at: [%i, %i]\n", latitude, longitude);
  return 0;
}
```

*The arguments will store pointers so they need to be int *.*

**lat can read the old value and set the new value.*

You need to find the address of the latitude and longitude variables with &.

&lon   *latitude   int   &lat   &lon   *longitude   lat   int   &lat   lon

Test Drive

Now if you compile and run the *new* version of the function, you get this:

This is southeast of the original location.

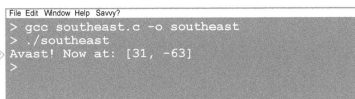

```
File Edit Window Help Savvy?
> gcc southeast.c -o southeast
> ./southeast
Avast! Now at: [31, -63]
>
```

Wind in the sails, cap'n!
Set sail for Cancun!
Arr! Spring break!

The code works.

Because the function takes pointer arguments, it's able to update the original `latitude` and `longitude` variables. That means that you now know how to create functions that not only return values, but can also update any memory locations that are passed to them.

BULLET POINTS

- Variables are allocated storage in memory.
- Local variables live in the stack.
- Global variables live in the globals section.
- Pointers are just variables that store memory addresses.
- The `&` operator finds the address of a variable.
- The `*` operator can read the contents of a memory address.
- The `*` operator can also set the contents of a memory address.

there are no Dumb Questions

Q: Are pointers actual address locations? Or are they some other kind of reference?

A: They're actual numeric addresses in the process's memory.

Q: What does that mean?

A: Each process is given a simplified version of memory to make it look like a single long sequence of bytes.

Q: And memory's not like that?

A: It's more complicated in reality. But the details are hidden from the process so that the operating system can move the process around in memory, or unload it and reload it somewhere else.

Q: Is memory not just a long list of bytes?

A: The computer will probably structure its physical memory in a more complex way. The machine will typically group memory addresses into separate banks of memory chips.

Q: Do I need to understand this?

A: For most programs, you don't need to worry about the details of how the machine arranges its memory.

Q: Why do I have to print out pointers using the `%p` format string?

A: You don't have to use the `%p` string. On most modern machines, you can use `%li`—although the compiler may give you a warning if you do.

Q: Why does the `%p` format display the memory address in hex format?

A: It's the way engineers typically refer to memory addresses.

Q: If reading the contents of a memory location is called *dereferencing*, does that mean that pointers should be called *references*?

A: Sometimes coders will call pointers *references*, because they refer to a memory location. However, C++ programmers usually reserve the word *reference* for a slightly different concept in C++.

Q: Oh yeah, C++. Are we going to look at that?

A: No, this book looks at C only.

How do you pass a string to a function?

Cookies make you fat

You know how to pass simple values as arguments to functions, but what if you want to send something more complex to a function, like a string? If you remember from the last chapter, strings in C are actually arrays of characters. That means if you want to pass a string to a function, you can do it like this:

```
void fortune_cookie(char msg[])
{
  printf("Message reads: %s\n", msg);
}

char quote[] = "Cookies make you fat";
fortune_cookie(quote);
```

The function will be passed a char array.

The msg argument is defined like an array, but because you won't know how long the string will be, the msg argument doesn't include a length. That *seems* straightforward, but there's something a little strange going on...

Honey, who shrank the string?

C has an operator called **sizeof** that can tell you how many bytes of space something takes in memory. You can either call it with a data type or with a piece of data:

On most machines, this will return the value 4.

```
sizeof(int)
sizeof("Turtles!")
```

This will return 9, which is 8 characters plus the \0 end character.

But a strange thing happens if you look at the length of the string you've passed in the function:

```
void fortune_cookie(char msg[])
{
  printf("Message reads: %s\n", msg);
  printf("msg occupies %i bytes\n", sizeof(msg));
}
```

File Edit Window Help TakeAByte

```
> ./fortune_cookie
Message reads: Cookies make you fat
msg occupies 8 bytes
>
```

8??? And on some machines, this might even say 4! What gives?

Instead of displaying the full length of the string, the code returns just 4 or 8 bytes. What's happened? Why does it think the string we passed in is shorter?

BRAIN POWER

Why do you think sizeof(msg) is shorter than the length of the whole string? What is msg? Why would it return different sizes on different machines?

Array variables are like pointers...

When you create an array, the array variable can be used as a **pointer** to the start of the array in memory. When C sees a line of code in a function like this:

```
char quote[] = "Cookies make you fat";
```

The quote variable will represent the address of the first character in the string.

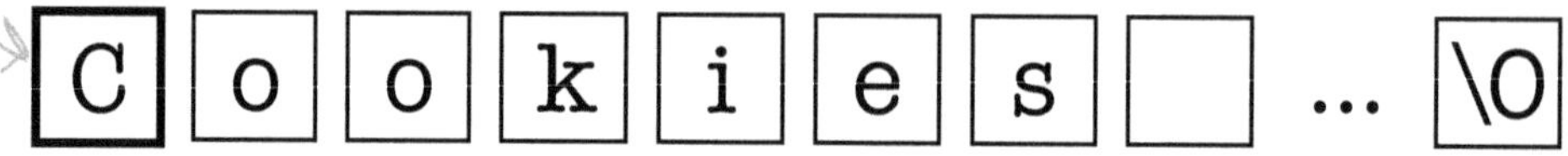
C
o
o
k
i
e
s
...
\0

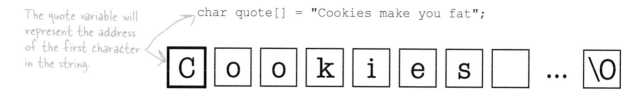

The computer will set aside space on the stack for each of the characters in the string, plus the `\0` end character. But it will also associate the **address of the first character** with the `quote` variable. Every time the `quote` variable is used in the code, the computer will substitute it with the address of the first character in the string. In fact, the array variable is *just like a pointer*:

```
printf("The quote string is stored at: %p\n", quote);
```

You can use "quote" as a pointer variable, even though it's an array.

If you write a test program to display the address, you will see something like this.

```
File Edit Window Help TakeAByte
> ./where_is_quote
The quote string is stored at: 0x7fff69d4bdd7
>
```

...so our function was passed a pointer

That's why that weird thing happened in the `fortune_cookie()` code. Even though it looked like you were passing a string to the `fortune_cookie()` function, you were actually just passing a pointer to it:

```
void fortune_cookie(char msg[])
{
  printf("Message reads: %s\n", msg);
  printf("msg occupies %i bytes\n", sizeof(msg));
}
```

msg is actually a pointer variable.

msg **points** to the message.

sizeof(msg) is just the size of a **pointer**.

And that's why the `sizeof` operator returned a weird result. It was just returning the size of a **pointer to a string**. On 32-bit operating systems, a pointer takes 4 bytes of memory and on 64-bit operating systems, a pointer takes 8 bytes.

What the computer thinks when it runs your code

1 The computer sees the function.

```
void fortune_cookie(char msg[])
{
  ...
}
```

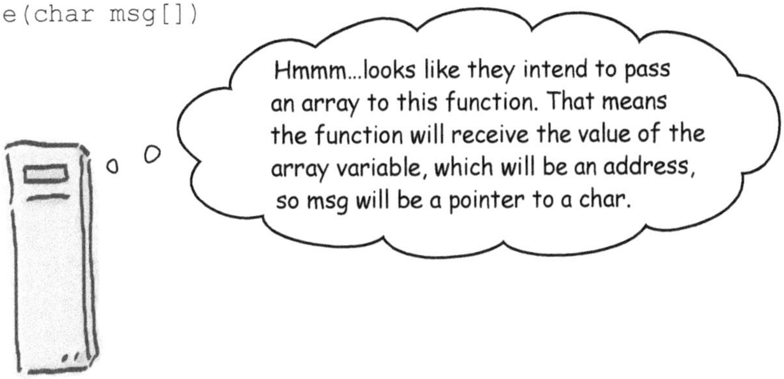
Hmmm...looks like they intend to pass an array to this function. That means the function will receive the value of the array variable, which will be an address, so msg will be a pointer to a char.

2 Then it sees the function contents.

```
printf("Message reads: %s\n", msg);
printf("msg occupies %i bytes\n", sizeof(msg));
```

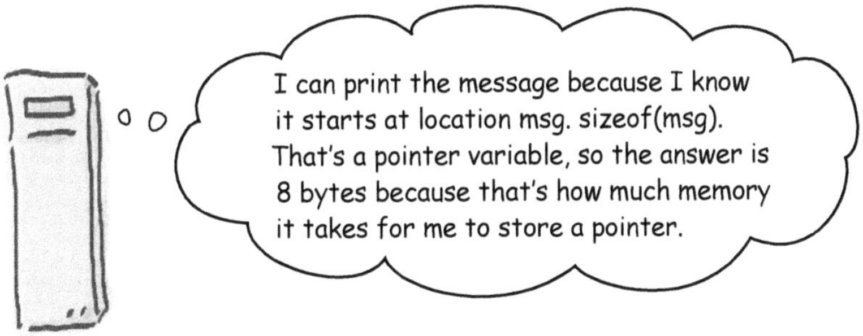
I can print the message because I know it starts at location msg. sizeof(msg). That's a pointer variable, so the answer is 8 bytes because that's how much memory it takes for me to store a pointer.

3 The computer calls the function.

```
char quote[] = "Cookies make you fat";
fortune_cookie(quote);
```

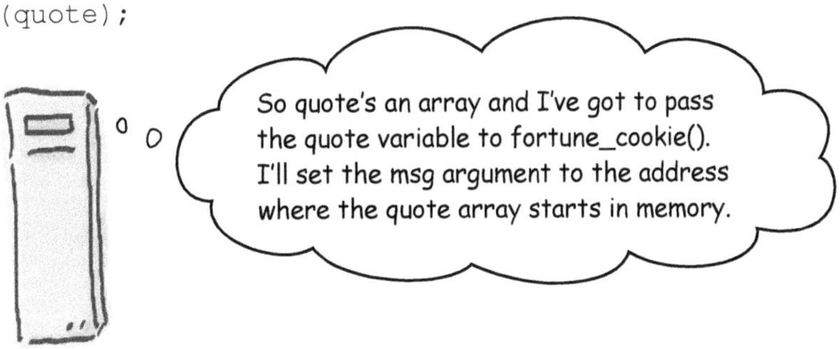
So quote's an array and I've got to pass the quote variable to fortune_cookie(). I'll set the msg argument to the address where the quote array starts in memory.

BULLET POINTS

- An array variable can be used as a pointer.
- The array variable points to the first element in the array.
- If you declare an array argument to a function, it will be treated as a pointer.
- The `sizeof` operator returns the space taken by a piece of data.
- You can also call `sizeof` for a data type, such as `sizeof(int)`.
- `sizeof(a pointer)` returns 4 on 32-bit operating systems and 8 on 64-bit.

there are no Dumb Questions

Q: Is `sizeof` a function?

A: No, it's an operator.

Q: What's the difference?

A: An operator is compiled to a sequence of instructions by the compiler. But if the code calls a function, it has to jump to a separate piece of code.

Q: So is `sizeof` calculated when the program is compiled?

A: Yes. The compiler can determine the size of the storage at compile time.

Q: Why are pointers different sizes on different machines?

A: On 32-bit operating systems, a memory address is stored as a 32-bit number. That's why it's called a 32-bit system. 32 bits == 4 bytes. That's why a 64-bit system uses 8 bytes to store an address.

Q: If I create a pointer variable, does the pointer variable live in memory?

A: Yes. A pointer variable is just a variable storing a number.

Q: So can I find the address of a pointer variable?

A: Yes—using the `&` operator.

Q: Can I convert a pointer to an ordinary number?

A: On most systems, yes. C compilers typically make the long data type the same size as a memory address. So if `p` is a pointer and you want to store it in a `long` variable `a`, you can type `a = (long)p`. We'll look at this in a later chapter.

Q: On *most* systems? So it's not guaranteed?

A: It's not guaranteed.

The Mating Game

We have a classic trio of bachelors ready to play *The Mating Game* today.

Tonight's lucky lady is going to pick one of these fine contestants. Who will she choose?

Contestant 1
Contestant 2
Contestant 3
I'm going to pick contestant number ....
Look at the code below, and write your answer here.

```
#include <stdio.h>

int main()
{
  int contestants[] = {1, 2, 3};
  int *choice = contestants;
  contestants[0] = 2;
  contestants[1] = contestants[2];
  contestants[2] = *choice;
  printf("I'm going to pick contestant number %i\n", contestants[2]);
  return 0;
}
```

The Mating Game Solution

We had a classic trio of bachelors ready to play *The Mating Game* today.

Tonight's lucky lady picked one of these fine contestants. Who did she choose?

Contestant 1
Contestant 2
Contestant 3
I'm going to pick contestant number
2

```
#include <stdio.h>

int main()
{
  int contestants[] = {1, 2, 3};
  int *choice = contestants;
  contestants[0] = 2;
  contestants[1] = contestants[2];
  contestants[2] = *choice;
  printf("I'm going to pick contestant number %i\n", contestants[2]);
  return 0;
}
```

"choice" is now the address of the "contestants" array.

contestants[2]
== *choice
== contestants[0]
== 2

But array variables aren't quite pointers

Even though you can use an array variable as a pointer, there are still a few differences. To see the differences, think about this piece of code.

```
char s[] = "How big is it?";
char *t = s;
```

1. **`sizeof(an array)` is...the size of an array.**
You've seen that `sizeof(a pointer)` returns the value 4 or 8, because that's the size of pointers on 32- and 64-bit systems. But if you call `sizeof` on an array variable, C is smart enough to understand that what you want to know is **how big the array is in memory**.

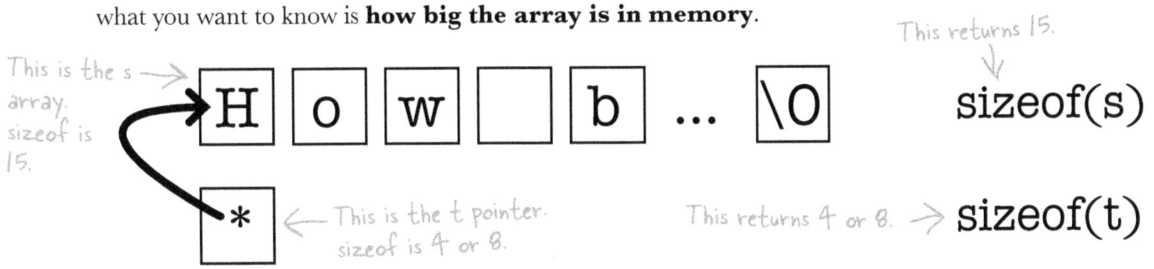

This is the s array. sizeof is 15.
H
o
w
b
...
\0
*
This is the t pointer. sizeof is 4 or 8.
This returns 15.
sizeof(s)
This returns 4 or 8.
sizeof(t)

2. **The address of the array...is the address of the array.**
A pointer variable is just a variable that stores a memory address. But what about an array variable? If you use the & operator on an array variable, the result equals the array variable itself.

&s == s **&t != t**

If a coder writes `&s`, that means "What is the address of the `s` array?" The address of the `s` array is just...`s`. But if someone writes `&t`, that means "What is the address of the `t` variable?"

3. **An array variable can't point anywhere else.**
When you create a pointer variable, the machine will allocate 4 or 8 bytes of space to store it. But what if you create an array? The computer will allocate space to store the array, but it won't allocate *any* memory to store the array variable. The compiler simply plugs in the address of the start of the array.

But because array variables don't have allocated storage, it means you can't point them at anything else.

This will give a compile error. →
```
s = t;
```

Pointer decay

Because array variables are slightly different from pointer variables, you need to be careful when you assign arrays to pointers. If you assign an array to a pointer variable, then the pointer variable will only contain the **address** of the array. The pointer doesn't know anything about the size of the array, so a little information has been lost. That loss of information is called **decay**.

Every time you pass an array to a function, you'll decay to a pointer, so it's unavoidable. But you need to keep track of where arrays decay in your code because it can cause very subtle bugs.

The Case of the Lethal List

The mansion had all the things he'd dreamed of: landscaped grounds, chandeliers, its own bathroom. The 94-year-old owner, Amory Mumford III, had been found dead in the garden, apparently of a heart attack. Natural causes? The doc thought it was an overdose of heart medication. Something stank here, and it wasn't just the dead guy in the gazebo. Walking past the cops in the hall, he approached Mumford's newly widowed 27-year-old wife, Bubbles.

Five-Minute
Mystery

"I don't understand. He was always so careful with his medication. Here's the list of doses." She showed him the code from the drug dispenser.

```
int doses[] = {1, 3, 2, 1000};
```

"The police say I reprogrammed the dispenser. But I'm no good with technology. They say I wrote this code, but I don't even think it'll compile. Will it?"

She slipped her manicured fingers into her purse and handed him a copy of the program the police had found lying by the millionaire's bed. It certainly didn't look like it would compile…

```
printf("Issue dose %i", 3[doses]);
```

What did the expression `3[doses]` mean? 3 wasn't an array. Bubbles blew her nose. "I could never write that. And anyway, a dose of 3 is not so bad, is it?"

A dose of size 3 wouldn't have killed the old guy. But maybe there was more to this code than met the eye…

Why arrays <u>really</u> start at 0

An array variable can be used as a pointer to the first element in an array. That means you can read the first element of the array either by using the brackets notation *or* using the * operator like this:

```
int drinks[] = {4, 2, 3};
printf("1st order: %i drinks\n", drinks[0]);
printf("1st order: %i drinks\n", *drinks);
```

These lines of code are equivalent.

drinks[0] == *drinks

But because an address is just a number, that means you can do **pointer arithmetic** and actually ***add*** values to a pointer value and find the next address. So you can either use brackets to read the element with index 2, or you can just add 2 to the address of the first element:

```
printf("3rd order: %i drinks\n", drinks[2]);
printf("3rd order: %i drinks\n", *(drinks + 2));
```

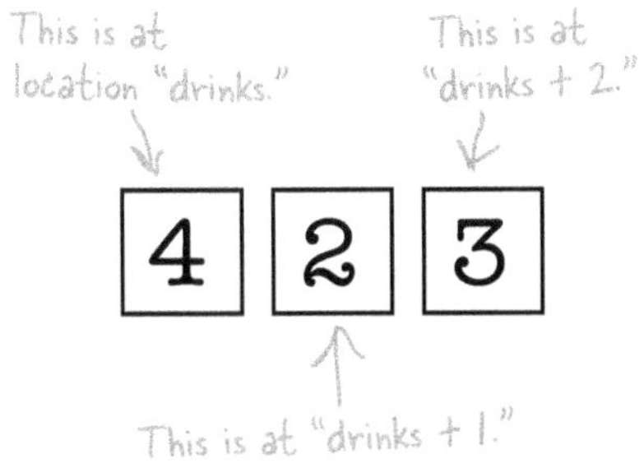
This is at location "drinks."
This is at "drinks + 2."
4
2
3
This is at "drinks + 1."

In general, the two expressions `drinks[i]` and `*(drinks + i)` are equivalent. That's why arrays begin with index 0. The index is just the number that's added to the pointer to find the location of the element.

Sharpen your pencil

Use the power of pointer arithmetic to mend a broken heart. This function will skip the first six characters of the text message.

```
void skip(char *msg)
{
  puts(.........................);
}

char *msg_from_amy = "Don't call me";
skip(msg_from_amy);
```

What expression do you need here to print from the seventh character?

The function needs to print this message from the 'c' character on.

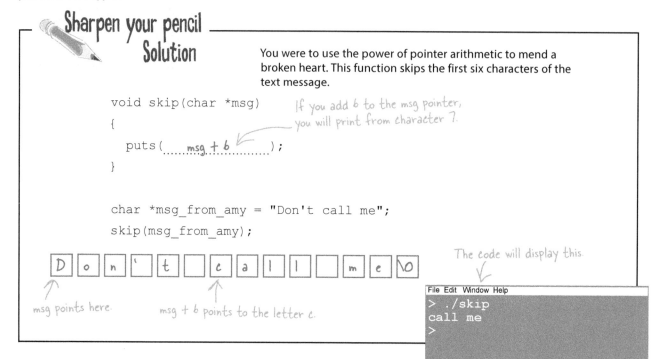

Sharpen your pencil Solution

You were to use the power of pointer arithmetic to mend a broken heart. This function skips the first six characters of the text message.

```
void skip(char *msg)
{
  puts( msg + 6 );
}

char *msg_from_amy = "Don't call me";
skip(msg_from_amy);
```

If you add 6 to the msg pointer, you will print from character 7.

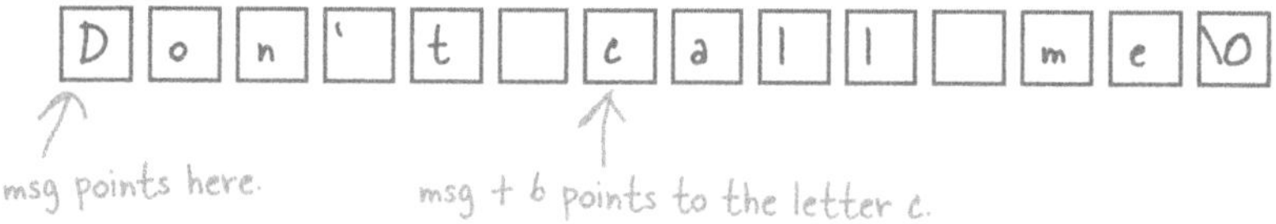

D
o
n
'
t
c
a
l
l
m
e
\0
msg points here.
msg + 6 points to the letter c.

The code will display this.

```
File Edit Window Help
> ./skip
call me
>
```

Why pointers have types

If pointers are just addresses, then why do pointer variables have types? Why can't you just store all pointers in some sort of general pointer variable?

The reason is that pointer arithmetic is *sneaky*. If you add **1** to a `char` pointer, the pointer will point to the very next memory address. But that's just because a `char` occupies **1 byte of memory**.

What if you have an `int` pointer? `int`s usually take 4 bytes of space, so if you add 1 to an `int` pointer, the compiled code will actually add 4 to the memory address.

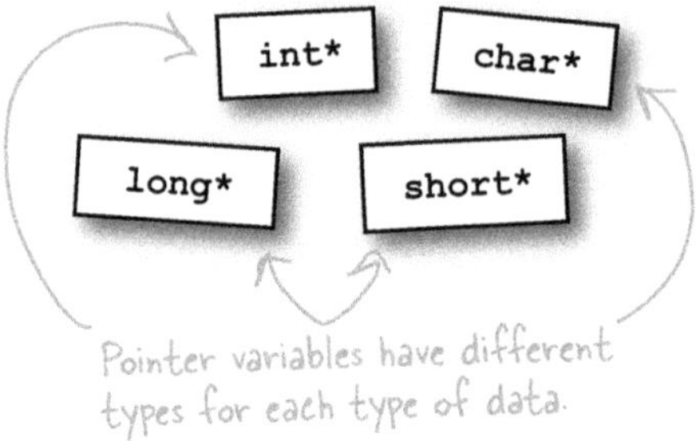

int*
char*
long*
short*
Pointer variables have different types for each type of data.


```
int nums[] = {1, 2, 3};
printf("nums is at %p\n", nums);
printf("nums + 1 is at %p\n", nums + 1);
```

If you run this code, the two memory address will be *more* than one byte apart. So pointer types exist so that **the compiler knows how much to adjust the pointer arithmetic**.

(nums + 1) is 4 bytes away from nums.

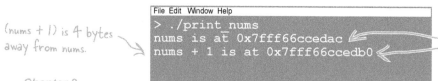

```
File Edit Window Help
> ./print_nums
nums is at 0x7fff66ccedac
nums + 1 is at 0x7fff66ccedb0
```

Remember, these addresses are printed in **hex** format.

The Case of the Lethal List

Last time we left our hero interviewing Bubbles Mumford, whose husband had been given an overdose as a result of suspicious code. Was Bubbles the coding culprit or just a patsy? To find out, read on...

He put the code into his pocket. "It's been a pleasure, Mrs. Mumford. I don't think I need to bother you anymore." He shook her by the hand. "Thank you," she said, wiping the tears from her baby blue eyes, "You've been so kind."

Five-Minute
Mystery
Solved

"Not so fast, sister." Bubbles barely had time to gasp before he'd slapped the bracelets on her. "I can tell from your hacker manicure that you know more than you say about this crime." No one gets fingertip calluses like hers without logging plenty of time on the keyboard.

"Bubbles, you know a lot more about C than you let on. Take a look at this code again."

```
int doses[] = {1, 3, 2, 1000};
printf("Issue dose %i", 3[doses]);
```

"I knew something was wrong when I saw the expression `3[doses]`. You knew you could use an array variable like `doses` as a pointer. The fatal 1,000 dose could be written down like this..." He scribbled down a few coding options on his second-best Kleenex:

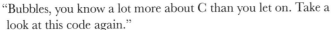

```
doses[3] == *(doses + 3) == *(3 + doses) == 3[doses]
```

"Your code was a dead giveaway, sister. It issued a dose of 1,000 to the old guy. And now you're going where you can never corruptly use C syntax again..."

BULLET POINTS

- Array variables can be used as pointers...
- ...but array variables are not quite the same.
- `sizeof` is different for array and pointer variables.
- Array variables can't point to anything else.
- Passing an array variable to a pointer decays it.
- Arrays start at zero because of pointer arithmetic.
- Pointer variables have types so they can adjust pointer arithmetic.

there are no Dumb Questions

Q: Do I really need to understand pointer arithmetic?

A: Some coders avoid using pointer arithmetic because it's easy to get it wrong. But it can be used to process arrays of data efficiently.

Q: Can I subtract numbers from pointers?

A: Yes. But be careful that you don't go back before the start of the allocated space in the array.

Q: When does C adjust the pointer arithmetic calculations?

A: It happens when the compiler is generating the executable. It looks at the type of the variable and then multiplies the pluses and minuses by the size of the underlying variable.

Q: Go on...

A: If the compiler sees that you are working with an `int` array and you are adding 2, the compiler will multiply that by 4 (the length of an `int`) and add 8.

Q: Does C use the `sizeof` operator when it is adjusting pointer arithmetic?

A: Effectively. The `sizeof` operator is also resolved at compile time, and both `sizeof` and the pointer arithmetic operations will use the same sizes for different data types.

Q: Can I multiply pointers?

A: No.

Using pointers for data entry

You already know how to get the user to enter a string from the keyboard. You can do it with the `scanf()` function:

You're going to store a name in this array.

```
char name[40];
printf("Enter your name: ");
scanf("%39s", name);
```

scanf will read up to 39 characters plus the string terminator \0.

How does `scanf()` work? It accepts a `char` pointer, and in this case you're passing it an array variable. By now, you might have an idea **why** it takes a pointer. It's because the `scanf()` function is going to *update* the contents of the array. Functions that need to update a variable don't want the value of the variable itself—they want its **address**.

Entering numbers with scanf()

So how do you enter data into a **numeric field**? You do it by passing a *pointer* to a number variable.

```
int age;
printf("Enter your age: ");
scanf("%i", &age);
```

%i means the user will enter an int value.

Use the & operator to get the address of the int.

Because you pass the address of a number variable into the function, `scanf()` can update the contents of the variable. And to help you out, you can pass a format string that contains the same kind of format codes that you pass to the `printf()` function. You can even use `scanf()` to enter more than one piece of information at a time:

`%i` ← Enter an integer.

`%29s` ← Enter up to 29 characters (+ '\0').

`%f` ← Enter a floating-point number.

```
char first_name[20];
char last_name[20];
printf("Enter first and last name: ");
scanf("%19s %19s", first_name, last_name);
printf("First: %s Last:%s\n", first_name, last_name);
```

This reads a first name, then a **space**, then the second name.

The first and last names are stored in separate arrays.

```
File Edit Window Help Meerkats
> ./name_test
Enter first and last name: Sanders Kleinfeld
First: Sanders Last: Kleinfeld
>
```

Be careful with scanf()

SECURITY ALERT!
SECURITY ALERT!
SECURITY ALERT!!

There's a little...problem with the `scanf()` function. So far, all of the code you've written has very carefully put a limit on the number of characters that `scanf()` will read into a function:

```
scanf("%39s", name);
```

```
scanf("%2s", card_name);
```

Why is that? After all, `scanf()` uses the same kind of format strings as `printf()`, but when we print a string with `printf()`, you just use `%s`. Well, if you just use `%s` in `scanf()`, there can be a problem if someone gets a little type-happy:

```
char food[5];
printf("Enter favorite food: ");
scanf("%s", food);
printf("Favorite food: %s\n", food);
```

```
File Edit Window Help TakeAByte
> ./food
Enter favorite food: liver-tangerine-raccoon-toffee
Favorite food: liver-tangerine-raccoon-toffee
Segmentation fault: 11
>
```

The program crashes. The reason is because `scanf()` writes data way beyond the end of the space allocated to the food array.

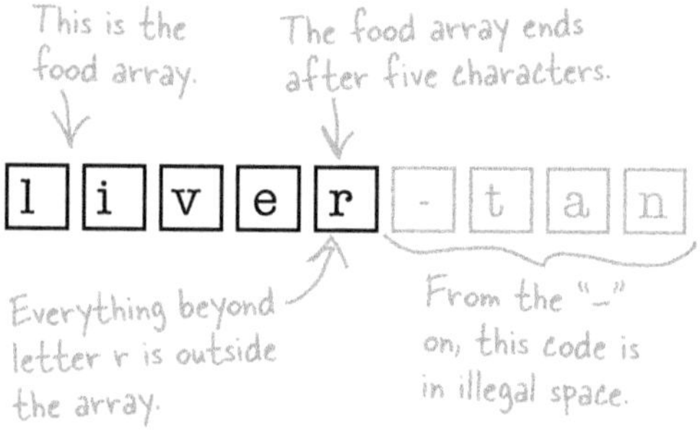
This is the food array.
The food array ends after five characters.
l i v e r - t a n
Everything beyond letter r is outside the array.
From the "-" on, this code is in illegal space.

scanf() can cause buffer overflows

If you forget to limit the length of the string that you read with `scanf()`, then any user can enter far more data than the program has space to store. The extra data then gets written into memory that has not been properly allocated by the computer. Now, you might get lucky and the data will simply be stored and not cause any problems.

But it's *very* likely that buffer overflows will cause bugs. It might be called a *segmentation fault* or an *abort trap*, but whatever the error message that appears, the result will be a ***crash***.

fgets() is an alternative to scanf()

There's another function you can use to enter text data: **fgets()**. Just like the `scanf()` function, it takes a `char` pointer, but *unlike* the `scanf()` function, the `fgets()` function must be given a maximum length:

This is the same program as before.

```
char food[5];
printf("Enter favorite food: ");
fgets(food, sizeof(food), stdin);
```

First, it takes a pointer to a buffer.

Next, it takes a maximum size of the string ('\0' included).

stdin just means the data will be coming from the keyboard.

You'll find out more about stdin later.

That means that you can't accidentally forget to set a length when you call `fgets()`; it's right there in the function signature as a mandatory argument. Also, notice that the `fgets()` buffer size **includes** the final `\0` character. So you don't need to subtract 1 from the length as you do with `scanf()`.

OK, what else do you need to know about fgets()?

Using sizeof with fgets()

The code above sets the maximum length using the `sizeof` operator. Be careful with this. Remember: `sizeof` returns the amount of space occupied by a variable. In the code above, `food` is an array variable, so `sizeof` returns the size of the array. If `food` was just a simple pointer variable, the `sizeof` operator would have just returned the size of a pointer.

If you know that you are passing an array variable to `fgets()` function, then using `sizeof` is fine. If you're just passing a simple pointer, you should just enter the size you want:

If food was a simple pointer, you'd give an explicit length, rather than using sizeof.

```
printf("Enter favorite food: ");
fgets(food, 5, stdin);
```

Tales from the Crypt

The fgets() function actually comes from an older function called gets().

Even though `fgets()` *is seen as a safer-to-use function than* `scanf()`*, the truth is that the older* `gets()` *function is far more dangerous than either of them. The reason? The* `gets()` *function has* ***no limits at all****:*

Noooooooo!!!!! Seriously, don't use this.

```
char dangerous[10];
gets(dangerous);
```

`gets()` *is a function that's been around for a long time. But all you really need to know is that you* ***really shouldn't use it****.*

Title Fight

Roll up! Roll up! It's time for the title fight we've all been waiting for. In the red corner: nimble light, flexible but oh-so-slightly dangerous. It's the bad boy of data input: `scanf()`. And in the blue corner, he's simple, he's safe, he's the function you'd want to introduce to your mom: it's `fgets()`!

Round 1: Limits

	scanf():	**fgets():**
Do you limit the number of characters that a user can enter?	`scanf()` can limit the data entered, so long as you remember to add the size to the format string.	`fgets()` has a mandatory limit. Nothing gets past him.

Result: fgets() takes this round on points.

Round 2: Multiple fields

	scanf():	**fgets():**
Can you be used to enter more than one field?	Yes! `scanf()` will not only allow you to enter more than one field, but it also allows you to enter **structured data** including the ability to specify what characters appear between fields.	Ouch! `fgets()` takes this one on the chin. `fgets()` allows you to enter just one string into a buffer. No other data types. Just strings. Just one buffer.

Result: scanf() clearly wins this round.

Round 3: Spaces in strings

	scanf():	**fgets():**
If someone enters a string, can it contain spaces?	Oof! `scanf()` gets hit badly by this one. When `scanf()` reads a string with the `%s`, it stops as soon as it hits a space. So if you want to enter more than one word, you either have to call it more than once, or use some fancy regular expression trick.	No problem with spaces at all. `fgets()` can read the whole string every time.

Result: A fightback! Round to fgets().

A good clean fight between these two feisty functions. Clearly, if you need to enter **structured data** with *several* fields, you'll want to use `scanf()`. If you're entering a **single unstructured string**, then `fgets()` is probably the way to go.

Anyone for three-card monte?

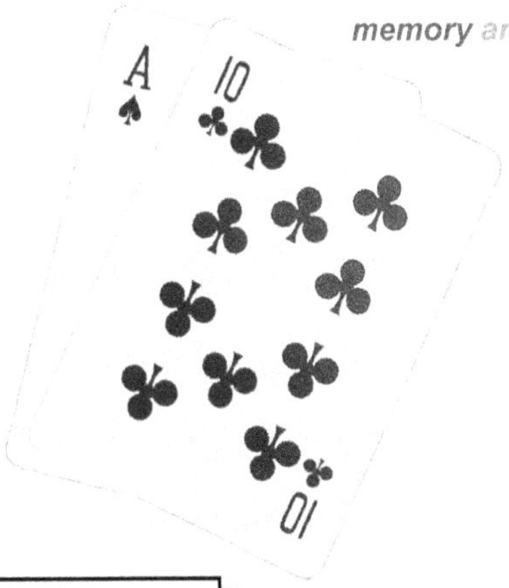

In the back room of the Head First Lounge, there's a game of three-card monte going on. Someone shuffles three cards around, and you have to watch carefully and decide where you think the Queen card went. Of course, being the Head First Lounge, they're not using real cards; they're using *code*. Here's the program they're using:

```
#include <stdio.h>

int main()
{
  char *cards = "JQK";
  char a_card = cards[2];
  cards[2] = cards[1];
  cards[1] = cards[0];
  cards[0] = cards[2];
  cards[2] = cards[1];
  cards[1] = a_card;
  puts(cards);
  return 0;
}
```

Find the Queen.

The code is designed to shuffle the letters in the three-letter string "JQK." Remember: in C, a string is just an array of characters. The program switches the characters around and then displays what the string looks like.

The players place their bets on where they think the "Q" letter will be, and then the code is compiled and run.

Oops...there's a memory problem...

It seems there's a problem with the card shark's code. When the code is compiled and run on the Lounge's notebook computer, this happens:

Darn it. I knew that card shark couldn't be trusted...

```
File Edit Window Help PlaceBet
> gcc monte.c -o monte && ./monte
bus error
```

What's more, if the guys try the same code on different machines and operating systems, they get a whole bunch of different errors:

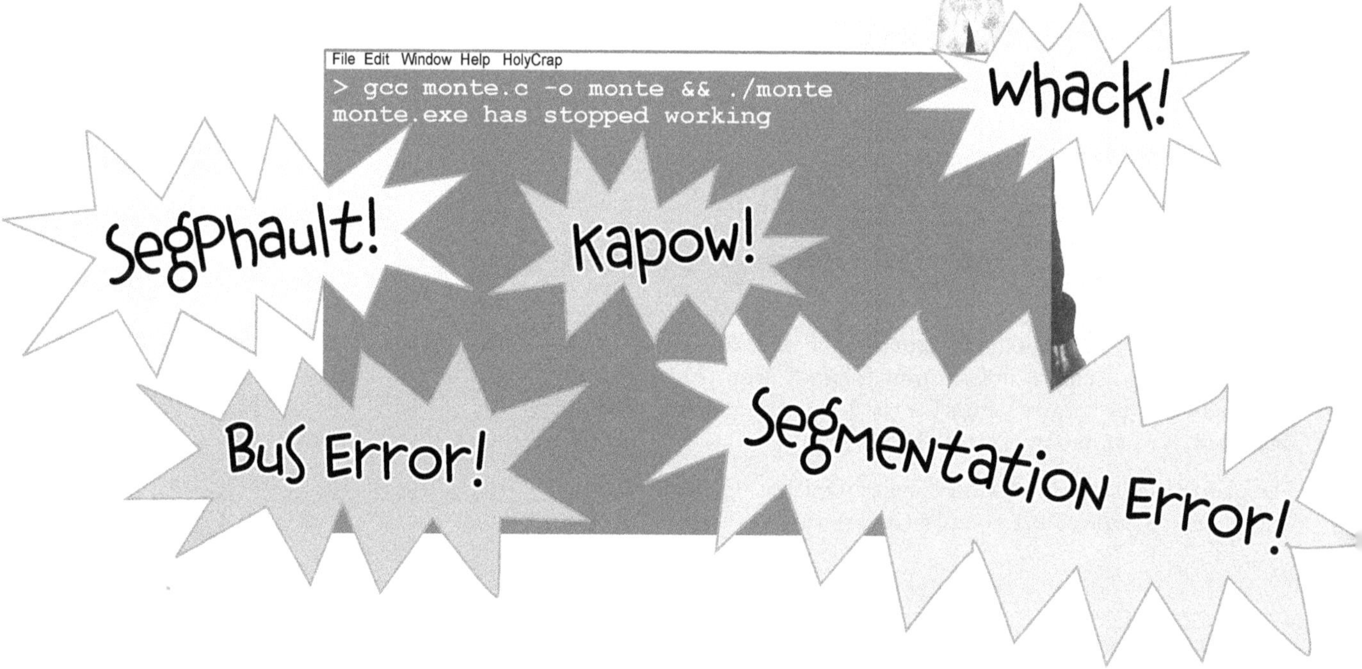
File Edit Window Help HolyCrap
> gcc monte.c -o monte && ./monte
monte.exe has stopped working
Whack!
SegPhault!
Kapow!
Bus Error!
Segmentation Error!

What's wrong with the code?

What's your hunch?

It's time to use your **intuition**. Don't overanalyze. Just **take a guess**. *Read* through these possible answers and select *only* the one you think is correct.

What do **you** think the problem is?

The string can't be updated.	
We're swapping characters outside the string.	
The string isn't in memory.	
Something else.	

What's your hunch? Solution

It was time to use your **intuition**. You were to read through these possible answers and select *only* the one you think is correct.

What did **you** think the problem was?

The string can't be updated.	✓
We're swapping characters outside the string.	
The string isn't in memory.	
Something else.	

String literals can never be updated

A variable that points to a string literal can't be used to change the contents of the string:

```
char *cards = "JQK";
```

← This variable can't modify this string.

But if you create an array from a string literal, then you **can** modify it:

```
char cards[] = "JQK";
```

It all comes down to how C uses memory...

In memory: char *cards="JQK";

To understand why this line of code causes a memory error, we need to dig into the memory of the computer and see exactly what the computer will do.

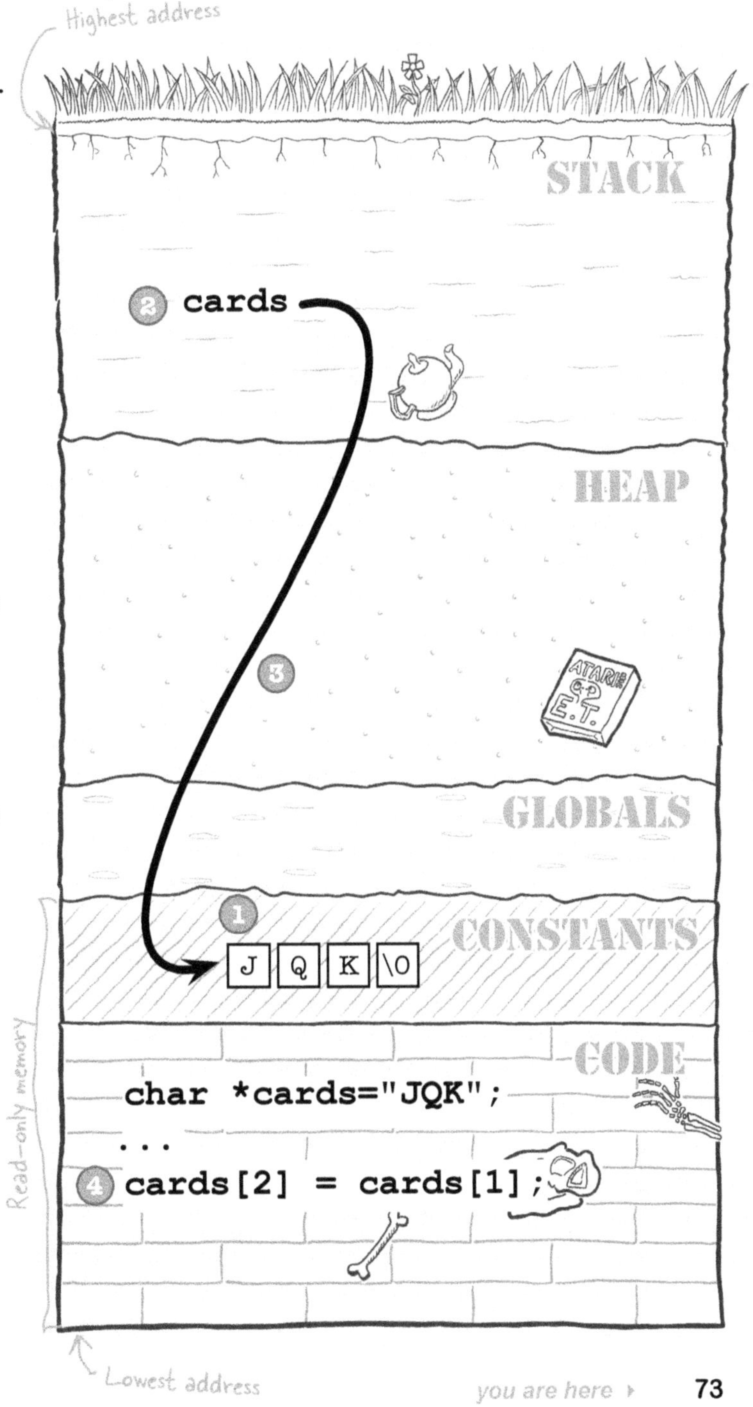
Highest address
STACK
2 cards
HEAP
3
GLOBALS
CONSTANTS
1
J Q K \0
CODE
char *cards="JQK";
...
4 cards[2] = cards[1];
Read-only memory
Lowest address

1. **The computer loads the string literal.**
When the computer loads the program into memory, it puts all of the constant values—like the string literal "JQK"—into the constant memory block. This section of memory is **read only**.

2. **The program creates the cards variable on the stack.**
The stack is the section of memory that the computer uses for local variables: variables inside functions. The cards variable will live here.

3. **The cards variable is set to the address of "JQK."**
The cards variable will contain the address of **the string literal "JQK**." String literals are usually stored in read-only memory to prevent anyone from changing them.

4. **The computer tries to change the string.**
When the program tries to change the contents of the string pointed to by the cards variable, it can't; the string is read-only.

I can't update that, buddy. It's in the constant memory block, so it's read-only.

So the problem is that string literals like "JQK" are held in read only memory. They're constants.

But if that's the problem, how do you fix it?

If you're going to change a string, make a copy

The truth is that if you want to change the contents of a string, you'll need to work on a ***copy***. If you create a copy of the string in an area of memory that's *not* read-only, there won't be a problem if you try to change the letters it contains.

But how do you make a copy? Well, just create the string as a *new array*.

```
char cards[] = "JQK";
```

← cards is not just a pointer. cards is now an **array**.

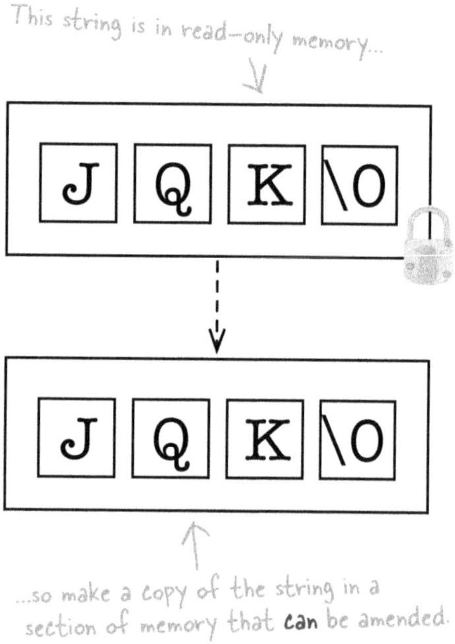

This string is in read-only memory...
J
Q
K
\0
J
Q
K
\0
...so make a copy of the string in a section of memory that **can** be amended.

It's probably not too clear why this changes anything. *All* strings are arrays. But in the old code, `cards` was just a *pointer*. In the new code, it's an ***array***. If you declare an array called `cards` and then set it to a string literal, the `cards` array will be a completely new copy. The variable isn't just *pointing* at the string literal. It's a brand-new array that contains a fresh ***copy*** of the string literal.

To see how this works in practice, you'll need to look at what happens in memory.

Geek Bits

cards[] or cards*?

If you see a declaration like this, what does it *really* mean?

```
char cards[]
```

Well, it **depends on where you see it**. If it's a normal variable declaration, then it means that `cards` is an array, and you have to set it to a value immediately:

```
int my_function()
{
  char cards[] = "JQK";
  ...
}
```

cards is an array. → `char cards[]`

There's no array size given, so you have to set it to something immediately.

But if cards is being declared as a *function argument*, it means that `cards` is a **pointer**:

```
void stack_deck(char cards[])
{
  ...
}
```

cards is a char pointer.

```
void stack_deck(char *cards)
{
  ...
}
```

These two functions are equivalent.

In memory: char cards[]="JQK";

We've already seen what happens with the *broken code*, but what about our new code? Let's take a look.

1. **The computer loads the string literal.** As before, when the computer loads the program into memory, it stores the constant values—like the string "JQK"—into read-only memory.

2. **The program creates a new array on the stack.** We're declaring an array, so the program will create one large enough to store the "JQK" string—four characters' worth.

3. **The program initializes the array.** But as well as allocating the space, the program will also **copy the contents** of the string literal "JQK" into the stack memory.

So the difference is that the original code used a pointer to point to a read-only string literal. But if you initialize an array with a string literal, you then have a *copy* of the letters, and you can change them as much as you like.

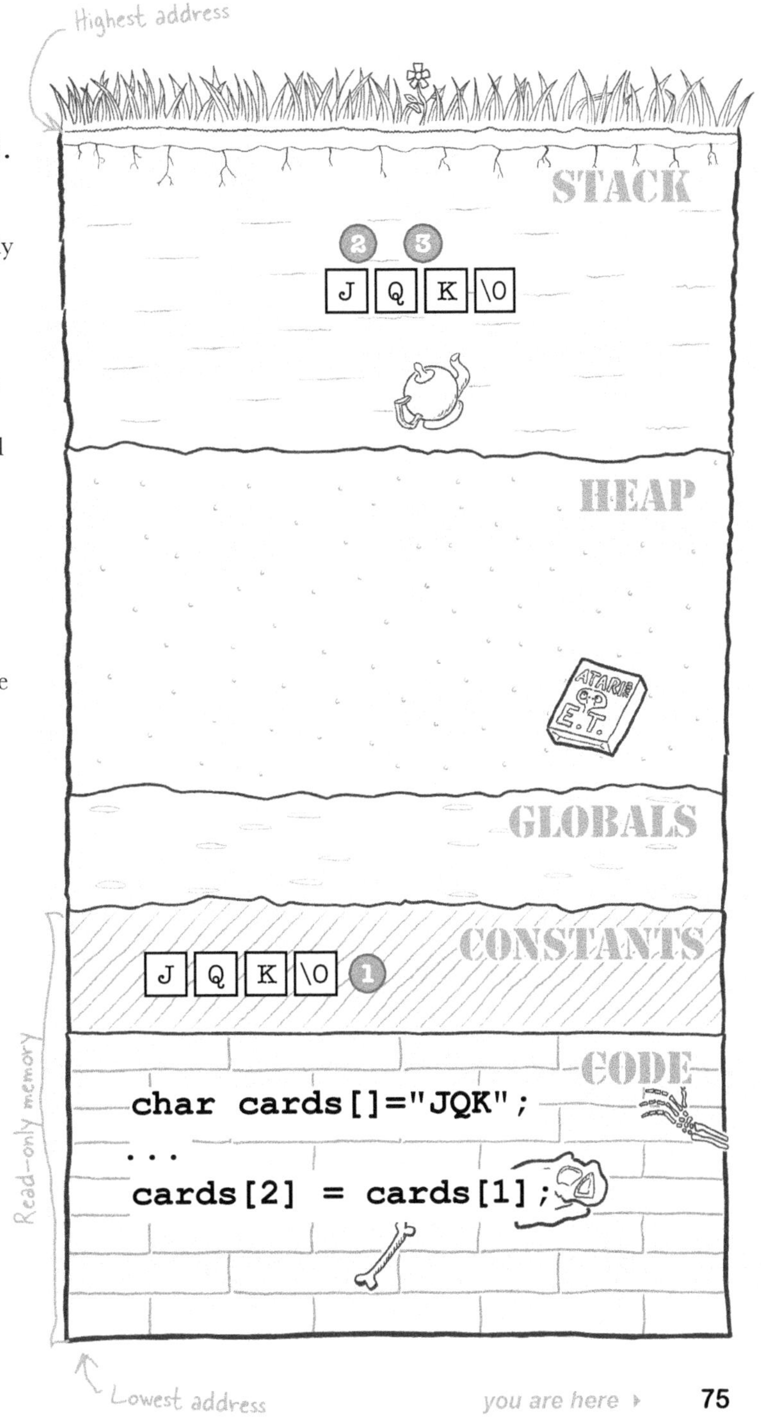
Highest address
STACK
2
3
J
Q
K
\0
HEAP
ATARI
E.T.
GLOBALS
CONSTANTS
J
Q
K
\0
1
CODE
char cards[]="JQK";
...
cards[2] = cards[1];
Read-only memory
Lowest address

Test Drive

See what happens if you construct a **new array** in the code.

```
#include <stdio.h>

int main()
{
  char cards[] = "JQK";
  char a_card = cards[2];
  cards[2] = cards[1];
  cards[1] = cards[0];
  cards[0] = cards[2];
  cards[2] = cards[1];
  cards[1] = a_card;
  puts(cards);
  return 0;
}
```

File Edit Window Help Where'sTheLady?

```
> gcc monte.c -o monte && ./monte
QKJ
```

Yes! The Queen was the first card. I knew it...

The code works! Your `cards` variable now points to a string in an unprotected section of memory, so we are free to modify its contents.

Geek Bits

One way to avoid this problem in the future is to never write code that sets a simple `char` pointer to a string literal value like:

```
char *s = "Some string";
```

There's nothing wrong with setting a pointer to a string literal—the problems only happen when you try to *modify* a string literal. Instead, if you want to set a pointer to a literal, always make sure you use the `const` keyword:

```
const char *s = "some string";
```

That way, if the compiler sees some code that tries to modify the string, it will give you a compile error:

```
s[0] = 'S';
monte.c:7: error: assignment of read-only location
```

The Case of the Magic Bullet

He was scanning his back catalog of *Guns 'n' Ammo* into Delicious Library when there was a knock at the door and she walked in: 5' 6", blonde, with a good laptop bag and cheap shoes. He could tell she was a code jockey. "You've gotta help me…you gotta clear his name! Jimmy was innocent, I tells you. Innocent!" He passed her a tissue to wipe the tears from her baby blues and led her to a seat.

It was the old story. She'd met a guy, who knew a guy. Jimmy Blomstein worked tables at the local Starbuzz and spent his weekends cycling and working on his taxidermy collection. He hoped one day to save up enough for an elephant. But he'd fallen in with the wrong crowd. The Masked Raider had met Jimmy in the morning for coffee and they'd both been alive:

```
char masked_raider[] = "Alive";
char *jimmy = masked_raider;
  printf("Masked raider is %s, Jimmy is %s\n", masked_raider,
    jimmy);
```

Five-Minute Mystery

```
File Edit Window Help
Masked raider is Alive, Jimmy is Alive
```

Then, that afternoon, the Masked Raider had gone off to pull a heist, like a hundred heists he'd pulled before. But this time, he hadn't reckoned on the crowd of G-Men enjoying their weekly three-card monte session in the back room of the Head First Lounge. You get the picture. A rattle of gunfire, a scream, and moments later the villain was lying on the sidewalk, creating a public health hazard:

```
masked_raider[0] = 'D';
masked_raider[1] = 'E';
masked_raider[2] = 'A';
masked_raider[3] = 'D';
masked_raider[4] = '!';
```

Problem is, when Toots here goes to check in with her boyfriend at the coffee shop, she's told he's served his last orange mocha frappuccino:

```
printf("Masked raider is %s, Jimmy is %s\n", masked_raider, jimmy);
```

```
File Edit Window Help
Masked raider is DEAD!, Jimmy is DEAD!
```

So what gives? How come a single magic bullet killed Jimmy and the Masked Raider? What do you think happened?

The Case of the Magic Bullet

How come a single magic bullet killed Jimmy and the Masked Raider?

Jimmy, the mild-mannered barista, was mysteriously gunned down at the same time as arch-fiend the Masked Raider:

```
#include <stdio.h>
int main()
{
  char masked_raider[] = "Alive";
  char *jimmy = masked_raider;
  printf("Masked raider is %s, Jimmy is %s\n", masked_raider, jimmy);
  masked_raider[0] = 'D';
  masked_raider[1] = 'E';
  masked_raider[2] = 'A';
  masked_raider[3] = 'D';
  masked_raider[4] = '!';
  printf("Masked raider is %s, Jimmy is %s\n", masked_raider, jimmy);
  return 0;
}
```

Note from Marketing: ditch the product placement for the Brain Booster drink; the deal fell through.

Five-Minute
Mystery
Solved

It took the detective a while to get to the bottom of the mystery. While he was waiting, he took a long refreshing sip from a Head First Brain Booster Fruit Beverage. He sat back in his seat and looked across the desk at her blue, blue eyes. She was like a rabbit caught in the headlights of an oncoming truck, and he knew that he was at the wheel.

"I'm afraid I got some bad news for you. Jimmy and the Masked Raider…were one and the same man!"

"No!"

She took a sharp intake of breath and raised her hand to her mouth. "Sorry, sister. I have to say it how I see it. Just look at the memory usage." He drew a diagram:

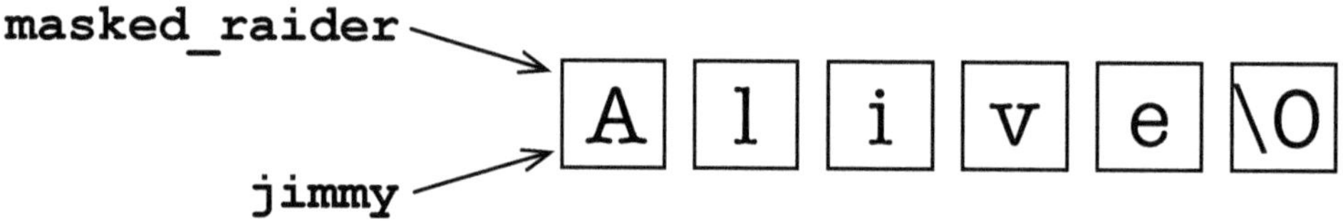
masked_raider
jimmy
A
l
i
v
e
\0

"`jimmy` and `masked_raider` are just aliases for the same memory address. They're pointing to the same place. When the `masked_raider` stopped the bullet, so did Jimmy. Add to that this invoice from the San Francisco elephant sanctuary and this order for 15 tons of packing material, and it's an open and shut case."

BULLET POINTS

- If you see a `*` in a variable declaration, it means the variable will be a pointer.
- String literals are stored in read-only memory.
- If you want to modify a string, you need to make a copy in a new array.
- You can declare a `char` pointer as `const char *` to prevent the code from using it to modify a string.

there are no Dumb Questions

Q: Why didn't the compiler just tell me I couldn't change the string?

A: Because we declared the `cards` as a simple `char *`, the compiler didn't know that the variable would always be pointing at a string literal.

Q: Why are string literals stored in read-only memory?

A: Because they are designed to be constant. If you write a function to print "Hello World," you don't want some other part of the program modifying the "Hello World" string literal.

Q: Do all operating systems enforce the read-only rule?

A: The vast majority do. Some versions of `gcc` on Cygwin actually allow you to modify a string literal without complaining. But it is *always* wrong to do that.

Q: What does `const` actually mean? Does it make the string read-only?

A: String literals are read-only anyway. The `const` modifier means that the compiler will complain if you try to modify an array with that particular variable.

Q: Do the different memory segments always appear in the same order in memory?

A: They will always appear in the same order for a given operating system. But different operating systems can vary the order slightly. For example, Windows doesn't place the code in the lowest memory addresses.

Q: I still don't understand why an array variable isn't stored in memory. If it exists, surely it lives somewhere?

A: When the program is compiled, all the references to array variables are replaced with the addresses of the array. So the truth is that the array variable won't exist in the final executable. That's OK because the array variable will never be needed to point anywhere else.

Q: If I set a new array to a string literal, will the program really copy the contents each time?

A: It's down to the compiler. The final machine code will either copy the bytes of the string literal to the array, or else the program will simply set the values of each character every time it reaches the declaration.

Q: You keep saying "declaration." What does that mean?

A: A *declaration* is a piece of code that declares that something (a variable, a function) exists. A definition is a piece of code that says what something is. If you declare a variable and set it to a value (e.g., `int x = 4;`), then the code is both a declaration and a definition.

Q: Why is `scanf()` called `scanf()`?

A: `scanf()` means "scan formatted" because it's used to scan formatted input.

Memory memorizer

Highest address
STACK
HEAP
ATARI E.T.
GLOBALS
CONSTANTS
Read-only memory
LINK A6, #VARSIZE
MOVEM.L D0-D7/A1-A5,-(SP)
MOVE.L SP, SAVESTK(A6)
MOVE.L SP, SAVEAS(A6)
MOVE.L GRAFGLOBALS(A5),A0
...
CODE
Lowest address

Stack

This is the section of memory used for **local variable storage**. Every time you call a function, all of the function's local variables get created on the stack. It's called the *stack* because it's like a stack of plates: variables get added to the stack when you enter a function, and get taken off the stack when you leave. Weird thing is, the stack actually works upside down. It starts at the top of memory and **grows downward**.

Heap

This is a section of memory we haven't really used yet. The heap is for **dynamic memory:** pieces of data that get created when the program is running and then hang around a long time. You'll see later in the book how you'll use the heap.

Globals

A global variable is a variable that lives outside all of the functions and is visible to all of them. Globals get created when the program first runs, and you can update them freely. But that's unlike…

Constants

Constants are *also* created when the program first runs, but they are stored in **read-only** memory. Constants are things like *string literals* that you will need when the program is running, but you'll never want them to change.

Code

Finally, the code segment. A lot of operating systems place the code right down in the lowest memory addresses. The code segment is also read-only. This is the part of the memory where the actual assembled code gets loaded.

Your C Toolbox

You've got Chapter 2 under your belt, and now you've added pointers and memory to your toolbox. For a complete list of tooltips in the book, see Appendix ii.

scanf("%i", &x) will allow a user to enter a number x directly.

ints are different sizes on different machines.

&x returns the address of x.

&x is called a pointer to x.

A char pointer variable x is declared as char *x.

String literals are stored in read-only memory.

Local variables are stored on the stack.

Initialize a new array with a string, and it will copy it.

Read the contents of an address a with *a.

Array variables can be used as pointers.

fgets(buf, size, stdin) is a simpler way to enter text.

2.5 strings

String theory

strcmp() says we're identical.
I thought it called you short and said your butt was bigger.

There's more to strings than reading them.

You've seen how strings in C are actually `char` *arrays* but what does C allow you to *do* with them? That's where ***string.h*** comes in. *string.h* is part of the C Standard Library that's dedicated to **string manipulation**. If you want to ***concatenate*** strings together, ***copy*** one string to another, or ***compare*** two strings, the functions in *string.h* are there to help. In this chapter, you'll see how to create an **array of strings**, and then take a close look at how to ***search within strings*** using the `strstr()` function.

Desperately seeking ~~Susan~~ Frank

There are so many tracks on the retro jukebox that people can't find the music they are looking for. To help the customers, the guys in the Head First Lounge want you to write another program.

This is the track list:

Tracks from the new album "Little Known Sinatra."

Track list:

I left my heart in Harvard med school

Newark, Newark - a wonderful town

Dancing with a Dork

From here to maternity

The girl from Iwo Jima

The guys say that there will be lots more tracks in the future, but they'll never be more than 79 characters long.

Gah! Wayne Newton... again! We need a search program to help people find tracks on the jukebox.

The list is likely to get longer, so there's just the first few tracks for now. You'll need to write a C program that will ask the user which track she is looking for, and then get it to search through all of the tracks and display any that match.

BRAIN POWER

There'll be lots of strings in this program. How do you think you can record that information in C?

Create an array of arrays

There are several track names that you need to record. You can record several things at once in an array. But remember: *each string is itself an array*. That means you need to create an array of arrays, like this:

This first set of brackets is for the array of **all** strings.

The second set of brackets is used for each individual string.

The compiler can tell that you have five strings, so you don't need a number between these brackets.

You know that track names will never get longer than 79 characters, so set the value to 80.

```
char tracks[][80] = {
  "I left my heart in Harvard Med School",
  "Newark, Newark - a wonderful town",
  "Dancing with a Dork",
  "From here to maternity",
  "The girl from Iwo Jima",
};
```

Each string is an array, so this is an array of arrays.

The array of arrays looks something like this in memory:

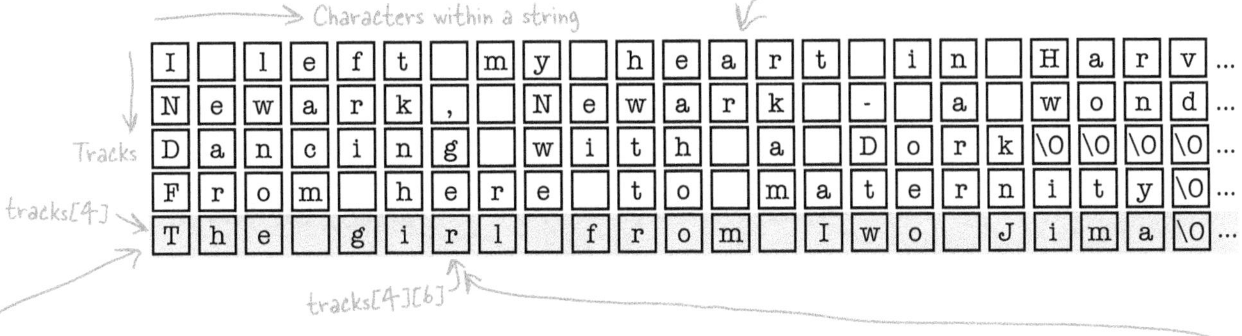

Each song title will be allocated 80 characters.
Characters within a string
Tracks
tracks[4]
tracks[4][6]
I left my heart in Harv...
Newark, Newark - a wond...
Dancing with a Dork\0\0\0\0...
From here to maternity\0...
The girl from Iwo Jima\0...

That means that you'll be able to find an individual track name like this:

This has this value. This is the **fifth** string. ← Remember: arrays begin at **zero**.

tracks[4] ⟶ "The girl from Iwo Jima"

But you can also read the individual characters of each of the strings if you want to:

tracks[4][6] ⟶ 'r' ← This is the **seventh** character in the **fifth** string.

So now that you know how to record the data in C, what do you need to do with it?

Find strings containing the search text

The guys have helpfully given you a spec.

> Ask the user for the text she's looking for.
>
> Loop through all of the track names.
>
> If a track name contains the search text, display the track name.

Well, you know how to record the tracks. You also know how to read the value of an individual track name, so it shouldn't be too difficult to loop through each of them. You even know how to ask the user for a piece of text to search for. But how do you look to see if the track name contains a given piece of text?

Using string.h

The **C Standard Library** is a bunch of useful code that you get for free when you install a C compiler. The library code does useful stuff like opening files, or doing math, or managing memory. Now, chances are, you won't want to use the *whole* of the Standard Library at once, so the library is broken up into several sections, and each one has a **header** file. The header file lists all of the functions that live in a particular section of the library.

So far, you have only really used the *stdio.h* header file. *stdio.h* lets you use the standard *input/output* functions like `printf` and `scanf`.

But the Standard Library also contains code to *process strings*. String processing is required by a lot of the programs, and the string code in the Standard Library is tested, stable, and fast.

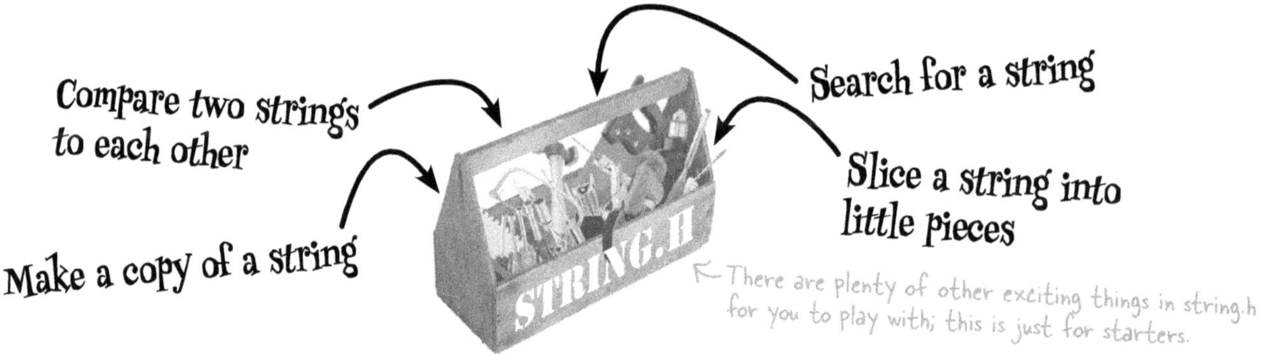

Compare two strings to each other
Search for a string
Slice a string into little pieces
Make a copy of a string
STRING.H
There are plenty of other exciting things in string.h for you to play with; this is just for starters.

You include the string code into your program using the ***string.h*** header file. You add it at the top of your program, just like you include *stdio.h*.

```
#include <stdio.h>
#include <string.h>
```

You'll use **both** stdio.h **and** string.h in your jukebox program.

What's my purpose?

See if you can match up each *string.h* function with the description of what it does.

strchr()	Concatenate two strings.
strcmp()	Find the location of a string inside another string.
strstr()	Find the location of a character inside a string.
strcpy()	Find the length of a string.
strlen()	Compare two strings.
strcat()	Copy one string to another.

Sharpen your pencil

Which of the functions above should you use for the jukebox program? Write your answer below.

....

What's My Purpose? Solution

You were to match up each *string.h* function with the description of what it does.

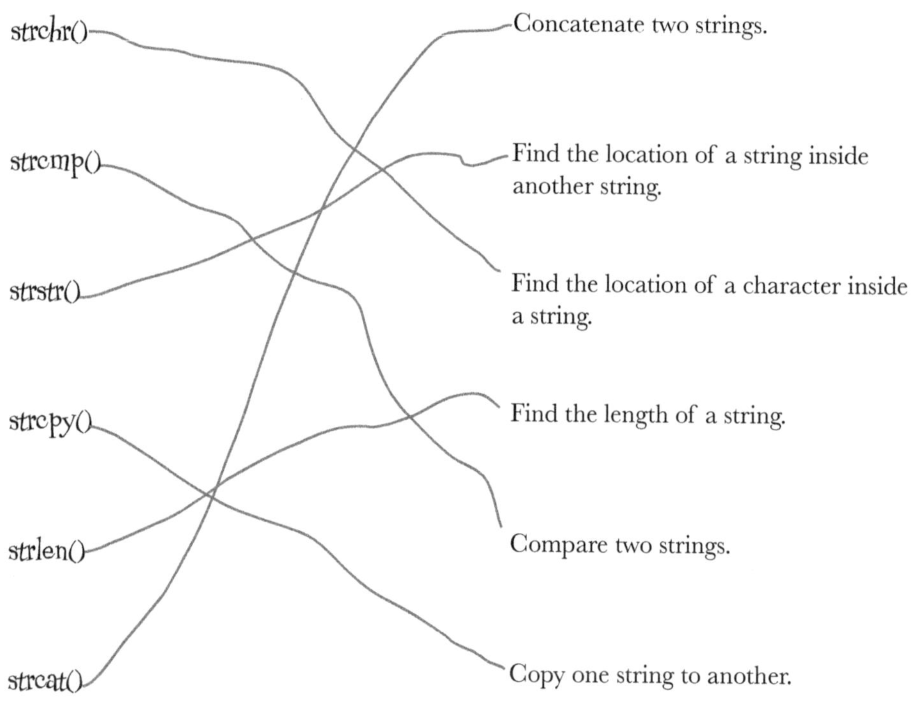
strchr()
strcmp()
strstr()
strcpy()
strlen()
strcat()
Concatenate two strings.
Find the location of a string inside another string.
Find the location of a character inside a string.
Find the length of a string.
Compare two strings.
Copy one string to another.

Sharpen your pencil Solution

You were to write which of the above functions you should use for the jukebox program.

strstr()

Using the strstr() function

So how exactly does the `strstr()` function work? Let's look at an example. Let's say you're looking for the string "fun" inside a larger string, "dysfunctional." You'd call it like this:

```
strstr("dysfunctional", "fun")
```

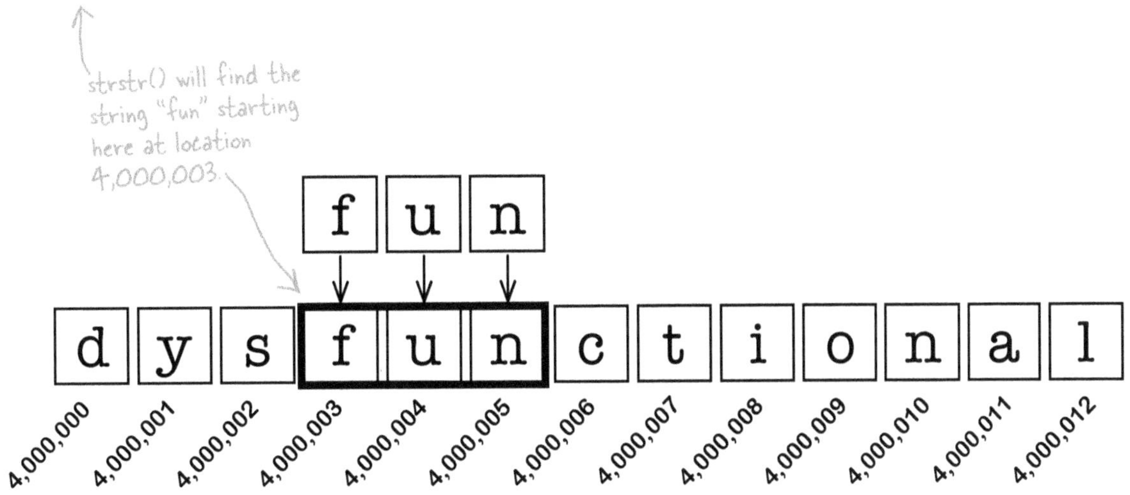
strstr() will find the string "fun" starting here at location 4,000,003.
f
u
n
d
y
s
f
u
n
c
t
i
o
n
a
l
4,000,000
4,000,001
4,000,002
4,000,003
4,000,004
4,000,005
4,000,006
4,000,007
4,000,008
4,000,009
4,000,010
4,000,011
4,000,012

The `strstr()` function will *search for the second string in the first string*. If it finds the string, it will return the address of the located string in memory. In the example here, the function would find that the `fun` substring begins at memory location 4,000,003.

But what if the `strstr()` can't find the substring? What then? In that case, `strstr()` returns the value 0. Can you think why that is? Well, if you remember, C treats zero as *false*. That means you can use `strstr()` to check for the *existence* of one string inside another, like this:

```
char s0[] = "dysfunctional";
char s1[] = "fun";
if (strstr(s0, s1))
  puts("I found the fun in dysfunctional!");
```

Let's see how we can use strstr() in the jukebox program.

Pool Puzzle

The guys in the Lounge had already started to write the code to search through the track list, but—oh no!—some of the paper they were writing the code on has fallen into the pool. Do you think you can select the correct pieces of code to complete the search function? It's been a while since the pool was cleaned, so be warned: some of the code in the pool might not be needed for this program.

Note: the guys have slipped in a couple of new pieces of code they found in a book somewhere.

Hey, look: you're creating a separate function. Presumably, when you get around to writing the main() function, it will call this.

"void" just means this function won't return a value.

```
void find_track(char search_for[])
{
  int i;
  for (i = 0; i < 5; i++) {
    if (............... (..............., ...............))
      printf("Track %i: '%s'\n", ..............., ...............);
  }
}
```

This is the "for loop." We'll look at this in more detail in a while, but for now you just need to know that it will run this piece of code five times.

This is where you're checking to see if the search term is contained in the track name.

If the track name matches our search, you'll display it here.

You're going to be printing out **two** values here.

One value will need to be an integer.

The other will be a string.

Note: each thing from the pool can be used only once!

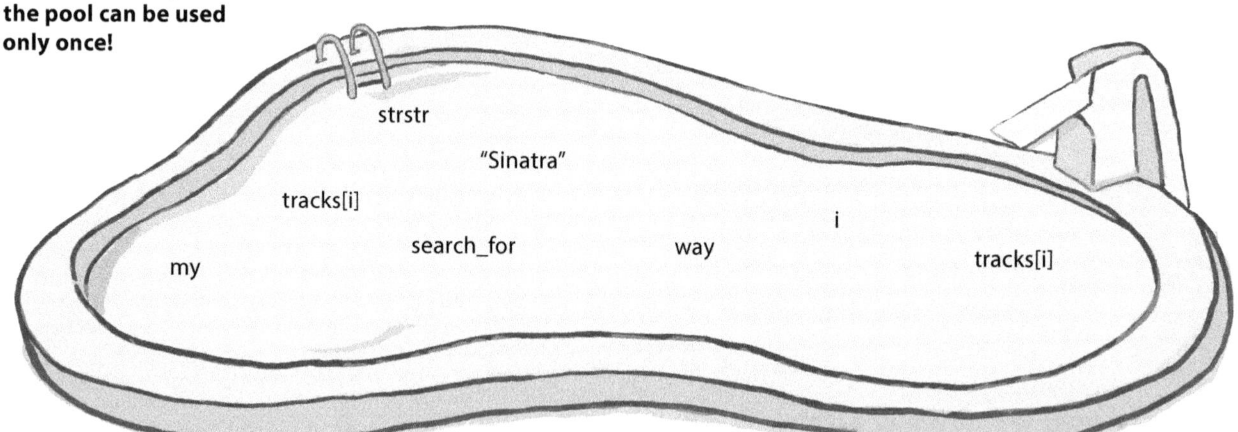

strstr
"Sinatra"
tracks[i]
i
search_for
way
tracks[i]
my

BE the Compiler

The jukebox program needs a main() function that reads input from the user and calls the find_track() function on the opposite page. Your job is to play like you're the compiler and say which of the following main() functions is the one you need for the jukebox program.

```
int main()
{
  char search_for[80];
  printf("Search for: ");
  fgets(search_for, 80, stdin);
  search_for[strlen(search_for) - 1] =
   '\0';
  find_track();
  return 0;
}
```

```
int main()
{
  char search_for[80];
  printf("Search for: ");
  fgets(search_for, 79, stdin);
  search_for[strlen(search_for)
   - 1] = '\0';
  find_track(search_for);
  return 0;
}
```

```
int main()
{
  char search_for[80];
  printf("Search for: ");
  scanf("%79s", search_for);
  search_for[strlen(search_for)
   - 1] = '\0';
  find_track(search_for);
  return 0;
}
```

```
int main()
{
  char search_for[80];
  printf("Search for: ");
  scanf("%80s", search_for);
  find_track(search_for);
  return 0;
}
```

Pool Puzzle Solution

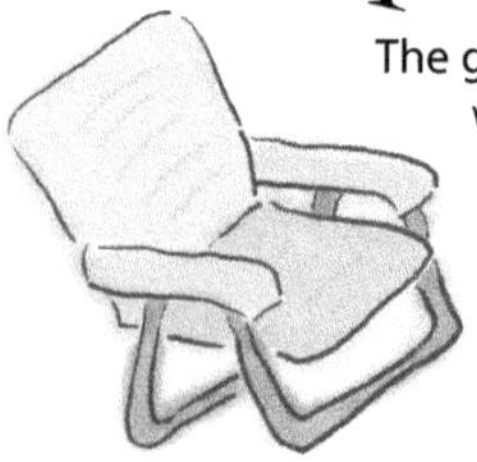

The guys in the Lounge had already started to write the code to search through the track list, but—oh no!—some of the paper they were writing the code on has fallen into the pool. You were to select the correct pieces of code to complete the search function.

Note: the guys have slipped in a couple of new pieces of code they found in a book somewhere.

```
void find_track(char search_for[])
{
  int i;
  for (i = 0; i < 5; i++) {
    if ( strstr ( tracks[i] , search_for ))
      printf("Track %i: '%s'\n", i , tracks[i] );
  }
}
```

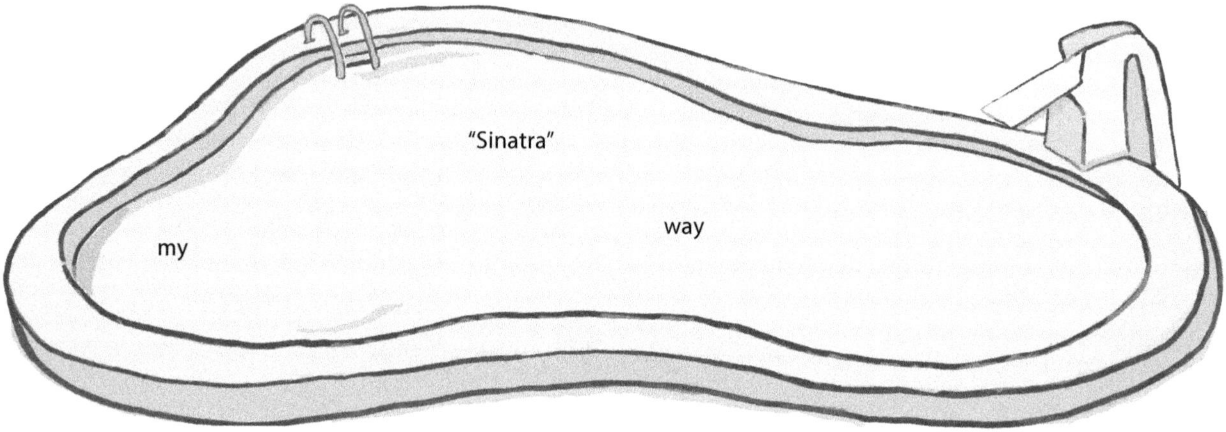
"Sinatra"
way
my

BE the Compiler Solution

The jukebox program needs a main() function that reads input from the user and calls the find_track() function on the opposite page. Your job was to play like you're the compiler and say which of the following main() functions is the one you need for the jukebox program.

```
int main()
{
  char search_for[80];
  printf("Search for: ");
  fgets(search_for, 80, stdin);
  search_for[strlen(search_for) - 1] =
   '\0';
  find_track();
  return 0;
}
```

find_track() is being called without passing the search term.

```
int main()
{
  char search_for[80];
  printf("Search for: ");
  fgets(search_for, 79, stdin);
  search_for[strlen(search_for)
   - 1] = '\0';
  find_track(search_for);
  return 0;
}
```

This version isn't using the full length of the array. The coder has subtracted one from the length, like you would with scanf().

```
int main()
{
  char search_for[80];
  printf("Search for: ");
  scanf("%79s", search_for);
  search_for[strlen(search_for)
   - 1] = '\0';
  find_track(search_for);
  return 0;
}
```

This is the correct main() function.

```
int main()
{
  char search_for[80];
  printf("Search for: ");
  scanf("%80s", search_for);
  find_track(search_for);
  return 0;
}
```

This version is using scanf() and would allow the user to enter 81 characters into the array.

It's time for a code review

Let's bring the code together and review what you've got so far:

You still need stdio.h for the printf() and scanf() functions.

You will also need the string.h header, so you can search with the strstr() function.

You'll set the tracks array outside of the main() and find_track() functions; that way, the tracks will be usable everywhere in the program.

This is your new find_track() function. You'll need to declare it here before you call it from main().

i++ means "increase the value of i by 1."

This code will display all the matching tracks.

And this is your main() function, which is the starting point of the program.

You're asking for the search text here.

Now you call your new find_track() function and display the matching tracks.

```
#include <stdio.h>
#include <string.h>

char tracks[][80] = {
  "I left my heart in Harvard Med School",
  "Newark, Newark - a wonderful town",
  "Dancing with a Dork",
  "From here to maternity",
  "The girl from Iwo Jima",
};

void find_track(char search_for[])
{
  int i;
  for (i = 0; i < 5; i++) {
    if (strstr(tracks[i], search_for))
      printf("Track %i: '%s'\n", i, tracks[i]);
  }
}

int main()
{
  char search_for[80];
  printf("Search for: ");
  scanf("%79s", search_for);
  search_for[strlen(search_for) - 1] = '\0';
  find_track(search_for);
  return 0;
}
```

It's important that you assemble the code in this order. The headers are included at the top so that the compiler will have all the correct functions before it compiles your code. Then you define the `tracks` *before* you write the functions. This is called putting the `tracks` array in **global scope**. A global variable is one that lives outside any particular function. Global variables like `tracks` are available to all of the functions in the program.

Finally, you have the functions: `find_track()` first, followed by `main()`. The `find_track()` function needs to come first, *before* you call it from `main()`.

Test Drive

It's time to fire up the terminal and see if the code works.

```
File Edit Window Help string.h
> gcc text_search.c -o text_search && ./text_search
Search for: town
Track 1: 'Newark, Newark - a wonderful town'
>
```

And the great news is, the program works!

Even though this program is a little longer than any code you've written so far, it's actually doing a lot more. It creates an array of strings and then uses the string library to search through all of them to find the music track that the user was looking for.

Hey, hey, hey! That code's a rockin' success. The cats in the bar are groovin' on down to a whole heap of Sinatra goodness!

Geek Bits

For more information about the functions available in *string.h*, see *http://tinyurl.com/82acwue*.

If you are using a Mac or a Linux machine, you can find out more about each of the *string.h* functions like `strstr()` by typing:

```
man strstr
```

there are no Dumb Questions

Q: Why is the list of tracks defined as `tracks[][80]`? Why not `tracks[5][80]`?

A: You *could* have defined it that way, but the compiler can tell there are five items in the list, so you can skip the `[5]` and just put `[]`.

Q: But in that case, why couldn't we just say `tracks[][]`?

A: The track names are all different lengths, so you need to tell the compiler to allocate enough space for even the largest.

Q: Does that mean each string in the `tracks` array is 80 characters, then?

A: The program will *allocate* 80 characters for each string, even though each of them is much smaller.

Q: So the `tracks` array takes 80 × 5 characters = 400 characters' worth of space in memory?

A: Yes.

Q: What happens if I forget to include a header file like *string.h*?

A: For some header files, the compiler will give you a warning and then include them anyway. For other header files, the compiler will simply give a compiler error.

Q: Why did we put the `tracks` array definition outside of the functions?

A: We put it into global scope. Global variables can be used by all functions in the program.

Q: Now that we've created two functions, how does the computer know which one to run first?

A: The program will always run the `main()` function first.

Q: Why do I have to put the `find_track()` function before `main()`?

A: C needs to know what parameters a function takes and what its return type is before it can be called.

Q: What would happen if I put the functions in a different order?

A: In that case, you'd just get a few warnings.

BULLET POINTS

- You can create an array of arrays with `char strings[...][...]`.
- The first set of brackets is used to access the outer array.
- The second set of brackets is used to access the details of each of the inner arrays.
- The *string.h* header file gives you access to a set of string manipulation functions in the C Standard Library.
- You can create several functions in a C program, but the computer will always run `main()` first.

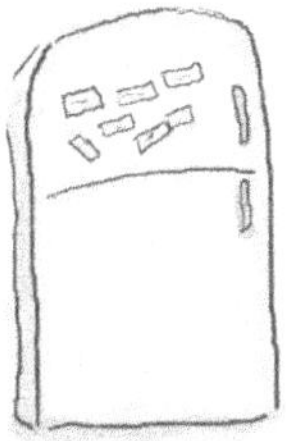

Code Magnets

The guys are working on a new piece of code for a game. They've created a function that will display a string backward on the screen. Unfortunately, some of the fridge magnets have moved out of place. Do you think you can help them to reassemble the code?

```
void print_reverse(char *s)
{
  size_t len = strlen(s);

  char *t = ........... + ........... - 1;

  while ( ........... >= ........... ) {
    printf("%c", *t);

    t = ...........  ...........  ...........;
  }
  puts("");
}
```

size_t is just an integer used for storing the sizes of things. → (size_t len = strlen(s);)

This works out the length of a string, so strlen("ABC") == 3.

Magnets: `s` `t` `len` `s` `-` `1` `t`

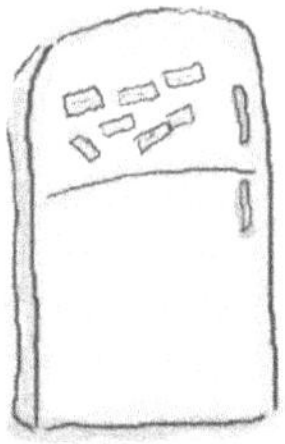

Code Magnets Solution

The guys are working on a new piece of code for a game. They've created a function that will display a string backward on the screen. Unfortunately, some of the fridge magnets have moved out of place. You were to help them to reassemble the code.

```
void print_reverse(char *s)
{
  size_t len = strlen(s);
  char *t = s + len - 1;
  while ( t >= s ) {
    printf("%c", *t);
    t = t - 1 ;
  }
  puts("");
}
```

← Calculating addresses like this is called "pointer arithmetic."

Array of arrays vs. array of pointers

You've seen how to use an array of arrays to store a sequence of strings, but another option is to use an **array of pointers**. An array of pointers is actually what it sounds like: a list of memory addresses stored in an array. It's very useful if you want to quickly create a list of string literals:

```
char *names_for_dog[] = {"Bowser", "Bonza", "Snodgrass"};
```

This is an array that stores pointers.

There will be one pointer pointing at each string literal.

You can access the array of pointers just like you accessed the array of arrays.

C-Cross

Now that the guys have the **print_reverse()** function working, they've used it to create a crossword. The answers are displayed by the output lines in the code.

5
6
1
7
2
8
3
4

Across

```
int main()
{
  char *juices[] = {
    "dragonfruit", "waterberry", "sharonfruit", "uglifruit",
    "rumberry", "kiwifruit", "mulberry", "strawberry",
    "blueberry", "blackberry", "starfruit"
  };
  char *a;
(1) puts(juices[6]);
(2) print_reverse(juices[7]);
  a = juices[2];
  juices[2] = juices[8];
  juices[8] = a;
(3) puts(juices[8]);
(4) print_reverse(juices[(18 + 7) / 5]);
```

Down

```
(5) puts(juices[2]);
(6) print_reverse(juices[9]);
    juices[1] = juices[3];
(7) puts(juices[10]);
(8) print_reverse(juices[1]);
    return 0;
}
```

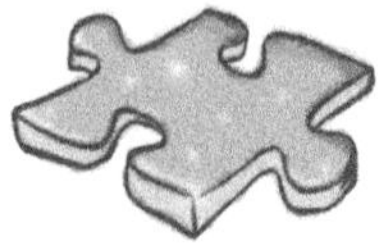

C-Cross Solution

Now that the guys have the **`print_reverse()`** function working, they've used it to create a crossword. The answers are displayed by the output lines in the code.

1 MULBERRY
2 YRREBWARTS
3 SHARONFRUIT
4 TIURFIWIK
5 BLUEBERRY
6 YRREBKCALB
7 STARFRUIT
8 TIURFILGU

Across

```
 int main()
 {
   char *juices[] = {
     "dragonfruit", "waterberry", "sharonfruit", "uglifruit",
     "rumberry", "kiwifruit", "mulberry", "strawberry",
     "blueberry", "blackberry", "starfruit"
   };
   char *a;
1  puts(juices[6]);
2  print_reverse(juices[7]);
   a = juices[2];
   juices[2] = juices[8];
   juices[8] = a;
3  puts(juices[8]);
4  print_reverse(juices[(18 + 7) / 5]);
```

Down

```
5  puts(juices[2]);
6  print_reverse(juices[9]);
   juices[1] = juices[3];
7  puts(juices[10]);
8  print_reverse(juices[1]);
   return 0;
 }
```

Your C Toolbox

You've got Chapter 2.5 under your belt, and now you've added strings to your toolbox. For a complete list of tooltips in the book, see Appendix ii.

An array of strings is an array of arrays.

The string.h header contains useful string functions.

You create an array of arrays using char strings [...][...]

strcmp() compares two strings.

strstr(a, b) will return the address of string b in string a.

strchr() finds the location of a character inside a string.

strcat() concatenates two strings.

strcpy() copies one string to another.

strlen() finds the length of a string.

3 creating small tools

Do one thing and do it well

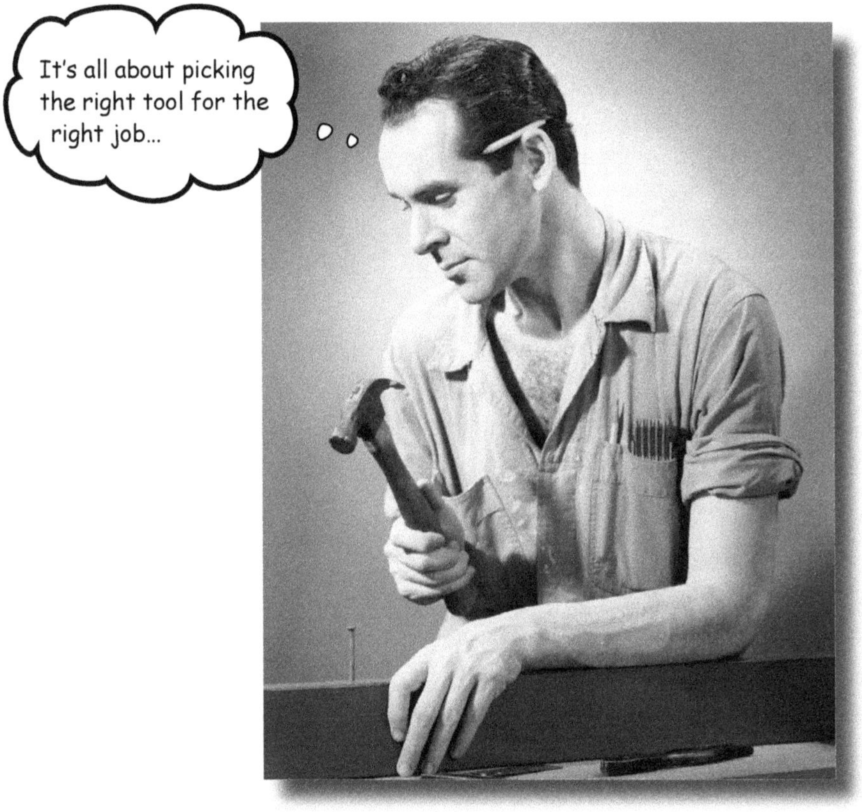
It's all about picking the right tool for the right job...

Every operating system includes small tools.

Small tools written in C perform **specialized small tasks**, such as reading and writing files, or filtering data. If you want to perform more complex tasks, you can even *link several tools together*. But how are these small tools built? In this chapter, you'll look at the building blocks of creating small tools. You'll learn how to control **command-line options**, how to manage **streams of information**, and **redirection**, getting tooled up in no time.

Small tools can solve big problems

A **small tool** is a C program that does *one* task and *does it well.* It might display the contents of a file on the screen or list the processes running on the computer. Or it might display the first 10 lines of a file or send it to the printer. Most operating systems come with a whole set of small tools that you can run from the command prompt or the terminal. Sometimes, when you have a *big* problem to solve, you can break it down into a series of *small* problems, and then write small tools for each of them.

Operating systems like Linux are mostly made up of hundreds and hundreds of small tools.

A small tool does one task and does it well.

Someone's written me a map web application, and I'd love to publish my route data with it. Trouble is, the format of the data coming from my GPS is wrong.

This is the data from the cyclist's GPS. It's a comma-separated format.

This is a latitude.

This is a longitude.

```
42.363400,-71.098465,Speed = 21
42.363327,-71.097588,Speed = 23
42.363255,-71.096710,Speed = 17
```

This is the data format the map needs. It's in JavaScript Object Notation, or JSON.

The data's the same, but the format's a little different.

```
data=[
{latitude: 42.363400, longitude: -71.098465, info: 'Speed = 21'},
{latitude: 42.363327, longitude: -71.097588, info: 'Speed = 23'},
{latitude: 42.363255, longitude: -71.096710, info: 'Speed = 17'},
...
]
```

If one small part of your program needs to convert data from one format to another, that's the perfect kind of task for a small tool.

Pocket Code

Hey, who hasn't taken a code printout on a long ride only to find that it soon becomes... unreadable? Sure, we all have. But with a little thought, you should be able to piece together the original version of some code.

This program can read comma-separated data from the command line and then display it in JSON format. See if you can figure out what the missing code is.

```
#include <stdio.h>

int main()
{
  float latitude;
  float longitude;
  char info[80];
  int started = ................;

  puts("data=[");
  while (scanf("%f,%f,%79[^\n]", ................, ................, ................) == 3) {
    if (started)
      printf(",\n");
    else
      started = ................;
    printf("{latitude: %f, longitude: %f, info: '%s'}", ............, ..............., ........);
  }
  puts("\n]");
  return 0;
}
```

We're using scanf() to enter **more than one** piece of data.

What will these values be? Remember: scanf() always uses **pointers**

The scanf() function returns the number of values it was able to read.

This is just a way of saying, "Give me every character up to the end of the line."

Be careful how you set "started."

What values need to be displayed?

Pocket Code Solution

Hey, who hasn't taken a code printout on a long ride only to find that it soon becomes... unreadable? Sure, we all have. But with a little thought, you should have been able to piece together the original version of some code.

This program can read comma-separated data from the command line and then display it in JSON format. You were to figure out what the missing code is.

```
#include <stdio.h>

int main()
{
  float latitude;
  float longitude;
  char info[80];
  int started = 0;

  puts("data=[");
  while (scanf("%f,%f,%79[^\n]", &latitude, &longitude, info) == 3) {
    if (started)
      printf(",\n");
    else
      started = 1;
    printf("{latitude: %f, longitude: %f, info: '%s'}", latitude, longitude, info);
  }
  puts("\n]");
  return 0;
}
```

We need to begin with "started" set to 0, which means **false**.

Did you remember the "&"s on the number variables? scanf() needs pointers.

You'll display a comma only if you've already displayed a previous line.

Once the loop has started, you can set "started" to 1, which is **true**.

You don't need & here because printf() is using the values, not the addresses of the numbers.

Test Drive

So what happens when you compile and run this code? What will it do?

This is the data that's printed out. This is the data you type in. The input and the output are mixed up.

```
File Edit Window Help JSON
>./geo2json
data=[
42.363400,-71.098465,Speed = 21
{latitude: 42.363400, longitude: -71.098465, info: 'Speed = 21'}42.363327,-71.097588,Speed = 23
,
{latitude: 42.363327, longitude: -71.097588, info: 'Speed = 23'}42.363255,-71.096710,Speed = 17
,
{latitude: 42.363255, longitude: -71.096710, info: 'Speed = 17'}42.363182,-71.095833,Speed = 22
,
...
...
...
{latitude: 42.363182, longitude: -71.095833, info: 'Speed = 22'}42.362385,-71.086182,Speed = 21
,
{latitude: 42.362385, longitude: -71.086182, info: 'Speed = 21'}^D
]
>
```

Several more hours' worth of typing...

In the end, you need to press Ctrl-D just to stop the program.

The program lets you enter GPS data at the keyboard and then it displays the JSON-formatted data on the screen. Problem is, the *input* and the *output* are all *mixed up together*. Also, there's a **lot of data**. If you are writing a small tool, you don't want to type in the data; you want to get large amounts of data by reading a **file**.

Also, how is the JSON data going to be used? Surely it can't be much use on the *screen*?

So is the program running OK? Is it doing the right thing? **Do you need to change the code?**

We really don't want the output on the screen. We need it in a file so we can use it with the mapping application. Here, let me show you...

Here's how the program should work

1. **Take the GPS from the bike and download the data.**
It creates a file called *gpsdata.csv* with one line of data for every location.

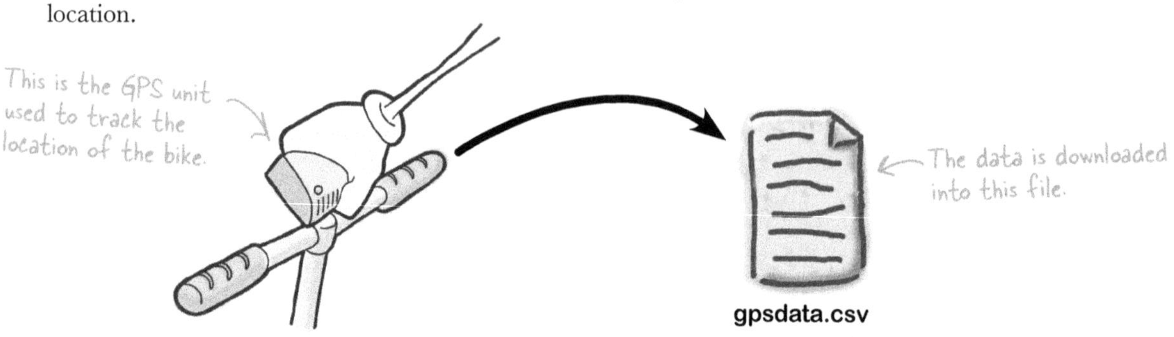
This is the GPS unit used to track the location of the bike.
The data is downloaded into this file.
gpsdata.csv

2. **The geo2json tool needs to read the contents of the gpsdata.csv line by line...**

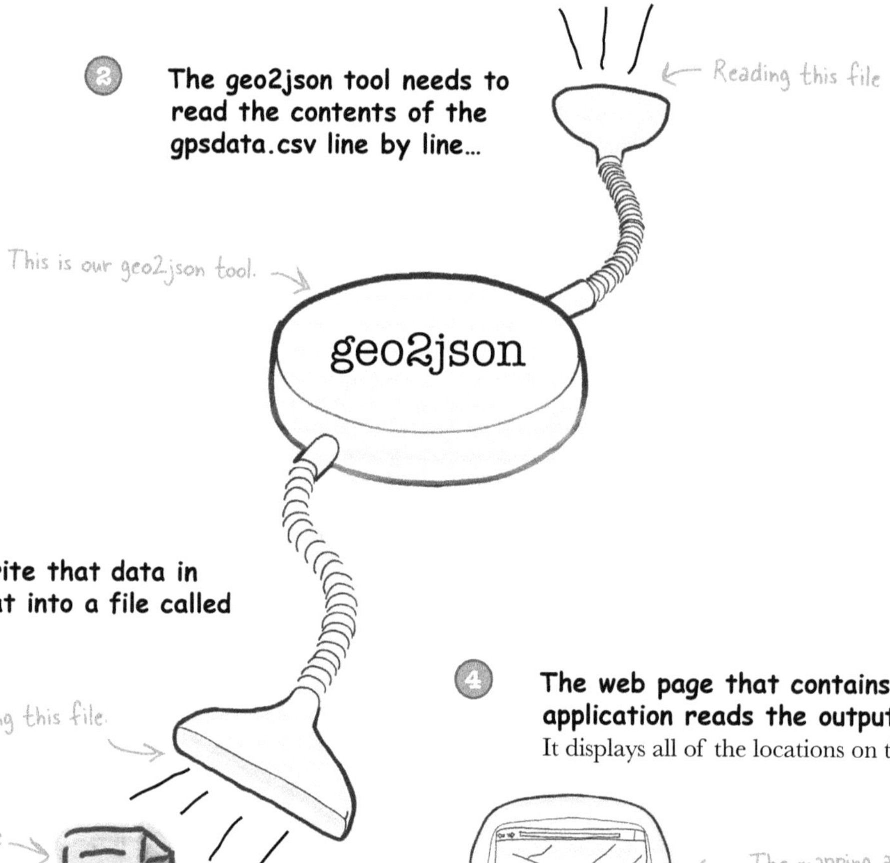
Reading this file
This is our geo2json tool.
geo2json
Writing this file.

3. **...and then write that data in JSON format into a file called output.json.**

4. **The web page that contains the map application reads the output.json file.**
It displays all of the locations on the map.

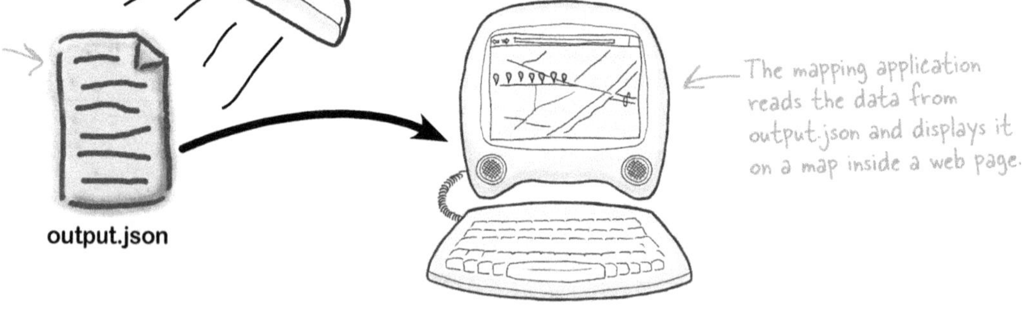
Your tool will write data to this file.
output.json
The mapping application reads the data from output.json and displays it on a map inside a web page.

But you're not using files...

The problem is, instead of reading and writing files, your program is currently reading data from the *keyboard* and writing it to the *display*.

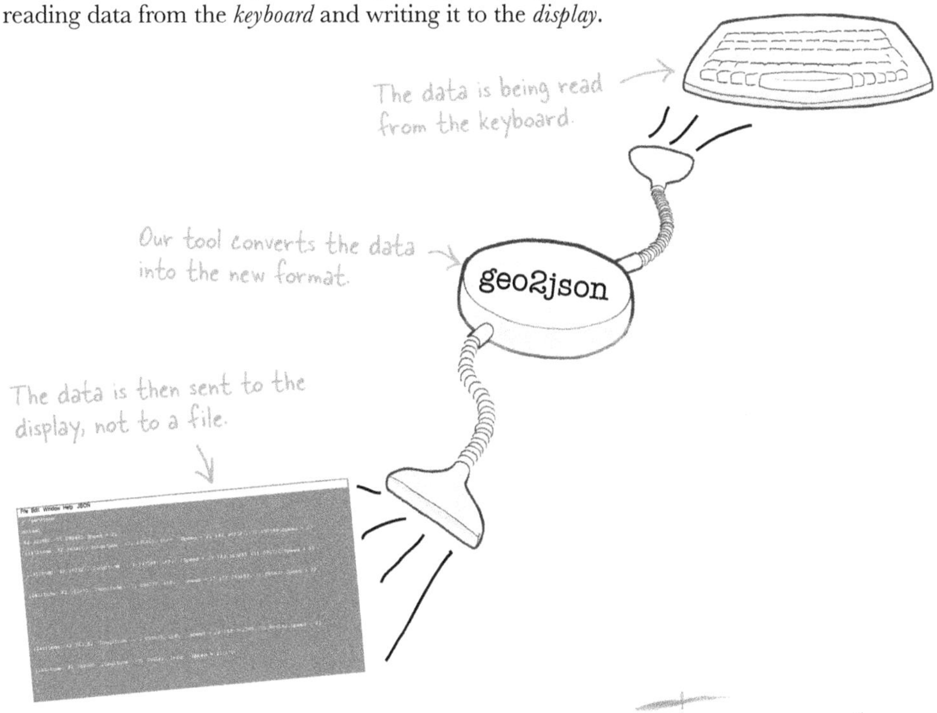
The data is being read from the keyboard.
Our tool converts the data into the new format.
geo2json
The data is then sent to the display, not to a file.

But that isn't good enough. The user won't want to type in all of the data if it's already stored in a file somewhere. And if the data in JSON format is just displayed on the screen, there's no way the map within the web page will be able to read it.

You need to make the program work with **files**. But how do you do that? If you want to use *files* instead of the keyboard and the display, what code will you have to change? Will you have to change any code at all?

BRAIN POWER

Is there a way of making our program use files without changing code? Without even *recompiling* it?

Geek Bits

Tools that read data line by line, process it, and write it out again are called **filters**. If you have a Unix machine, or you've installed Cygwin on Windows, you already have a few filter tools installed.

head: This tool displays the first few lines of a file.

tail: This filter displays the lines at the end of a file.

sed: The *stream editor* lets you do things like search and replace text.

You'll see later how to combine filters together to form **filter chains**.

You can use redirection

You're using `scanf()` and `printf()` to read from the keyboard and write to the display. But the truth is, they don't talk *directly* to the keyboard and display. Instead, they use the **Standard Input and Standard Output**. The *Standard Input* and *Standard Output* are created by the operating system when the program runs.

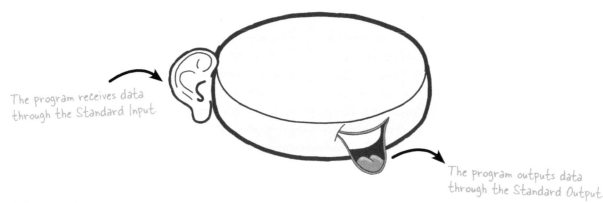

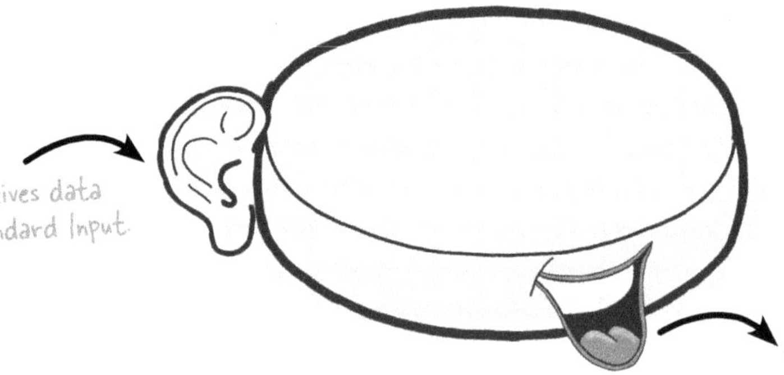
The program receives data through the Standard Input.
The program outputs data through the Standard Output.

The operating system controls how data gets into and out of the Standard Input and Output. If you run a program from the command prompt or terminal, the operating system will send all of the keystrokes from the keyboard into the Standard Input. If the operating system reads any data from the Standard Output, by default it will send that data to the display.

The `scanf()` and `printf()` functions don't know, or care, where the data comes from or goes to. They just read and write Standard Input and the Standard Output.

Now this might sound like it's kind of complicated. After all, why not just have your program talk directly to the keyboard and screen? Wouldn't that be simpler?

Well, there's a very good reason why operating systems communicate with programs using the Standard Input and the Standard Output:

You can redirect the Standard Input and Standard Output so that they read and write data somewhere else, such as to and from files.

You can redirect the Standard Input with <...

Instead of entering data at the keyboard, you can use the < operator to read the data from a file.

```
42.363400,-71.098465,Speed = 21
42.363327,-71.097588,Speed = 23
42.363255,-71.096710,Speed = 17
42.363182,-71.095833,Speed = 22
42.363110,-71.094955,Speed = 14
42.363037,-71.094078,Speed = 16
42.362965,-71.093201,Speed = 18
42.362892,-71.092323,Speed = 22
42.362820,-71.091446,Speed = 17
42.362747,-71.090569,Speed = 23
42.362675,-71.089691,Speed = 14
42.362602,-71.088814,Speed = 19
42.362530,-71.087936,Speed = 16
42.362457,-71.087059,Speed = 16
42.362385,-71.086182,Speed = 21
```

This is the file containing the data from the GPS device.

This is telling the operating system to send the data from the file into the Standard Input of the program.

You don't have to type in the GPS data, so you don't see it mixed up with the output.

File Edit Window Help Don'tCrossTheStreams

```
> ./geo2json < gpsdata.csv
data=[
{latitude: 42.363400, longitude: -71.098465, info: 'Speed = 21'},
{latitude: 42.363327, longitude: -71.097588, info: 'Speed = 23'},
{latitude: 42.363255, longitude: -71.096710, info: 'Speed = 17'},
{latitude: 42.363182, longitude: -71.095833, info: 'Speed = 22'},
{latitude: 42.363110, longitude: -71.094955, info: 'Speed = 14'},
{latitude: 42.363037, longitude: -71.094078, info: 'Speed = 16'},
...
...
{latitude: 42.362385, longitude: -71.086182, info: 'Speed = 21'}
]
>
```

Now you just see the JSON data coming from the program.

The < operator tells the operating system that the Standard Input of the program should be connected to the *gpsdata.csv* file instead of the keyboard. So you can send the program data from a file. Now you just need to redirect its **output**.

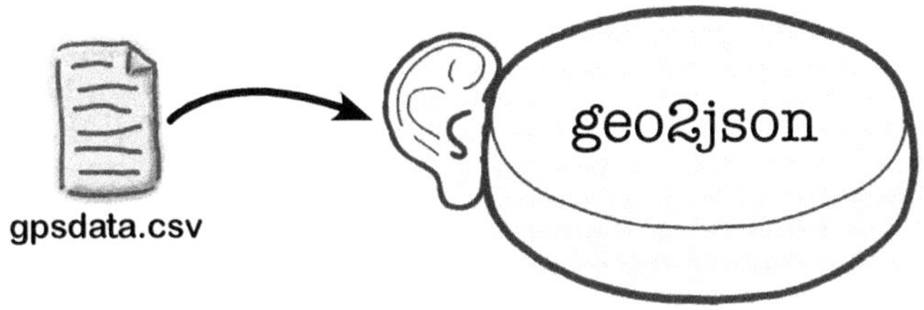
gpsdata.csv
geo2json

...and redirect the Standard Output with >

To redirect the Standard Output to a file, you need to use the > operator:

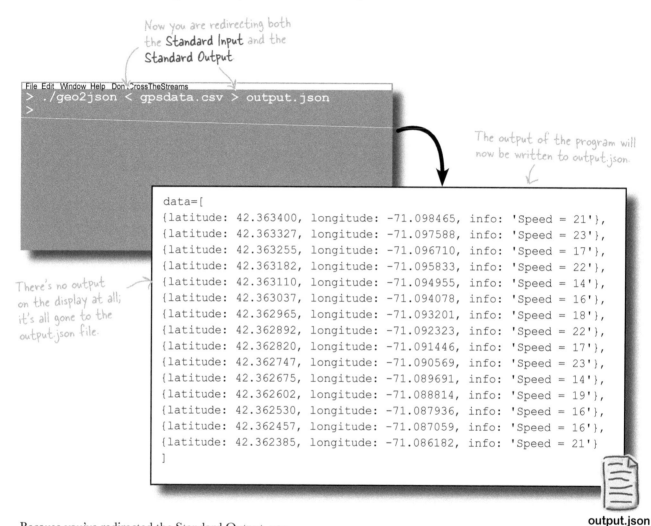

Now you are redirecting both the Standard Input and the Standard Output.

```
File Edit Window Help Don'tCrossTheStreams
> ./geo2json < gpsdata.csv > output.json
>
```

The output of the program will now be written to output.json.

```
data=[
{latitude: 42.363400, longitude: -71.098465, info: 'Speed = 21'},
{latitude: 42.363327, longitude: -71.097588, info: 'Speed = 23'},
{latitude: 42.363255, longitude: -71.096710, info: 'Speed = 17'},
{latitude: 42.363182, longitude: -71.095833, info: 'Speed = 22'},
{latitude: 42.363110, longitude: -71.094955, info: 'Speed = 14'},
{latitude: 42.363037, longitude: -71.094078, info: 'Speed = 16'},
{latitude: 42.362965, longitude: -71.093201, info: 'Speed = 18'},
{latitude: 42.362892, longitude: -71.092323, info: 'Speed = 22'},
{latitude: 42.362820, longitude: -71.091446, info: 'Speed = 17'},
{latitude: 42.362747, longitude: -71.090569, info: 'Speed = 23'},
{latitude: 42.362675, longitude: -71.089691, info: 'Speed = 14'},
{latitude: 42.362602, longitude: -71.088814, info: 'Speed = 19'},
{latitude: 42.362530, longitude: -71.087936, info: 'Speed = 16'},
{latitude: 42.362457, longitude: -71.087059, info: 'Speed = 16'},
{latitude: 42.362385, longitude: -71.086182, info: 'Speed = 21'}
]
```

There's no output on the display at all; it's all gone to the output.json file.

output.json

Because you've redirected the Standard Output, you don't see any data appearing on the screen at all. But the program has now created a file called *output.json*.

The *output.json* file is the one you needed to create for the mapping application. Let's see if it works.

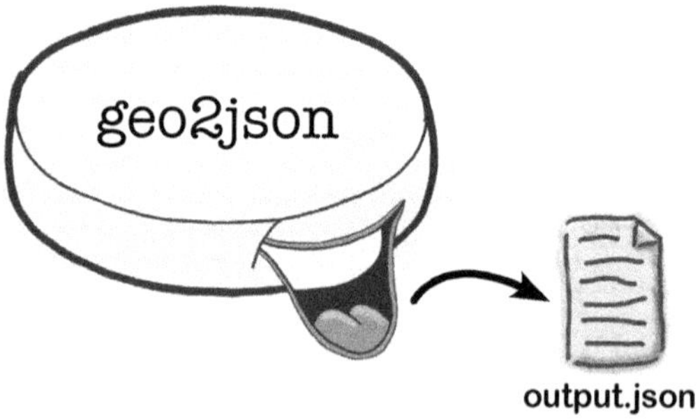
geo2json
output.json

Test Drive

Now it's time to see if the new data file you've created can be used to plot the location data on a map. You'll take a copy of the web page containing the mapping program and put it into the same folder as the *output.json* file. Then you need to open the web page in a browser:

Do this!

Download the web page from *https://github.com/dogriffiths/HeadFirstC*.

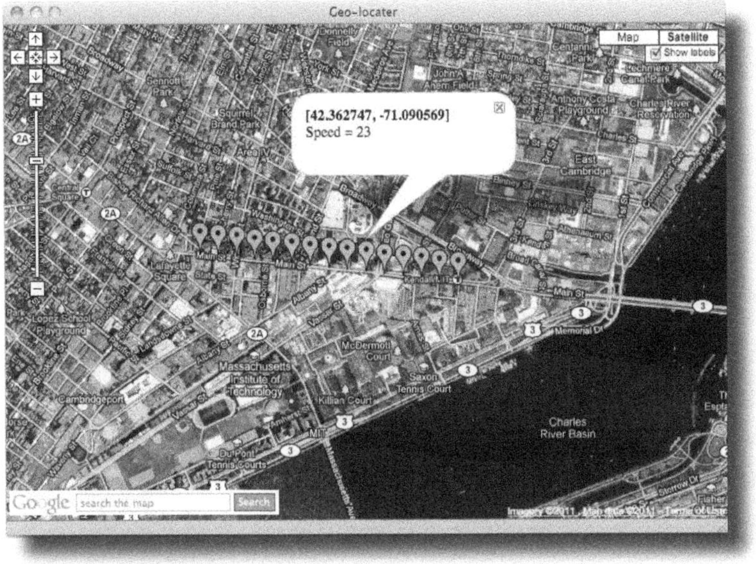
Geo-locater
Map
Satellite
Show labels
[42.362747, -71.090569]
Speed = 23
Charles River Basin
Search

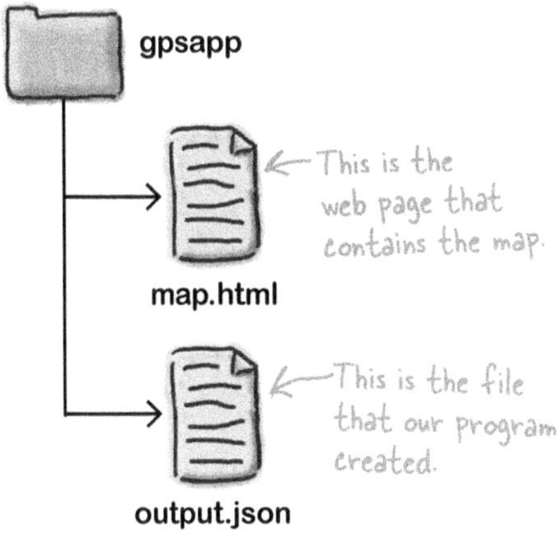
gpsapp
map.html
This is the web page that contains the map.
output.json
This is the file that our program created.

The map works.

The map inside the web page is able to read the data from the output file.

Great! Now I can publish my journeys on the Web!

But there's a problem with some of the data...

Your program seems to be able to read GPS data and format it correctly for the mapping application. But after a few days, a problem creeps in.

Geo-locater
JavaScript
Invalid latitude: '423.631805'
OK
Loading "file:///Users/davidg/Desktop/website/static/map.html", completed 5 of 6 items

I dropped the GPS unit on a ride a couple of times, and now the map won't display.

So what happened here? The problem is that there was some **bad data** in the GPS data file:

```
{latitude: 42.363255, longitude: -71.096710, info: 'Speed = 17'},
{latitude: 423.63182, longitude: -71.095833, info: 'Speed = 22'},
```

The decimal point is in the wrong place in this number.

But the `geo2json` program doesn't do any checking of the data it reads; it just reformats the numbers and sends them to the output.

That should be easy to fix. You need to validate the data.

Exercise

You need to add some code to the `geo2json` program that will check for bad latitude and longitude values. You don't need anything fancy. If a latitude or longitude falls outside the expected numeric, just display an error message and exit the program with an error status of 2:

```
#include <stdio.h>

int main()
{
  float latitude;
  float longitude;
  char info[80];
  int started = 0;

  puts("data=[");
  while (scanf("%f,%f,%79[^\n]", &latitude, &longitude, info) == 3) {
    if (started)
      printf(",\n");
    else
      started = 1;
...........................................................................
...........................................................................
...........................................................................
...........................................................................
...........................................................................
...........................................................................
...........................................................................
...........................................................................
...........................................................................
    printf("{latitude: %f, longitude: %f, info: '%s'}", latitude, longitude, info);
  }
  puts("\n]");
  return 0;
}
```

If the latitude is < -90 or > 90, then error with status 2. If the longitude is < -180 or > 180, then error with status 2.

Exercise
Solution

You needed to add some code to the `geo2json` program to check for bad latitude and longitude values. If a latitude or longitude falls outside the expected numeric, just display an error message and exit the program with an error status of 2:

```
#include <stdio.h>

int main()
{
  float latitude;
  float longitude;
  char info[80];
  int started = 0;

  puts("data=[");
  while (scanf("%f,%f,%79[^\n]", &latitude, &longitude, info) == 3) {
    if (started)
      printf(",\n");
    else
      started = 1;
    if ((latitude < -90.0) || (latitude > 90.0)) {
      printf("Invalid latitude: %f\n", latitude);
      return 2;
    }
    if ((longitude < -180.0) || (longitude > 180.0)) {
      printf("Invalid longitude: %f\n", longitude);
      return 2;
    }

    printf("{latitude: %f, longitude: %f, info: '%s'}", latitude, longitude, info);
  }
  puts("\n]");
  return 0;
}
```

These lines check that the latitude and longitude are in the correct range.

These lines display simple error messages.

These lines will exit from the main() function with an error status of 2.

Test Drive

OK, so you now have the code in place to check that the latitude and longitude are in range. But will it be enough to make our program cope with bad data? Let's see.

Compile the code and then run the bad data through the program:

This line will recompile the program.

Then run the program again with the bad data.

WTF??? No error message?

This means "Welcome To Finland."

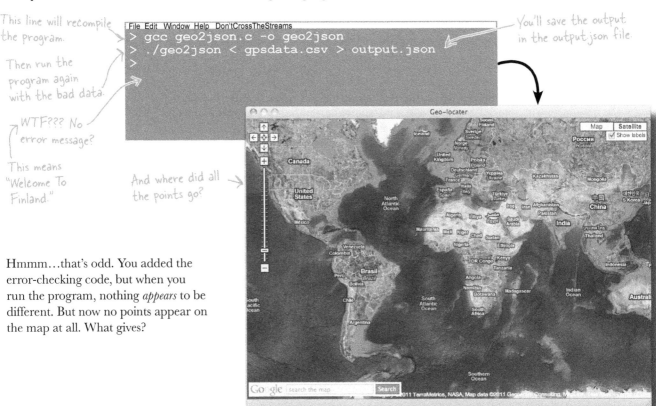

```
File Edit Window Help Don'tCrossTheStreams
> gcc geo2json.c -o geo2json
> ./geo2json < gpsdata.csv > output.json
>
```

You'll save the output in the output.json file.

And where did all the points go?

Geo-locater
Map
Satellite
Show labels
Canada
United States
Mexico
North Atlantic Ocean
South Atlantic Ocean
Brasil
Argentina
India
China
Indian Ocean
Southern Ocean
Search

Hmmm…that's odd. You added the error-checking code, but when you run the program, nothing *appears* to be different. But now no points appear on the map at all. What gives?

Brain Power

Study the code. What do **you** think happened? Is the code doing what you asked it to? Why weren't there any error messages? Why did the mapping program think that the entire *output.json* file was corrupt?

Code Deconstruction

The mapping program is complaining about the *output.json* file, so let's open it up and see what's inside:

This is the output.json file.

```
data=[
{latitude: 42.363400, longitude: -71.098465, info: 'Speed = 21'},
{latitude: 42.363327, longitude: -71.097588, info: 'Speed = 23'},
{latitude: 42.363255, longitude: -71.096710, info: 'Speed = 17'},
Invalid latitude: 423.631805
```

Oh, the error message was also redirected to the output file.

Once you open the file, you can see *exactly* what happened. The program saw that there was a problem with some of the data, and it exited right away. It didn't process any more data and it *did* output an error message. Problem is, because you were **redirecting the Standard Output** into the *output.json*, that meant you were also redirecting the error message. So the program ended silently, and you never saw what the problem was.

Now, you *could* have checked the exit status of the program, but you really want to be able to see the error messages.

But how can you still display error messages if you are redirecting the output?

Geek Bits

If your program finds a problem in the data, it exits with a status of 2. But how can you check that error status after the program has finished? Well, it depends on what operating system you're using. If you're running on a Mac, Linux, some other kind of Unix machine, or if you're using Cygwin on a Windows machine, you can display the error status like this:

```
File Edit Window Help
$ echo $?
2
```

If you're using the Command Prompt in Windows, then it's a little different:

```
File Edit Window Help
C:\> echo %ERRORLEVEL%
2
```

Both commands do the same thing: they display the number returned by the program when it finished.

Wouldn't it be dreamy if there were a special output for errors so that I didn't have to mix my errors in with Standard Output? But I know it's just a fantasy...

Introducing the Standard Error

The **Standard Output** is the *default* way of outputting data from a program. But what if something *exceptional* happens, like an error? You'll probably want to deal with things like error messages a little differently from the usual output.

That's why the **Standard Error** was invented. The Standard Error is a *second output* that was created for sending error messages.

Human beings generally have two ears and one mouth, but processes are wired a little differently. Every process has **one ear** (the Standard Input) and **two mouths** (the Standard Output and the Standard Error).

Human

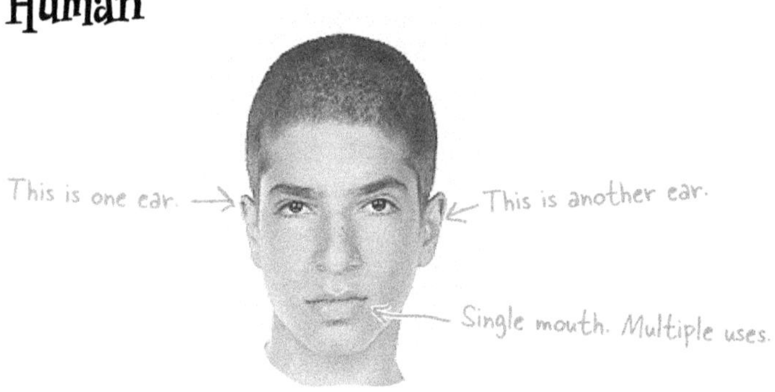
This is one ear.
This is another ear.
Single mouth. Multiple uses.

Process

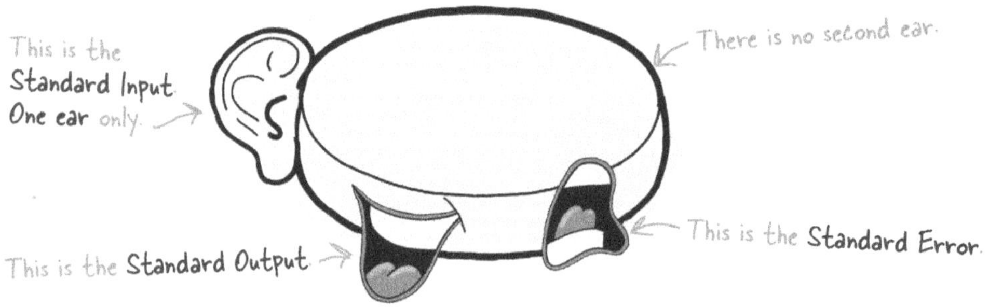
This is the Standard Input. One ear only.
There is no second ear.
This is the Standard Output.
This is the Standard Error.

Let's see how the operating system sets these up.

By default, the Standard Error is sent to the display

Remember how when a new process is created, the operating system points the Standard Input at the keyboard and the Standard Output at the screen? Well, the operating system creates the Standard Error at the same time and, like the Standard Output, the Standard Error is sent to the display by default.

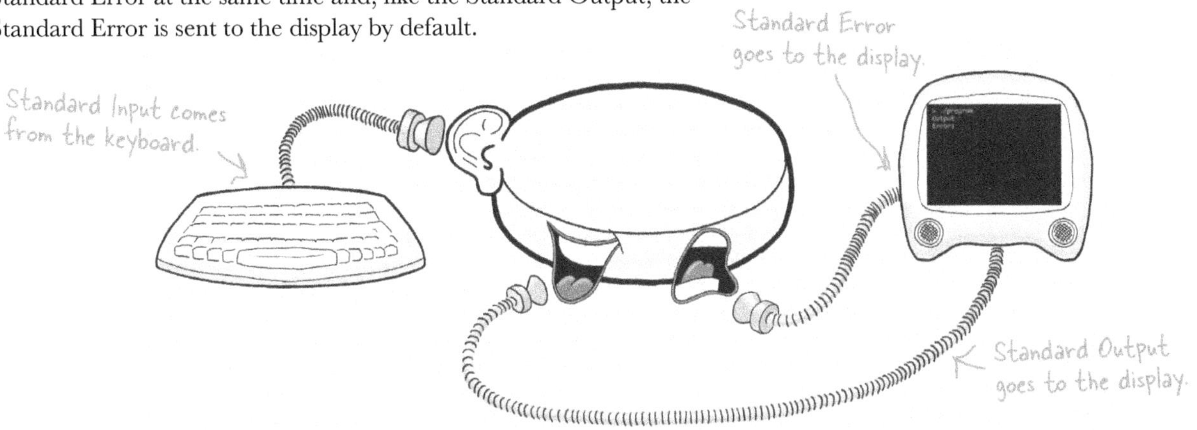
Standard Error goes to the display.
Standard Input comes from the keyboard.
Standard Output goes to the display.

That means that if someone redirects the Standard Input and Standard Output so they use files, the Standard Error will continue to send data to the display.

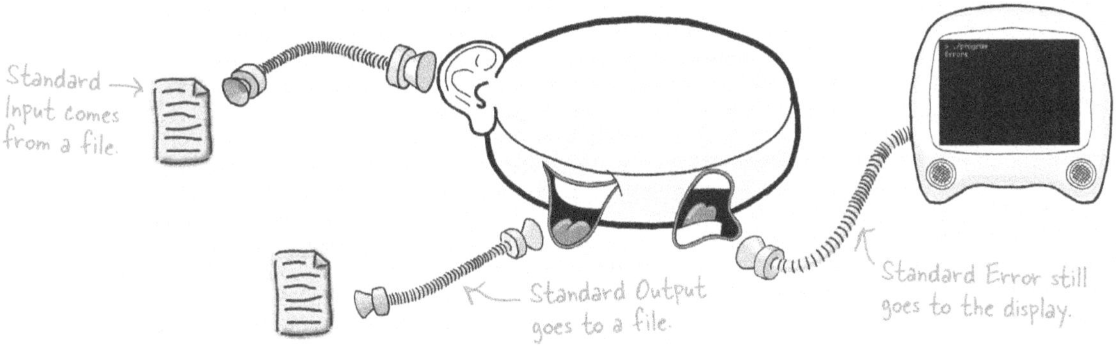
Standard Input comes from a file.
Standard Output goes to a file.
Standard Error still goes to the display.

And that's really cool, because it means that even if the Standard Output is redirected somewhere else, by default, **any messages sent down the Standard Error will still be visible on the screen**.

So you can fix the problem of our hidden error messages by simply displaying them on the Standard Error.

But how do you do that?

fprintf() prints to a data stream

You've already seen that the `printf()` function sends data to the Standard Output. What you *didn't* know is that the `printf()` function is just a version of a more general function called `fprintf()`:

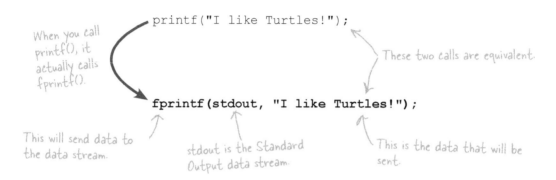

```
printf("I like Turtles!");
```

When you call printf(), it actually calls fprintf().

These two calls are equivalent.

```
fprintf(stdout, "I like Turtles!");
```

This will send data to the data stream.

stdout is the Standard Output data stream.

This is the data that will be sent.

The `fprintf()` function allows you to choose where you want to send text to. You can tell `fprintf()` to send text to **`stdout`** (the Standard Output) or **`stderr`** (the Standard Error).

there are no Dumb Questions

Q: There's a `stdout` and a `stderr`. Is there a `stdin`?

A: Yes, and as you probably guessed, it refers to the Standard Input.

Q: Can I print to it?

A: No, the Standard Input can't be printed to.

Q: Can I read from it?

A: Yes, by using `fscanf()`, which is just like `scanf()`, but you can specify the data stream.

Q: So is `fscanf(stdin, ...)` exactly the same as `scanf(...)`?

A: Yes, they're identical. In fact, behind the scenes, `scanf(...)` just calls `fscanf(stdin, ...)`.

Q: Can I redirect the Standard Error?

A: Yes; > redirects the Standard Output. But 2> redirects the Standard Error.

Q: So I could write `geo2json 2> errors.txt`?

A: Yes.

Let's update the code to use fprintf()

With just a couple of small changes, you can get our error messages printing on the Standard Error.

```
#include <stdio.h>

int main()
{
  float latitude;
  float longitude;
  char info[80];
  int started = 0;

  puts("data=[");
  while (scanf("%f,%f,%79[^\n]", &latitude, &longitude, info) == 3) {
    if (started)
      printf(",\n");
    else
      started = 1;
    if ((latitude < -90.0) || (latitude > 90.0)) {
      printf("Invalid latitude: %f\n", latitude);
      fprintf(stderr, "Invalid latitude: %f\n", latitude);
      return 2;
    }
    if ((longitude < -180.0) || (longitude > 180.0)) {
      printf(stderr, "Invalid longitude: %f\n", longitude);
      fprintf(stderr, "Invalid longitude: %f\n", longitude);
      return 2;
    }
    printf("{latitude: %f, longitude: %f, info: '%s'}", latitude, longitude, info);
  }
  puts("\n]");
  return 0;
}
```

Instead of printf(), we use fprintf().

We need to specify stderr as the first parameter.

That means that the code should now work in exactly the same way, *except* the error messages should appear on the Standard Error instead of the Standard Output.

Let's run the code and see.

Test Drive

If you recompile the program and then run the corrupted GPS data through it again, this happens.

```
File Edit Window Help ControlErrors
> gcc geo2json.c -o geo2json
> ./geo2json-page21  < gpsdata.csv > output.json
Invalid latitude: 423.631805
```

That's excellent. This time, even though you are redirecting the Standard Output into the *output.json* file, the error message is still visible on the screen.

The Standard Error was created with exactly this in mind: to separate the error messages from the usual output. But remember: `stderr` and `stdout` are both just output streams. And there's nothing to prevent you from using them for anything.

Let's try out your newfound Standard Input and Standard Error skills.

BULLET POINTS

- The `printf()` function sends data to the *Standard Output*.
- The Standard Output goes to the display by default.
- You can *redirect* the Standard Output to a file by using > on the command line.
- `scanf()` reads data from the *Standard Input*.
- The Standard Input reads data from the keyboard by default.
- You can redirect the Standard Input to read a file by using < on the command line.
- The *Standard Error* is reserved for outputting error messages.
- You can redirect the Standard Error using 2>.

TOP SECRET

We have reason to believe that the following program has been used in the transmission of secret messages:

```
#include <stdio.h>

int main()
{
  char word[10];
  int i = 0;
  while (scanf("%9s", word) == 1) {
    i = i + 1;
    if (i % 2)
      fprintf(stdout, "%s\n", word);
    else
      fprintf(stderr, "%s\n", word);
  }
  return 0;
}
```

i % 2 means "The remainder left when you divide by 2."

We have intercepted a file called *secret.txt* and a scrap of paper with instructions:

```
THE BUY SUBMARINE
SIX WILL EGGS
SURFACE AND AT
SOME NINE MILK PM
```

secret.txt

Run with:
secret_messages < secret.txt > message1.txt 2> message2.txt

> will redirect the Standard Output.

2> will redirect the Standard Error.

Your mission is to decode the two secret messages. Write your answers below.

Message 1	Message 2
....	....
....	....
....	....
....	....
....	....
....	....
....	....

TOP SECRET — SOLVED

We have reason to believe that the following program has been used in the transmission of secret messages:

```
#include <stdio.h>

int main()
{
  char word[10];
  int i = 0;
  while (scanf("%9s", word) == 1) {
    i = i + 1;
    if (i % 2)
      fprintf(stdout, "%s\n", word);
    else
      fprintf(stderr, "%s\n", word);
  }
  return 0;
}
```

We have intercepted a file called *secret.txt* and a scrap of paper with instructions:

```
THE BUY SUBMARINE
SIX WILL EGGS
SURFACE AND AT
SOME NINE MILK PM
```

secret.txt

```
Run with:
secret_messages < secret.txt > message1.txt 2> message2.txt
```

Your mission was to decode the two secret messages.

Message 1	Message 2
THE	BUY
SUBMARINE	SIX
WILL	EGGS
SURFACE	AND
AT	SOME
NINE	MILK
PM	

The Operating System Exposed

This week's interview: Does the Operating System Matter?

Head First: Operating System, we're so pleased you've found time for us today.

O/S: Time sharing: it's what I'm good at.

Head First: Now you've agreed to appear under conditions of anonymity, is that right?

O/S: Don't Ask/Don't Tell. Just call me O/S.

Head First: Does it matter what kind of O/S you are?

O/S: A lot of people get pretty heated over which operating system to use. But for simple C programs, we all behave pretty much the same way.

Head First: Because of the C Standard Library?

O/S: Yeah, if you're writing C, then the basics are the same everywhere. Like I always say, we're all the same with the lights out. Know what I'm saying?

Head First: Oh, of course. Now, you are in charge of loading programs into memory?

O/S: I turn them into processes, that's right.

Head First: Important job?

O/S: I like to think so. You can't just throw a program into memory and let it struggle, you know? There's a whole bunch of setup. I need to allocate memory for the programs and connect them to their standard data streams so they can use things like displays and keyboards.

Head First: Like you just did for the `geo2json` program?

O/S: That guy's a real tool.

Head First: Oh, I'm sorry.

O/S: No, I mean he's a real tool: a simple, text-based program.

Head First: Ah, I see. And do you deal with a lot of tools?

O/S: Ain't that life? It depends on the operating system. Unix-style systems use a lot of tools to get the work done. Windows uses them less, but they're still important.

Head First: Creating small tools that work together is almost a philosophy, isn't it?

O/S: It's a way of life. Sometimes when you've got a big problem to solve, it can be easier to break it down into a set of simpler tasks.

Head First: Then write a tool for each task?

O/S: Exactly. Then use the operating system—that's me—to connect the tools together.

Head First: Are there any advantages to that approach?

O/S: The big one is simplicity. If you have a set of small programs, they are easier to test. The other thing is that once you've built a tool, you can use it in other projects.

Head First: Any downsides?

O/S: Well, tools don't look that great. They work on the command line usually, so they don't have a lot of what you might call Eye Appeal.

Head First: Does that matter?

O/S: Not as much as you'd think. As long as you have a set of solid tools to do the important work, you can always connect them to a nice interface, whether it's a desktop application or a website. But, hey, look at the time. Sorry, I've got to preempt you.

Head First: Oh, well, thank you, O/S; it's been a pleas...*zzzzzz*...

Small tools are flexible

One of the great things about small tools is their flexibility. If you write a program that does one thing really well, chances are you will be able to use it in lots of contexts. If you create a program that can search for text inside a file, say, then chances are you're going to find that program useful in more than one place.

For example, think about your `geo2json` tool. You created it to help display cycling data, right? But there's no reason you can't use it for some other purpose…like investigating…the…

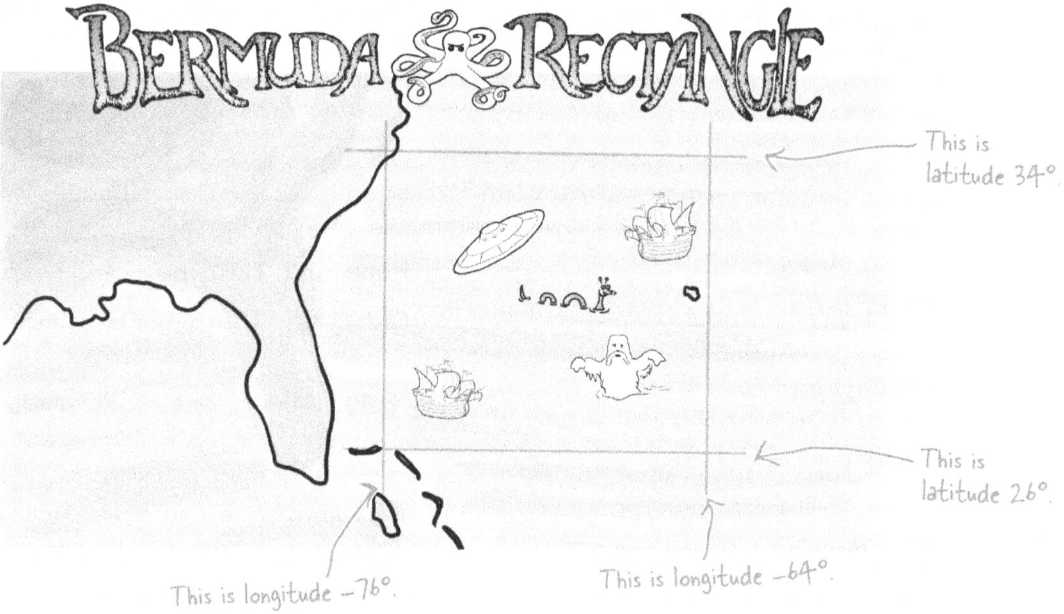
BERMUDA RECTANGLE
This is latitude 34°.
This is latitude 26°.
This is longitude -76°.
This is longitude -64°.

To see how flexible our tool is, let's use it for a completely different problem. Instead of just displaying data on a map, let's try to use it for something a little more complex. Say you want to read in a whole set of GPS data like before, but instead of just displaying everything, let's just display the information that falls inside the Bermuda Rectangle.

That means you will display only data that matches these conditions:

```
((latitude > 26) && (latitude < 34))

((longitude > -76) && (longitude < -64))
```

So where do you need to begin?

Don't change the geo2json tool

Our `geo2json` tool displays all of the data it's given. So what should we do? Should we *modify* `geo2json` so that it *exports* data and also *checks* the data?

Well, we *could*, but remember, a small tool:

does one job and does it well

You don't really want to modify the `geo2json` tool, because you want it to do just one task. If you make the program do something more complex, you'll cause problems for your users who expect the tool to keep working in exactly the same way.

I really don't want to filter data. I need to keep on displaying everything.

So if you don't want to change the geo2json tool, what should you do?

Tips for Designing Small Tools

Small tools like `geo2json` all follow these design principles:

* They can read data from the Standard Input.
* They can display data on the Standard Output.
* They deal with *text* data rather than obscure binary formats.
* They each perform *one simple task*.

A different task needs a different tool

If you want to skip over the data that falls outside the Bermuda Rectangle, you should build a separate tool that does just that.

So, you'll have **two** tools: a new **bermuda** tool that filters out data that is outside the Bermuda Rectangle, and then your original geo2json tool that will convert the remaining data for the map.

This is how you'll connect the programs together:

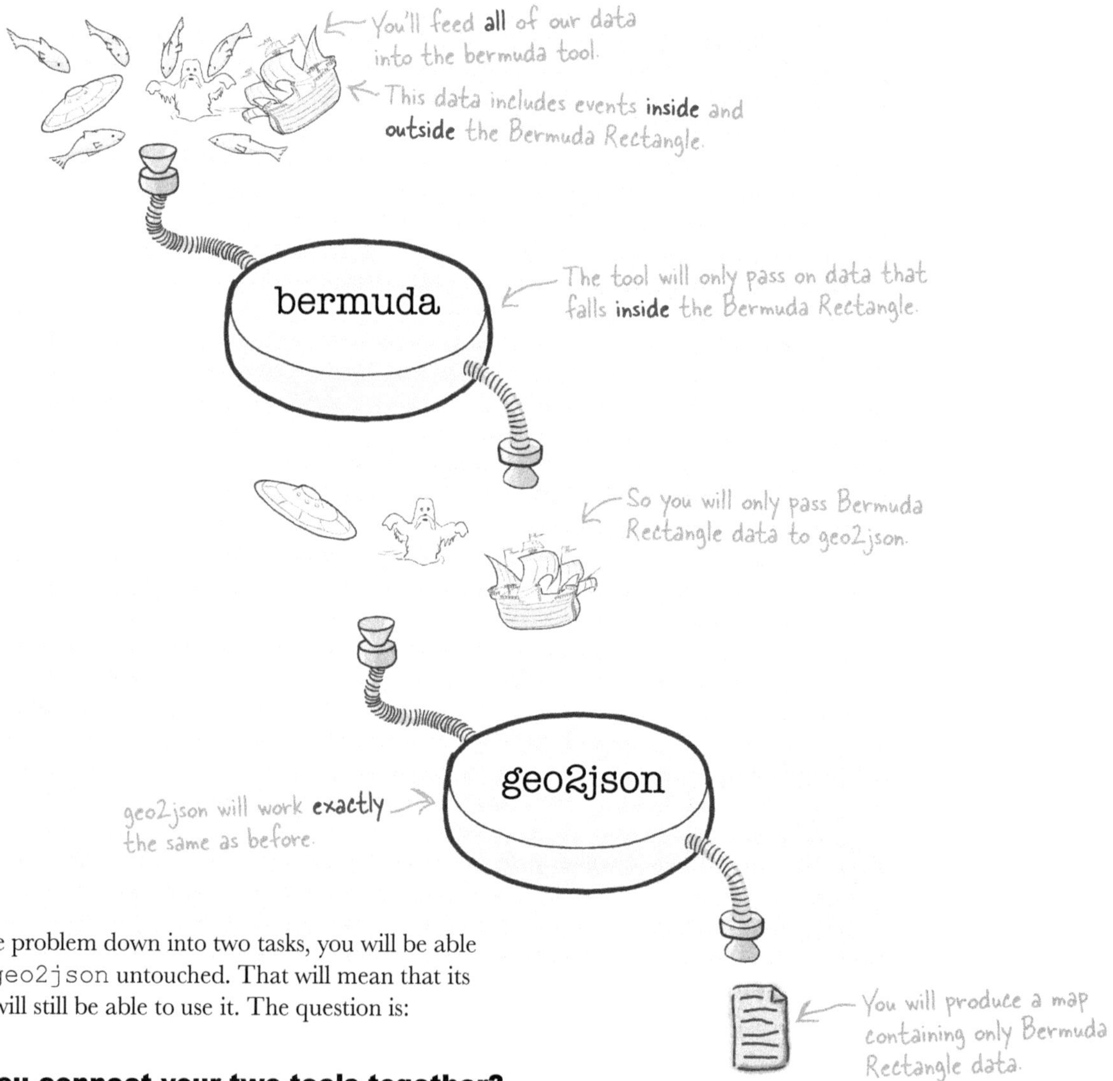
You'll feed all of our data into the bermuda tool.
This data includes events inside and outside the Bermuda Rectangle.
bermuda
The tool will only pass on data that falls inside the Bermuda Rectangle.
So you will only pass Bermuda Rectangle data to geo2json.
geo2json
geo2json will work exactly the same as before.
You will produce a map containing only Bermuda Rectangle data.

By splitting the problem down into two tasks, you will be able to leave your geo2json untouched. That will mean that its current users will still be able to use it. The question is:

How will you connect your two tools together?

Connect your input and output with a pipe

You've already seen how to use redirection to connect the *Standard Input* and the *Standard Output* of a program file. But now you'll connect the **Standard Output** of the **bermuda** tool to the **Standard Input** of the `geo2json`, like this:

The | symbol is a pipe that connects the Standard Output of one process to the Standard Input of another process.

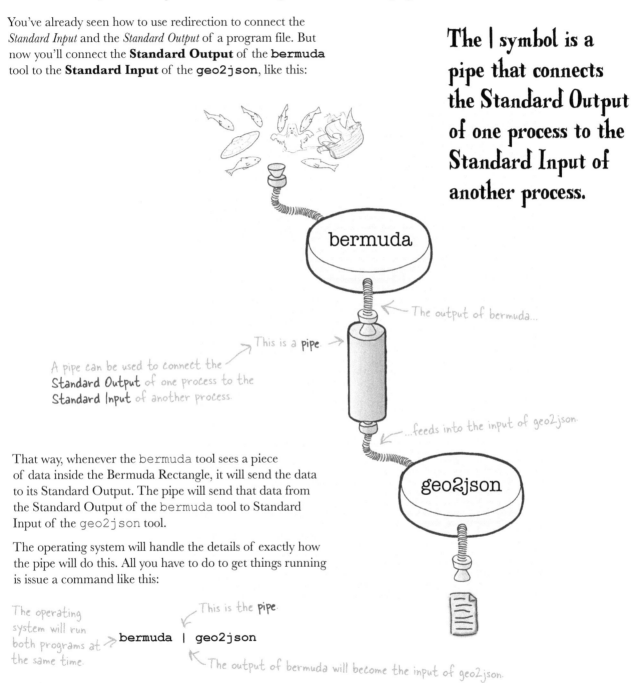

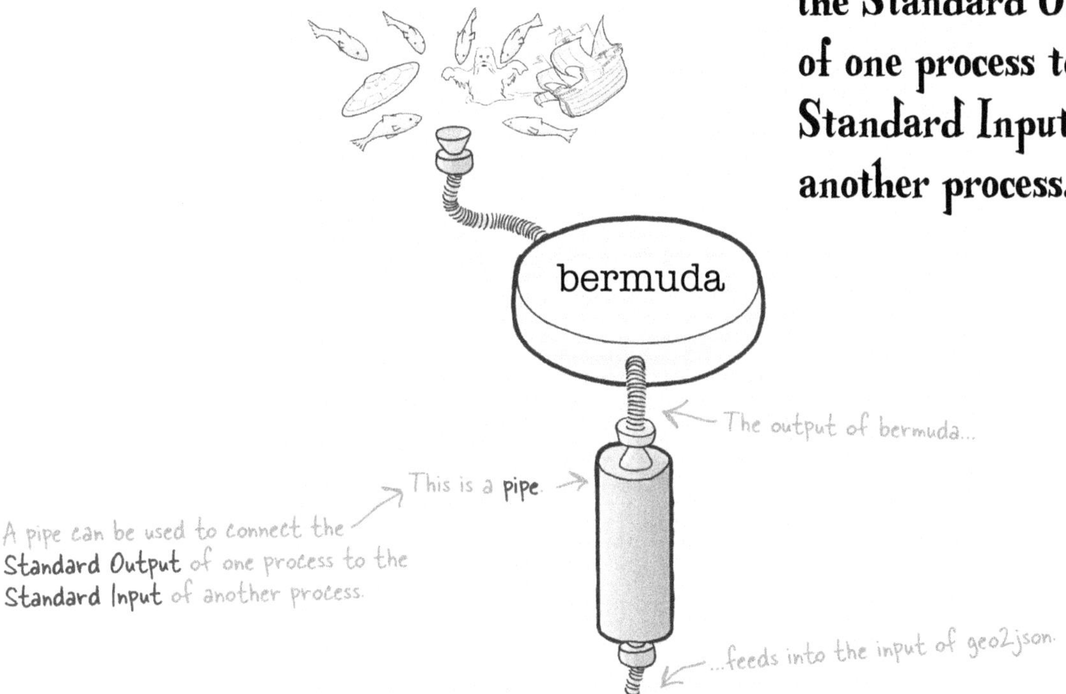
bermuda
The output of bermuda...
This is a pipe.
A pipe can be used to connect the Standard Output of one process to the Standard Input of another process.
...feeds into the input of geo2json.

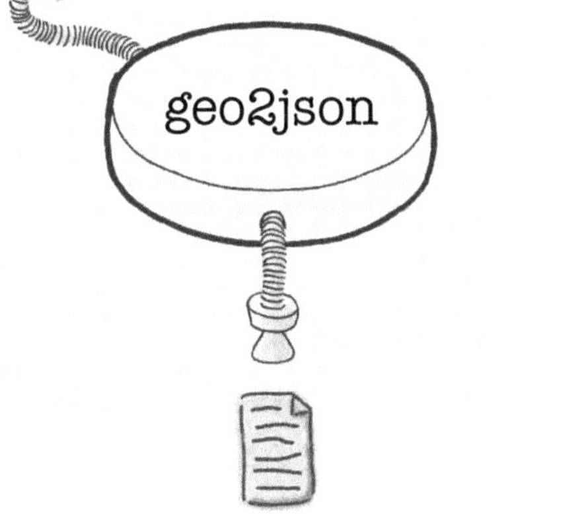
geo2json

That way, whenever the `bermuda` tool sees a piece of data inside the Bermuda Rectangle, it will send the data to its Standard Output. The pipe will send that data from the Standard Output of the `bermuda` tool to Standard Input of the `geo2json` tool.

The operating system will handle the details of exactly how the pipe will do this. All you have to do to get things running is issue a command like this:

The operating system will run both programs at the same time.

This is the pipe.

```
bermuda | geo2json
```

The output of bermuda will become the input of geo2json.

So now it's time to build the `bermuda` tool.

The bermuda tool

The `bermuda` tool will work in a very similar way to the `geo2json` tool: it will read through a set of GPS data, line by line, and then send data to the Standard Output.

But there will be two big differences. First, it won't send *every* piece of data to the Standard Output, just the lines that are inside the Bermuda Rectangle. The second difference is that the `bermuda` tool will always output data in the same CSV format used to store GPS data.

This is what the pseudocode for the tool looks like:

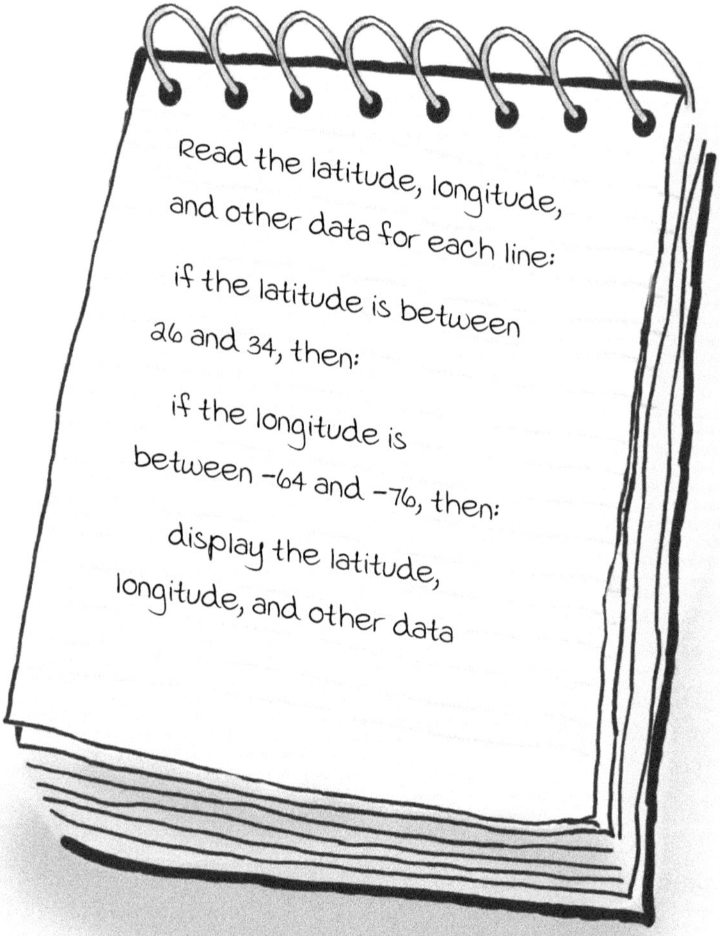
Read the latitude, longitude, and other data for each line:
if the latitude is between 26 and 34, then:
if the longitude is between -64 and -76, then:
display the latitude, longitude, and other data

Let's turn the pseudocode into C.

Pool Puzzle

Your **goal** is to complete the code for the `bermuda` program. Take code snippets from the pool and place them into the blank lines below. You won't need to use all the snippets of code in the pool.

```
#include <stdio.h>

int main()
{
  float latitude;
  float longitude;
  char info[80];
  while (scanf("%f,%f,%79[^\n]",.................,.................,.................) == 3)
    if ((.................>.................).................(.................<.................))
      if ((.................>.................).................(.................<.................))
        printf("%f,%f,%s\n",.................,.................,.................);

  return 0;
}
```

Note: each thing from the pool can be used only once!

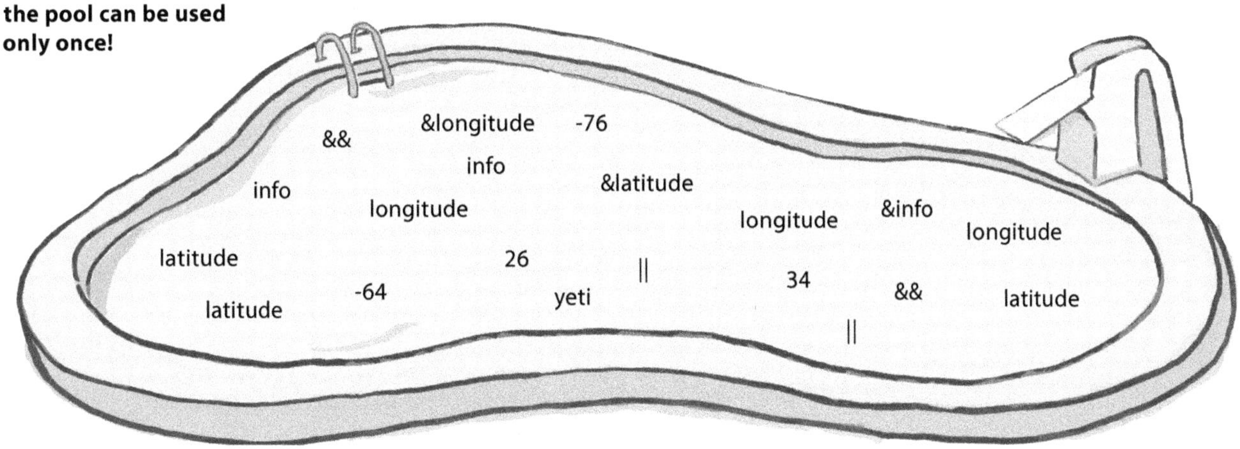

&&
&longitude
-76
info
info
&latitude
longitude
longitude
&info
longitude
latitude
26
||
34
latitude
-64
yeti
&&
latitude
||

Pool Puzzle Solution

Your **goal** was to complete the code for the `bermuda` program by taking code snippets from the pool and placing them into the blank lines below.

```
#include <stdio.h>

int main()
{
  float latitude;
  float longitude;
  char info[80];
  while (scanf("%f,%f,%79[^\n]", &latitude , &longitude , info ) == 3)
    if ((latitude > 26 ) && (latitude < 34 ))
      if ((longitude > -76 ) && (longitude < -64 ))
        printf("%f,%f,%s\n", latitude , longitude , info );

  return 0;
}
```

Note: each thing from the pool can be used only once!

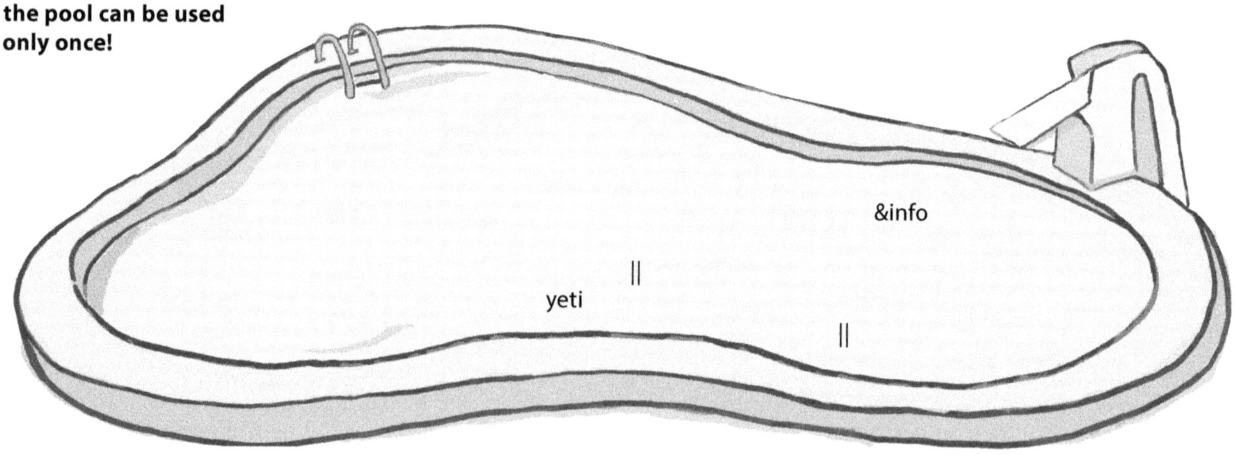
&info
||
yeti
||

Test Drive

Do this!

You can download the *spooky.csv* file at *https://github.com/dogriffiths/HeadFirstC*.

Now that you've completed the `bermuda` tool, it's time to use it with the `geo2json` tool and see if you can map any weird occurrences inside the Bermuda Rectangle.

Once you've compiled both of the tools, you can fire up a console and then run the two programs together like this:

```
(./bermuda | ./geo2json) < spooky.csv > output.json
```

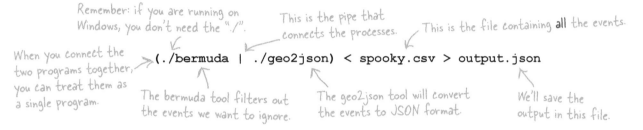

- Remember: if you are running on Windows, you don't need the "./".
- This is the pipe that connects the processes.
- This is the file containing **all** the events.
- When you connect the two programs together, you can treat them as a single program.
- The bermuda tool filters out the events we want to ignore.
- The geo2json tool will convert the events to JSON format.
- We'll save the output in this file.

By connecting the two programs together with a pipe, you can treat these two separate programs as if they were a single program, so you can redirect the Standard Input and Standard Output like you did before.

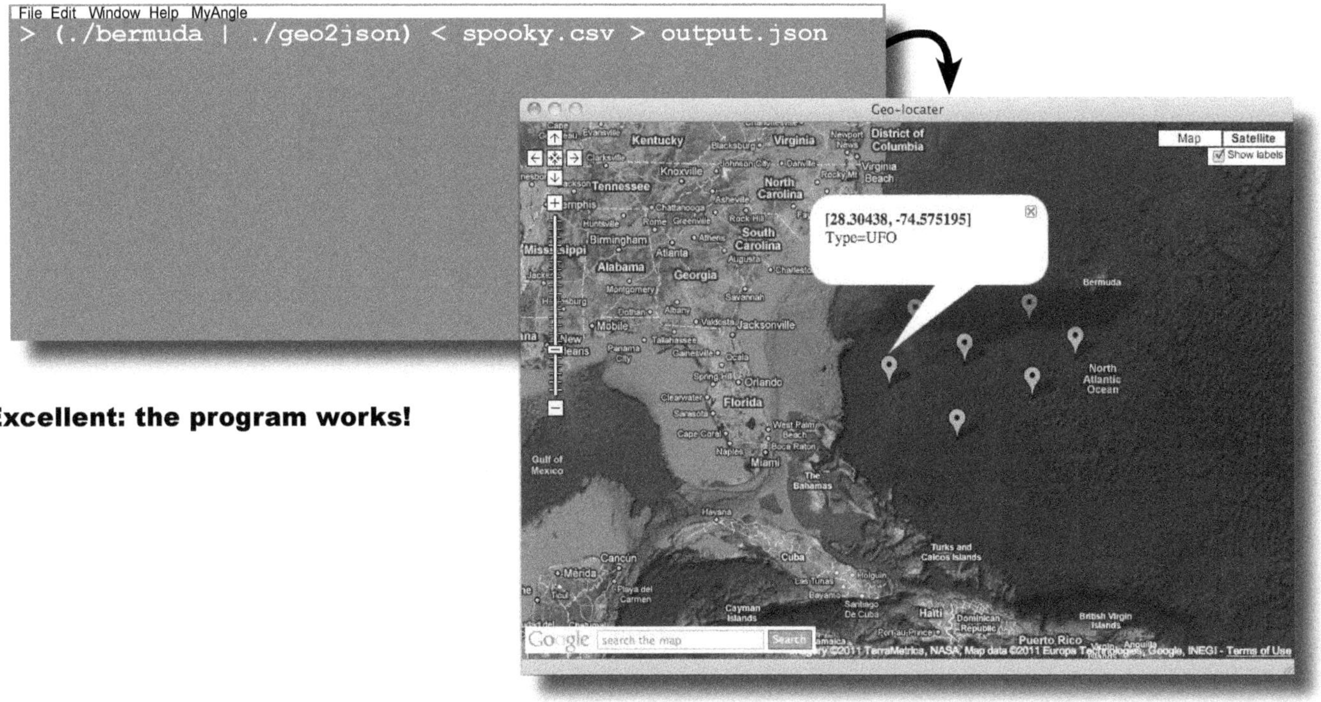
File Edit Window Help MyAngle
> (./bermuda | ./geo2json) < spooky.csv > output.json
Geo-locater
[28.30438, -74.575195]
Type=UFO

Excellent: the program works!

there are no Dumb Questions

Q: Why is it important that small tools use the Standard Input and Standard Output?

A: Because it makes it easier to connect tools together with pipes.

Q: Why does that matter?

A: Small tools usually don't solve an entire problem on their own, just a small technical problem, like converting data from one format to another. But if you can combine them together, then you can solve large problems.

Q: What is a pipe, actually?

A: The exact details depend on the operating system. Pipes might be made from sections of memory or temporary files. The important thing is that they accept data in one end, and send the data out of the other in sequence.

Q: So if two programs are piped together, does the first program have to finish running before the second program can start?

A: No. Both of the programs will run at the same time; as output is produced by the first program, it can be consumed by the second program.

Q: Why do small tools use text?

A: It's the most open format. If a small tool uses text, it means that any other programmer can easily read and understand the output just by using a text editor. Binary formats are normally obscure and hard to understand.

Q: Can I connect several programs together with pipes?

A: Yes, just add more `|` between each program name. A series of connected processes is called a *pipeline*.

Q: If several processes are connected together with pipes and then I use > and < to redirect the Standard Input and Output, which processes will have their input and output redirected?

A: The < will send a file's contents to the first process in the pipeline. The > will capture the Standard Output from the last process in the pipeline.

Q: Are the parentheses really necessary when I run the `bermuda` program with `geo2json`?

A: Yes. The parentheses will make sure the data file is read by the Standard Input of the `bermuda` program.

BULLET POINTS

- If you want to perform a different task, consider writing a separate small tool.
- Design tools to work with Standard Input and Standard Output.
- Small tools normally read and write text data.
- You can connect the Standard Output of one process to the Standard Input of another process using a **pipe**.

But what if you want to output to more than one file?

We've looked at how to read data from one file and write to another file using redirection, but what if the program needs to do something a little more complex, like send data to **more than one file?**

Imagine you need to create another tool that will read a set of data from a file, and then split it into other files.

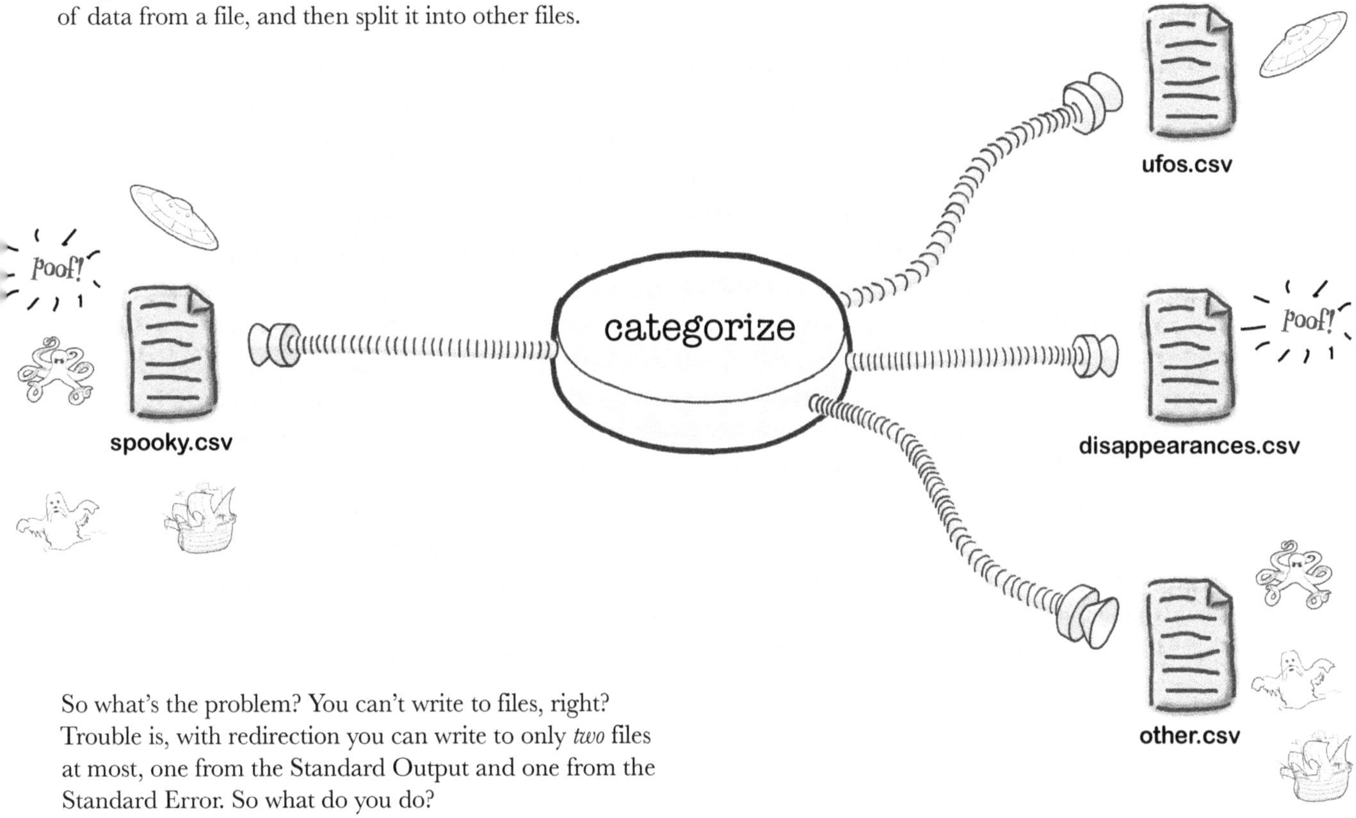
Poof!
spooky.csv
categorize
ufos.csv
Poof!
disappearances.csv
other.csv

So what's the problem? You can't write to files, right? Trouble is, with redirection you can write to only *two* files at most, one from the Standard Output and one from the Standard Error. So what do you do?

Roll your own data streams

When a program runs, the operating system gives it three file data streams: the Standard Input, the Standard Output, and the Standard Error. But sometimes you need to create other data streams on the fly.

The good news is that the operating system doesn't limit you to the ones you are dealt when the program starts. You can roll your own as the program runs.

Each data stream is represented by a pointer to a file, and you can create a new data stream using the **fopen()** function:

This will create a data stream to read **from** a file. This is the name of the file. This is the **mode**: "r" means "read."

```
FILE *in_file = fopen("input.txt", "r");
```

This will create a data stream to write **to** a file. This is the name of the file. This is the **mode**: "w" means "write."

```
FILE *out_file = fopen("output.txt", "w");
```

The fopen() function takes **two** parameters: a *filename* and a *mode*. The mode can be **w** to write to a file, **r** to read from a file, or **a** to append data to the *end* of a file.

The mode is:
"w" = write,
"r" = read, or
"a" = append.

Once you've created a data stream, you can print to it using **fprintf()**, just like before. But what if you need to read from a file? Well, there's also an **fscanf()** function to help you do that too:

```
fprintf(out_file, "Don't wear %s with %s", "red", "green");

fscanf(in_file, "%79[^\n]\n", sentence);
```

Finally, when you're finished with a data stream, you need to *close it*. The truth is that all data streams are automatically closed when the program ends, but it's still a good idea to always close the data stream yourself:

```
fclose(in_file);
fclose(out_file);
```

Let's try this out now.

Sharpen your pencil

This is the code for a program to read all of the data from a GPS file and then write the data into one of three other files. See if you can fill in the blanks.

```
#include <stdio.h>
#include <stdlib.h>
#include <string.h>

int main()
{
  char line[80];
  FILE *in = fopen("spooky.csv", ...............);
  FILE *file1 = fopen("ufos.csv", ...............);
  FILE *file2 = fopen("disappearances.csv", ...............);
  FILE *file3 = fopen("others.csv", ...............);
  while (............... (in, "%79[^\n]\n", line) == 1) {
    if (strstr(line, "UFO"))
      ............... (file1, "%s\n", line);
    else if (strstr(line, "Disappearance"))
      ............... (file2, "%s\n", line);
    else
      ............... (file3, "%s\n", line);
  }
  ...............(file1);
  ...............(file2);
  ...............(file3);
  fclose(in);
  return 0;
}
```

there are no Dumb Questions

Q: How many data streams can I have?

A: It depends on the operating system, but usually a process can have up to 256. The key thing is there's a limited number of them, so make sure you close them when you're done using them.

Q: Why is `FILE` in uppercase?

A: It's historic. `FILE` used to be defined using a macro. Macros are usually given uppercase names. You'll hear about macros later on.

Sharpen your pencil Solution

This is the code for a program to read all of the data from a GPS file and then write the data into one of three other files. You were to fill in the blanks.

```
#include <stdio.h>
#include <stdlib.h>
#include <string.h>

int main()
{
  char line[80];
  FILE *in = fopen("spooky.csv", "r");
  FILE *file1 = fopen("ufos.csv", "w");
  FILE *file2 = fopen("disappearances.csv", "w");
  FILE *file3 = fopen("others.csv", "w");
  while (fscanf(in, "%79[^\n]\n", line) == 1) {
    if (strstr(line, "UFO"))
      fprintf(file1, "%s\n", line);
    else if (strstr(line, "Disappearance"))
      fprintf(file2, "%s\n", line);
    else
      fprintf(file3, "%s\n", line);
  }
  fclose(file1);
  fclose(file2);
  fclose(file3);
  fclose(in);
  return 0;
}
```

The program runs, but...

If you compile and run the program with:

```
gcc categorize.c -o categorize && ./categorize
```

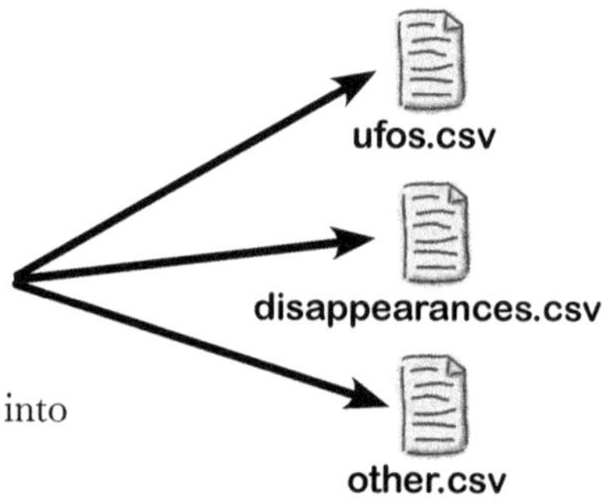

ufos.csv
disappearances.csv
other.csv

the program will read the *spooky.csv* file and split up the data, line by line, into three other files—*ufos.csv*, *disappearances.csv*, and *other.csv*.

That's great, but what if a user wanted to split up the data differently? What if he wanted to search for different words or write to different files? Could he do that without needing to recompile the program each time?

There's more to main()

The thing is, any program you write will need to give the user the ability to change the way it works. If it's a GUI program, you will probably need to give it preferences. And if it's a command-line program, like our `categorize` tool, it will need to give the user the ability to pass it **command-line arguments**:

This is the first word to filter for.

All of the mermaid data will be stored in this file.

This means you want to check for Elvis.

```
./categorize mermaid mermaid.csv Elvis elvises.csv the_rest.csv
```

Everything else goes into this file.

All the Elvis sightings will be stored here.

But how do you read command-line arguments from **within the program**? So far, every time you've created a **`main()`** function, you've written it without any arguments. But the truth is, there are actually *two* forms of the `main()` function we can use. This is the second version:

```
int main(int argc, char *argv[])
{
    .... Do stuff....
}
```

The `main()` function can read the command-line arguments as an **array of strings**. Actually, of course, because C doesn't really have strings built-in, it reads them as *an array of character pointers to strings*. Like this:

```
"./categorize"  "mermaid"  "mermaid.csv"  "Elvis"  "elvises.csv"  "the_rest.csv"
```

This is argv[0]. This is argv[1]. This is argv[2]. This is argv[3]. This is argv[4]. This is argv[5].

The first argument is actually the name of the program being run.

Like any array in C, you need some way of knowing how long the array is. That's why the `main()` function has two parameters. The `argc` value is a count of the number of elements in the array.

Command-line arguments really give your program a lot more flexibility, and it's worth thinking about which things you want your users to *tweak* at runtime. It will make your program a lot more valuable to them.

OK, let's see how you can add a little flexibility to the categorize program.

Watch it!

The first argument contains the name of the program as it was run by the user.

That means that the first ***proper*** *command-line argument is* `argv[1]`.

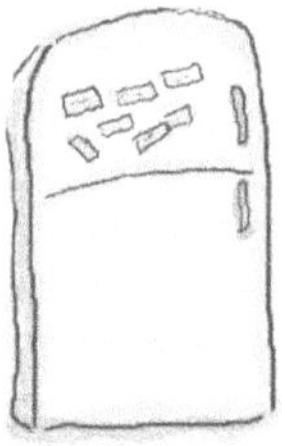

Code Magnets

This is a modified version of the `categorize` program that can read the keywords to search for and the files to use from the command line. See if you can fit the correct magnets into the correct slots.

The program runs using:

```
./categorize mermaid mermaid.csv Elvis elvises.csv the_rest.csv
```

```
#include <stdio.h>
#include <stdlib.h>
#include <string.h>

int main(int argc, char *argv[])
{
  char line[80];

  if ( .................. != .................. ) {
    fprintf(stderr, "You need to give 5 arguments\n");
    return 1;
  }
  FILE *in = fopen("spooky.csv", "r");

  FILE *file1 = fopen( .................. , "w");

  FILE *file2 = fopen( .................. , "w");

  FILE *file3 = fopen( .................. , "w");
```

```
  while (fscanf(in, "%79[^\n]\n", line) == 1) {

    if (strstr(line, .................... ))
      fprintf(file1, "%s\n", line);

    else if (strstr(line, .................... ))
      fprintf(file2, "%s\n", line);
    else
      fprintf(file3, "%s\n", line);
  }
  fclose(file1);
  fclose(file2);
  fclose(file3);
  fclose(in);
  return 0;
}
```

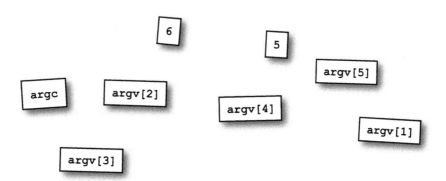

- **6**
- **5**
- **argv[5]**
- **argc**
- **argv[2]**
- **argv[4]**
- **argv[1]**
- **argv[3]**

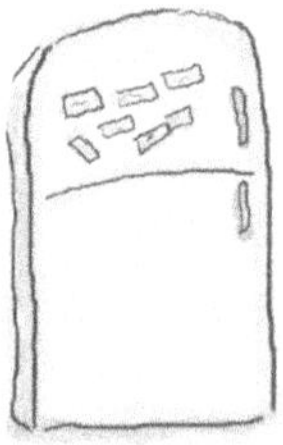

Code Magnets Solution

This is a modified version of the `categorize` program that can read the keywords to search for and the files to use from the command line. You were to fit the correct magnets into the correct slots.

The program runs using:

```
./categorize mermaid mermaid.csv Elvis elvises.csv the_rest.csv
```

```
#include <stdio.h>
#include <stdlib.h>
#include <string.h>

int main(int argc, char *argv[])
{
  char line[80];
  if ( argc != 6 ) {
    fprintf(stderr, "You need to give 5 arguments\n");
    return 1;
  }
  FILE *in = fopen("spooky.csv", "r");

  FILE *file1 = fopen( argv[2] , "w");

  FILE *file2 = fopen( argv[4] , "w");

  FILE *file3 = fopen( argv[5] , "w");
```

```
  while (fscanf(in, "%79[^\n]\n", line) == 1) {

    if (strstr(line, argv[1]))
      fprintf(file1, "%s\n", line);

    else if (strstr(line, argv[3]))
      fprintf(file2, "%s\n", line);
    else
      fprintf(file3, "%s\n", line);
  }
  fclose(file1);
  fclose(file2);
  fclose(file3);
  fclose(in);
  return 0;
}
```

5

Test Drive

OK, let's try out the new version of the code. You'll need a test data file called *spooky.csv*.

```
30.685163,-68.137207,Type=Yeti
28.304380,-74.575195,Type=UFO
29.132971,-71.136475,Type=Ship
28.343065,-62.753906,Type=Elvis
27.868217,-68.005371,Type=Goatsucker
30.496017,-73.333740,Type=Disappearance
26.224447,-71.477051,Type=UFO
29.401320,-66.027832,Type=Ship
37.879536,-69.477539,Type=Elvis
22.705256,-68.192139,Type=Elvis
27.166695,-87.484131,Type=Elvis
```

spooky.csv

Now you'll need to run the `categorize` program with a few command-line arguments saying what text to look for and what filenames to use:

File Edit Window Help ThankYouVeryMuch

```
> categorize UFO aliens.csv Elvis elvises.csv the_rest.csv
```

When the program runs, the following files are produced:

```
28.304380,-74.575195,Type=UFO
26.224447,-71.477051,Type=UFO
```

aliens.csv

```
30.685163,-68.137207,Type=Yeti
29.132971,-71.136475,Type=Ship
27.868217,-68.005371,Type=Goatsucker
30.496017,-73.333740,Type=Disappearance
29.401320,-66.027832,Type=Ship
```

the_rest.csv

```
28.343065,-62.753906,Type=Elvis
37.879536,-69.477539,Type=Elvis
22.705256,-68.192139,Type=Elvis
27.166695,-87.484131,Type=Elvis
```

elvises.csv

If you run elvises.csv through geo2json, you can display it on a map.

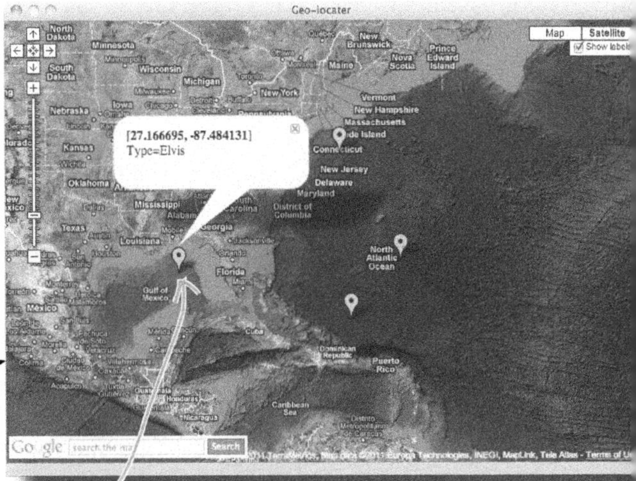
Geo-locater
Map
Satellite
[27.166695, -87.484131]
Type=Elvis
Search

Elvis has left the building.

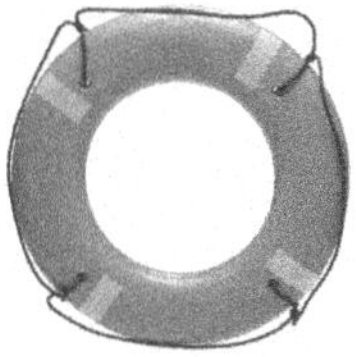

Safety Check

Although at Head First Labs we never make mistakes (cough), it's important in real-world programs to check for problems when you open a file for reading or writing. Fortunately, if there's a problem opening a data stream, the `fopen()` function will return the value 0. That means if you want to check for errors, you should change code like:

```
FILE *in = fopen("i_dont_exist.txt", "r");
```

to this:

```
FILE *in;
if (!(in = fopen("dont_exist.txt", "r"))) {
  fprintf(stderr, "Can't open the file.\n");
  return 1;
}
```

Overheard at the Head First Pizzeria

Anchovy and pineapple, thick crust! Make it snappy; we need it for immediate delivery.

Chances are, any program you write is going to need options. If you create a chat program, it's going to need preferences. If you write a game, the user will want to change the shape of the blood spots. And if you're writing a command-line tool, you are probably going to need to add **command-line options**.

Command-line options are the little switches you often see with command-line tools:

```
ps -ae
```

← Display all the processes, including their environments.

```
tail -f logfile.out
```

← Display the end of the file, but wait for new data to be added to the end of the file.

Let the library do the work for you

Many programs use command-line options, so there's a special library function you can use to make dealing with them a little easier. It's called **getopt()**, and each time you call it, it returns the next option it finds on the command line.

Let's see how it works. Imagine you have a program that can take a set of different options:

Use four engines. → Awesomeness mode enabled.

```
rocket_to -e 4 -a Brasilia Tokyo London
```

This program needs one option that will take a value (`-e` = engines) and another that is simply *on* or *off* (`-a` = awesomeness). You can handle these options by calling `getopt()` in a loop like this:

The Polite Guide to Standards

The *unistd.h* header is not actually part of the standard C library. Instead, it gives your programs access to some of the POSIX libraries. POSIX was an attempt to create a common set of functions for use across all popular operating systems.

You will need to include this header. →

```
#include <unistd.h>

...

while ((ch = getopt(argc, argv, "ae:")) != EOF)
  switch(ch) {
  ...
  case 'e':
    engine_count = optarg;
  ...
  }

argc -= optind;
argv += optind;
```

This means "The a option is valid; so is the e option."

The ":" means that the e option needs an argument.

The code to handle each option goes here.

You're reading the argument for the "e" option here.

optind stores the number of strings read from the command line to get past the options.

These final two lines make sure we skip past the options we read.

Inside the loop, you have a `switch` statement to handle each of the valid options. The string **ae:** tells the `getopt()` function that `a` and `e` are valid options. The `e` is followed by a colon to tell `getopt()` that the `-e` needs to be followed by an extra argument. `getopt()` will point to that argument with the **optarg** variable.

When the loop finishes, you tweak the `argv` and `argc` variables to skip past all of the options and get to the main command-line arguments. That will make your `argv` array look like this:

```
Brasilia Tokyo London
```

This is argv[0]. This is argv[1]. This is argv[2].

BANG!
Watch it!

After processing the arguments, the 0th argument will no longer be the program name.

`argv[0]` *will instead point to the first command-line argument that follows the options.*

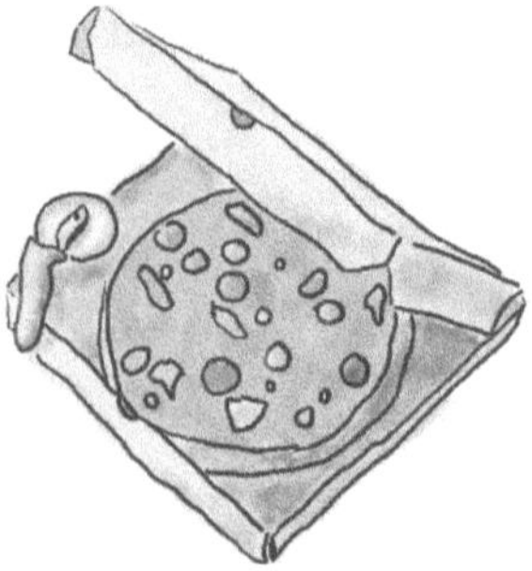

Pizza Pieces

Looks like someone's been taking a bite out of the pizza code. See if you can replace the pizza slices and rebuild the `order_pizza` program.

```
#include <stdio.h>
#include <unistd.h>

int main(int argc, char *argv[])
{
  char *delivery = "";
  int thick = 0;
  int count = 0;
  char ch;


  while ((ch = getopt(argc, argv, "d .............................  ..............................")) != EOF)
    switch (ch) {
    case 'd':


      ............................. = ............................. ;
      break;
    case 't':


      ............................. = ............................. ;
      break;
    default:
      fprintf(stderr, "Unknown option: '%s'\n", optarg);


      return ............................. ;
    }
```

```
  argc -= optind;
  argv += optind;

  if (thick)
    puts("Thick crust.");

  if (delivery[0])
    printf("To be delivered %s.\n", delivery);

  puts("Ingredients:");




  for (count = ..............................; count < ..............................; count++)
    puts(argv[count]);
  return 0;
}
```

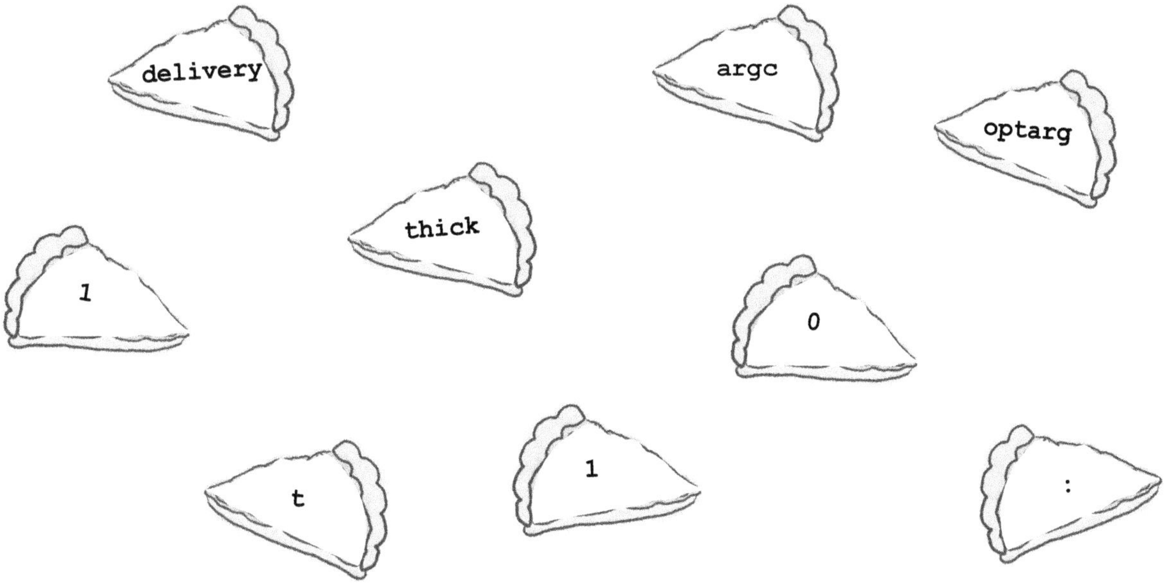
delivery
argc
optarg
thick
1
0
t
1
:

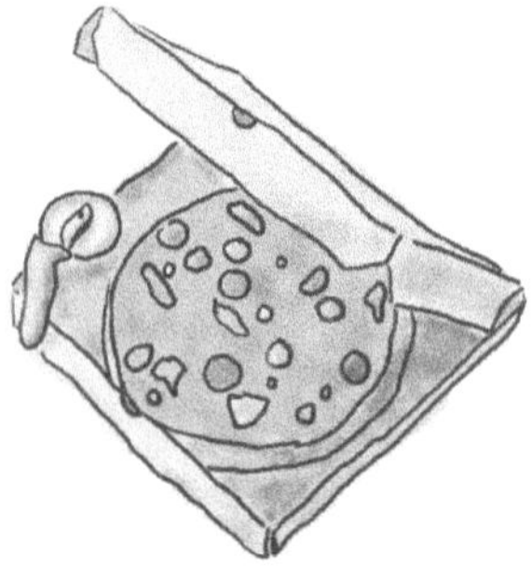

Pizza Pieces Solution

Looks like someone's been taking a bite out of the pizza code. You were to replace the pizza slices and rebuild the `order_pizza` program.

```
#include <stdio.h>
#include <unistd.h>

int main(int argc, char *argv[])
{
  char *delivery = "";
  int thick = 0;
  int count = 0;
  char ch;

  while ((ch = getopt(argc, argv, "d:t")) != EOF)
    switch (ch) {
    case 'd':
      delivery = optarg;
      break;
    case 't':
      thick = 1;
      break;
    default:
      fprintf(stderr, "Unknown option: '%s'\n", optarg);
      return 1;
    }
```

The 'd' is followed by a **colon** because it takes an argument.

We'll point the delivery variable to the argument supplied with the 'd' option.

Remember: in C, setting something to 1 is equivalent to setting it to true.

```
  argc -= optind;
  argv += optind;

  if (thick)
    puts("Thick crust.");

  if (delivery[0])
    printf("To be delivered %s.\n", delivery);

  puts("Ingredients:");

  for (count = 0; count < argc; count++)
    puts(argv[count]);
  return 0;
}
```

After processing the options, the first ingredient is argv[0].

We'll keep looping while we're less than argc.

Test Drive

Now you can try out the pizza-order program:

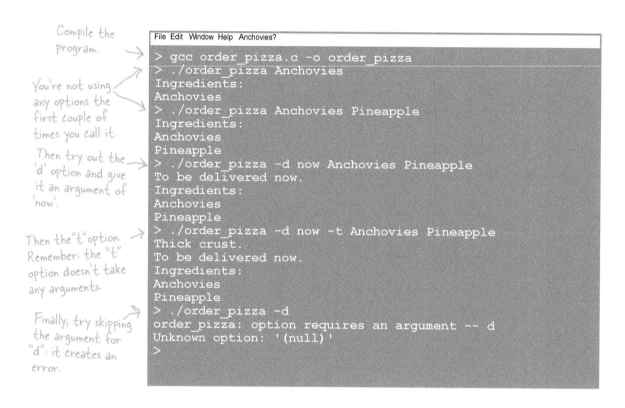

Compile the program.

You're not using any options the first couple of times you call it.

Then try out the 'd' option and give it an argument of 'now'.

Then the "t" option. Remember: the "t" option doesn't take any arguments.

Finally, try skipping the argument for "d": it creates an error.

File Edit Window Help Anchovies?

```
> gcc order_pizza.c -o order_pizza
> ./order_pizza Anchovies
Ingredients:
Anchovies
> ./order_pizza Anchovies Pineapple
Ingredients:
Anchovies
Pineapple
> ./order_pizza -d now Anchovies Pineapple
To be delivered now.
Ingredients:
Anchovies
Pineapple
> ./order_pizza -d now -t Anchovies Pineapple
Thick crust.
To be delivered now.
Ingredients:
Anchovies
Pineapple
> ./order_pizza -d
order_pizza: option requires an argument -- d
Unknown option: '(null)'
>
```

It works!

Well, you've learned a lot in this chapter. You got deep into the Standard Input, Standard Output, and Standard Error. You learned how to talk to files using redirection and your own custom data streams. Finally, you learned how to deal with command-line arguments and options.

A lot of C programmers spend their time creating small tools, and most of the small tools you see in operating systems like Linux are written in C. If you're careful in how you design them, and if you make sure that you design tools that **do one thing** and **do that one thing well**, you're well on course to becoming a kick-ass C coder.

there are no Dumb Questions

Q: Can I combine options like `-td now` instead of `-d now -t`?

A: Yes, you can. The `getopt()` function will handle all of that for you.

Q: What about changing the order of the options?

A: Because of the way we read the options, it won't matter if you type in `-d now -t` or `-t -d now` or `-td now`.

Q: So if the program sees a value on the command line beginning with "-", it will treat it as an option?

A: If it reads it before it gets to the main command-line arguments, it will, yes.

Q: But what if I want to pass negative numbers as command-line arguments like `set_temperature -c -4`? Won't it think that the 4 is an option, not an argument?

A: In order to avoid ambiguity, you can split your main arguments from the options using `--`. So you would write `set_temperature -c -- -4`. `getopt()` will stop reading options when it sees the `--`, so the rest of the line will be read as simple arguments.

BULLET POINTS

- There are two versions of the `main()` function—one with command-line arguments, and one without.
- Command-line arguments are passed to `main()` as an argument count and an array of pointers to the argument strings.
- Command-line options are command-line arguments prefixed with "-".
- The `getopt()` function helps you deal with command-line options.
- You define valid options by passing a string to `getopt()` like `ae:`.
- A "`:`" (colon) following an option in the string means that the option takes an additional argument.
- `getopt()` will record the options argument using the `optarg` variable.
- After you have read all of the options, you should skip past them using the `optind` variable.

Your C Toolbox

You've got Chapter 3 under your belt, and now you've added small tools to your toolbox. For a complete list of tooltips in the book, see Appendix ii.

C functions like printf() and scanf() use the Standard Output and Standard Input to communicate.

The Standard Output goes to the display by default.

The Standard Input reads from the keyboard by default.

The Standard Error is a separate output intended for error messages.

You can print to the Standard Error using fprintf(stderr,...).

You can change where the Standard Input, Output, and Error are connected to using redirection.

Command-line arguments are passed to main() as an array of string pointers.

The getopt() function makes it easier to read command-line options.

You can create custom data streams with fopen("filename", mode).

The mode can be "w" to write, "r" to read, or "a" to append.

4 using multiple source files

Break it down, build it up

Who's he calling "short"?

If you create a big program, you don't want a big source file.

Can you imagine how difficult and time-consuming a single source file for an enterprise-level program would be to maintain? In this chapter, you'll learn how C allows you to break your source code into **small, manageable chunks** and then rebuild them into **one huge program**. Along the way, you'll learn a bit more about **data type subtleties** and get to meet your new best friend: `make`.

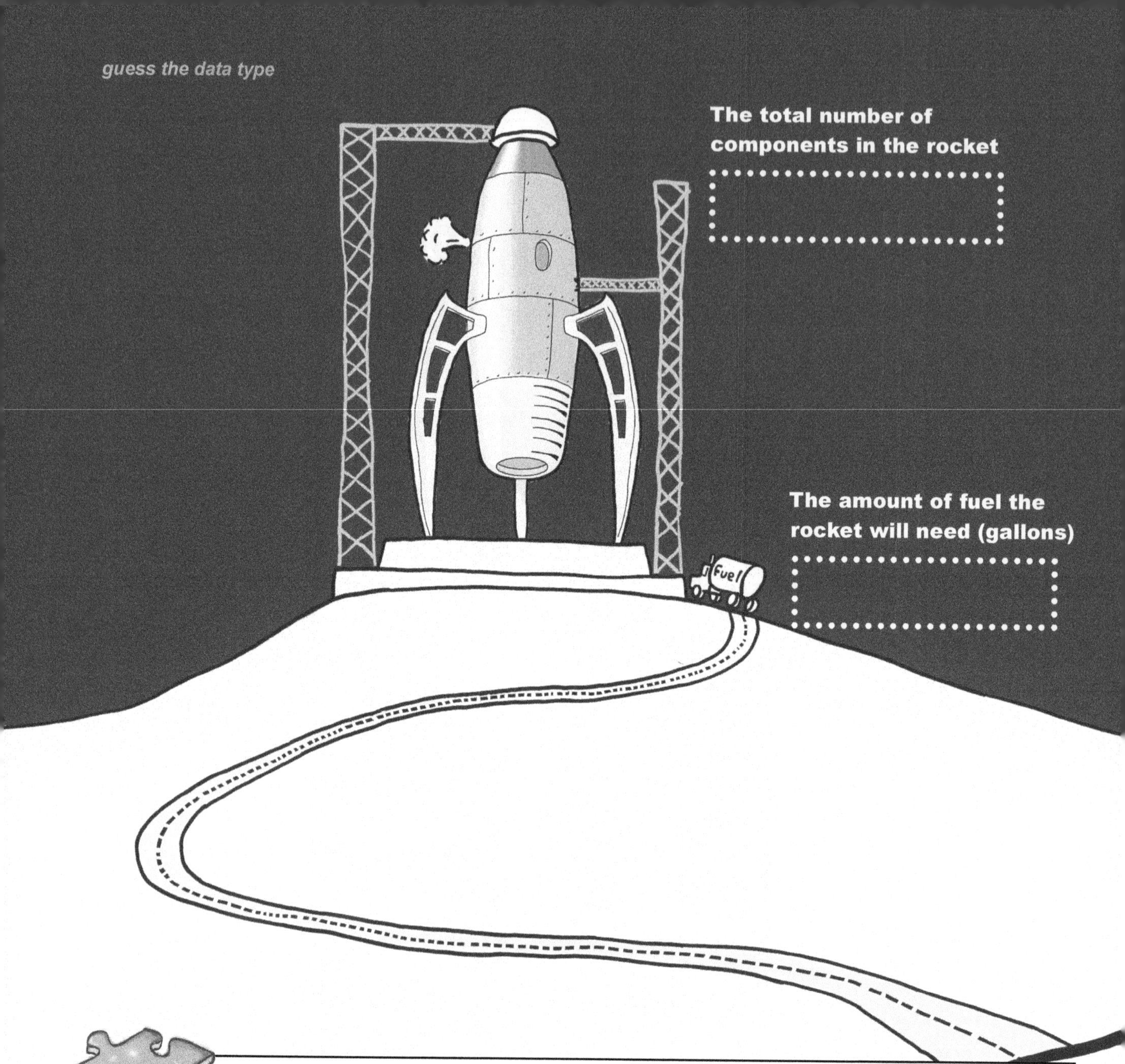
The total number of components in the rocket
Fuel
The amount of fuel the rocket will need (gallons)

Guess the Data Type

C can handle quite a few different types of data: characters and whole numbers, floating-point values for everyday values, and floating-point numbers for really precise scientific calculations. You can see a few of these data types listed on the opposite page. See if you can figure out which data type was used in each example.

Remember: each example uses a different data type.

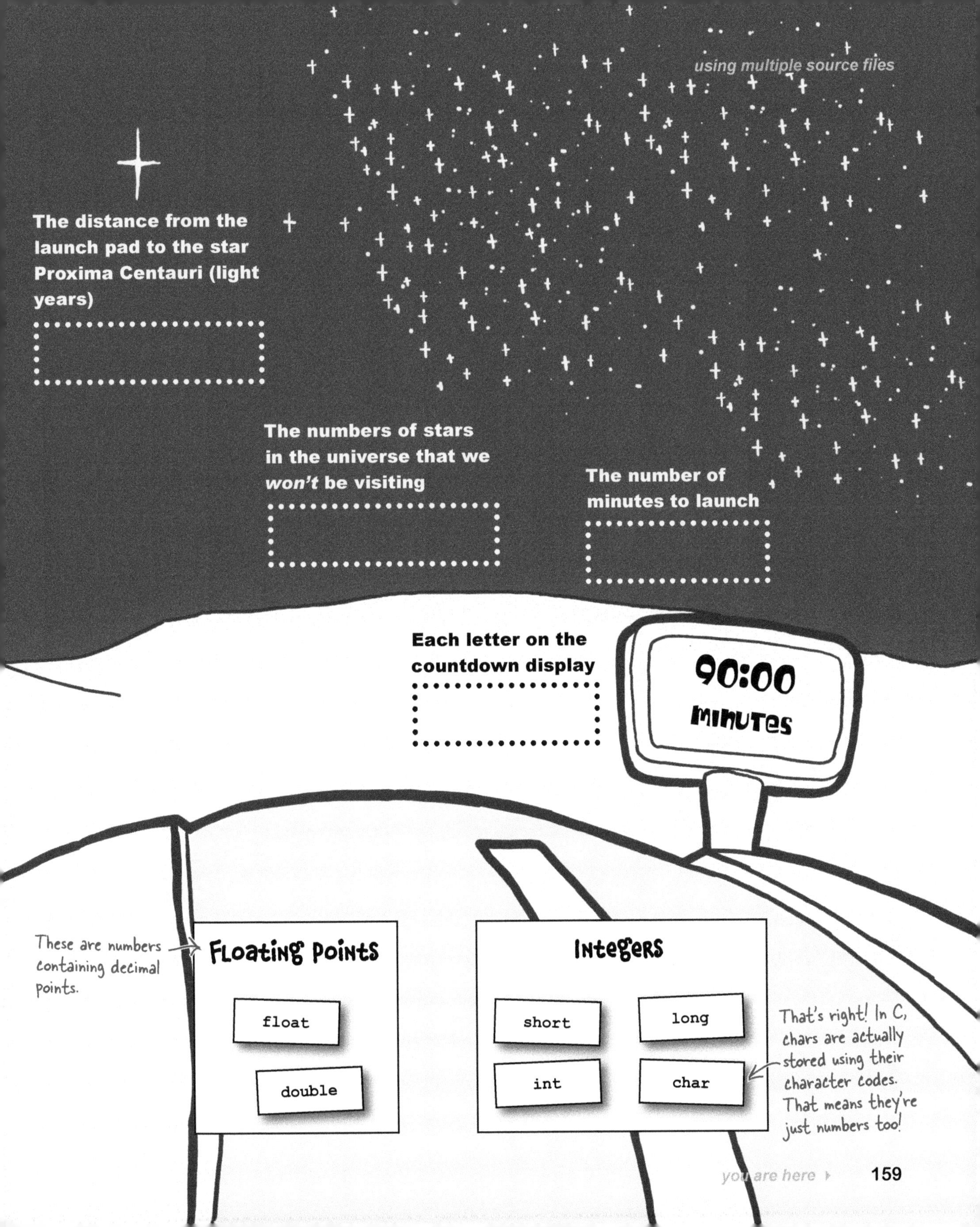
The distance from the launch pad to the star Proxima Centauri (light years)
The numbers of stars in the universe that we *won't* be visiting
The number of minutes to launch
Each letter on the countdown display
90:00
minutes
These are numbers containing decimal points.
Floating Points
float
double
Integers
short
long
int
char
That's right! In C, chars are actually stored using their character codes. That means they're just numbers too!

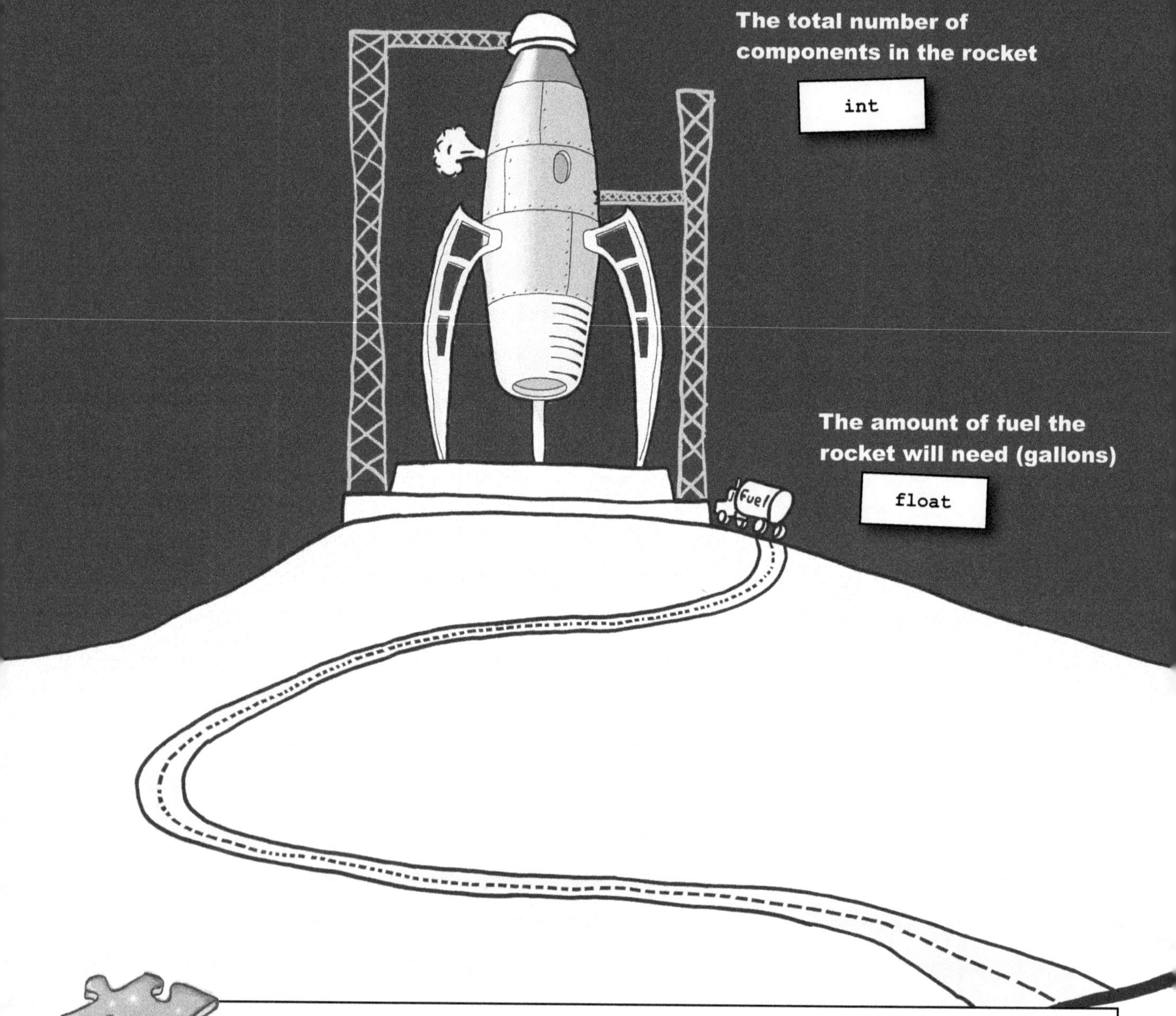
The total number of components in the rocket
int
Fuel
The amount of fuel the rocket will need (gallons)
float

Guess the Data Type Solution

C can handle quite a few different types of data: characters and whole numbers, floating-point values for everyday values, and floating-point numbers for really precise scientific calculations. You can see a few of these data types listed on the opposite page. You were to figure out which data type was used in each example.

Remember: each example uses a different data type.

The distance from the launch pad to the star Proxima Centauri (light years)
double
The numbers of stars in the universe that we *won't* be visiting
long
The number of minutes to launch
short
Each letter on the countdown display
char
90:00
MINUTES
Let's see why...

Your quick guide to data types

char

Each character is stored in the computer's memory as a character code. And that's just a number. So when the computer sees `A`, to the computer it's the same as seeing the literal number `65`.

65 is the ASCII code for A.

int

If you need to store a whole number, you can generally just use an `int`. The exact maximum size of an `int` can vary, but it's guaranteed to be at least 16 bits. In general, an `int` can store numbers up to a few million.

short

But sometimes you want to save a little memory. Why use an `int` if you just want to store numbers up to few hundreds or thousands? That's what a `short` is for. A `short` number usually takes up about half the space of an `int`.

long

Yes, but what if you want to store a **really large count**? That's what the `long` data type was invented for. On some machines, the `long` data type takes up *twice* the memory of an `int`, and it can hold numbers up in the **billions**. But because most computers can deal with really large `int`s, on a lot of machines, the `long` data type is *exactly the same size* as an `int`. The maximum size of a `long` is guaranteed to be at least 32 bits.

float

`float` is the basic data type for storing floating-point numbers. For most everyday floating-point numbers—like the amount of fluid in your orange mocha frappuccino—you can use a `float`.

double

Yes, but what if you want to get really **precise**? If you want to perform calculations that are accurate to a large number of **decimal places**, then you might want to use a `double`. A `double` takes up twice the memory of a `float`, and it uses that extra space to store numbers that are *larger and more precise*.

Don't put something big into something small

When you're passing around values, you need to be careful that the type of the value matches the type of the variable you are going to store it in.

Different data types use different amounts of memory. So you need to be careful that you don't try to store a value that's too large for the amount of space allocated to a variable. `short` variables take up less memory than `int`s, and `int`s take up less memory than `long`s.

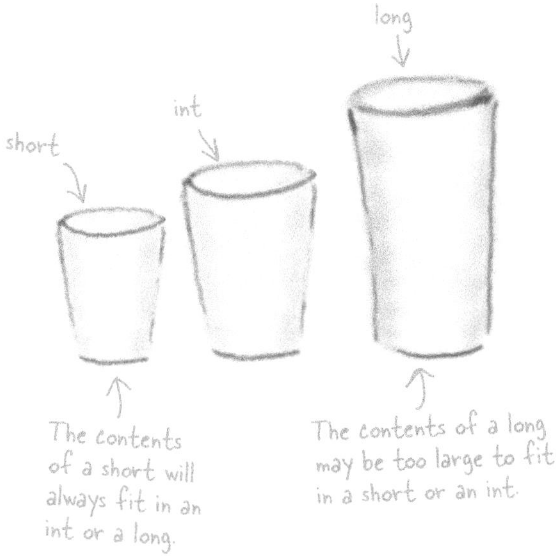
long
int
short
The contents of a short will always fit in an int or a long.
The contents of a long may be too large to fit in a short or an int.

Now there's no problem storing a `short` value inside an `int` or a `long` variable. There is plenty of space in memory, and your code will work correctly:

```
short x = 15;
int y = x;
printf("The value of y = %i\n", y);
```

This will say that y = 15.

The problems start to happen if you go the other way around—if, say, you try to store an `int` value into a `short`.

```
int x = 100000;
short y = x;
print("The value of y = %hi\n", y);
```

%hi is the proper code to format a short value.

Sometimes, the compiler will be able to spot that you're trying to store a really big value into a small variable, and then give you a warning. But a lot of the time the compiler won't be smart enough for that, and it will compile the code without complaining. In that case, when you try to run the code, the computer won't be able to store a number 100,000 into a `short` variable. The computer will fit in as many 1s and 0s as it can, but the number that ends up stored inside the y variable will be *very different* from the one you sent it:

```
The value of y = -31072
```

Geek Bits

So why did putting a large number into a `short` go negative? Numbers are stored in binary. This is what 100,000 looks like in binary:

```
x <- 0001 1000 0110 1010 0000
```

But when the computer tried to store that value into a `short`, it only allowed the value a couple of bytes of storage. The program stored just the *righthand side* of the number:

```
y <- 1000 0110 1010 0000
```

Signed values in binary beginning with a 1 in highest bit are treated as negative numbers. And this shortened value is equal to this in decimal:

```
-31072
```

Use casting to put floats into whole numbers

What do you think this piece of code will display?

```
int x = 7;
int y = 2;
float z = x / y;
printf("z = %f\n", z);
```

I've been cast a float.

The answer? **3.0000**. Why is that? Well, x and y are both integers, and if you divide integers you always get a rounded-off whole number—in this case, **3**.

What do you do if you want to perform calculations on whole numbers and you want to get floating-point results? You could store the whole numbers into float variables first, but that's a little wordy. Instead, you can use a **cast** to convert the numbers on the fly:

```
int x = 7;
int y = 2;
float z = (float)x / (float)y;
printf("z = %f\n", z);
```

The **(float)** will *cast* an integer value into a float value. The calculation will then work just as if you were using floating-point values the entire time. In fact, if the compiler sees you are adding, subtracting, multiplying, or dividing a floating-point value with a whole number, it will automatically cast the numbers for you. That means you can cut down the number of explicit casts in your code:

```
float z = (float)x / y;
```

← The compiler will automatically cast y to a float.

You can put some other keywords before data types to change the way that the numbers are interpreted:

unsigned

The number will always be positive. Because it doesn't need to worry about recording negative numbers, unsigned numbers can store larger numbers since there's now one more bit to work with. So an unsigned int stores numbers from 0 to a maximum value that is about twice as large as the maximum number that can be stored inside an int. There's also a signed keyword, but you almost never see it, because all data types are signed by default.

```
unsigned char c;
```

↑ This will probably store numbers from 0 to 255.

long

That's right, you can prefix a data type with the word long and make it longer. So a long int is a longer version of an int, which means it can store a larger range of numbers. And a long long is longer than a long. You can also use long with floating-point numbers.

← long long is C99 and C11 only.

```
long double d;
```

← A really REALLY precise number.

Exercise

There's a new program helping the waiters bus tables at the Head First Diner. The code automatically totals a bill and adds sales tax to each item. See if you can figure out what needs to go in each of the blanks.

Note: there are several data types that could be used for this program, but which would you use for the kind of figures you'd expect?

```
#include <stdio.h>

.................. total = 0.0;
.................. count = 0;
.................. tax_percent = 6;

.................. add_with_tax(float f)
{
  ..................tax_rate = 1 + tax_percent / 100 .................. ;
  total = total + (f * tax_rate);
  count = count + 1;
  return total;
}

int main()
{
  ..................val;
  printf("Price of item: ");
  while (scanf("%f", &val) == 1) {
    printf("Total so far: %.2f\n", add_with_tax(val));
    printf("Price of item: ");
  }
  printf("\nFinal total: %.2f\n", total);
  printf("Number of items: %hi\n", count);
  return 0;
}
```

%.2f formats a floating-point number to two decimal places.

%hi is used to format shorts.

Exercise Solution

There's a new program helping the waiters bus tables at the Head First Diner. The code automatically totals a bill and adds sales tax to each item. You were to figure out what needs to go in each of the blanks.

Note: there are several data types that could be used for this program, but which would you use for the kind of figures you'd expect?

```
#include <stdio.h>

float total = 0.0;
short count = 0;
short tax_percent = 6;

float add_with_tax(float f)
{
  float tax_rate = 1 + tax_percent / 100.0;
  total = total + (f * tax_rate);
  count = count + 1;
  return total;
}

int main()
{
  float val;
  printf("Price of item: ");
  while (scanf("%f", &val) == 1) {
    printf("Total so far: %.2f\n", add_with_tax(val));
    printf("Price of item: ");
  }
  printf("\nFinal total: %.2f\n", total);
  printf("Number of items: %hi\n", count);
  return 0;
}
```

You need a small floating-point number to total the cash. (→ float total)

There won't be many items on an order, so we'll choose a short. (→ short count)

We're returning a small cash value, so it'll be a float. (→ float add_with_tax)

A float will be OK for this fraction. (→ float tax_rate)

By adding .0, you make the calculation work as a float. If you left it as 100, it would have returned a whole number.

1 + tax_percent / 100; would return the value 1 because 6/100 == 0 in integer arithmetic.

Each price will easily fit in a float. (→ float val)

Data Type Sizes Up Close

Data types are different sizes on different platforms. But how do you find out how big an `int` is, or how many bytes a `double` takes up? Fortunately, the C Standard Library has a couple of headers with the details. This program will tell you about the sizes of `int`s and `float`s:

```
#include <stdio.h>
#include <limits.h>
#include <float.h>

int main()
{
  printf("The value of INT_MAX is %i\n", INT_MAX);
  printf("The value of INT_MIN is %i\n", INT_MIN);
  printf("An int takes %zu bytes\n", sizeof(int));

  printf("The value of FLT_MAX is %f\n", FLT_MAX);
  printf("The value of FLT_MIN is %.50f\n", FLT_MIN);
  printf("A float takes %zu bytes\n", sizeof(float));

  return 0;
}
```

This contains the values for the integer types like int and char.

This contains the values for floats and doubles.

This is the highest value.

This is the lowest value.

sizeof returns the number of bytes a data type occupies.

When you compile and run this code, you will see something like this:

```
File Edit Window Help HowBigIsBig
The value of INT_MAX is 2147483647
The value of INT_MIN is -2147483648
An int takes 4 bytes
The value of FLT_MAX is 340282346638528859811704183484516925440.000000
The value of FLT_MIN is 0.00000000000000000000000000000000000001175494350822
A float takes 4 bytes
```

The values you see on your particular machine will probably be different.

What if you want to know the details for `char`s or `double`s? Or `long`s? No problem. Just replace `INT` and `FLT` with `CHAR` (`char`s), `DBL` (`double`s), `SHRT` (`short`s), or `LNG` (`long`s).

there are no Dumb Questions

Q: Why are data types different on different operating systems? Wouldn't it be less confusing to make them all the same?

A: C uses different data types on different operating systems and processors because that allows it to make the most out of the hardware.

Q: In what way?

A: When C was first created, most machines were 8-bit. Now, most machines are 32- or 64-bit. Because C doesn't specify the exact size of its data types, it's been able to adapt over time. And as newer machines are created, C will be able to make the most of them as well.

Q: What do 8-bit and 64-bit actually mean?

A: Technically, the bit size of a computer can refer to several things, such as the size of its CPU instructions or the amount of data the CPU can read from memory. The bit size is really the favored size of numbers that the computer can deal with.

Q: So what does that have to do with the size of `int`s and `double`s?

A: If a computer is optimized best to work with 32-bit numbers, it makes sense if the basic data type—the `int`—is set at 32 bits.

Q: I understand how whole numbers like `int`s work, but how are `float`s and `double`s stored? How does the computer represent a number with a decimal point?

A: It's complicated. Most computers used a standard published by the IEEE (*http://tinyurl.com/6defkv6*).

Q: Do I really need to understand how floating-point numbers work?

A: No. The vast majority of developers use `float`s and `double`s without worrying about the details.

Oh no...it's the out-of-work actors...

Some people were never really cut out to be programmers. It seems that some aspiring actors are filling in their time *between roles* and making a little extra cash by cutting code, and they've decided to spend some time freshening up the code in the bill-totalling program.

By the time they rejiggered the code, the actors were much happier about the way everything looked...but there's just a tiny problem.

The code doesn't compile anymore.

To you, it's code.
To us, it's art.
Aspiring actors

Let's see what's happened to the code

This is what the actors did to the code. You can see they really just did a couple of things.

```
#include <stdio.h>

float total = 0.0;
short count = 0;
/* This is 6%. Which is a lot less than my agent takes...*/
short tax_percent = 6;

int main()
{
  /* Hey - I was up for a movie with Val Kilmer */
  float val;
  printf("Price of item: ");
  while (scanf("%f", &val) == 1) {
    printf("Total so far: %.2f\n", add_with_tax(val));
    printf("Price of item: ");
  }
  printf("\nFinal total: %.2f\n", total);
  printf("Number of items: %hi\n", count);
  return 0;
}

float add_with_tax(float f)
{
  float tax_rate = 1 + tax_percent / 100.0;
  /* And what about the tip? Voice lessons ain't free */
  total = total + (f * tax_rate);
  count = count + 1;
  return total;
}
```

The code has had some comments added, and they also **changed the order of the functions**. They made no other changes.

So there really shouldn't be a problem. The code should be good to go, right? Well, everything was great, right up until the point that they **compiled the code...**

Test Drive

If you open up the console and try to compile the program, this happens:

```
File Edit Window Help StickToActing
> gcc totaller.c -o totaller && ./totaller
totaller.c: In function "main":
totaller.c:14: warning: format "%.2f" expects type
"double", but argument 2 has type "int"
totaller.c: At top level:
totaller.c:23: error: conflicting types for "add_with_tax"
totaller.c:14: error: previous implicit declaration of
"add_with_tax" was here
```

Bummer.

That's not good. What does `error: conflicting types for 'add_with_tax'` mean? What is a *previous implicit declaration*? And why does it think the line that prints out the current total is now an `int`? Didn't we design that to be floating point?

The compiler will ignore the changes made to the comments, so that shouldn't make any difference. That means the problem must be caused by **changing the order of the functions**. But if the order is the problem, why doesn't the compiler just return a message saying something like:

Dude, the order of the functions is busted. Fix it.

Seriously, why doesn't the compiler give us a little help here?

To understand exactly what's happening here, you need to get inside the head of the compiler for a while and look at things from its point of view. You'll see that what's happening is that the compiler is actually trying to be a little *too helpful*.

Compilers don't like surprises

So what happens when the compiler sees this line of code?

```
printf("Total so far: %.2f\n", add_with_tax(val));
```

1. **The compiler sees a call to a function it doesn't recognize.**
Rather than complain about it, the compiler figures that it will find out more about the function later in the source file. The compiler simply remembers to look out for the function later on in the file. Unfortunately, this is where the problem lies…

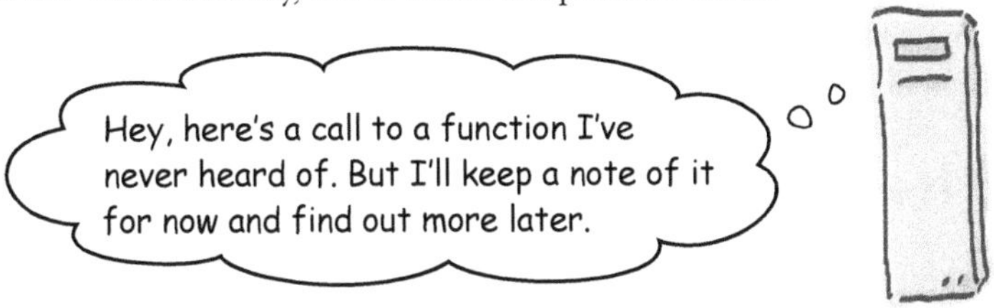
Hey, here's a call to a function I've never heard of. But I'll keep a note of it for now and find out more later.

2. **The compiler needs to know what data type the function will return.**
Of course, the compiler can't know what the function will return just yet, so it makes an ***assumption***. The compiler assumes it will return an `int`.

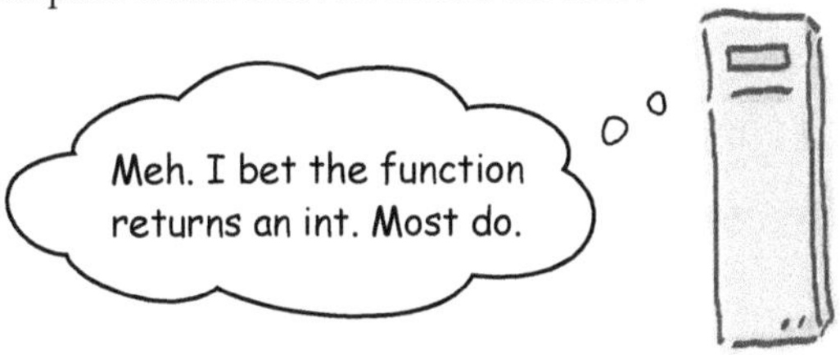
Meh. I bet the function returns an int. Most do.

3. **When it reaches the code for the actual function, it returns a "conflicting types for 'add_with_tax'" error.**
This is because the compiler thinks it has two functions with the same name. One function is the real one in the file. The other is the one that the compiler assumed would return an `int`.

A function called add_with_tax() that returns a **float**??? But in my notes it says we've already got one of these returning an int...

BRAIN POWER

The computer makes an assumption that the function returns an `int`, when in reality it returns a `float`. If you were designing the C language, how would you fix the problem?

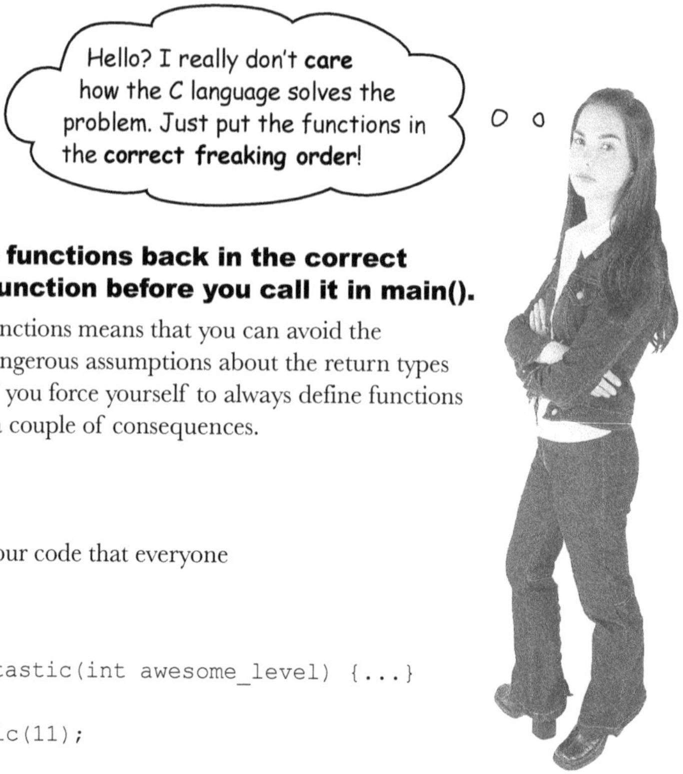
Hello? I really don't care how the C language solves the problem. Just put the functions in the correct freaking order!

You could just put the functions back in the correct order and define the function before you call it in main().

Changing the order of the functions means that you can avoid the compiler ever making any dangerous assumptions about the return types of unknown functions. But if you force yourself to always define functions in a specific order, there are a couple of consequences.

Fixing function order is a pain

Say you've added a cool new function to your code that everyone thinks is fantastic:

```
int do_whatever(){...}
float do_something_fantastic(int awesome_level) {...}
int do_stuff() {
  do_something_fantastic(11);
}
```

What happens if you *then* decide your program will be even *better* if you add a call to the `do_something_fantastic()` function in the existing `do_whatever()` code? You will have to **move the function** earlier in the file. Most coders want to spend their time improving what their code can do. It would be better if you didn't have to shuffle the order of the code just to keep the compiler happy.

In some situations, there is no correct order

Over to you, Cecil!

OK, so this situation is kind of rare, but occasionally you might write some code that is **mutually recursive**:

There is no way to reorder these functions.
float ping() {
...
pong();
...
}
float pong() {
...
ping();
...
}

If you have two functions that call *each other*, then **one of them will always be called in the file before it's defined**.

For both of those reasons, it's really useful to be able to define functions in whatever order is easiest at the time. But how?

Split the declaration from the definition

Remember how the compiler made a note to itself about the function it was expecting to find later in the file? You can avoid the compiler making assumptions by ***explicitly telling it what functions it should expect***. When you tell the compiler about a function, it's called a **function declaration**:

The declaration tells the compiler what return value to expect. →

```
float add_with_tax();
```

← A declaration has no body code.

← It just ends with a ; (semicolon).

The declaration is just a function **signature**: a record of what the function will be called, what kind of parameters it will accept, and **what type of data it will return**.

Once you've declared a function, the compiler won't need to make any assumptions, so it won't matter if you define the function after you call it.

So if you have a whole bunch of functions in your code and you don't want to worry about their order in the file, you can put a list of function declarations at the start of your C program code:

```
float do_something_fantastic();
double awesomeness_2_dot_0();
int stinky_pete();
char make_maguerita(int count);
```

Declarations don't have a body.

But even better than that, C allows you to take that whole set of declarations *out of your code* and put them in a **header file**. You've already used header files to include code from the C Standard Library:

```
#include <stdio.h>
```

← This line will include the contents of the header file called stdio.h.

Let's go see how you can create your own header files.

Creating your first header file

To create a header, you just need to do **two things**:

1. **Create a new file with a .h extension.**
If you are writing a program called `totaller`, then create a file called *totaller.h* and write your declarations inside it:

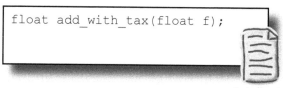

```
float add_with_tax(float f);
```

totaller.h

You won't need to include the `main()` function in the header file, because nothing else will need to call it.

2. **Include your header file in your main program.**
At the top of your program, you should add an extra `include` line:

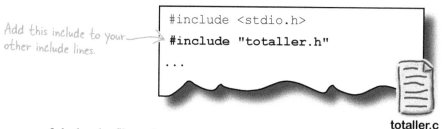

Add this include to your other include lines.

```
#include <stdio.h>
#include "totaller.h"
...
```

totaller.c

When you write the name of the header file, make sure you surround it with double quotes rather than angle brackets. Why the difference? When the compiler sees an `include` line with angle brackets, it assumes it will find the header file somewhere off in the directories where the library code lives. But **your** header file is in the same directory as your ***.c*** file. By wrapping the header filename in quotes, you are telling the compiler to look for a local file.

Local header files can also include directory names, but you will normally put them in the same directory as the C file.

When the compiler reads the `#include` in the code, it will read the contents of the header file, just as if it had been typed into the code.

Separating the declarations into a separate header file keeps your main code a little shorter, and it has another *big advantage* that you'll find out about in a few pages.

For now, let's see if the header file fixed the mess.

#include is a preprocessor instruction.

Test Drive

Now when you compile the code, this happens:

```
File Edit Window Help UseHeaders
> gcc totaller.c -o totaller
>
```

No error messages this time.

The compiler reads the function declarations from the header file, which means it doesn't have to make any guesses about the return type of the function. The order of the functions doesn't matter.

Just to check that everything is OK, you can run the generated program to see if it works the same as before.

```
File Edit Window Help UseHeaders
> ./totaller
Price of item: 1.23
Total so far: 1.30
Price of item: 4.57
Total so far: 6.15
Price of item: 11.92
Total so far: 18.78
Price of item: ^D
Final total: 18.78
Number of items: 3
```

Press Ctrl-D here to stop the program from asking for more prices.

BE the Compiler

Look at the program below. Part of the program is missing. Your job is to play like you're the compiler and say what you would do if each of the candidate code fragments on the right were slotted into the missing space.

Candidate code goes here.

```
#include <stdio.h>



  printf("A day on Mercury is %f hours\n", day);
  return 0;
}

float mercury_day_in_earth_days()
{
  return 58.65;
}

int hours_in_an_earth_day()
{
  return 24;
}
```

Here are the code fragments.

Mark the boxes that you think are correct.

```
float mercury_day_in_earth_days();
int hours_in_an_earth_day();

int main()
{
  float length_of_day = mercury_day_in_earth_days();
  int hours = hours_in_an_earth_day();
  float day = length_of_day * hours;
```

- [ ] You can compile the code.
- [ ] You should display a warning.
- [ ] The program will work.

```
float mercury_day_in_earth_days();

int main()
{
  float length_of_day = mercury_day_in_earth_days();
  int hours = hours_in_an_earth_day();
  float day = length_of_day * hours;
```

- [ ] You can compile the code.
- [ ] You should display a warning.
- [ ] The program will work.

```
int main()
{
  float length_of_day = mercury_day_in_earth_days();
  int hours = hours_in_an_earth_day();
  float day = length_of_day * hours;
```

- [ ] You can compile the code.
- [ ] You should display a warning.
- [ ] The program will work.

```
float mercury_day_in_earth_days();
int hours_in_an_earth_day();

int main()
{
  int length_of_day = mercury_day_in_earth_days();
  int hours = hours_in_an_earth_day();
  float day = length_of_day * hours;
```

- [ ] You can compile the code.
- [ ] You should display a warning.
- [ ] The program will work.

BE the Compiler Solution

Look at the program below. Part of the program is missing. Your job was to play like you're the compiler and say what you would do if each of the candidate code fragments on the right were slotted into the missing space.

```
#include <stdio.h>

[                                        ]

  printf("A day on Mercury is %f hours\n", day);
  return 0;
}

float mercury_day_in_earth_days()
{
  return 58.65;
}

int hours_in_an_earth_day()
{
  return 24;
}
```

```
float mercury_day_in_earth_days();
int hours_in_an_earth_day();

int main()
{
  float length_of_day = mercury_day_in_earth_days();
  int hours = hours_in_an_earth_day();
  float day = length_of_day * hours;
```

- [x] You can compile the code.
- [ ] You should display a warning.
- [x] The program will work.

There will be a warning, beause you haven't declared the hours_in_an_earth_day() before calling it. The program will still work because it will guess the function returns an int.

```
float mercury_day_in_earth_days();

int main()
{
  float length_of_day = mercury_day_in_earth_days();
  int hours = hours_in_an_earth_day();
  float day = length_of_day * hours;
```

- [x] You can compile the code.
- [x] You should display a warning.
- [x] The program will work.

```
int main()
{
  float length_of_day = mercury_day_in_earth_days();
  int hours = hours_in_an_earth_day();
  float day = length_of_day * hours;
```

The program won't compile, because you're calling a float function without declaring it first.

- [ ] You can compile the code.
- [x] You should display a warning.
- [ ] The program will work.

The program will compile without warnings, but it won't work because there will be a rounding problem.

```
float mercury_day_in_earth_days();
int hours_in_an_earth_day();

int main()
{
  int length_of_day = mercury_day_in_earth_days();
  int hours = hours_in_an_earth_day();
  float day = length_of_day * hours;
```

The length_of_day variable should be a float.

- [x] You can compile the code.
- [ ] You should display a warning.
- [ ] The program will work.

there are no Dumb Questions

Q: So I don't need to have declarations for `int` functions?

A: Not necessarily, unless you are sharing code. You'll see more about this soon.

Q: I'm confused. You talk about the compiler *preprocessing*? Why does the *compiler* do that?

A: Strictly speaking, the compiler just does the compilation step: it converts the C source code into assembly code. But in a looser sense, all of the stages that convert the C source code into the final executable are normally called *compilation*, and the `gcc` tool allows you to control those stages. The `gcc` tool does preprocessing and compilation.

Q: What is the preprocessor?

A: Preprocessing is the first stage in converting the raw C source code into a working executable. Preprocessing creates a modified version of the source just before the *proper* compilation begins. In your code, the preprocessing step read the contents of the header file into the main file.

Q: Does the preprocessor create an actual file?

A: No, compilers normally just use pipes for sending the stuff through the phases of the compiler to make things more efficient.

Q: Why do some headers have quotes and others have angle brackets?

A: Strictly speaking, it depends on the way your compiler works. Usually quotes mean to simply look for a file using a relative path. So if you just include the name of a file, without including a directory name, the compiler will look in the current directory. If angle brackets are used, it will search for the file along a path of directories.

Q: What directories will the compiler search when it is looking for header files?

A: The `gcc` compiler knows where the standard headers are stored. On a Unix-style operating system, the header files are normally in places like */usr/local/include*, */usr/include*, and a few others.

Q: So that's how it works for standard headers like *stdio.h*?

A: Yes. You can read through the *stdio.h* file on a Unix-style machine in */usr/include/stdio.h*. If you have the MinGW compiler on Windows, it will probably be in *C:\MinGW\include\stdio.h*.

Q: Can I create my own libraries?

A: Yes; you'll learn how to do that later in the book.

BULLET POINTS

- If the compiler finds a call to a function it hasn't heard of, it will assume the function returns an `int`.
- So if you try to call a function before you define it, there can be problems.
- Function declarations tell the compiler what your functions will look like before you define them.
- If function declarations appear at the top of your source code, the compiler won't get confused about return types.
- Function declarations are often put into header files.
- You can tell the compiler to read the contents of a header file using `#include`.
- The compiler will treat `include`d code the same as code that is typed into the source file.

Reserved

This Table's Reserved...

C is a very small language. Here is the entire set of reserved words (in no useful order).

Every C program you ever see will break into just these words and a few symbols. If you use these for names, the compiler will be very, very upset.

auto	if	break
int	case	long
char	register	continue
return	default	short
do	sizeof	double
static	else	struct
entry	switch	extern
typedef	float	union
for	unsigned	goto
while	enum	void
const	signed	volatile

If you have common features...

file_hider

Read the contents of a file and create an encrypted version using XOR encryption.

message_hider

Read a series of strings from the Standard Input and display an encrypted version on the Standard Output using XOR encryption.

Chances are, when you begin to write several programs in C, you will find that there are some functions and features that you will want to reuse from other programs. For example, look at the specs of the two programs on the right.

XOR encryption is a very simple way of disguising a piece of text by XOR-ing each character with some value. It's not very secure, but it's very easy to do. And the same code that can encrypt text can also be used to decrypt it. Here's the code to encrypt some text:

```
void encrypt(char *message)
{
  while (*message) {
    *message = *message ^ 31;
    message++;
  }
}
```

void means don't return anything.

Pass a pointer to an array into the function.

Loop through the array and update each character with an encrypted version.

This means you'll XOR each character with the number 31.

Doing math with a character? You can because char is a numeric data type.

...it's good to share code

Clearly, both of those programs are going to need to use the same `encrypt()` function. So you could just copy the code from one program to the other, right? That's not so bad if there's just a small amount of code to copy, but what if there's a really large amount of code? Or what if the way the `encrypt()` function works needs to change in the future? If there are two copies of the `encrypt()` function, you will have to change it in more than one place.

For your code to scale properly, you really need to find some way to reuse common pieces of code—some way of taking a set of functions and making them available in a bunch of different programs.

How would you do that?

BRAIN POWER

Imagine you have a set of functions that you want to share between programs. If you had created the C programming language, how would you allow code to be shared?

You can split the code into separate files

If you have a set of code that you want to share among several files, it makes a lot of sense to put that shared code into a separate ***.c*** file. If the compiler can somehow include the shared code when it's compiling the program, you can use the same code in multiple applications at once. So if you ever need to change the shared code, you only have to do it in one place.

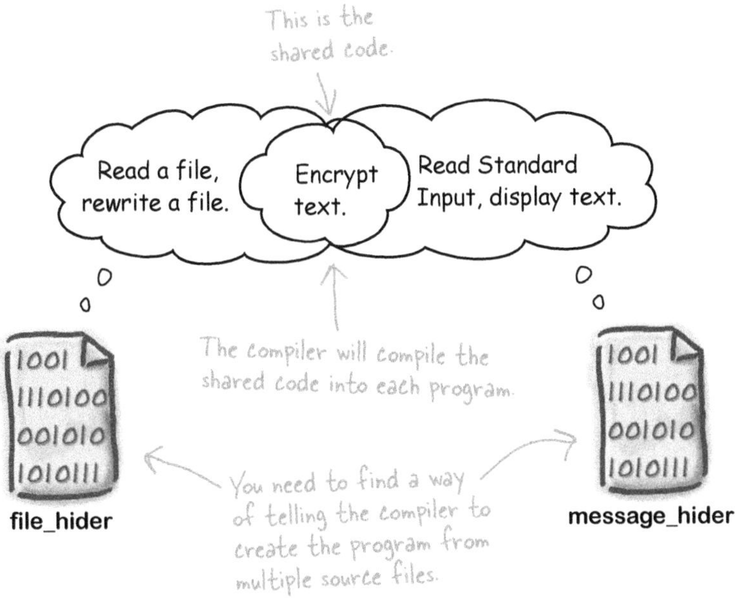
This is the shared code.
Read a file, rewrite a file.
Encrypt text.
Read Standard Input, display text.
The compiler will compile the shared code into each program.
file_hider
message_hider
You need to find a way of telling the compiler to create the program from multiple source files.

If you want to use a separate *.c* file for the shared code, that gives us a *problem*. So far, you have only created programs from single *.c* source files. So if you had a C program called `blitz_hack`, you would have created it from a single source code file called *blitz_hack.c*.

But now you want some way to give the compiler a **set of source code files** and say, "Go make a program from those." How do you do that? What syntax do you use with the `gcc` compiler? And more importantly, what does it *mean* for a compiler to create a single executable program from several files? How would it work? How would it stitch them together?

To understand how the C compiler can create a single program from multiple files, let's take a look at how compilation works...

Compilation behind the scenes

To understand how a compiler can compile several source files into a single program, you'll need to pull back the curtain and see how compilation really works.

Hmmmm...so I need to compile the source files into a program? Let's see what I can cook up...

1 Preprocessing: fix the source.
The first thing the compiler needs to do is fix the source. It needs to add in any extra header files it's been told about using the `#include` **directive**. It might also need to expand or skip over some sections of the program. Once it's done, the source code will be ready for the actual compilation.

"directive" is just a fancy word for "command."

It can do this with commands like #define and #ifdef. You'll see how to use them later in the book.

First, I'll just add some extra ingredients into the source.

2 Compilation: translate into assembly.
The C programming language probably seems pretty low level, but the truth is it's *not low level enough* for the computer to understand. The computer only really understands very low-level **machine code** instructions, and the first step to generate machine code is to convert the C source code into **assembly language symbols** like this:

```
movq   -24(%rbp), %rax
movzbl(%rax), %eax
movl   %eax, %edx
```

So for this "if" statement I need to begin by adding onto the stack...

Looks pretty obscure? Assembly language describes the individual instructions the central processor will have to follow when running the program. The C compiler has a whole set of recipes for each of the different parts of the C language. These recipes will tell the compiler how to convert an `if` statement or a function call into a sequence of assembly language instructions. But even assembly isn't low level enough for the computer. That's why it needs…

3 **Assembly: generate the object code.**
The compiler will need to *assemble* the symbol codes into *machine* or **object code**. This is the actual binary code that will be executed by the circuits inside the CPU.

Time to bake that assembly into something edible.

This is a really dirty joke in machine code.

```
10010101 00100101 11010101 01011100
```

So are you all done? After all, you've taken the original C source code and converted it into the 1s and 0s that the computer's circuits need. But no, there's still one more step. If you give the computer several files to compile for a program, the compiler will generate a piece of object code for each source file. But in order for these separate object files to form a single executable program, one more thing has to occur…

4 **Linking: put it all together.**
Once you have all of the separate pieces of object code, you need to fit them together like jigsaw pieces to form the **executable program**. The compiler will connect the code in one piece of object code that calls a function in another piece of object code. Linking will also make sure that the program is able to call library code properly. Finally, the program will be written out into the executable program file using a format that is supported by the operating system. The file format is important, because it will allow the operating system to load the program into memory and make it run.

Finally, I need to put everything together for the final result...

So how do you actually tell gcc that we want to make one executable program from several separate source files?

The shared code needs its own header file

If you are going to share the *encrypt.c* code between programs, you need some way to tell those programs about the encrypt code. You do that with a header file.

You'll include the header inside encrypt.c.

```
void encrypt(char *message);
```

encrypt.h

```
#include "encrypt.h"

void encrypt(char *message)
{
  while (*message) {
    *message = *message ^ 31;
    message++;
  }
}
```

encrypt.c

Include encrypt.h in your program

You're not using a header file here to be able to reorder the functions. You're using it to **tell other programs about the `encrypt()` function**:

```
#include <stdio.h>
#include "encrypt.h"

int main()
{
  char msg[80];
  while (fgets(msg, 80, stdin)) {
    encrypt(msg);
    printf("%s", msg);
  }
}
```

You'll include encrypt.h so that the program has the declaration of the encrypt() function.

message_hider.c

Having *encrypt.h* inside the main program will mean the compiler will know enough about the `encrypt()` function to compile the code. At the linking stage, the compiler will be able to connect the call to `encrypt(msg)` in *message_hider.c* to the actual `encrypt()` function in *encrypt.c.*

Finally, to compile everything together you just need to pass the source files to `gcc`:

```
gcc message_hider.c encrypt.c -o message_hider
```

Sharing variables

You've seen how to share functions between different files. But what if you want to share variables? Source code files normally contain their own separate variables to prevent a variable in one file affecting a variable in another file with the same name. But if you genuinely want to share variables, you should declare them in your header file and prefix them with the keyword **`extern`**:

```
extern int passcode;
```

Test Drive

Let's see what happens when you compile the `message_hider` program:

You need to compile the code with both source files.

When you run the program, you can enter text and see the encrypted version.

You can even pass it the contents of the encrypt.h file to encrypt it.

```
File Edit Window Help Shhh...
> gcc message_hider.c encrypt.c -o message_hider
> ./message_hider
I am a secret message
V?~r?~?lz|mzk?rzll~xz
> ./message_hider < encrypt.h
ipv{?zq|mfok7|w~m5?rzll~xz6$
>
```

The message_hider program is using the encrypt() function from encrypt.c.

The program works. Now that you have the `encrypt()` function in a separate file, you can use it in any program you like. If you ever change the `encrypt()` function to be something a little more secure, you will need to amend only the *encrypt.c* file.

BULLET POINTS

- You can share code by putting it into a separate C file.
- You need to put the function declarations in a separate *.h* header file.
- Include the header file in every C file that needs to use the shared code.
- List all of the C files needed in the compiler command.

Go Off Piste

Write your own program using the `encrypt()` function. Remember, you can call the same function to decrypt text.

Fuel
Man! Every time I make a simple change in **one** file, it takes an age to recompile! And I'm working on a schedule...
ullage_motor.

It's not rocket science...or is it?

Breaking your program out into separate source files not only means that you can *share code* between different programs, but it also means you can start to create *really large* programs. Why? Well, because you can start to break your program down into smaller **self-contained** pieces of code. Rather than being forced to have one *huge* source file, you can have lots of *simpler* files that are easier to understand, maintain, and test.

So on the plus side, you can start to create really large programs. The downside? The downside is…you can start to create really large programs. C compilers are really efficient pieces of software. They take your software through some very complex transformations. They can modify your source, link hundreds of files together without blowing your memory, and even optimize the code you wrote, along the way. And even though they do all that, they still manage to run quickly.

But if you create programs that use more than a few files, the time it takes to compile the code starts to become important. Let's say it takes a minute to compile a large project. That might not sound like a lot of time, but it's more than long enough to break your train of thought. If you try out a change in a single line of code, you want to see the result of that change as quickly as possible. If you have to wait a full minute to see the result of every change, that will really start to slow you down.

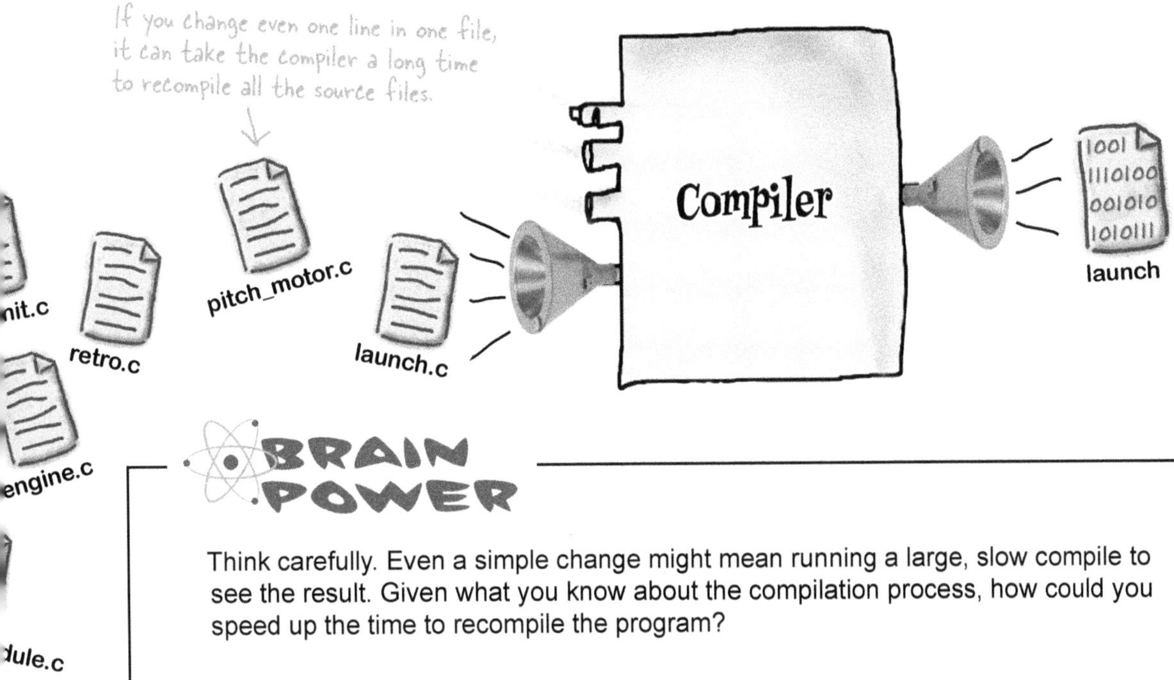
If you change even one line in one file, it can take the compiler a long time to recompile all the source files.
nit.c
retro.c
pitch_motor.c
launch.c
engine.c
dule.c
Compiler
1001
1110100
001010
1010111
launch

BRAIN POWER

Think carefully. Even a simple change might mean running a large, slow compile to see the result. Given what you know about the compilation process, how could you speed up the time to recompile the program?

Don't recompile every file

If you've just made a change to one or two of your source code files, it's a waste to recompile every source file for your program. Think what happens when you issue a command like this:

Skipping a few filenames here.

```
gcc reaction_control.c pitch_motor.c ... engine.c -o launch
```

What will the compiler do? It will run the preprocessor, compiler, and assembler for *each source code file*. Even the ones that haven't changed. And if the source code hasn't changed, the **object code** that's generated for that file won't change either. So if the compiler is generating the object code for every file, every time, what do you need to do?

Save copies of the compiled code

If you tell the compiler to save the object code it generates into a file, it shouldn't need to recreate it unless the source code changes. If a file *does* change, you can recreate the object code for that **one file** and then pass the whole set of object files to the compiler so they can be linked.

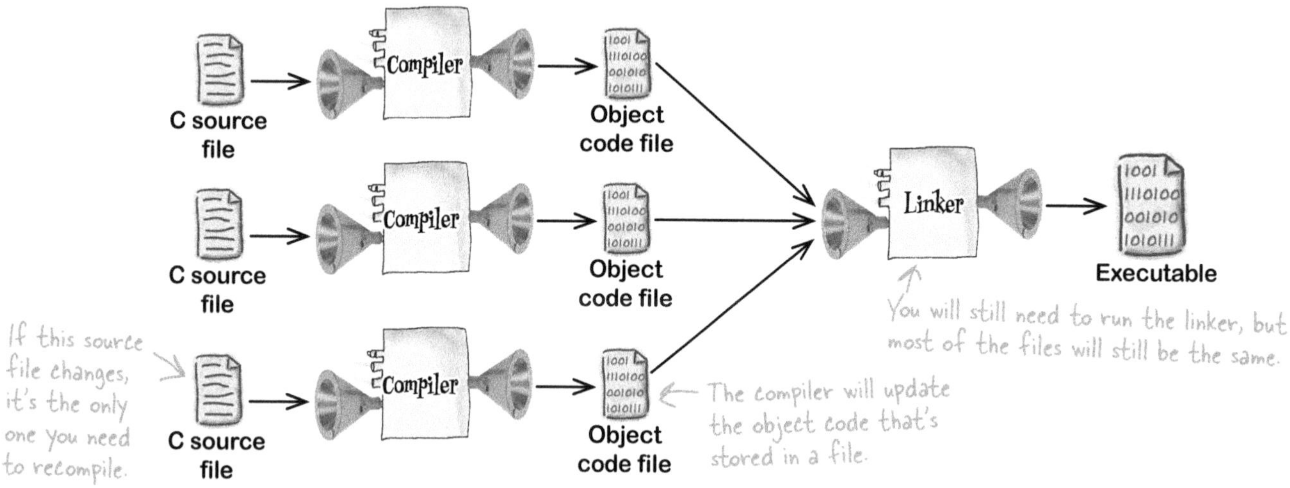
C source file
Compiler
Object code file
C source file
Compiler
Object code file
If this source file changes, it's the only one you need to recompile.
C source file
Compiler
Object code file
The compiler will update the object code that's stored in a file.
Linker
Executable
You will still need to run the linker, but most of the files will still be the same.

If you change a single file, you will have to recreate the object code file from it, but you *won't* need to create the object code for any other file. Then you can pass all the object code files to the linker and create a new version of the program.

So how do you tell gcc to save the object code in a file? And how do you then get the compiler to link the object files together?

First, compile the source into object files

You want object code for each of the source files, and you can do that by typing this command:

This will create object code for every file. →

```
gcc -c *.c
```

← The operating system will replace *.c with all the C filenames.

The *.c will match every C file in the current directory, and the -c will tell the compiler that you want to create an object file for each source file, but you don't want to link them together into a full executable program.

gcc -c will compile the code but won't link it.

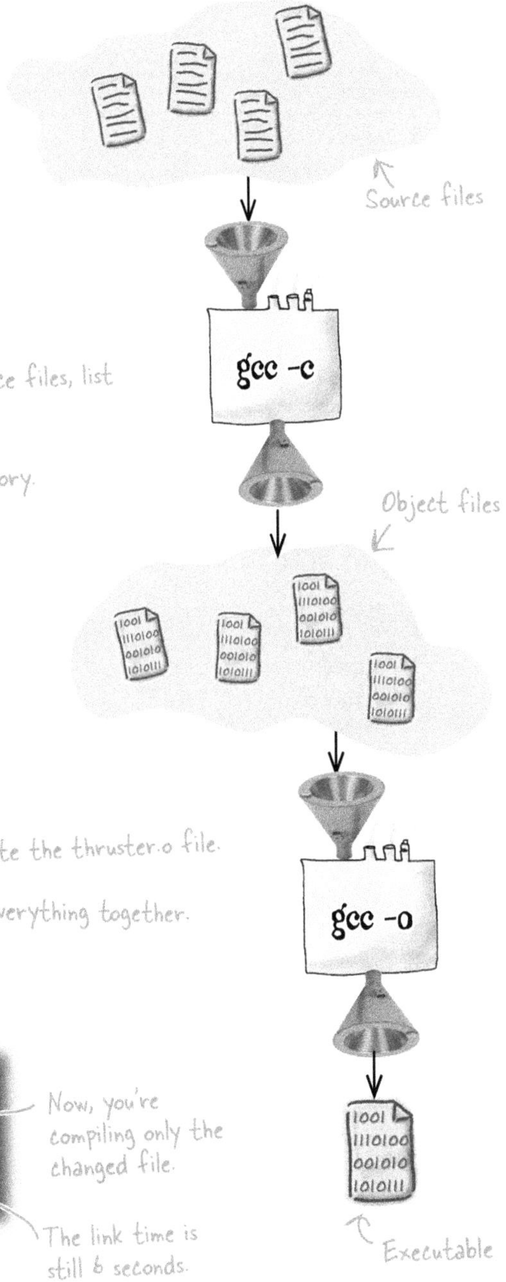

Source files
gcc -c
Object files
gcc -o
Executable

Then, link them together

Now that you have a set of object files, you can link them together with a simple compile command. But instead of giving the compiler the names of the C source files, you tell it the names of the object files:

This is similar to the compile commands you've used before. →

```
gcc *.o -o launch
```

← Instead of C source files, list the object files.

↑ This will match all the object files in the directory.

The compiler is smart enough to recognize the files as object files, rather than source files, so it will skip most of the compilation steps and just link them together into an executable program called launch.

OK, so now you have a compiled program, just like before. But you also have a set of object files that are ready to be linked together if you need them again. So if you change just one of the files, you'll only need to recompile that single file and then relink the program:

This is the only file that's changed. →

```
gcc -c thruster.c
gcc *.o -o launch
```

← This will recreate the thruster.o file. (gcc -c thruster.c)

← This will link everything together. (gcc *.o -o launch)

Even though you have to type two commands, you're saving a *lot* of time:

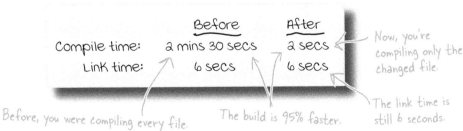

	Before	After
Compile time:	2 mins 30 secs	2 secs
Link time:	6 secs	6 secs

Now, you're compiling only the changed file.

Before, you were compiling every file.

The build is 95% faster.

The link time is still 6 seconds.

Long Exercise

Here is some of the code that's used to control the engine management system on the craft. There's a timestamp on each file. Which files do you think need to be recreated to make the `ems` executable up to date? Circle the files you think need to be updated.

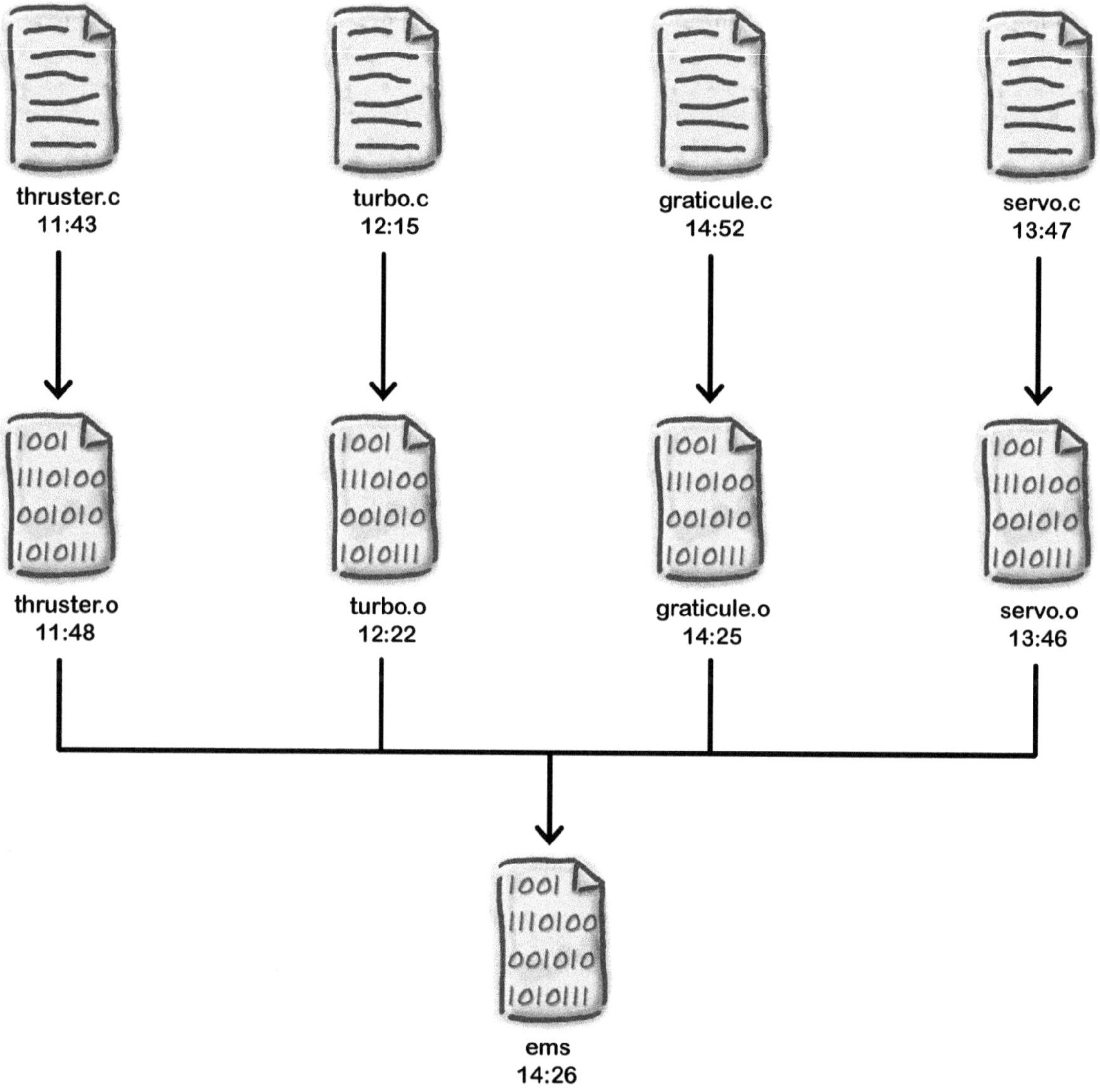
thruster.c
11:43
turbo.c
12:15
graticule.c
14:52
servo.c
13:47
thruster.o
11:48
turbo.o
12:22
graticule.o
14:25
servo.o
13:46
ems
14:26

And in the galley, they need to check that their code's up to date as well. Look at the times against the files. Which of these files need to be updated?

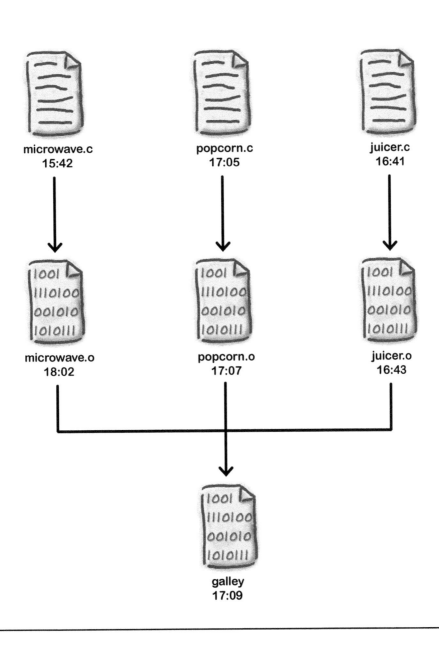

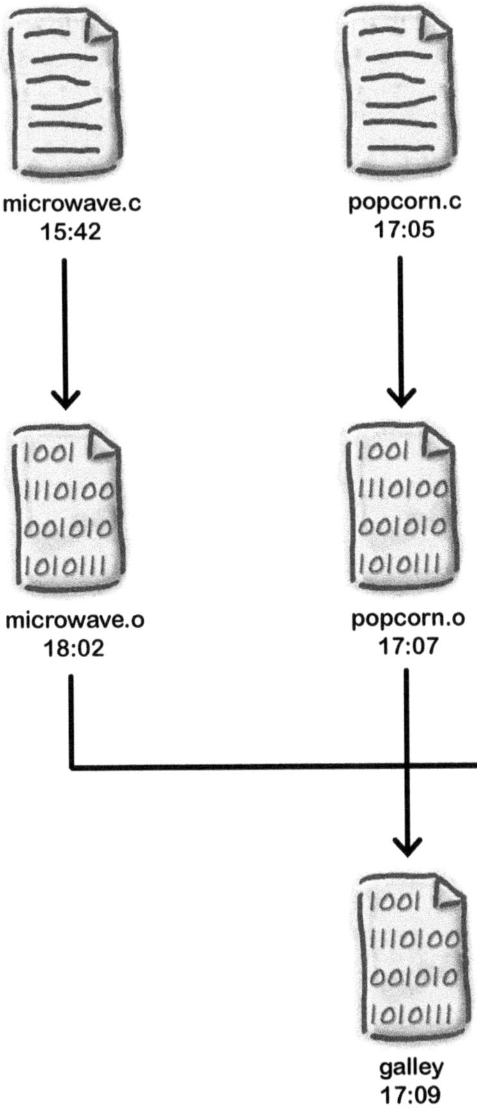
microwave.c
15:42
popcorn.c
17:05
juicer.c
16:41
microwave.o
18:02
popcorn.o
17:07
juicer.o
16:43
galley
17:09

Long Exercise Solution

Here is some of the code that's used to control the engine management system on the craft. There's a timestamp on each file. You were to circle the files you think need to be recreated to make the `ems` executable up to date.

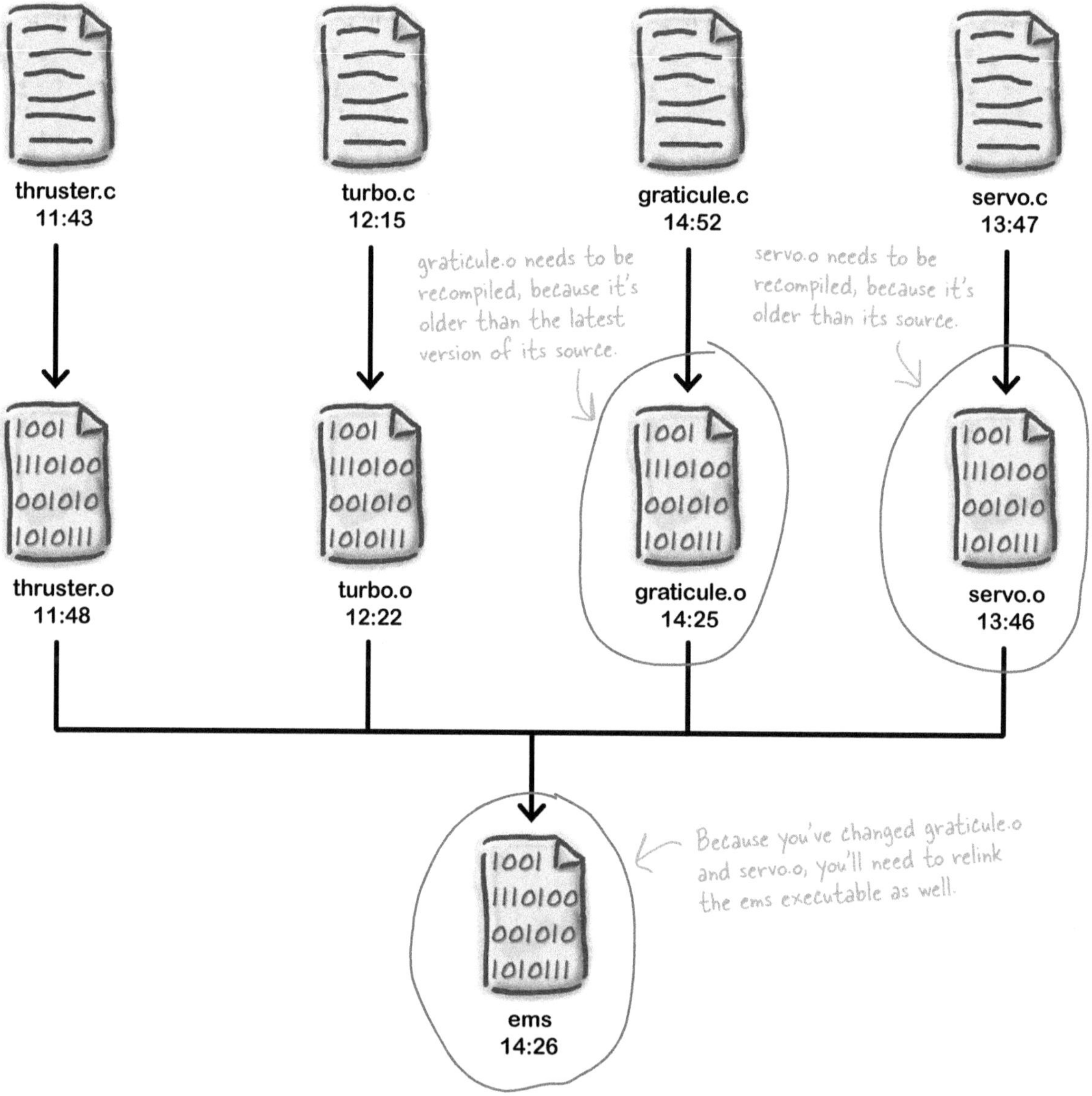

thruster.c
11:43
turbo.c
12:15
graticule.c
14:52
servo.c
13:47
graticule.o needs to be recompiled, because it's older than the latest version of its source.
servo.o needs to be recompiled, because it's older than its source.
thruster.o
11:48
turbo.o
12:22
graticule.o
14:25
servo.o
13:46
ems
14:26
Because you've changed graticule.o and servo.o, you'll need to relink the ems executable as well.

And in the galley, they need to check that their code's up to date as well. Look at the times against the files. Which of these files need to be updated?

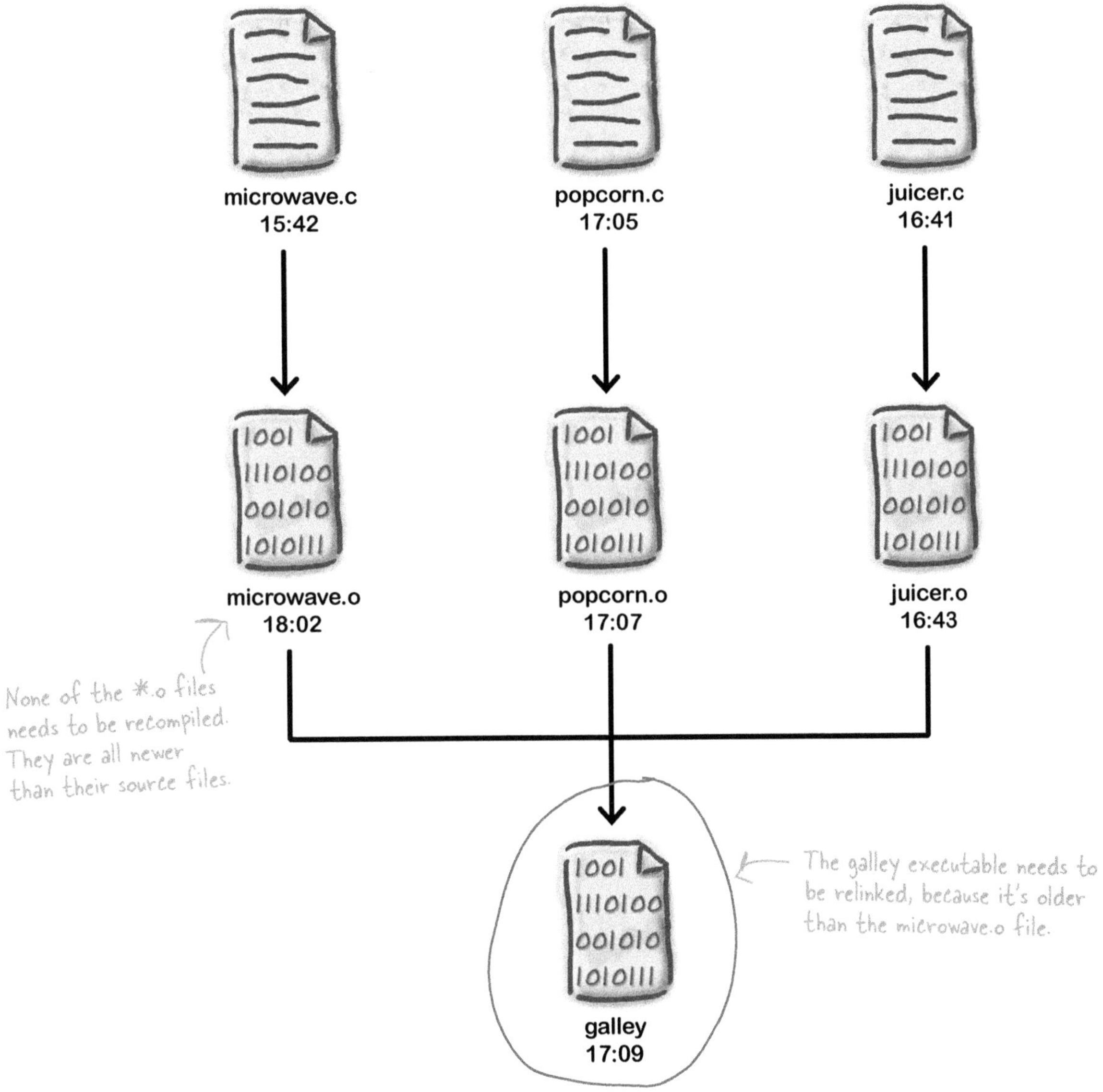
microwave.c
15:42
popcorn.c
17:05
juicer.c
16:41
1001
1110100
001010
1010111
microwave.o
18:02
popcorn.o
17:07
juicer.o
16:43
None of the *.o files needs to be recompiled. They are all newer than their source files.
galley
17:09
The galley executable needs to be relinked, because it's older than the microwave.o file.

It's hard to keep track of the files

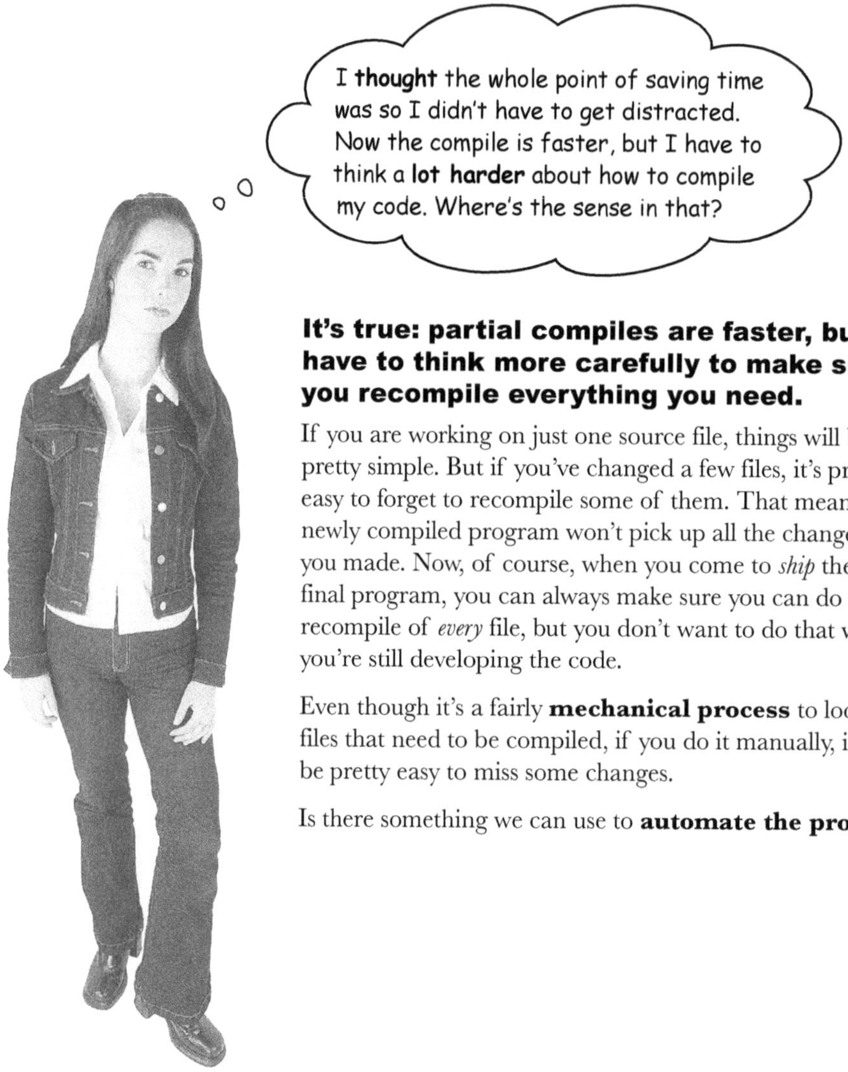
I **thought** the whole point of saving time was so I didn't have to get distracted. Now the compile is faster, but I have to think a **lot harder** about how to compile my code. Where's the sense in that?

It's true: partial compiles are faster, but you have to think more carefully to make sure you recompile everything you need.

If you are working on just one source file, things will be pretty simple. But if you've changed a few files, it's pretty easy to forget to recompile some of them. That means the newly compiled program won't pick up all the changes you made. Now, of course, when you come to *ship* the final program, you can always make sure you can do a full recompile of *every* file, but you don't want to do that while you're still developing the code.

Even though it's a fairly **mechanical process** to look for files that need to be compiled, if you do it manually, it will be pretty easy to miss some changes.

Is there something we can use to **automate the process**?

Wouldn't it be dreamy if there were a tool that could automatically recompile just the source that's changed? But I know it's just a fantasy...

Automate your builds with the make tool

This is make, your new best friend.

You can compile your applications really quickly in `gcc`, as long as you keep track of which files have changed. That's a tricky thing to do, but it's also pretty straightforward to automate. Imagine you have a file that is generated from some other file. Let's say it's an object file that is compiled from a source file:

If the thruster.c file is newer, you need to recompile. → **thruster.c** ⟶ **thruster.o** ← If the thruster.o file is newer, you don't need to recompile.

How do you tell if the *thruster.o* file needs to be recompiled? You just look at the timestamps of the two files. If the *thruster.o* file is older than the *thruster.c* file, then the *thruster.o* file needs to be recreated. Otherwise, it's up to date.

That's a pretty simple rule. And if you have a simple rule for something, then don't think about it—**automate it**...

make is a tool that can run the compile command for you. The `make` tool will check the timestamps of the source files and the generated files, and then it will only recompile the files if things have gotten out of date.

But before you can do all these things, you need to tell `make` about your source code. It needs to know the details of which files depend on which files. And it also needs to be told exactly how you want to build the code.

What does make need to know?

Every file that `make` compiles is called a **target**. Strictly speaking, `make` isn't limited to compiling files. A target is any file that is *generated* from some other files. So a target might be a zip archive that is generated from the set of files that need to be compressed.

For every target, `make` needs to be told *two things*:

- **The dependencies.**
  Which files the target is going to be generated from.
- **The recipe.**
  The set of instructions it needs to run to generate the file.

Hmm...this file's OK.
And this one. And this one.
And...ah, this one's out of date. I'd better send that to the compiler.

Together, the dependencies and the recipe form a **rule**. A rule tells `make` all it needs to know to create the target file.

How make works

Let's say you want to compile *thruster.c* into some object code in *thruster.o*. What are the dependencies and what's the recipe?

```
thruster.c ──> thruster.o
```

The *thruster.o* file is called the ***target***, because it's the file you want to generate. *thruster.c* is a dependency, because it's a file the compiler will need in order to create *thruster.o*. And what will the recipe be? That's the compile command to convert *thruster.c* into *thruster.o*.

```
gcc -c thruster.c
```

This is the rule for creating thruster.o.

Make sense? If you tell the `make` tool about the dependencies and the recipe, you can leave it to `make` to decide when it needs to recompile *thruster.o*.

But you can go further than that. Once you build the *thruster.o* file, you're going to use it to create the `launch` program. That means the `launch` file can also be set up as a target, because it's a file you want to generate. The dependency files for `launch` are all of the *.o* object files. The recipe is this command:

```
gcc *.o -o launch
```

Once `make` has been given the details of all of the dependencies and rules, all you have to do is tell it to create the `launch` file. `make` will work out the details.

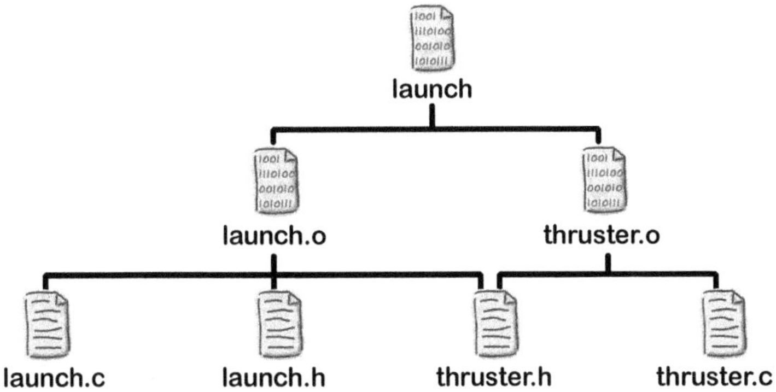
launch
launch.o
thruster.o
launch.c
launch.h
thruster.h
thruster.c

But how do you tell make about the dependencies and recipes? Let's find out.

Watch it!

The `make` tool may have a different name on Windows.

Because `make` *came from the Unix world, there are different flavors of it available in Windows. MinGW includes a version of* `make` *called* `mingw32-make` *and Microsoft produce their own version called* `NMAKE`*.*

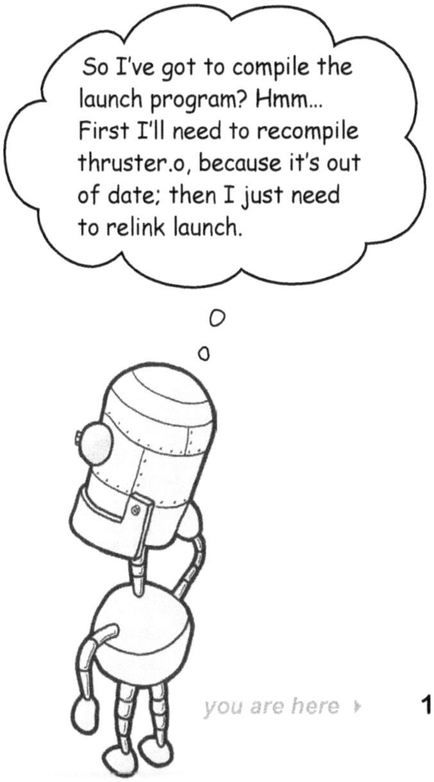
So I've got to compile the launch program? Hmm... First I'll need to recompile thruster.o, because it's out of date; then I just need to relink launch.

Tell make about your code with a makefile

All of the details about the targets, dependencies, and recipes need to be stored in a file called either *makefile* or *Makefile*. To see how it works, imagine you have a pair of source files that together create the `launch` program:

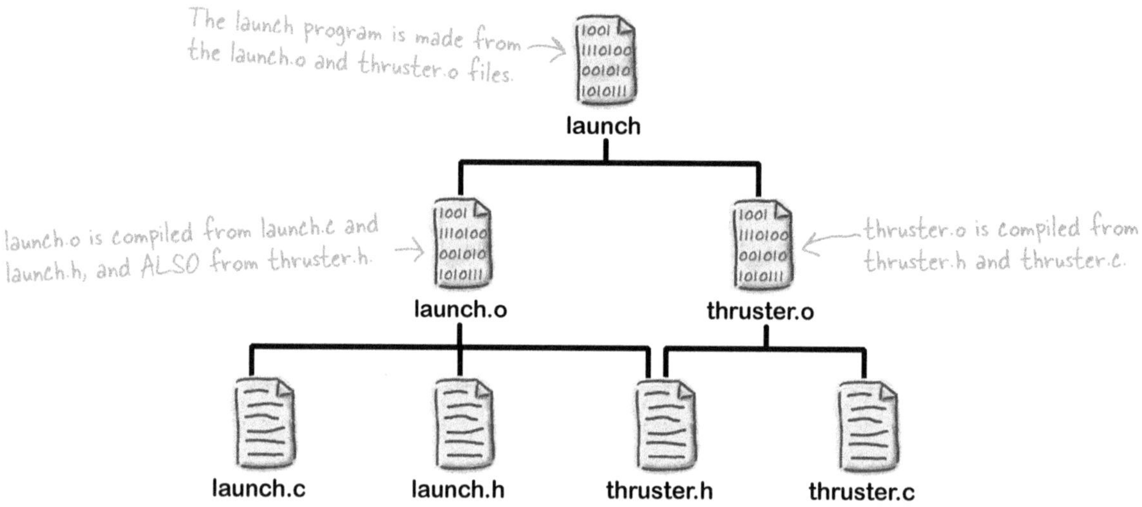
The launch program is made from the launch.o and thruster.o files.
launch
launch.o is compiled from launch.c and launch.h, and ALSO from thruster.h.
thruster.o is compiled from thruster.h and thruster.c.
launch.o
thruster.o
launch.c
launch.h
thruster.h
thruster.c

The `launch` program is made by linking the *launch.o* and *thruster.o* files. Those files are compiled from their matching C and header files, but the *launch.o* file *also* depends on the *thruster.h* file because it contains code that will need to call a function in the `thruster` code.

This is how you'd describe that build in a makefile:

A target is a file that is going to be generated.

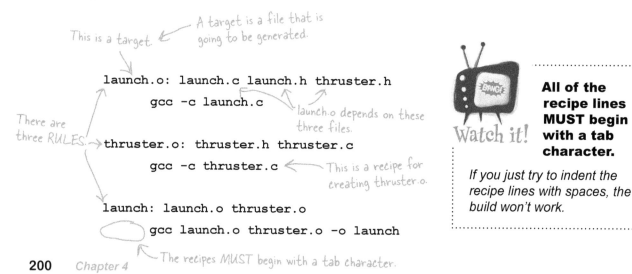

This is a target.

```
launch.o: launch.c launch.h thruster.h
	gcc -c launch.c

thruster.o: thruster.h thruster.c
	gcc -c thruster.c

launch: launch.o thruster.o
	gcc launch.o thruster.o -o launch
```

launch.o depends on these three files.

There are three RULES.

This is a recipe for creating thruster.o.

The recipes MUST begin with a tab character.

Watch it!

All of the recipe lines MUST begin with a tab character.

If you just try to indent the recipe lines with spaces, the build won't work.

Test Drive

Save your make rules into a text file called *Makefile* in the same directory; then, open up a console and type the following:

You are telling make to create the launch file.

make first needs to create a launch.o with this line.

make then needs to create thruster.o with this line.

Finally, make links the object files to create the launch program.

```
File Edit Window Help MakeItSo
> make launch
gcc -c launch.c
gcc -c thruster.c
gcc launch.o thruster.o -o launch
```

You can see that make was able to work out the sequence of commands required to create the launch program. But what happens if you make a change to the *thruster.c* file and then run make again?

make no longer needs to compile launch.c.

launch.o is already up to date.

```
File Edit Window Help MakeItSo
> make launch
gcc -c thruster.c
gcc launch.o thruster.o -o launch
```

make is able to skip creating a new version of *launch.o*. Instead, it just compiles *thruster.o* and then relinks the program.

there are no Dumb Questions

Q: Is `make` just like `ant`?

A: It's probably better to say that build tools like `ant` and `rake` are like `make`. `make` was one of the earliest tools used to automatically build programs from source code.

Q: This seems like a lot of work just to compile source code. Is it really that useful?

A: Yes, `make` is amazingly useful. For small projects, `make` might not appear to save you that much time, but once you have more than a handful of files, compiling and linking code together can become very painful.

Q: If I write a makefile for a Windows machine, will it work on a Mac? Or a Linux machine?

A: Because makefiles calls commands in the underlying operating system, sometimes makefiles don't work on different operating systems.

Q: Can I use `make` for things other than compiling code?

A: Yes. `make` is most commonly used to compile code. But it can also be used as a command-line installer, or a source control tool. In fact, you can use `make` for almost any task that you can perform on the command line.

Tales from the Crypt

Why indent with tabs?

It's easy to indent recipes with spaces instead of tabs. So why does `make` insist on using tabs? This is a quote from `make`'s creator, Stuart Feldman:

"Why the tab in column 1? ... It worked, it stayed. And then a few weeks later I had a user population of about a dozen, most of them friends, and I didn't want to screw up my embedded base. The rest, sadly, is history."

Geek Bits

`make` takes away a lot of the pain of compiling files. But if you find that even it is not automatic enough, take a look at a tool called **`autoconf`**:

http://www.gnu.org/software/autoconf/

`autoconf` is used to generate makefiles. C programmers often create tools to automate the creation of software. An increasing number of them are available on the GNU website.

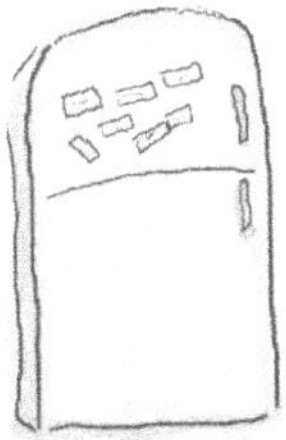

Make Magnets

Hey, baby, if you don't groove to the latest tunes, then you'll *love* the program the guys in the Head First Lounge just wrote! `oggswing` is a program that reads an Ogg Vorbis music file and creates a swing version. Sweet! See if you can complete the makefile that compiles `oggswing` and then uses it to convert a *.ogg* file:

This converts whitennerdy.ogg to swing.ogg.

```
oggswing: ....................................................

..............................................................

swing.ogg: ...................................................

..............................................................
```

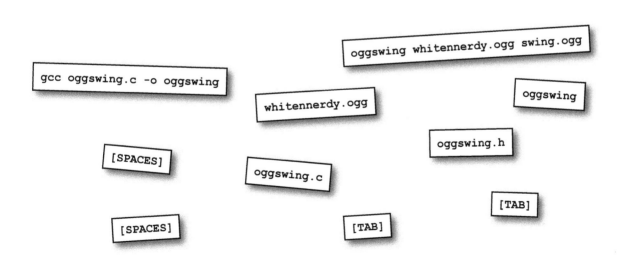

`oggswing whitennerdy.ogg swing.ogg`

`gcc oggswing.c -o oggswing`

`whitennerdy.ogg`

`oggswing`

`oggswing.h`

`[SPACES]`

`oggswing.c`

`[TAB]`

`[SPACES]`

`[TAB]`

Make Magnets Solution

Hey, baby, if you don't groove to the latest tunes, then you'll *love* the program the guys in the Head First Lounge just wrote! `oggswing` is a program that reads an Ogg Vorbis music file and creates a swing version. Sweet! You were to complete the makefile that compiles `oggswing` and then uses it to convert a *.ogg* file:

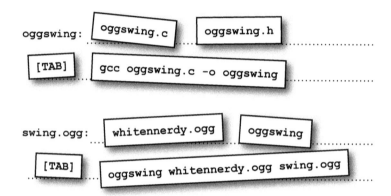

```
oggswing: oggswing.c oggswing.h
[TAB] gcc oggswing.c -o oggswing

swing.ogg: whitennerdy.ogg oggswing
[TAB] oggswing whitennerdy.ogg swing.ogg
```

[SPACES]

[SPACES]

Geek Bits

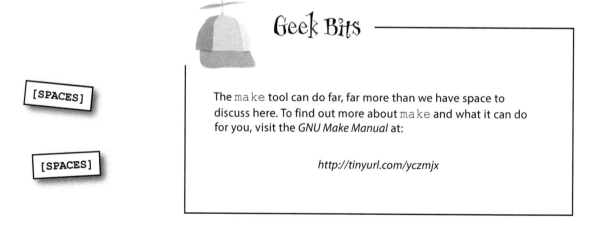

The `make` tool can do far, far more than we have space to discuss here. To find out more about `make` and what it can do for you, visit the *GNU Make Manual* at:

http://tinyurl.com/yczmjx

Liftoff!

If you have a very slow build, `make` will really speed things up. Most developers are so used to building their code with `make` that they even use it for small programs. `make` is like having a really careful developer sitting alongside you. If you have a large amount of code, `make` will always take care to build just the code you need at just the time you need it.

And sometimes getting things done in time is important...

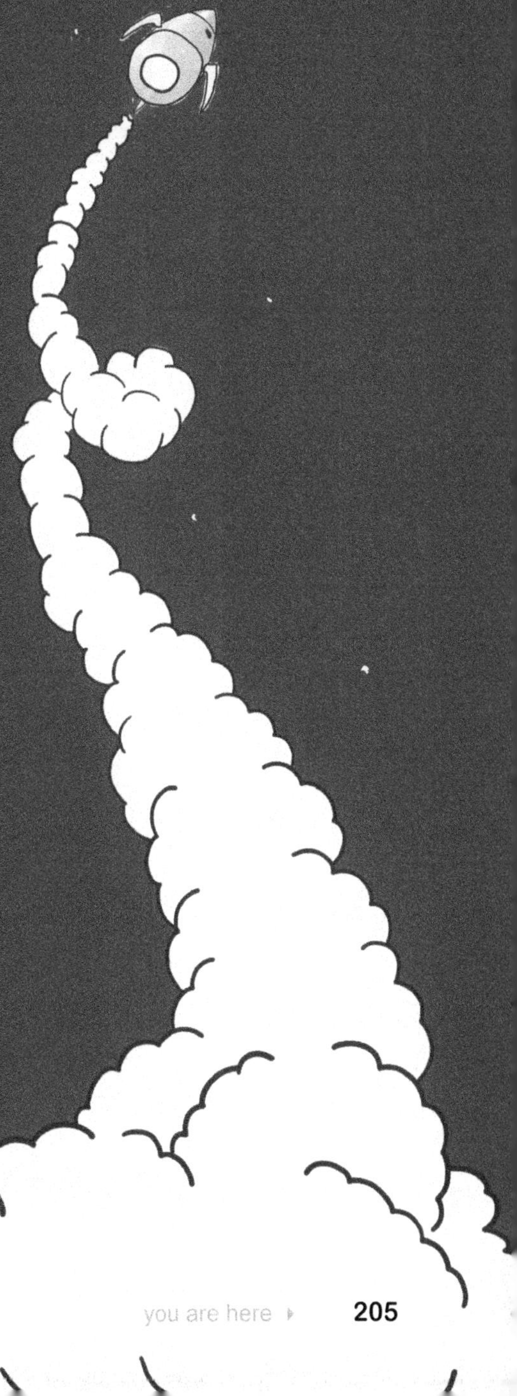

BULLET POINTS

- It can take a long time to compile a large number of files.
- You can speed up compilation time by storing object code in **.o* files.
- The `gcc` can compile programs from object files as well as source files.
- The `make` tool can be used to automate your builds.
- `make` knows about the dependencies between files, so it can compile just the files that change.
- `make` needs to be told about your build with a makefile.
- Be careful formatting your makefile: don't forget to indent lines with tabs instead of spaces.

Your C Toolbox

You've got Chapter 4 under your belt, and now you've added data types and header files to your toolbox. For a complete list of tooltips in the book, see Appendix ii.

chars are numbers.

Use shorts for small whole numbers.

Use ints for most whole numbers.

Use longs for really big whole numbers.

Use floats for most floating points.

Use doubles for really precise floating points.

Split function declarations from definitions.

Put declarations in a header file.

#include <> for library headers.

#include "" for local headers.

Save object code into files to speed up your builds.

Use make to manage your builds.

Name:

Date:

C Lab 1

Arduino

This lab gives you a spec that describes a program for you to build, using the knowledge you've gained over the last few chapters.

This project is bigger than the ones you've seen so far. So read the whole thing before you get started, and give yourself a little time. And don't worry if you get stuck. There are no new C concepts in here, so you can move on in the book and come back to the lab later.

We've filled in a few design details for you, and we've made sure you've got all the pieces you need to write the code. You can even build the physical device.

It's up to you to finish the job, but we won't give you the code for the answer.

The spec: make your houseplant talk

Ever wished your plants could tell you when they need watering? Well, with an Arduino they can! In this lab, you'll create an Arduino-powered plant monitor, all coded in C.

Here's what you're going to build.

Feed me! Feed me now!

The physical device

The plant monitor has a moisture sensor that measures how wet your plant's soil is. If the plant needs watering, an LED lights up until the plant's been watered, and the string "Feed me!" is repeatedly sent to your computer.

When the plant has been watered, the LED switches off and the string "Thank you, Seymour!" is sent once to your computer.

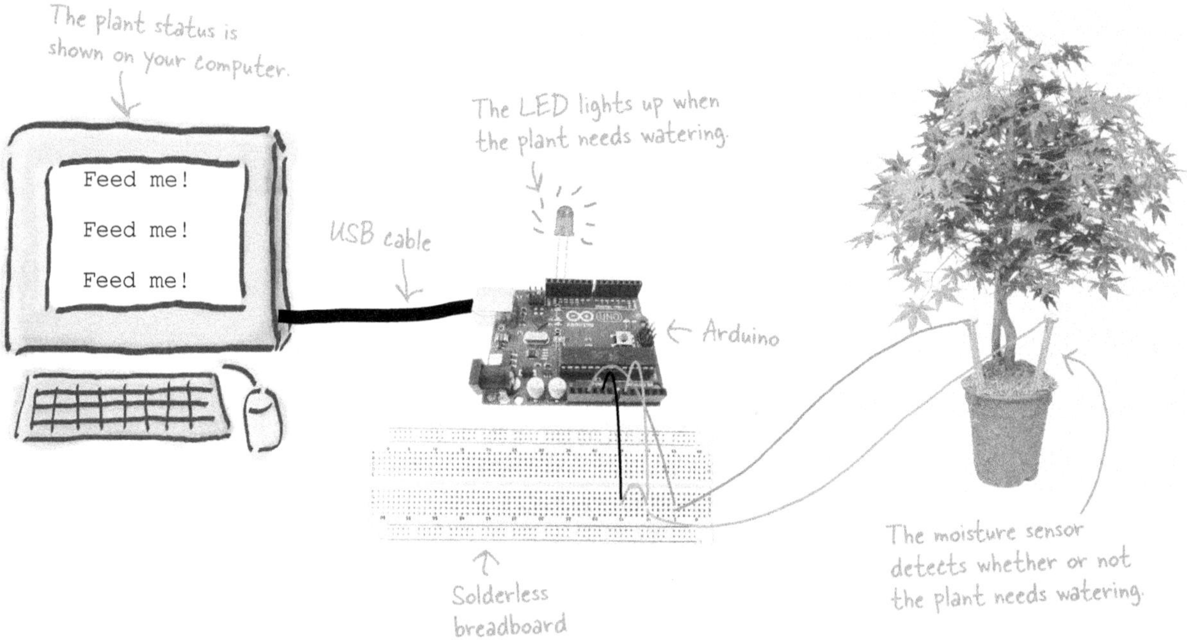
The plant status is shown on your computer.
Feed me!
Feed me!
Feed me!
USB cable
The LED lights up when the plant needs watering.
Arduino
Solderless breadboard
The moisture sensor detects whether or not the plant needs watering.

The Arduino

The brains of the plant monitor is an **Arduino**. An Arduino is a small micro-controller-based open source platform for electronic prototyping. You can connect it to sensors that pick up information about the world around it, and actuators that respond. All of this is controlled by code you write in C.

The Arduino board has 14 digital IO pins, which can be inputs or outputs. These tend to be used for reading on or off values, or switching actuators on or off.

The board also has six analog input pins, which take voltage readings from a sensor.

The board can take power from your computer's USB port.

USB
An Arduino board
Analog input pins 0 to 5
Digital pins 0 to 13

The Arduino IDE

You write your C code in an Arduino IDE. The IDE allows you to verify and compile your code, and then upload it to the Arduino itself via your USB port. The IDE also has a built-in serial monitor so that you can see what data the Arduino is sending back (if any).

The Arduino IDE is free, and you can get hold of a copy from *www.arduino.cc/en/Main/Software.*

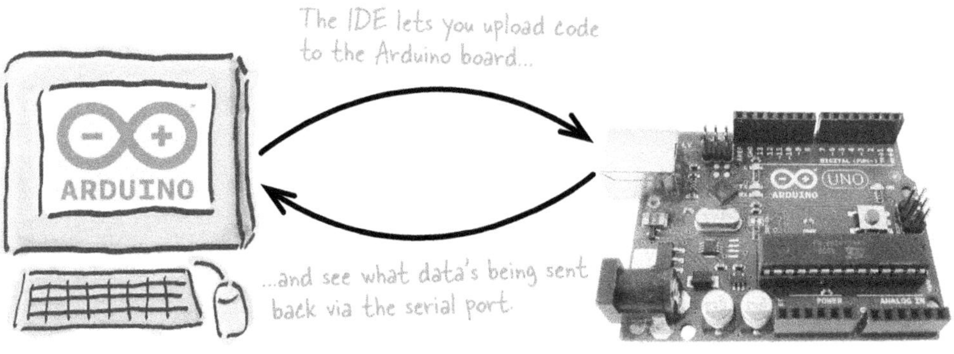
The IDE lets you upload code to the Arduino board...
ARDUINO
...and see what data's being sent back via the serial port.

Build the physical device

You start by building the physical device. While this bit's optional, we really recommend that you give it a go. Your plants will thank you for it.

We used an Arduino Uno.

You will need:

- 1 Arduino
- 1 solderless breadboard
- 1 LED
- 1 10K Ohm resistor
- 2 galvanized nails
- 3 short pieces of jumper wire
- 2 long pieces of jumper wire

Build the moisture sensor

Take a long piece of jumper wire and attach it to the head of one of the galvanized nails. You can either wrap the wire around the nail or solder it in place.

Once you've done that, attach another long piece of jumper wire to the second galvanized nail.

The moisture sensor works by checking the conductivity between the two nails. If the conductivity is high, the moisture content must be high. If it's low, the moisture content must be low.

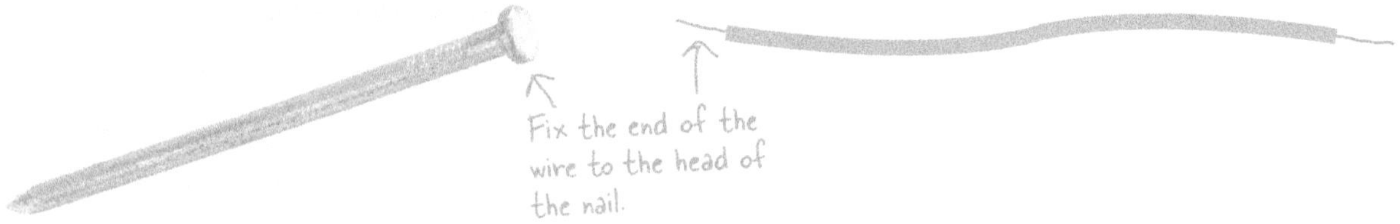
Fix the end of the wire to the head of the nail.

Connect the LED

Look at the LED. You will see that it has one longer (positive) lead and one shorter (negative) lead.

Now take a close look at the Arduino. You will see that along one edge there are slots for 14 digital pins labeled 0–13, and another one next to it labeled GND. Put the long positive lead of the LED into the slot labeled 13, and the shorter negative lead into the slot labeled GND.

This means that the LED can be controlled through digital pin 13.

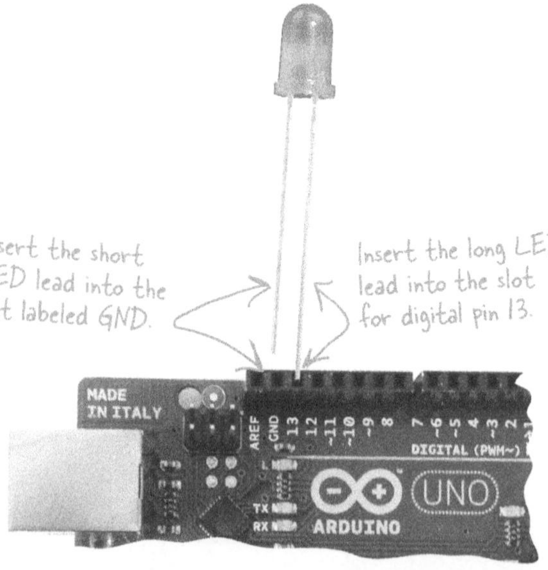
Insert the short LED lead into the slot labeled GND.
Insert the long LED lead into the slot for digital pin 13.
MADE IN ITALY
AREF
GND
DIGITAL (PWM~)
TX
RX
UNO
ARDUINO

Connect the moisture sensor

Connect the moisture sensor as shown below:

1. Connect a short jumper wire from the GND pin on the Arduino to slot D15 on the breadboard.
2. Connect the 10K Ohm resistor from slot C15 on the breadboard to slot C10.
3. Connect a short jumper wire from the 0 analog input pin to slot D10 on the breadboard.
4. Take one of the galvanized nails, and connect the wire attached to it to slot B10.
5. Connect a short jumper wire from the 5V pin on the Arduino to slot C5 on the breadboard.
6. Take the other galvanized nail, and connect the wire attached to it to slot B5.

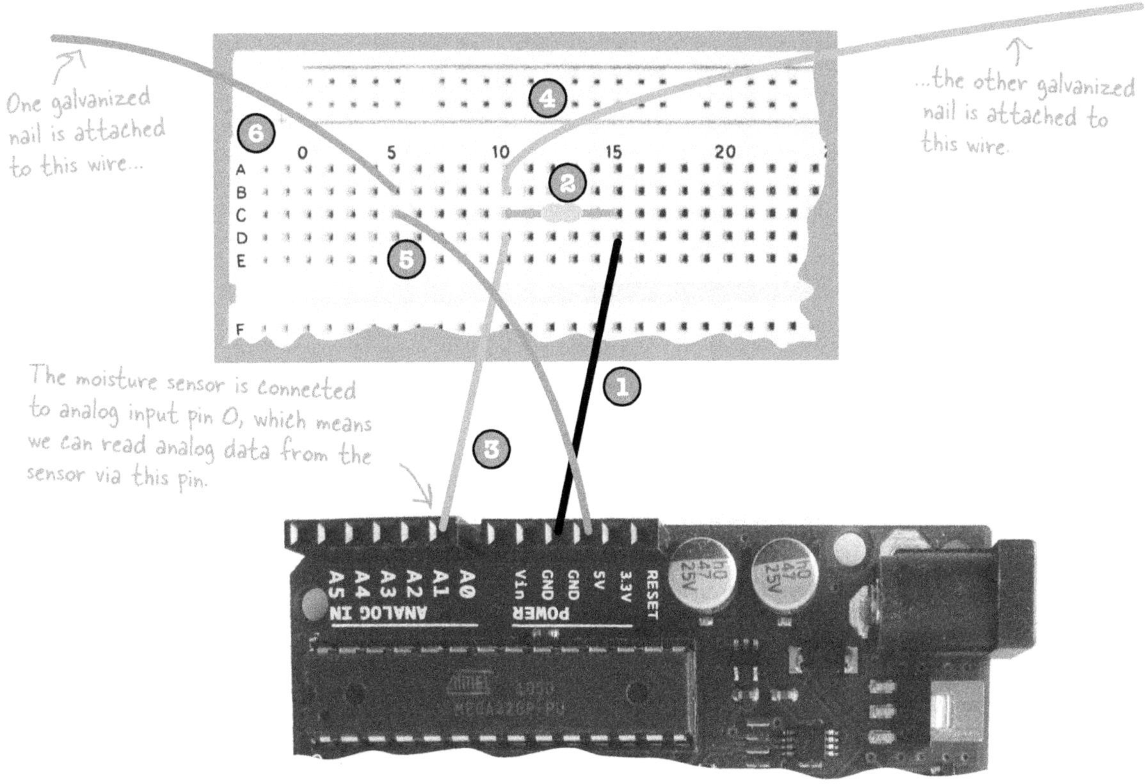
One galvanized nail is attached to this wire...
...the other galvanized nail is attached to this wire.
The moisture sensor is connected to analog input pin 0, which means we can read analog data from the sensor via this pin.
1
2
3
4
5
6
0
5
10
15
20
A
B
C
D
E
F
A0
A1
A2
A3
A4
A5
ANALOG IN
Vin
GND
GND
5V
3.3V
RESET
POWER

That's the physical Arduino built. Now for the C code...

Here's what your code should do

Your Arduino C code should do the following.

Read from the moisture sensor

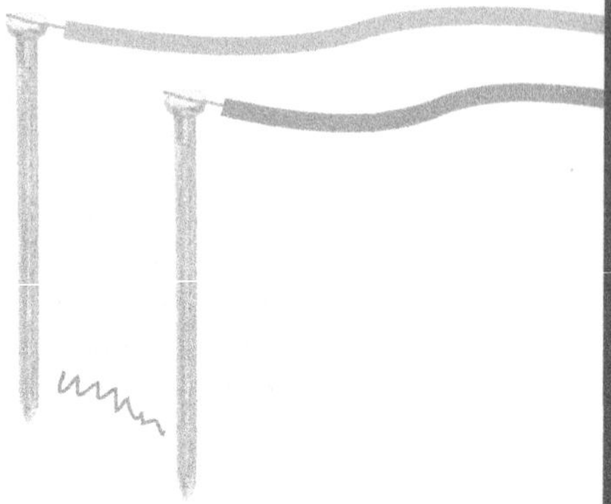

The moisture sensor is connected to an analog input pin. You will need to read analog values from this pin.

Here at the lab, we've found that our plants generally need watering when the value goes below 800, but your plant's requirements may be different—say, if it's a cactus.

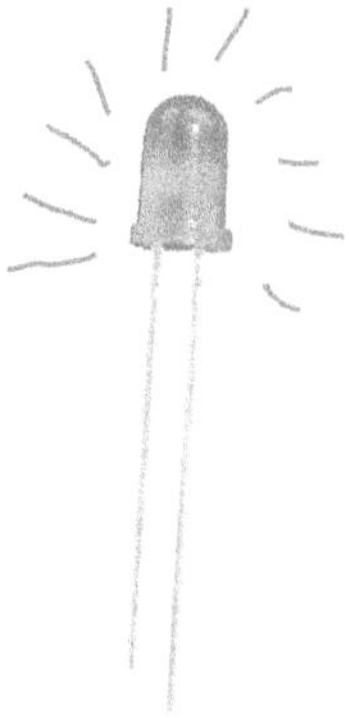

Write to the LED

The LED is connected to a digital pin.

When the plant doesn't need any more water, write to the digital pin the LED is connected to, and get it to switch off the LED.

When the plant needs watering, write to the digital pin and get it to switch on the LED. For extra credit, get it to flash. Even better, get it to flash when the conditions are borderline.

Write to the serial port

When the plant needs watering, repeatedly write the string "Feed me!" to the computer serial port.

When the plant has enough water, write the string "Thank you, Seymour!" to the serial port once.

Assume that the Arduino is plugged in to the computer USB socket.

Thank you, Seymour!
ARDUINO

Here's what your C code should look like

An Arduino C program has a specific structure. Your program must implement the following:

```
void setup()

{

/*This is called when the program starts. It
basically sets up the board. Put any initialization
code here.*/

}

void loop()

{

/*This is where your main code goes. This function
loops over and over, and allows you to respond to
input from your sensors. It only stops running when
the board is switched off*/

}
```

You can add extra functions and declarations if you like, but without these two functions the code won't work.

The easiest way of writing the Arduino C code is with the Arduino IDE. The IDE allows you to verify and compile your code, and then upload your completed program to the Arduino board, where you'll be able to see it running.

The Arduino IDE comes with a library of Arduino functions and includes lots of handy code examples. Turn the page to see a list of the functions you'll find most useful when creating Arduino.

Here are some useful Arduino functions

You'll need some of these to write the program.

`void pinMode(int pin, int mode)`

Tells the Arduino whether the digital `pin` is an input or output. `mode` can be either `INPUT` or `OUTPUT`.

`int digitalRead(int pin)`

Reads the value from the digital pin. The return value can be either `HIGH` or `LOW`.

`void digitalWrite(int pin, int value)`

Writes a value to a digital pin. *`value`* can be either `HIGH` or `LOW`.

`int analogRead(int pin)`

Reads the value from an analog pin. The return value is between 0 and 1023.

`void analogWrite(int pin, int value)`

Writes an analog value to a pin. *`value`* is between 0 and 255.

`void Serial.begin(long speed)`

Tells the Arduino to start sending and receiving serial data at *`speed`* bits per second. You usually set *`speed`* to 9600.

`void Serial.println(val)`

Prints data to the serial port. *`val`* can be any data type.

`void delay(long interval)`

Pauses the program for *`interval`* milliseconds.

The finished product

You'll know your Arduino project is complete when you put the moisture sensor in your plant's soil, connect the Arduino to your computer, and start getting status updates about your plant.

This end gets plugged into the computer.
Our fully assembled Arduino

If you have a Mac and want to make your plant *really* talk, you can download a script from the Head First Labs website that will read out the stream of serial data: www.headfirstlabs.com/books/hfc

5 structs, unions, and bitfields

Roll your own structures

struct tea quila =
{"tealeaves", "milk",
"sugar", "water", "tequila"};

Most things in life are more complex than a simple number.

So far, you've looked at the basic data types of the C language, but what if you want to go beyond numbers and pieces of text, and **model things in the real world**? `structs` allow you to model **real-world complexities** by writing your own structures. In this chapter, you'll learn how to **combine the basic data types** into `structs`, and even **handle life's uncertainties** with `unions`. And if you're after a simple yes or no, ***bitfields*** may be just what you need.

Sometimes you need to hand around a lot of data

Head First Aquarium

You've seen that C can handle a lot of different types of data: small numbers and large numbers, floating-point numbers, characters, and text. But quite often, when you are recording data about something in the real world, you'll find that you need to use more than one piece of data. Take a look at this example. Here you have two functions that *both* need the same set of data, because they are both dealing with the same real-world *thing*:

```
/* Print out the catalog entry */
void catalog(const char *name, const char *species, int teeth, int age)
{
  printf("%s is a %s with %i teeth. He is %i\n",
    name, species, teeth, age);
}

/* Print the label for the tank */
void label(const char *name, const char *species, int teeth, int age)
{
  printf("Name:%s\nSpecies:%s\n%i years old, %i teeth\n",
    name, species, age, teeth);
}
```

"const char *" just means you're going to pass string literals.

Both of these functions take the same set of parameters.

Now that's not really so bad, is it? But even though you're just passing four pieces of data, the code's starting to look a little messy:

```
int main()
{
  catalog("Snappy", "Piranha", 69, 4);
  label("Snappy", "Piranha", 69, 4);
  return 0;
}
```

You are passing the same four pieces of data **twice**.

There's only **one fish**, but you're passing **four** pieces of data.

That's me!

So how do you get around this problem? What can you do to avoid passing around lots and lots of data if you're really only using it to describe a single thing?

Cubicle conversation

I don't really see the problem. It's only **four** pieces of data.
Frank
Jill
Joe

Joe: Sure, it's four pieces of data *now*, but what if we change the system to record another piece of data for the fish?

Frank: That's only *one more parameter.*

Jill: Yes, it's just one piece of data, but we'll have to add that to *every function* that needs data about a fish.

Joe: Yeah, for a big system, that might be *hundreds* of functions. And all because we add *one more piece of data.*

Frank: That's a good point. But how do we get around it?

Joe: Easy, we just group the data into a *single thing*. Something like an array.

Jill: I'm not sure that would work. Arrays normally store a list of data of the *same type*.

Joe: Good point.

Frank: I see. We're recording strings and `int`s. Yeah, we can't put those into the same array.

Jill: I don't think we can.

Joe: But come on, there must be some way of doing this in C. Let's think about what we need.

Frank: OK, we want something that lets us refer to a whole set of data of different types all at once, as if it were a single piece of data.

Jill: I don't think we've seen anything like that yet, have we?

What you need is something that will let you record several pieces of data into *one large piece of data.*

Create your own structured data types with a struct

If you have a set of data that you need to bundle together into a *single thing*, then you can use a **struct**. The word struct is short for **structured data type**. A struct will let you take all of those different pieces of data into the code and wrap them up into one large new data type, like this:

```
struct fish {
  const char *name;
  const char *species;
  int teeth;
  int age;
};
```

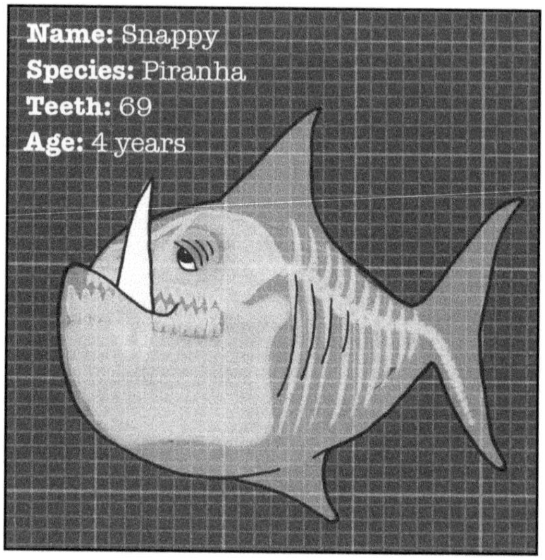
Name: Snappy
Species: Piranha
Teeth: 69
Age: 4 years

This will create a new custom data type that is made up of a collection of other pieces of data. In fact, it's a little bit like an array, except:

- **It's fixed length.**
- **The pieces of data inside the struct are given names.**

But once you've defined what your new struct looks like, how do you create pieces of data that use it? Well, it's quite similar to creating a new array. You just need to make sure the individual pieces of data are in the order that they are defined in the struct:

```
struct fish snappy = {"Snappy", "Piranha", 69, 4};
```

"struct fish" is the data type.
"snappy" is the variable name.
This is the name.
This is the species.
This is the number of teeth.
This is Snappy's age.

there are no Dumb Questions

Q: Hey, wait a minute. What's that const char thing again?

A: const char * is used for strings that you don't want to change. That means it's often used to record string literals.

Q: OK. So does this struct store the string?

A: In this case, no. The struct here just stores a pointer to a string. That means it's just recording an address, and the string lives somewhere else in memory.

Q: But you can store the whole string in there if you want?

A: Yes, if you define a char array in the struct, like char name[20];.

Just give them the fish

Now, instead of having to pass around a whole collection of individual pieces of data to the functions, you can just pass your new custom piece of data:

```
/* Print out the catalog entry */
void catalog(struct fish f)
{
  ...
}

/* Print the label for the tank */
void label(struct fish f)
{
  ...
}
```

Looks a lot simpler, doesn't it? Not only does it mean the functions now only need a *single piece of data*, but the code that calls them is easier to read:

```
struct fish snappy = {"Snappy", "Piranha", 69, 4};
catalog(snappy);
label(snappy);
```

So that's how you can define your custom data type, but how do you *use* it? How will our functions be able to read the individual pieces of data stored inside the `struct`?

Wrapping parameters in a struct makes your code more stable.

Hey, I'm goooood!

Why the fish is good for you

One of the great things about data passing around inside `struct`s is that you can change the contents of your `struct` without having to change the functions that use it. For example, let's say you want to add an extra field to `fish`:

```
struct fish {
  const char *name;
  const char *species;
  int teeth;
  int age;
  int favorite_music;
};
```

All the `catalog()` and `label()` functions have been told is they they're going to be handed a `fish`. They don't know (and don't care) that the `fish` now contains more data, so long as it has all the fields they need.

That means that `struct`s don't just make your code easier to read, they also make it better able to cope with change.

Read a struct's fields with the "." operator

Because a `struct`'s a little like an array, you might think you can read its fields like an array:

```
struct fish snappy = {"Snappy", "piranha", 69, 4};
printf("Name = %s\n", snappy[0]);
```

← If snappy was a pointer to an array, you would access the first field like this.

You get an error if you try to read a struct field like it's an array.

```
File Edit Window Help Fish
> gcc fish.c -o fish
fish.c: In function 'main':
fish.c:12: error: subscripted value is neither array nor pointer
>
```

But you can't. Even though a `struct` stores fields like an array, the only way to access them is ***by name***. You can do this using the "." operator. If you've used another language, like JavaScript or Ruby, this will look familiar:

```
struct fish snappy = {"Snappy", "piranha", 69, 4};
printf("Name = %s\n", snappy.name);
```

This is the name attribute in snappy.

This will return the string "Snappy."

```
File Edit Window Help Fish
> gcc fish.c -o fish
> ./fish
Name = Snappy
>
```

OK, now that you know a few things about using structs, let's see if you can go back and update that code...

Piranha ~~Pool~~ Puzzle

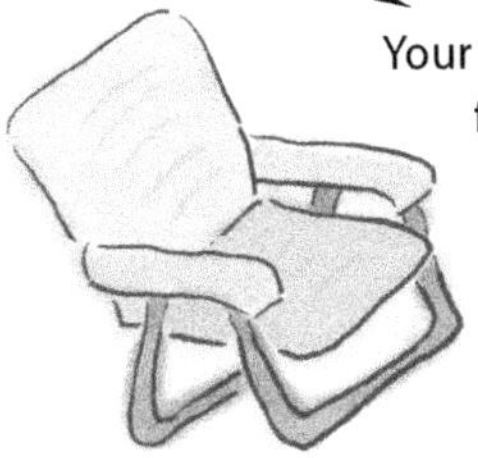

Your job is to write a new version of the `catalog()` function using the `fish struct`. Take fragments of code from the pool and place them in the blank lines below. You may not use the same fragment more than once, and you won't need to use all the fragments.

```
void catalog(struct fish f)
{
  printf("%s is a %s with %i teeth. He is %i\n",
    ______.______, ______.______, ______.______, ______.______);
}

int main()
{
  struct fish snappy = {"Snappy", "Piranha", 69, 4};
  catalog(snappy);
  /* We're skipping calling label for now */
  return 0;
}
```

Note: each thing from the pool can be used only once!

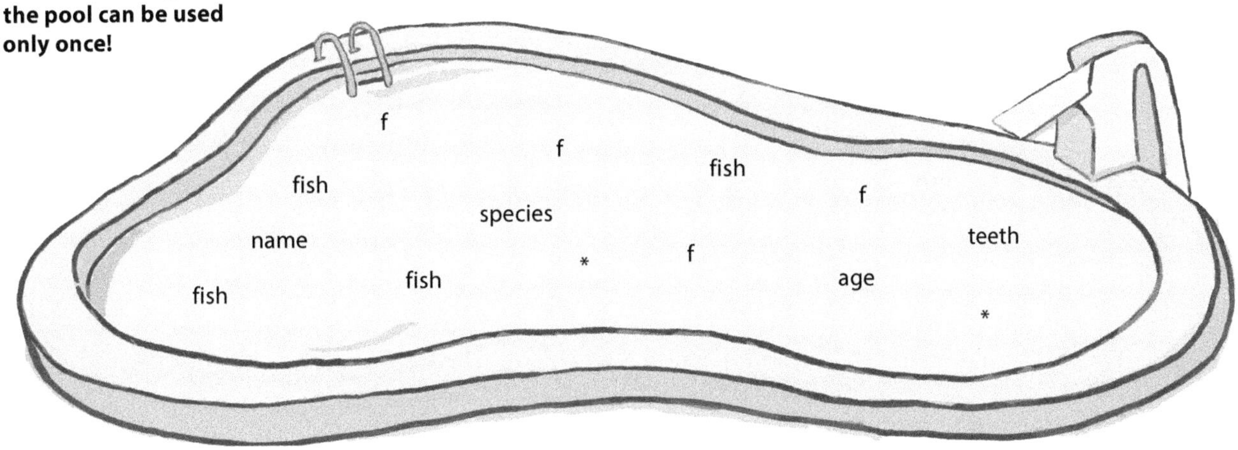
f
f
fish
fish
f
species
teeth
name
f
*
fish
age
fish
*

Piranha ~~Pool~~ Puzzle Solution

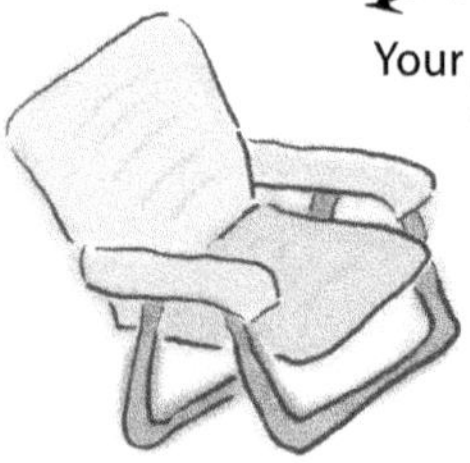

Your job was to write a new version of the `catalog()` function using the `fish struct`. You were to take fragments of code from the pool and place them in the blank lines below.

```
void catalog(struct fish f)
{
  printf("%s is a %s with %i teeth. He is %i\n",
     f.name, f.species, f.teeth, f.age);
}

int main()
{
  struct fish snappy = {"Snappy", "Piranha", 69, 4};
  catalog(snappy);
  /* We're skipping calling label for now */
  return 0;
}
```

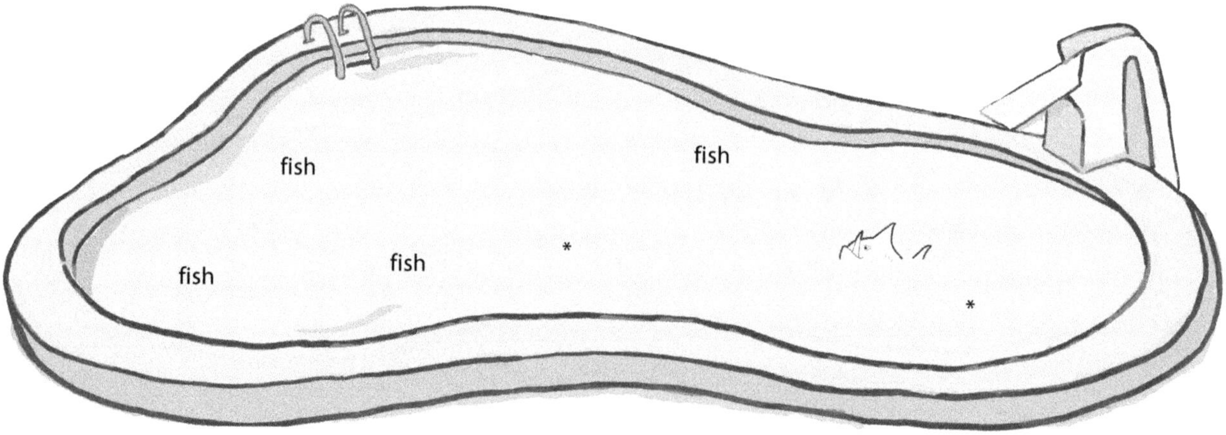
fish
fish
fish
fish
*
*

Test Drive

You've rewritten the `catalog()` function, so it's pretty easy to rewrite the `label()` function as well. Once you've done that, you can compile the program and check that it still works:

Hey, look, someone's using make...

This line is printed out by the catalog() function.

These lines are printed by the label() function.

```
File Edit Window Help FishAreFriendsNotFood
> make pool_puzzle && ./pool_puzzle
gcc pool_puzzle.c -o pool_puzzle
Snappy is a Piranha with 69 teeth. He is 4
Name:Snappy
Species:Piranha
4 years old, 69 teeth
>
```

That's great. The code works the same as it did before, but now you have really simple lines of code that call the two functions:

```
catalog(snappy);

label(snappy);
```

Not only is the code more readable, but if you ever decide to record some extra data in the `struct`, you won't have to change anything in the functions that use it.

there are no Dumb Questions

Q: So is a `struct` just an array?

A: No, but *like* an array, it groups a number of pieces of data together.

Q: An array variable is just a pointer to the array. Is a `struct` variable a pointer to a `struct`?

A: No, a `struct` variable is a name for the `struct` itself.

Q: I know I don't have to, but could I use `[0]`, `[1]`,... to access the fields of a `struct`?

A: No, you can only access fields by name.

Q: Are `structs` like classes in other languages?

A: They're similar, but it's not so easy to add methods to `structs`.

Structs In Memory Up Close

When you define a `struct`, you're not telling the computer to create anything in memory. You're just giving it a **template** for how you want a new type of data to look.

```
struct fish {
  const char *name;
  const char *species;
  int teeth;
  int age;
};
```

But when you define a new variable, the computer will need to create some space in memory for an **instance** of the `struct`. That space in memory will need to be big enough to contain all of the fields within the `struct`:

```
struct fish snappy = {"Snappy", "Piranha", 69, 4};
```

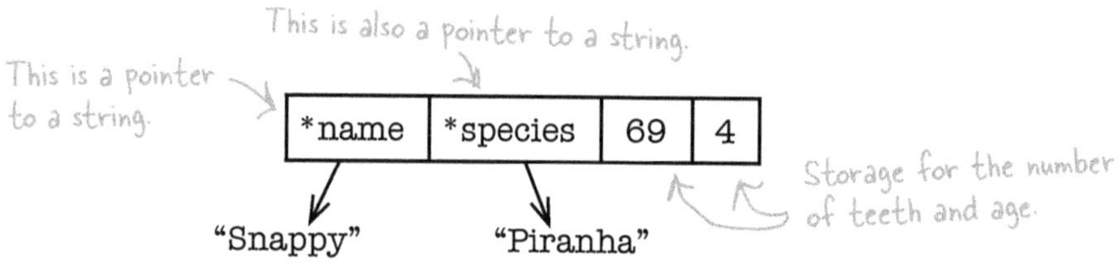
This is also a pointer to a string.
This is a pointer to a string.
*name
*species
69
4
"Snappy"
"Piranha"
Storage for the number of teeth and age.

So what do you think happens when you assign a `struct` to another variable? Well, the computer will create a **brand-new copy of the struct**. That means it will need to allocate another piece of memory of the same size, and then copy over each of the fields.

```
struct fish snappy = {"Snappy", "Piranha", 69, 4};
struct fish gnasher = snappy;
```

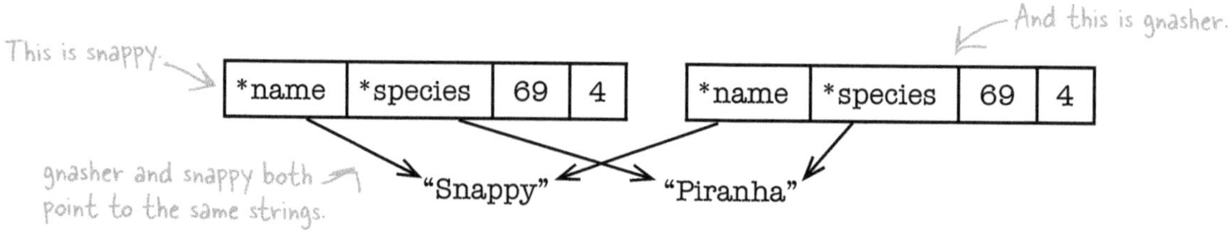
This is snappy.
And this is gnasher.
*name
*species
69
4
*name
*species
69
4
"Snappy"
"Piranha"
gnasher and snappy both point to the same strings.

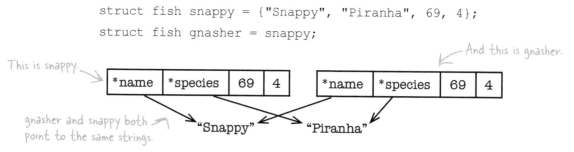

Remember: when you're assigning struct variables, you are telling the computer to *copy* data.

Watch it!

The assignment copies the pointers to strings, not the strings themselves.

When you assign one `struct` *to another, the contents of the* `struct` *will be copied. But if, as here, that includes* ***pointers****, the assignment will just copy the pointer values. That means the* `name` *and* `species` *fields of* `gnasher` *and* `snappy` *both point to the same strings.*

Can you put one struct inside another?

Remember that when you define a `struct`, you're actually creating a *new data type*. C gives us lots of built-in data types like `int`s and `short`s, but a `struct` lets us combine existing types together so that you can describe *more complex objects* to the computer.

But if a `struct` creates a data type from existing data types, that means you can also **create `struct`s from other `struct`s**. To see how this works, let's look at an example.

```
struct preferences {          <- These are things our fish likes.
  const char *food;
  float exercise_hours;
};

struct fish {
  const char *name;
  const char *species;
  int teeth;
  int age;
  struct preferences care;    <- This is called nesting.
};
```

This is a struct inside a struct.

This is a new field.

Our new field is called "care," but it will contain fields defined by the "preferences" struct.

Why nest structs?

Why would you want to do this? So you can cope with **complexity**. `struct`s give us bigger *building blocks* of data. By combining `struct`s together, you can create larger and larger data structures. You might have to begin with just `int`s and `short`s, but with `struct`s, you can describe hugely complex things, like **network streams** or **video images**.

This code tells the computer one `struct` will contain another `struct`. You can then create variables using the same array-like code as before, but now you can include the data for one `struct` *inside another*:

```
struct fish snappy = {"Snappy", "Piranha", 69, 4, {"Meat", 7.5}};
```

This is the struct data for the care field.

This is the value for care.food.

This is the value for care.exercise_hours.

Once you've combined `struct`s together, you can access the fields using a *chain* of "." operators:

```
printf("Snappy likes to eat %s", snappy.care.food);
printf("Snappy likes to exercise for %f hours", snappy.care.exercise_hours);
```

OK, let's try out your new struct skillz...

Long Exercise

The guys at the Head First Aquarium are starting to record lots of data about each of their fish guests. Here are their `struct`s:

```
struct exercise {
  const char *description;
  float duration;
};

struct meal {
  const char *ingredients;
  float weight;
};

struct preferences {
  struct meal food;
  struct exercise exercise;
};

struct fish {
  const char *name;
  const char *species;
  int teeth;
  int age;
  struct preferences care;
};
```

This is the data that will be recorded for one of the fish:

```
Name: Snappy
Species: Piranha
Food ingredients: meat
Food weight: 0.2 lbs
Exercise description: swim in the jacuzzi
Exercise duration 7.5 hours
```

Question 0: How would you write this data in C?

```
struct fish snappy = ..........................................................
```

Question 1: Complete the code of the `label()` function so it produces output like this:

```
Name:Snappy
Species:Piranha
4 years old, 69 teeth
Feed with 0.20 lbs of meat and allow to swim in the jacuzzi for 7.50 hours
```

```
void label(struct fish a)
{
  printf("Name:%s\nSpecies:%s\n%i years old, %i teeth\n",
         a.name, a.species, a.teeth, a.age);
  printf("Feed with %2.2f lbs of %s and allow to %s for %2.2f hours\n",
         ............................ , ............................ ,
         ............................ , ............................ );
}
```

Long Exercise Solution

The guys at the Head First Aquarium are starting to record lots of data about each of their fish guests. Here are their `struct`s:

```
struct exercise {
  const char *description;
  float duration;
};

struct meal {
  const char *ingredients;
  float weight;
};

struct preferences {
  struct meal food;
  struct exercise exercise;
};

struct fish {
  const char *name;
  const char *species;
  int teeth;
  int age;
  struct preferences care;
};
```

This is the data that will be recorded for one of the fish:

```
Name: Snappy
Species: Piranha
Food ingredients: meat
Food weight: 0.2 lbs
Exercise description: swim in the jacuzzi
Exercise duration 7.5 hours
```

Question 0: How would you write this data in C?

```
struct fish snappy = {"Snappy", "Piranha", 69, 4, {{"meat", 0.2}, {"swim in the jacuzzi", 7.5}}};
```

Question 1: Complete the code of the `label()` function so it produces output like this:

```
Name:Snappy
Species:Piranha
4 years old, 69 teeth
Feed with 0.20 lbs of meat and allow to swim in the jacuzzi for 7.50 hours
```

```
void label(struct fish a)
{
  printf("Name:%s\nSpecies:%s\n%i years old, %i teeth\n",
         a.name, a.species, a.teeth, a.age);
  printf("Feed with %2.2f lbs of %s and allow to %s for %2.2f hours\n",
         a.care.food.weight , a.care.food.ingredients ,
         a.care.exercise.description , a.care.exercise.duration );
}
```

Hmmm...all these struct commands seem kind of wordy. I have to use the struct keyword when I define a struct, and then I have to use it again when I define a variable. I wonder if there's some way of simplifying this.

You can give your struct a proper name using typedef.
When you create variables for built-in data types, you can use simple short names like `int` or `double`, but so far, every time you've created a variable containing a `struct` you've had to include the `struct` keyword.

```
struct cell_phone {
  int cell_no;
  const char *wallpaper;
  float minutes_of_charge;
};
...
struct cell_phone p = {5557879, "sinatra.png", 1.35};
```

But C allows you to create an **alias** for any `struct` that you create. If you add the word **typedef** *before* the `struct` keyword, and a **type name** *after* the closing brace, you can call the new type whatever you like:

typedef means you are going to give the struct type a new name.

```
typedef struct cell_phone {
  int cell_no;
  const char *wallpaper;
  float minutes_of_charge;
} phone;
...
phone p = {5557879, "sinatra.png", 1.35};
```

phone will become an alias for "struct cell_phone."

Now, when the compiler sees "phone," it will treat it like "struct cell_phone."

`typedef`s can shorten your code and make it easier to read. Let's see what your code will look like if you start to add `typedef`s to it…

What should I call my new type?

If you use `typedef` to create an alias for a `struct`, you will need to decide what your ***alias*** will be. The alias is just the name of your type. That means there are *two names* to think about: the name of the `struct` (`struct` **`cell_phone`**) and the name of the ***type*** (**phone**). Why have two names? You usually don't need both. The compiler is quite happy for you to skip the `struct` name, like this:

```
typedef struct {
  int cell_no;
  const char *wallpaper;
  float minutes_of_charge;
} phone;
phone p = {5557879, "s.png", 1.35};
```

This is the alias.

Exercise

It's time for the scuba diver to make his daily round of the tanks, and he needs a new label on his suit. Trouble is, it looks like some of the code has gone missing. Can you work out what the missing words are?

```
#include <stdio.h>

 ........................... struct {
   float tank_capacity;
   int tank_psi;
   const char *suit_material;
} ...........................;

 ........................... struct scuba {
   const char *name;
   equipment kit;
} diver;

void badge(........................... d)
{
   printf("Name: %s Tank: %2.2f(%i) Suit: %s\n",
     d.name, d.kit.tank_capacity, d.kit.tank_psi, d.kit.suit_material);
}

int main()
{
   ........................... randy = {"Randy", {5.5, 3500, "Neoprene"}};
   badge(randy);
   return 0;
}
```

Exercise Solution

It's time for the scuba diver to make his daily round of the tanks, and he needs a new label on his suit. Trouble is, it looks like some of the code has gone missing. Could you work out what the missing words were?

```
#include <stdio.h>

  typedef struct {
  float tank_capacity;
  int tank_psi;
  const char *suit_material;
} equipment;

  typedef struct scuba {
  const char *name;
  equipment kit;
} diver;

void badge(diver d)
{
  printf("Name: %s Tank: %2.2f(%i) Suit: %s\n",
    d.name, d.kit.tank_capacity, d.kit.tank_psi, d.kit.suit_material);
}

int main()
{
  diver randy = {"Randy", {5.5, 3500, "Neoprene"}};
  badge(randy);
  return 0;
}
```

The coder decided to give the struct the name "scuba" here. But you'll just use the diver type name.

BULLET POINTS

- A `struct` is a data type made from a sequence of other data types.
- `struct`s are fixed length.
- `struct` *fields* are accessed by name, using the <*struct*>.<*field name*> syntax (aka *dot notation*).
- `struct` fields are stored in memory in the same order they appear in the code.
- You can nest `struct`s.
- `typedef` creates an *alias* for a data type.
- If you use `typedef` with a `struct`, then you can skip giving the `struct` a name.

there are no Dumb Questions

Q: Do `struct` fields get placed next to each other in memory?

A: Sometimes there are small gaps between the fields.

Q: Why's that?

A: The computer likes data to fit inside word boundaries. So if a computer uses 32-bit words, it won't want a `short`, say, to be split over a 32-bit boundary.

Q: So it would leave a gap and start the `short` in the next 32-bit word?

A: Yes.

Q: Does that mean each field takes up a whole word?

A: No. The computer leaves gaps only to prevent fields from splitting across word boundaries. If it can fit several fields into a single word, it will.

Q: Why does the computer care so much about word boundaries?

A: It will read complete words from the memory. If a field was split across more than one word, the CPU would have to read several locations and somehow stitch the value together.

Q: And that'd be slow?

A: That'd be slow.

Q: In languages like Java, if I assign an object to a variable, it doesn't copy the object, it just copies a reference. Why is it different in C?

A: In C, *all* assignments copy data. If you want to copy a reference to a piece of data, you should assign a pointer.

Q: I'm really confused about `struct` names. What's the `struct` name and what's the alias?

A: The `struct` name is the word that follows the `struct` keyword. If you write `struct peter_parker { ... };`, then the name is `peter_parker`, and when you create variables, you would say `struct peter_parker x`.

Q: And the alias?

A: Sometimes you don't want to keep using the `struct` keyword when you declare variables, so `typedef` allows you to create a single word alias. In `typedef struct peter_parker { ... } spider_man;`, `spider_man` is the alias.

Q: So what's an anonymous `struct`?

A: One without a name. So `typedef struct { ... } spider_man;` has an alias of `spider_man`, but no name. Most of the time, if you create an alias, you don't need a name.

How do you update a struct?

A `struct` is really just a bundle of variables, grouped together and treated like a single piece of data. You've already seen how to create a `struct` object, and how to access its values using dot notation. But how do you *change* the value of a `struct` that already exists? Well, you can change the fields just like any other variable:

```
fish snappy = {"Snappy", "piranha", 69, 4};
printf("Hello %s\n", snappy.name);
snappy.teeth = 68;
```

This creates a struct. → `fish snappy = {"Snappy", "piranha", 69, 4};`

This reads the value of the name field. ← `printf("Hello %s\n", snappy.name);`

This **sets** the value of the teeth field. → `snappy.teeth = 68;` ← Ouch! Looks like Snappy bit something hard.

That means if you look at this piece of code, you should be able to work out what it does, right?

```
#include <stdio.h>

typedef struct {
  const char *name;
  const char *species;
  int age;
} turtle;

void happy_birthday(turtle t)
{
  t.age = t.age + 1;
  printf("Happy Birthday %s! You are now %i years old!\n",
    t.name, t.age);
}

int main()
{
  turtle myrtle = {"Myrtle", "Leatherback sea turtle", 99};
  happy_birthday(myrtle);
  printf("%s's age is now %i\n", myrtle.name, myrtle.age);
  return 0;
}
```

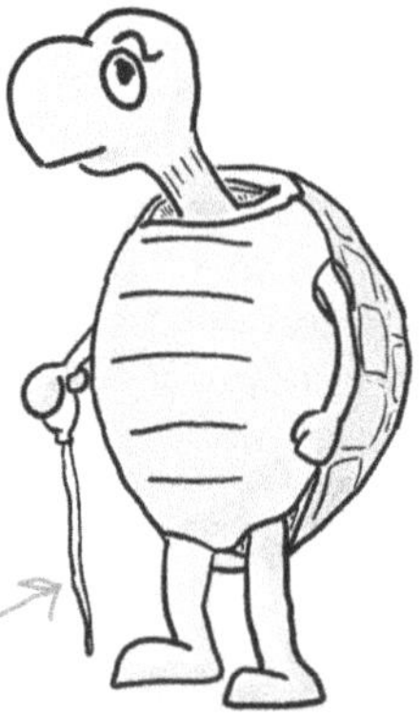

Myrtle the turtle

But there's something odd about this code...

Test Drive

This is what happens when you compile and run the code.

```
File Edit Window Help ILikeTurtles
> gcc turtle.c -o turtle && ./turtle
Happy Birthday Myrtle! You are now 100 years old!
Myrtle's age is now 99
>
```

WTF????

Wicked Turtle Feet

Something weird has happened.

The code creates a new `struct` and then passes it to a function that was *supposed* to increase the value of one of the fields by 1. And *that's exactly what the code did*...at least, for a while.

Inside the `happy_birthday()` function, the `age` field was updated, and you know that it worked because the `printf()` function displayed the new increased `age` value. But that's when the weird thing happened. Even though the `age` was updated by the function, when the code returned to the `main()` function, the `age` seemed to reset itself.

Brain Power

This code is doing something weird. But you've already been given enough information to tell you exactly ***what*** happened. Can you work out what it is?

The code is cloning the turtle

Let's take a closer look at the code that called the `happy_birthday()` function:

```
void happy_birthday(turtle t)
{
   ...
}
...
happy_birthday(myrtle);
```

This is the turtle that we are passing to the function.

The myrtle struct will be **copied** to this parameter.

When you assign a struct, its values get copied to the new struct.

In C, parameters are passed to functions **by value**. That means that when you call a function, the values you pass into it are *assigned* to the parameters. So in this code, it's almost as if you had written something like this:

```
turtle t = myrtle;
```

But *remember*: when you assign `structs` in C, the values are copied. When you call the function, the parameter `t` will contain a *copy* of the `myrtle struct`. It's as if the function ***has a clone of the original turtle***. So the code inside the function *does* update the age of the turtle, **but it's a different turtle**.

What happens when the function returns? The `t` parameter disappears, and the rest of the code in `main()` uses the `myrtle struct`. But the value of `myrtle` was never changed by the code. It was always a completely separate piece of data.

This is Myrtle...
...but her clone is sent to the function.
Turtle "t"

So what do you do if you want pass a struct to a function that needs to update it?

You need a pointer to the struct

When you passed a variable to the `scanf()` function, you couldn't pass the variable itself to `scanf()`; you had to pass a **pointer**:

```
scanf("%f", &length_of_run);
```

Why did you do that? Because if you tell the `scanf()` function where the variable lives in memory, then the function will be able to update the data stored at that place in memory, which means it can update the variable.

And you can do just the same with `structs`. If you want a function to update a `struct` variable, you can't just pass the `struct` as a parameter because that will simply send a *copy* of the data to the function. Instead, you can pass the address of the `struct`:

```
void happy_birthday(turtle *t)
{
   ...
}

...
happy_birthday(&myrtle);
```

This means "Someone is going to give me a pointer to a struct."

Remember: an address is a pointer.

This means you will pass the address of the myrtle variable to the function.

Sharpen your pencil

See if you can figure out what *expression* needs to fit into each of the gaps in this new version of the `happy_birthday()` function.

Be careful. Don't forget that `t` is now a **pointer variable**.

```
void happy_birthday(turtle *t)
{
  .............age = .............age + 1;
  printf("Happy Birthday %s! You are now %i years old!\n",
         .............name, .............age);
}
```

Sharpen your pencil Solution

You were to figure out what *expression* needs to fit into each of the gaps in this new version of the `happy_birthday()` function.

```
void happy_birthday(turtle *t)
{
   (*t).age = (*t).age + 1;
   printf("Happy Birthday %s! You are now %i years old!\n",
        (*t).name, (*t).age);
}
```

You need to put a * before the variable name, because you want the value it points to.

The parentheses are really important. The code will break without them.

(*t).age vs. *t.age

So why did you need to make sure that `*t` was wrapped in parentheses? It's because the two expressions, `(*t).age` and `*t.age`, are very different.

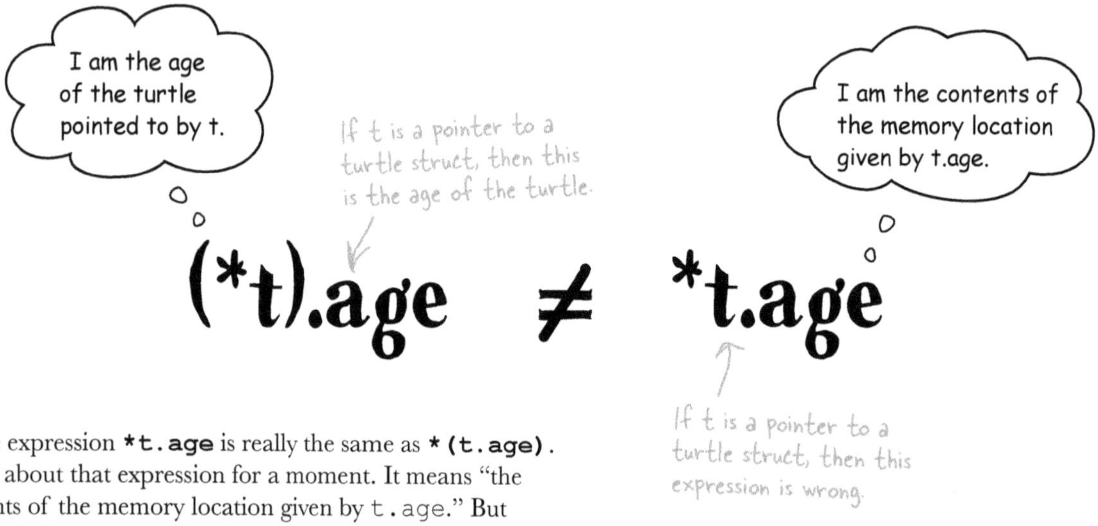
I am the age of the turtle pointed to by t.
If t is a pointer to a turtle struct, then this is the age of the turtle.
I am the contents of the memory location given by t.age.
(*t).age ≠ *t.age
If t is a pointer to a turtle struct, then this expression is wrong.

So the expression **`*t.age`** is really the same as **`*(t.age)`**. Think about that expression for a moment. It means "the contents of the memory location given by `t.age`." But `t.age` isn't a memory location.

So be careful with your parentheses when using structs—parentheses really matter.

Test Drive

Let's check if you got around the bug:

```
File Edit Window Help ILikeTurtles
> gcc happy_birthday_turtle_works.c -o happy_birthday_turtle_works
Happy Birthday Myrtle! You are now 100 years old!
Myrtle's age is now 100
>
```

That's great. The function now works.
By passing a pointer to the `struct`, you allowed the function to update the *original data* rather than taking a local copy.

t->age means (*t).age

I can see how the new code works. But the stuff about parentheses and * notation doesn't make the code all that readable. I wonder if there's something that would help with that.

Yes, there is another struct pointer notation that is more readable.
Because you need to be careful to use parentheses in the right way when you're dealing with pointers, the inventors of the C language came up with a simpler and easier-to-read piece of syntax. These two expressions mean the same thing:

```
(*t).age

t->age
```

These two mean the same.

So, `t->age` means, "The `age` field in the `struct` that `t` points to," That means you can also write the function like this:

```
void happy_birthday(turtle *a)
{
  a->age = a->age + 1;
  printf("Happy Birthday %s! You are now %i years old!\n",
         a->name, a->age);
}
```

Safe Cracker

Shhh...it's late at night in the bank vault. Can you spin the correct combination to crack the safe? Study these pieces of code and then see if you can find the correct combination that will allow you to get to the gold. Be careful! There's a `swag` type *and* a `swag` field.

You need to crack this combination.

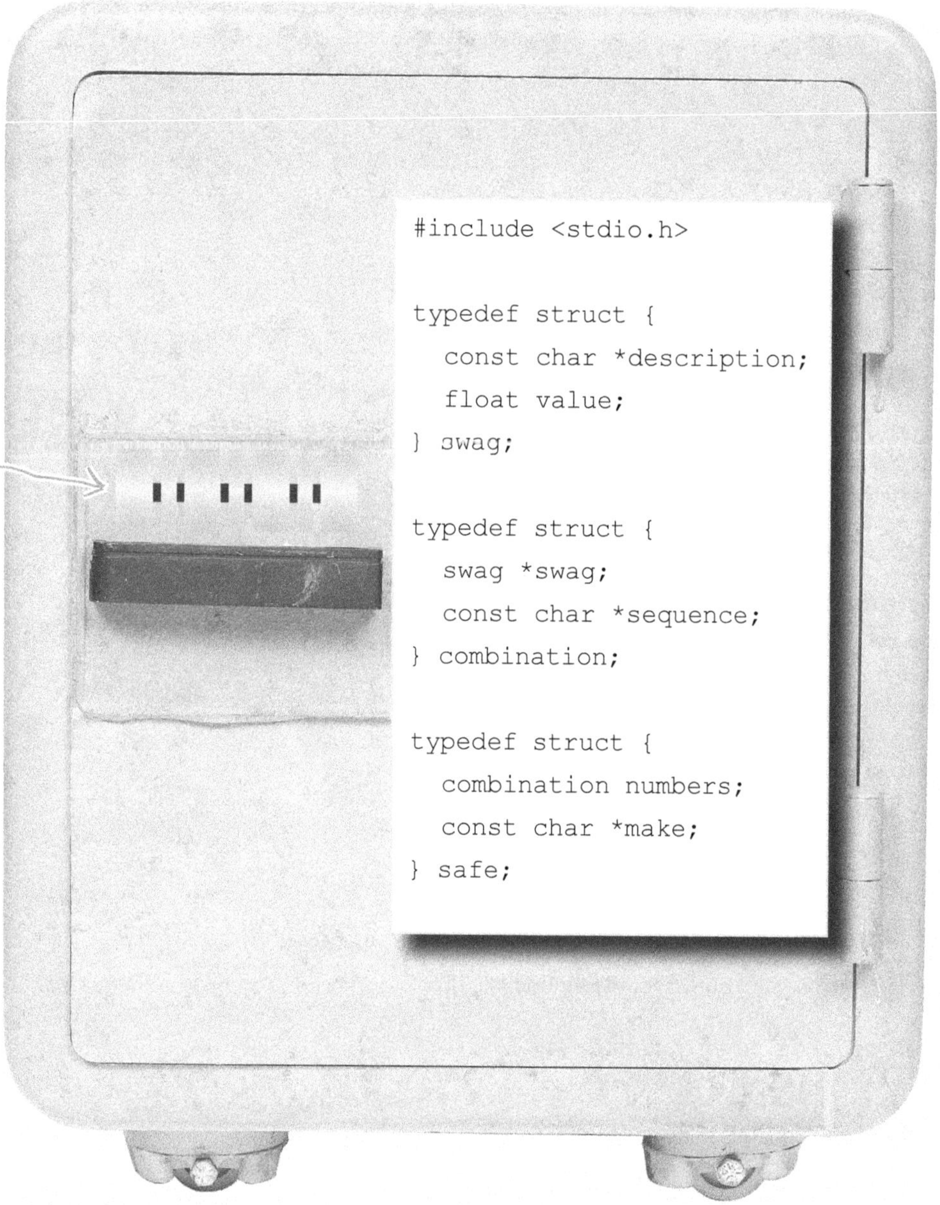

```
#include <stdio.h>

typedef struct {
  const char *description;
  float value;
} swag;

typedef struct {
  swag *swag;
  const char *sequence;
} combination;

typedef struct {
  combination numbers;
  const char *make;
} safe;
```

The bank created its safe like this:

```
swag gold = {"GOLD!", 1000000.0};
combination numbers = {&gold, "6502"};
safe s = {numbers, "RAMACON250"};
```

What combination will get you to the string "GOLD!"? Select one symbol or word from each column to assemble the expression.

con	.	s	+	swag	.	value
s	->	numbers	.	description	-	swag
numbers	:	swag	->	value	->	description
swap	-	gold	-	sequence	+	gold

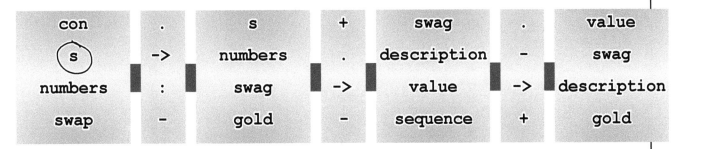

there are no Dumb Questions

Q: Why are values copied to parameter variables?

A: The computer will pass values to a function by assigning values to the function's parameters. And all assignments copy values.

Q: Why isn't `*t.age` just read as `(*t).age`?

A: Because the computer evaluates the dot operator before it evaluates the *.

Safe Cracker Solution

Shhh…it's late at night in the bank vault. You were to spin the correct combination to crack the safe. You needed to study these pieces of code and then find the correct combination that would allow you to get to the gold.

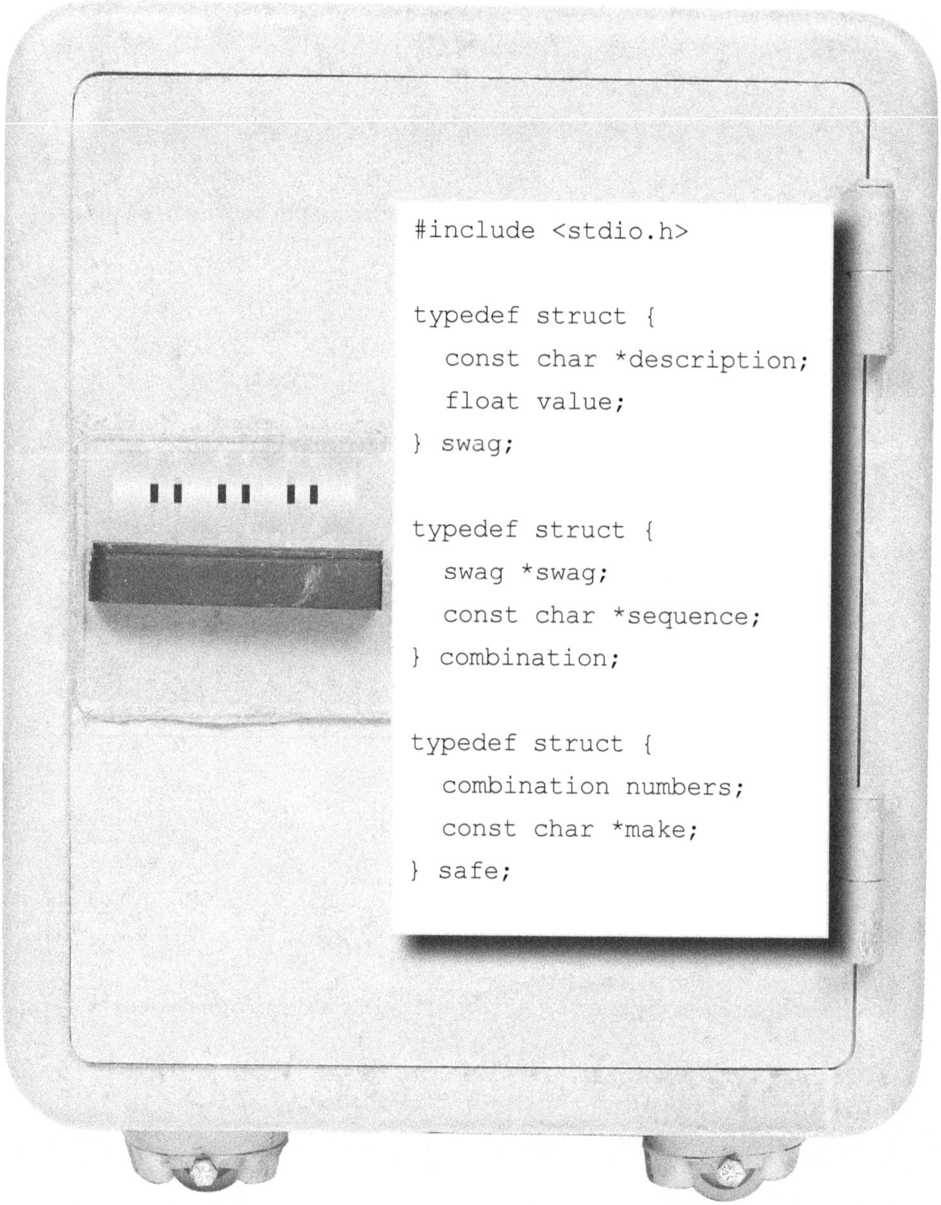

```
#include <stdio.h>

typedef struct {
  const char *description;
  float value;
} swag;

typedef struct {
  swag *swag;
  const char *sequence;
} combination;

typedef struct {
  combination numbers;
  const char *make;
} safe;
```

The bank created its safe like this:

```
swag gold = {"GOLD!", 1000000.0};
combination numbers = {&gold, "6502"};
safe s = {numbers, "RAMACON250"};
```

What combination will get you to the string "GOLD!"? You were to select one symbol or word from each column to assemble the expression.

con	. (circled)	s	+	swag (circled)	.	value
s (circled)	->	numbers (circled)	. (circled)	description	-	swag
numbers	:	swag	->	value	-> (circled)	description (circled)
swap	-	gold	-	sequence	+	gold

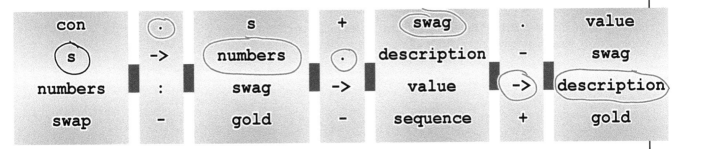

So you can display the gold in the safe with:

```
printf("Contents = %s\n", s.numbers.swag->description);
```

BULLET POINTS

- When you call a function, the values are ***copied*** to the parameter variables.
- You can create pointers to `struct`s, just like any other type.
- `pointer->field` is the same as `(*pointer).field`.
- The -> notation cuts down on parentheses and makes the code more readable.

Sometimes the same type of thing needs different types of data

`structs` enable you to model more complex things from the real world. But there are pieces of data that don't have a single data type:

An integer
Floating point
Floating point
Sale today:
6 apples
1.5 lb strawberries
0.5 pint orange juice
All of these describe a quantity.

So if you want to record, say, a *quantity* of something, and that quantity might be a **count**, a **weight**, or a **volume**, how would you do that? Well, you *could* create several fields with a `struct`, like this:

```
typedef struct {
  ...
  short count;
  float weight;
  float volume;
  ...
} fruit;
```

But there are a few reasons why this is not a good idea:

- **It will take up more space in memory.**
- **Someone might set more than one value.**
- **There's nothing called "quantity."**

It would be *really useful* if you could specify something called `quantity` in a data type and then decide for each particular piece of data whether you are going to record a count, a weight, or a volume against it.

In C, you can do just that by using a union.

A union lets you reuse memory space

Every time you create an instance of a `struct`, the computer will lay out the fields in memory, one after the other:

This is space for the age as an int.

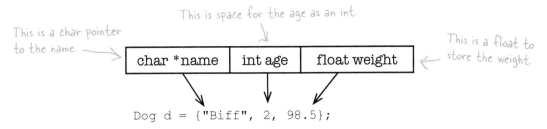

This is a char pointer to the name.

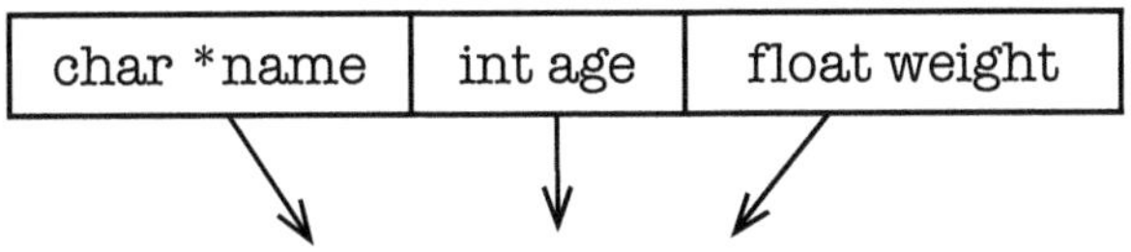
char *name
int age
float weight

This is a float to store the weight.

```
Dog d = {"Biff", 2, 98.5};
```

A **`union`** is different. A `union` will use the space for just one of the fields in its definition. So, if you have a `union` called `quantity`, with fields called `count`, `weight`, and `volume`, the computer will give the `union` enough space for its largest field, and then leave it up to you which value you will store in there. Whether you set the `count`, `weight`, or `volume` field, the data will go into the same space in memory:

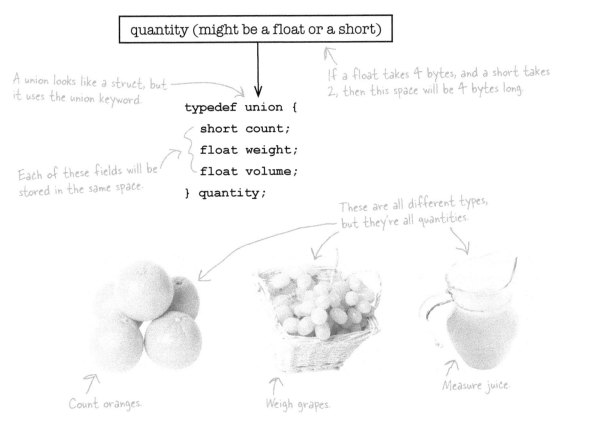

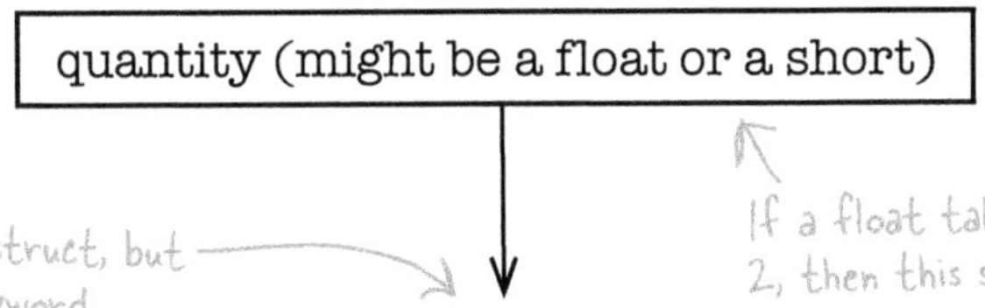
quantity (might be a float or a short)

If a float takes 4 bytes, and a short takes 2, then this space will be 4 bytes long.

A union looks like a struct, but it uses the union keyword.

```
typedef union {
  short count;
  float weight;
  float volume;
} quantity;
```

Each of these fields will be stored in the same space.

These are all different types, but they're all quantities.

Count oranges.

Weigh grapes.

Measure juice.

How do you use a union?

When you declare a `union` variable, there are a few ways of setting its value.

C89 style for the first field

If the `union` is going to store a value for the **first field**, then you can use C89 notation. To give the `union` a value for its first field, just wrap the value in braces:

```
quantity q = {4};
```

← This means the quantity is a **count** of 4.

Designated initializers set other values

A **designated initializer** sets a `union` field value by **name**, like this:

```
quantity q = {.weight=1.5};
```

← This will set the union for a floating-point weight value.

Set the value with dot notation

The third way of setting a `union` value is by creating the variable on one line, and setting a field value on another line:

```
quantity q;
q.volume = 3.7;
```

Remember: whichever way you set the `union`'s value, there will only ever be **one piece of data stored**. The `union` just gives you a way of creating a variable that supports ***several different data types***.

there are no Dumb Questions

Q: Why is a `union` always set to the size of the *largest* field?

A: The computer needs to make sure that a `union` is always the same size. The only way it can do that is by making sure it is large enough to contain any of the fields.

Q: Why does the C89 notation only set the first field? Why not set it to the first `float` if I pass it a `float` value?

A: To avoid ambiguity. If you had, say, a `float` and a `double` field, should the computer store `{2.1}` as a `float` or a `double`? By always storing the value in the first field, you know exactly how the data will be initialized.

The Polite Guide to Standards

Designated initializers allow you to set `struct` and `union` fields by name and are part of the C99 C standard. They are supported by most modern compilers, but be careful if you are using some *variant* of the C language. For example, *Objective C* supports designated initializers, but C++ **does not**.

Those designated initializers look like they could be useful for structs as well. I wonder if I can use them there.

Yes, designated initializers can be used to set the initial values of fields in structs as well.

They can be very useful if you have a `struct` that contains a large number of fields and you initially just want to set a few of them. It's also a good way of making your code more readable:

```
typedef struct {
  const char *color;
  int gears;
  int height;
} bike;
bike b = {.height=17, .gears=21};
```

This will set the gears and the height fields, but won't set the color field.

unions are often used with structs

Once you've created a `union`, you've created a *new data type*. That means you can use its values anywhere you would use another data type like an `int` or a `struct`. For example, you can combine them with `struct`s:

```
typedef struct {
  const char *name;
  const char *country;
  quantity amount;
} fruit_order;
```

And you can access the values in the `struct/union` combination using the dot or `->` notation you used before:

It's amount because that's the name of the struct quantity variable.

Here, you're using a double designated identifier. It accesses the weight field of the amount union.

```
fruit_order apples = {"apples", "England", .amount.weight=4.2};
printf("This order contains %2.2f lbs of %s\n", apples.amount.weight, apples.name);
```

This will print "This order contains 4.20 lbs of apples."

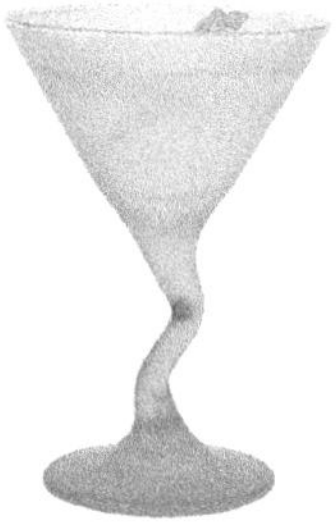

Mixed-Up Mixers

It's Margarita Night at the Head First Lounge, but after one too many samples, it looks like the guys have mixed up their recipes. See if you can find the matching code fragments for the different margarita mixes.

Here are the basic ingredients:

```
typedef union {
  float lemon;
  int lime_pieces;
} lemon_lime;

typedef struct {
  float tequila;
  float cointreau;
  lemon_lime citrus;
} margarita;
```

Here are the different margaritas:

```
margarita m = {2.0, 1.0, {0.5}};
```

```
margarita m = {2.0, 1.0, .citrus.lemon=2};
```

```
margarita m = {2.0, 1.0, 0.5};
```

```
margarita m = {2.0, 1.0, {.lime_pieces=1}};
```

```
margarita m = {2.0, 1.0, {1}};
```

```
margarita m = {2.0, 1.0, {2}};
```

And finally, here are the different mixes and the drink recipes they produce. Which of the margaritas need to be added to these pieces of code to generate the correct recipes?

```
..................................................................................................

printf("%2.1f measures of tequila\n%2.1f measures of cointreau\n%2.1f
    measures of juice\n", m.tequila, m.cointreau, m.citrus.lemon);
```

```
2.0 measures of tequila
1.0 measures of cointreau
2.0 measures of juice
```

```
..................................................................................................

printf("%2.1f measures of tequila\n%2.1f measures of cointreau\n%2.1f
    measures of juice\n", m.tequila, m.cointreau, m.citrus.lemon);
```

```
2.0 measures of tequila
1.0 measures of cointreau
0.5 measures of juice
```

```
..................................................................................................

printf("%2.1f measures of tequila\n%2.1f measures of cointreau\n%i pieces
    of lime\n", m.tequila, m.cointreau, m.citrus.lime_pieces);
```

```
2.0 measures of tequila
1.0 measures of cointreau
1 pieces of lime
```

BE the Compiler

One of these pieces of code compiles; the other doesn't. Your job is to play like you're the compiler and say which one compiles, and why the other one doesn't.

```
margarita m = {2.0, 1.0, {0.5}};
```

```
margarita m;
m = {2.0, 1.0, {0.5}};
```

Mixed-Up Mixers Solution

It's Margarita Night at the Head First Lounge, but after one too many samples, it looks like the guys have mixed up their recipes. You were to find the matching code fragments for the different margarita mixes.

Here are the basic ingredients:

```
typedef union {
  float lemon;
  int lime_pieces;
} lemon_lime;

typedef struct {
  float tequila;
  float cointreau;
  lemon_lime citrus;
} margarita;
```

Here are the different margaritas:

```
margarita m = {2.0, 1.0, .citrus.lemon=2};
```

```
margarita m = {2.0, 1.0, 0.5};
```

None of these lines was used.

```
margarita m = {2.0, 1.0, {1}};
```

And finally, here are the different mixes and the drink recipes they produce. Which of the margaritas need to be added to these pieces of code to generate the correct recipes?

```
margarita m = {2.0, 1.0, {2}};

printf("%2.1f measures of tequila\n%2.1f measures of cointreau\n%2.1f
    measures of juice\n", m.tequila, m.cointreau, m.citrus.lemon);
```

```
2.0 measures of tequila
1.0 measures of cointreau
2.0 measures of juice
```

```
margarita m = {2.0, 1.0, {0.5}};

printf("%2.1f measures of tequila\n%2.1f measures of cointreau\n%2.1f
    measures of juice\n", m.tequila, m.cointreau, m.citrus.lemon);
```

```
2.0 measures of tequila
1.0 measures of cointreau
0.5 measures of juice
```

```
margarita m = {2.0, 1.0, {.lime_pieces=1}};

printf("%2.1f measures of tequila\n%2.1f measures of cointreau\n%i pieces
    of lime\n", m.tequila, m.cointreau, m.citrus.lime_pieces);
```

```
2.0 measures of tequila
1.0 measures of cointreau
1 pieces of lime
```

BE the Compiler Solution

One of these pieces of code compiles; the other doesn't. Your job is to play like you're the compiler and say which one compiles, and why the other one doesn't.

```
margarita m = {2.0, 1.0, {0.5}};
```

This one compiles perfectly. It's actually just one of the drinks above!

```
margarita m;
m = {2.0, 1.0, {0.5}};
```

This one doesn't compile because the compiler will only know that {2.0, 1.0, {0.5}} represents a struct if it's used on the same line that a struct is declared. When it's on a separate line, the compiler thinks it's an array.

Hey, wait a minute... You're setting **all** these different values with all these different types and you're storing them in **the same place in memory**... How do I know if I stored a float in there once I've stored it? What's to stop me from reading it as a short or something??? **Hello?**

That's a really good point: you can store lots of possible values in a union, but you have *no way of knowing* what type it was once it's stored.

The compiler won't be able to keep track of the fields that are set and read in a `union`, so there's nothing to stop us setting one field and reading another. Is that a problem? Sometimes it can be a **BIG PROBLEM**.

```
#include <stdio.h>
typedef union {
  float weight;
  int count;
} cupcake;

int main()
{
  cupcake order = {2};
  printf("Cupcakes quantity: %i\n", order.count);
  return 0;
}
```

By mistake, the programmer has set the weight, **not** the count.

She set the weight, but she's reading the count.

This is what the program did.

File Edit Window Help

```
> gcc badunion.c -o badunion && ./badunion
Cupcakes quantity: 1073741824
```

That's a **lot** of cupcakes...

You need some way, then, of keeping track of the values we've stored in a `union`. One trick that some C coders use is to create an **`enum`**.

An enum variable stores a symbol

Sometimes you don't want to store a number or a piece of text. Instead, you want to store something from a list of **symbols**. If you want to record a day of the week, you only want to store MONDAY, TUESDAY, WEDNESDAY, etc. You don't need to store the text, because there are only ever going to be seven different values to choose from.

That's why `enums` were invented.

`enum` lets you create a list of symbols, like this:

The values are separated by commas.

Possible colors in your enum.

```
enum colors {RED, GREEN, PUCE};
```

You could have given the type a proper name with typedef.

Any variable that is defined with a type of **`enum colors`** can then only be set to one of the keywords in the list. So you might define an `enum colors` variable like this:

```
enum colors favorite = PUCE;
```

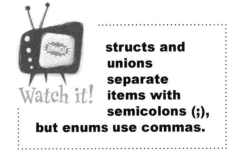

Watch it! **structs and unions separate items with semicolons (;), but enums use commas.**

Under the covers, the computer will just assign numbers to each of the symbols in your list, and the `enum` will just store a number. But you don't need to worry about what the numbers are; your C code can just refer to the symbols. That'll make your code easier to read, and it will prevent storing values like `REB` or `PUSE`:

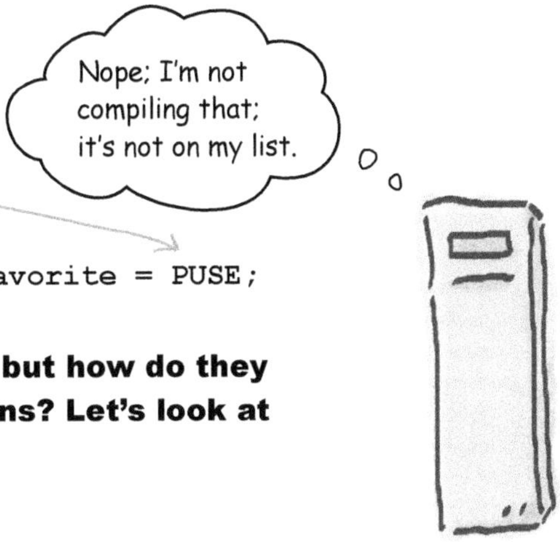
Nope; I'm not compiling that; it's not on my list.

The computer will spot that this is not a legal value, so it won't compile.

```
enum colors favorite = PUSE;
```

So that's how enums work, but how do they help you keep track of unions? Let's look at an example...

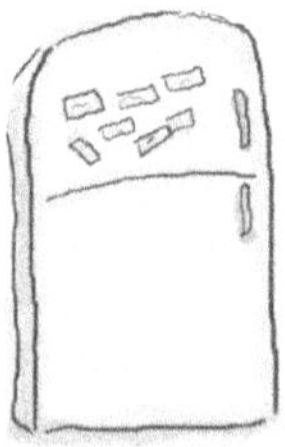

Code Magnets

Because you can create new data types with enums, you can store them inside structs and unions. In this program, an enum is being used to track the kinds of quantities being stored. Do you think you can work out where the missing pieces of code go?

```
#include <stdio.h>

typedef enum {
  COUNT, POUNDS, PINTS
} unit_of_measure;

typedef union {
  short count;
  float weight;
  float volume;
} quantity;

typedef struct {
  const char *name;
  const char *country;
  quantity amount;
  unit_of_measure units;
} fruit_order;

void display(fruit_order order)
{
  printf("This order contains ");

  if (.......................... == PINTS)

    printf("%2.2f pints of %s\n", order.amount.........................., order.name);
```

```
  else if (.............. == ..............)
    printf("%2.2f lbs of %s\n", order.amount.weight, order.name);
  else
    printf("%i %s\n", order.amount. .............. , order.name);
}

int main()
{
  fruit_order apples = {"apples", "England", .amount.count=144, ..............};

  fruit_order strawberries = {"strawberries", "Spain", .amount.........=17.6, POUNDS};

  fruit_order oj = {"orange juice", "U.S.A.", .amount.volume=10.5, ..............};
  display(apples);
  display(strawberries);
  display(oj);
  return 0;
}
```

POUNDS

order.units

COUNT

weight

volume

count

PINTS

order.units

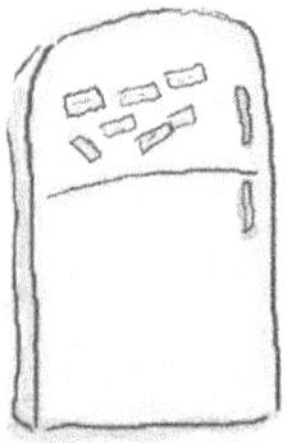

Code Magnets Solution

Because you can create new data types with `enum`s, you can store them inside `struct`s and `union`s. In this program, an `enum` is being used to track the kinds of quantities being stored. Were you able to work out where the missing pieces of code go?

```
#include <stdio.h>

typedef enum {
  COUNT, POUNDS, PINTS
} unit_of_measure;

typedef union {
  short count;
  float weight;
  float volume;
} quantity;

typedef struct {
  const char *name;
  const char *country;
  quantity amount;
  unit_of_measure units;
} fruit_order;

void display(fruit_order order)
{
  printf("This order contains ");

  if (order.units == PINTS)

    printf("%2.2f pints of %s\n", order.amount.volume, order.name);
```

```
  else if (order.units == POUNDS)
    printf("%2.2f lbs of %s\n", order.amount.weight, order.name);
  else
    printf("%i %s\n", order.amount.count, order.name);
}

int main()
{
  fruit_order apples = {"apples", "England", .amount.count=144, COUNT};
  fruit_order strawberries = {"strawberries", "Spain", .amount.weight=17.6, POUNDS};
  fruit_order oj = {"orange juice", "U.S.A.", .amount.volume=10.5, PINTS};
  display(apples);
  display(strawberries);
  display(oj);
  return 0;
}
```

When you run the program, you get this:

```
File Edit Window Help
> gcc enumtest.c -o enumtest
This order contains 144 apples
This order contains 17.60 lbs of strawberries
This order contains 10.50 pints of orange juice
```

Overheard at Head First Lounge

union: …so I said to the code, "Hey, look. I don't care if you gave me a `float` or not. You asked for an `int`. You got an `int`."

struct: Dude, that was totally uncalled for.

union: That's what I said. It's totally uncalled for.

struct: Everyone knows you only have one storage location.

union: Exactly. Everything is one. I'm, like, Zen that way…

enum: What happened, dude?

struct: Shut up, `enum`. I mean, the guy was crossing the line.

union: I mean, if he had just left a record. You know, said, I stored this as an `int`. It just needed an `enum` or something.

enum: You want me to do what?

struct: Shut up, `enum`.

union: I mean, if he'd wanted to store several things at once, he should have called you, am I right?

struct: Order. That's what these people don't grasp.

enum: Ordering what?

struct: Separation and sequencing. I keep several things alongside each other. All at the same time, dude.

union: That's just my point.

struct: All. At. The. Same. Time.

enum: (Pause) So has there been a problem?

union: Please, `enum`? I mean these people just need to make a decision. Wanna store several things, use you. But store just one thing with different possible types? Dude's your man.

struct: I'm calling him.

union: Hey, wait…

enum: Who's he calling, dude?

struct/union: Shut up, `enum`.

union: Look, let's not cause any more problems here.

struct: Hello? Could I speak to the Bluetooth service, please?

union: Hey, let's just think about this.

struct: What do you mean, he'll give me a callback?

union: I'm just. This doesn't seem like a good idea.

struct: No, let me leave you a message, my friend.

union: Please, just put the phone down.

enum: Who's on the phone, dude?

struct: Be quiet, `enum`. Can't you see I'm on the phone here? Listen, you just tell him that if he wants to store a `float` and an `int`, he needs to come see me. Or I'm going to come see him. Understand me? Hello? Hello?

union: Easy, man. Just try to keep calm.

struct: On hold? They put me on ^*&^ing hold!

union: They what? Pass me the phone… Oh…that… man. The Eagles! I hate the Eagles…

enum: So if you pack your fields, is that why you're so fat?

struct: You are entering a world of pain, my friend.

Sometimes you want control at the bit level

Let's say you need a `struct` that will contain a lot of yes/no values. You *could* create the `struct` with a series of `short`s or `int`s:

```
typedef struct {
  short low_pass_vcf;
  short filter_coupler;
  short reverb;
  short sequential;
  ...
} synth;
```

Each of these fields will contain 1 for true or 0 for false.

There are a lot more fields that follow this.

Each field will use many bits.

0000000000000001	0000000000000001	0000000000000001	...

And that would work. The problem? The `short` fields will take up a lot more space than the *single bit* that you need for **true/false** values. It's wasteful. It would be much better if you could create a `struct` that could hold a sequence of single bits for the values.

That's why **`bitfields`** were created.

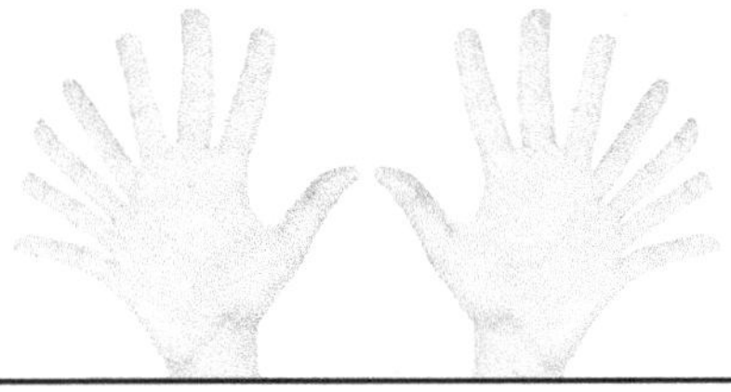

Geek Binary Digits

When you're dealing with binary value, it would be great if you had some way of specifying the 1s and 0s in a literal, like:

```
int x = 01010100;
```

Unfortunately, C doesn't support **binary literals**, but it *does* support **hexadecimal literals**. Every time C sees a number beginning with 0x, it treats the number as **base 16**:

```
int x = 0x54;
```

This is **not** decimal 54.

But how do you convert back and forth between hexadecimal and binary? And is it any easier than converting binary and **decimal**? The good news is that you can convert hex to binary **one digit at a time**:

```
        0x54
       /    \
    0101    0100
```

This is 5. → 0101   This is 4. → 0100

Each hexadecimal digit matches a binary digit of length 4. All you need to learn are the binary patterns for the numbers 0–15, and you will soon be able to convert binary to hex and back again in your head within seconds.

Bitfields store a custom number of bits

A **bitfield** lets you specify *how many bits* an individual field will store. For example, you could write your `struct` like this:

```
typedef struct {
  unsigned int low_pass_vcf:1;
  unsigned int filter_coupler:1;
  unsigned int reverb:1;
  unsigned int sequential:1;
  ...
} synth;
```

Each field should be an unsigned int.

This means the field will only use 1 bit of storage.

By using bitfields, you can make sure each field takes up only one bit.

1	1	1	...

If you have a sequence of bitfields, the computer can **squash them together** to save space. So if you have eight single-bit bitfields, the computer can store them in a single byte.

BANG!
Watch it!

Bitfields can save space if they are collected together in a struct.

But if the compiler finds a single bitfield on its own, it might still have to pad it out to the size of a word. That's why bitfields are usually grouped together.

Let's see how how good you are at using bitfields.

How many bits do I need?

Bitfields can be used to store a sequence of true/false values, but they're also useful for other short-range values, like months of the year. If you want to store a month number in a `struct`, you know it will have a value of, say, 0–11. You can store those values in **4 bits**. Why? Because 4 bits let you store 0–15, but 3 bits only store 0–7.

```
...
 unsigned int month_no:4;
...
```

Exercise

Back at the Head First Aquarium, they're creating a customer satisfaction survey. Let's see if you can use bitfields to create a matching `struct`.

Head First Aquarium

Aquarium Questionnaire

Is this your first visit?	
Will you come again?	
Number of fingers lost in the piranha tank:	
Did you lose a child in the shark exhibit?	
How many days a week would you visit if you could?	

```
typedef struct {
  unsigned int first_visit: .......... ;
  unsigned int come_again: .......... ;
  unsigned int fingers_lost: .......... ;
  unsigned int shark_attack: .......... ;
  unsigned int days_a_week: .......... ;
} survey;
```

You need to decide how many bits to use.

Exercise Solution

Back at the Head First Aquarium, they're creating a customer satisfaction survey. You were to use bitfields to create a matching `struct`.

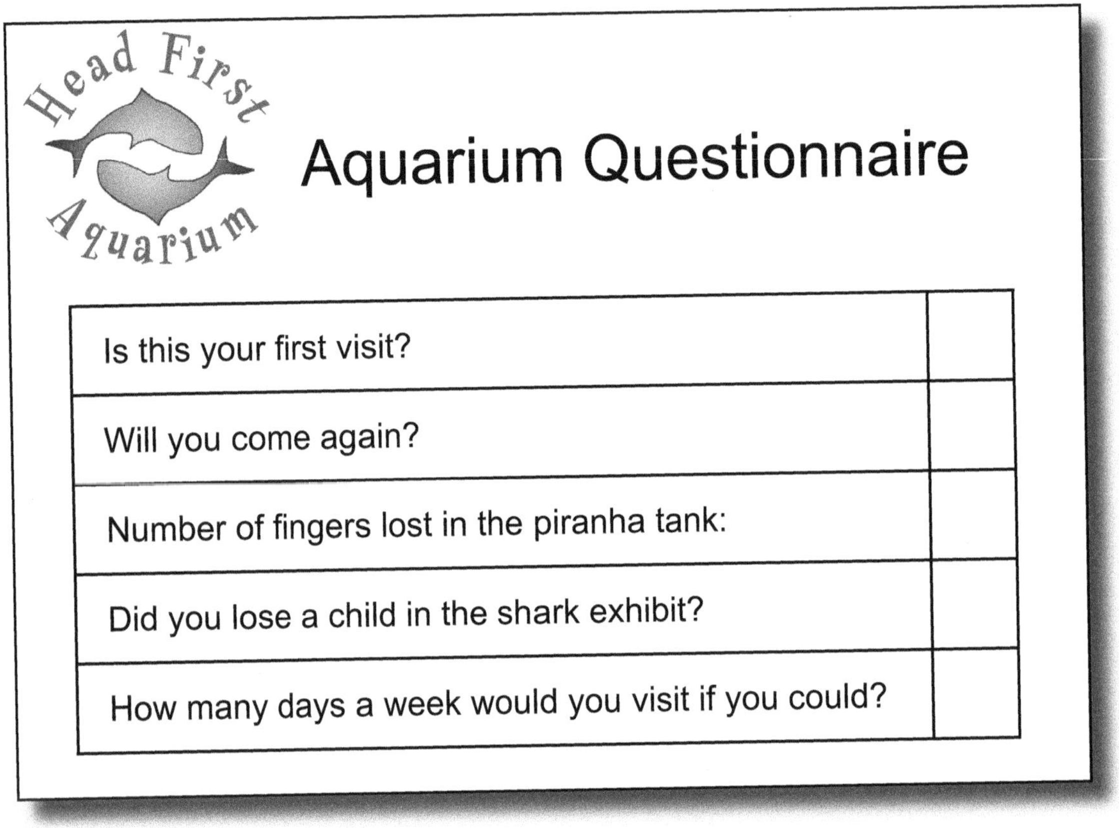
Head First Aquarium
Aquarium Questionnaire
Is this your first visit?
Will you come again?
Number of fingers lost in the piranha tank:
Did you lose a child in the shark exhibit?
How many days a week would you visit if you could?

```
typedef struct {
  unsigned int first_visit: 1;
  unsigned int come_again: 1;
  unsigned int fingers_lost: 4;
  unsigned int shark_attack: 1;
  unsigned int days_a_week: 3;
} survey;
```

1 bit can store 2 values: true/false.

4 bits are needed to store up to 10.

3 bits can store numbers up to 7.

there are no Dumb Questions

Q: Why doesn't C support binary literals?

A: Because they take up a lot of space, and it's usually more efficient to write hex values.

Q: Why do I need 4 bits to store a value up to 10?

A: Four bits can store values from 0 to binary 1111, which is 15. But 3 bits can only store values up to binary 111, which is 7.

Q: So what if I try to put the value 9 into a 3-bit field?

A: The computer will store a value of 1 in it, because 9 is 1001 in binary, so the computer transfers 001.

Q: Are bitfields really just used to save space?

A: No. They're important if you need to read low-level binary information.

Q: Such as?

A: If you're reading or writing some sort of custom binary file.

BULLET POINTS

- A `union` allows you to store different data types in the same memory location.
- A designated initializer sets a field value by name.
- Designated initializers are part of the C99 standard. They are not supported in C++.
- If you declare a `union` with a value in {braces}, it will be stored with the type of the first field.
- The compiler will let you store one field in a `union` and read a completely different field. But be careful! This can cause bugs.
- `enum`s store symbols.
- Bitfields allow you to store a field with a custom number of bits.
- Bitfields should be declared as `unsigned int`.

Your C Toolbox

You've got Chapter 5 under your belt, and now you've added structs, unions, and bitfields to your toolbox. For a complete list of tooltips in the book, see Appendix ii.

typedef lets you create an alias for a data type.

A struct combines data types together.

You can read struct fields with dot notation.

You can initialize structs with {array, like, notation}.

-> notation lets you easily update fields using a struct pointer.

Designated initializers let you set struct and union fields by name.

unions can hold different data types in one location.

enums let you create a set of symbols.

Bitfields give you control over the exact bits stored in a struct.

6 data structures and dynamic memory

Building bridges

I heard that Ted left Judy on the heap.
That's so sad.

Sometimes, a single struct is simply not enough.

To model complex data requirements, you often need to **link `structs` together**. In this chapter, you'll see how to use **`struct` pointers** to connect custom data types into **large, complex data structures**. You'll explore *key principles* by creating **linked lists**. You'll also see how to make your data structures cope with flexible amounts of data by **dynamically allocating memory on the heap**, and freeing it up when you're done. And if good housekeeping becomes tricky, you'll also learn how `valgrind` can help.

Do you need flexible storage?

Coconut Airways flies C planes between the islands.

You've looked at the different kinds of data that you can store in C, and you've also seen how you can store multiple pieces of data in an array. But sometimes you need to be a little more flexible.

Imagine you're running a travel company that arranges flying tours through the islands. Each tour contains a sequence of short flights from one island to the next. For each of those islands, you will need to record a few pieces of information, such as the name of the island and the hours that its airport is open. So how would you record that?

You could create a `struct` to represent a single island:

```
typedef struct {
  char *name;
  char *opens;
  char *closes;
} island;
```

Now if a tour passes through a *sequence* of islands, that means you'll need to record a list of islands, and you can do that with an array of `islands`:

```
island tour[4];
```

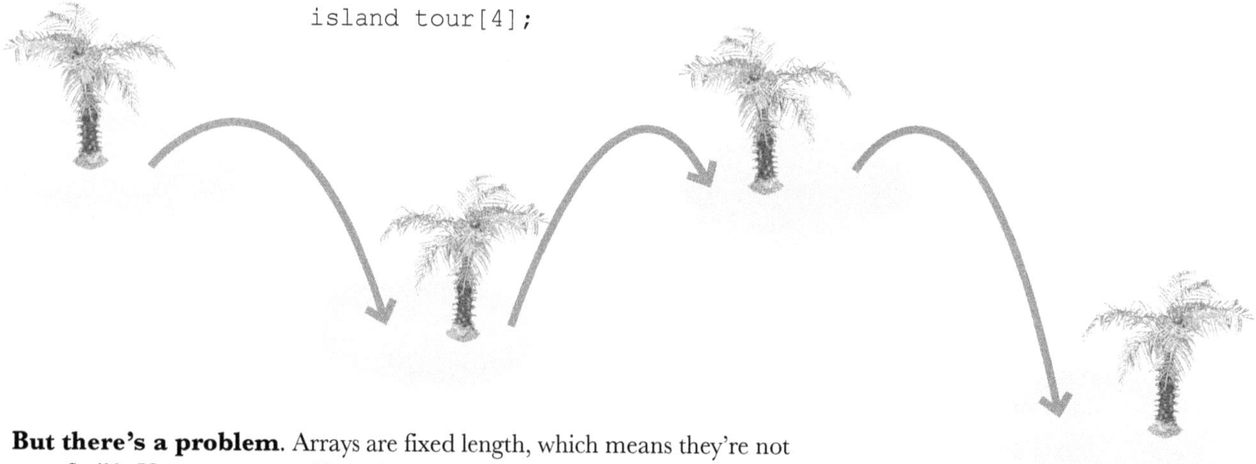

But there's a problem. Arrays are fixed length, which means they're not very *flexible*. You can use one if you know **exactly** how *long* a tour will be. But what if you need to change the tour? What if you want to add an extra destination to the middle of the tour?

To store a flexible amount of data, you need something more extensible than an array. You need a *linked list*.

Linked lists are like chains of data

A **linked list** is an example of an **abstract data structure**. It's called an *abstract* data structure because a linked list is *general*: it can be used to store a lot of different kinds of data.

To understand how a linked list works, think back to our tour company. A linked list stores a piece of data, and a link to *another* piece of data.

Sharpen your pencil

In a linked list, as long as you know where the list starts, you can travel along the list of links, from one piece of data to the next, until you reach the end of the list. Using a pencil, change the list so that the tour includes a trip to Skull Island between Craggy Island and Isla Nublar.

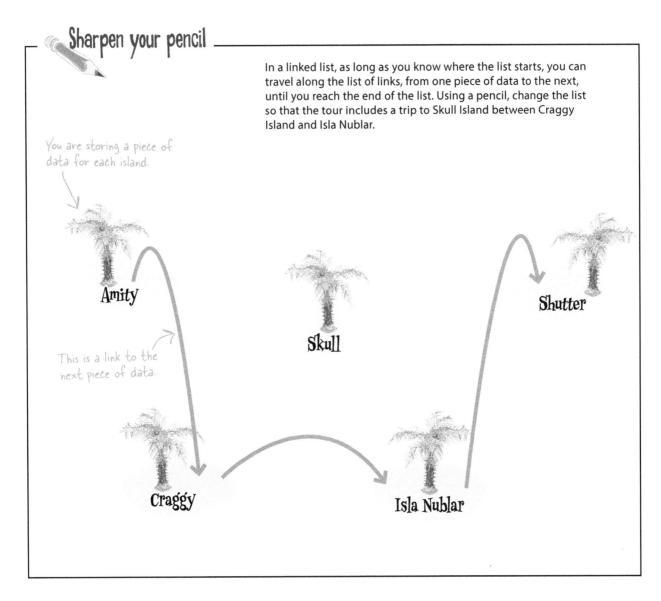

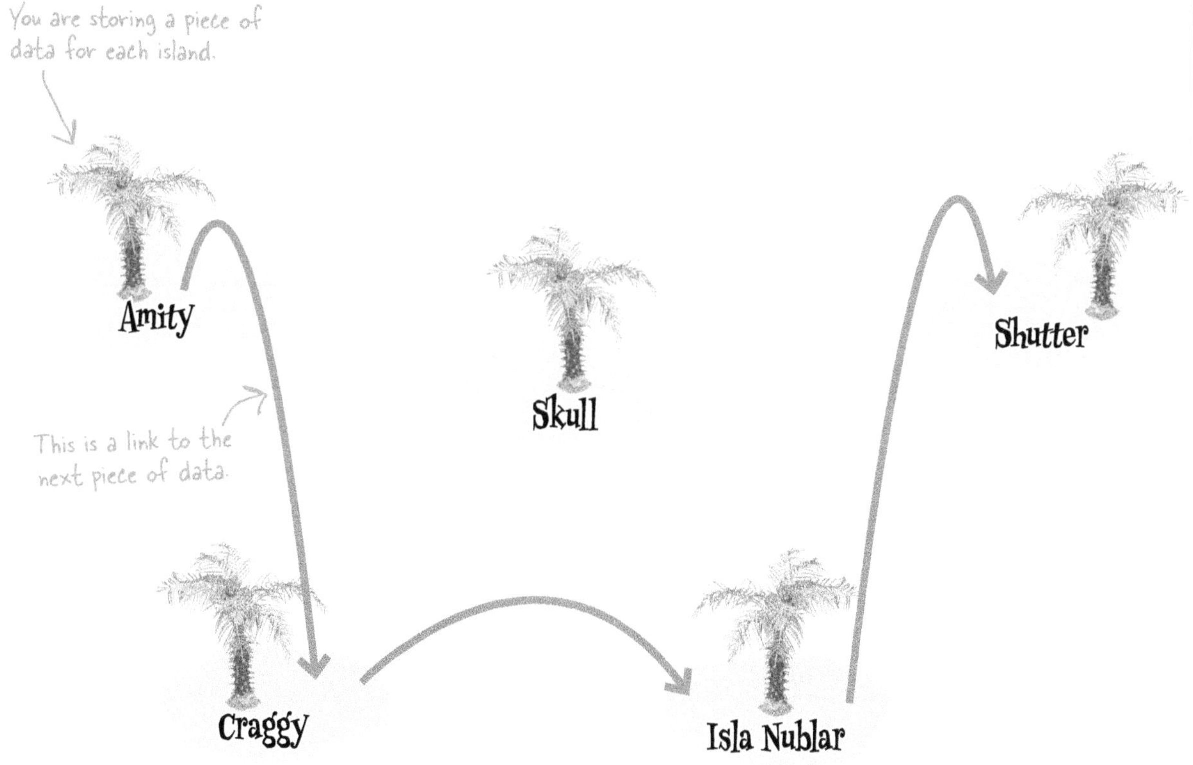
You are storing a piece of data for each island.
Amity
This is a link to the next piece of data.
Skull
Shutter
Craggy
Isla Nublar

Sharpen your pencil Solution

In a linked list, as long as you know where the list starts, you can travel along the list of links, from one piece of data to the next, until you reach the end of the list. Using a pencil, you were to change the list so that the tour includes a trip to Skull Island between Craggy Island and Isla Nublar.

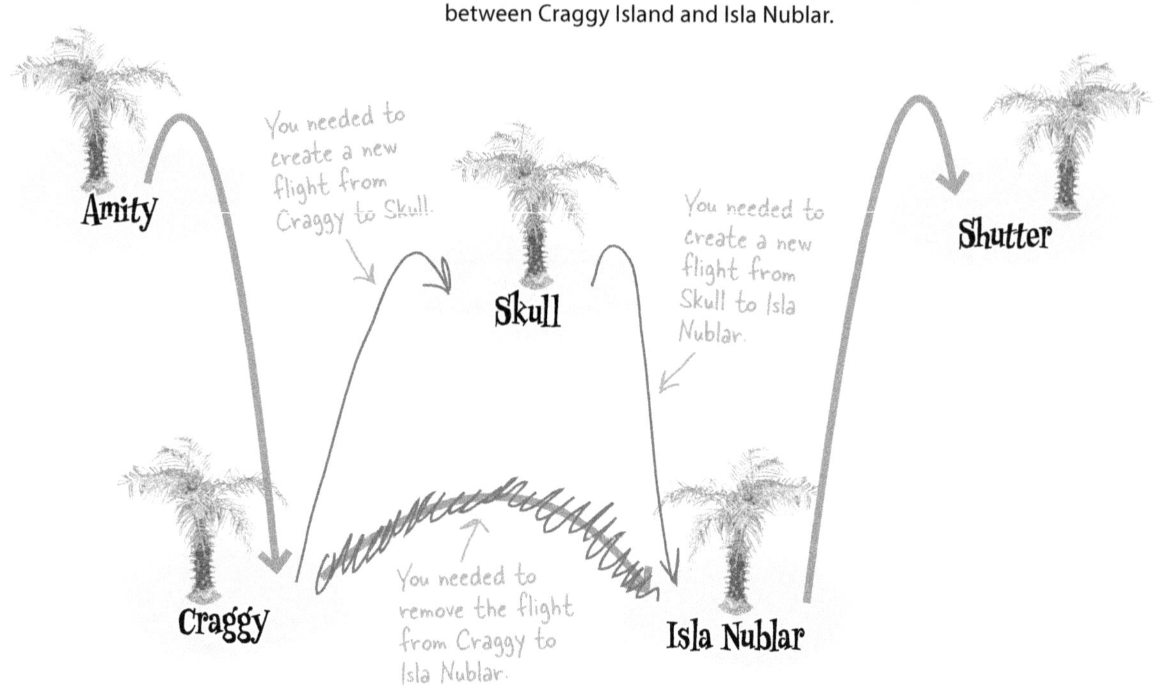

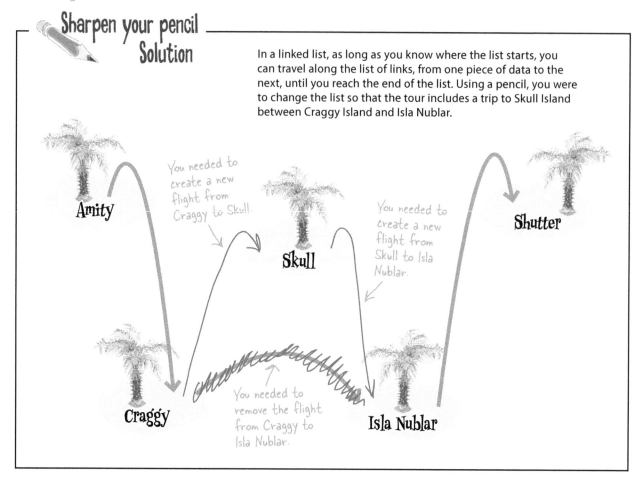

Amity
You needed to create a new flight from Craggy to Skull.
Skull
You needed to create a new flight from Skull to Isla Nublar.
Shutter
Craggy
You needed to remove the flight from Craggy to Isla Nublar.
Isla Nublar

Linked lists allow inserts

With just a few changes, you were able to add an extra step to the tour. That's another advantage linked lists have over arrays: **inserting data is very quick**. If you wanted to insert a value into the middle of an *array*, you would have to shuffle all the pieces of data that follow it along by one:

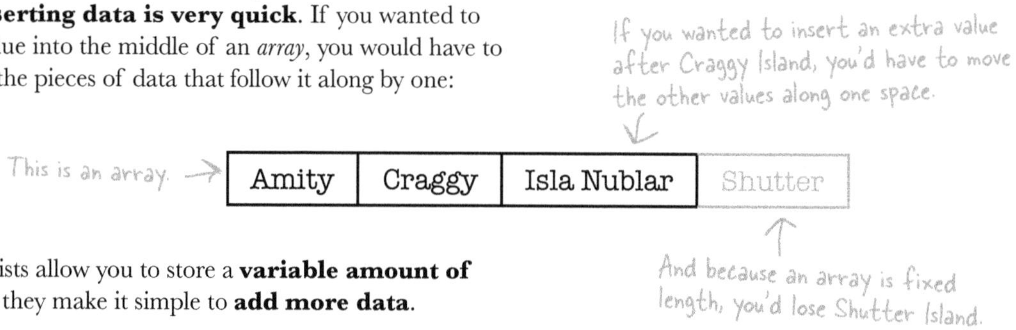

If you wanted to insert an extra value after Craggy Island, you'd have to move the other values along one space.
This is an array.
Amity
Craggy
Isla Nublar
Shutter
And because an array is fixed length, you'd lose Shutter Island.

So linked lists allow you to store a **variable amount of data**, and they make it simple to **add more data**.

But how do you create a linked list in C?

Create a recursive structure

Each one of the `structs` in the list will need to connect to the one next to it. A `struct` that contains a link to another `struct` of the same type is called a **recursive structure**.

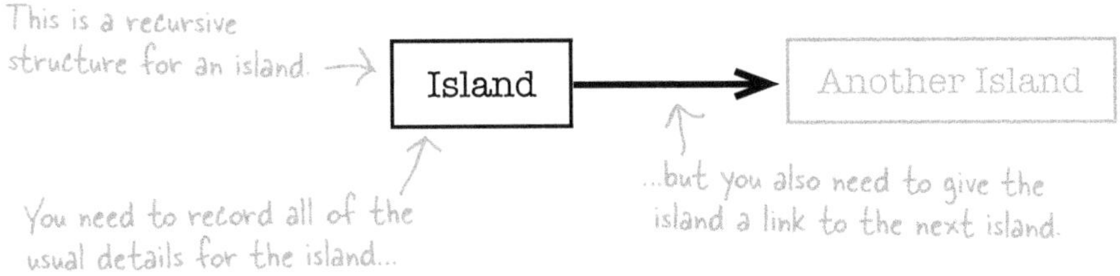
This is a recursive structure for an island.
Island
Another Island
You need to record all of the usual details for the island...
...but you also need to give the island a link to the next island.

Recursive structures contain pointers to other structures of the same type. So if you have a flight schedule for the list of islands that you're going to visit, you can use a recursive structure for each `island`. Let's look at how that works in more detail:

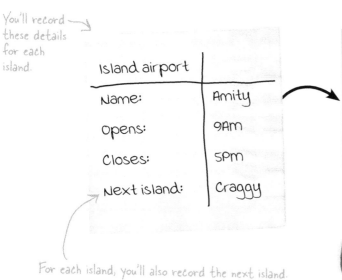

You'll record these details for each island.

Island airport	
Name:	Amity
Opens:	9AM
Closes:	5PM
Next island:	Craggy

For each island, you'll also record the next island.

You must give the struct a name.

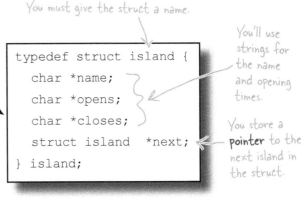

```
typedef struct island {
  char *name;
  char *opens;
  char *closes;
  struct island  *next;
} island;
```

You'll use strings for the name and opening times.

You store a **pointer** to the next island in the struct.

How do you store a link from one `struct` to the next? With a pointer. That way, the `island` data will contain the *address* of the next `island` that we're going to visit. So, whenever our code is at one `island`, it will always be able to hop over to the next `island`.

Let's write some code and start island hopping.

Watch it!

Recursive structures need names.

If you use the `typedef` command, you can normally skip giving the `struct` a proper name. But in a recursive structure, you need to include a pointer to the same type. C syntax won't let you use the `typedef` alias, so you need to give the `struct` a proper name. That's why the `struct` here is called `struct island`.

Create islands in C...

Once you have defined an island data type, you can create the first set of islands like this:

This code will create island structs for each of the islands.

```
island amity = {"Amity", "09:00", "17:00", NULL};
island craggy = {"Craggy", "09:00", "17:00", NULL};
island isla_nublar = {"Isla Nublar", "09:00", "17:00", NULL};
island shutter = {"Shutter", "09:00", "17:00", NULL};
```

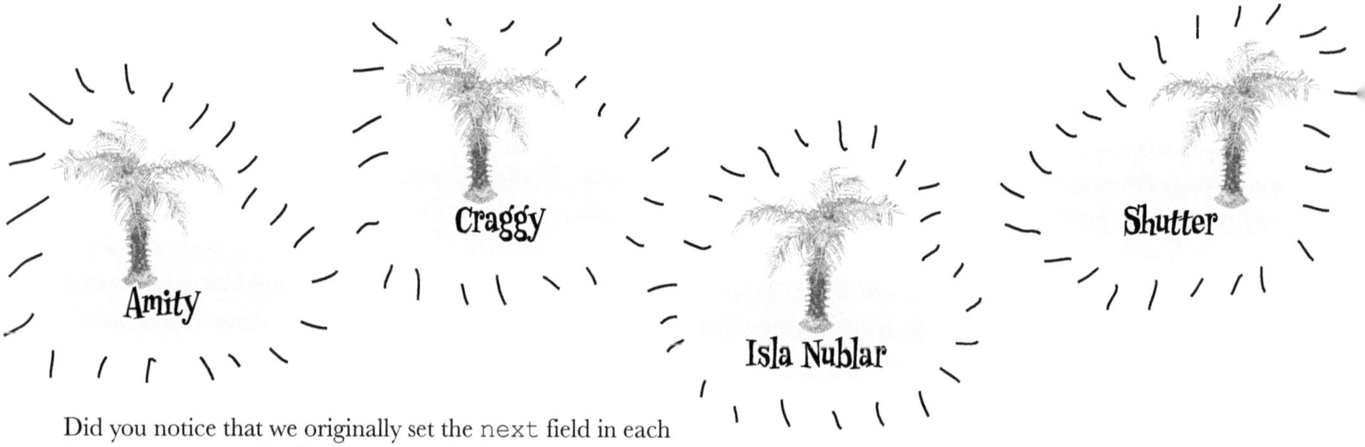
Amity
Craggy
Isla Nublar
Shutter

Did you notice that we originally set the next field in each island to NULL? In C, NULL actually has the value 0, but it's set aside specially to set *pointers* to 0.

...and link them together to form a tour

Once you've created each island, you can then connect them together:

```
amity.next = &craggy;
craggy.next = &isla_nublar;
isla_nublar.next = &shutter;
```

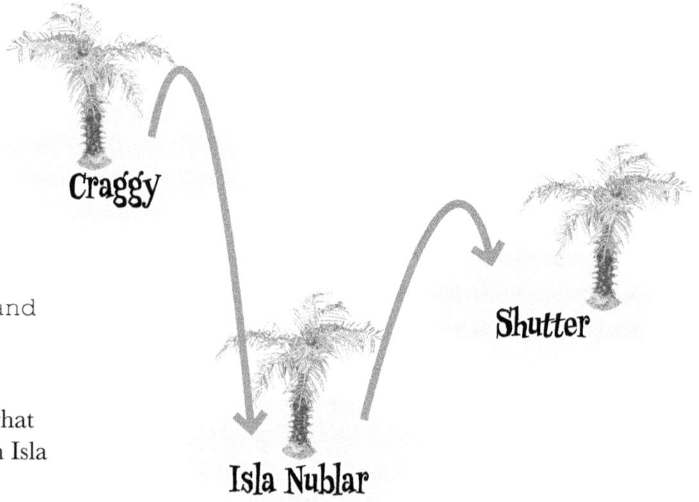
Craggy
Isla Nublar
Shutter

You have to be careful to set the next field in each island to the *address* of the next island. You'll use struct variables for each of the islands.

So now you've created a complete island tour in C, but what if you want to insert an excursion to Skull Island between Isla Nublar and Shutter Island?

Inserting values into the list

You can insert `islands` just like you did earlier, by changing the values of the pointers between `islands`:

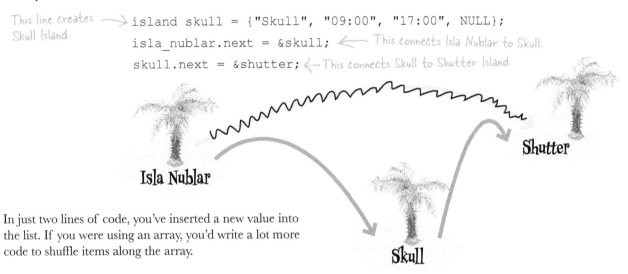

This line creates Skull Island.

```
island skull = {"Skull", "09:00", "17:00", NULL};
isla_nublar.next = &skull;   <- This connects Isla Nublar to Skull.
skull.next = &shutter;   <- This connects Skull to Shutter Island.
```

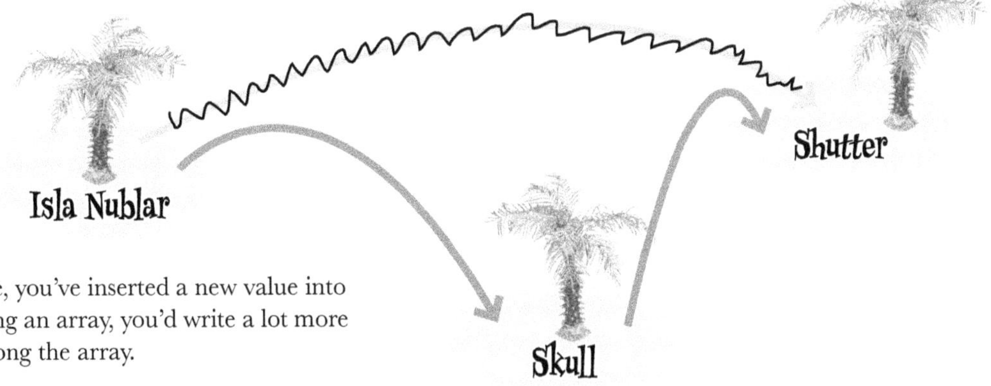
Isla Nublar
Shutter
Skull

In just two lines of code, you've inserted a new value into the list. If you were using an array, you'd write a lot more code to shuffle items along the array.

OK, you've seen how to create and use linked lists. Now let's try out your new skills...

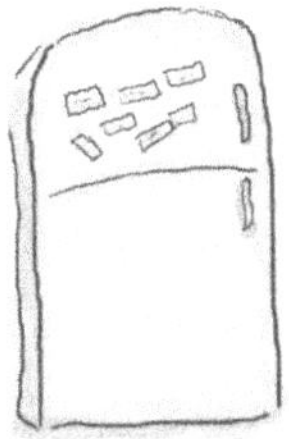

Code Magnets

Oh, no, the code for the `display()` function was on the fridge door, but someone's mixed up the magnets. Do you think you can reassemble the code?

```
void display(island *start)
{
  island *i = start;

  for (; i ........ ........ ; i ........ ........ ) {
    printf("Name: %s open: %s-%s\n", ........ , ........ , ........ );
  }
}
```

`i->closes` `!=` `i->opens` `i->name` `NULL` `i->next` `=`

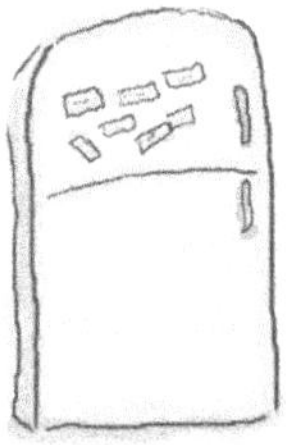

Code Magnets Solution

Oh, no, the code for the `display()` function was on the fridge door, but someone's mixed up the magnets. Were you able to reassemble the code?

```
void display(island *start)
{
  island *i = start;
  for (; i != NULL ; i = i->next ) {
    printf("Name: %s open: %s-%s\n", i->name , i->opens , i->closes );
  }
}
```

You don't need any extra code at the start of the loop.

You need to keep looping until the current island has no next value.

At the end of each loop, skip to the next island.

there are no Dumb Questions

Q: Other languages, like Java, have linked lists built in. Does C have any data structures?

A: C doesn't really come with any data structures built in. You have to create them yourself.

Q: What if I want to use the 700th item in a really long list? Do I have to start at the first item and then read all the way through?

A: Yes, you do.

Q: That's not very good. I thought a linked list was better than an array.

A: You shouldn't think of data structures as being *better* or *worse*. They are either *appropriate* or *inappropriate* for what you want to use them for.

Q: So if I want a data structure that lets me insert things quickly, I need a linked list, but if I want direct access I might use an array?

A: Exactly.

Q: You've shown a `struct` that contains a pointer to another `struct`. Can a `struct` contain a whole recursive `struct` inside itself?

A: No.

Q: Why not?

A: C needs to know the exact amount of space a `struct` will occupy in memory. If it allowed full recursive copies of the same `struct`, then one piece of data would be a different size than another.

Test Drive

Let's use the `display()` function on the linked list of `islands` and compile the code together into a program called `tour`.

```
island amity = {"Amity", "09:00", "17:00", NULL};
island craggy = {"Craggy", "09:00", "17:00", NULL};
island isla_nublar = {"Isla Nublar", "09:00", "17:00", NULL};
island shutter = {"Shutter", "09:00", "17:00", NULL};
amity.next = &craggy;
craggy.next = &isla_nublar;
isla_nublar.next = &shutter;
island skull = {"Skull", "09:00", "17:00", NULL};
isla_nublar.next = &skull;
skull.next = &shutter;
display(&amity);
```

```
File Edit Window Help GetBiggerBoat
> gcc tour.c -o tour && ./tour
Name: Amity
Open: 09:00-17:00
Name: Craggy
Open: 09:00-17:00
Name: Isla Nublar
Open: 09:00-17:00
Name: Skull
Open: 09:00-17:00
Name: Shutter
Open: 09:00-17:00
>
```

Excellent. The code creates a linked list of `islands`, and you can insert items with very little work.

OK, so now that you know the basics of how to work with recursive `structs` and lists, you can move on to the main program. You need to read the tour data from a file that looks like this:

```
Delfino Isle
Angel Island
Wild Cat Island
Neri's Island
Great Todday
```

There will be some more lines after this.

The folks at the airline are still creating the file, so you won't know how long it is until runtime. Each line in the file is the name of an island. It should be pretty straightforward to turn this file into a linked list. Right?

The Polite Guide to Standards

The code on this page declares a new variable, `skull`, right in the middle of the code. This is allowed only in C99 and C11. In ANSI C, you need to declare all your local variables at the top of a function.

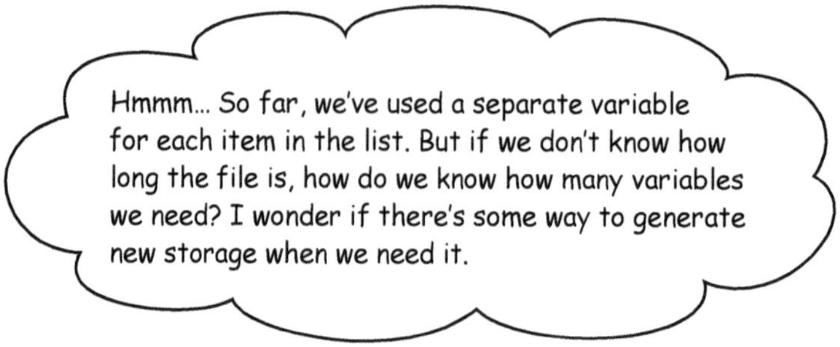
Hmmm... So far, we've used a separate variable for each item in the list. But if we don't know how long the file is, how do we know how many variables we need? I wonder if there's some way to generate new storage when we need it.

Yes, you need some way to create *dynamic storage*.

All of the programs you've written so far have used static storage. Every time you wanted to store something, you've added a variable to the code. Those variables have generally been stored in the stack. Remember: the stack is the area of memory set aside for storing local variables.

So when you created the first four islands, you did it like this:

```
island amity = {"Amity", "09:00", "17:00", NULL};
island craggy = {"Craggy", "09:00", "17:00", NULL};
island isla_nublar = {"Isla Nublar", "09:00", "17:00", NULL};
island shutter = {"Shutter", "09:00", "17:00", NULL};
```

Each `island struct` needed its own variable. This piece of code will always create exactly four `islands`. If you wanted the code to store more than four `islands`, you would need another local variable. That's fine if you know how much data you need to store at compile time, but quite often, programs don't know how much storage they need until runtime. If you're writing a web browser, for instance, you won't know how much data you'll need to store a web page until, well, you read the web page. So C programs need some way to tell the operating system that they need a little extra storage, at the moment that they need it.

Programs need *dynamic* storage.

Wouldn't it be dreamy if there were a way to allocate as much space as I needed with code at runtime? But I know that's just a fantasy...

Use the heap for dynamic storage

Heap storage is like saving valuables in a locker.

Most of the memory you've been using so far has been in the **stack**. The stack is the area of memory that's used for local variables. Each piece of data is stored in a variable, and each variable disappears as soon as you leave its function.

The trouble is, it's harder to get more storage on the stack at runtime, and that's where the **heap** comes in. The heap is the place where a program stores data that will need to be available longer term. It won't automatically get cleared away, so that means it's the perfect place to store data structures like our linked list. You can think of heap storage as being a bit like reserving a locker in a locker room.

First, get your memory with malloc()

Imagine your program suddenly finds it has a large amount of data that it needs to store at runtime. This is a bit like asking for a large storage locker for the data, and in C you do that with a function called **`malloc()`**. You tell the `malloc()` function exactly how much memory you need, and it asks the operating system to set that much memory aside in the heap. The `malloc()` function then returns a **pointer** to the new heap space, a bit like getting a key to the locker. It allows you access to the memory, and it can also be used to keep track of the storage locker that's been allocated.

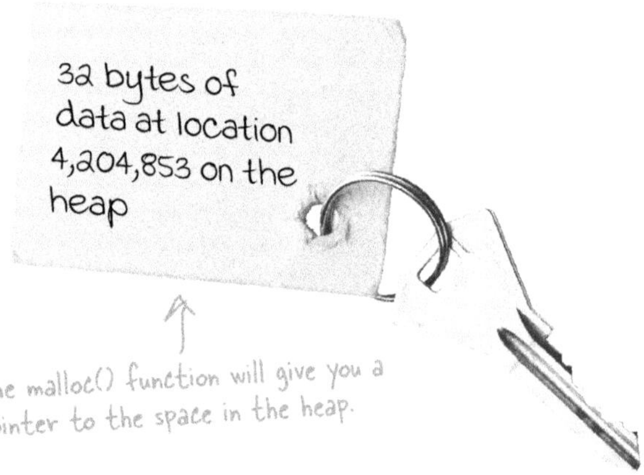
32 bytes of data at location 4,204,853 on the heap

The malloc() function will give you a pointer to the space in the heap.

The heap

STACK
HEAP
GLOBALS
CONSTANTS
LINK A6, #VARSIZE
MOVEM.L D0-D7/A1-A5,-(SP)
MOVE.L SP, SAVESTK(A6)
MOVE.L SP, SAVEAS(A6)
MOVE.L GRAFGLOBALS(A5),A0
...
CODE

Give the memory back when you're done

The good news about heap memory is that you can keep hold of it for a really long time. The bad news is…you can keep hold of it for a really long time.

When you were just using the stack, you didn't need to worry about returning memory; it all happened automatically. Every time you leave a function, the local storage is freed from the stack.

The heap is different. Once you've asked for space on the heap, it will never be available for anything else until you tell the C Standard Library that you're finished with it. There's only so much heap memory available, so if your code keeps asking for more and more heap space, your program will quickly start to develop memory leaks.

A memory leak happens when a program asks for more and more memory without releasing the memory it no longer needs. Memory leaks are among the most common bugs in C programs, and they can be really hard to track down.

The heap has only a fixed amount of storage available, so be sure you use it wisely.

Free memory by calling the free() function

The `malloc()` function allocates space and gives you a pointer to it. You'll need to use this pointer to access the data and then, when you're finished with the storage, you need to release the memory using the **`free()`** function. It's a bit like handing your locker key back to the attendant so that the locker can be reused.

Thanks for the storage. I'm done with it now.

Every time some part of your code requests heap storage with the `malloc()` function, there should be some other part of your code that hands the storage back with the `free()` function. When your program stops running, all of its heap storage will be released automatically, but it's always good practice to explicitly call `free()` on every piece of dynamic memory you've created.

Let's see how malloc() and free() work.

Ask for memory with malloc()...

The function that asks for memory is called `malloc()` for *memory allocation*. `malloc()` takes a single parameter: the number of bytes that you need. Most of the time, you probably don't know exactly how much memory you need in bytes, so `malloc()` is almost always used with an operator called `sizeof`, like this:

```
#include <stdlib.h>
...
malloc(sizeof(island));
```

You need to include the stdlib.h header file to pick up the malloc() and free() functions.

This means, "Give me enough space to store an island struct."

`sizeof` tells you how many bytes a particular data type occupies on your system. It might be a `struct`, or it could be some base data type, like `int` or `double`.

The `malloc()` function sets aside a chunk of memory for you, then returns a pointer containing the start address. But what kind of pointer will that be? `malloc()` actually returns a *general-purpose pointer*, with type **`void*`**.

```
island *p = malloc(sizeof(island));
```

This means, "Create enough space for an island, and store the address in variable p."

...and free up the memory with free()

Once you've created the memory on the heap, you can use it for as long as you like. But once you've finished, you need to release the memory using the `free()` function.

`free()` needs to be given the address of the memory that `malloc()` created. As long as the library is told where the chunk of memory starts, it will be able to check its records to see how much memory to free up. So if you wanted to free the memory you allocated above, you'd do it like this:

```
free(p);
```

This means, "Release the memory you allocated from heap address p."

OK, now that we know more about dynamic memory, we can start to write some code.

Remember: if you allocated memory with malloc() in one part of your program, you should always release it later with the free() function.

Oh, no! It's the out-of-work actors...

The aspiring actors are currently between jobs, so they've found some free time in their busy schedules to help you out with the coding. They've created a utility function to create a new `island struct` with a name that you pass to it. The function looks like this:

```
island* create(char *name)
{
  island *i = malloc(sizeof(island));
  i->name = name;
  i->opens = "09:00";
  i->closes = "17:00";
  i->next = NULL;
  return i;
}
```

This is the new function.

The name of the island is passed as a char pointer.

It's using the malloc() function to create space on the heap.

This will create a new island struct on the heap.

The sizeof operator works out how many bytes are needed.

These lines set the fields on the new struct.

The function returns the address of the new struct.

That's a pretty cool-looking function. The actors have spotted that most of the island airports have the same opening and closing times, so they've set the `opens` and `closes` fields to default values. The function returns a pointer to the newly created `struct`.

BRAIN POWER

Look carefully at the code for the `create()` function. Do you think there might be any problems with it? Once you've thought about it good and hard, turn the page to see it in action.

The Case of the Vanishing Island

Five-Minute
Mystery

Captain's Log. 11:00. Friday. Weather clear. A `create()` function using dynamic allocation has been written, and the coding team says it is ready for air trials.

```
island* create(char *name)
{
  island *i = malloc(sizeof(island));
  i->name = name;
  i->opens = "09:00";
  i->closes = "17:00";
  i->next = NULL;
  return i;
}
```

14:15. Weather cloudy. Northwest headwind 15kts near Bermuda. Landing at first stop. Software team on board providing basic code. Name of island entered at the command line.

```
char name[80];
fgets(name, 80, stdin);
island *p_island0 = create(name);
```

Create an array to store an island name. → `char name[80];`

Ask the user for the name of an island. → `fgets(name, 80, stdin);`

```
File Edit Window Help
> ./test_flight
Atlantis
```

14:45. Take off from landing strip rocky due to earth tremors. Software team still on board. Supplies of Jolt running low.

15:35. Arrival at second island. Weather good. No wind. Entering details into new program.

Ask the user to enter the name of the second island.

```
fgets(name, 80, stdin);
island *p_island1 = create(name);
p_island0->next = p_island1;
```

This creates the second island.

This connects the first island to the second island.

```
File Edit Window Help
Titchmarsh Island
```

17:50 Back at headquarters tidying up on paperwork. Strange thing. The flight log produced by the test program appears to have a bug. When the details of today's flight are logged, the trip to the first island has been mysteriously renamed. Asking software team to investigate.

This will display the details of the list of islands using the function we created earlier.

```
display(p_island0);
```

What happened to Atlantis????

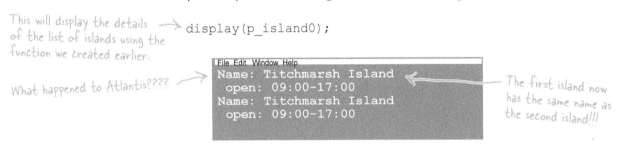

```
File Edit Window Help
Name: Titchmarsh Island
 open: 09:00-17:00
Name: Titchmarsh Island
 open: 09:00-17:00
```

The first island now has the same name as the second island!!!

What happened to the name of the first island? Is there a bug in the* `create()` *function? Does the way it was called give any clues?

The Case of the Vanishing Island

What happened to the name of the first island?

Look at the code of the `create()` function again:

```
island* create(char *name)
{
  island *i = malloc(sizeof(island));
  i->name = name;
  i->opens = "09:00";
  i->closes = "17:00";
  i->next = NULL;
  return i;
}
```

Five-Minute
Mystery
Solved

When the code records the name of the island, it doesn't take a copy of the whole `name` string; it just records the address where the `name` string lives in memory. Is that important? Where did the `name` string live? We can find out by looking at the code that was calling the function:

```
char name[80];
 fgets(name, 80, stdin);
 island *p_island0 = create(name);
 fgets(name, 80, stdin);
 island *p_island1 = create(name);
```

The program asks the user for the name of each island, but *both times* it uses the `name` local `char` array to store the name. That means that **the two islands share the same `name` string**. As soon as the local `name` variable gets updated with the name of the second island, the name of the first island changes as well.

String Copying Up Close

In C, you often need to make copies of strings. You *could* do that by calling the `malloc()` function to create a little space on the heap and then manually copying each character from the string you are copying to the space on the heap. But guess what? Other developers got there ahead of you. They created a function in the **`string.h`** header called **`strdup()`**.

Let's say that you have a pointer to a character array that you want to copy:

```
char *s = "MONA LISA";
```

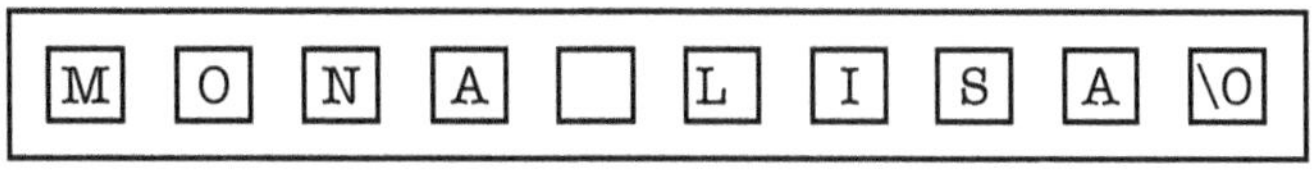
M
O
N
A
L
I
S
A
\0

The **`strdup()`** function can reproduce a complete copy of the string somewhere on the heap:

```
char *copy = strdup(s);
```

1. **The strdup() function works out how long the string is, and then calls the malloc() function to allocate the correct number of characters on the heap.**

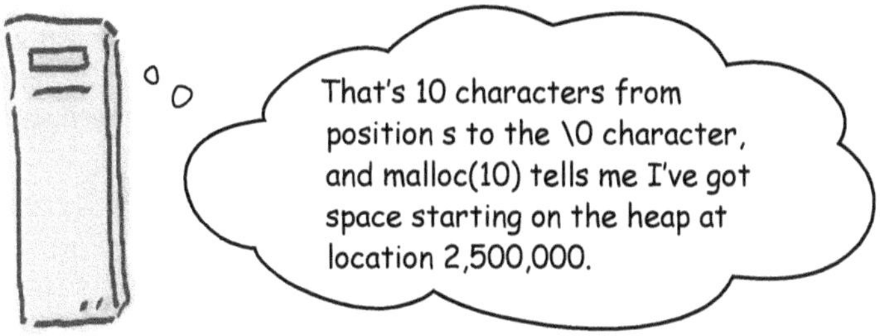
That's 10 characters from position s to the \0 character, and malloc(10) tells me I've got space starting on the heap at location 2,500,000.

2. **It then copies each of the characters to the new space on the heap.**

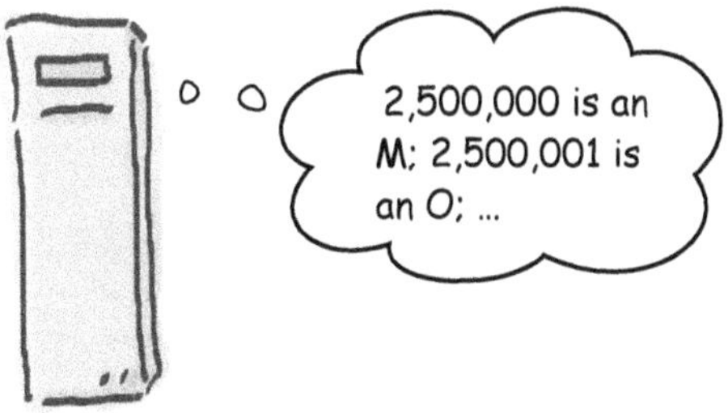
2,500,000 is an M; 2,500,001 is an O; ...

That means that `strdup()` always creates space **on the heap**. It can't create space on the stack because that's for *local variables*, and local variables get cleared away too often.

But because `strdup()` puts new strings on the heap, that means you must **always remember to release their storage with the `free()` function**.

Let's fix the code using the strdup() function

You can fix up the original `create()` function using the `strdup()` function, like this:

```
island* create(char *name)
{
  island *i = malloc(sizeof(island));
  i->name = strdup(name);
  i->opens = "09:00";
  i->closes = "17:00";
  i->next = NULL;
  return i;
}
```

You can see that we only need to put the `strdup()` function on the `name` field. Can you figure out why that is?

It's because we are setting the `opens` and `closes` fields to *string literals*. Remember way back when you saw where things were stored in memory? String literals are stored in a **read-only** area of memory set aside for **constant values**. Because you always set the `opens` and `closes` fields to constant values, you don't need to take a defensive copy of them, because they'll never change. But you had to take a defensive copy of the `name` array, because something might come and update it later.

So does it fix the code?

To see if the change to the `create()` function fixed the code, let's run your original code again:

```
File Edit Window Help CoconutAirways
> ./test_flight
Atlantis
Titchmarsh Island
Name: Atlantis
 open: 09:00-17:00
Name: Titchmarsh Island
 open: 09:00-17:00
```

Now that code works. Each time the user enters the name of an island, the `create()` function is storing it in a brand-new string.

OK, now that you have a function to create island data, let's use it to create a linked list from a file.

there are no Dumb Questions

Q: If the `island struct` had a name array rather than a character pointer, would I need to use `strdup()` here?

A: No. Each `island struct` would store its own copy, so you wouldn't need to make your own copy.

Q: So why would I want to use `char` pointers rather than `char` arrays in my data structures?

A: `char` pointers won't limit the amount of space you need to set aside for strings. If you use `char` arrays, you will need to decide in advance exactly how long your strings might need to be.

Pool Puzzle

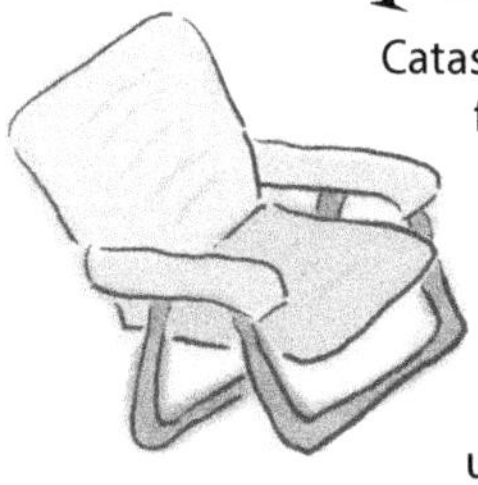

Catastrophe! The code to create an island tour has fallen into the pool! Your **job** is to take code snippets from the pool and place them into the blank lines in the code below. Your **goal** is to reconstruct the program so that it can read a list of names from Standard Input and then connect them together to form a linked list. You may **not** use the same code snippet more than once, and you won't need to use all the pieces of code.

```
island *start = NULL;
island *i = NULL;
island *next = NULL;
char name[80];
for(; .................. != .................. ; i = .................. ) {
  next = create(name);
  if (start == NULL)
    start = .................. ;
  if (i != NULL)
    i .................. .................. = next;
}
display(start);
```

Note: each thing from the pool can be used only once!

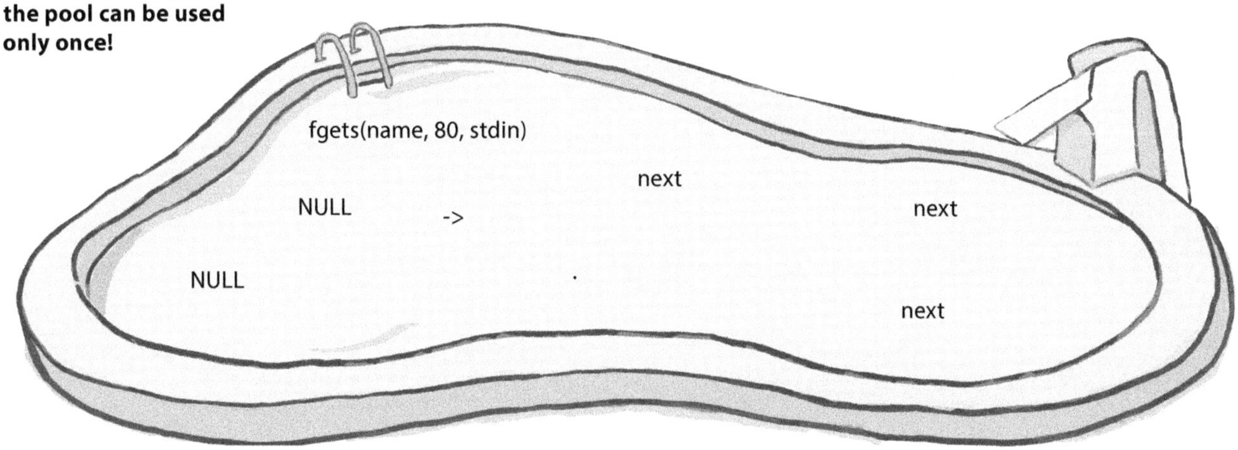
fgets(name, 80, stdin)
next
NULL
->
next
NULL
.
next

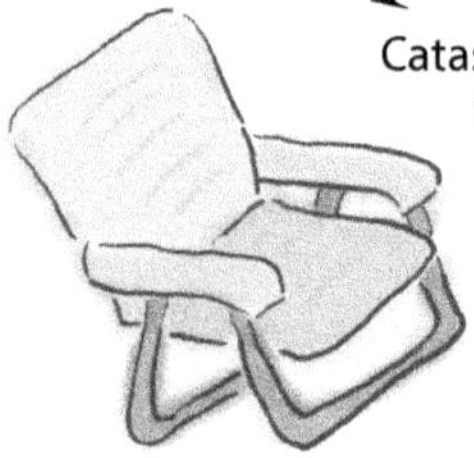

Pool Puzzle Solution

Catastrophe! The code to create an island tour has fallen into the pool! Your **job** was to take code snippets from the pool and place them into the blank lines in the code below. Your **goal** was to reconstruct the program so that it can read a list of names from Standard Input and then connect them together to form a linked list.

```
island *start = NULL;
island *i = NULL;
island *next = NULL;
char name[80];
for(; fgets(name, 80, stdin) != NULL ; i = next ) {
  next = create(name);
  if (start == NULL)
    start = next ;
  if (i != NULL)
    i -> next = next;
}
display(start);
```

Read a string from the Standard Input.

At the end of each loop, set i to the next island we created.

This creates an island.

We'll keep looping until we don't get any more strings.

The first time through, start is set to NULL, so set it to the first island.

Don't forget: i is a pointer, so we'll use -> notation.

Note: each thing from the pool can be used only once!

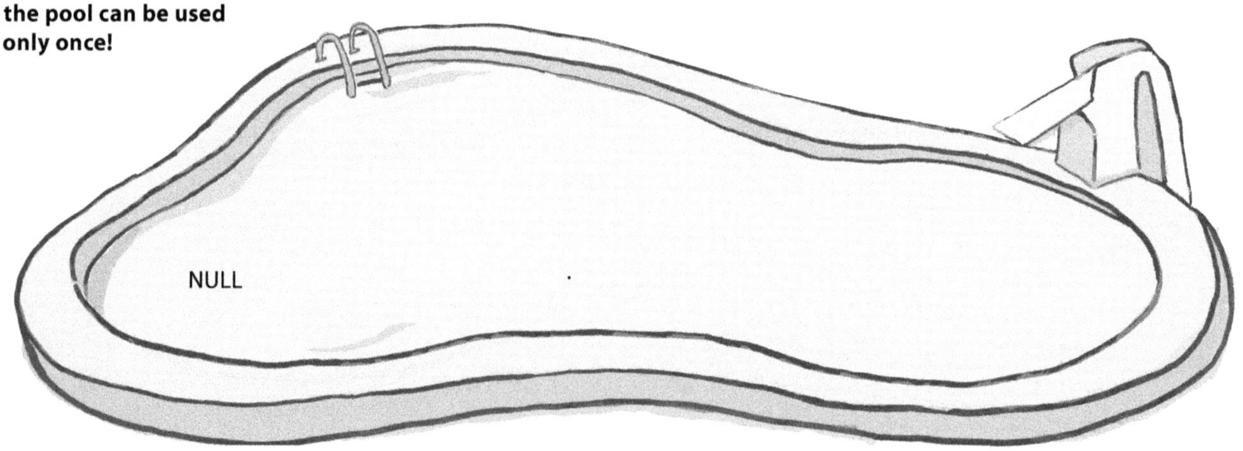
NULL

Sharpen your pencil

But wait! You're not done yet. Don't forget that if you ever **allocate space** with the `malloc()` function, you need to **release the space** with the `free()` function. The program you've written so far creates a linked list of islands in heap memory using `malloc()`, but now it's time to write some code to release that space once you're done with it.

Here's a start on a function called `release()` that will release all of the memory used by a linked list, if you pass it a pointer to the first `island`:

```
void release(island *start)
{
  island *i = start;
  island *next = NULL;
  for (; i != NULL; i = next) {
    next = ......................;
     ......................;
     ......................;
  }
}
```

Think very carefully. When you release the memory, what will you need to free? Just the `island`, or something more? In what sequence should you free them?

Sharpen your pencil Solution

But wait! You're not done yet. Don't forget that if you ever **allocate space** with the `malloc()` function, you need to **release the space** with the `free()` function. The program you've written so far creates a linked list of islands in heap memory using `malloc()`, but now it's time to write some code to release that space once you're done with it.

Here's a start on a function called `release()` that will release all of the memory used by a linked list, if you pass it a pointer to the first `island`:

```
void release(island *start)
{
  island *i = start;
  island *next = NULL;
  for (; i != NULL; i = next) {
    next = i->next;
    free(i->name);
    free(i);
  }
}
```

Set next to point to the next island.

First, you need to free the name string that you created with strdup().

Only **after** freeing the name should you free the island struct.

If you'd freed the island first, you might not have been able to reach the name to free it.

When you release the memory, what will you need to free? Just the `island`, or something more? In what sequence should you free them?

Free the memory when you're done

Now that you have a function to free the linked list, you'll need to call it when you've finished with it. Your program only needs to display the contents of the list, so once you've done that, you can release it:

```
display(start);
release(start);
```

Once that's done, you can test the code.

Test Drive

So, if you compile the code and then run the file through it, what happens?

```
File Edit Window Help FreeSpaceYouDon'tNeed
> ./tour < trip1.txt
Name: Delfino Isle
 Open: 09:00-17:00
Name: Angel Island
 Open: 09:00-17:00
Name: Wild Cat Island
 Open: 09:00-17:00
Name: Neri's Island
 Open: 09:00-17:00
Name: Great Todday
 Open: 09:00-17:00
Name: Ramita de la Baya
 Open: 09:00-17:00
Name: Island of the Blue Dolphins
 Open: 09:00-17:00
Name: Fantasy Island
 Open: 09:00-17:00
Name: Farne
 Open: 09:00-17:00
Name: Isla de Muert
 Open: 09:00-17:00
Name: Tabor Island
 Open: 09:00-17:00
Name: Haunted Isle
 Open: 09:00-17:00
Name: Sheena Island
 Open: 09:00-17:00
```

It works. Remember: you had no way of knowing how long that file was going to be. In this case, because you are just printing out the file, you *could* have simply printed it out without storing it all in memory. But because you *do* have it in memory, you're free to manipulate it. You could add in extra steps in the tour, or remove them. You could reorder or extend the tour.

Dynamic memory allocation lets you create the memory you need at RUNTIME. And the way you access dynamic heap memory is with `malloc()` and `free()`.

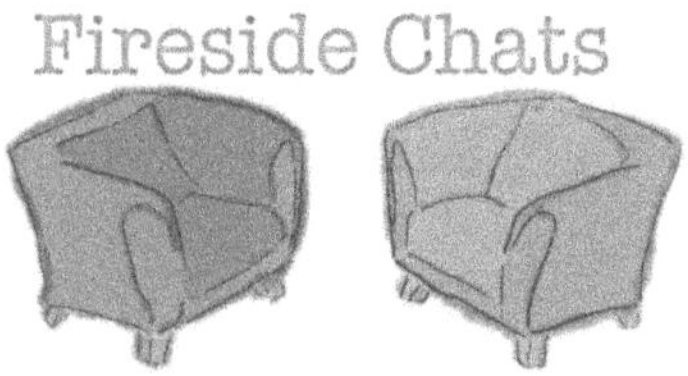
Fireside Chats

Tonight's Talk: **Stack and Heap Discuss Their Differences**

Stack: Heap? Are you there? I'm home.

Heap: Don't see you too often this time of day. Got a little something going on?

Stack: Deep regression. Oops…excuse me…Just tidy that up…

Heap: What're you doing?

Stack: The code just exited a function. Just need to free up the storage from those local variables.

Heap: You should take life a little easier. Relax a little…

Stack: Perhaps you're right. Mind if I sit?

Heap: Beer? Don't worry about the cap; throw it anywhere.

Stack: I…think this is yours?

Heap: Hey, you found the pizza! That's great. I've been looking for that all week.

Stack: You really should consider getting somebody in to take care of this place.

Heap: Don't worry about it. That online ordering application left it lying around. It'll probably be back for it.

Stack: How do you know? I mean, how do you know it hasn't just forgotten about it?

Heap: He'd have been back in touch. He'd have called `free()`.

Stack: Hmmm? Are you sure? Wasn't it written by the same woman who wrote that dreadful Whack-a-bunny game? Memory leaks everywhere. I could barely move for rabbit `structs`. Droppings everywhere. It was terrible.

Stack:	**Heap:**
	Hey, it's not my responsibility to clear up the memory. Someone asks me for space, I give him space. I'll leave it there until he tells me to clean it up.
That's irresponsible.	
	Yeah, maybe. But I'm easy to use. Not like you and your…fussing.
Fussing? I don't fuss! You might want to use a napkin…	
	<belches>What? I'm just saying you're difficult to keep track of.
I just believe that memory should be properly maintained.	
	Whatever. I'm a live-and-let-live type. If a program wants to make a mess, it's not my responsibility.
You're messy.	
	I'm easygoing.
Why don't you do garbage collection?!	
	Ah, here we go again…
I mean, just a little…tidying up. You don't do anything!!!	
	Easy, now.
<crying>I'm sorry. I just can't cope with this level of disorganization.	
	Hey, you're overflowing. Take this…
<blows nose>Thank you. Wait, what is this?	
	It's the high score table from Whack-a-Bunny. Don't worry; I don't think the program needs it anymore.

there are no Dumb Questions

Q: Why is the heap called the heap?

A: Because the computer doesn't automatically organize it. It's just a big heap of data.

Q: What's garbage collection?

A: Some languages track when you allocate data on a heap and then, when you're no longer using the data, they free the data from the heap.

Q: Why doesn't C contain garbage collection?

A: C is quite an old language; when it was invented, most languages didn't do automatic garbage collection.

Q: I understand why I needed to copy the `name` of the `island` in the example. Why didn't I need to copy the `opens` and `closes` values?

A: The `opens` and `closes` values are set to string literals. String literals can't be updated, so it doesn't matter if several data items refer to the same string.

Q: Does `strdup()` actually call the `malloc()` function?

A: It will depend on how the C Standard Library is implemented, but most of the time, yes.

Q: Do I need to free all my data before the program ends?

A: You don't have to; the operating system will clear away all of the memory when the program exits. But it's good practice to always explicitly free anything you've created.

BULLET POINTS

- Dynamic data structures allow you to store a variable number of data items.
- A linked list is a data structure that allows you to easily insert items.
- Dynamic data structures are normally defined in C with recursive `struct`s.
- A recursive `struct` contains one or more pointers to a similar `struct`.
- The stack is used for local variables and is managed by the computer.
- The heap is used for long-term storage. You allocate space with `malloc()`.
- The `sizeof` operator will tell you how much space a `struct` needs.
- Data will stay on the heap until you release it with `free()`.

What's My Data Structure?

You've seen how to create a linked list in C. But linked lists aren't the only data structures you might need to build. Below are some other example data structures. See if you can match up the data structure with the description of how it can be used.

Data structure

Description

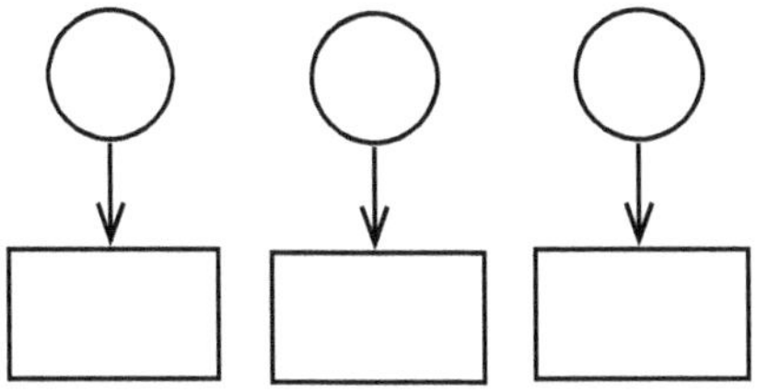

I can be used to store a sequence of items, and I make it easy to insert new items. But you can process me in only one direction.

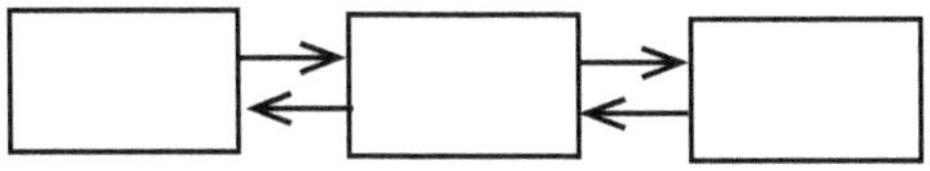

Each item I store can connect to up to two other items. I am useful for storing hierarchical information.

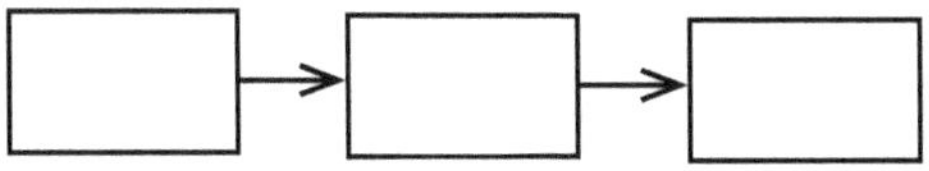

I can be used to associate two different types of data. For example, you could use me to associate people's names to their phone numbers.

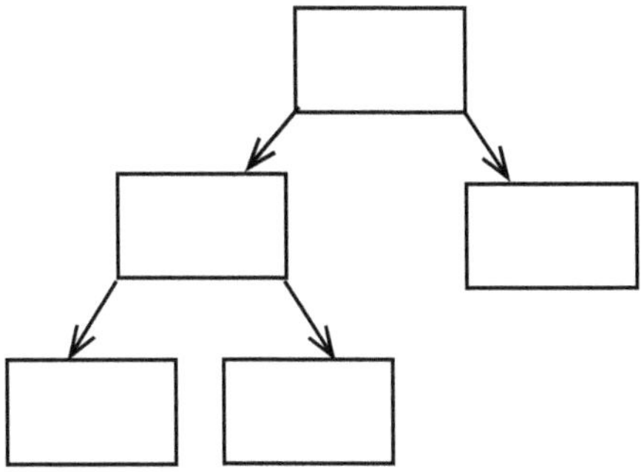

Each item I store connects to up to two other items. You can process me in two directions.

What's My Data Structure? Solution

You've seen how to create a linked list in C. But linked lists aren't the only data structures you might need to build. Below are some other example data structures. You were to match up the data structure with the description of how it can be used.

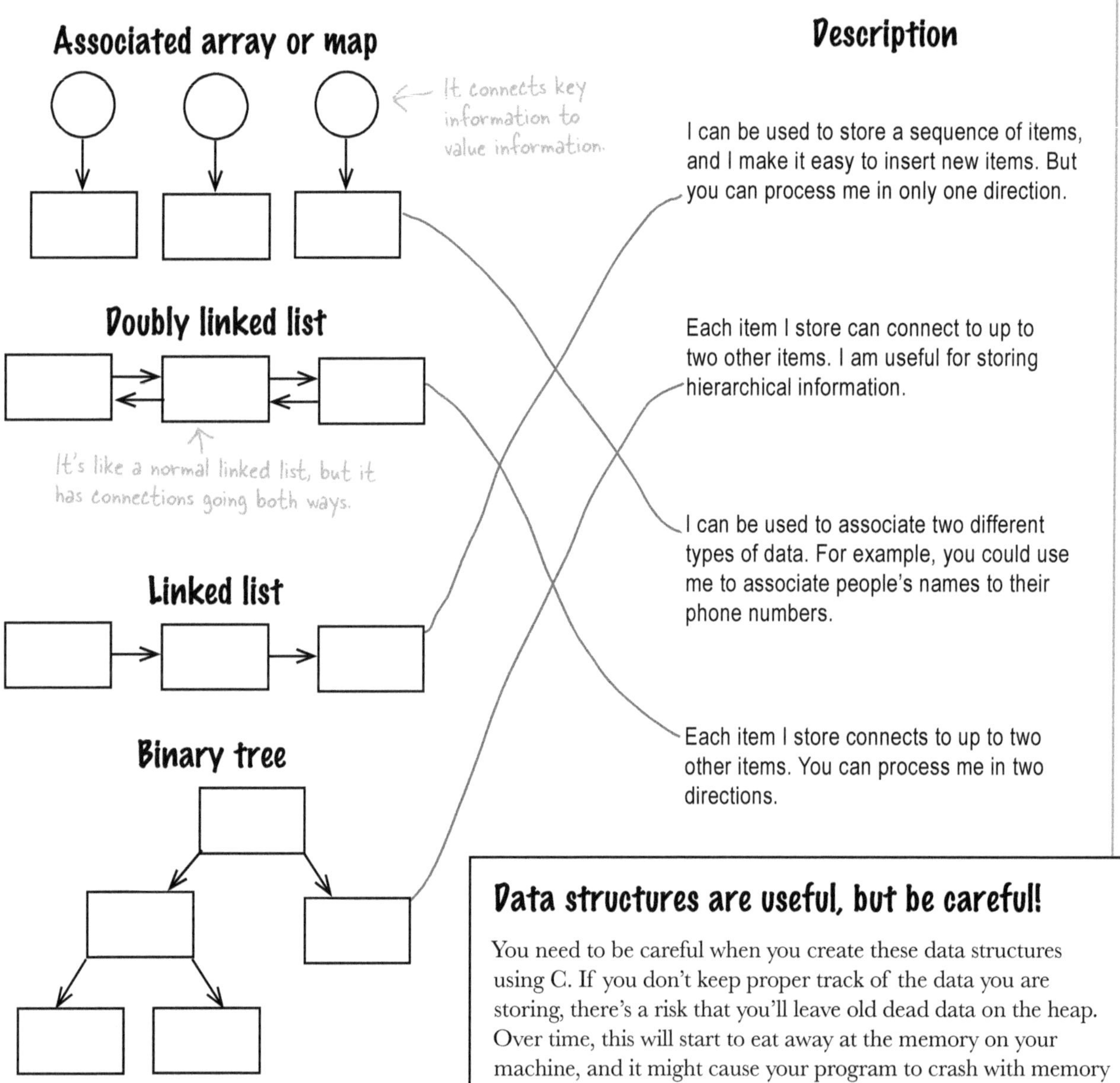
Associated array or map
It connects key information to value information.
Doubly linked list
It's like a normal linked list, but it has connections going both ways.
Linked list
Binary tree
Description
I can be used to store a sequence of items, and I make it easy to insert new items. But you can process me in only one direction.
Each item I store can connect to up to two other items. I am useful for storing hierarchical information.
I can be used to associate two different types of data. For example, you could use me to associate people's names to their phone numbers.
Each item I store connects to up to two other items. You can process me in two directions.

Data structures are useful, but be careful!

You need to be careful when you create these data structures using C. If you don't keep proper track of the data you are storing, there's a risk that you'll leave old dead data on the heap. Over time, this will start to eat away at the memory on your machine, and it might cause your program to crash with memory errors. **That means it's really important that you learn to track down and fix memory leaks in your code...**

TOP SECRET

Federal Bureau of Investigations United States Department of Justice, Washington, D. C.

From: J. Edgar Hoover, Director

Subject: SUSPECTED LEAK IN GOVERNMENT EXPERT SYSTEM

Our Cambridge, MA, office advised that there is a suspected leak somewhere inside the new Suspicious Persons Identification Expert System (SPIES). Our sources and informants familiar with software matters advise that the supposed leak is the result of shoddy coding by person or persons unknown.

An informant who has furnished reliable information in the past and who claims to be close to the people concerned has advised that the leak is the result of careless management of data in the area of memory known to the hacker fraternity as "The Heap."

You are hereby given access to the expert system source code and have, by my order, been given access to the full resources of the FBI's software engineering lab. Consider the evidence and analyze the details of the case carefully. I want this leak found, and I want this leak fixed.

Failure is not an option.

Very truly yours,

J. Edgar Hoover

Exhibit A: the source code

What follows is the source code for the Suspicious Persons Identification Expert System (SPIES). This software can be used to record and identify persons of interest. You are not required to read this code in detail now, but please keep a copy in your records so that you may refer to it during the ongoing investigation.

```
#include <stdio.h>
#include <stdlib.h>
#include <string.h>

typedef struct node {
  char *question;
  struct node  *no;
  struct node  *yes;
} node;

int yes_no(char *question)
{
  char answer[3];
  printf("%s? (y/n): ", question);
  fgets(answer, 3, stdin);
  return answer[0] == 'y';
}

node* create(char *question)
{
  node *n = malloc(sizeof(node));
  n->question = strdup(question);
  n->no = NULL;
  n->yes = NULL;
  return n;
}

void release(node *n)
{
  if (n) {
    if (n->no)
      release(n->no);
    if (n->yes)
      release(n->yes);
    if (n->question)
      free(n->question);
    free(n);
  }
}
```

```
int main()
{
  char question[80];
  char suspect[20];
  node *start_node = create("Does suspect have a mustache");
  start_node->no = create("Loretta Barnsworth");
  start_node->yes = create("Vinny the Spoon");

  node *current;
  do {
    current = start_node;
    while (1) {
      if (yes_no(current->question))
      {
        if (current->yes) {
          current = current->yes;
        } else {
          printf("SUSPECT IDENTIFIED\n");
          break;
        }
      } else if (current->no) {
        current = current->no;
      } else {

         /* Make the yes-node the new suspect name */
         printf("Who's the suspect? ");
         fgets(suspect, 20, stdin);
         node *yes_node = create(suspect);
         current->yes = yes_node;

         /* Make the no-node a copy of this question */
         node *no_node = create(current->question);
         current->no = no_node;

         /* Then replace this question with the new question */
         printf("Give me a question that is TRUE for %s but not for %s? ", suspect,
            current->question);
         fgets(question, 80, stdin);
         current->question = strdup(question);

         break;
      }
    }
  } while(yes_no("Run again"));
  release(start_node);
  return 0;
}
```

An overview of the SPIES system

The SPIES program is an expert system that learns how to identify individuals using distinguishing features. The more people you enter into the system, the more the software learns and the smarter it gets.

The program builds a tree of suspects

The program records data using a **binary tree**. A *binary tree* allows each piece of data to connect to two other pieces of data like this:

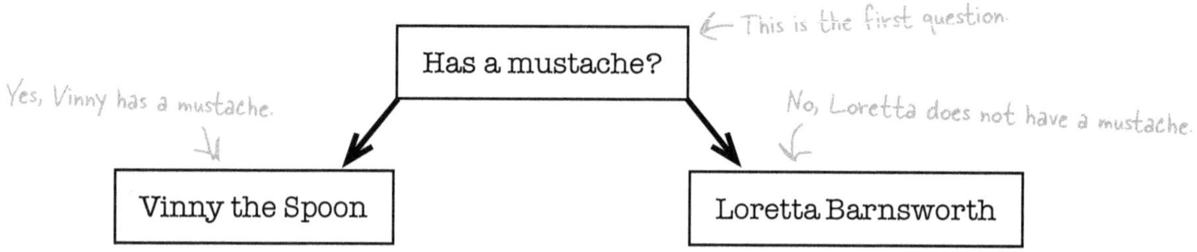

This is the first question.
Has a mustache?
Yes, Vinny has a mustache.
No, Loretta does not have a mustache.
Vinny the Spoon
Loretta Barnsworth

This is what the data looks like when the program starts. The first item (or **node**) in the tree stores a question: "Does the suspect have a mustache?" That's linked to two other nodes: one if the answer's ***yes***, and another if the answer's ***no***. The *yes* and *no* nodes store the name of a suspect.

The program will use this tree to ask the user a series of questions to identify a suspect. If the program can't find the suspect, it will ask the user for the name of the new suspect and some detail that can be used to identify him or her. It will store this information in the tree, which will gradually grow as it learns more things.

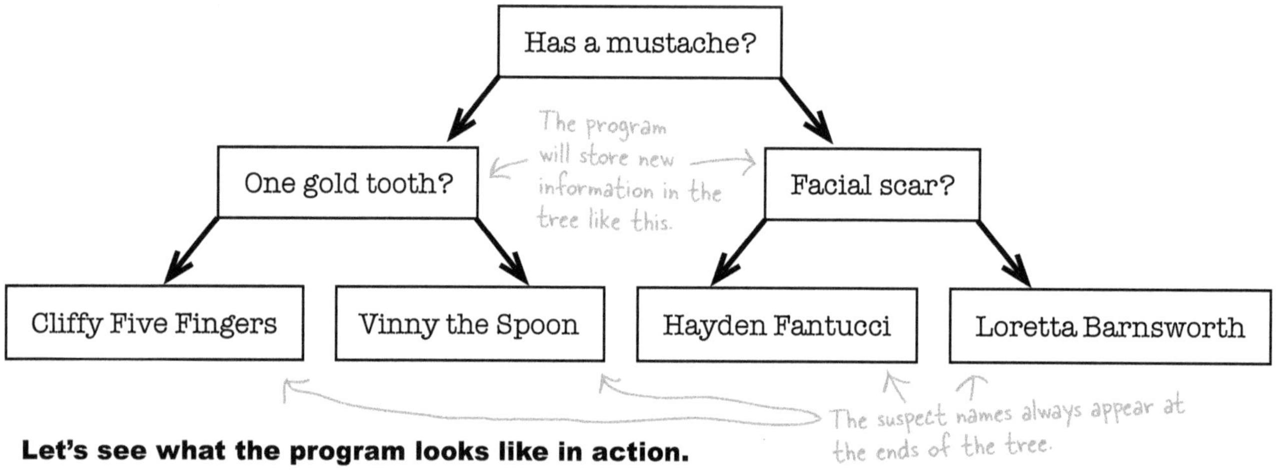

Has a mustache?
The program will store new information in the tree like this.
One gold tooth?
Facial scar?
Cliffy Five Fingers
Vinny the Spoon
Hayden Fantucci
Loretta Barnsworth
The suspect names always appear at the ends of the tree.

Let's see what the program looks like in action.

Test Drive

This is what happens if an agent compiles the SPIES program and then takes it on a test run:

```
File Edit Window Help TrustNoone
> gcc spies.c -o spies && ./spies
Does suspect have a mustache? (y/n): n
Loretta Barnsworth? (y/n): n
Who's the suspect? Hayden Fantucci
Give me a question that is TRUE for Hayden Fantucci
 but not for Loretta Barnsworth? Has a facial scar
Run again? (y/n): y
Does suspect have a mustache? (y/n): n
Has a facial scar
? (y/n): y
Hayden Fantucci
? (y/n): y
SUSPECT IDENTIFIED
Run again? (y/n): n
>
```

The first time through, the program fails to identify the suspect Hayden Fantucci. But once the suspect's details are entered, the program learns enough to identify Mr. Fantucci on the second run.

Pretty smart. So what's the problem?

Someone was using the system for a few hours in the lab and noticed that even though the program appeared to be working correctly, it was using almost **twice the amount of memory** it needed.

That's why **you** have been called in. Somewhere deep in the source code, something is allocating memory on the heap and *never freeing it*. Now, you could just sit and read through all of the code and hope that you see what's causing the problem. But memory leaks can be awfully difficult to track down.

So maybe you should pay a trip to the software lab...

Software forensics: using valgrind

It can take an achingly long time to track down bugs in large, complex programs like SPIES. So C hackers have written tools that can help you on your way. One tool used on the **Linux** operating system is called **`valgrind`**.

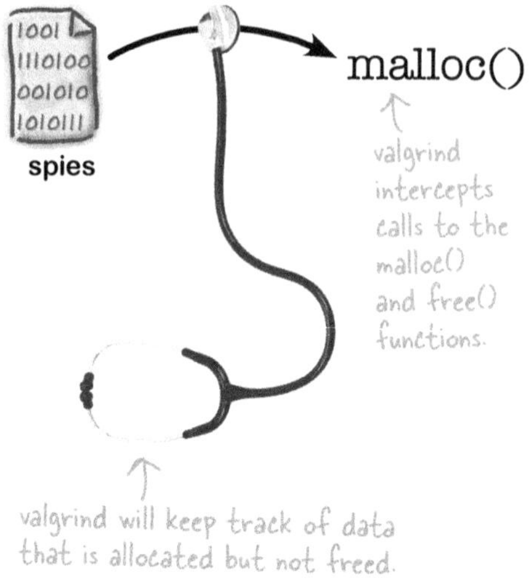
1001
1110100
0010100
1010111
spies
malloc()
valgrind intercepts calls to the malloc() and free() functions.
valgrind will keep track of data that is allocated but not freed.

`valgrind` can monitor the pieces of data that are allocated space on the heap. It works by creating its own **fake version of `malloc()`**. When your program wants to allocate some heap memory, `valgrind` will intercept your calls to `malloc()` and `free()` and run its own versions of those functions. The `valgrind` version of `malloc()` will take note of which piece of code is calling it and which piece of memory it allocated. When your program ends, `valgrind` will report back on any data that was left on the heap and tell you where in your code the data was created.

Prepare your code: add debug info

You don't *need* to do anything to your code before you run it through `valgrind`. You don't even need to recompile it. But to really get the most out of `valgrind`, you need to make sure your executable contains **debug information**. Debug information is extra data that gets packed into your executable when it's compiled—things like the line number in the source file that a particular piece of code was compiled from. If the debug info is present, `valgrind` will be able to give you a lot more details about the source of your memory leak.

To add debug info into your executable, you need to recompile the source with the `-g` switch:

```
gcc -g spies.c -o spies
```

The -g switch tells the compiler to record the line numbers against the code it compiles.

Just the facts: interrogate your code

To see how `valgrind` works, let's fire it up on a Linux box and use it to interrogate the SPIES program a couple times.

You can find out if valgrind is available on your operating system and how to install it at http://valgrind.org.

The first time, use the program to identify one of the built-in suspects: Vinny the Spoon. You'll start `valgrind` on the command line with the `--leak-check=full` option and then pass it the program you want to run:

File Edit Window Help valgrindRules

```
> valgrind --leak-check=full ./spies
==1754== Copyright (C) 2002-2010, and GNU GPL'd, by Julian Seward et al.
Does suspect have a mustache? (y/n): y
Vinny the Spoon? (y/n): y
SUSPECT IDENTIFIED
Run again? (y/n): n
==1754== All heap blocks were freed -- no leaks are possible
```

Use valgrind repeatedly to gather more evidence

When the SPIES program exited, there was nothing left on the heap. But what if you run it a second time and teach the program about a new suspect called Hayden Fantucci?

```
File Edit Window Help valgrindRules
> valgrind --leak-check=full ./spies
==2750== Copyright (C) 2002-2010, and GNU GPL'd, by Julian Seward et al.
Does suspect have a mustache? (y/n): n
Loretta Barnsworth? (y/n): n
Who's the suspect? Hayden Fantucci
Give me a question that is TRUE for Hayden Fantucci
 but not for Loretta Barnsworth? Has a facial scar
Run again? (y/n): n
==2750== HEAP SUMMARY:
==2750==     in use at exit: 19 bytes in 1 blocks
==2750==   total heap usage: 11 allocs, 10 frees, 154 bytes allocated
==2750== 19 bytes in 1 blocks are definitely lost in loss record 1 of 1
==2750==    at 0x4026864: malloc (vg_replace_malloc.c:236)
==2750==    by 0x40B3A9F: strdup (strdup.c:43)
==2750==    by 0x8048587: create (spies.c:22)
==2750==    by 0x804863D: main (spies.c:46)
==2750== LEAK SUMMARY:
==2750==    definitely lost: 19 bytes in 1 blocks
>
```

19 bytes was left on the heap.

Upi allocated new pieces of memory 11 times, but only freed 10 of them.

Do these lines give us any clues?

Why 19 bytes? Is that a clue?

This time, valgrind found a memory leak

It looks like there were 19 bytes of information left on the heap at the end of the program. `valgrind` is telling you the following things:

- **19 bytes of memory were allocated but not freed.**
- **Looks like we allocated new pieces of memory 11 times, but freed only 10 of them.**
- **Do these lines give us any clues?**
- **Why 19 bytes? Is that a clue?**

That's quite a few pieces of information. Let's take these facts and analyze them.

Look at the evidence

OK, now that you've run `valgrind`, you've collected quite a few pieces of evidence. It's time to analyze that evidence and see if you can draw any conclusions.

1. Location

You ran the code *two times*. The first time, there was no problem. The memory leak only happened when you entered a new suspect name. Why is that significant? Because that means the leak can't be in the code that ran the first time. Looking back at the source code, that means the problem lies in this section of the code:

```
} else if (current->no) {
  current = current->no;
} else {

   /* Make the yes-node the new suspect name */
   printf("Who's the suspect? ");
   fgets(suspect, 20, stdin);
   node *yes_node = create(suspect);
   current->yes = yes_node;

   /* Make the no-node a copy of this question */
   node *no_node = create(current->question);
   current->no = no_node;

   /* Then replace this question with the new question */
   printf("Give me a question that is TRUE for %s but not for %s? ",
           suspect, current->question);
   fgets(question, 80, stdin);
   current->question = strdup(question);

   break;
}
```

2. Clues from valgrind

When you ran the code through `valgrind` and added a single suspect, the program allocated memory 11 times, but only released memory 10 times. What does that tell you?

`valgrind` told you that there were 19 bytes of data left on the heap when the program ended. If you look at the source code, what piece of data is likely to take up 19 bytes of space?

Finally, what does this output from `valgrind` tell you?

```
==2750== 19 bytes in 1 blocks are definitely lost in loss record 1 of 1
==2750==    at 0x4026864: malloc (vg_replace_malloc.c:236)
==2750==    by 0x40B3A9F: strdup (strdup.c:43)
==2750==    by 0x8048587: create (spies.c:22)
==2750==    by 0x804863D: main (spies.c:46)
```

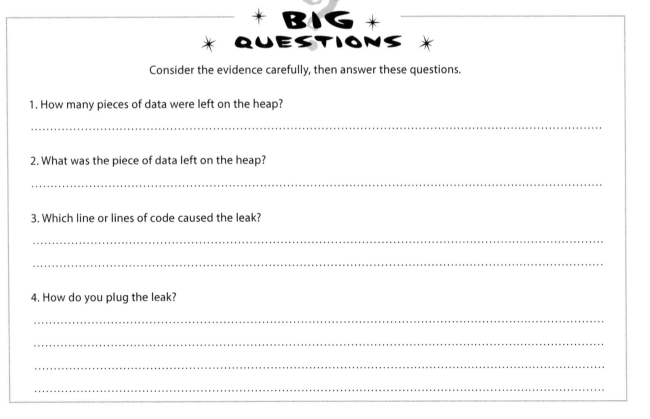

THE BIG QUESTIONS

Consider the evidence carefully, then answer these questions.

1. How many pieces of data were left on the heap?

2. What was the piece of data left on the heap?

3. Which line or lines of code caused the leak?

4. How do you plug the leak?

THE BIG ANSWERS

You were to consider the evidence carefully and answer these questions.

1. How many pieces of data were left on the heap?

There is one piece of data.

2. What was the piece of data left on the heap?

The string "Loretta Barnsworth". It's 18 characters with a string terminator.

3. Which line or lines of code caused the leak?

The create() functions themselves don't cause leaks because they didn't on the first pass, so it must be this strdup() line:

```
current->question = strdup(question);
```

4. How do you plug the leak?

If current->question is already pointing to something on the heap, free that before allocating a new question:

```
free(current->question);
current->question = strdup(question);
```

The fix on trial

Now that you've added the fix to the code, it's time to run the code through `valgrind` again.

```
File Edit Window Help valgrindRules
> valgrind --leak-check=full ./spies
==1800== Copyright (C) 2002-2010, and GNU GPL'd, by Julian Seward et al.
Does suspect have a mustache? (y/n): n
Loretta Barnsworth? (y/n): n
Who's the suspect? Hayden Fantucci
Give me a question that is TRUE for Hayden Fantucci
 but not for Loretta Barnsworth? Has a facial scar
Run again? (y/n): n
==1800== All heap blocks were freed -- no leaks are possible
>
```

The leak is fixed

You ran exactly the same test data through the program, and this time the program cleared everything away from the heap.

How did you do? Did you crack the case? Don't worry if you didn't manage to find and fix the leak this time. Memory leaks are some of the hardest bugs to find in C programs. The truth is that many of the C programs available probably have some memory bugs buried deep inside them, but that's why tools like `valgrind` are important.

- **Spot when leaks happen.**
- **Identify the location where they happen.**
- **Check to make sure the leak is fixed.**

there are no Dumb Questions

Q: `valgrind` said the leaked memory was created on line 46, but the leak was fixed on a completely different line. How come?

A: The "Loretta..." data was put onto the heap on line 46, but the leak happened when the variable pointing to it (`current->question`) was reassigned without freeing it. Leaks don't happen when data is created; they happen when the program loses all references to the data.

Q: Can I get `valgrind` on my Mac/Windows/FreeBSD system?

A: Check *http://valgrind.org* for details on the latest release.

Q: How does `valgrind` intercept calls to `malloc()` and `free()`?

A: The `malloc()` and `free()` functions are contained in the C Standard Library. But `valgrind` contains a library with its own versions of `malloc()` and `free()`. When you run a program with `valgrind`, your program will be using `valgrind`'s functions, rather than the ones in the C Standard Library.

Q: Why doesn't the compiler always include debug information when it compiles code?

A: Because debug information will make your executable larger, and it may also make your program slightly slower.

Q: Where did the name `valgrind` come from?

A: Valgrind is the name of the entrance to Valhalla. `valgrind` (the program) gives you access to the computer's heap.

BULLET POINTS

- `valgrind` checks for memory leaks.
- `valgrind` works by intercepting the calls to `malloc()` and `free()`.
- When a program stops running, `valgrind` prints details of what's left on the heap.
- If you compile your code with debug information, `valgrind` can give you more information.
- If you run your program several times, you can narrow the search for the leak.
- `valgrind` can tell you which lines of code in your source put the data on the heap.
- `valgrind` can be used to check that you've fixed a leak.

Your C Toolbox

You've got Chapter 6 under your belt, and now you've added data structures and dynamic memory to your toolbox. For a complete list of tooltips in the book, see Appendix ii.

- A linked list is more extensible than an array.
- Data can be inserted easily into a linked list.
- A linked list is a dynamic data structure.
- Dynamic data structures use recursive structs.
- Recursive structs contain one or more links to similar data.
- malloc() allocates memory on the heap.
- free() releases memory on the heap.
- Unlike the stack, heap memory is not automatically released.
- The stack is used for local variables.
- strdup() will create a copy of a string on the heap.
- A memory leak is allocated memory you can no longer access.
- valgrind can help you track down memory leaks.

7 advanced functions

Turn your functions up to 11

My go_on_date() is awesome now that I've discovered variadic functions.

Basic functions are great, but sometimes you need more.

So far, you've focused on the basics, but what if you need even more *power* and *flexibility* to achieve what you want? In this chapter, you'll see how to **up your code's IQ** by **passing functions as parameters**. You'll find out how to **get things sorted with comparator functions**. And finally, you'll discover how to make your code *super stretchy* with **variadic functions**.

Looking for Mr. Right...

You've used a lot of C functions in the book so far, but the truth is that there are still some ways to make your C functions a lot more powerful. If you know how to use them correctly, C functions can make your code **do more things** but *without* writing a lot more code.

To see how this works, let's look at an example. Imagine you have an array of strings that you want to filter down, displaying some strings and not displaying others:

```
int NUM_ADS = 7;
char *ADS[] = {
  "William: SBM GSOH likes sports, TV, dining",
  "Matt: SWM NS likes art, movies, theater",
  "Luis: SLM ND likes books, theater, art",
  "Mike: DWM DS likes trucks, sports and bieber",
  "Peter: SAM likes chess, working out and art",
  "Josh: SJM likes sports, movies and theater",
  "Jed: DBM likes theater, books and dining"
};
```

I want someone into sports, but definitely not into Bieber...

Let's write some code that uses string functions to filter this array down.

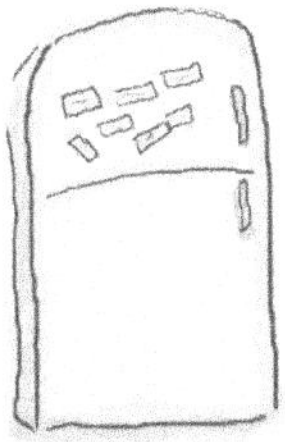

Code Magnets

Complete the `find()` function so it can track down all the sports fans in the list who **don't** also share a passion for Bieber.

Beware: you might not need all the fragments to complete the function.

```
void find()
{
  int i;
  puts("Search results:");
  puts("------------------------------------");

  for (i = 0; i .......... .......... ; i++) {

    if (.......... (.........., ..........)

        .......... .......... ..........(.........., ..........)) {

      printf("%s\n", ADS[i]);
    }
  }
  puts("------------------------------------");
}
```

`strcmp` `strstr` `ADS[i]` `ADS[i]` `"sports"` `NUM_ADS` `<` `!` `strstr` `&&` `||` `"bieber"` `strcmp`

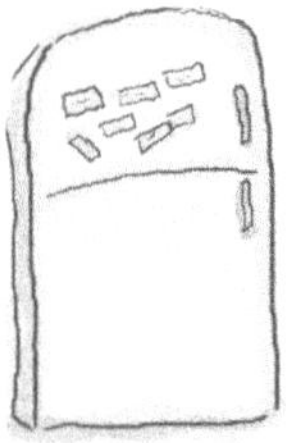

Code Magnets Solution

You were to complete the `find()` function so it can track down all the sports fans in the list who **don't** also share a passion for Bieber.

```
void find()
{
  int i;
  puts("Search results:");
  puts("------------------------------------");

  for (i = 0; i < NUM_ADS ; i++) {
    if ( strstr ( ADS[i] , "sports" )
      && ! strstr ( ADS[i] , "bieber" )) {
      printf("%s\n", ADS[i]);
    }
  }
  puts("------------------------------------");
}
```

strcmp

||

strcmp

Test Drive

Now, if you take the function and the data, and wrap everything up in a program called `find.c`, you can compile and run it like this:

```
File Edit Window Help FindersKeepers
> gcc find.c -o find && ./find
Search results:
------------------------------------
William: SBM GSOH likes sports, TV, dining
Josh: SJM likes sports, movies and theater
------------------------------------
>
```

I want a non-smoker who likes the theater.
Find someone who likes sports or working out.
Find someone who likes the art, theater, or dining.

And sure enough, the `find()` function loops through the array and finds the matching strings. Now that you have the basic code, it would be easy to create *clones* of the function that could perform different kinds of searches.

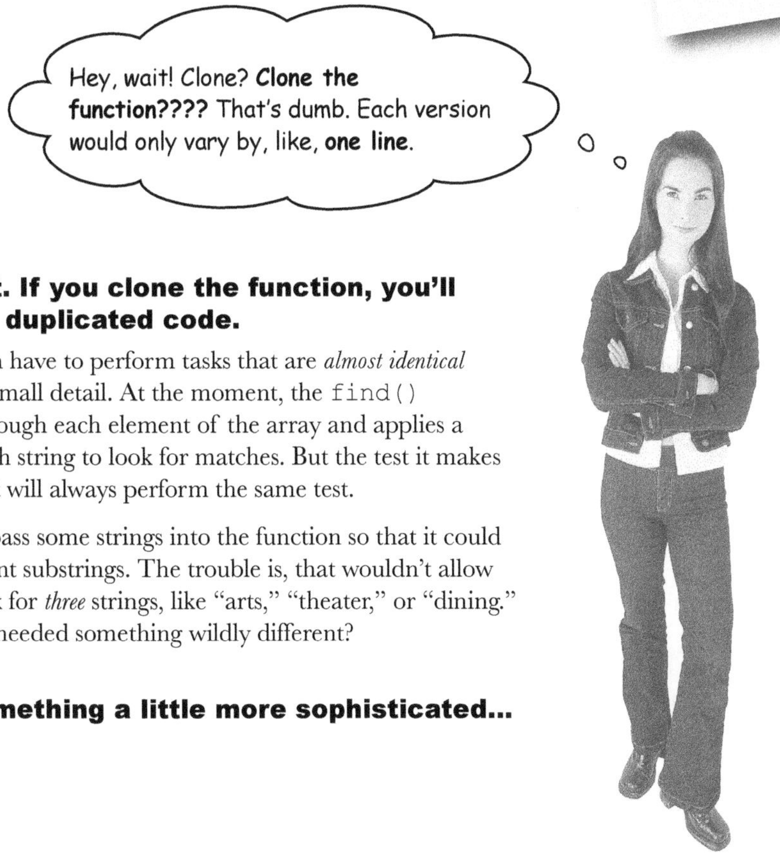
Hey, wait! Clone? **Clone the function????** That's dumb. Each version would only vary by, like, **one line**.

Exactly right. If you clone the function, you'll have a lot of duplicated code.

C programs often have to perform tasks that are *almost identical* except for some small detail. At the moment, the `find()` function runs through each element of the array and applies a simple test to each string to look for matches. But the test it makes is **hardwired**. It will always perform the same test.

Now, you could pass some strings into the function so that it could search for different substrings. The trouble is, that wouldn't allow `find()` to check for *three* strings, like "arts," "theater," or "dining." And what if you needed something wildly different?

You need something a little more sophisticated...

Pass code to a function

What you need is some way of **passing the code for the test to the `find()` function**. If you had some way of wrapping up a piece of code and handing that code to the function, it would be like passing the `find()` function a *testing machine* that it could apply to each piece of data.

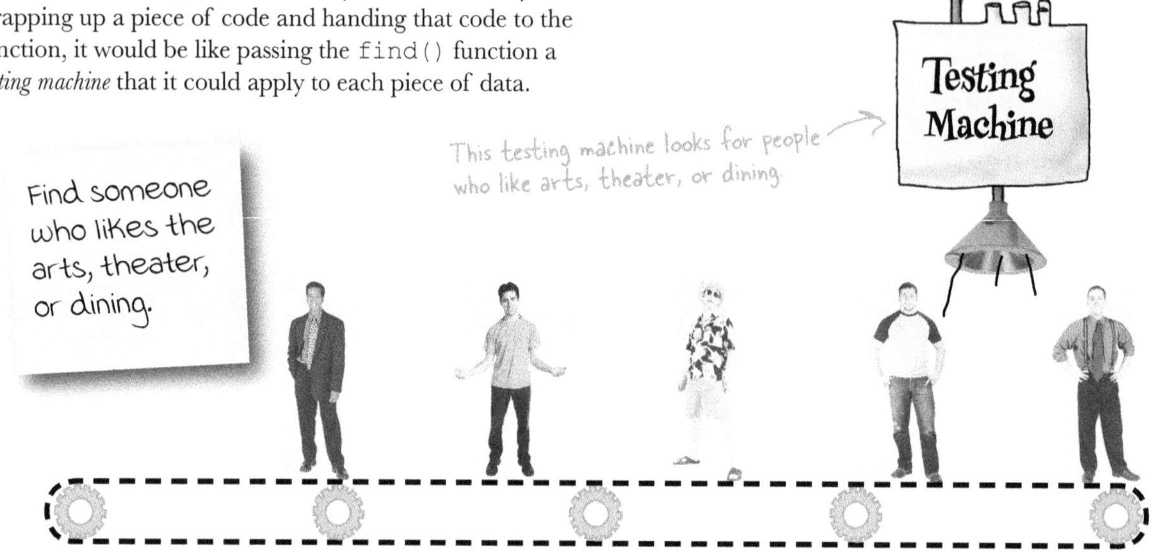
Find someone who likes the arts, theater, or dining.
This testing machine looks for people who like arts, theater, or dining.
Testing Machine

Find someone who likes sports or working out.
This testing machine looks for people who like sports or working out.
Testing Machine

This means the bulk of the `find()` function would stay **exactly the same**. It would still contain the code to check each element in an array and display the same kind of output. But the test it applies against each element in the array would be done *by the code that you pass to it.*

You need to tell find() the name of a function

Imagine you take our original search condition and rewrite it as a function:

```
int sports_no_bieber(char *s)
{
  return strstr(s, "sports") && !strstr(s, "bieber");
}
```

I want someone into sports, but definitely not into Bieber...

Now, if you had some way of passing **the name of the function** to `find()` as a *parameter*, you'd have a way of **injecting** the test:

```
void find( function-name match )
{
  int i;
  puts("Search results:");
  puts("------------------------------------");
  for (i = 0; i < NUM_ADS; i++) {
    if ( call-the-match-function (ADS[i])) {
      printf("%s\n", ADS[i]);
    }
  }
  puts("------------------------------------");
}
```

match would specify the name of the function containing the test.

Here, you'd need some way of calling the function whose name was given by the match parameter.

If you could find a way of passing a function name to `find()`, there would be no limit to the kinds of tests that you could make in the future. As long as you can write a function that will return *true* or *false* to a string, you can reuse the same `find()` function.

```
find(sports_no_bieber);
find(sports_or_workout);
find(ns_theater);
find(arts_theater_or_dining);
```

But how do you say that a parameter stores the name of a function? And if you have a function name, how do you use it to call the function?

Every function name is a pointer to the function...

You probably guessed that pointers would come into this somewhere, right? Think about what the **name of a function** *really is*. It's a way of *referring* to the piece of code. And that's just what a pointer is: ***a way of referring to something in memory***.

That's why, in C, function names are also pointer variables. When you create a function called `go_to_warp_speed(int speed)`, you are also creating a pointer variable called `go_to_warp_speed` that contains the address of the function. So, if you give `find()` a parameter that has a *function pointer* type, you should be able to use the parameter to call the function it points to.

STACK
HEAP
GLOBALS
CONSTANTS
"go_to_warp_speed"
CODE

```
int go_to_warp_speed(int speed)
{
  dilithium_crystals(ENGAGE);
  warp = speed;
  reactor_core(c, 125000 * speed, PI);
  clutch(ENGAGE);
  brake(DISENGAGE);
  return 0;
}
```

Whenever you create a function, you also create a function pointer with the same name.

The pointer contains the address of the function.

```
go_to_warp_speed(4);
```

When you call the function, you are using the function pointer.

Let's look at the C syntax you'll need to work with function pointers.

...but there's no function data type

Usually, it's pretty easy to declare pointers in C. If you have a data type like `int`, you just need to add an asterisk to the end of the data type name, and you declare a pointer with `int *`. Unfortunately, C doesn't have a `function` data type, so you can't declare a function pointer with anything like `function *`.

```
int *a;
```
← This declares an int pointer...

```
function *f;
```
← ...but this **won't** declare a function pointer.

Why doesn't C have a function data type?

C doesn't have a `function` data type because there's not just one *type* of function. When you create a function, you can vary a lot of things, such as the return type or the list of parameters it takes. That combination of things is what defines the *type* of the function.

```
int go_to_warp_speed(int speed)
{
   ...
}

char** album_names(char *artist, int year)
{
   ...
}
```

There are many different types of functions. These functions are different types because they have different return types and parameters.

So, for function pointers, you'll need to use slightly more complex notation…

How to create function pointers

Say you want to create a pointer variable that can store the address of each of the functions on the previous page. You'd have to do it like this:

```
int (*warp_fn)(int);
warp_fn = go_to_warp_speed;
warp_fn(4);
```

This will create a variable called warp_fn that can store the address of the go_to_warp_speed() function.

This is just like calling go_to_warp_speed(4).

```
char** (*names_fn)(char*,int);
names_fn = album_names;
char** results = names_fn("Sacha Distel", 1972);
```

This will create a variable called names_fn that can store the address of the album_names() function.

That looks pretty complex, doesn't it?

Unfortunately, it has to be, because you need to tell C the return type and the parameter types the function will take. But once you've declared a function pointer variable, you can use it like any other variable. You can assign values to it, you can add it to arrays, and you can also pass it to functions…

…which brings us back to your `find()` code…

there are no Dumb Questions

Q: What does `char**` mean? Is it a typing error?

A: `char**` is a pointer normally used to point to an array of strings.

Exercise

Take a look at those other types of searches that people have asked for. See if you can create a function for each type of search. Remember: the first is already written.

Someone who likes sports but not Bieber

```
int sports_no_bieber(char *s)
{
  return strstr(s, "sports") && !strstr(s, "bieber");
}
```

Find someone who likes sports or working out.

```
int sports_or_workout(char *s)
{
  ..........................................................
}
```

I want a non-smoker who likes the theater.

```
int ns_theater(char *s)
{
  ..........................................................
}
```

Find someone who likes the arts, theater, or dining.

```
int arts_theater_or_dining(char *s)
{
  ..........................................................
}
```

Then, see if you can complete the `find()` function:

```
void find( ........................................ )
{
  int i;
  puts("Search results:");
  puts("------------------------------------");
  for (i = 0; i < NUM_ADS; i++) {
    if (match(ADS[i])) {
      printf("%s\n", ADS[i]);
    }
  }
  puts("------------------------------------");
}
```

find() will need a function pointer passing to it called match.

This will call the match() function that was passed in.

Exercise Solution

You were to take a look at those other types of searches that people have asked for and create a function for each type of search.

Someone who likes sports but not Bieber

```
int sports_no_bieber(char *s)
{
  return strstr(s, "sports") && !strstr(s, "bieber");
}
```

Find someone who likes sports or working out.

```
int sports_or_workout(char *s)
{
  return strstr(s, "sports") || strstr(s, "working out");
}
```

I want a non-smoker who likes the theater.

```
int ns_theater(char *s)
{
  return strstr(s, "NS") && strstr(s, "theater");
}
```

Find someone who likes the arts, theater, or dining.

```
int arts_theater_or_dining(char *s)
{
  return strstr(s, "arts") || strstr(s, "theater") || strstr(s, "dining");
}
```

Then, you were to complete the `find()` function:

```
void find( int (*match)(char*) )
{
  int i;
  puts("Search results:");
  puts("------------------------------------");
  for (i = 0; i < NUM_ADS; i++) {
    if (match(ADS[i])) {
      printf("%s\n", ADS[i]);
    }
  }
  puts("------------------------------------");
}
```

Test Drive

Let's take those functions out on the road and see how they perform. You'll need to create a program to call `find()` with each function in turn:

```
int main()
{
  find(sports_no_bieber);
  find(sports_or_workout);
  find(ns_theater);
  find(arts_theater_or_dining);
  return 0;
}
```

```
File Edit Window Help FindersKeepers
> ./find
Search results:
------------------------------------
William: SBM GSOH likes sports, TV, dining
Josh: SJM likes sports, movies and theater
------------------------------------
Search results:
------------------------------------
William: SBM GSOH likes sports, TV, dining
Mike: DWM DS likes trucks, sports and bieber
Peter: SAM likes chess, working out and art
Josh: SJM likes sports, movies and theater
------------------------------------
Search results:
------------------------------------
Matt: SWM NS likes art, movies, theater
------------------------------------
Search results:
------------------------------------
William: SBM GSOH likes sports, TV, dining
Matt: SWM NS likes art, movies, theater
Luis: SLM ND likes books, theater, art
Josh: SJM likes sports, movies and theater
Jed: DBM likes theater, books and dining
------------------------------------
>
```

This is find(sports_no_bieber).

This is find(sports_or_workout).

This is find(ns_theater).

This is find(arts_theater_or_dining).

Each call to the `find()` function is performing a very different search. That's why function pointers are one of the most powerful features in C: they allow you to mix functions together. Function pointers let you build programs with a lot **more power** and a lot **less code**.

The Hunter's Guide to Function Pointers

When you're out in the reeds, identifying those function pointers can be pretty tricky. But this simple, easy-to-carry guide will fit in the ammo pocket of any C user.

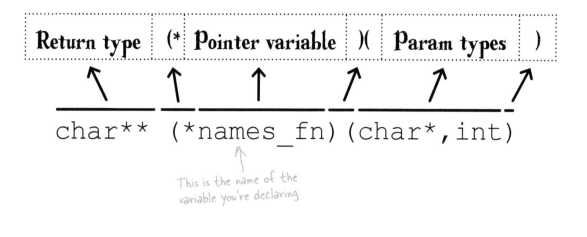

Return type	(*	Pointer variable	)(	Param types	)

```
char** (*names_fn)(char*,int)
```

This is the name of the variable you're declaring.

there are no Dumb Questions

Q: If function pointers are just pointers, why don't you need to prefix them with a * when you call the function?

A: You can. In the program, instead of writing `match(ADS[i])`, you could have written `(*match)(ADS[i])`.

Q: And could I have used & to get the address of a method?

A: Yes. Instead of `find(sports_or_workout)`, you could have written `find(&sports_or_workout)`.

Q: Then why didn't I?

A: Because it makes the code easier to read. If you skip the `*` and `&`, C will still understand what you're saying.

Get it sorted with the C Standard Library

Lots of programs need to sort data. And if the data's something simple like a set of numbers, then sorting is pretty easy. Numbers have their own natural order. But it's not so easy with other types of data.

Imagine you have a set of people. How would you put them in order? By height? By intelligence? By *hotness*?

When the people who wrote the C Standard Library wanted to create a sort function, they had a problem:

How could a sort function sort any type of data at all?

Use function pointers to set the order

You probably guessed the solution: the C Standard Library has a sort function that accepts a pointer to a **comparator function**, which will be used to decide if one piece of data is **the same as**, **less than,** or **greater than** another piece of data.

This is what the `qsort()` function looks like:

```
qsort(void *array,
      size_t length,
      size_t item_size,
      int (*compar)(const void *, const void *));
```

This is a pointer to an array. (`void *array`)

This is the length of the array. (`size_t length`)

This is the size of each element in the array. (`size_t item_size`)

Remember, a void* pointer can point to anything.

This is a pointer to a function that compares two items in the array.

The `qsort()` function compares pairs of values over and over again, and if they are in the wrong order, the computer will switch them.

And that's what the comparator function is for. It will tell `qsort()` which order a pair of elements should be in. It does this by returning three different values:

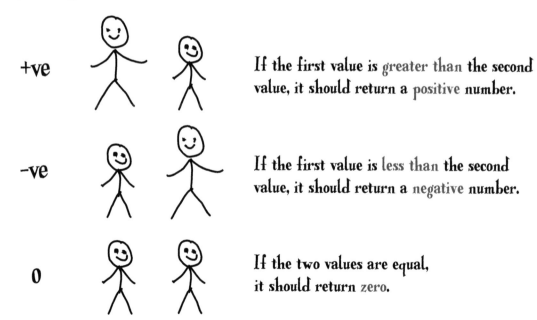

+ve  If the first value is greater than the second value, it should return a positive number.

-ve  If the first value is less than the second value, it should return a negative number.

0  If the two values are equal, it should return zero.

To see how this works in practice, let's look at an example.

Sorting ints Up Close

Let's say you have an array of integers and you want to sort them in increasing order. What does the comparator function look like?

```
int scores[] = {543,323,32,554,11,3,112};
```

If you look at the **signature** of the comparator function that `qsort()` needs, it takes two **void pointers** given by **`void*`**. Remember `void*` when we used `malloc()`? A void pointer can store the address of **any kind of data**, but you always need to *cast* it to something more specific before you can use it.

A void pointer void* can store a pointer to anything.

The `qsort()` function works by comparing pairs of elements in the array and then placing them in the correct order. It compares the values by calling the comparator function that you give it.

```
int compare_scores(const void* score_a, const void* score_b)
{
    ...
}
```

Values are always passed to the function as pointers, so the first thing you need to do is get the integer values from the pointers:

You need to **cast** the void pointer to an integer pointer.

```
int a = *(int*)score_a;
int b = *(int*)score_b;
```

This first * then gets the int stored at address score_b.

Then you need to return a positive, negative, or zero value, depending on whether `a` is greater than, less than, or equal to `b`. For integers, that's pretty easy to do—you just subtract one number from the other:

The comparator function returned the value -21. That means 11 needs to be before 32.

```
return a - b;
```

If a > b, this is positive. If a < b, this is negative. If a and b are equal, this is zero.

And this is how you ask `qsort()` to sort the array:

```
qsort(scores, 7, sizeof(int), compare_scores);
```

Long Exercise

Now it's your turn. Look at these different sort descriptions. See if you can write a comparator function for each one. To get you started, the first one is already completed.

Sort integer scores, with the smallest first.

```
int compare_scores(const void* score_a, const void* score_b)
{
  int a = *(int*)score_a;
  int b = *(int*)score_b;
  return a - b;
}
```

Sort integer scores, with the largest first.

```
int compare_scores_desc(const void* score_a, const void* score_b)
{
...................................................................
...................................................................
...................................................................
}
```

Sort the rectangles in area order, smallest first.

```
typedef struct {   <- This is the rectangle type.
  int width;
  int height;
} rectangle;

int compare_areas(const void* a, const void* b)
{
...................................................................
...................................................................
...................................................................
...................................................................
...................................................................
}
```

Warning: this one is **really** tricky.

Sort a list of names in alphabetical order. Case-sensitive.

```
int compare_names(const void* a, const void* b)
{
..........................................................................
..........................................................................
..........................................................................
}
```

Here's a hint: strcmp("Abc", "Def") < 0

If a string is a pointer to a char, what will a pointer to it be?

And finally: if you already had the `compare_areas()` and `compare_names()` functions, how would you write these two comparator functions?

Sort the rectangles in area order, largest first.

```
int compare_areas_desc(const void* a, void* b)
{
..........................................................................
}
```

Sort a list of names in reverse alphabetical order. Case-sensitive.

```
int compare_names_desc(const void* a, const void* b)
{
..........................................................................
}
```

Long Exercise Solution

Now it's your turn. You were to look at these different sort descriptions and write a comparator function for each one.

Sort integer scores, with the smallest first.

```
int compare_scores(const void* score_a, const void* score_b)
{
  int a = *(int*)score_a;
  int b = *(int*)score_b;
  return a - b;
}
```

This is the one done before.

Sort integer scores, with the largest first.

```
int compare_scores_desc(const void* score_a, const void* score_b)
{
  int a = *(int*)score_a;
  int b = *(int*)score_b;
  return b - a;
}
```

If you subtract the numbers the other way around, you'll reverse the order of the final sort.

Sort the rectangles in area order, smallest first.

```
typedef struct {
  int width;
  int height;
} rectangle;
```

This is the rectangle type.

```
int compare_areas(const void* a, const void* b)
{
  rectangle* ra = (rectangle*)a;
  rectangle* rb = (rectangle*)b;
  int area_a = (ra->width * ra->height);
  int area_b = (rb->width * rb->height);
  return area_a - area_b;
}
```

First, convert the pointers to the correct type.

Then, calculate the areas.

Then, use the subtraction trick.

Sort a list of names in alphabetical order. Case-sensitive.

```
int compare_names(const void* a, const void* b)
{
  char** sa = (char**)a;
  char** sb = (char**)b;
  return strcmp(*sa, *sb);
}
```

A string is a pointer to a char, so the pointers you're given are pointers to pointers.

We need to use the * operator to find the actual strings.

Here's a hint: strcmp("Abc", "Def") < 0

And finally: if you already had the `compare_areas()` and `compare_names()` functions, how did you write these two comparator functions?

Sort the rectangles in area order, largest first.

```
int compare_areas_desc(const void* a, const void* b)
{
  return compare_areas(b, a);
}
```

Or you could have used -compare_areas(a, b).

Sort a list of names in reverse alphabetical order. Case-sensitive.

```
int compare_names_desc(const void* a, const void* b)
{
  return compare_names(b, a);
}
```

Or you could have used -compare_names(a, b).

Relax

Don't worry if this exercise caused you a few problems.

It involved pointers, function pointers, and even a little math. If you found it tough, take a break, drink a little water, and then try it again in an hour or two.

Test Drive

Some of the comparator functions were really pretty gnarly, so it's worth seeing how they run in action. This is the kind of code you need to call the functions.

```
#include <stdio.h>
#include <string.h>
#include <stdlib.h>
```

The comparator functions go here. →

```
int main()
{
  int scores[] = {543,323,32,554,11,3,112};
  int i;
  qsort(scores, 7, sizeof(int), compare_scores_desc);
  puts("These are the scores in order:");
  for (i = 0; i < 7; i++) {
    printf("Score = %i\n", scores[i]);
  }
  char *names[] = {"Karen", "Mark", "Brett", "Molly"};
  qsort(names, 4, sizeof(char*), compare_names);
  puts("These are the names in order:");
  for (i = 0; i < 4; i++) {
    printf("%s\n", names[i]);
  }
  return 0;
}
```

This is the line that sorts the scores.

qsort() changes the order of the elements in the array.

This will print out the array once it's been sorted.

This sorts the names.

Remember: an array of names is just an array of char pointers, so the size of each item is sizeof(char*).

This prints the sorted names out.

If you compile and run this code, this is what you get:

```
File Edit Window Help Sorted
> ./test_drive
These are the scores in order:
Score = 554
Score = 543
Score = 323
Score = 112
Score = 32
Score = 11
Score = 3
These are the names in order:
Brett
Karen
Mark
Molly
>
```

Great, it works.

Now try writing your own example code. The sorting functions can be incredibly useful, but the comparator functions they need can be tricky to write. But the more practice you get, the easier they become.

Do this!

there are no Dumb Questions

Q: I don't understand the comparator function for the array of strings. What does `char**` mean?

A: Each item in a string array is a `char` pointer (`char*`). When `qsort()` calls the comparator function, it sends pointers to two elements in the arrays. That means the comparator receives two pointers-to-pointers-to-char. In C notation, each value is a `char**`.

Q: OK, but when I call the `strcmp()` function, why does the code say `strcmp(*a, *b)`? Why not `strcmp(a, b)`?

A: `a` and `b` are of type `char**`. The `strcmp()` function needs values of type `char*`.

Q: Does `qsort()` create a sorted version of an array?

A: It doesn't make a copy, it actually modifies the original array.

Q: Why does my head hurt?

A: Don't worry about it. Pointers are really difficult to use sometimes. If you *don't* find them a little confusing, it probably means you aren't thinking hard enough about them.

Automating the Dear John letters

Imagine you're writing a mail-merge program to send out different types of messages to different people. One way of creating the data for each response is with a `struct` like this:

These are the three types of messages that will be sent to people.

```
enum response_type {DUMP, SECOND_CHANCE, MARRIAGE};
typedef struct {
  char *name;
  enum response_type type;
} response;
```

You'll record a response type with each piece of response data.

The `enum` gives you the names for each of the three types of response you'll be sending out, and that response type can be recorded against each response. Then you'll be able to use your new `response` data type by calling one of these three functions for each type of response:

```
void dump(response r)
{
  printf("Dear %s,\n", r.name);
  puts("Unfortunately your last date contacted us to");
  puts("say that they will not be seeing you again");
}

void second_chance(response r)
{
  printf("Dear %s,\n", r.name);
  puts("Good news: your last date has asked us to");
  puts("arrange another meeting. Please call ASAP.");
}

void marriage(response r)
{
  printf("Dear %s,\n", r.name);
  puts("Congratulations! Your last date has contacted");
  puts("us with a proposal of marriage.");
}
```

So, now that you know what the data looks like, and you have the functions to generate the responses, let's see how complex the code is to generate a set of responses from an array of data.

Pool Puzzle

Take code fragments from the pool and place them into the blank lines below. Your goal is to piece together the `main()` function so that it can generate a set of letters for the array of `response` data. You may **not** use the same code fragment more than once.

```
int main()
{
  response r[] = {
    {"Mike", DUMP}, {"Luis", SECOND_CHANCE},
    {"Matt", SECOND_CHANCE}, {"William", MARRIAGE}
  };
  int i;
  for (i = 0; i < 4; i++) {
    switch(..........................) {
    case ..........................:
      dump(..........................);
      break;
    case ..........................:
      second_chance(..........................);
      break;
    default:
      marriage(..........................);
    }
  }
  return 0;
}
```

Note: each thing from the pool can be used only once!

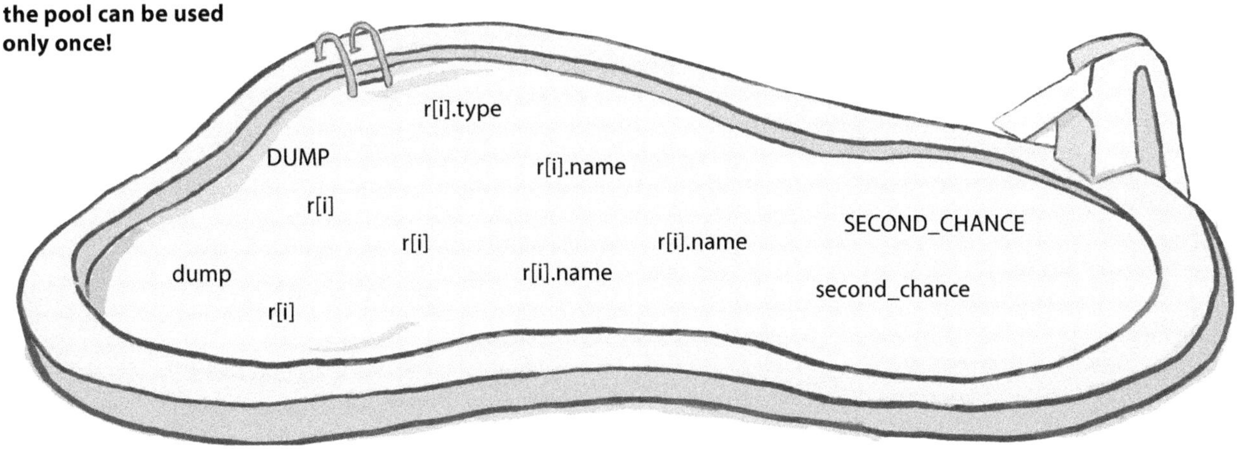

r[i].type
DUMP
r[i].name
r[i]
r[i]
r[i].name
SECOND_CHANCE
dump
r[i].name
second_chance
r[i]

Pool Puzzle Solution

Take code fragments from the pool and place them into the blank lines below. Your goal was to piece together the `main()` function so that it can generate a set of letters for the array of `response` data.

```
int main()
{
  response r[] = {
    {"Mike", DUMP}, {"Luis", SECOND_CHANCE},
    {"Matt", SECOND_CHANCE}, {"William", MARRIAGE}
  };
  int i;
  for (i = 0; i < 4; i++) {
    switch(r[i].type) {
    case DUMP:
      dump(r[i]);
      break;
    case SECOND_CHANCE:
      second_chance(r[i]);
      break;
    default:
      marriage(r[i]);
    }
  }
  return 0;
}
```

← Looping through the array

← Testing the type field each time

Call the method for each matching type.

Note: each thing from the pool can be used only once!

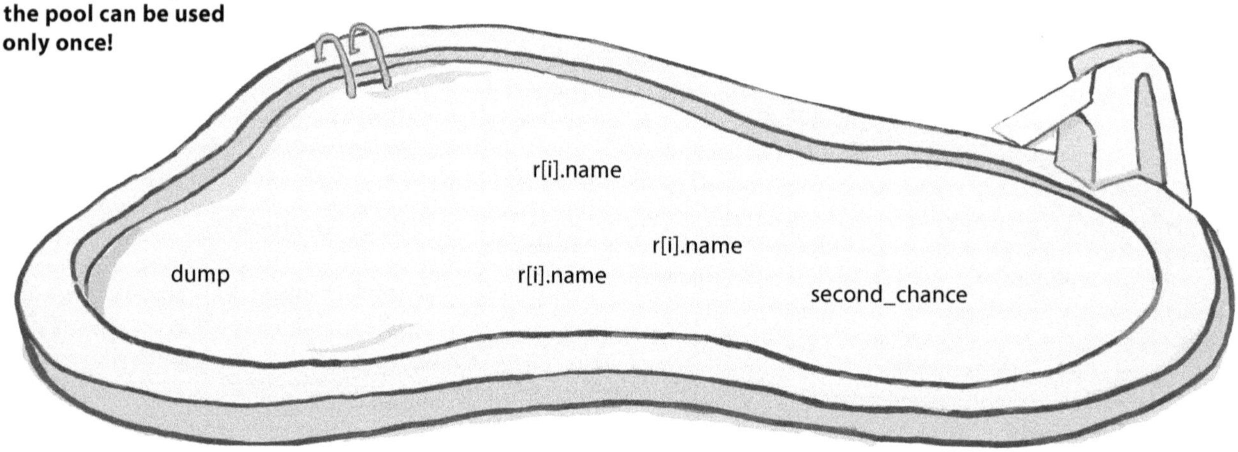
r[i].name
r[i].name
dump
r[i].name
second_chance

Test Drive

When you run the program, sure enough, it generates the correct response for each person:

```
File Edit Window Help DontForgetToBreak
./send_dear_johns
Dear Mike,
Unfortunately your last date contacted us to
say that they will not be seeing you again
Dear Luis,
Good news: your last date has asked us to
arrange another meeting. Please call ASAP.
Dear Matt,
Good news: your last date has asked us to
arrange another meeting. Please call ASAP.
Dear William,
Congratulations! Your last date has contacted
us with a proposal of marriage.
>
```

Well, it's good that it worked, but there is quite a lot of code in there just to call a function for each piece of `response` data. Every time you need call a function that matches a response type, it will look like this:

```
switch(r.type) {
case DUMP:
  dump(r);
  break;
case SECOND_CHANCE:
  second_chance(r);
  break;
default:
  marriage(r);
}
```

They told me a coder forgot a set of break statements, and that meant I ended up with this guy...

And what will happen if you add a **fourth** response type? You'll have to change every section of your program that looks like this. Soon, you will have a lot of code to maintain, and it might go wrong.

Fortunately, there is a trick that you can use in C, and it involves **arrays**...

Create an array of function pointers

The trick is to create an array of function pointers that match the different response types. Before seeing how that works, let's look at how to create an array of function pointers. If you had an array variable that could store a whole bunch of function names, you could use it like this:

```
replies[] = {dump, second_chance, marriage};
```

But that syntax doesn't quite work in C. You have to tell the compiler exactly what the functions will look like that you're going to store in the array: what their return types will be and what parameters they'll accept. That means you have to use this **much more complex** syntax:

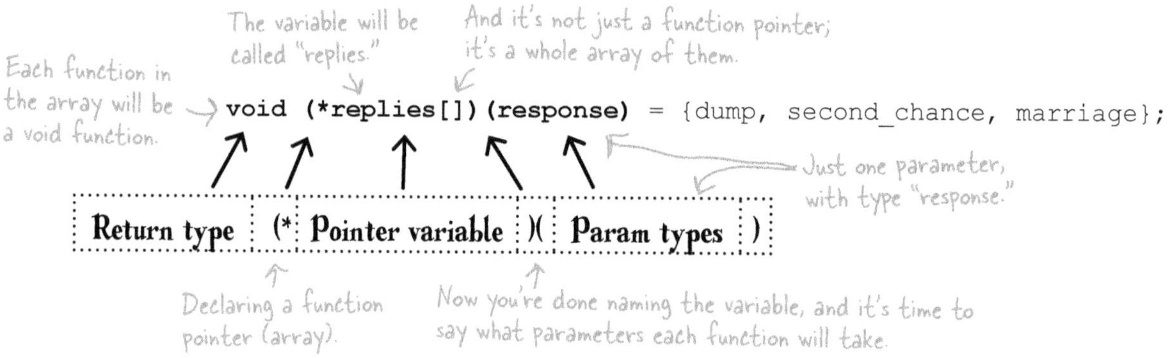
The variable will be called "replies."
And it's not just a function pointer; it's a whole array of them.
Each function in the array will be a void function.
void (*replies[])(response) = {dump, second_chance, marriage};
Just one parameter, with type "response."
Return type
(*
Pointer variable
)(
Param types
)
Declaring a function pointer (array).
Now you're done naming the variable, and it's time to say what parameters each function will take.

But how does an array help?

Look at that array. It contains a set of function names that are in **exactly the same order as the types in the enum**:

```
enum response_type {DUMP, SECOND_CHANCE, MARRIAGE};
```

This is *really important*, because when C creates an `enum`, it gives each of the symbols a number starting at 0. So `DUMP == 0`, `SECOND_CHANCE == 1`, and `MARRIAGE == 2`. And that's really neat, because it means you can get a pointer to one of your sets of functions using a **`response_type`**:

This is your "replies" array of functions. → `replies[SECOND_CHANCE] == second_chance` ← It's equal to the name of the second_chance function.

SECOND_CHANCE has the value 1.

Let's see if you can use the function array to replace your old main() function.

Sharpen your pencil

OK, this exercise is quite a tough one. But take your time with it, and you should be fine. You already have all the information you need to complete the code. In this new version of the `main()` function, the whole `switch/case` statement used before has been removed and needs to be replaced with a **single line of code**. This line of code will find the correct function name from the `replies` array and then use it to **call the function**.

```
void (*replies[])(response) = {dump, second_chance, marriage};

int main()
{
  response r[] = {
    {"Mike", DUMP}, {"Luis", SECOND_CHANCE},
    {"Matt", SECOND_CHANCE}, {"William", MARRIAGE}
  };
  int i;
  for (i = 0; i < 4; i++) {
    ..........................................................
  }
  return 0;
}
```

Sharpen your pencil Solution

OK, this exercise was quite a tough one. In this new version of the `main()` function, the whole `switch/case` statement used before was removed, and you needed to replace it. This line of code will find the correct function name from the `replies` array and then use it to **call the function**.

```
void (*replies[])(response) = {dump, second_chance, marriage};

int main()
{
  response r[] = {
    {"Mike", DUMP}, {"Luis", SECOND_CHANCE},
    {"Matt", SECOND_CHANCE}, {"William", MARRIAGE}
  };
  int i;
  for (i = 0; i < 4; i++) {
    (replies[r[i].type])(r[i]);
  }
  return 0;
}
```

If you wanted, you could have added a * after the opening parenthesis, but it would work the same way.

Let's break that down.

This whole thing is a function like "dump" or "marriage."

(replies[r[i].type])(r[i]);

This is your array of function names.

This is a value like 0 for DUMP or 2 for MARRIAGE.

You're calling the function and passing it the response data r[i].

Test Drive

Now, when you run the new version of the program, you get exactly the same output as before:

```
File Edit Window Help WhoIsJohn
> ./dear_johns
Dear Mike,
Unfortunately your last date contacted us to
say that they will not be seeing you again
Dear Luis,
Good news: your last date has asked us to
arrange another meeting. Please call ASAP.
Dear Matt,
Good news: your last date has asked us to
arrange another meeting. Please call ASAP.
Dear William,
Congratulations! Your last date has contacted
us with a proposal of marriage.
>
```

The difference? Now, instead of an entire `switch` statement, you just have this:

```
(replies[r[i].type])(r[i]);
```

If you have to call the response functions at several places in the program, you won't have to copy a lot of code. And if you decide to add a new type and a new function, you can just add it to the array:

```
enum response_type {DUMP, SECOND_CHANCE, MARRIAGE, LAW_SUIT};
void (*replies[])(response) = {dump, second_chance, marriage, law_suit};
```

You can add new types and functions like this.

Arrays of function pointers can make your code much easier to manage. They are designed to make your code *scalable* by making it shorter and easier to extend. Even though they are quite difficult to understand at first, function pointer arrays can really crank up your C programming skills.

BULLET POINTS

- Function pointers store the addresses of functions.
- The name of each function is actually a function pointer.
- If you have a function `shoot()`, then `shoot` and `&shoot` are both pointers to that function.
- You declare a new function pointer with `return-type(*var-name)(param-types)`.
- If `fp` is a function pointer, you can call it with `fp(params, ...)`.
- Or, you can use `(*fp)(params,...)`. C will work the same way.
- The C Standard Library has a sorting function called `qsort()`.
- `qsort()` accepts a pointer to a *comparator function* that can test for (in)equality.
- The comparator function will be passed **pointers** to two items in the array being sorted.
- If you have an array of data, you can associate functions with each data item using function pointer arrays.

there are no Dumb Questions

Q: Why is the function pointer array syntax so complex?

A: Because when you declare a function pointer, you need to say what the return and parameter types are. That's why there are so many parentheses.

Q: This looks a little like the sort of object-oriented code in other languages. Is it?

A: It's similar. Object-oriented languages associate a set of functions (called *methods*) with pieces of data. In the same way, you can use function pointers to associate functions with pieces of data.

Q: Hey, so does that mean that C is object oriented? Wow, that's awesome.

A: No. C is not object oriented, but other languages that are built on C, like Objective-C and C++, create a lot of their object-oriented features by using function pointers under the covers.

Make your functions streeeeeetchy

Sometimes, you want to write C functions that are really *powerful*, like your `find()` function that could search using function pointers. But other times, you just want to write functions that are *easy to use*. Take the `printf()` function. The `printf()` function has one really cool feature that you've used: it can take a **variable number of arguments**:

```
printf("%i bottles of beer on the wall, %i bottles of beer\n", 99, 99);
printf("Take one down and pass it around, ");
printf("%i bottles of beer on the wall\n", 98);
```

You can pass the printf() as many arguments as you need to print.

So how can YOU do that?

And you've got just the problem that needs it. Down in the Head First Lounge, they're finding it a little difficult to keep track of the drink totals. One of the guys has tried to make life easier by creating an `enum` with the list of cocktails available and a function that returns the prices for each one:

```
enum drink {
  MUDSLIDE, FUZZY_NAVEL, MONKEY_GLAND, ZOMBIE
};

double price(enum drink d)
{
  switch(d) {
  case MUDSLIDE:
    return 6.79;
  case FUZZY_NAVEL:
    return 5.31;
  case MONKEY_GLAND:
    return 4.82;
  case ZOMBIE:
    return 5.89;
  }
  return 0;
}
```

And that's pretty cool, if the Head First Lounge crew just wants the price of a drink. But what they want to do is get the price of a total drinks order:

Easy → `price(ZOMBIE)`

```
total(3, ZOMBIE, MONKEY_GLAND, FUZZY_NAVEL)
```

The number of drinks

A list of the drinks in the order

Not so easy

They want a function called `total()` that will accept a count of the drinks and then a list of drink names.

Variadic Functions Up Close

A function that takes a variable number of parameters is called a **variadic function**. The C Standard Library contains a set of **macros** that can help you create your own variadic functions. To see how they work, you'll create a function that can print out series of `ints`:

You can think of macros as a special type of function that can modify your source code.

```
print_ints(3, 79, 101, 32);
```

Number of ints to print

The ints that need to be printed

Here's the code:

The **variable** arguments will follow here.

The variable arguments will start after the args parameter.

```
#include <stdarg.h>

void print_ints(int args, ...)
{
  va_list ap;
  va_start(ap, args);
  int i;
  for (i = 0; i < args; i++) {
    printf("argument: %i\n", va_arg(ap, int));
  }
  va_end(ap);
}
```

This is a normal, ordinary argument that will always be passed.

va_start says where the variable arguments start.

This will loop through all of the other arguments.

args contains a count of how many variables there are.

Let's break it down and take a look at it, step by step.

1. **Include the stdarg.h header.**
All the code to handle variadic functions is in *stdarg.h*, so you need to make sure you include it.

2. **Tell your function there's more to come...**
Remember those books where the heroine drags the guy through the bedroom and then the chapter ends "..."? Well, that "..." is called an *ellipsis*, and it tells you that something else is going to follow. In C, an ellipsis after the argument of a function means there are more arguments to come.

No, we don't read those books either.

3. **Create a va_list.**
A `va_list` will be used to store the extra arguments that are passed to your function.

4. **Say where the variable arguments start.**
C needs to be told the name of the **last fixed argument**. In the case of our function, that'll be the `args` parameter.

5. **Then read off the variable arguments, one at a time.**
Now your arguments are all stored in the `va_list`, you can read them with `va_arg`. `va_arg` takes two values: the `va_list` and the **type** of the next argument. In your case, all of the arguments are `ints`.

6. **Finally...end the list.**
After you've finished reading all of the arguments, you need to tell C that you're finished. You do that with the `va_end` macro.

7. **Now you can call your function.**
Once the function is complete, you can call it:

```
print_ints(3, 79, 101, 32);
```

This will print out 79, 101, and 32 values.

Geek Bits

Functions vs. macros

A **macro** is used to rewrite your code before it's compiled. The macros you're using here (`va_start`, `va_arg`, and `va_end`) might look like functions, but they actually hide secret instructions that tell the *preprocessor* how to generate lots of extra smart code inside your program, just before compiling it.

there are no Dumb Questions

Q: Wait, why are `va_end` and `va_start` called *macros*? Aren't they just normal functions?

A: No, they are designed to look like ordinary functions, but they actually are replaced by the preprocessor with other code.

Q: And the preprocessor is?

A: The preprocessor runs just before the compilation step. Among other things, the preprocessor includes the headers into the code.

Q: Can I have a function with *just* variable arguments, and no fixed arguments at all?

A: No. You need to have at least one fixed argument in order to pass its name to `va_start`.

Q: What happens if I try to read more arguments from `va_arg` than have been passed in?

A: Random errors will occur.

Q: That sounds bad.

A: Yep, pretty bad.

Q: What if I try to read an `int` argument as a `double`, or something?

A: Random errors will occur.

Exercise

OK, now it's over to you. The guys in the Head First Lounge want to create a function that can return the total cost of a round of drinks, like this:

```
printf("Price is %.2f\n", total(3, MONKEY_GLAND, MUDSLIDE, FUZZY_NAVEL));
```

This will print "Price is 16.9".

Using the `price()` from a few pages back, complete the code for `total()`:

```
double total(int args, ...)
{
  double total = 0;
  ..........................................................................
  ..........................................................................
  ..........................................................................
  ..........................................................................
  ..........................................................................
  ..........................................................................
  ..........................................................................
  ..........................................................................
  return total;
}
```

Exercise Solution

OK, now it's over to you. The guys in the Head First Lounge want to create a function that can return the total cost of a round of drinks, like this:

```
printf("Price is %.2f\n", total(3, MONKEY_GLAND, MUDSLIDE, FUZZY_NAVEL));
```

This will print "Price is 16.9".

Using the `price()` from a few pages back, you were to complete the code for `total()`:

```
double total(int args, ...)
{
  double total = 0;
  va_list ap;
  va_start(ap, args);
  int i;
  for(i = 0; i < args; i++) {
    enum drink d = va_arg(ap, enum drink);
    total = total + price(d);
  }
  va_end(ap);
  return total;
}
```

Don't worry if your code doesn't look **exactly** like this. There are a few ways of writing it.

Test Drive

If you create a little test code to call the function, you can compile it and see what happens:

This is the test code.

```
main(){
  printf("Price is %.2f\n", total(2, MONKEY_GLAND, MUDSLIDE));
  printf("Price is %.2f\n", total(3, MONKEY_GLAND, MUDSLIDE, FUZZY_NAVEL));
  printf("Price is %.2f\n", total(1, ZOMBIE));
  return 0;
}
```

```
File Edit Window Help Cheers
> ./price_drinks
Price is 11.61
Price is 16.92
Price is 5.89
>
```

And this is the output.

Your code works!
Now you know how to use variable arguments to make your code simpler and more intuitive to use.

Yeah, baby! I could remember these even after one too many Monkey Glands...

BULLET POINTS

- Functions that accept a variable number of arguments are called **variadic functions**.
- To create variadic functions, you need to include the *stdarg.h* header file.
- The variable arguments will be stored in a `va_list`.
- You can control the `va_list` using `va_start()`, `va_arg()`, and `va_end()`.
- You will need at least one *fixed parameter*.
- Be careful that you don't try to read more parameters than you've been given.
- You will always need to know the data type of every parameter you read.

Your C Toolbox

You've got Chapter 7 under your belt, and now you've added advanced functions to your toolbox. For a complete list of tooltips in the book, see Appendix ii.

Function pointers let you pass functions around as if they were data.

Function pointers are the only pointers that don't need the * and & operators...

...but you can still use them if you want to.

The name of every function is a pointer to the function.

qsort() will sort an array.

Each sort function needs a pointer to a comparator function.

Functions with a variable number of arguments are called "variadic."

Comparator functions decide how to order two pieces of data.

Arrays of function pointers can help run different functions for different types of data.

stdarg.h lets you create variadic functions.

8 static and dynamic libraries

Hot-swappable code

The toe bone's statically linked to the foot bone, and the foot bone's statically linked to the ankle bone...

You've already seen the power of standard libraries.

Now it's time to use that power for your *own* code. In this chapter, you'll see how to create your **own libraries** and **reuse the same code across several programs**. What's more, you'll learn how to share code at runtime with **dynamic libraries**. You'll learn the secrets of the *coding gurus*. And by the end of the chapter, you'll be able to write code that you can scale and manage simply and efficiently.

Code you can take to the bank

Do you remember the `encrypt()` function you wrote a while back that encrypted the contents of a string? It was in a separate source code file that could be used by several programs:

```
#include "encrypt.h"

void encrypt(char *message)
{
  while (*message) {
    *message = *message ^ 31;
    message++;
  }
}
```

encrypt.c

```
void encrypt(char *message);
```

encrypt.h

Somebody else has written a function called `checksum()` that can be used to check if the contents of a string have been modified. Encrypting data and checking if data has been modified are both important for **security**. Separately, the two functions are useful, but together they could form the basis of a **security library**.

```
#include "checksum.h"

int checksum(char *message)
{
  int c = 0;
  while (*message) {
    c += c ^ (int)(*message);
    message++;
  }
  return c;
}
```

This function returns a number based on the contents of a string.

checksum.c

```
int checksum(char *message);
```

checksum.h

A security library? Hey, that's just what I'm looking for! The security at our bank is, well...kinda sloppy.

Head of security at the First Bank of Head First. He also cleans pools.

Sharpen your pencil

The guy at the bank has written a test program to see how the two functions work. He put all of the source into the same directory on his machine and then began to compile it.

He compiled the two security files into object files, and then wrote a test program:

```
File Edit Window Help
> gcc -c encrypt.c -o encrypt.o
> gcc -c checksum.c -o checksum.o
>
```

```
#include <stdio.h>
#include <encrypt.h>
#include <checksum.h>

int main()
{
  char s[] = "Speak friend and enter";
  encrypt(s);
  printf("Encrypted to '%s'\n", s);
  printf("Checksum is %i\n", checksum(s));
  encrypt(s);
  printf("Decrypted back to '%s'\n", s);
  printf("Checksum is %i\n", checksum(s));
  return 0;
}
```

encrypt() will encrypt your data. If you call it again, it will **decrypt** it.

And that's when the problems started. When he compiled the program, something went badly wrong…

```
File Edit Window Help
> gcc test_code.c encrypt.o checksum.o -o test_code
test_code.c:2:21: error: encrypt.h: No such file or directory
test_code.c:3:22: error: checksum.h: No such file or directory
>
```

Using a pencil, highlight which command or code made the compile fail.

Sharpen your pencil Solution

The problem is in the test program. All of the source files are stored in the same directory, but the test program includes the *encrypt.h* and *checksum.h* headers using **angle brackets** (< >).

```
#include <stdio.h>
#include <encrypt.h>
#include <checksum.h>

int main()
{
  char s[] = "Speak friend and enter";
  encrypt(s);
  printf("Encrypted to '%s'\n", s);
  printf("Checksum is %i\n", checksum(s));
  encrypt(s);
  printf("Decrypted back to '%s'\n", s);
  printf("Checksum is %i\n", checksum(s));
  return 0;
}
```

Angle brackets are for standard headers

If you use angle brackets in an `#include` statement, the compiler won't look for the headers in the *current* directory; instead, it will search for them in the **standard** header directories.

To get the program to compile with the **local** header files, you need to switch the angle brackets for simple quotes (" "):

stdio.h is stored in one of the standard header directories.

```
#include <stdio.h>
#include "encrypt.h"
#include "checksum.h"
```

encrypt.h and checksum.h are in the same directory as the program.

Now the code compiles correctly. It encrypts the test string to something unreadable.

```
File Edit Window Help <>
> gcc test_code.c encrypt.o checksum.o -o test_code
> ./test_code
Encrypted to 'Loz~t?ymvzq{?~q{?zqkzm'
Checksum is 89561741
Decrypted back to 'Speak friend and enter'
Checksum is 89548156
>
```

The checksum returns different values for different strings.

Calling the encrypt() function a second time returns the original string.

Where are the standard header directories?

So, if you include headers using angle brackets, where does the compiler go searching for the header files? You'll need to check the documentation that came with your compiler, but typically on a Unix-style system like the Mac or a Linux machine, the compiler will look for the files under these directories:

```
/usr/local/include
/usr/include
```

It will check /usr/local/include first.

/usr/local/include is often used for header files for third-party libraries.

/usr/include is normally used for operating system header files.

And if you're using the MinGW version of the gcc compiler, it will normally look here:

```
C:\MinGW\include
```

But what if you want to share code?

Sometimes you want to write code that will be available to lots of programs, in different folders, all over your computer. What do you do then?

Yeah, I gotta get security added to all these different programs. I don't want a separate copy of the security code for each one...

There are two sets of files that you want to share between programs: the ***.h* header files** and the ***.o* object files**. Let's look at how you can share each type.

Sharing .h header files

There are a few ways of sharing header files between different C projects:

1. **Store them in a standard directory.**
If you copy your header files into one of the standard directories like */usr/local/include*, you can include them in your source code using angle brackets.

```
#include <encrypt.h>
```

You can use angle brackets if your header files are in a standard directory.

2. **Put the full pathname in your include statement.**
If you want to store your header files somewhere else, such as ***/my_header_files***, you can add the directory name to your `include` statement:

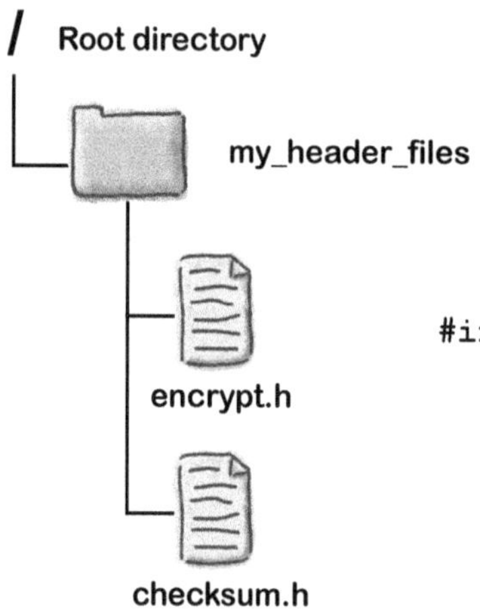
/ Root directory
my_header_files
encrypt.h
checksum.h

```
#include "/my_header_files/encrypt.h"
```

3. **You can tell the compiler where to find them.**
The final option is to tell the compiler where it can find your header files. You can do this with the **-I** option on `gcc`:

```
gcc -I/my_header_files test_code.c ... -o test_code
```

This tells the compiler to look in /my_header_files as well as the standard directories.

The `-I` option tells the `gcc` compiler that there's another place where it can find header files. It will still search in all the standard places, but first it will check the directory names in the `-I` option.

Share .o object files by using the full pathname

Now you can always put your *.o* object files into some sort of *shared directory*. Once you've done that, you can then just add the full path to the object files when you're compiling the program that uses them:

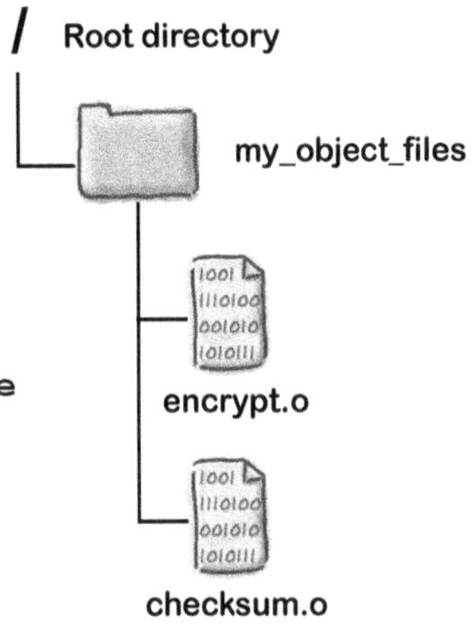
/
Root directory
my_object_files
1001
1110100
001010
1010111
encrypt.o
1001
1110100
001010
1010111
checksum.o

```
gcc -I/my_header_files test_code.c
      /my_object_files/encrypt.o
      /my_object_files/checksum.o -o test_code
```

Using the full pathname to the object files means you don't need a separate copy for each C project.

/my_object_files is like a **central store** for your object files.

If you compile your code with the *full pathname* to the object files you want to use, then *all* your C programs can share the same *encrypt.o* and *checksum.o* files.

Hmmm... That's OK if I just have one or two object files to share, but what if I have a lot of object files? I wonder if there's some way of telling the compiler about a bunch of them...

Yes, if you create an archive of object files, you can tell the compiler about a whole set of object files all at once.

An **archive** is just a bunch of object files wrapped up into a single file. By creating a single archive file of all of your security code, you can make it a lot easier to share the code between projects.

Let's see how to do it...

An archive contains .o files

Ever used a *.zip* or a *.tar* file? Then you know how easy it is to create a file that contains *other* files. That's exactly what a *.a* archive file is: a file containing other files.

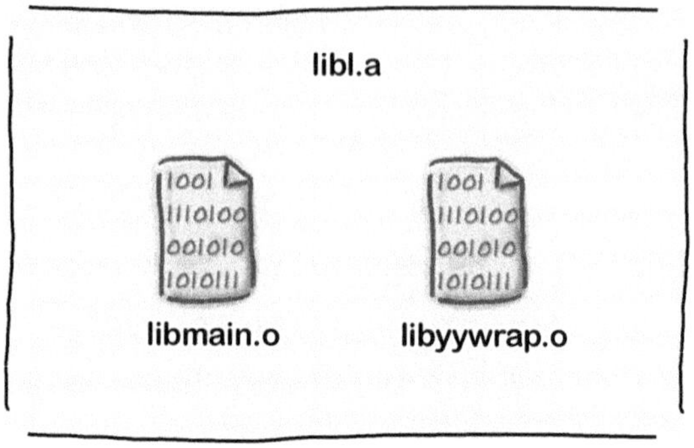
libl.a
1001
1110100
001010
1010111
libmain.o
1001
1110100
001010
1010111
libyywrap.o

Open up a terminal or a command prompt and change into one of the *library* directories. These are the directories like */usr/lib* or *C:\MinGW\lib* that contain the library code. In a library directory, you'll find a whole bunch of *.a* archives. And there's a command called nm that you can use to look inside them:

You might not have a libl.a on your machine, but you can try the command on any other .a file.

This is an archive called libl.a.

libmain.o

libyywrap.o

"T _main" means libmain.o contains a main() function.

```
File Edit Window Help SilenceInTheLibrary
> nm libl.a

libl.a(libmain.o):
00000000000003a8 s EH_frame0
                 U _exit
0000000000000000 T _main
00000000000003c0 S _main.eh
                 U _yylex

libl.a(libyywrap.o):
0000000000000350 s EH_frame0
0000000000000000 T _yywrap
0000000000000368 S _yywrap.eh
>
```

The nm command lists the **names** that are stored inside the archive. The *libl.a* archive shown here contains two object files: *libmain.o* and *libyywrap.o*. What these two object files are used for doesn't really matter; the point is that you can take a whole set of object files and turn them into a single archive file that you can use with gcc.

Before you see how to compile programs using *.a*, let's see how to store our *encrypt.o* and *checksum.o* files in an archive.

Create an archive with the ar command...

The **archive command** (`ar`) will store a set of object files in an archive file:

The r means the .a file will be updated if it already exists.

The s tells ar to create an index at the start of the .a file.

These are the files that will be stored in the archive.

```
ar -rcs libhfsecurity.a encrypt.o checksum.o
```

The c means that the archive will be created without any feedback.

This is the name of the .a file to create.

Did you notice that all of the *.a* files have names like ***lib<something>.a***? That's the standard way of naming archives. The names begin with *lib* because they are **static libraries**. You'll see what this means later on.

Watch it!

Make sure you always name your archives *lib<something>.a*.

If you don't name them this way, your compiler will have problems tracking them down.

...then store the .a in a library directory

Once you have an archive, you can store it in a library directory. Which library directory should you store it in? It's up to you, but you have a couple of choices:

- **You can put your .a file in a standard directory like /usr/local/lib.**
  Some coders like to install archives into a standard directory once they are sure it's working. On Linux, on Mac, and in Cygwin, the */usr/local/lib* directory is a good choice because that's the directory set aside for your own local custom libraries.

- **Put the .a file in some other directory.**
  If you are still developing your code, or if you don't feel comfortable installing your code in a system directory, you can always create your own library directory. For example: */my_lib*.

On most machines, you need to be an administrator to put files in /usr/local/lib.

Finally, compile your other programs

The whole point of creating a library archive was so you could use it with other programs. If you've installed your archive in a standard directory, you can compile your code using the `-l` switch:

Remember to list your source files **before** your -l libraries.

hfsecurity tells the compiler to look for an archive called libhfsecurity.a.

```
gcc test_code.c -lhfsecurity -o test_code
```

Do you need a -I option? It depends on where you put your headers.

If you're using several archives, you can set several -l options.

Can you see now why it's so important to name your archive *lib<something>.a*? The name that follows the `-l` option needs to match *part of the archive name*. So if your archive is called *libawesome.a*, you can compile your program with the `-lawesome` switch.

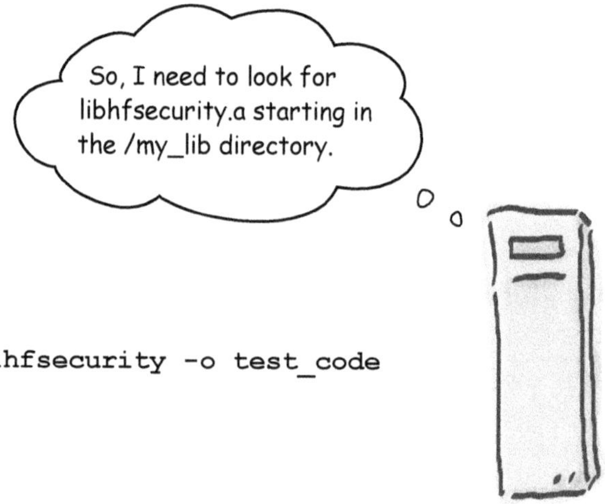
So, I need to look for libhfsecurity.a starting in the /my_lib directory.

But what if you put your archive somewhere else, like */my_lib*? In that case, you will need to use the `-L` option to say which directories to search:

```
gcc test_code.c -L/my_lib -lhfsecurity -o test_code
```

Geek Bits

The contents of the library directories can be *very* different from one machine to another. Why is that? It's because different operating systems have different *services* available. Each of the *.a* files is a separate library. There'll be libraries for connecting to the network, or creating GUI applications.

Try running the `nm` command on a few of the *.a* files. A lot of the names listed in each module will match compiled functions that you can use:

T means "Text," which means this is a function.

```
0000000000000000 T _yywrap
```

The name of the function is yywrap().

The `nm` command will tell you the name of each *.o* object file and then list the names that are available within the object file. If you see a **T** next to a name, that means it's the name of a function within the object file.

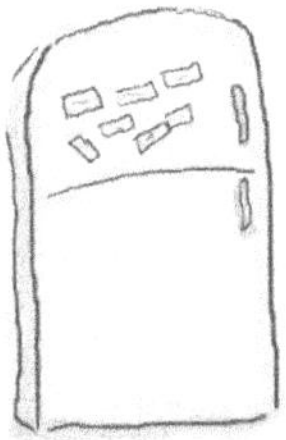

Make Magnets

The security guy is having trouble compiling one of the bank programs against the new security library. He has his source code as well as the `encrypt` and `checksum` source code in the same directory. For now, he wants to create the *libhfsecurity.a* archive in the same directory and then use it to compile his own program. Can you help him fix his makefile?

Note: the `bank_vault` program uses these `#include` statements:

```
#include <encrypt.h>
#include <checksum.h>
```

This is the makefile:

```
encrypt.o: encrypt.c
	gcc ................................ encrypt.c -o encrypt.o

checksum.o: checksum.c
	gcc ................................ checksum.c -o checksum.o

libhfsecurity.a: encrypt.o ................................
	ar -rcs ................................ encrypt.o ................................

bank_vault: bank_vault.c ................................
	gcc ................................ -I ............... -L ............... ................................ -o bank_vault
```

`-c` `-c` `checksum.o` `libhfsecurity.a` `bank_vault.c` `checksum.o` `-lhfsecurity` `.` `libhfsecurity.a` `/usr/lib` `/usr/local/include` `.` `-rcs` `/usr/local/lib` `-rcs`

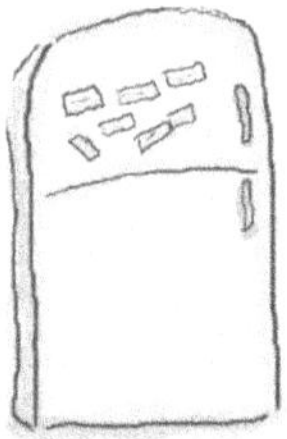

Make Magnets Solution

The security guy is having trouble compiling one of the bank programs against the new security library. He has his source code, as well as the `encrypt` and `checksum` source code in the same directory. For now, he wants to create the *libhfsecurity.a* archive in the same directory and then use it to compile his own program. You were to help him fix his makefile.

Note: the `bank_vault` program uses these `#include` statements:

```
#include <encrypt.h>
#include <checksum.h>
```

The #includes are using angle brackets. The compiler will need to be told where the header files are with a -I statement.

This is the makefile:

```
encrypt.o: encrypt.c
	gcc -c encrypt.c -o encrypt.o
```

This creates the object file from the encrypt.c source file.

```
checksum.o: checksum.c
	gcc -c checksum.c -o checksum.o
```

This creates the object file from the checksum.c source file.

```
libhfsecurity.a: encrypt.o checksum.o
	ar -rcs libhfsecurity.a encrypt.o checksum.o
```

You can't build the libhfsecurity.a archive until we've created encrypt.o and checksum.o.

This will create the libhfsecurity.a archive.

```
bank_vault: bank_vault.c libhfsecurity.a
	gcc bank_vault.c -I . -L . -lhfsecurity -o bank_vault
```

You need -lhfsecurity because the archive is called libhfsecurity.a.

The program's source code needs to be listed **before** the library code.

You need -I. because the header files are in the "." (current) directory.

You need the -L., because the archive is in the current directory.

`/usr/lib` `/usr/local/include` `-rcs` `/usr/local/lib` `-rcs`

BULLET POINTS

- Headers in angle brackets (< >) are read from the standard directories.
- Examples of standard header directories are */usr/include* and *C:\MinGW\include*.
- A library archive contains several object files.
- You can create an archive with `ar -rcs libarchive.a file0.o file1.o....`
- Library archive names should begin *lib.* and end *.a*.
- If you need to link to an archive called *libfred.a*, use `-lfred`.
- The `-L` flag should appear *after* the source files in the `gcc` command.

there are no Dumb Questions

Q: How do I know what the standard library directories are on my machine?

A: You need to check the documentation for your compiler. On most Unix-style machines, the library directories include */usr/lib* and */usr/local/lib*.

Q: When I try to put a library archive into my */usr/lib* directory, it won't let me. Why is that?

A: Almost certainly security. Many operating systems will prevent you from writing files to the standard directories in case you accidentally break one of the existing libraries.

Q: Is the `ar` format the same on all systems?

A: No. Different platforms can have slightly different archive formats. And the object code the archive contains will be completely different for different operating systems.

Q: If I've created a library archive, can I see what's inside it?

A: Yes. `ar -t <filename>` will list the contents of the archive.

Q: Are the object files in the archive linked together like an executable?

A: No. The object files are stored in the archive as distinct files.

Q: Can I put any kind of file in a library archive?

A: No. The `ar` command will check the file type before including it.

Q: Can I extract a single object file from an archive?

A: Yes. To extract the *encrypt.o* file from *libhfsecurity.a*, use `ar -x libhfsecurity.a encrypt.o`.

Q: Why is it called "static" linking?

A: Because it can't change once it's been done. When two files are linked together statically, it's like mixing coffee with milk: you can't separate them afterward.

Q: Should I use the HF security library to secure the data at my bank?

A: That's probably not a good idea.

The Linker Exposed

This week's interview:
What Exactly Do You Do?

Head First: Linker, thank you so much for making time for us today.

Linker: It's a pleasure.

Head First: I'd like to begin by asking if you ever feel overlooked by developers. Perhaps they don't understand exactly what it is you do?

Linker: I'm a very quiet person. A lot of people don't talk to me directly with the `ld` command.

Head First: `ld`?

Linker: Yes? See, that's me.

Head First: That's a lot of options on my screen.

Linker: Exactly. I have a lot of options. A lot of ways of joining programs together. That's why some people just use the `gcc` command.

Head First: So the compiler can link files together?

Linker: The compiler works out what needs to be done to join some files together and then calls me. And I do it. Quietly. You'd never know I was there.

Head First: I do have another question…

Linker: Yes?

Head First: I hate to sound foolish, but what exactly is it you do?

Linker: That's not a foolish question. I stitch pieces of compiled code together, a bit like a telephone operator.

Head First: I don't follow.

Linker: The old telephone operators would patch calls from one location to another so the two parties could talk. An object file is like that.

Head First: How so?

Linker: An object file might need to call a function that's stored in some other file. I link together the point in one file where the function call is made to the point in another file where the function lives.

Head First: You must have a lot of patience.

Linker: I like that kind of thing. I make lace in my spare time.

Head First: Really?

Linker: No.

Head First: Linker, thank you.

The Head First Gym is going global

The guys at the Head First Gym are going to spread their business **worldwide**. They are opening up outlets on four continents, and each one will contain their trademarked *Blood, Sweat, and Gears*™ gym equipment. So they're writing software for their ellipticals, treadmills, and exercise bikes. The software will read data from the sensors that are fitted on each device and then display information on a small LCD screen that will tell users what distance they've covered and how many calories they've burned.

That's the plan, anyway, but the guys need a little help. Let's look into the code in a little more detail.

Calculating calories

The team is still working on the software, but they've got one of the *key modules* ready. The *hfcal* library will generate the main data for the LCD display. If the code is told the user's weight, the virtual distance she's traveled on the machine, and then a special *coefficient*, it will generate the basic LCD details on the Standard Output:

```
#include <stdio.h>
#include <hfcal.h>

void display_calories(float weight, float distance, float coeff)
{
  printf("Weight: %3.2f lbs\n", weight);
  printf("Distance: %3.2f miles\n", distance);
  printf("Calories burned: %4.2f cal\n", coeff * weight * distance);
}
```

The hfcal.h header file just contains a declaration of the display_calories() function.

The weight is in pounds.

The distance is in miles.

This code will go into a file called hfcal.c.

hfcal.c

The team hasn't yet written the main code for each piece of equipment. When they do, there will be separate programs for the ellipticals, treadmills, and exercise bikes. Until then, they've created a *test program* that will call the *hfcal.c* code with some example data:

```
#include <stdio.h>
#include <hfcal.h>

int main()
{
  display_calories(115.2, 11.3, 0.79);
  return 0;
}
```

The test user weighs 115.2 pounds and has done 11.3 miles on the elliptical.

For this machine, the coefficient is 0.79.

elliptical.c

This is the test code.

The LCD display will capture the Standard Output.

Weight: 115.20 lbs
Distance: 11.30 miles
Calories burned: 1028.39 cal

This is what the display looks like for the test program.

Sharpen your pencil

Now that you've seen the source code for the test program and the *hfcal* library, it's time to build the code.

Let's see how well you remember the commands.

1. Start by creating an object file called *hfcal.o*. The *hfcal.h* header is going to be stored in *./includes*:

....

2. Next, you need to create an object file called *elliptical.o* from the *elliptical.c* test program:

....

3. Now, you need to create an archive library from *hfcal.o* and store it in *./libs*:

....

4. Finally, create the `elliptical` executable using *elliptical.o* and the *hfcal* archive:

....

Sharpen your pencil Solution

Now that you've seen the source code for the test program and the *hfcal* library, it's time to build the code.

Let's see how well you remembered the commands.

1. Start by creating an object file called *hfcal.o*. The *hfcal.h* header is going to be stored in *./includes*:

The hfcal.c program needs to know where the header file is.

```
gcc -I./includes -c hfcal.c -o hfcal.o
```

Did you remember to add the -I flag?

-c means "just create the object file; don't link it."

2. Next, you need to create an object file called *elliptical.o* from the *elliptical.c* test program:

```
gcc -I./includes -c elliptical.c -o elliptical.o
```

Again, you need to tell the compiler that the headers are in ./includes.

3. Now, you need to create an archive library from *hfcal.o* and store it in *./libs*:

The library needs to be named lib....a.

```
ar -rcs ./libs/libhfcal.a hfcal.o
```

The archive needs to go into the ./libs directory.

4. Finally, create the `elliptical` executable using *elliptical.o* and the *hfcal* archive:

-lhfcal tells the compiler to look for libhfcal.a.

```
gcc elliptical.o -L./libs -lhfcal -o elliptical
```

You're building the program using elliptical.o and the library.

-L./libs tells the compiler where the library is stored.

Now that you've built the elliptical program, you can run it on the console:

```
File Edit Window Help SilenceInTheLibrary
> ./elliptical
Weight: 115.20 lbs
Distance: 11.30 miles
Calories burned: 1028.39 cal
>
```

But things are a bit more complex...

Turns out, there's a problem. The Head First Gyms are expanding *everywhere*, in different countries that use different languages and different measures. For example, in England, the machines need to report information in **kilograms** and **kilometers**:

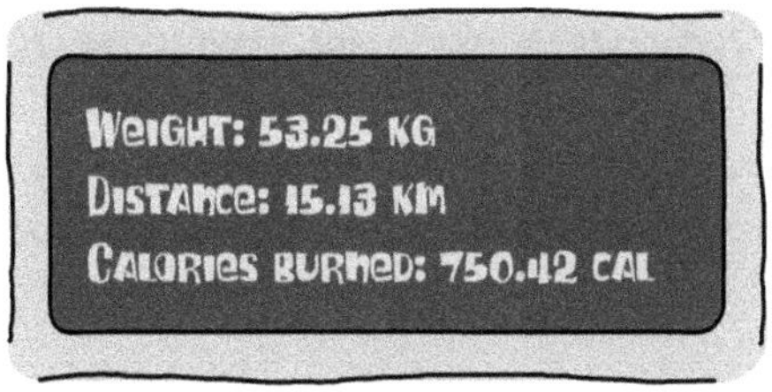
WEIGHT: 53.25 KG
DISTANCE: 15.13 KM
CALORIES BURNED: 750.42 CAL

In the US, measurements need to be in pounds and miles.

But in England, measurements need to be in kgs and kms.

The gyms have lots of different types of equipment. If they have 20 different types of machines, and they have gyms in 50 countries, that means there will be ***1,000*** different versions of the software. That's a *lot* of different versions.

And then there are other problems too:

- If an engineer upgrades the sensors used on a machine, she might need to upgrade the code that talks to them.
- If the displays ever change, the engineers might need to change the code that generates the output.
- Plus many, many other variations.

If you think about it, you get the same kinds of problems when you write any software. Different machines might require different *device driver code*, or they might need to talk to different *databases* or different *graphical user interfaces*. You probably won't be able to build a version of your code that will work on *every* machine, so what should you do?

Programs are made out of lots of pieces...

You've already seen that you can build programs using different pieces of **object code**. You've created *.o* files and *.a* archives, and you've linked them together into single executables.

Raisins, flour,
butter, anchovies...

...but once they're linked, you can't change them

The problem is that if you build programs like this, they are **static**. Once you've created a single executable file from those separate pieces of object code, you really have *no way* of changing any of the ingredients without rebuilding the whole program.

Hmmmm...maybe I
should have used
cranberries.

The program is just a large chunk of object code. There's no way to separate the **display code** from the **sensor code**; it's all lost in the mix.

Wouldn't it be dreamy if there were a way to run a program using switchable pieces of object code? But I guess that's just a fantasy...

Dynamic linking happens at runtime

The reason you can't change the different pieces of object code in an executable file is because, well, they are all contained in a single file. They were **statically linked** together when the program was compiled.

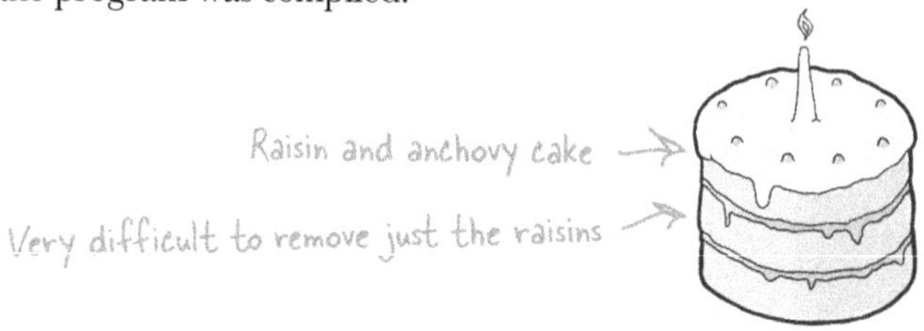
Raisin and anchovy cake
Very difficult to remove just the raisins

But if your program wasn't just a single file—if your program was made up of lots of separate files that only joined together when the program was run—you would avoid the problem.

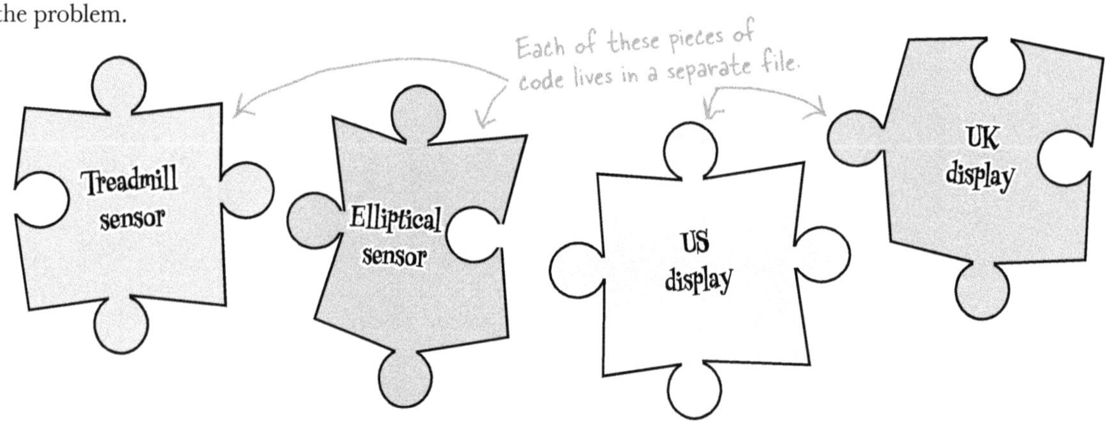
Each of these pieces of code lives in a separate file.
Treadmill sensor
Elliptical sensor
US display
UK display

The trick, then, is to find a way of storing pieces of object code in separate files and then ***dynamically linking them together*** only when the program runs.

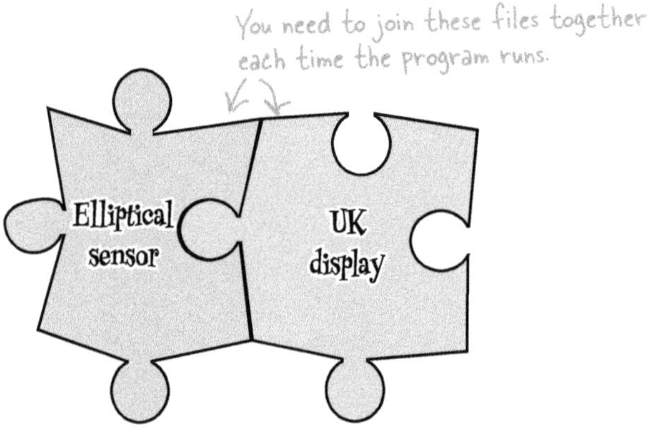
You need to join these files together each time the program runs.
Elliptical sensor
UK display

Can you link .a at runtime?

So you need to have separate files containing separate pieces of object code. But you've already got separate files containing object code: the *.o* object files and the *.a* archive files. Does that mean you just need to tell the computer not to link the *.o* files until you run the program?

Sadly, it's not that easy. Simple object files and archives don't have quite enough information in them to be linked together at runtime. There are other things our *dynamic library files* will need, like the names of the other files they need to link to.

Dynamic libraries are object files on steroids

So, dynamic libraries are *similar* to those *.o* object files you've been creating for a while, but they're not quite the same. Like an archive file, a dynamic library can be built from several *.o* object files, but unlike an archive, the object files are properly linked together in a dynamic library to form a single piece of object code.

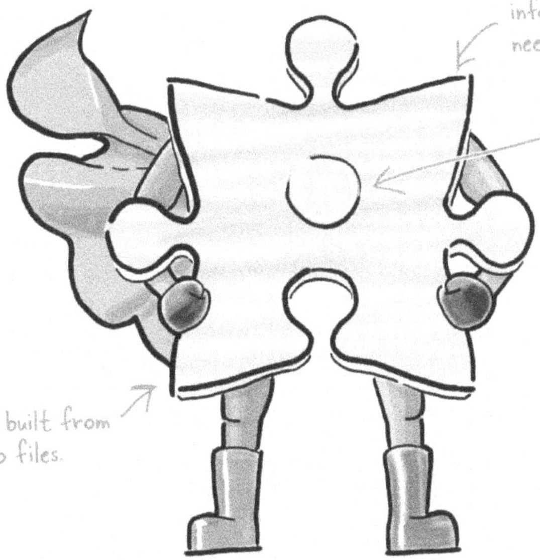

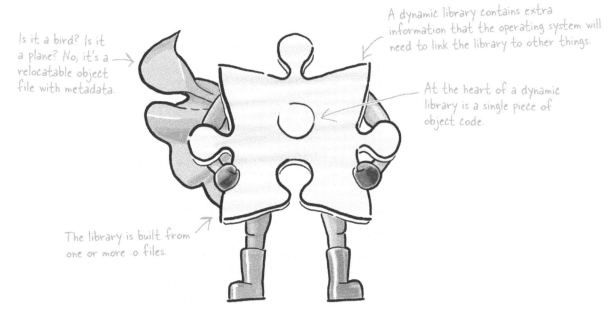

A dynamic library contains extra information that the operating system will need to link the library to other things.
Is it a bird? Is it a plane? No, it's a relocatable object file with metadata.
At the heart of a dynamic library is a single piece of object code.
The library is built from one or more .o files.

So how do you create your own dynamic libraries? Let's see.

First, create an object file

If you're going to convert the *hfcal.c* code into a dynamic library, then you need to begin by compiling it into a *.o* object file, like this:

-c means "Don't link the code."

```
gcc -I/includes -fPIC -c hfcal.c -o hfcal.o
```

The hfcal.h header is in /includes.

What does -fPIC mean?

Did you spot the difference? You're creating the *hfcal.o* exactly the same as before *except* you're adding an extra flag: **`-fPIC`**. This tells `gcc` that you want to create **position-independent code**. Some operating systems and processors need to build libraries from position-independent code so that they can decide at runtime where they want to load it into memory.

Now, the truth is that on *most* systems you don't need to specify this option. Try it out on your system. If it's not needed, it won't do any harm.

Position-independent code can be moved around in memory.

Geek Bits

So, what is **position-independent code**?

Position-independent code is code that doesn't mind where the computer loads it into memory. Imagine you had a dynamic library that expected to find the value of some piece of global data 500 bytes away from where the library is loaded. Bad things would happen if the operating system decided to load the library somewhere else in memory. If the compiler is told to create position-independent code, it will avoid problems like this.

Some operating systems, like Windows, use a technique called **memory mapping** when loading dynamic libraries, which means all code is effectively position-independent. If you compile your code on Windows, you might find that `gcc` will give you a warning that the `-fPIC` option is not needed. You can either remove the `-fPIC` flag, or ignore the warning. Either way, your code will be fine.

What you call your dynamic library depends on your platform

Dynamic libraries are available on most operating systems, and they all work in pretty much the same way. But what they're *called* can vary a lot. On Windows, dynamic libraries are usually called **dynamic link libraries** and they have the extension ***.dll***. On Linux and Unix, they're **shared object files** (***.so***), and on the Mac, they're just called **dynamic libraries** (***.dylib***). But even though the files have different extensions, you can create them in very similar ways:

```
gcc -shared hfcal.o -o  C:\libs\hfcal.dll          <- MinGW on Windows
                        /libs/libhfcal.dll.a       <- Cygwin on Windows
                        /libs/libhfcal.so          <- Linux or Unix
                        /libs/libhfcal.dylib       <- Mac
```

The `-shared` option tells `gcc` that you want to convert a *.o* object file into a dynamic library. When the compiler creates the dynamic library, it will store the name of the library inside the file. So, if you create a library called *libhfcal.so* on a Linux machine, the *libhfcal.so* file will remember that its library name is *hfcal*. Why is that important? It means that if you compile a library with one name, you can't just rename the file afterward.

If you need to rename a library, recompile it with the new name.

BANG!
Watch it!

On some older Mac systems, the -shared flag is not available.

But don't worry, on those machines, if you just replace it with `-dynamiclib`*, everything will work exactly the same way.*

Compiling the elliptical program

Once you've created the dynamic library, you can use it just like a static library. So, you can build the `elliptical` program like this:

```
gcc -I\include -c elliptical.c -o elliptical.o
gcc elliptical.o -L\libs -lhfcal -o elliptical
```

Even though these are the same commands you would use if *hfcal* were a static archive, the compile will work differently. Because the library's dynamic, the compiler won't include the library code into the executable file. Instead, it will insert some placeholder code that will track down the library and link to it at runtime.

Now, let's see if the program runs.

Library names in MinGW and Cygwin

Both MinGW and Cygwin let you use several name formats for dynamic libraries. The *hfcal* library can have any of these names:

libhfcal.dll.a

libhfcal.dll

hfcal.dll

Test Drive

You've created the dynamic library in the */libs* directory and built the elliptical test program. Now you need to run it. Because *hfcal* isn't in one of the standard library directories, you'll need to make sure the computer can find the library when you run the program.

On a Mac

On the Mac, you can just run the program. When the program is compiled on the Mac, the full path to the */libs/libhfcal.dylib* file is stored inside the executable, so when the program starts, it knows exactly where to find the library.

```
File Edit Window Help I'mAMac
> ./elliptical
Weight: 115.20 lbs
Distance: 11.30 miles
Calories burned: 1028.39 cal
>
```

← Mac

On Linux

That's not quite what happens on Linux.

On Linux, and most versions of Unix, the compiler just records the filename of the *libhfcal.so* library, *without* including the path name. That means if the library is stored outside the standard library directories (like */usr/lib*), the program won't have any way of finding the *hfcal* library. To get around this, Linux checks additional directories that are stored in the `LD_LIBRARY_PATH` variable. If you make sure your library directory is added to the `LD_LIBRARY_PATH`—and if you make sure you **export** it—then `elliptical` will find *libhfcal.so*.

On Linux, you need to set the LD_LIBRARY_PATH variable so the program can find the library. →

There's no need to do this if the library is somewhere standard, like /usr/lib.

You need to make sure the variable is exported.

```
File Edit Window Help I'mLinux
> export LD_LIBRARY_PATH=$LD_LIBRARY_PATH:/libs
> ./elliptical
Weight: 115.20 lbs
Distance: 11.30 miles
Calories burned: 1028.39 cal
>
```

↑ Linux

On Windows

Now let's take a look at how to run code that's been compiled using the Cygwin and MinGW versions of the `gcc` compiler. Both compilers create Windows DLL libraries and Windows executables. And just like Linux, Windows executables store the name of the *hfcal* library *without* the name of the directory where it's stored.

But Windows doesn't use a `LD_LIBRARY_PATH` variable to hunt the library down. Instead, Windows programs look for the library in the current directory, and if they don't find it there, the programs search for it using the directories stored in the `PATH` variable.

Using Cygwin

If you've compiled the program using Cygwin, you can run the program from the *bash shell* like this:

File Edit Window Help I'mCygwin

```
> PATH="$PATH:/libs"
> ./elliptical
Weight: 115.20 lbs
Distance: 11.30 miles
Calories burned: 1028.39 cal
>
```

← Windows using Cygwin

Using MinGW

And if you've compiled the program using the MinGW compiler, you can run it from the *command prompt* like this:

File Edit Window Help I'mMinGW

```
C:\code> PATH="%PATH%;C:\libs"
C:\code> ./elliptical
Weight: 115.20 lbs
Distance: 11.30 miles
Calories burned: 1028.39 cal
C:\code>
```

← Windows using MinGW

Does this seem a little complex? It is, which is why most programs that use dynamic libraries store them in one of the standard directories. That means on Linux and the Mac, they are normally in directories like */usr/lib* or */usr/local/lib*; and in Windows, developers normally keep *.DLLs* stored in the same directory as the executable.

Long Exercise

The guys at the Head First Gym are about to ship a treadmill over to England. The embedded server is running Linux, and it already has the US code installed.

The tech guys installed the library in */usr/local/lib.*

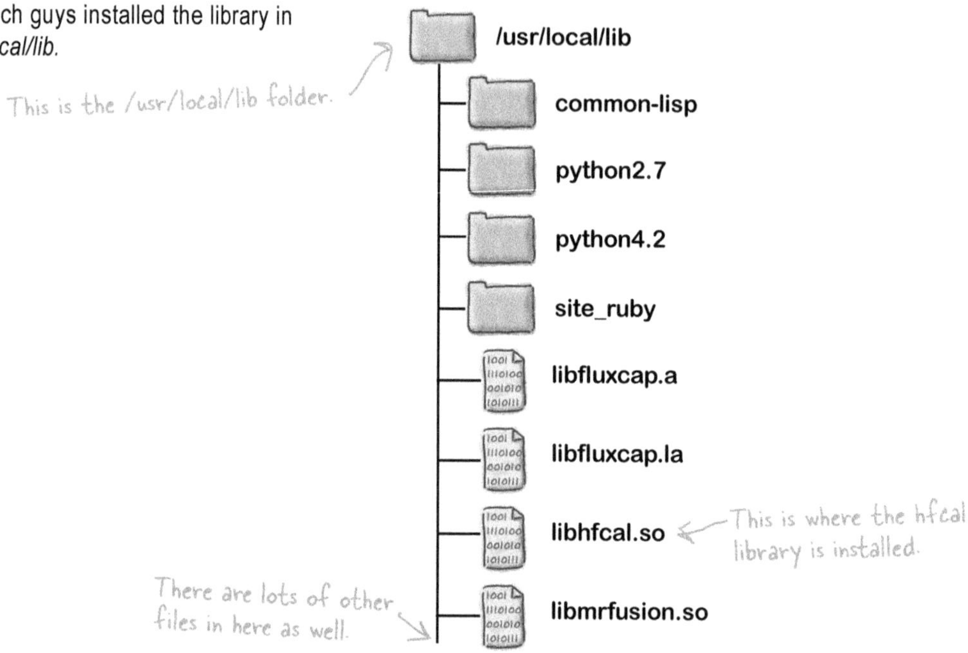
/usr/local/lib
This is the /usr/local/lib folder.
common-lisp
python2.7
python4.2
site_ruby
libfluxcap.a
libfluxcap.la
libhfcal.so
This is where the hfcal library is installed.
There are lots of other files in here as well.
libmrfusion.so

And this machine also has the header file for the *hfcal* library installed in */usr/local/include*:

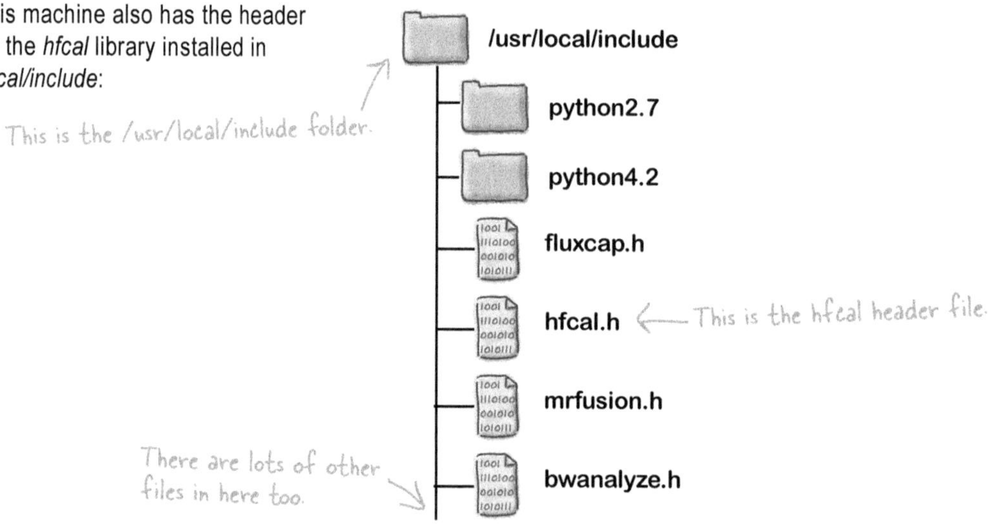
/usr/local/include
This is the /usr/local/include folder.
python2.7
python4.2
fluxcap.h
hfcal.h
This is the hfcal header file.
mrfusion.h
There are lots of other files in here too.
bwanalyze.h

The tech guys like to install libraries using these directories because it's a little more standard. The machine is all configured for use in the US, but things need to change.

The system needs to be updated for use in the gym it is being shipped to in England. That means the treadmill's display code needs to be switched from miles and pounds to kilometers and kilograms.

This is the code for the UK gym.

```
#include <stdio.h>
#include <hfcal.h>

void display_calories(float weight, float distance, float coeff)
{
  printf("Weight: %3.2f kg\n", weight / 2.2046);
  printf("Distance: %3.2f km\n", distance * 1.609344);
  printf("Calories burned: %4.2f cal\n", coeff * weight * distance);
}
```

This code displays the information in kms and kgs.

hfcal_UK.c

This file is in the /home/ebrown directory.

The software that's already installed on the machine needs to use this new version of the code. Because the applications connect to this code as a dynamic library, all you need to do is compile it into the */usr/local/lib* directory.

Assuming that you are already in the same directory as the *hfcal_UK.c* file and that you have write permissions on all the directories, what commands would you need to type to compile this new version of the library?

If the treadmill's main application is called */opt/apps/treadmill*, what would you need to type in to run the program?

Long Exercise Solution

The guys at the Head First Gym are about to ship a treadmill over to England. The embedded server is running Linux, and it already has the US code installed.

The tech guys installed the library in */usr/local/lib.*

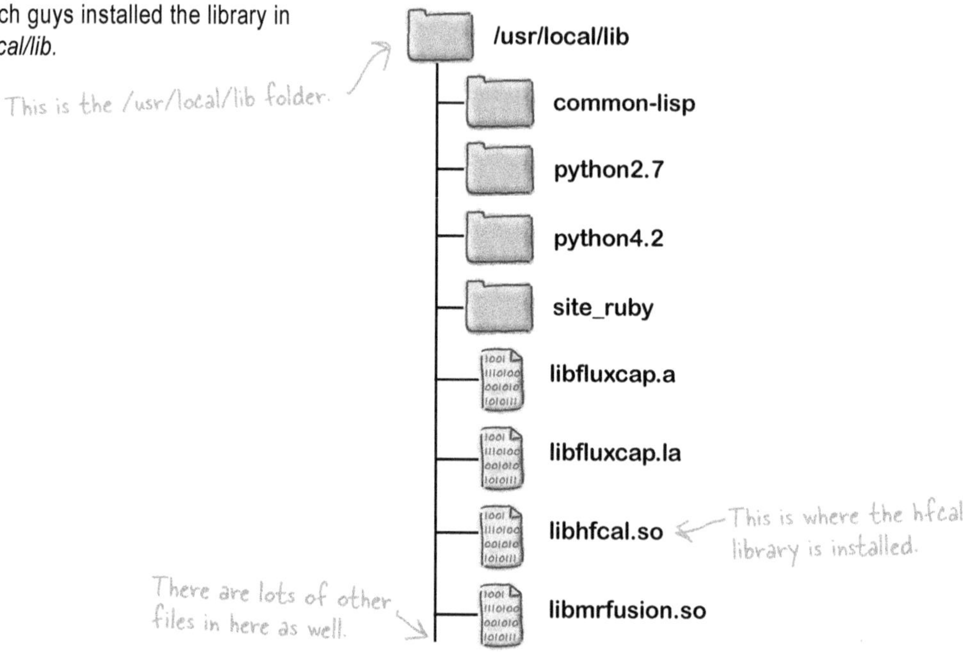
/usr/local/lib
This is the /usr/local/lib folder.
common-lisp
python2.7
python4.2
site_ruby
libfluxcap.a
libfluxcap.la
libhfcal.so
This is where the hfcal library is installed.
libmrfusion.so
There are lots of other files in here as well.

And this machine also has the header file for the *hfcal* library installed in */usr/local/include*:

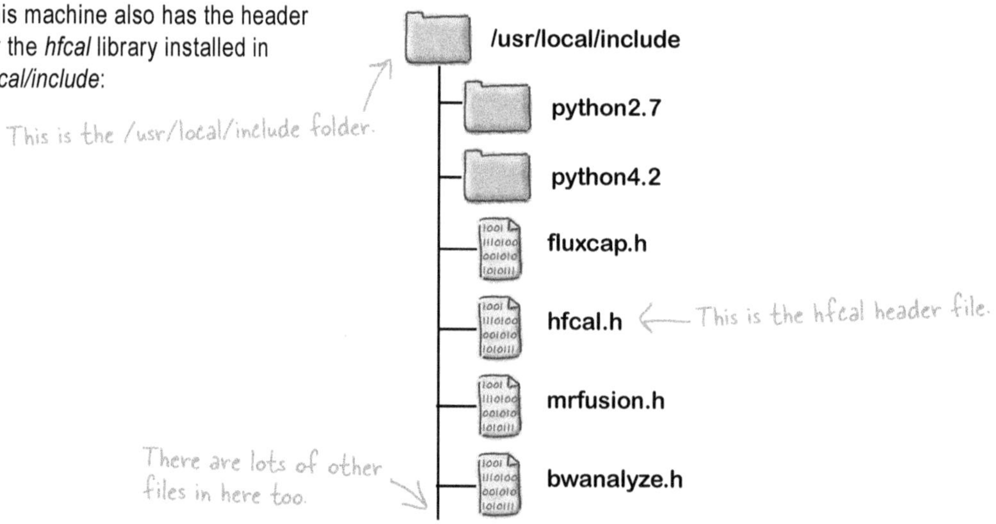
/usr/local/include
This is the /usr/local/include folder.
python2.7
python4.2
fluxcap.h
hfcal.h
This is the hfcal header file.
mrfusion.h
bwanalyze.h
There are lots of other files in here too.

The tech guys like to install libraries using these directories because it's a little more standard. The machine is all configured for use in the US, but things need to change.

The system needs to be updated for use in the gym it is being shipped to in England. That means the treadmill's display code needs to be switched from miles and pounds to kilometers and kilograms.

```
#include <stdio.h>
#include <hfcal.h>

void display_calories(float weight, float distance, float coeff)
{
  printf("Weight: %3.2f kg\n", weight / 2.2046);
  printf("Distance: %3.2f km\n", distance * 1.609344);
  printf("Calories burned: %4.2f cal\n", coeff * weight * distance);
}
```

hfcal_UK.c

The software that's already installed on the machine needs to use this new version of the code. Because the applications connect to this code as a dynamic library, all you need to do is compile it into the */usr/local/lib* directory.

Assuming that you are already in the same directory as the *hfcal_UK.c* file and that you have write permissions on all the directories, what commands would you need to type to compile this new version of the library?

You need to compile the source code to an object file. → `gcc -c -fPIC hfcal_UK.c -o hfcal.o` ← You don't need to set a -I option, because the header file is in a standard directory.

Then you need to convert the object file to a shared object. → `gcc -shared hfcal.o -o /usr/local/lib/libhfcal.so`

If the treadmill's main application is called */opt/apps/treadmill*, what would you need to type in to run the program?

`/opt/apps/treadmill` ← You don't need to set the LD_LIBRARY_PATH variable because the library is in a standard directory.

Did you spot that the library and headers had been installed in standard directories? That meant you didn't have to use a -I flag when you were compiling the code, and you didn't have to set the LD_LIBRARY_PATH variable when you were running the code.

Test Drive

Now that you've updated the library on the English treadmill, let's try it against an **American** machine. This is one of the unaltered US treadmills using the original version of *libhfcal.so* library:

This is an American treadmill.

The `treadmill` application starts when the machine boots up, so after using the machine for a while the display shows this:

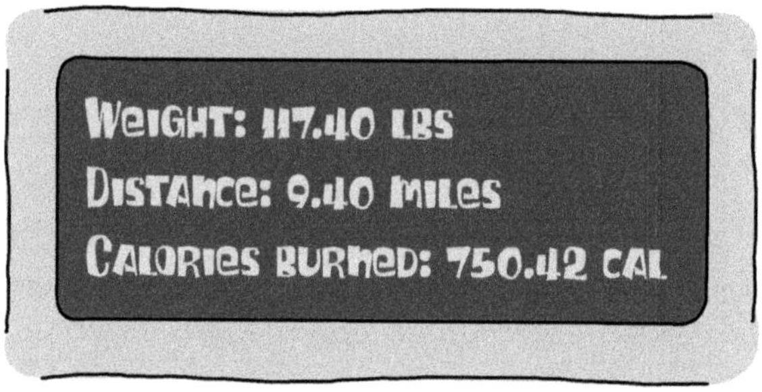
Weight: 117.40 lbs
Distance: 9.40 miles
Calories burned: 750.42 cal

The `treadmill` program on the US. machine is dynamically linking itself to the version of the *libhfcal.so* library that was compiled from the US version of the `hfcal` program.

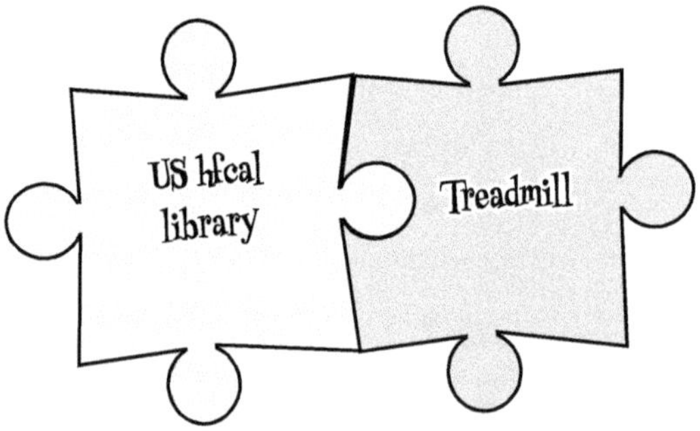
US hfcal library
Treadmill

But what about the treadmill in England?

The **English** machine has the same `treadmill` program installed, but on this machine you recompiled the *libhfcal.so* library from the source code in the *hfcal_UK.c* file.

This is an English treadmill.

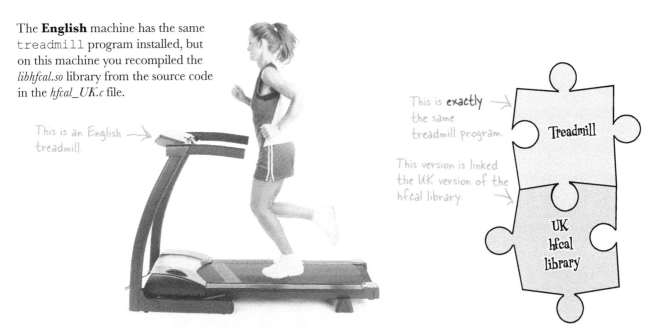

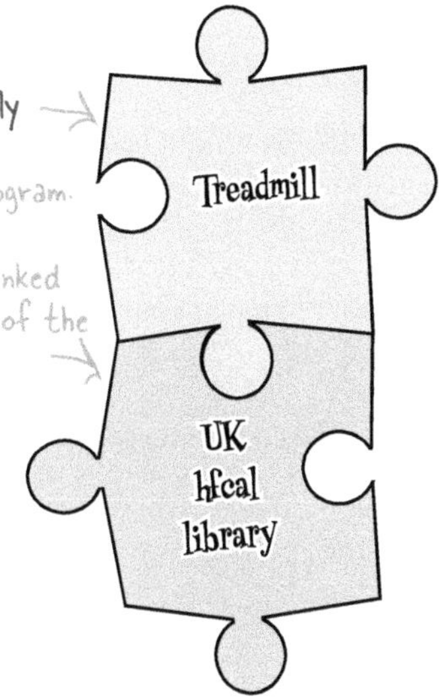
This is exactly the same treadmill program.
Treadmill
This version is linked the UK version of the hfcal library.
UK hfcal library

When the runner has been on the treadmill for a similar distance, the display looks like this:

The weight is displayed in kgs.
The distance is displayed in kms.
WEIGHT: 53.25 KG
DISTANCE: 15.13 KM
CALORIES BURNED: 750.42 CAL
The calories are still displayed in calories.

It worked.

Even though the `treadmill` program was never recompiled, it was able to pick up the code from the new library **dynamically**.

Dynamic libraries make it easier to change code at **runtime**. You can update an application without needing to recompile it. If you have several programs that share the same piece of code, you can update them *all at the same time*. Now that you know how to create dynamic libraries, you've become a much more powerful C developer.

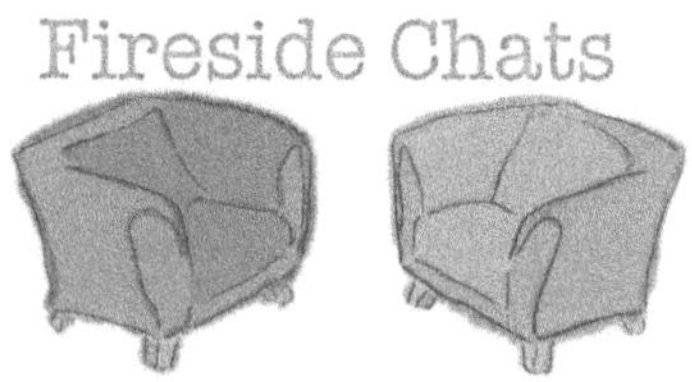
Fireside Chats

Tonight's talk: **Two renowned proponents of modular software discuss the pros and cons of static and dynamic linking.**

Static: Well, I think we can both agree that creating code in smaller modules is a good idea.

Dynamic: Absolutely.

Static: It makes so much sense, doesn't it?

Dynamic: Yes.

Static: Keeps the code manageable.

Dynamic: Yes.

Static: Nice, large programs.

Dynamic: Large?

Static: Yes. Nice BIG programs with their dependencies fixed.

Dynamic: That doesn't sound like a good idea.

Static: What do you mean, old friend?

Dynamic: I think programs should be made of lots of small files that link together only when the program is run.

Static: Well… <laughs>…that's a very…but no, seriously.

Dynamic: I'm being serious.

Static: What? Lots of separate files? Joined together *willy-nilly*?!

Dynamic: I prefer the term *dynamically* to *willy-nilly*.

Static: But that's…that's…a recipe for ***chaos***!

Dynamic: It means I can change my mind later.

Static: You should get things right in the first place.

Dynamic: But that's not always possible. All large programs should use dynamic linking.

Static: *All* programs?

Dynamic: I think so.

Static: What about the Linux kernel, hmmm? That large enough? And I believe that's…

Dynamic: …statically linked. Yeah, I know. That's your one.

Static: Static linking might not be as *loose* and *informal*, but you know what? Static programs are simple to use. Single files. Want to install one? Just copy the executable. No need for DLL hell.

Dynamic: Look, we'll just have to agree to disagree.

Static: I can't change your mind?

Dynamic: No.

Static: So, you're telling me your mind is statically linked?

BULLET POINTS

- Dynamic libraries are linked to programs at runtime.
- Dynamic libraries are created from one or more object files.
- On some machines, you need to compile them with the `-fPIC` option.
- `-fPIC` makes the object code position-independent.
- You can skip `-fPIC` on many systems.
- The `-shared` compiler option creates a dynamic library.
- Dynamic libraries have different names on different systems.
- Life is simpler if your dynamic libraries are stored in standard directories.
- Otherwise, you might need to set `PATH` and `LD_LIBRARY_PATH` variables.

there are no Dumb Questions

Q: Why are dynamic libraries so different on different operating systems?

A: Operating systems like to optimize the way they load dynamic libraries, so they've each evolved different requirements for dynamic libraries.

Q: I tried to change the name of my library by renaming the file, but the compiler couldn't find it anymore. Why not?

A: When the compiler creates a dynamic library, it stores the name of the library inside the file. If you rename the file, it will then have the wrong name inside the file and will get confused. If you want to change its name, you should recompile the library.

Q: Why does Cygwin support so many different naming conventions for dynamic library files?

A: Cygwin makes it easy to compile Unix software on a Windows machine. Because Cygwin creates a Unix-style environment, it borrows a lot of Unix conventions. So it prefers to give libraries *.a* extensions, even if they're dynamic DLLs.

Q: Are Cygwin dynamic libraries real DLLs?

A: Yes. But because they depend on the Cygwin system, you'll need to do a little work before non-Cygwin code can use them.

Q: Why does the MinGW compiler support the same dynamic library name format as Cygwin?

A: Because the two projects are closely associated and share a lot of code. The big difference is that MinGW programs can run on machines that don't have Cygwin installed.

Q: Why doesn't Linux just store library pathnames in executables? That way, you wouldn't need to set `LD_LIBRARY_PATH`.

A: It was a design choice. By not storing the pathname, it gives you a lot more control over which version of a library a program can use—which is great when you're developing new libraries.

Q: Why doesn't Cygwin use `LD_LIBRARY_PATH` to find libraries?

A: Because it needs to use Windows DLLs. Windows DLLs are loaded using the `PATH` variable.

Q: Which is better? Static or dynamic linking?

A: It depends. Static linking means you get a small, fast executable file that is easier to move from machine to machine. Dynamic linking means that you can configure the program at runtime more.

Q: If different programs use the same dynamic library, does it get loaded more than once? Or is it shared in memory?

A: That depends on the operating system. Some operating systems will load separate copies for each process. Others load shared copies to save memory.

Q: Are dynamic libraries the best way of configuring an application?

A: Usually, it's simpler to use configuration files. But if you're going to connect to some external device, you'd normally need separate dynamic libraries to act as drivers.

Your C Toolbox

You've got Chapter 8 under your belt, and now you've added static and dynamic libraries to your toolbox. For a complete list of tooltips in the book, see Appendix ii.

-L<name> adds a directory to the list of standard library directories.

#include <> looks in standard directories such as /usr/include.

-l<name> links to a file in standard directories such as /usr/lib.

-I<name> adds a directory to the list of standard include directories.

The ar command creates a library archive of object files.

Library archives have names like libsomething.a.

gcc -shared converts object files into dynamic libraries.

Dynamic libraries are linked at runtime.

Library archives are statically linked.

Dynamic libraries have different names on different operating systems.

Dynamic libraries have .so, .dylib, .dll, or .dll.a extensions.

Name:

Date:

C Lab 2

OpenCV

This lab gives you a spec that describes a program for you to investigate and build, using the knowledge you've gained over the last few chapters.

This project is bigger than the ones you've seen so far. So read the whole thing before you get started, and give yourself a little time. And don't worry if you get stuck; there are no new C concepts in here, so you can move on in the book and come back to the lab later.

It's up to you to finish the job, but we won't give you the code for the answer.

The spec: turn your computer into an intruder detector

Imagine if your computer could keep an eye on your house while you're out and tell you who's been prowling around. Well, using its default webcam and the cleverness of *OpenCV*, it can!

Here's what you're going to create.

The intruder detector

Your computer will constantly survey its surroundings using its webcam. When it detects movement, it will write the current webcam image to a file. And if you store this file on a network drive or use a file synchronization service such as Dropbox, you'll have instant evidence of any intruders.

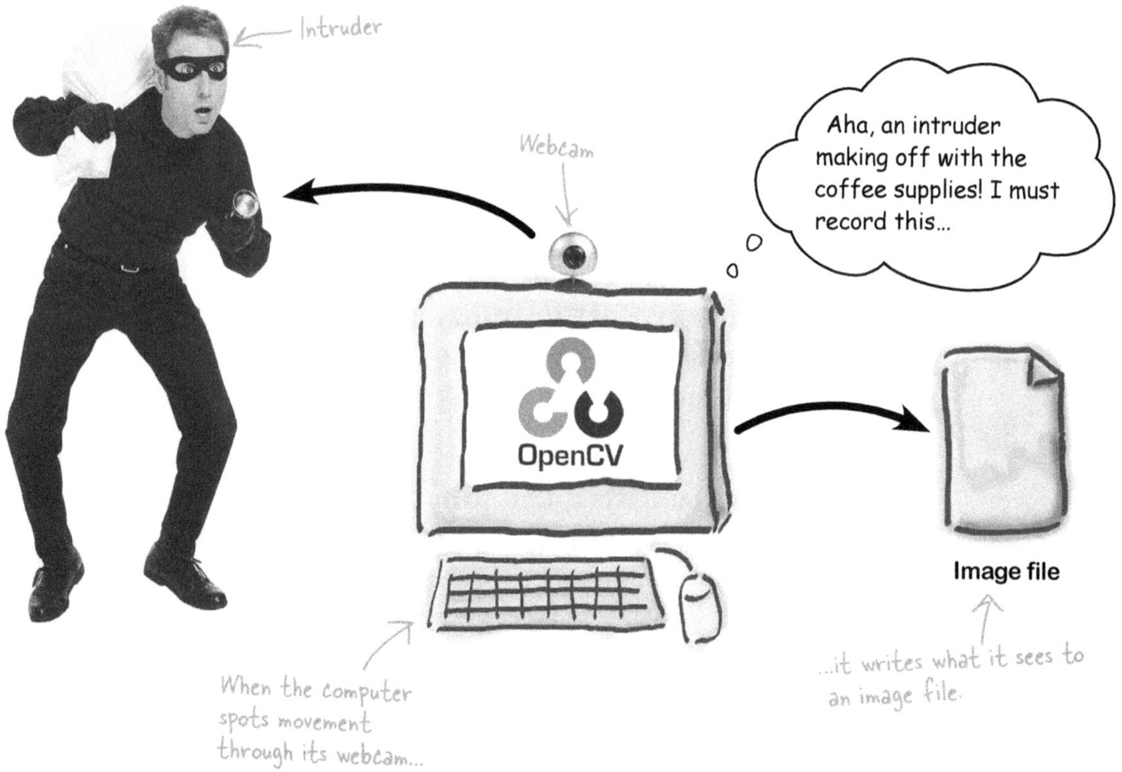
Intruder
Webcam
Aha, an intruder making off with the coffee supplies! I must record this...
OpenCV
Image file
When the computer spots movement through its webcam...
...it writes what it sees to an image file.

OpenCV

OpenCV is an open source computer vision library. It allows you to take input from your computer camera, process it, and analyze real-time image data and make decisions based on what your computer sees. What's more, you can do all of this using C code.

OpenCV is available on Window, Linux, and Mac platforms.

You can find the OpenCV wiki here:

http://opencv.willowgarage.com/wiki/FullOpenCVWiki

Installing OpenCV

You can install OpenCV on Windows, Linux, or Mac. The install guide is here, and includes links to the latest stable releases:

http://opencv.willowgarage.com/wiki/InstallGuide

Once you've installed OpenCV, you should see a folder on your computer labeled *samples*. It's worth taking a look at these. There are also links to tutorials on the OpenCV wiki. You'll need to investigate OpenCV in order to complete this lab.

If you want to get deep into OpenCV, we recommend the book *Learning OpenCV* by Gary Bradski and Adrian Kaehler (O'Reilly).

We found the book Learning OpenCV inspirational.

Learning
OpenCV
O'REILLY

What your code should do

Your C code should do the following.

Take input from your computer camera

You need to work with real-time data that comes in from your computer camera, so the first thing you need to do is capture that data. There's an OpenCV function that will help you with this called **`cvCreateCameraCapture(0)`**. It returns a pointer to a `CvCapture struct`. This pointer is your hotline to the webcam device, and you'll use it to grab images.

Remember to check for errors in case your computer can't find a camera. If you can't contact the webcam, you'll receive a `NULL` pointer from `cvCreateCameraCapture(0)`.

Image file

Grab an image from the webcam

You can read the latest image from the webcam using the `cvQueryFrame()` function. It takes the `CvCapture` pointer as a parameter. The `cvQueryFrame()` function returns a pointer to the latest image, so your code will probably start with something a little like this:

```
CvCapture* webcam = cvCreateCameraCapture(0);
if (!webcam)  <— This means "Couldn't find the webcam."
  /* Exit with an error */
while (1) {  <— Loop forever.
  IplImage* image = cvQueryFrame(webcam);  <— Read an image from the webcam.
  if (image) {
    <— If you read an image, you'll need to process it here.
  }
}
```

If you decide that there's a thief in the image, you can save the image to a file with:

```
cvSaveImage("somefile.jpg", image, 0);
```

- "somefile.jpg" — The name of the image file
- image — The image you read from the webcam
- 0 — Unless you want a grayscale image, set this flag to 0.

Maybe if I move
reeeaaaally slooooowly,
it won't spot me...

Detect an intruder

Now you come to the really clever part of the code. How do you decide if there's an intruder in the frame?

One way is to check for movement in the image. OpenCV has functions to create a **Farneback optical flow**. An optical flow compares two images and tells you how much movement there's been at each pixel.

This part, you'll need to research yourself. You'll probably want to use the `cvCalcOpticalFlowFarneback()` to compare two consecutive images from the webcam and create the optical flow. From that, you'll need to write some code that measures the amount of movement between the two frames. If the movement's above a threshold level, you'll know that something large is moving in front of the webcam.

Make a clean getaway

When you start the program, you don't want the camera to record you walking away, so you might want to add a delay to give you time to leave the room.

Optional: show the current webcam output

During our tests here at the lab, we found it useful to check on the current images the program is seeing. To do this, we opened a window and displayed the current webcam output.

You can easily create a window in OpenCV with:

```
cvNamedWindow("Thief", 1);
```

To display the current image in the window, use this:

```
cvShowImage("Thief", image);
```

The finished product

You'll know your OpenCV project is complete when your computer is able to automatically take pictures of people trying to sneak up on it.

Busted.
OpenCV

Why stop there? We're sure you have all kinds of exciting ideas for what you could do with OpenCV. Drop us a line at Head First Labs and let us know how OpenCV is working out for you.

It's time to become a C ninja...

The final part of the book covers ***advanced topics***.

As you're going to be digging into some of the more advanced functions in C, you'll need to make sure that you have all of these features available on your computer. If you're using Linux or Mac, you'll be fine, but if you're using Windows, you need to have Cygwin installed.

Once you're ready, turn the page and enter the gate...

9 processes and system calls

Breaking boundaries

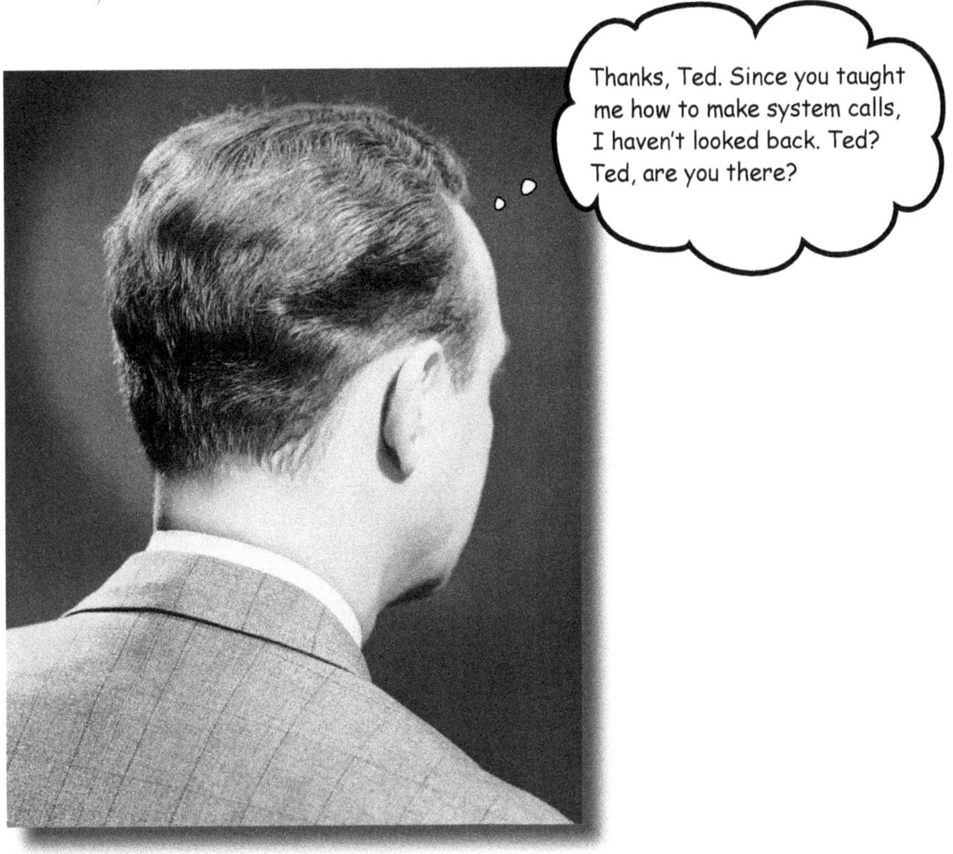
Thanks, Ted. Since you taught me how to make system calls, I haven't looked back. Ted? Ted, are you there?

It's time to think outside the box.

You've already seen that you can build complex applications by connecting small tools together on the command line. But what if you want to *use other programs* from inside your own code? In this chapter, you'll learn how to use **system services** to create and control ***processes***. That will give your programs access to *email*, the *Web,* and *any other tool you've got installed*. By the end of the chapter, you'll have the power to go ***beyond C.***

System calls are your hotline to the OS

C programs rely on the operating system for pretty much everything. They make **system calls** if they want to talk to the hardware. System calls are just functions that live *inside* the operating system's **kernel**. Most of the code in the C Standard Library depends on them. Whenever you call `printf()` to display something on the command line, somewhere at the back of things, a system call will be made to the operating system to send the string of text to the screen.

I want to display this on the command line, then play this music track, then send this message to the network...
Certainly. I shall perform those tasks immediately.

Let's look at an example of a system call. We'll begin with one called (appropriately) **`system()`**.

`system()` takes a single string parameter and executes it as if you had typed it on the command line:

```
system("dir D:");
```

This will print out the contents of the D: drive.

```
system("gedit");
```

This will launch an editor on Linux.

```
system("say 'End of line'");
```

This will read to you on the Mac.

The `system()` function is an easy way of running other programs from your code—particularly if you're creating a quick prototype and you'd sooner call external programs rather than write lots and lots of C code.

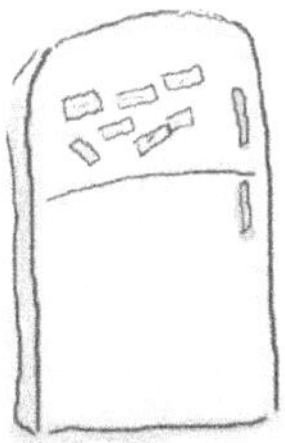

Code Magnets

This is a program that writes timestamped text to the end of a logfile. It would have been perfectly possible to write this entire program in C, but the programmer has used a call to `system()` as a quick way of dealing with the file handling.

See if you can complete the code that creates the operating system command string that displays the text comment, followed by the timestamp.

```
#include <stdio.h>
#include <stdlib.h>
#include <time.h>

char* now()  <-- This function returns a string
                 containing the current date and time.
{
  time_t t;
  time (&t);
  return asctime(localtime (&t));
}

/* Master Control Program utility.
   Records guard patrol check-ins. */
int main()
{
  char comment[80];
  char cmd[120];

  ..................(..................., ..................., ...................);

  ..................................( ..................................,

            .............................................. ,

            .................................... , ....................................);
  system(cmd);
  return 0;
}
```

`sprintf` `"echo '%s %s' >> reports.log"` `80` `stdin` `cmd` `printf` `120` `comment` `fgets` `comment` `now()` `scanf` `stdout`

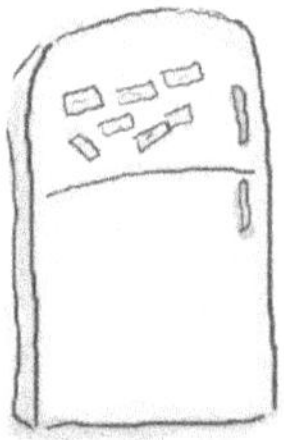

Code Magnets Solution

This is a program that writes timestamped text to the end of a logfile. It would have been perfectly possible to write this entire program in C, but the programmer has used a call to `system()` as a quick way of dealing with the file handling.

You were to complete the code that creates the operating system command string that displays the text comment, followed by the timestamp.

```
#include <stdio.h>
#include <stdlib.h>
#include <time.h>

char* now()
{
  time_t t;
  time (&t);
  return asctime(localtime (&t));
}

/* Master Control Program utility.
   Records guard patrol check-ins. */
int main()
{
  char comment[80];
  char cmd[120];
  fgets( comment , 80 , stdin );
  sprintf( cmd ,
  "echo '%s %s' >> reports.log" ,
  comment , now() );
  system(cmd);
  return 0;
}
```

Using fgets for unstructured text.

It needs to store the text in the comment array.

There is room for only 80 characters.

The data will come from the Standard Input: the keyboard.

sprintf will print the characters to a string.

The formatted string will be stored in the cmd array.

This is the command template.

The command will append the comment to a file.

This runs the contents of the cmd string.

The comment will appear first.

The timestamp appears second.

printf

120

scanf

stdout

Test Drive

Let's compile the program and then watch it in action:

This will compile the program.

This runs the program.

Running it a second time

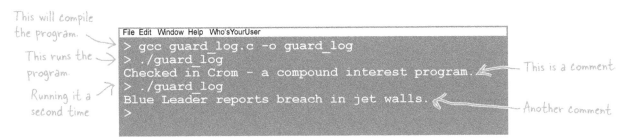

```
File Edit Window Help Who'sYourUser
> gcc guard_log.c -o guard_log
> ./guard_log
Checked in Crom - a compound interest program.
> ./guard_log
Blue Leader reports breach in jet walls.
>
```

This is a comment.

Another comment

Now, when you look in the same directory as the program, there's a new file that's been created called *reports.log*:

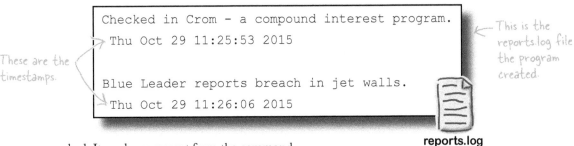

```
Checked in Crom - a compound interest program.
 Thu Oct 29 11:25:53 2015

Blue Leader reports breach in jet walls.
 Thu Oct 29 11:26:06 2015
```

These are the timestamps.

reports.log

This is the reports.log file the program created.

The program worked. It read a comment from the command line and called the `echo` command to add the comment to the end of the file.

Even though you could have written the whole program in C, by using `system()`, you simplified the program and got it working with very little work.

there are no Dumb Questions

Q: Does the `system()` function get compiled into my program?

A: No. The `system()` function—like all system calls—doesn't live in your program. It lives in the main operating system.

Q: So, when I make a system call, I'm making a call to some external piece of code, like a library?

A: Kind of. But the details depend on the operating system. On some operating systems, the code for a system call lives inside the kernel of the operating system. On other operating systems, it might simply be stored in some dynamic library.

Then someone busted into the system...

ALERT! ALERT! Main system security has been breached!

There's a downside to the `system()` function. It's quick and easy to use, but it's also kinda sloppy. Before getting into the problems with `system()`, let's see what it takes to break the program.

The code worked by stitching together a string containing a command, like this:

echo '	<comment>		<timestamp>	' >> reports.log

But what if someone entered a comment like this?

echo '	' && ls / && echo '		<timestamp>	' >> reports.log

By *injecting* some command-line code into the text, you can make the program run **whatever code you like**:

The user can use the program to run any command she likes on the computer.

```
File Edit Window Help Yikes
> ./guard_log
' && ls / && echo '

Applications               System   dev           private
Developer                  Users    etc           sbin
Library                    Volumes  home          tmp
Network                    bin      mach_kernel   usr
Space Paranoids Source     cores    net           var
>
```

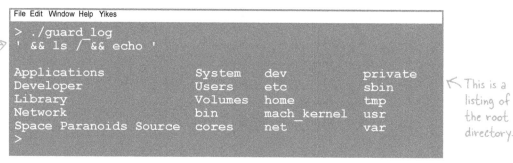

This is a listing of the root directory.

Is this a big problem? If a user can run `guard_log`, she can just as easily run some other program. But what if your code has been called from a *web server*? Or if it's processing data from a *file*?

Security's not the only problem

This example injects a piece of code to list the contents of the root directory, but it could have *deleted files* or *launched a virus*. But you shouldn't just worry about security.

- **What if the comments contain apostrophes?**
  That might break the quotes in the command.

- **What if the PATH variable causes the system() function to call the wrong program?**

- **What if the program we're calling needs to have a specific set of environment variables set up first?**

The `system()` function is easy to use, but most of the time, you're going to need something more structured—some way of calling a *specific* program, with a set of command-line arguments and maybe even some *environment variables*.

Geek Bits

What's the kernel?

On most machines, system calls are functions that live inside the **kernel** of the operating system. But what is the kernel? You never actually *see* the kernel on the screen, but it's always there, controlling your computer. The kernel is the most important program on your computer, and it's in charge of **three things:**

Processes
No program can run on the system without the kernel loading it into memory. The kernel creates processes and makes sure they get the resources they need. The kernel also watches for processes that become too greedy or crash.

Memory
Your machine has a limited supply of memory, so the kernel has to carefully ration the amount of memory each process can take. The kernel can increase the **virtual memory size** by quietly loading and unloading sections of memory to disk.

Hardware
The kernel uses **device drivers** to talk to the equipment that's plugged into the computer. Your program can use the keyboard and the screen and the graphics processor without knowing too much about them, because the kernel talks to them on your behalf.

System calls are the functions that your program uses to talk to the kernel.

The exec() functions give you more control

When you call the `system()` function, the operating system has to interpret the command string and decide which programs to run and how to run them. And that's where the problem is: the operating system needs to *interpret* the string, and you've already seen how easy it is to get that wrong. So, the solution is to remove the **ambiguity** and tell the operating system precisely which program you want to run. That's what the **`exec()`** functions are for.

exec() functions replace the current process

A process is just a program running in memory. If you type **`taskmgr`** on Windows or **`ps -ef`** on most other machines, you'll see the processes running on your system. The operating system tracks each process with a number called the **process identifier** (**PID**).

A process is a program running in memory.

The `exec()` functions **replace the current process** by running some other program. You can say which *command-line arguments* or *environment variables* to use, and when the new program starts it will have exactly the same PID as the old one. It's like a relay race, where your program hands over its process to the new program.

OK, I'm handing over to you now, sendmail. This is the data you need. Don't let me down.
I'm all over it.

There are many exec() functions

Over time, programmers have created several different versions of `exec()`. Each version has a slightly different name and its own set of parameters. Even though there are lots of versions, there are really just two groups of `exec()` functions: the **list** functions and the **array** functions.

The exec() functions are in unistd.h.

The list functions: execl(), execlp(), execle()

The list functions accept command-line arguments as a list of parameters, like this:

- **The program.**
  This might be the full pathname of the program—`execl()`/`execle()`—or just a command name to search for—`execlp()`—but the first parameter tells the `exec()` function what program it will run.

- **The command-line arguments.**
  You need to list one by one the command-line arguments you want to use. Remember: the ***first*** command-line argument is always the name of the program. That means the first two parameters passed to a list version of `exec()` should always be the ***same string***.

- **NULL.**
  That's right. After the last command-line argument, you need a **NULL**. This tells the function that there are no more arguments.

- **Environment variables (maybe).**
  If you call an `exec()` function whose name ends with `...e()`, you can also pass an array of environment variables. This is just an array of strings like `"POWER=4", "SPEED=17", "PORT=OPEN", ....`

BANG!
Watch it!

Spaces in command line arguments can confuse MinGW.

If you pass two arguments "I like" and "turtles," MinGW programs might send ***three*** *arguments: "I," "like," and "turtles."*

execL = a LIST of arguments.

These are the arguments.

```
execl("/home/flynn/clu", "/home/flynn/clu", "paranoids", "contract", NULL)
```

The second parameter should be the same as the first.

execLP = a LIST of arguments + search on the PATH.

These are the arguments.

```
execlp("clu", "clu", "paranoids", "contract", NULL)
```

You should end the list with NULL.

These are the arguments.

```
execle("/home/flynn/clu", "/home/flynn/clu", "paranoids", "contract", NULL, env_vars)
```

execLE = a LIST of arguments + ENVIRONMENT variables.

env_vars is an array of strings containing environment variables.

The array functions: execv(), execvp(), execve()

If you already have your command-line arguments stored in an array, you might find these two versions easier to use:

execV = an array or VECTOR of arguments.

```
execv("/home/flynn/clu", my_args);
```

The arguments need to be stored in the my_args string array.

execVP = an array/VECTOR of arguments + search on the PATH.

```
execvp("clu", my_args);
```

The only difference between these two functions is that **execvp** will search for the program using the PATH variable.

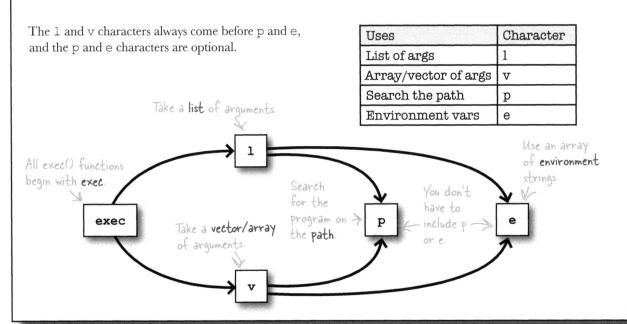

How to remember the exec() functions

You can figure out which exec() function you need by constructing the name. Each exec() function can be followed by one or two characters that must be **l**, **v**, **p**, or **e**. The characters tell you which feature you want to use. So, for the execle() function:

execle = exec + l + e = LIST of arguments + an ENVIRONMENT

The l and v characters always come before p and e, and the p and e characters are optional.

Uses	Character
List of args	l
Array/vector of args	v
Search the path	p
Environment vars	e

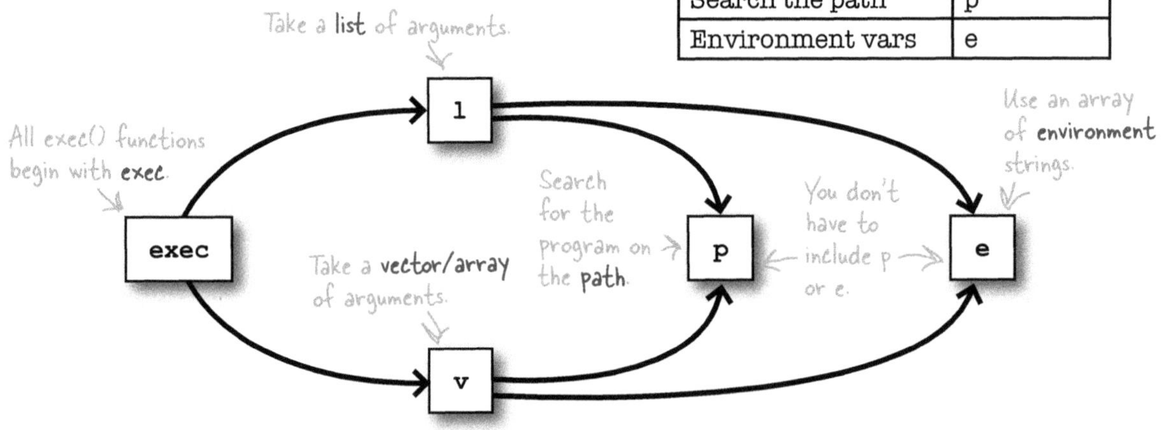
Take a list of arguments.
All exec() functions begin with exec.
exec
l
v
p
e
Search for the program on the path.
Take a vector/array of arguments.
You don't have to include p or e.
Use an array of environment strings.

Passing environment variables

Every process has a set of *environment variables*. These are the values you see when you type `set` or `env` on the command line, and they usually tell the process useful information, such as the location of the home directory or where to find the commands. C programs can read environment variables with the **`getenv()`** system call. You can see `getenv()` being used in the `diner_info` program on the right.

```
#include <stdio.h>
#include <stdlib.h>

int main(int argc, char *argv[])
{
  printf("Diners: %s\n", argv[1]);
  printf("Juice: %s\n", getenv("JUICE"));
  return 0;
}
```

getenv() in stdlib.h lets you read environment variables.

diner_info.c

If you want to run a program using command-line arguments *and* environment variables, you can do it like this:

You can create a set of environment variables as an array of string pointers.

Each variable in the environment is **name=value**.

The last item in the array must be NULL.

```
char *my_env[] = {"JUICE=peach and apple", NULL};

execle("diner_info", "diner_info", "4", NULL, my_env);
```

execle passes a list of arguments **and** an environment.

my_env contains the environment.

The `execle()` function will set the command-line arguments and environment variables and then replace the current process with `diner_info`.

```
File Edit Window Help MoreOJ
> ./my_exec_program
Diners: 4
Juice: peach and apple
>
```

But what if there's a problem?

If there's a problem calling the program, the existing process will keep running. That's useful, because it means that if you can't start that second process, you'll be able to recover from the error and give the user more information on what went wrong. And luckily, the C Standard Library provides some built-in code to help you with that.

Watch it!

If you're passing an environment on Cygwin, be sure to include a PATH variable.

On Cygwin, the `PATH` variable is needed when programs are loaded. So, if you're passing environment variables on Cygwin, be sure to include `PATH=/usr/bin`.

Most system calls go wrong in the same way

Because system calls depend on something *outside* your program, they might go wrong in some way that you can't control. To deal with this problem, most system calls go wrong in the same way.

Guaranteed Standard of Failure

Take the `execle()` call, for example. It's really easy to see when an `exec()` call goes wrong. If an `exec()` call is successful, the current program stops running. So, if the program runs *anything* after the call to `exec()`, there must have been a problem:

```
execle("diner_info", "diner_info", "4", NULL, my_env);
puts("Dude - the diner_info code must be busted");
```

If execle() worked, this line of code would never run.

But just telling *if* a system call worked is not enough. You normally want to know *why* a system call failed. That's why most system calls follow the **golden rules of failure**.

The Golden Rules of Failure

* Tidy up as much as you can.
* Set the errno variable to an error value.
* Return -1.

The **errno** variable is a global variable that's defined in *errno.h*, along with a whole bunch of standard error values, like:

EPERM=1	Operation not permitted
ENOENT=2	No such file or directory
ESRCH=3	No such process
EMULLET=81	Bad haircut

This value is not available on all systems.

Now you *could* check the value of `errno` against each of these values, or you could look up a standard piece of error text using a function in *string.h* called **`strerror()`**:

```
puts(strerror(errno));
```

strerror() converts an error number into a message.

So, if the system can't find the program you are running and it sets the `errno` variable to ENOENT, the above code will display this message:

```
No such file or directory
```

Exercise

Different machines have different commands to tell you about their network configuration. On Linux and Mac machines, there's the `/sbin/ifconfig` program, and on Windows there's a command called `ipconfig` that's stored somewhere on the **command path**.

This program tries to run the `/sbin/ifconfig` program and, if that fails, it will try the `ipconfig` command. There's no need to pass arguments to either command. Think carefully. What type of `exec()` commands will you need?

```
#include <stdio.h>
..............................................
..............................................
..............................................

int main()
{
  if (..........................................................................)
    if (execlp(..................................................................) {
      fprintf(stderr, "Cannot run ipconfig: %s", ..............................);
      return 1;
    }
  return 0;
}
```

What headers will you need?

This will need to run /sbin/ifconfig. What should we test for?

This will need to run the ipconfig command and check if it fails.

What do you think goes here?

Exercise Solution

Different machines have different commands to tell you about their network configuration. On Linux and Mac machines, there's the `/sbin/ifconfig` program, and on Windows there's a command called `ipconfig` that's stored somewhere on the **command path**.

This program tries to run the `/sbin/ifconfig` program and, if that fails, it will try the `ipconfig` command. There's no need to pass arguments to either command. Think carefully. What type of `exec()` commands will you need?

```
#include <stdio.h>
#include <unistd.h>
#include <errno.h>
#include <string.h>

int main()
{
  if (execl("/sbin/ifconfig", "/sbin/ifconfig", NULL) == -1)
    if (execlp("ipconfig", "ipconfig", NULL) == -1) {
      fprintf(stderr, "Cannot run ipconfig: %s", strerror(errno));
      return 1;
    }
  return 0;
}
```

- #include <unistd.h> — You need this for the exec() functions.
- #include <errno.h> — You need this for the errno variable.
- #include <string.h> — This will let you display errors with strerror().
- Use execl() because you have the path to the program file.
- If execl() returns -1, it failed, so we should probably look for ipconfig.
- execlp() will let us find the ipconfig command on the path.
- Checking for the value -1 in case the command failed.
- The strerror() function will display any problems.

there are no Dumb Questions

Q: Isn't `system()` just easier to use than `exec()`?

A: Yes. But because the operating system needs to interpret the string you pass to `system()`, it can be a bit buggy. Particularly if you create the command string dynamically.

Q: Why are there so many `exec()` functions?

A: Over time, people wanted to create processes in different ways. The different versions of `exec()` were created for more flexibility.

Q: Do I always have to check the return value of a system call? Doesn't it make the program really long?

A: If you make system calls and don't check for errors, your code will be shorter. But it will probably also have more bugs. It is better to think about errors when you first write code. It will make it much easier to catch bugs later on.

Q: If I call an `exec()` function, can I do anything afterward?

A: No. If the `exec()` function is successful, it will change the process so that it runs the new program instead of your program. That means the program containing the `exec()` call will stop as soon as it runs the `exec()` function.

BULLET POINTS

- System calls are functions that live in the operating system.
- When you make a system call, you are calling code outside your program.
- `system()` is a system call to run a command string.
- `system()` is easy to use, but it can cause bugs.
- The `exec()` system calls let you run programs with more control.
- There are several versions of the `exec()` system call.
- System calls usually, but not always, return –1 if there's a problem.
- They will also set the `errno` variable to an error number.

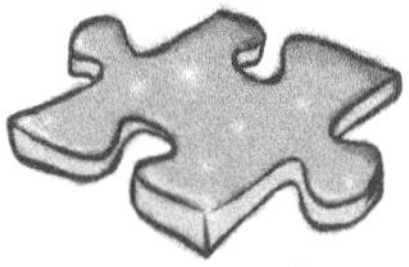

Mixed Messages

The guys over at Starbuzz have come up with a new order-generation program that they call **`coffee`**:

```
#include <stdio.h>
#include <stdlib.h>

int main(int argc, char *argv[])
{
  char *w = getenv("EXTRA");
  if (!w)
    w = getenv("FOOD");
  if (!w)
    w = argv[argc - 1];
  char *c = getenv("EXTRA");
  if (!c)
    c = argv[argc - 1];
  printf("%s with %s\n", c, w);
  return 0;
}
```

To try it out, they've created this test program. Can you match up these code fragments to the output they produce?

```
#include <string.h>
#include <stdio.h>
#include <errno.h>
int main(int argc, char *argv[]){

    [                                        ]

}
```

Candidate code goes here.

Candidates:

Match each candidate with one of the possible outputs.

Possible output:

```
char *my_env[] = {"FOOD=coffee", NULL};
if(execle("./coffee", "./coffee", "donuts", NULL, my_env) == -1){
  fprintf(stderr,"Can't run process 0: %s\n", strerror(errno));
  return 1;
}
```

```
char *my_env[] = {"FOOD=donuts", NULL};
if(execle("./coffee", "./coffee", "cream", NULL, my_env) == -1){
  fprintf(stderr,"Can't run process 0: %s\n", strerror(errno));
  return 1;
}
```

```
if(execl("./coffee", "coffee", NULL) == -1){
  fprintf(stderr,"Can't run process 0: %s\n", strerror(errno));
  return 1;
}
```

```
char *my_env[] = {"FOOD=donuts", NULL};
if(execle("./coffee", "coffee", NULL, my_env) == -1){
  fprintf(stderr,"Can't run process 0: %s\n", strerror(errno));
  return 1;
}
```

```
coffee with donuts
```

```
cream with donuts
```

```
donuts with coffee
```

```
coffee with coffee
```

Mixed Messages Solution

The guys over at Starbuzz have come up with a new order-generation program that they call **coffee**:

```
#include <stdio.h>
#include <stdlib.h>

int main(int argc, char *argv[])
{
  char *w = getenv("EXTRA");
  if (!w)
    w = getenv("FOOD");
  if (!w)
    w = argv[argc - 1];
  char *c = getenv("EXTRA");
  if (!c)
    c = argv[argc - 1];
  printf("%s with %s\n", c, w);
  return 0;
}
```

To try it out, they've created this test program. Can you match up these code fragments to the output they produce?

```
#include <string.h>
#include <stdio.h>
#include <errno.h>
int main(int argc, char *argv[]){

    [                                  ]

}
```

Candidate code goes here.

Candidates:

```
char *my_env[] = {"FOOD=coffee", NULL};
if(execle("./coffee", "./coffee", "donuts", NULL, my_env) == -1){
  fprintf(stderr,"Can't run process 0: %s\n", strerror(errno));
  return 1;
}
```

```
char *my_env[] = {"FOOD=donuts", NULL};
if(execle("./coffee", "./coffee", "cream", NULL, my_env) == -1){
  fprintf(stderr,"Can't run process 0: %s\n", strerror(errno));
  return 1;
}
```

```
if(execl("./coffee", "coffee", NULL) == -1){
  fprintf(stderr,"Can't run process 0: %s\n", strerror(errno));
  return 1;
}
```

```
char *my_env[] = {"FOOD=donuts", NULL};
if(execle("./coffee", "coffee", NULL, my_env) == -1){
  fprintf(stderr,"Can't run process 0: %s\n", strerror(errno));
  return 1;
}
```

Possible output:

```
coffee with donuts
```

```
cream with donuts
```

```
donuts with coffee
```

```
coffee with coffee
```

Read the news with RSS

RSS feeds are a common way for websites to publish their latest news stories. Each RSS feed is just an XML file containing a summary of stories and links. Of course, it's possible to write a C program that will read RSS files straight off the Web, but it involves a few programming ideas that you haven't seen yet. But that's not a problem if you can find another program that will handle the RSS processing for you.

Do this!

Download RSS Gossip from *https://github.com/dogriffiths/rssgossip/zipball/master*. Also, if you don't have Python installed, you can get it here: *http://www.python.org/*.

I want all the latest stories on Pajama Death.
Editor

RSS Gossip is a small **Python script** that can search RSS feeds for stories containing a piece of text. To run the script, you will need Python installed. Once you have Python and *rssgossip.py*, you can search for stories like this:

This is running in a Unix environment.

You need to create an environment variable containing the address of an RSS feed.

This runs the rssgossip script with a search string.

This isn't a real feed. You should replace it with one you find online.

File Edit Window Help ReadAllAboutIt

```
> export RSS_FEED=http://www.cnn.com/rss/celebs.xml
> python rssgossip.py 'pajama death'
Pajama Death launch own range of kitchen appliances.
Lead singer of Pajama Death has new love interest.
"I never ate the bat" says Pajama Death's Hancock.
```

Ooh, I just had a great idea. Why not write a program that can search **a lot of** RSS feeds all at once! Can you do that?

Exercise

The editor wants a program on his machine that can search a lot of RSS feeds all at the same time. You could do that if you ran the *rssgossip.py* several times for different RSS feeds. Fortunately, the **out-of-work actors** have made a start on the program for you. Trouble is, they're having problems creating the call to `exec()` the *rssgossip.py* script. Think carefully about what you need to do to run the script, and then complete the **newshound** code.

To save space, this listing doesn't show the #include lines.

These are RSS feeds the editor wants (you might want to choose your own).

We'll pass the search terms in as an argument.

Loop through each of the feeds.

This is an environment array.

On the editor's Mac, Python is installed here.

You need to insert the function name here.

You need to insert the other parameters to the function here.

```
int main(int argc, char *argv[])
{
  char *feeds[] = {"http://www.cnn.com/rss/celebs.xml",
                   "http://www.rollingstone.com/rock.xml",
                   "http://eonline.com/gossip.xml"};
  int times = 3;
  char *phrase = argv[1];
  int i;
  for (i = 0; i < times; i++) {
    char var[255];
    sprintf(var, "RSS_FEED=%s", feeds[i]);
    char *vars[] = {var, NULL};
    if (..................("/usr/bin/python", "/usr/bin/python",
          ............................................................) == -1) {
      fprintf(stderr, "Can't run script: %s\n", strerror(errno));
      return 1;
    }
  }
  return 0;
}
```

newshound.c

And for extra bonus points...

What will the program do when it runs?

Exercise Solution

The editor wants a program on his machine that can search a lot of RSS feeds all at the same time. You could do that if you ran the *rssgossip.py* several times for different RSS feeds. Fortunately, the **out-of-work actors** have made a start on the program for you. Trouble is, they're having problems creating the call to `exec()` the *rssgossip.py* script. You were to think carefully about what you need to do to run the script, and then complete the **newshound** code.

```
int main(int argc, char *argv[])
{
  char *feeds[] = {"http://www.cnn.com/rss/celebs.xml",
                   "http://www.rollingstone.com/rock.xml",
                   "http://eonline.com/gossip.xml"};
  int times = 3;
  char *phrase = argv[1];
  int i;
  for (i = 0; i < times; i++) {
    char var[255];
    sprintf(var, "RSS_FEED=%s", feeds[i]);
    char *vars[] = {var, NULL};
    if ( execle ("/usr/bin/python", "/usr/bin/python",
            "./rssgossip.py", phrase, NULL, vars ) == -1) {
      fprintf(stderr, "Can't run script: %s\n", strerror(errno));
      return 1;
    }
  }
  return 0;
}
```

You're using a LIST of args and an ENVIRONMENT, so it's execLE.

This is the name of the Python script.

This is the search phrase, as a command-line argument.

Pass the environment as an extra parameter.

newshound.c

But what will the program do when you run it?

Test Drive

When you compile and run the program, it looks like it works:

```
File Edit Window Help ReadAllAboutIt
> ./newshound 'pajama death'
Pajama Death ex-drummer tells all.
New Pajama Death album due next month.
```

The newshound program has the *rssgossip.py* script using data from the array of RSS feeds.

Worked!? Worked?!? It didn't work! What about the announcement of the surprise concert? That was on every other news site! I coulda sent my photographers down there. As it is, I was beaten to the story by everyone else in town!

Actually there *is* a problem.

Although the newshound program managed to run the *rssgossip.py* script, it looks like it didn't manage to run the script for *all of the feeds*. In fact, the only news it displayed came from the **first feed on the list**. That meant the other news stories matching the search terms were missed.

Brain Power

Look at the code of the newshound program again and think about how it works. Why do you think it failed to run the *rssgossip.py* script for any of the other newsfeeds?

exec() is the end of the line for your program

The `exec()` functions *replace* the current function by running a new program. But what happens to the original program? It terminates, and it terminates **immediately**. That's why the program only ran the *rssgossip.py* script for the first newsfeed. After it had called `execle()` the first time, the `newshound` program terminated.

Once the newshound program hands over the process to the rssgossip.py program, newshound quits.
newshound
rssgossip.py

The loop will run only once.

```
for (i = 0; i < times; i++) {
  ...
  if (execle("/usr/bin/python", "/usr/bin/python",
             "./rssgossip.py", phrase, NULL, vars) == -1) {
  ...
  }
}
```

Once execle() is called, the whole program quits.

But if you want to start *another* process and keep your original process running, how do you do it?

BANG!

Watch it!

Unlike Linux and the Mac, Windows doesn't support `fork()` natively.

To use `fork()` on a Windows machine, you should first install Cygwin.

fork() will clone your process

You're going to get around this problem by using a system call named **`fork()`**.

`fork()` makes a complete **copy** of the current process. The brand-new copy will be running the same program, on the same line number. It will have exactly the same variables that contain exactly the same values. The only difference is that the copy process will have a different process identifier from the original.

The original process is called the **parent process**, and the newly created copy is called the **child process**.

But how can cloning the current process fix the problems with `exec()`? Let's see.

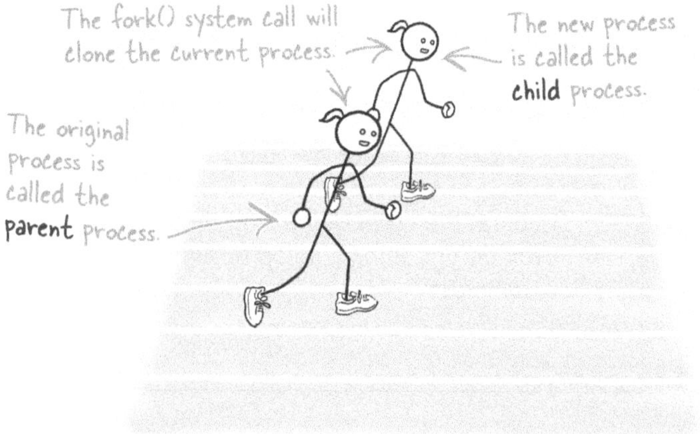
The fork() system call will clone the current process.
The new process is called the child process.
The original process is called the parent process.

Running a child process with fork() + exec()

The trick is to only call an `exec()` function on a *child process*. That way, your original parent process will be able to continue running. Let's look at the process step by step.

1. Make a copy

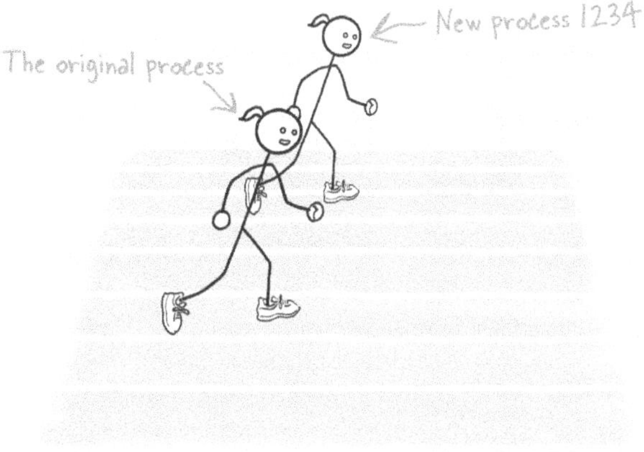
New process 1234
The original process

Begin by making a copy of your current process by calling the `fork()` system call.

The processes need some way of telling which of them is the parent process and which is the child, so the `fork()` function returns 0 to the child process, and it will return a **nonzero** value to the parent process.

2. If you're the child process, call exec()

At this point, you have two identical processes running, both of them using identical code. But the child process (the one that received a 0 from the `fork()` call) now needs to replace itself by calling `exec()`:

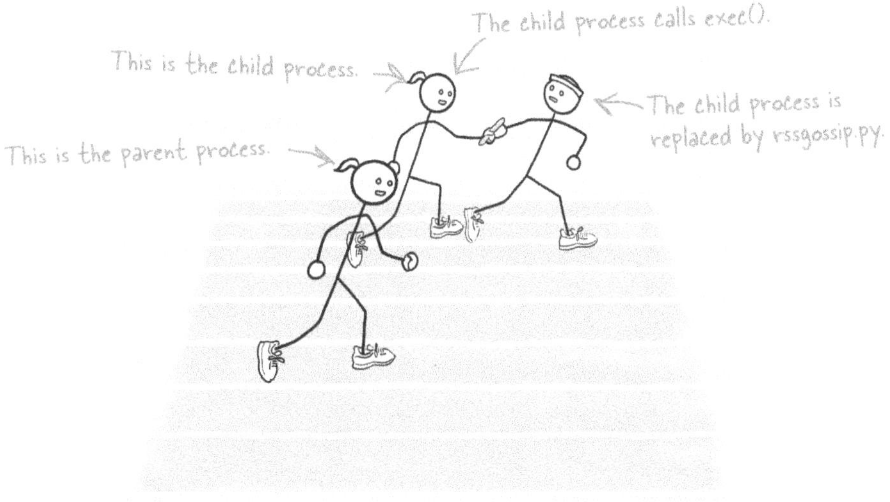
The child process calls exec().
This is the child process.
The child process is replaced by rssgossip.py.
This is the parent process.

Now you have two separate processes: the child process is running the *rssgossip.py* script, and the original parent process is free to continue doing something else.

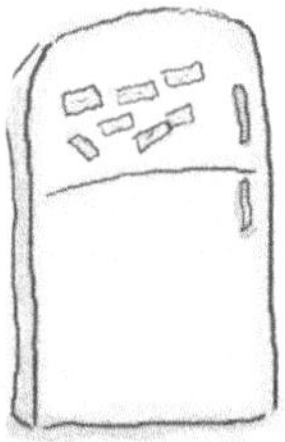

Code Magnets

It's time to update the newshound program. The code needs to run the *rssgossip.py* script in a separate process for each of the RSS feeds. The code is reduced, so you only have to worry about the main loop. Be careful to check for errors, and don't get the parent and child processes mixed!

Put your magnets in this space.

```
for (i = 0; i < times; i++) {
  char var[255];
  sprintf(var, "RSS_FEED=%s", feeds[i]);
  char *vars[] = {var, NULL};









}
```

What the fork()?

You call `fork()` like this:

```
pid_t pid = fork();
```

`fork()` will actually return an integer value that is 0 for the child process and positive for the parent process. The parent process will receive the process identifier of the child process.

But what is `pid_t`? Different operating systems use different kinds of integers to store process IDs: some might use `short`s and some might use `int`s. So `pid_t` is always set to the type that the operating system uses.

```
fprintf(stderr, "Can't fork process: %s\n", strerror(errno));
```

```
fprintf(stderr, "Can't run script: %s\n", strerror(errno));
```

```
if (execle("/usr/bin/python", "/usr/bin/python", "./rssgossip.py",
          phrase, NULL, vars) == -1) {
```

```
pid_t pid = fork();
```

```
return 1;
```

```
}
```

```
if (pid == -1) {
```

```
if (!pid) {
```

```
}
```

```
}
```

```
return 1;
```

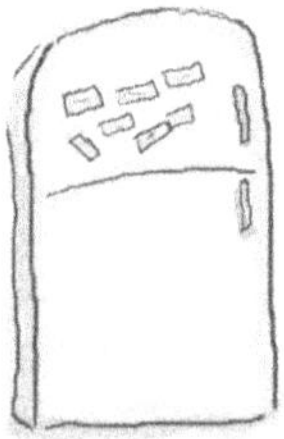

Code Magnets Solution

It's time to update the newshound program. The code needs to run the *rssgossip.py* script in a separate process for each of the RSS feeds. The code is reduced, so you only had to worry about the main loop. Be careful to check for errors, and don't get the parent and child processes mixed!

```
for (i = 0; i < times; i++) {
  char var[255];
  sprintf(var, "RSS_FEED=%s", feeds[i]);
  char *vars[] = {var, NULL};
  pid_t pid = fork();
  if (pid == -1) {
    fprintf(stderr, "Can't fork process: %s\n", strerror(errno));
    return 1;
  }
  if (!pid) {
    if (execle("/usr/bin/python", "/usr/bin/python", "./rssgossip.py",
               phrase, NULL, vars) == -1) {
      fprintf(stderr, "Can't run script: %s\n", strerror(errno));
      return 1;
    }
  }
}
```

First, call fork() to clone the process. (`pid_t pid = fork();`)

If fork() returned -1, there was a problem cloning the process. (`if (pid == -1) {`)

This is the same as if (pid == 0). ← *If fork() returned a 0, the code is running in the child process.* (`if (!pid) {`)

If you get here, you're the child process, so we should exec() the script. (`if (execle(...`)

Test Drive

Now, if you compile and run the code, this happens:

File Edit Window Help ReadAllAboutIt

```
> ./newshound 'pajama death'
Pajama Death ex-drummer tells all.
New Pajama Death album due next month.
Photos from the surprise Pajama Death concert.
Official Pajama Death pajamas go on sale.
"When Pajama Death jumped the shark" by HenryW.
Breaking News: Pajama Death attend premiere.
```

Hey! That's great! I'll send my photographers down to the premiere.

By `fork`-ing a copy of itself and then `exec`-ing the Python script in a separate process, the `newshound` program is able to run a separate process for each of the RSS feeds. And the great thing is that these processes will all run **at the same time**.

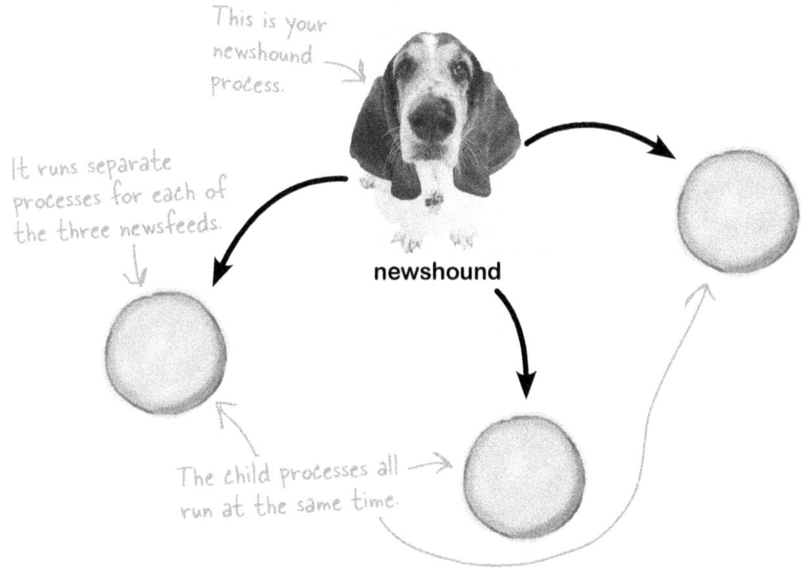
This is your newshound process.
It runs separate processes for each of the three newsfeeds.
newshound
The child processes all run at the same time.

That's a lot faster than reading the newsfeeds one at a time. By learning how to create and run separate processes with `fork()` and `exec()`, not only can you make the most of your existing software, but you can also improve the performance of your code.

there are no Dumb Questions

Q: Does `system()` run programs in a separate process?

A: Yes. But `system()` gives you less control over exactly how the program runs.

Q: Isn't `fork`-ing processes really inefficient? I mean, it copies an entire process, and then a moment later we replace the child process by doing an `exec()`?

A: Operating systems use lots of tricks to make `fork`-ing processes really quick. For example, the operating system cheats and avoids making an actual copy of the parent process's data. Instead, the child and parent processes share the same data.

Q: But what if one of the processes changes some data in memory? Won't that screw things up?

A: It would, but the operating system will catch that a piece of memory is going to change, and then it will make a separate copy of that piece of memory for the child process.

Q: That technique sounds quite cool. Does it have a name?

A: Yes; it's called "copy-on-write."

Q: Is a `pid_t` just an `int`?

A: It depends on the platform. The only thing you know is that it will be some integer type.

Q: I stored the result of a `fork()` call in an `int`, and it worked just fine.

A: It's best to always use `pid_t` to store process IDs. If you don't, you might cause problems with other system calls or if your code is compiled on another machine.

Q: Why doesn't Windows support the `fork()` system call?

A: Windows manages processes very differently from other operating systems, and the kinds of tricks `fork()` needs to do in order to work efficiently are very hard to do on Windows. This may be why there isn't a version of `fork()` built in.

Q: But Cygwin lets me do `fork()`s on Windows, right?

A: Yes. The gurus who work on Cygwin did a lot of work to make Windows processes look like processes that are used on Unix, Linux, and the Mac. But because they still need to rely on Windows to create the underlying processes, `fork()` on Cygwin can be a little slower than `fork()` on other platforms.

Q: So, if I'm just interested in writing code to work on Windows, is there something else I should use instead?

A: Yes. There's a function called `CreateProcess()` that's like an enhanced version of `system()`. To find out more, go to *http://msdn.microsoft.com* and search for "CreateProcess."

Q: Won't the output of the various feeds get mixed up?

A: The operating system will make sure that each string is printed completely.

BULLET POINTS

- System calls are functions that live in the kernel.
- The `exec()` functions give you more control than `system()`.
- The `exec()` functions replace the current process.
- The `fork()` function duplicates the current process.
- System calls usually return –1 if they fail.
- Failed system calls set the `errno` variable to the error number.

Your C Toolbox

You've got Chapter 9 under your belt, and now you've added processes and system calls to your toolbox. For a complete list of tooltips in the book, see Appendix ii.

system() will run a string like a console command.

execl() = list of args.

execle() = list of args + environment.

execlp() = list of args + search on path.

execv() = array of args.

execve() = array of args + environment.

execvp() = array of args + search on path.

fork() duplicates the current process.

fork() + exec() creates a child process.

10 interprocess communication

It's good to talk

Creating processes is just half the story.

What if you want to *control* the process once it's running? What if you want to *send it data*? Or *read its output*? **Interprocess communication** lets processes work together to *get the job done*. We'll show you how to multiply the **power** of your code by letting it ***talk*** to other programs on your system.

Redirecting input and output

When you run programs from the command line, you can redirect the Standard Output to a file using the > operator:

```
python ./rssgossip.py Snooki > stories.txt
```

You can redirect output using the > operator.

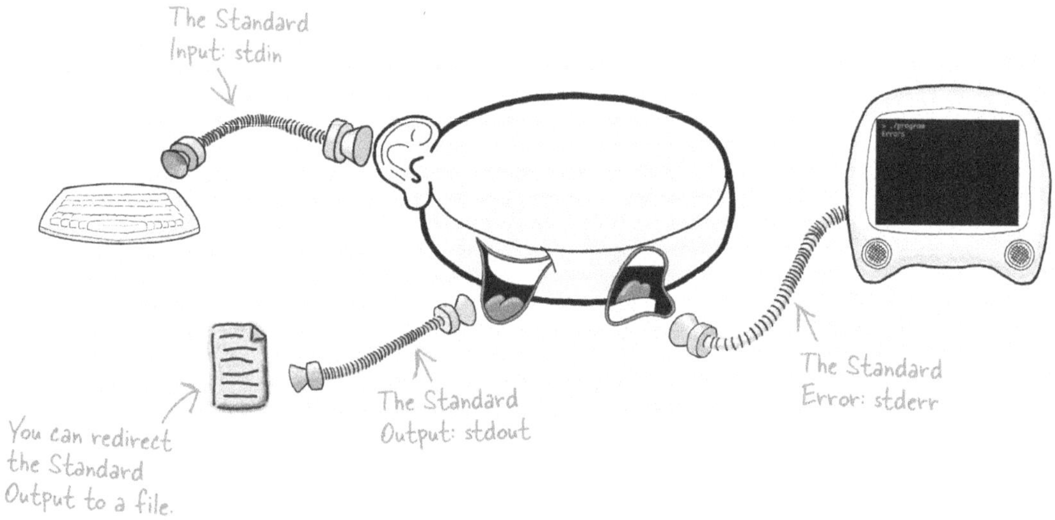
The Standard Input: stdin
The Standard Output: stdout
The Standard Error: stderr
You can redirect the Standard Output to a file.

The Standard Output is one of the three default **data streams**. A *data stream* is exactly what it sounds like: a stream of data that goes into, or comes out of, a process. There are data streams for the Standard Input, Output, and Error, and there are also data streams for other things, like files or network connections. When you redirect the output of a process, you change where the data is sent. So, instead of the Standard Output sending data to the screen, you can make it send the data to a file.

Redirection is really useful on the command line, but is there a way of making a process ***redirect itself***?

A look inside a typical process

Every process will contain the program it's running, as well as space for stack and heap data. But it will also need somewhere to record where data streams like the Standard Output are connected. Each data stream is represented by a **file descriptor**, which, under the surface, is just a number. The process keeps everything straight by storing the file descriptors and their data streams in a **descriptor table**.

A file descriptor is a number that represents a data stream.

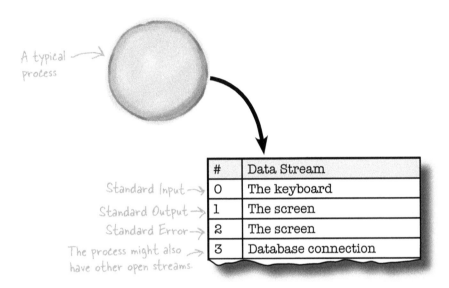

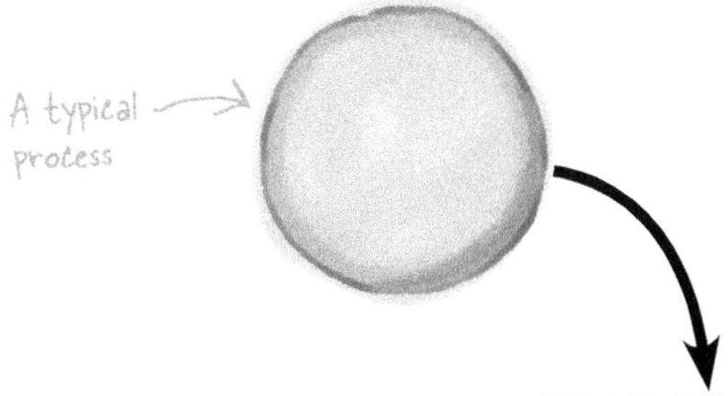
A typical process

	#	Data Stream
Standard Input →	0	The keyboard
Standard Output →	1	The screen
Standard Error →	2	The screen
The process might also have other open streams. →	3	Database connection

The descriptor table has one column for each of the file descriptor numbers. Even though these are called **file** descriptors, they might not be connected to an actual file on the hard disk. Against every file descriptor, the table records the associated data stream. That data stream might be a connection to the keyboard or screen, a file pointer, or a connection to the network.

The first three slots in the table are always the same. Slot 0 is the Standard Input, slot 1 is the Standard Output, and slot 2 is the Standard Error. The other slots in the table are either empty or connected to data streams that the process has opened. For example, every time your code opens a file for reading or writing, another slot is filled in the descriptor table.

File descriptors don't necessarily refer to files.

When the process is created, the Standard Input is connected to the keyboard, and the Standard Output and Error are connected to the screen. And they will stay connected that way until something redirects them somewhere else.

Redirection just replaces data streams

The Standard Input, Output, and Error are always fixed in the same places in the descriptor table. But the data streams they point to can change.

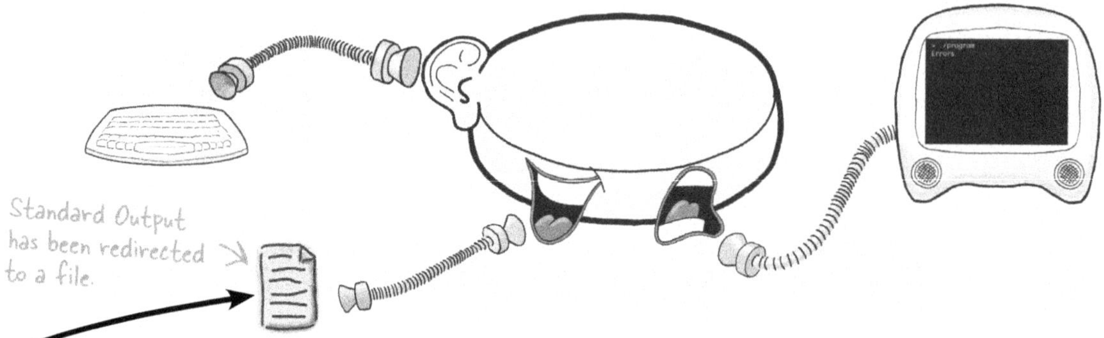
Standard Output has been redirected to a file.

That means if you want to redirect the Standard Output, you just need to switch the data stream against descriptor 1 in the table.

#	Data Stream
0	The keyboard
1	~~The screen~~ File stories.txt
2	The screen
3	Database connection

All of the functions, like `printf()`, that send data to the Standard Output will first look in the descriptor table to see where descriptor 1 is pointing. They will then write data out to the correct data stream.

Processes can redirect themselves

Every time you've used redirection so far, it's been from the command line using the > and < operators. But processes can do their *own redirection* by **rewiring the descriptor table.**

Geek Bits

So, that's why it's 2>...

You can redirect the Standard Output and Standard Error on the command line using the > and 2> operators:

```
./myprog > output.txt 2> errors.log
```

Now you can see why the Standard Error is redirected with **2**>. The **2** refers to the number of the Standard Error in the descriptor table. On most operating systems, you can use **1**> as an alternative way of redirecting the Standard Output, and on Unix-based systems you can even redirect the Standard Error to the same place as the Standard Output like this:

```
./myprog 2>&1
```

2> means "redirect Standard Error."

&1 means "to the Standard Output."

fileno() tells you the descriptor

Every time you open a file, the operating system registers a new item in the descriptor table. Let's say you open a file with something like this:

```
FILE *my_file = fopen("guitar.mp3", "r");
```

Hmmm...looks
like slot 4 is free;
I'll record the music
file there.

The operating system will open the *guitar.mp3* file and return a pointer to it, but it will also skim through the descriptor table until it finds an empty slot and register the new file there.

#	Data Stream
0	The keyboard
1	The screen
2	The screen
3	Database connection
4	File guitar.mp3

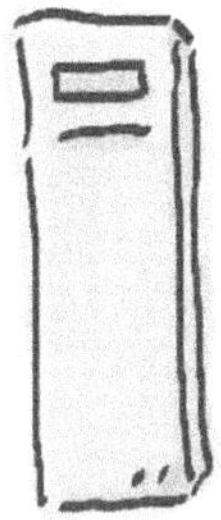

But once you've got a file pointer, how do you find it in the descriptor table? The answer is by calling the **fileno()** function.

```
int descriptor = fileno(my_file);
```

This will return the value 4.

`fileno()` is one of the few system functions that doesn't return –1 if it fails. As long as you pass `fileno()` the pointer to an open file, it should always return the descriptor number.

dup2() duplicates data streams

Opening a file will fill a slot in the descriptor table, but what if you want to *change* the data stream already registered against a descriptor? What if you want to change file descriptor 3 to point to a different data stream? You can do it with the **dup2()** function. `dup2()` duplicates a data stream from one slot to another. So, if you have a file pointer to *guitar.mp3* plugged in to file descriptor 4, the following code will connect it to file descriptor 3 as well.

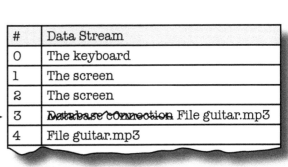

```
dup2(4, 3);
```

#	Data Stream
0	The keyboard
1	The screen
2	The screen
3	~~Database connection~~ File guitar.mp3
4	File guitar.mp3

There's still just one *guitar.mp3* file, and there's still just one data stream connected to it. But the data stream (the `FILE*`) is now registered with file descriptors 3 and 4.

Now that you know how to find and change things in the descriptor table, you should be able to redirect the Standard Output of a process to point to a file.

Does your error code worry you?

Do you find that you're writing duplicate error-handling code every time you make a system call? Then fear no more! Using our patented method, we'll show you how to make the most out of your error code without writing the same thing over and over.

Look at these two troublesome pieces of code:

```
pid_t pid = fork();
if (pid == -1) {
  fprintf(stderr, "Can't fork process: %s\n", strerror(errno));
  return 1;
}

if (execle(...) == -1) {
  fprintf(stderr, "Can't run script: %s\n", strerror(errno));
  return 1;
}
```

Duplicated code can be the cause of unwarranted coding stress.

Is there some way of removing the duplicated code block? **Why, yes, there is!** By creating a simple fire-and-forget error() function, you'll make your duplicated code a thing of the past.

What's that, you say? How do you handle that troublesome return statement? After all, you can't move **that** into a function, can you?

There's no need! The exit() system call is the fastest way to stop your program in its tracks. No more worrying about returning to main(); just call exit(), and your program's history!

This is how it works. First, remove all of your error code into a separate function called error() and replace that tricky return with a call to exit().

To ensure you have the exit system call available, you need to include stdlib.h.

```
void error(char *msg)
{
  fprintf(stderr, "%s: %s\n", msg, strerror(errno));
  exit(1);
}
```

exit(1) will terminate your program with status 1 IMMEDIATELY!

Now you can replace that troublesome error-checking code with something much simpler:

```
pid_t pid = fork();
if (pid == -1) {
  error("Can't fork process");
}

if (execle(...) == -1) {
  error("Can't run script");
}
```

Warning: offer limited to one exit() call per program execution. Do not operate exit() if you have a fear of sudden program termination.

Sharpen your pencil

This is a program that saves the output of the *rssgossip.py* script into a file called *stories.txt*. It's similar to the `newshound` program, except it searches through a single RSS feed only. Using what you've learned about the descriptor table, see if you can find the missing line of code that will redirect the **Standard Output** of the child process to the *stories.txt* file.

The #includes and the error() function have been removed to save space.

```
int main(int argc, char *argv[])
{
  char *phrase = argv[1];
  char *vars[] = {"RSS_FEED=http://www.cnn.com/rss/celebs.xml", NULL};
  FILE *f = fopen("stories.txt", "w");
  if (!f) {      <- If we can't write to stories.txt, then f will be zero.
    error("Can't open stories.txt");   <- We'll report errors using the error()
  }                                       function we wrote earlier.
  pid_t pid = fork();
  if (pid == -1) {
    error("Can't fork process");
  }
  if (!pid) {                     <- What do you think goes here?
    if (............................................) {
      error("Can't redirect Standard Output");
    }
    if (execle("/usr/bin/python", "/usr/bin/python", "./rssgossip.py",
                        phrase, NULL, vars) == -1) {
      error("Can't run script");
    }
  }
  return 0;
}
```

newshound2.c

Sharpen your pencil Solution

This is a program that saves the output of the *rssgossip.py* script into a file called *stories.txt*. It's similar to the `newshound` program, except it searches through a single RSS feed only. Using what you've learned about the descriptor table, you were to find the missing line of code that will redirect the **Standard Output** of the child process to the *stories.txt* file.

```
int main(int argc, char *argv[])
{
  char *phrase = argv[1];
  char *vars[] = {"RSS_FEED=http://www.cnn.com/rss/celebs.xml", NULL};
  FILE *f = fopen("stories.txt", "w"); <- This opens stories.txt for writing.
  if (!f) {  <- If f was zero, we couldn't open the file.
    error("Can't open stories.txt");
  }
  pid_t pid = fork();
  if (pid == -1) {
    error("Can't fork process");
  }
  if (!pid) {  <- This code changes the child process because the pid is zero.
    if (dup2(fileno(f), 1) == -1) {  <- This points descriptor #1 to the stories.txt file.
      error("Can't redirect Standard Output");
    }
    if (execle("/usr/bin/python", "/usr/bin/python", "./rssgossip.py",
                        phrase, NULL, vars) == -1) {
      error("Can't run script");
    }
  }
  return 0;
}
```

newshound2.c

Did you get the right answer? The program will change the descriptor table in the child script to look like this:

#	Data Stream
0	The keyboard
1	File stories.txt
2	The screen
3	File stories.txt

That means that when the *rssgossip.py* script sends data to the Standard Output, it should appear in the *stories.txt* file.

Test Drive

This is what happens when the program is compiled and run:

```
File Edit Window Help ReadAllAboutIt
> ./newshound2 'pajama death'
> cat stories.txt
Pajama Death ex-drummer tells all.
New Pajama Death album due next month.
```

This runs the program.

This displays the contents of the stories.txt file.

If you're on a Windows machine, you'll need to be running Cygwin.

The stories are saved in the stories.txt file.

What happened?

When the program opened the *stories.txt* file with `fopen()`, the operating system registered the file `f` in the descriptor table. `fileno(f)` was the descriptor number it used. The `dup2()` function set the Standard Output descriptor (1) to point to the same file.

I think there might be a problem with the program. See, I just tried the same thing, but on **my** machine the file was empty. So what happened?

```
File Edit Window Help ReadAllAboutIt
> ./newshound2 'pajama death'
> cat stories.txt
>
```

No data in the file? WTF?!?

Where's The Facts?

Brain Power

Assuming you're searching for stories that exist on the feed, why was *stories.txt* empty after the program finished?

Sometimes you need to wait...

The `newshound2` program fires off a separate process to run the *rssgossip.py* script. But once that child process gets created, it's **independent** of its parent. You could run the `newshound2` program and still have an empty *stories.txt*, just because the *rssgossip.py* isn't finished yet. That means the operating system has to give you some way of **waiting** for the child process to complete.

Can you save these stories to the file?
Might take a while...
That's OK, I can wait.
newshound
child process

The waitpid() function

The **`waitpid()`** function won't return until the child process dies. That means you can add a little code to your program so that it won't exit until the *rssgossip.py* script has stopped running:

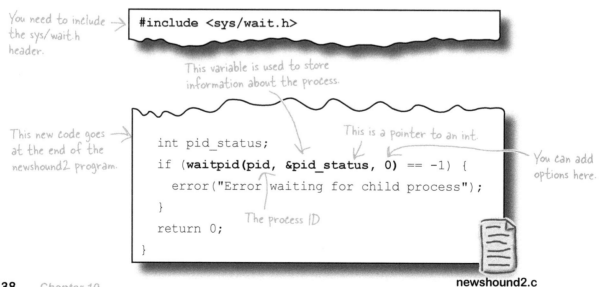

You need to include the sys/wait.h header.

```
#include <sys/wait.h>
```

This variable is used to store information about the process.

This new code goes at the end of the newshound2 program.

This is a pointer to an int.

You can add options here.

```
  int pid_status;
  if (waitpid(pid, &pid_status, 0) == -1) {
    error("Error waiting for child process");
  }
  return 0;
}
```

The process ID

newshound2.c

waitpid() Up Close

`waitpid()` takes three parameters:

waitpid(pid, pid_status, options)

- **pid**
  This is the process ID that the parent process was given when it `fork`ed the child.

- **pid_status**
  This will store *exit information* about the process. `waitpid()` will update it, so it needs to be a pointer.

- **options**
  There are several options you can pass to `waitpid()`, and typing `man waitpid` will give you more info. If you set the options to **0**, the function waits until the process finishes.

What's the status?

When the `waitpid()` function has finished waiting, it stores a value in `pid_status` that tells you how the process did. To find the *exit status* of the child process, you'll have to pass the `pid_status` value through a macro called **`WEXITSTATUS()`**:

```
if (WEXITSTATUS(pid_status))   <- If the exit status is not zero
  puts("Error status non-zero");
```

Why do you need the macro? Because the `pid_status` contains several pieces of information, and only the first 8 bits represent the exit status. The macro tells you the value of just those 8 bits.

Test Drive

Now, when you run the newshound2 program, it checks that the *rssgossip.py* script finishes before newshound2 itself ends:

```
File Edit Window Help ReadAllAboutIt
> ./newshound2 'pajama death'
> cat stories.txt
Pajama Death ex-drummer tells all.
New Pajama Death album due next month.
```

The stories.txt file now contains the stories as soon as newshound2 is run.

That's great. Now I'll never miss another story again.

Adding a waitpid() to the program was easy to do and it made the program more reliable. Before, you couldn't be sure that the subprocess had finished writing, and that meant there was no way you could use the newshound2 program as a proper tool. You couldn't use it in scripts and you couldn't create a GUI frontend for it.

Redirecting input and output, and making processes wait for each other, are all simple forms of **interprocess communication**. When processes are able to cooperate—by sharing data or by waiting for each other—they become much more powerful.

BULLET POINTS

- exit() is a quick way of ending a program.
- All open files are recorded in the descriptor table.
- You can redirect input and output by changing the descriptor table.
- fileno() will find a descriptor in the table.
- dup2() can be used to change the descriptor table.
- waitpid() will wait for processes to finish.

there are no Dumb Questions

Q: Does `exit()` end the program faster than just returning from `main()`?

A: No. But if you call `exit()`, you don't need to structure your code to get back to the `main()` function. As soon as you call `exit()`, your program is dead.

Q: Should I check for –1 when I call `exit()`, in case it doesn't work?

A: No. `exit()` doesn't return a value, because `exit()` never fails. `exit()` is the only function that is guaranteed never to return a value and never to fail.

Q: Is the number I pass to `exit()` the exit status?

A: Yes.

Q: Are the Standard Input, Output, and Error always in slots 0, 1, and 2 of the descriptor table?

A: Yes, they are.

Q: So, if I open a new file, it is automatically added to the descriptor table?

A: Yes.

Q: Is there a rule about which slot it gets?

A: New files are always added to the available slot with the lowest number. So, if slot number 4 is the first available one, that's the one your new file will use.

Q: How big is the descriptor table?

A: It has slots from 0 to 255.

Q: The descriptor table seems kinda complicated. Why is it there?

A: Because it allows you to rewire the way a program works. Without the descriptor table, redirection isn't possible.

Q: Is there a way of sending data to the screen without using the Standard Output?

A: On some systems. For example, on Unix-based machines, if you open */dev/tty*, it will send data directly to the terminal.

Q: Can I use `waitpid()` to wait for any process? Or just the processes I started?

A: You can use `waitpid()` to wait for any process.

Q: Why isn't the `pid_status` in `waitpid(..., &pid_status, ...)` just an exit status?

A: Because the `pid_status` contains other information.

Q: Such as?

A: For example, `WIFSIGNALED(pid_status)` will be false if a process ended naturally, or true if something killed it off.

Q: How can an integer variable like `pid_status` contain several pieces of information?

A: It stores different things in different bits. The first 8 bits store the exit status. The other information is stored in the other bits.

Q: So, if I can extract the first 8 bits of the `pid_status` value, I don't have to use `WEXITSTATUS()`?

A: It is always best to use `WEXITSTATUS()`. It's easier to read and it will work on whatever the native `int` size is on the platform.

Q: Why is `WEXITSTATUS()` in uppercase?

A: Because it is a macro rather than a function. The compiler replaces macro statements with small pieces of code at runtime.

Stay in touch with your child

You've seen how to run a separate process using `exec()` and `fork()`, and you know how to redirect the output of a child process into a file. But what if you want to listen to a child process directly? Is that possible? Rather than waiting for a child process to send all of its data into a file and then reading the file afterward, is there some way to start a process running and read the data it generates ***in real time***?

Reading story links from rssgossip

As an example, there's an option on the *rssgossip.py* script that allows you to display the URLs for any stories that it finds:

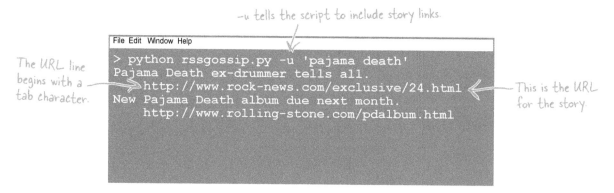

-u tells the script to include story links.

```
File Edit Window Help
> python rssgossip.py -u 'pajama death'
Pajama Death ex-drummer tells all.
	http://www.rock-news.com/exclusive/24.html
New Pajama Death album due next month.
	http://www.rolling-stone.com/pdalbum.html
```

The URL line begins with a tab character.

This is the URL for the story.

Now, you *could* run the script and save its output to a file, but that would be slow. It would be much better if the parent and child process could talk to each other while the child process is still running.

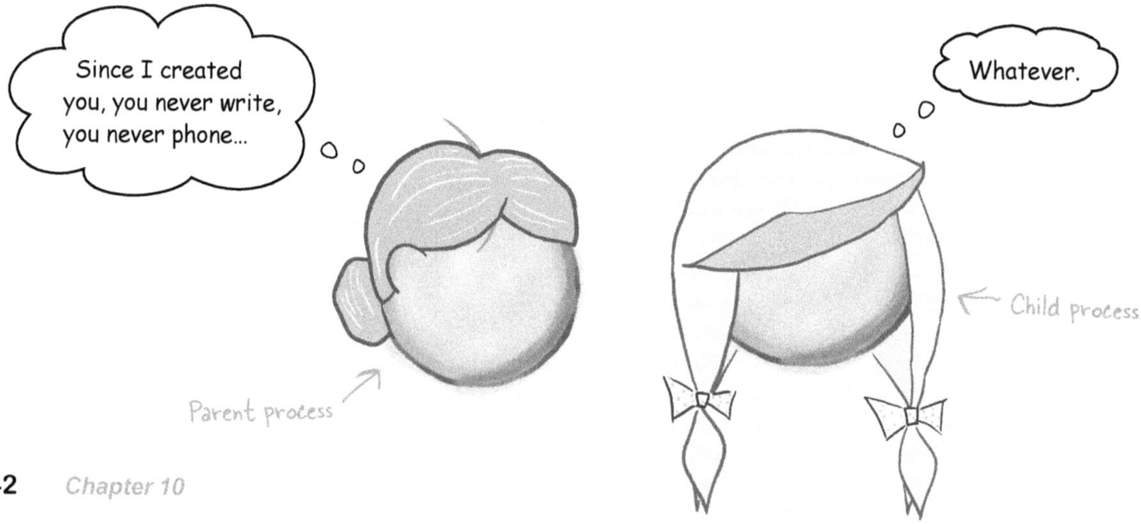
Since I created you, you never write, you never phone...
Whatever.
Child process
Parent process

Connect your processes with pipes

You've already used something that makes live connections between processes: pipes.

rssgossip.py sends its output into the pipe.

The two processes are connected with a pipe.

grep filters the output of the script.

```
File Edit Window Help ReadAllAboutIt
python rssgossip.py -u 'pajama death' | grep 'http'
     http://www.rock-news.com/exclusive/24.html
     http://www.rolling-stone.com/pdalbum.html
```

Pipes are used on the command line to connect the **output** of one process with the **input** of another process. In the example here, you're running the *rssgossip.py* script manually and then passing its output through a command called **grep**. The grep command finds all the lines containing **http**.

Piped commands are parents and children

Whenever you *pipe* commands together on the command line, you are actually connecting them together as parent and child processes. So, in the above example, the grep command is the **parent** of the *rssgossip.py* script.

1. **The command line creates the parent process.**
2. **The parent process forks the rssgossip.py script in a child process.**
3. **The parent connects the output of the child with the input of the parent using a pipe.**
4. **The parent process execs the grep command.**

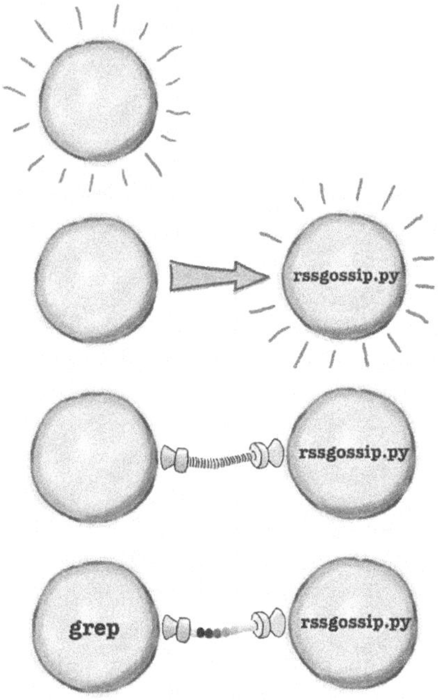
rssgossip.py
rssgossip.py
grep
rssgossip.py

Pipes are used a lot on the command line to allow users to connect processes together. But what if you're just using C code? How do you connect a pipe to your child process so that you can read its output as soon as it's generated?

Case study: opening stories in a browser

Let's say you want to run the *rssgossip.py* script and then open the stories it finds in a web browser. Your program will run in the parent process and *rssgossip.py* will run in the child. You need to create a pipe that connects the output of *rssgossip.py* to the input of your program.

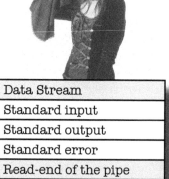

I want a program
that opens stories in
my browser as soon
as they're found.

But how do you create a pipe?

pipe() opens two data streams

Because the child is going to send data to the parent, you need a pipe that's connected to the Standard Output of the child and the Standard Input of the parent. You'll create the pipe using the **`pipe()`** function. Remember how we said that every time you open a data stream to something like a file, it gets added to the descriptor table? Well, that's exactly what the `pipe()` functions does: it creates two connected streams and adds them to the table. Whatever is written into one stream can be read from the other.

#	Data Stream
0	Standard input
1	Standard output
2	Standard error
3	Read-end of the pipe
4	Write-end of the pipe

This is fd[0]. → 3

This is fd[1]. → 4

Calling pipe() creates these two descriptors.

Whatever is written here... →

← ...can be read from here.

When `pipe()` creates the two lines in the descriptor table, it will store their file descriptors in a two-element array:

The descriptors will be stored in this array.

You pass the name of the array to the pipe() function.

```
int fd[2];
if (pipe(fd) == -1) {
  error("Can't create the pipe");
}
```

The `pipe()` command creates a pipe and tells you two descriptors: `fd[1]` is the descriptor that **writes** to the pipe, and `fd[0]` is the descriptor that **reads** from the pipe. Once you've got the descriptors, you'll need to use them in the parent and child processes.

fd[1] writes to the pipe; fd[0] reads from it.

In the child

In the child process, you need to **close** the `fd[0]` end of the pipe and then change the child process's Standard Output to point to the same stream as descriptor `fd[1]`.

```
close(fd[0]);
dup2(fd[1], 1);
```

The child won't read from the pipe. → `close(fd[0]);`

This will close the read end of the pipe.

The child then connects the write end to the Standard Output.

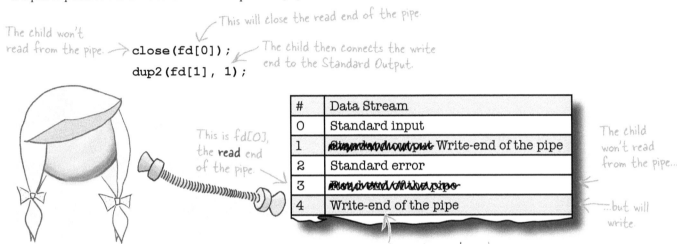

This is fd[0], the **read** end of the pipe.

#	Data Stream
0	Standard input
1	~~Standard output~~ Write-end of the pipe
2	Standard error
3	~~Read-end of the pipe~~
4	Write-end of the pipe

The child won't read from the pipe...

...but will write.

This is fd[1], the **write** end of the pipe.

That means that everything the child sends to the Standard Output will be written to the pipe.

In the parent

In the parent process, you need to close the `fd[1]` end of the pipe (because you won't be writing to it) and then redirect the parent process's Standard Input to read its data from the same place as descriptor `fd[0]`:

```
dup2(fd[0], 0);
close(fd[1]);
```

fd[0] is the read end of the pipe.

The parent connects the read end to the Standard Output. → `dup2(fd[0], 0);`

This will close the write end of the pipe.

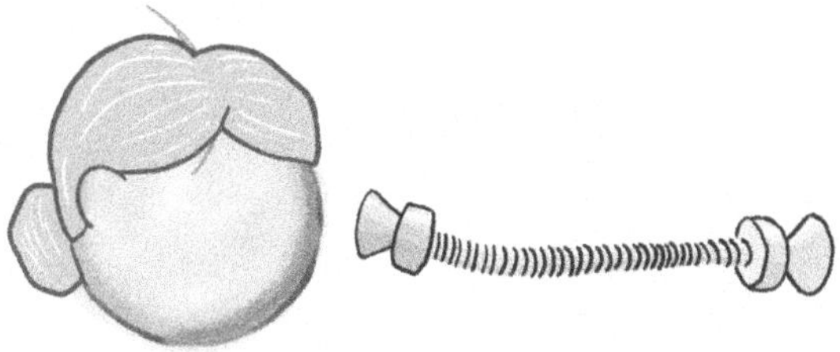

#	Data Stream
0	~~Standard input~~ Read-end of the pipe
1	Standard output
2	Standard error
3	Read-end of the pipe
4	~~Write-end of the pipe~~

The parent will read from the pipe...

...but won't write

Everything that the child writes to the pipe will be read through the Standard Input of the parent process.

Opening a web page in a browser

Your program will need to open up a web page using the machine's browser. That's kind of hard to do, because different operating systems have different ways of talking to programs like web browsers.

Fortunately, the out-of-work actors have hacked together some code that will open web pages on most systems. It looks like they were in a rush to go do something else, so they've put together something pretty simple using `system()`:

Ready-Bake Code

```
void open_url(char *url)
{
  char launch[255];
  sprintf(launch, "cmd /c start %s", url);
  system(launch);
  sprintf(launch, "x-www-browser '%s' &", url);
  system(launch);
  sprintf(launch, "open '%s'", url);
  system(launch);
}
```

This will open a web page on Windows.

This will open a web page on Linux.

This will open a web page on the Mac.

The code runs **three separate commands** to open a URL: that's one command each for the Mac, Windows, and Linux. Two of the commands will always fail, but as long as the third command works, that'll be fine.

Go Off Piste

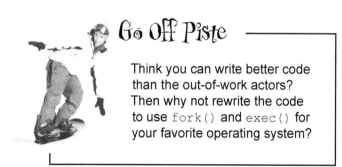

Think you can write better code than the out-of-work actors? Then why not rewrite the code to use `fork()` and `exec()` for your favorite operating system?

Exercise

It looks like most of the program is already written. All you need to do is complete the code that connects the *parent* and *child* processes to a pipe. To save space, the `#include` lines and the `error()` and `open_url()` functions have been removed. Remember, in this program the *child* is going to talk to the *parent*, so make sure that pipe's connected the right way!

```
int main(int argc, char *argv[])
{
  char *phrase = argv[1];
  char *vars[] = {"RSS_FEED=http://www.cnn.com/rss/celebs.xml", NULL};
  int fd[2];
  ..........................................................................
  ..........................................................................
  ..........................................................................
  pid_t pid = fork();
  if (pid == -1) {
    error("Can't fork process");
  }
  if (!pid) {
    ..........................................................................
    ..........................................................................
    if (execle("/usr/bin/python", "/usr/bin/python", "./rssgossip.py",
                          "-u", phrase, NULL, vars) == -1) {
      error("Can't run script");
    }
  }
  ..........................................................................
  ..........................................................................
  char line[255];
  while (fgets(line, 255, ........................................)) {
    if (line[0] == '\t')
      open_url(line + 1);
  }
  return 0;
}
```

You might want to replace this with another RSS newsfeed.

`int fd[2];` ← This array will store the descriptors for your pipe.

Create your pipe here.

Are you parent or child? What code goes in these lines?

"-u" tells the script to display URLs for the stories.

Are you in the parent or the child here? What do you need to do to the pipe?

What needs to go here? What will you read from?

If the line starts with a tab...

...then it's a URL.

"line + 1" is the string starting **after** the tab character.

news_opener.c

Exercise Solution

It looks like most of the program is already written. You were to complete the code that connects the *parent* and *child* processes to a pipe. To save space, the `#include` lines and the `error()` and `open_url()` functions have been removed.

```
int main(int argc, char *argv[])
{
  char *phrase = argv[1];
  char *vars[] = {"RSS_FEED=http://www.cnn.com/rss/celebs.xml", NULL};
  int fd[2];   <- This will create the pipe and store its descriptors in fd[0] and fd[1].
  if (pipe(fd) == -1) {
    error("Can't create the pipe");   <- Need to check that return code,
  }                                      in case we can't create the pipe.
  pid_t pid = fork();
  if (pid == -1) {
    error("Can't fork process");
  }       <- You're in the child process here.
  if (!pid) {
    dup2(fd[1], 1);   <- This will set the Standard Output to the write end of the pipe.
    close(fd[0]);     <- The child won't read from the pipe, so we'll close the read end.
    if (execle("/usr/bin/python", "/usr/bin/python", "./rssgossip.py",
                        "-u", phrase, NULL, vars) == -1) {
      error("Can't run script");
    }
  }    <- You're in the parent process down here.
  dup2(fd[0], 0);   <- This will redirect the Standard Input to the read end of the pipe.
  close(fd[1]);     <- This will close the write end of the pipe,
  char line[255];      because the parent won't write to it.
  while (fgets(line, 255, stdin)) {
    if (line[0] == '\t')
      open_url(line + 1);
  }
  return 0;
}
```

You're reading from the **Standard Input**, because that's connected to the pipe. <- You could also have put fd[0].

news_opener.c

Test Drive

When you compile and run the code, this happens:

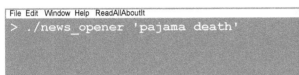

```
File Edit Window Help ReadAllAboutIt
> ./news_opener 'pajama death'
```

New Pajama Death album due next month
O'REILLY
Strata
CONFERENCE
Feb 28-Mar 1, 2012
Making Data Work
Santa Clara, CA
Save 60% Today
Most Popular
STORY HIGHLIGHTS

The program opens all the news stories it can find in the browser.

That's great. It worked.

The `news_opener` program ran the *rssgossip.py* in a separate process and told it to display URLs for each story it found. All of the output of the screen was redirected through a **pipe** that was connected to the `news_opener` parent process. That meant the `news_opener` process could search for any URLs and then open them in the browser.

Pipes are a great way of connecting processes together. Now, you have the ability to not only **run** processes and **control** their environments, but you also have a way of **capturing their output**. That opens up a huge amount of functionality to you. Your C code can now use and control ***any program*** that you can use from the command line.

Go Off Piste

Now that you know how to control *rssgossip.py*, why not try controlling some of these programs? You can get all of them for Unix-style machines or any Windows machine using Cygwin:

curl/wget
These programs let you talk to web servers. If you call them from C code, you can write programs that can talk to the Web.

mail/mutt
These programs let you send email from the command line. If they're on your machine, it means your C programs can send mail too.

convert
This command can convert one image format to another image format. Why not create a C program that outputs SVG charts in text format, and then use the convert command to create PNG images from them?

there are no Dumb Questions

Q: Is a pipe a file?

A: It's up to the operating system how it creates pipes, but pipes created with the `pipe()` function are not normally files.

Q: So pipes *might* be files?

A: It is possible to create pipes based on files, which are normally called *named pipes* or *FIFO* (first-in/first-out) files.

Q: Why would anyone want a pipe that uses a file?

A: Pipes based on files have names. That means they are useful if two processes need to talk to each other and they are not parent and child processes. As long as both processes know the name of the pipe, they can talk with it.

Q: Great! So how do I use named pipes?

A: Using the `mkfifo()` system call. For more information, see *http://tinyurl.com/cdf6ve5*.

Q: If most pipes are not files, what are they?

A: Usually, they are just pieces of memory. Data is written at one point and read at another.

Q: What happens if I try to read from a pipe and there's nothing in there?

A: Your program will wait until something is there.

Q: How does the parent know when the child is finished?

A: When the child process dies, the pipe is closed and the `fgets()` command receives an end-of-file, which means the `fgets()` function returns 0, and the loop ends.

Q: Can parents speak to children?

A: Absolutely. There is no reason why you can't connect your pipes the other way around, so that the parent sends data to the child process.

Q: Can you have a pipe that works in both directions at once? That way, my parent and child processes could have a two-way conversation.

A: No, you can't do that. Pipes always work in only one direction. But you can create two pipes: one from the parent to the child, and one from the child to the parent.

BULLET POINTS

- Parent and child processes can communicate using pipes.
- The `pipe()` function creates a pipe and two descriptors.
- The descriptors are for the read and write ends of the pipe.
- You can redirect Standard Input and Output to the pipe.
- The parent and child processes use different ends of the pipe.

The death of a process

You've seen how processes are created, how their environments are configured, and even how processes talk to each other. But what about how processes die? For example, if your program is reading data from the keyboard and the user hits Ctrl-C, the program stops running.

How does that happen? You can tell from the output that the program never got as far as running the second `printf()`, so the Ctrl-C didn't just stop the `fgets()` command. Instead, the whole program just stopped in its tracks. Did the operating system just unload the program? Did the `fgets()` function call `exit()`? What happened?

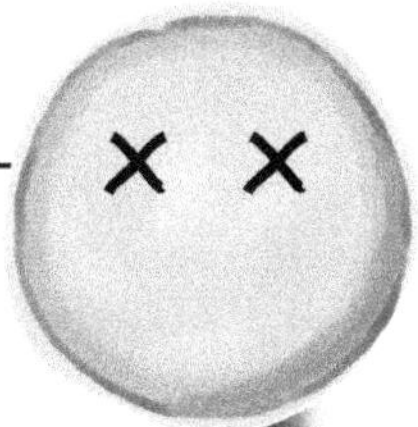

```
#include <stdio.h>

int main()
{
  char name[30];
  printf("Enter your name: ");
  fgets(name, 30, stdin);
  printf("Hello %s\n", name);
  return 0;
}
```

```
File Edit Window Help
> ./greetings
Enter your name: ^C
>
```

If you press Ctrl-C, the program stops running. But why?

The O/S controls your program with signals

The magic all happens in the operating system. When you call the `fgets()` function, the operating system reads the data from the keyboard, and when it sees the user hit Ctrl-C, sends an interrupt signal to the program.

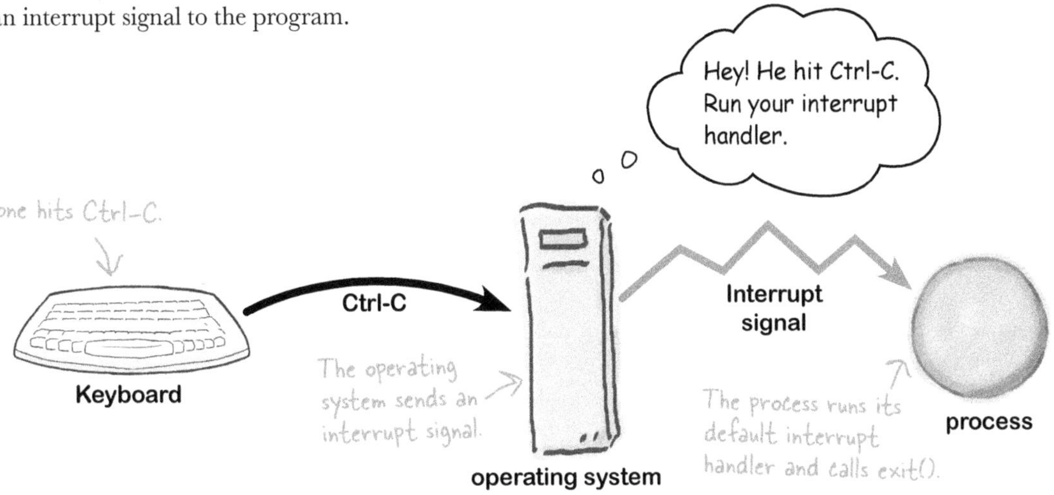
Hey! He hit Ctrl-C.
Run your interrupt handler.
Someone hits Ctrl-C.
Ctrl-C
Keyboard
The operating system sends an interrupt signal.
operating system
Interrupt signal
The process runs its default interrupt handler and calls exit().
process

A signal is just a short message: a single integer value. When the signal arrives, the process has to stop whatever it's doing and go deal with the signal. The process looks at a table of *signal mappings* that link each signal with a function called the **signal handler**. The default signal handler for the interrupt signal just calls the `exit()` function.

So, why doesn't the operating system just kill the program? Because the signal table lets you run your ***own code*** when your process receives a signal.

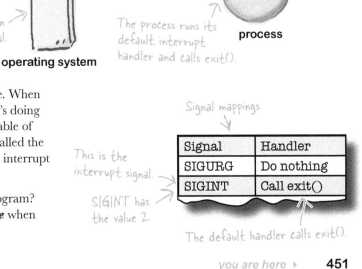

Signal mappings

Signal	Handler
SIGURG	Do nothing
SIGINT	Call exit()

This is the interrupt signal. SIGINT has the value 2.

The default handler calls exit().

Catching signals and running your own code

Sometimes you'll want to run your own code if someone interrupts your program. For example, if your process has files or network connections open, it might want to close things down and tidy up before exiting. But how do you tell the computer to run your code when it sends you a signal? You can do it with **`sigaction`**s.

A sigaction is a function wrapper

A `sigaction` is a `struct` that contains a pointer to a function. `sigaction`s are used to tell the operating system which function it should call when a signal is sent to a process. So, if you have a function called `diediedie()` that you want the operating system to call if someone sends an *interrupt* signal to your process, you'll need to wrap the `diediedie()` function up as a `sigaction`.

This is how you create a `sigaction`:

```
struct sigaction action;
action.sa_handler = diediedie;
sigemptyset(&action.sa_mask);
action.sa_flags = 0;
```

Create a new action.

This is the name of the function you want the computer to call.

The function that the sigaction wraps is called a **handler**.

The mask is a way of filtering the signals that the sigaction will handle.

You'll usually want to use an empty mask, like here.

These are some additional flags. You can just set them to zero.

The function wrapped by a `sigaction` is called the **handler**, because it will be used to deal with (or *handle*) a signal that's sent to it. If you want to create a handler, it will need to be written in a certain way.

All handlers take signal arguments

Signals are just integer values, and if you create a custom handler function, it will need to accept an `int` argument, like this:

```
void diediedie(int sig)
{
  puts ("Goodbye cruel world....\n");
  exit(1);
}
```

This is the signal number the handler has caught.

Because the handler is passed the number of the signal, you can *reuse* the same handler for several signals. Or, you can have a separate handler for each signal. How you choose to program it is up to you.

Handlers are intended to be short, fast pieces of code. They should do *just enough* to deal with the signal that's been received.

BANG!
Watch it!

Be careful when writing to Standard Output and Error in handler functions.

Even though the example code you'll use will display text on the Standard Output, be careful about doing that in more complex programs. Signals can arrive because something bad has happened to the program. That might mean that Standard Output isn't available, so be careful.

sigactions are registered with sigaction()

Once you've create a `sigaction`, you'll need to tell the operating system about it. You do that with the **`sigaction()`** function:

```
sigaction(signal_no, &new_action, &old_action);
```

`sigaction()` takes three parameters:

- **The signal number.**
  The integer value of the signal you want to handle. Usually, you'll pass one of the standard signal symbols, like `SIGINT` or `SIGQUIT`. ← You'll find out more about the standard signals in a while.

- **The new action.**
  This is the **address** of the new `sigaction` you want to register.

- **The old action.**
  If you pass a pointer to another `sigaction`, it will be filled with details of the *current* handler that you're about to replace. If you don't care about the existing signal handler, you can set this to `NULL`.

The `sigaction()` function will return –1 if it fails and will also set the `errno` variable. To keep the code short, some of the code you'll see in this book will skip checking for errors, but you should ***always*** check for errors in your own code.

Ready-Bake Code

This is a function that will make it a little easier to register functions as signal handlers:

The signal number → `sig`
A pointer to the handler function → `(*handler)`

```
int catch_signal(int sig, void (*handler)(int))
{
  struct sigaction action;
  action.sa_handler = handler;
  sigemptyset(&action.sa_mask);
  action.sa_flags = 0;
  return sigaction (sig, &action, NULL);
}
```

- `struct sigaction action;` ← Create an action.
- `action.sa_handler = handler;` ← Set the action's handler to the handler function that was passed in.
- Use an empty mask. → `sigemptyset(&action.sa_mask);`
- `return sigaction (...)` ← Return the value of sigaction(), so you can check for errors.

This function will allow you to set a signal handler by calling `catch_signal()` with a signal number and a function name:

```
catch_signal(SIGINT, diedieie)
```

Rewriting the code to use a signal handler

You now have all the code to make your program do something if someone hits the Ctrl-C key:

```
#include <stdio.h>
#include <signal.h>     <- You need to include the signal.h header.
#include <stdlib.h>
                        This our new signal handler.
void diediedie(int sig) <- The operating system passes the signal to the handler.
{
  puts ("Goodbye cruel world....\n");
  exit(1);
}
                        This is the function to register a handler.
int catch_signal(int sig, void (*handler)(int))
{
  struct sigaction action;
  action.sa_handler = handler;
  sigemptyset(&action.sa_mask);
  action.sa_flags = 0;
  return sigaction (sig, &action, NULL);
}

int main()
{
  if (catch_signal(SIGINT, diediedie) == -1) {
    fprintf(stderr, "Can't map the handler");
    exit(2);
  }
  char name[30];
  printf("Enter your name: ");
  fgets(name, 30, stdin);
  printf("Hello %s\n", name);
  return 0;
}
```

Handlers have void return types. (points to `void diediedie(int sig)`)

SIGINT means we are capturing the **interrupt** signal. (points to `SIGINT`)

This sets the **interrupt** handler to the diediedie() function. (points to `diediedie`)

The program will ask for the user's name and then wait for her to type. But if instead of typing her name, the user just hits the Ctrl-C key, the operating system will automatically send the process an *interrupt signal* (`SIGINT`). That interrupt signal will be handled by the `sigaction` that was registered in the `catch_signal()` function. The `sigaction` contains a pointer to the `diediedie()` function. This will then be called, and the program will display a message and `exit()`.

Test Drive

When you run the new version of the program and press Ctrl-C, this happens:

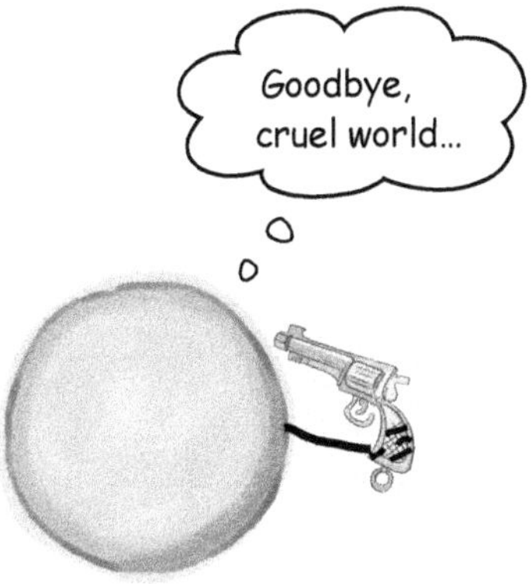
Goodbye,
cruel world...

```
File Edit Window Help
> ./greetings
Enter your name: ^CGoodbye cruel world....
>
```

The operating system received the Ctrl-C and sent a `SIGINT` signal to the process, which then ran ***your*** `diediedie()` function.

What's my purpose?

There are a bunch of different signals the operating system can send to your process. Match each signal to its cause.

`SIGINT`	The process was interrupted.
`SIGQUIT`	The terminal window changed size.
`SIGFPE`	The process tried to access illegal memory.
`SIGTRAP`	Someone just asked the kernel to kill the process.
`SIGSEGV`	The process wrote to a pipe that nothing's reading.
`SIGWINCH`	Floating-point error.
`SIGTERM`	Someone asked the process to stop and dump the memory in a core dump file.
`SIGPIPE`	The debugger asks where the process is.

What's My Purpose? Solution

There are a bunch of different signals the operating system can send to your process. You were to match each signal to its cause.

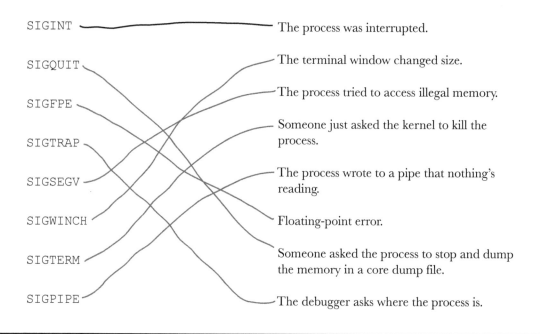

Signal	Cause
SIGINT	The process was interrupted.
SIGQUIT	Someone asked the process to stop and dump the memory in a core dump file.
SIGFPE	Floating-point error.
SIGTRAP	The debugger asks where the process is.
SIGSEGV	The process tried to access illegal memory.
SIGWINCH	The terminal window changed size.
SIGTERM	Someone just asked the kernel to kill the process.
SIGPIPE	The process wrote to a pipe that nothing's reading.

there are no Dumb Questions

Q: If the interrupt handler didn't call `exit()`, would the program still have ended?

A: No.

Q: So, I could write a program that completely ignores interrupts?

A: You could, but it's not a good idea. In general, if your program receives an error signal, it's best to exit with an error, even if you run some of your own code first.

Use kill to send signals

If you've written some signal-handling code, how do you test it? Fortunately, on Unix-style systems, there's a command called **kill**. It's called kill because it's normally used to kill off processes, but in fact, kill just sends a signal to a process. By default, the command sends a SIGTERM signal to the process, but you can use it to send any signal you like.

Including Cygwin on Windows

To try it out, open *two terminals*. In one terminal, you can run your program. Then, in the second terminal, you can send signals to your program with the kill command:

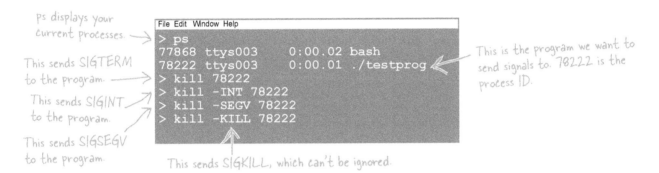

ps displays your current processes.

This sends SIGTERM to the program.

This sends SIGINT to the program.

This sends SIGSEGV to the program.

```
File Edit Window Help
> ps
77868 ttys003    0:00.02 bash
78222 ttys003    0:00.01 ./testprog
> kill 78222
> kill -INT 78222
> kill -SEGV 78222
> kill -KILL 78222
```

This is the program we want to send signals to. 78222 is the process ID.

This sends SIGKILL, which can't be ignored.

Each of these kill commands will send signals to the process and run whatever handler the process has configured. The exception is the **SIGKILL** signal. The SIGKILL signal can't be caught by code, and it can't be ignored. That means if you have a bug in your code and it is ignoring every signal, you can **always** stop the process with kill -KILL.

SIGSTOP can't be ignored either. It's used to pause your process.

kill -KILL <pid> will always kill your program.

Send signals with raise()

Sometimes you might want a process to send a signal to itself, which you can do with the raise() command.

```
raise(SIGTERM);
```

Normally, the raise() command is used inside your own custom signal handlers. It means your code can receive a signal for something minor and then choose to raise a more serious signal.

This is called **signal escalation**.

Sending your code a wake-up call

The operating system sends signals to a process when something has happened that the process needs to know about. It might be that the user has tried to interrupt the process, or someone has tried to kill it, or even that the process has tried to do something it shouldn't have, like trying to access a restricted piece of memory.

But signals are not just used when things go wrong. Sometimes a process might actually want to generate its own signals. One example of that is the **alarm signal**, **`SIGALRM`**. The alarm signal is usually created by the process's **interval timer**. The interval timer is like an alarm clock: you set it for some time in the future, and in the meantime your program can go and do something else:

Tick, tick, tick, just a couple of minutes...
Calling alarm(120) sets the alarm for 120 seconds in the future.

This will make the timer fire in 120 seconds. →

```
alarm(120);
do_important_busy_work();
do_more_busy_work();
```

Meanwhile, your code does something else. →

But even though your program is busy doing other things, the timer is still running in the background. That means that when the 120 seconds are up…

...the timer fires a SIGALRM signal

When a process receives a signal, it **stops doing everything else** and handles the signal. But what does a process do with an alarm signal by default? It ***stops the process***. It's really unlikely that you would ever want a timer to kill your program for you, so most of the time you will set the handler to do something else:

This will catch the signal using the function you created earlier. →

```
catch_signal(SIGALRM, pour_coffee);
alarm(120);
```

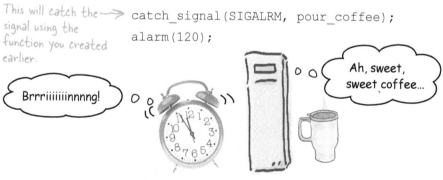

Brrriiiiiiinnnng!
Ah, sweet, sweet coffee...

Alarm signals let you **multitask**. If you need to run a particular job every few seconds, or if you want to limit the amount of time you spend doing a job, then alarm signals are a great way of getting a program to ***interrupt itself***.

Watch it!

Don't use alarm() and sleep() at the same time.

The `sleep()` function puts your program to sleep for a few seconds, but it works by using the same interval timer as the `alarm()` function, so if you try to use the two functions at the same time, they will interfere with each other.

Resetting and Ignoring Signals Up Close

You've seen how to set custom signal handlers, but what if you want to restore the default signal handler? Fortunately, the *signal.h* header has a special symbol **SIG_DFL**, which means ***handle it the default way***.

OK, so if I receive TERM signal, I should just exit() like before...

```
catch_signal(SIGTERM, SIG_DFL);
```

Also, there's another symbol, **SIG_IGN**, that tells the process to completely **ignore** a signal.

Ctrl-C? Talk to the hand; I'm doing nothing.

```
catch_signal(SIGINT, SIG_IGN);
```

But you should be *very careful* before you choose to ignore a signal. Signals are an important way of controlling—and stopping—processes. If you ignore them, your program will be harder to stop.

there are no Dumb Questions

Q: Can I set an alarm for less than a second?

A: Yes, but it's a little more complicated. You need to use a different function called `setitimer()`. It lets you set the process's interval timer directly in either seconds or fractions of a second.

Q: How do I do that?

A: Go to *http://tinyurl.com/3o7hzbm* for more details.

Q: Why is there only one timer for a process?

A: The timers have to be managed by the operating system kernel, and if processes had lots of timers, the kernel would go slower and slower. To prevent this from happening, the operating system limits each process to one timer.

Q: Timers let me multitask?! Great, so I can use them to do lots of things at once?

A: No. Remember, your process will always stop whatever it's doing when it handles a signal. That means it is still only doing one thing at a time. You'll see later how you can really make your code do more than one thing at a time.

Q: What happens if I set one timer and it had already been set?

A: Whenever you call the `alarm()` function, you reset the timer. That means if you set the alarm for 10 seconds, then a moment later you set it for 10 minutes, the alarm won't fire until 10 minutes are up. The original 10-second timer will be lost.

Long Exercise

This is the source code for a program that tests the user's math skills. It asks the user to work the answer to a simple multiplication problem and keeps track of how many answers he got right. The program will keep running forever, unless:

1. The user presses Ctrl-C, or
2. The user takes more than **five seconds** to answer the question.

When the program ends, it will display the final score and set the exit status to 0.

```
#include <stdio.h>
#include <stdlib.h>
#include <unistd.h>
#include <time.h>
#include <string.h>
#include <errno.h>
#include <signal.h>

int score = 0;

void end_game(int sig)
{
  printf("\nFinal score: %i\n", score);
  ..........................................................................................
}

int catch_signal(int sig, void (*handler)(int))
{
  struct sigaction action;
  action.sa_handler = handler;
  sigemptyset(&action.sa_mask);
  action.sa_flags = 0;
  return sigaction (sig, &action, NULL);
}
```

What should happen once the score is displayed?

```
void times_up(int sig)
{
  puts("\nTIME'S UP!");
  raise(.........................................);
}
```

Raise what?

```
void error(char *msg)
{
  fprintf(stderr, "%s: %s\n", msg, strerror(errno));
  exit(1);
}

int main()
{
  catch_signal(SIGALRM, ..............................);
  catch_signal(SIGINT, ...............................);
  srandom (time (0));
  while(1) {
    int a = random() % 11;
    int b = random() % 11;
    char txt[4];
    ................................................................
    printf("\nWhat is %i times %i? ", a, b);
    fgets(txt, 4, stdin);
    int answer = atoi(txt);
    if (answer == a * b)
      score++;
    else
      printf("\nWrong! Score: %i\n", score);
  }
  return 0;
}
```

What will the catch_signal() functions do?

This makes sure you get different random numbers each time.

a and b will be random numbers from 0 to 10.

Hmmm...what line is missing? Need to check the spec...

Long Exercise Solution

This is the source code for a program that tests the user's math skills. It asks the user to work the answer to a simple multiplication problem and keeps track of how many answers he got right.The program will keep running forever, unless:

1. The user presses Ctrl-C, or
2. The user takes more than **five seconds** to answer the question.

When the program ends, it will display the final score and set the exit status to 0.

```
#include <stdio.h>
#include <stdlib.h>
#include <unistd.h>
#include <time.h>
#include <string.h>
#include <errno.h>
#include <signal.h>

int score = 0;

void end_game(int sig)
{
  printf("\nFinal score: %i\n", score);
  exit(0);
}

int catch_signal(int sig, void (*handler)(int))
{
  struct sigaction action;
  action.sa_handler = handler;
  sigemptyset(&action.sa_mask);
  action.sa_flags = 0;
  return sigaction (sig, &action, NULL);
}
```

You need to set the exit status to 0 and stop. (annotation pointing to `exit(0);`)

```
void times_up(int sig)
{
  puts("\nTIME'S UP!");
  raise(SIGINT);
}

void error(char *msg)
{
  fprintf(stderr, "%s: %s\n", msg, strerror(errno));
  exit(1);
}

int main()
{
  catch_signal(SIGALRM, times_up);
  catch_signal(SIGINT, end_game);
  srandom (time (0));
  while(1) {
    int a = random() % 11;
    int b = random() % 11;
    char txt[4];
    alarm(5);
    printf("\nWhat is %i times %i? ", a, b);
    fgets(txt, 4, stdin);
    int answer = atoi(txt);
    if (answer == a * b)
      score++;
    else
      printf("\nWrong! Score: %i\n", score);
  }
  return 0;
}
```

Raising SIGINT will make the program display the final score in end_game().

The signal() functions set the handlers.

This makes sure you get different random numbers each time.

Set the alarm to fire in 5 seconds.

As long as you go through the loop in less than 5 seconds, the timer will be reset and it will never fire.

Test Drive

To see if the program works, you need to run it a couple of times.

Test 1: hit Ctrl-C

The first time, you'll answer a few questions and then hit Ctrl-C.

Ctrl-C sends the process an interrupt signal (`SIGINT`) that makes the program display the final score and then `exit()`.

```
File Edit Window Help
> ./math_master
What is 0 times 1? 0
What is 6 times 1? 6
What is 4 times 10? 40
What is 2 times 3? 6
What is 7 times 4? 28
What is 4 times 10? ^C
Final score: 5
>
```

The user hit Ctrl-C here.

The program displayed the final score before ending.

Test 2: wait five seconds

The second time, instead of hitting Ctrl-C, wait for at least five seconds on one of the answers and see what happens.

The alarm signal (`SIGALRM`) fires. The program was waiting for the user to enter an answer, but because he took so long, the timer signal was sent; the process immediately switches to the `times_up()` handler function. The handler displays the "TIME'S UP!" message and then escalates the signal to a `SIGINT` that causes the program to display the final score.

```
File Edit Window Help
> ./math_master
What is 5 times 9? 45
What is 2 times 8? 16
What is 9 times 1? 9
What is 9 times 3?
TIME'S UP!
Final score: 3
>
```

Uh, oh...looks like someone was a little slow.

Signals are a little complex, but incredibly useful. They allow your programs to end gracefully, and the interval timer can help you deal with tasks that are taking too long.

there are no Dumb Questions

Q: Are signals always received in the same order they are sent?

A: Not if they are sent very close together. The operating system might choose to reorder the signals if it thinks one is more important than the others.

Q: Is that always true?

A: It depends on the platform. On most versions of Cygwin, for example, the signals will always be sent and received in the same order. But in general, you shouldn't rely on it.

Q: If I send the same signal twice, will it be received twice by the process?

A: Again, it depends. On Linux and the Mac, if the same signal is repeated very quickly, the kernel might choose to only send the signal once to the process. On Cygwin, it will always send both signals. But again, you should not assume that just because you sent the same signal twice, it will be received twice.

BULLET POINTS

- The operating system talks to processes using signals.
- Programs are normally stopped using signals.
- When a process receives a signal, it runs a handler.
- For most error signals, the default handler stops the program.
- Handlers can be replaced with the `signal()` function.
- You can send signals to yourself with `raise()`.
- The interval timer sends `SIGALRM` signals.
- The `alarm()` function sets the interval timer.
- There is one timer per process.
- Don't use `sleep()` and `alarm()` at the same time.
- `kill` sends signals to a process.
- `kill -KILL` will always kill a process.

CHAPTER 10

Your C Toolbox

You've got Chapter 10 under your belt, and now you've added interprocess communication to your toolbox. For a complete list of tooltips in the book, see Appendix ii.

exit() stops the program immediately.

fileno() finds the descriptor.

dup2() duplicates a data stream.

waitpid() waits for a process to finish.

pipe() creates a communication pipe.

Processes can communicate using pipes.

Signals are messages from the O/S.

sigaction() lets you handle signals.

A program can send signals to itself with raise().

The kill command sends a signal.

alarm() sends a SIGALRM after a few seconds.

11 sockets and networking

There's no place like 127.0.0.1

Servers-R-Us, how can I help you?
A new client, darling? I always knew your BLABing would come in useful one day.

Programs on different machines need to talk to each other.

You've learned how to use I/O to communicate with files and how processes on the same machine can communicate with each other. Now you're going to *reach out to the rest of the world*, and learn how to write C programs that can talk to other programs **across the network** and **across the *world***. By the end of this chapter, you'll be able to create **programs that behave as servers** and **programs that behave as clients**.

The Internet knock-knock server

C is used to write most of the low-level networking code on the Internet. Most networked applications need two separate programs: a **server** and a **client**.

You're going to build a server in C that tells jokes over the Internet. You'll be able to start the server on one machine like this:

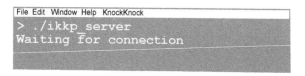

```
File Edit Window Help KnockKnock
> ./ikkp_server
Waiting for connection
```

Other than telling you it's running, the server won't display anything else on the screen. However, if you open a second console, you'll be able to connect to the server using a client program called **telnet**. Telnet takes two parameters: the *address* of the server, and the *port* the server is running on. If you are running telnet on the same machine as the server, you can use `127.0.0.1` for the address:

Watch it!

You'll be using telnet quite a lot in this chapter to test our server code.

If you try to use the built-in Windows telnet, you might have problems because of the way it communicates with the network. If you install the Cygwin version of telnet, you should be fine.

30000 is the number of the network **port**.

Use 127.0.0.1 if you're running the server on the same machine.

The server has responded.

You type in these responses.

```
File Edit Window Help Who'sThere?
> telnet 127.0.0.1 30000
Trying 127.0.0.1...
Connected to localhost.
Escape character is '^]'.
Internet Knock-Knock Protocol Server
Version 1.0
Knock! Knock!
> Who's there?
Oscar
> Oscar who?
Oscar silly question, you get a silly answer
Connection closed by foreign host.
>
```

Do this!

You will need a **telnet** program in order to connect to the server. Most systems come with telnet already installed. You can check that you have telnet by typing:

```
telnet
```

on the command line.

If you *don't* have telnet, you can install it in one of these ways:

Cygwin:
Run the `setup.exe` program for Cygwin and search for *telnet*.

Linux:
Search for *telnet* in your package manager. On many systems, the package manager is called **Synaptic**.

Mac:
If you don't have telnet, you can install it from *www.macports.org* or *www.finkproject.org*.

Knock-knock server overview

The server will be able to talk to several clients at once. The client and the server will have a *structured conversation* called a **protocol**. There are different protocols used on the Internet. Some of them are *low-level* protocols, like the *internet protocol* (IP), which are used to control how binary 1s and 0s are sent around the Internet. Other protocols are *high-level* protocols, like the *hypertext transfer protocol* (HTTP), which controls how web browsers talk to web servers. The joke server is going to use a custom high-level protocol called the *Internet knock-knock protocol* (IKKP).

A protocol is a structured conversation.

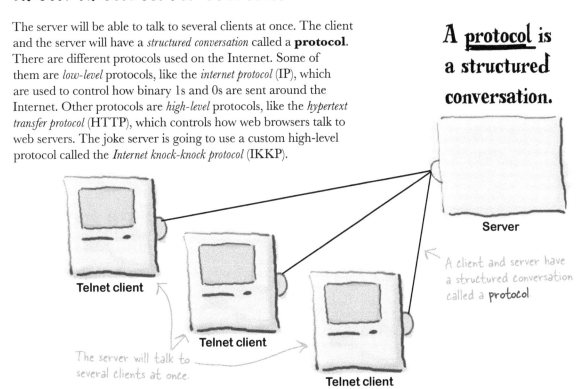

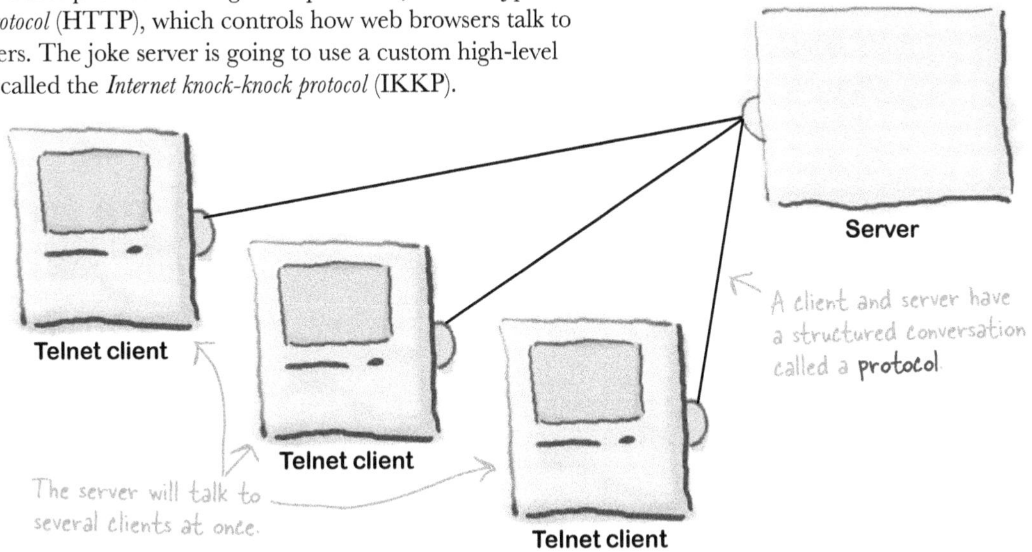
Server
A client and server have a structured conversation called a protocol
Telnet client
Telnet client
Telnet client
The server will talk to several clients at once.

The client and the server will exchange messages like this:

Server:	Client:
Knock knock!	
	Who's there?
Oscar.	
	Oscar who?
Oscar silly question, you get a silly answer.	

Protocol demands that you reply with "Who's there?" I shall therefore terminate this conversation forthwith.

A **protocol** always has a strict set of rules. As long as the client and the server both follow those rules, everything is fine. But if one of them breaks the rules, the conversation usually stops pretty abruptly.

BLAB: how servers talk to the Internet

When C programs need to talk to the outside world, they use **data streams** to read and write bytes. You've used data streams that are connected to the files or Standard Input and Output. But if you're going to write a program to talk to the network, you need a new kind of data stream called a ***socket***.

```
#include <sys/socket.h>
...
int listener_d = socket(PF_INET, SOCK_STREAM, 0);
if (listener_d == -1)
  error("Can't open socket");
```

You'll need this header.

listener_d is a descriptor for the socket.

It's an Internet socket.

This is a protocol number. You can leave it as 0.

This is the error() function you created in the last chapter.

Before a server can use a socket to talk to a client program, it needs to go through four stages that you can remember with the acronym **BLAB**: **Bind, Listen, Accept, Begin**.

Bind to a port.
Listen.
Accept a connection.
Begin talking.

1. Bind to a port

A computer might need to run several server programs at once. It might be sending out web pages, posting email, and running a chat server all at the same time. To prevent the different conversations from getting confused, each server uses a different **port**. A port is just like a channel on a TV. Different ports are used for different network services, just like different channels are used for different content.

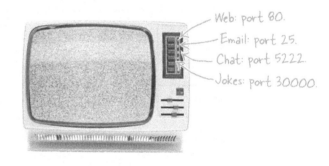

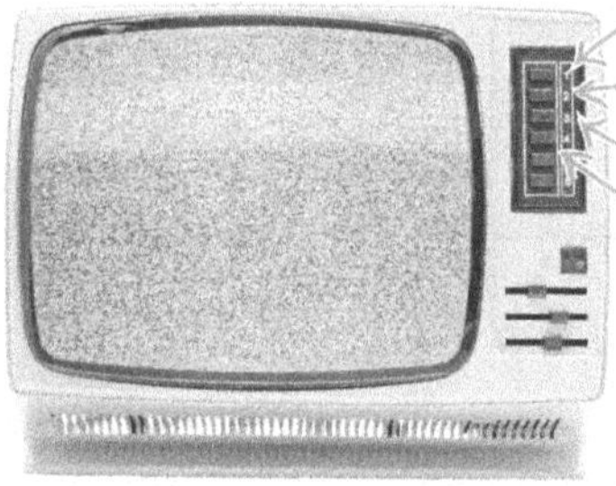
Web: port 80.
Email: port 25.
Chat: port 5222.
Jokes: port 30000.

When a server starts up, it needs to tell the operating system which port it's going to use. This is called ***binding the port***. The knock-knock server is going to use port 30000, and to bind it you'll need two things: the **socket descriptor** and a **socket name**. A socket name is just a `struct` that means "Internet port 30000."

```
#include <arpa/inet.h>
...
struct sockaddr_in name;
name.sin_family = PF_INET;
name.sin_port = (in_port_t)htons(30000);
name.sin_addr.s_addr = htonl(INADDR_ANY);
int c = bind (listener_d, (struct sockaddr *) &name, sizeof(name));
if (c == -1)
  error("Can't bind to socket");
```

You'll need this header for creating Internet addresses.

These lines create a name for the port meaning "Internet port 30000."

2. Listen

If your server becomes popular, you'll probably get lots of clients connecting to it at once. Would you like the clients to wait in a queue for a connection? The `listen()` system call tells the operating system how long you want the queue to be:

You'll use a queue with a length of 10.

```
if (listen(listener_d, 10) == -1)
  error("Can't listen");
```

Calling `listen()` with a queue length of 10 means that up to 10 clients can try to connect to the server at once. They won't all be immediately answered, but they'll be able to wait. The 11th client will be told the server is too busy.

The first 10 clients will be able to wait.

The 11th and 12th will be told the server is too busy.

3. Accept a connection

Once you've bound a port and set up a listen queue, you then just have to…wait. Servers spend most of their lives waiting for clients to contact them. The `accept()` system call waits until a client contacts the server, and then it returns a **second socket descriptor** that you can use to hold a conversation on.

client_addr will store details about the client who's just connected.

```
struct sockaddr_storage client_addr;
unsigned int address_size = sizeof(client_addr);
int connect_d = accept(listener_d, (struct sockaddr *)&client_addr, &address_size);
if (connect_d == -1)
  error("Can't open secondary socket");
```

This new **connection descriptor** (`connect_d`) is the one that the server will use to…

Begin talking.

BRAIN BARBELL

Why do you think the `accept()` system call creates the descriptor for a new socket? Why don't servers just use the socket they created to listen to the port?

A socket's not your typical data stream

So far, data streams have all been the same. Whether you're connected to files or Standard Input/Output, you've been able to use functions like `fprintf()` and `fscanf()` to talk to them. But sockets are a little different. A socket is *two way*: it can be used for input *and* output. That means it needs different functions to talk to it.

If you want to output data on a socket, you can't use `fprintf()`. Instead, you use a function called **`send()`**:

This is the message you're going to send over the network.

```
char *msg = "Internet Knock-Knock Protocol Server\r\nVersion 1.0\r\nKnock! Knock!\r\n> ";
if (send(connect_d, msg, strlen(msg), 0) == -1)
  error("send");
```

This is the socket descriptor.

This is the message and its length.

The final parameter is used for advanced options. This can be left as 0.

Remember: it's important to always check the return value of system calls like `send()`. Network errors are really common, and your servers will have to cope with them.

Geek Bits

What port should I use?

You need to be careful when you choose a port number for a server application. There are lots of different servers available, and you need to make sure you don't use a port number that's normally used for some other program. On Cygwin and most Unix-style machines, you'll find a file called ***/etc/services*** that lists the ports used by most of the common servers. When you choose a port, make sure there isn't another application that already uses the same one.

Port numbers can be between 0 and 65535, and you need to decide whether you want to use a low number (< 1024) or a high one. Port numbers that are lower than 1024 are usually only available to the superuser or administrator on most systems. This is because the low port numbers are reserved for well-known services, like web servers and email servers. Operating systems restrict these ports to administrators only, to prevent ordinary users from starting unwanted services.

Most of the time, you'll probably want to use a port number greater than 1024.

Sharpen your pencil

This server generates random advice for any client that connects to it, but it's not quite complete. You need to fill in the missing system calls. Also, this version of the code will send back a single piece of advice and then end. Part of the code needs to be inside a loop. Which part?

The includes are removed to save space.

```
int main(int argc, char *argv[])
{
  char *advice[] = {
    "Take smaller bites\r\n",
     "Go for the tight jeans. No they do NOT make you look fat.\r\n",
     "One word: inappropriate\r\n",
     "Just for today, be honest. Tell your boss what you *really* think\r\n",
     "You might want to rethink that haircut\r\n"
  };
  int listener_d = ......................(PF_INET, SOCK_STREAM, 0);

  struct sockaddr_in name;
  name.sin_family = PF_INET;
  name.sin_port = (in_port_t)htons(30000);
  name.sin_addr.s_addr = htonl(INADDR_ANY);
  ......................(listener_d, (struct sockaddr *) &name, sizeof(name));

  ......................(listener_d, 10);
  puts("Waiting for connection");

  struct sockaddr_storage client_addr;
  unsigned int address_size = sizeof(client_addr);
  int connect_d = ................(listener_d, (struct sockaddr *)&client_addr, &address_size);
  char *msg = advice[rand() % 5];

  ......................(connect_d, msg, strlen(msg), 0);
  close(connect_d);

  return 0;
}
```

And for a bonus point, if you add in the missing `#include` statements, the program will work. But what has the programmer missed out? **Hint: look at the system calls.**

The programmer has forgotten to ....

Sharpen your pencil Solution

This server generates random advice for any client that connects to it, but it's not quite complete. You needed to fill in the missing system calls. Also, this version of the code will send back a single piece of advice and then end. Part of the code needs to be inside a loop. Which part?

```
int main(int argc, char *argv[])
{
  char *advice[] = {
    "Take smaller bites\r\n",
    "Go for the tight jeans. No they do NOT make you look fat.\r\n",
    "One word: inappropriate\r\n",
    "Just for today, be honest. Tell your boss what you *really* think\r\n",
    "You might want to rethink that haircut\r\n"
  };
  int listener_d = socket(PF_INET, SOCK_STREAM, 0);   <- Create a socket.

  struct sockaddr_in name;
  name.sin_family = PF_INET;
  name.sin_port = (in_port_t)htons(30000);            Bind the socket to port 30000.
  name.sin_addr.s_addr = htonl(INADDR_ANY);
  bind(listener_d, (struct sockaddr *) &name, sizeof(name));

  listen(listener_d, 10);   <- Set to the listen queue depth to 10.
  puts("Waiting for connection");
  while (1) {   <- You need to loop the accept/begin talking section.
    struct sockaddr_storage client_addr;
    unsigned int address_size = sizeof(client_addr);
    int connect_d = accept(listener_d, (struct sockaddr *)&client_addr, &address_size);
    char *msg = advice[rand() % 5];   <- Accept a connection from a client.

    send(connect_d, msg, strlen(msg), 0);
    close(connect_d);   <- Begin talking to the client.
  }
  return 0;
}
```

And for a bonus point, if you add in the missing `#include` statements, the program will work. But what has the programmer missed out? **Hint: look at the system calls.**

The programmer has forgotten to check for errors. ← You should always check if socket, bind, listen, accept, or send return -1.

Test Drive

Let's compile the advice server and see what happens.

```
File Edit Window Help I'mTheServer
> gcc advice_server.c -o advice_server
> ./advice_server
Waiting for connection
```

Then, while the server is still running, open a second console and connect to the server using telnet a couple of times.

```
File Edit Window Help I'mTelnet
> telnet 127.0.0.1 30000
Trying 127.0.0.1...
Connected to localhost.
Escape character is '^]'.
One word: inappropriate
Connection closed by foreign host.
> telnet 127.0.0.1 30000
Trying 127.0.0.1...
Connected to localhost.
Escape character is '^]'.
You might want to rethink that haircut
Connection closed by foreign host.
>
```

That's great, the server works. Here, you're using 127.0.0.1 as the IP address, because the client is running on the same machine as the server. But you could have connected to the server from anywhere on the network and we'd have gotten the same response.

Working, you say? Hmm...I think there might be a problem...

Sometimes the server doesn't start properly

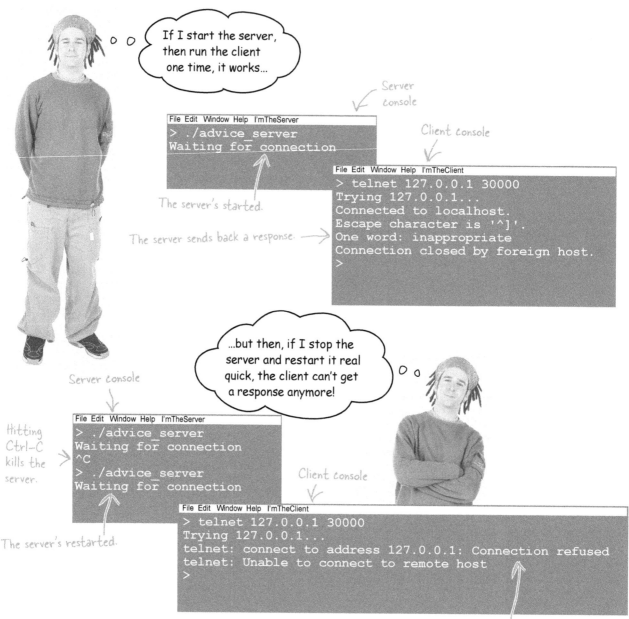

If I start the server, then run the client one time, it works...

Server console

```
File Edit Window Help I'mTheServer
> ./advice_server
Waiting for connection
```

The server's started.

Client console

```
File Edit Window Help I'mTheClient
> telnet 127.0.0.1 30000
Trying 127.0.0.1...
Connected to localhost.
Escape character is '^]'.
One word: inappropriate
Connection closed by foreign host.
>
```

The server sends back a response.

...but then, if I stop the server and restart it real quick, the client can't get a response anymore!

Server console

```
File Edit Window Help I'mTheServer
> ./advice_server
Waiting for connection
^C
> ./advice_server
Waiting for connection
```

Hitting Ctrl-C kills the server.

The server's restarted.

Client console

```
File Edit Window Help I'mTheClient
> telnet 127.0.0.1 30000
Trying 127.0.0.1...
telnet: connect to address 127.0.0.1: Connection refused
telnet: Unable to connect to remote host
>
```

WTF??!?!??

Where's The Feedback????

The server *looks* like it's starting correctly the second time, but the client can't get any response from it. Why is that?

Remember that the code was written **without any error checking**. Let's add a little error check into the code and see if we can figure out what's happening.

Why your mom always told you to check for errors

If you add an error check on the line that binds the socket to a port:

From this...

~~bind (listener_d, (struct sockaddr *) &name, sizeof (name));~~

...to this

```
if (bind (listener_d, (struct sockaddr *) &name, sizeof(name)) == -1)
  error("Can't bind the port");
```

This is calling the error function you wrote a while back. It will display the cause of the error and exit.

Then you'll get a little more information from the server if it is stopped and restarted quickly:

```
File Edit Window Help I'mTheServer
> ./advice_server
Waiting for connection
^C
> ./advice_server
Can't bind the port: Address already in use
>
```

The bind fails!

If the server has responded to a client and then gets stopped and restarted, the call to the bind system call fails. But because the original version of the program never checked for errors, the rest of the server code ran even though it couldn't use the server port.

Bound ports are sticky

When you bind a socket to a port, the operating system will prevent anything else from rebinding to it for the next 30 seconds or so, and that includes the program that bound the port in the first place. To get around the problem, you just need to set an option on the socket before you bind it:

ALWAYS check for errors on system calls.

You need an int variable to store the option. Setting it to 1 means "Yes, reuse the port."

```
int reuse = 1;
if (setsockopt(listener_d, SOL_SOCKET, SO_REUSEADDR, (char *)&reuse, sizeof(int)) == -1)
  error("Can't set the reuse option on the socket");
```

This makes the socket reuse the port.

This code makes the socket **reuse the port** when it's bound. That means you can stop and restart the server and there will be no errors when you bind the port a second time.

Reading from the client

You've learned how to send data to the client, but what about *reading* from the client? In the same way that sockets have a special `send()` function to write data, they also have a **`recv()`** function to read data.

```
<bytes read> = recv(<descriptor>, <buffer>, <bytes to read>, 0);
```

If someone types in a line of text into a client and hits return, the `recv()` function stores the text into a character array like this:

W	h	o	'	s		t	h	e	r	e	?	\r	\n

recv() will return the value 14, because there are 14 characters sent from the client.

There are a few things to remember:

- **The characters are not terminated with a \0 character.**
- **When someone types text in telnet, the string always ends \r\n.**
- **The recv() will return the number of characters, or -1 if there's an error, or 0 if the client has closed the connection.**
- **You're not guaranteed to receive all the characters in a single call to recv().**

This last point is important. It means you might have to call `recv()` more than once:

[W][h][o][']   [s][ ][t]   [h][e][r][e][?][\r][\n]

You might need to call recv() a few times to get all the characters.

That means `recv()` can be tricky to use. It's best to wrap `recv()` in a function that stores a simple `\0`-terminated string in the array it's given. Something like this:

```
int read_in(int socket, char *buf, int len)
{
  char *s = buf;
  int slen = len;
  int c = recv(socket, s, slen, 0);
  while ((c > 0) && (s[c-1] != '\n')) {
    s += c; slen -= c;
    c = recv(socket, s, slen, 0);
  }
  if (c < 0)
    return c;
  else if (c == 0)
    buf[0] = '\0';
  else
    s[c-1]='\0';
  return len - slen;
}
```

This reads all the characters until it reaches '\n'.

Keep reading until there are no more characters or you reach '\n'.

In case there's an error

Nothing read; send back an empty string.

Replace the '\r' character with a '\0'.

-Go Off Piste

This is one way of simplifying `recv()`, but could *you* do better? Why not write your own version of `read_in()` and let us know at *headfirstlabs.com*.

Ready-Bake Code

Here are some other functions that are useful when you are writing a server. Do you understand how each of them works?

You've used this error function a LOT in this book.

Don't call this function if you want the program to keep running.

```
void error(char *msg)
{
  fprintf(stderr, "%s: %s\n", msg, strerror(errno));
  exit(1);
}
```

Display the error... ...then stop the program.

```
int open_listener_socket()
{
  int s = socket(PF_INET, SOCK_STREAM, 0);
  if (s == -1)
    error("Can't open socket");

  return s;
}
```

Create an Internet streaming socket.

Yes, reuse the socket (so you can restart the server without problems).

```
void bind_to_port(int socket, int port)
{
  struct sockaddr_in name;
  name.sin_family = PF_INET;
  name.sin_port = (in_port_t)htons(port);
  name.sin_addr.s_addr = htonl(INADDR_ANY);
  int reuse = 1;
  if (setsockopt(socket, SOL_SOCKET, SO_REUSEADDR, (char *)&reuse, sizeof(int)) == -1)
    error("Can't set the reuse option on the socket");
  int c = bind (socket, (struct sockaddr *) &name, sizeof(name));
  if (c == -1)
    error("Can't bind to socket");
}
```

Grab port.

```
int say(int socket, char *s)
{
  int result = send(socket, s, strlen(s), 0);
  if (result == -1)
    fprintf(stderr, "%s: %s\n", "Error talking to the client", strerror(errno));
  return result;
}
```

Send a string to a client.

Don't call error() if there's a problem. You won't want to stop the server if there's just a problem with one client.

Now that you have a set of server functions, let's try them out...

Long Exercise

Now it's time to write the code for the **Internet knock-knock server**. You're going to write a little more code than usual, but you'll be able to use the ready-bake code from the previous page. Here's the start of the program.

```
#include <stdio.h>
#include <string.h>
#include <errno.h>
#include <stdlib.h>
#include <sys/socket.h>
#include <arpa/inet.h>
#include <unistd.h>
#include <signal.h>
```

← The ready-bake functions from the previous page go here.

This will store the main listener socket for the server. →

```
int listener_d;

void handle_shutdown(int sig)
{
  if (listener_d)
    close(listener_d);

  fprintf(stderr, "Bye!\n");
  exit(0);
}
```

↖ If someone hits Ctrl-C when the server is running, this function will close the socket before the program ends.

Now it's over to you to write the main function. You'll need to create a new server socket and store it in `listener_d`. The socket will be bound to port 30000, and the queue depth should be set to 10. Once that's done, you need to write code that works like this:

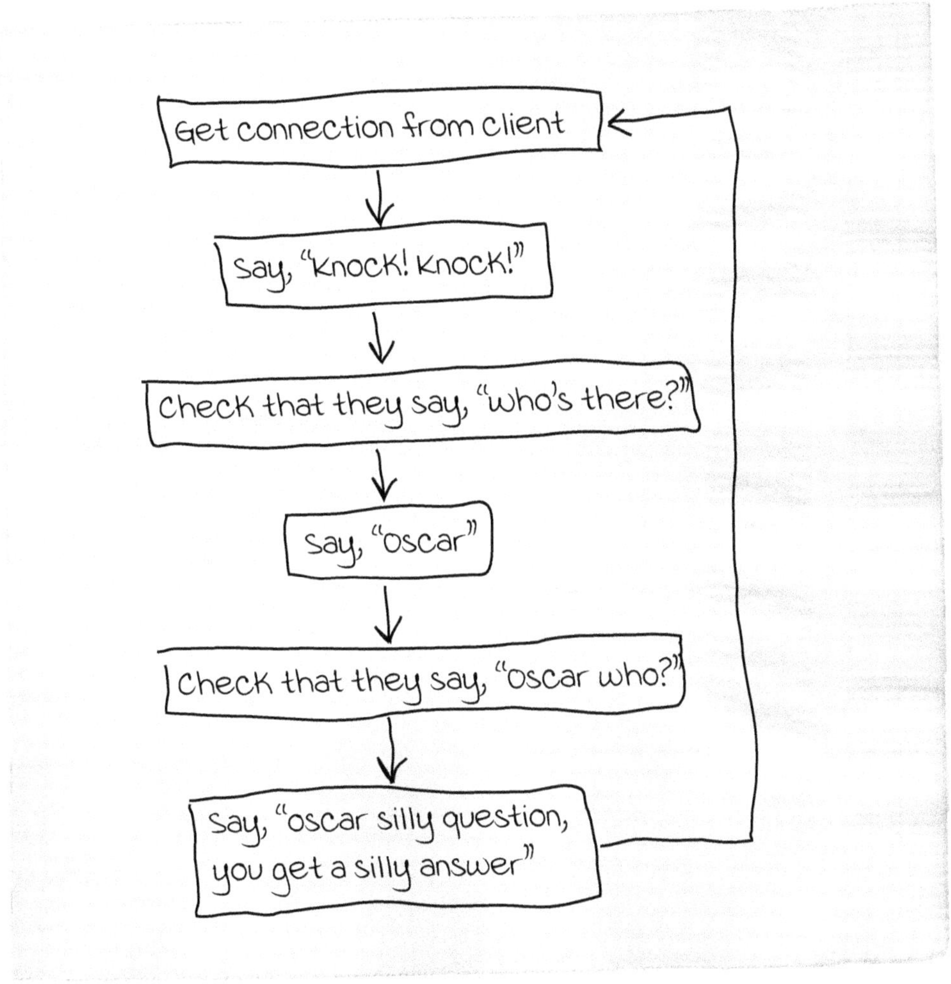
Get connection from client
Say, "Knock! Knock!"
Check that they say, "Who's there?"
Say, "Oscar"
Check that they say, "Oscar who?"
Say, "Oscar silly question, you get a silly answer"

Try to check error codes and if the user says the wrong thing, just send an error message, close the connection, and then wait for another client.

Good luck!

Long Exercise Solution

Now it's time to write the code for the **Internet knock-knock server**. You were to write a little more code than usual, but you'll be able to use the ready-bake code from the previous page. Here's the start of the program.

```
#include <stdio.h>
#include <string.h>
#include <errno.h>
#include <stdlib.h>
#include <sys/socket.h>
#include <arpa/inet.h>
#include <unistd.h>
#include <signal.h>
```

← The ready-bake functions from the previous page go here.

This will store the main listener socket for the server. →

```
int listener_d;

void handle_shutdown(int sig)
{
  if (listener_d)
    close(listener_d);

  fprintf(stderr, "Bye!\n");
  exit(0);
}
```

If someone hits Ctrl-C when the server is running, this function will close the socket before the program ends.

This is the kind of code you should have written. Is yours similar? It doesn't matter if the code is *exactly* the same. The important thing is that your code can tell the joke in the right way, and cope with errors.

```
int main(int argc, char *argv[])
{
  if (catch_signal(SIGINT, handle_shutdown) == -1)
    error("Can't set the interrupt handler");   <-- This will call handle_shutdown() if Ctrl-C is hit.
  listener_d = open_listener_socket();
  bind_to_port(listener_d, 30000);   <-- Create a socket on port 30000.
  if (listen(listener_d, 10) == -1)   <-- Set the listen-queue length to 10.
    error("Can't listen");
  struct sockaddr_storage client_addr;
  unsigned int address_size = sizeof(client_addr);
  puts("Waiting for connection");
  char buf[255];
  while (1) {
    int connect_d = accept(listener_d, (struct sockaddr *)&client_addr, &address_size);   <-- Listen for a connection.
    if (connect_d == -1)
      error("Can't open secondary socket");
    if (say(connect_d,   <-- Send data to the client.
          "Internet Knock-Knock Protocol Server\r\nVersion 1.0\r\nKnock! Knock!\r\n> ") != -1) {
      read_in(connect_d, buf, sizeof(buf));   <-- Read data from the client.
      if (strncasecmp("Who's there?", buf, 12))
        say(connect_d, "You should say 'Who's there?'!");   <-- Checking the user's answers.
      else {
        if (say(connect_d, "Oscar\r\n> ") != -1) {
          read_in(connect_d, buf, sizeof(buf));
          if (strncasecmp("Oscar who?", buf, 10))
            say(connect_d, "You should say 'Oscar who?'!\r\n");
          else
            say(connect_d, "Oscar silly question, you get a silly answer\r\n");
        }
      }
    }
    close(connect_d);   <-- Close the secondary socket we used for the conversation.
  }
  return 0;
}
```

Test Drive

Now that you've written the knock-knock server, it's time to compile it and fire it up.

Server console

```
File Edit Window Help I'mTheServer
> gcc ikkp_server.c -o ikkp_server
> ./ikkp_server
Waiting for connection
```

The server's waiting for a connection, so open a separate console and connect to it with telnet:

Client console

```
File Edit Window Help I'mTheClient
> telnet 127.0.0.1 30000
Trying 127.0.0.1...
Connected to localhost.
Escape character is '^]'.
Internet Knock-Knock Protocol Server
Version 1.0
Knock! Knock!
> Who's there?
Oscar
> Oscar who?
Oscar silly question, you get a silly answer
Connection closed by foreign host.
```

The server can tell you a joke, but what happens if you break the protocol and send back an invalid response?

Client console

```
File Edit Window Help I'mTheClient
> telnet 127.0.0.1 30000
Trying 127.0.0.1...
Connected to localhost.
Escape character is '^]'.
Internet Knock-Knock Protocol Server
Version 1.0
Knock! Knock!
> Come in
You should say 'Who's there?'!Connection closed by foreign host.
>
```

The server is able to validate the data you send it and close the connection immediately. Once you're done running the server, you can switch back to the server window and hit Ctrl-C to close it down neatly. It even sends you a farewell message:

Server console

```
File Edit Window Help I'mTheServer
> gcc ikkp_server.c -o ikkp_server
> ./ikkp_server
Waiting for connection
^CBye!
>
```

That's great! The server does everything you need it to do.

Or does it?

The server can only talk to one person at a time

There's a problem with the current server code. Imagine someone connects to it and he is a little slow with his responses:

The server is running on a machine out on the Internet.

```
File Edit Window Help I'mTheClient
> telnet knockknockster.com 30000
Trying knockknockster.com...
Connected to localhost.
Escape character is '^]'.
Internet Knock-Knock Protocol Server
Version 1.0
Knock! Knock!
> Who's there?
Oscar
>
```

Oh, wait! Oscar! Oh, I know this one... Oh, it's so funny... It's... Oscar...Oscar who? Hey,that's like... no, wait...don't tell me...

Then, if someone else tries to get through to the server, she can't; it's busy with the first guy:

```
File Edit Window Help I'mAnotherClient
> telnet knockknockster.com 30000
Trying knockknockster.com...
Connected to localhost.
Escape character is '^]'.
```

Oh, great! I can't get through to the server and I can't even Ctrl-C my way out of telnet. What gives?

The problem is that the server is still busy talking to the first guy. The main server socket will keep the client waiting until the server calls the `accept()` system call again. But because of the guy already connected, it will be some time before that happens.

BRAIN POWER

The server can't respond to the second user, because it is busy dealing with the first. What have you learned that might help you deal with *both* clients *at once*?

You can fork() a process for each client

When the clients connect to the server, they start to have a conversation on a separate, newly created socket. That means the main server socket is free to go and find another client. So let's do that.

When a client connects, you can `fork()` a separate child process to deal with the conversation between the server and the client.

Child process
Hey, great to see you! I'll just hand you over to someone who can deal with you.
Parent process
Client

While the client is talking to the child process, the server's parent process can go connect to the next client.

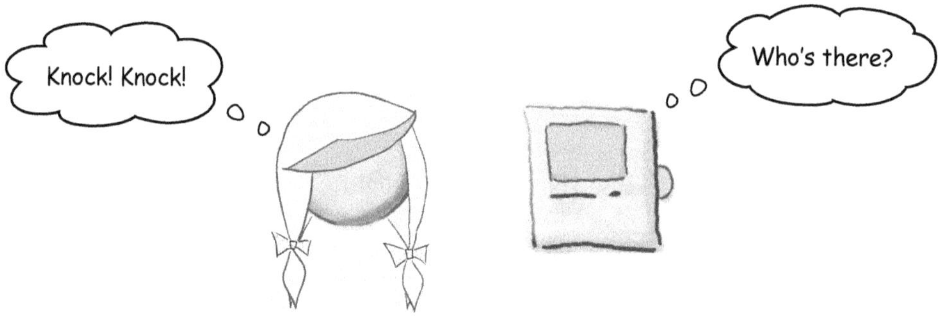
Knock! Knock!
Who's there?

The parent and child use different sockets

One thing to bear in mind is that the parent server process will only need to use the main listener socket. That's because the main listener socket is the one that's used to `accept()` new connections. On the other hand, the child process will only ever need to deal with the secondary socket that gets created by the `accept()` call. That means once the parent has `fork`ed the child, the parent can close the secondary socket and the child can close the main listener socket.

After forking the child, the parent can close this socket.

```
close(connect_d);
close(listener_d);
```

Once the child gets created, it can close this socket.

there are no Dumb Questions

Q: If I create a new process for each client, what happens if hundreds of clients connect? Will my machine create hundreds of processes?

A: Yes. If you think your server will get a lot of clients, you need to control how many processes you create. The child can signal you when it's finished with a client, and you can use that to maintain a count of current child processes.

Sharpen your pencil

This is a version of the server code that has been changed to `fork` a separate child process to talk to each client…except it's not quite finished. See if you can figure out the missing pieces of code.

```
while (1) {
  int connect_d = accept(listener_d, (struct sockaddr *)&client_addr,
                         &address_size);
  if (connect_d == -1)
    error("Can't open secondary socket");

  if (........................) {
    close(........................);
    if (say(connect_d,
        "Internet Knock-Knock Protocol Server\r\nVersion 1.0\r\nKnock! Knock!\r\n> ")
      != -1) {
      read_in(connect_d, buf, sizeof(buf));

      if (strncasecmp("Who's there?", buf, 12))
        say(connect_d, "You should say 'Who's there?'!");
      else {
        if (say(connect_d, "Oscar\r\n> ") != -1) {
          read_in(connect_d, buf, sizeof(buf));

          if (strncasecmp("Oscar who?", buf, 10))
            say(connect_d, "You should say 'Oscar who?'!\r\n");
          else
            say(connect_d, "Oscar silly question, you get a silly answer\r\n");
        }
      }
    }
    close(........................);
    ........................  <-- What should the child do when the conversation is done?
  }
  close(........................);
}
```

Sharpen your pencil Solution

This is a version of the server code that has been changed to `fork` a separate child process to talk to each client—except it's not quite finished. You were to figure out the missing pieces of code.

```
while (1) {
  int connect_d = accept(listener_d, (struct sockaddr *)&client_addr,
                         &address_size);
  if (connect_d == -1)
    error("Can't open secondary socket");

  if ( !fork() ) {
    close( listener_d );
    if (say(connect_d,
          "Internet Knock-Knock Protocol Server\r\nVersion 1.0\r\nKnock! Knock!\r\n> ")
        != -1) {
      read_in(connect_d, buf, sizeof(buf));

      if (strncasecmp("Who's there?", buf, 12))
        say(connect_d, "You should say 'Who's there?'!");
      else {
        if (say(connect_d, "Oscar\r\n> ") != -1) {
          read_in(connect_d, buf, sizeof(buf));

          if (strncasecmp("Oscar who?", buf, 10))
            say(connect_d, "You should say 'Oscar who?'!\r\n");
          else
            say(connect_d, "Oscar silly question, you get a silly answer\r\n");
        }
      }
    }
    close( connect_d );
    exit(0);
  }
  close( connect_d );
}
```

Annotations:

- `!fork()`: This creates the child process, and you know that if the fork() call returns 0, you must be in the child.
- `close( listener_d );`: In the child, you need to close the main listener socket. The child will use only the connect_d socket to talk to the client.
- `close( connect_d );` (in the child): Once the conversation's over, the child can close the socket to the client.
- `exit(0);`: Once the child process has finished talking, it should exit. That will prevent it from falling into the main server loop.

Test Drive

Let's try the modified version of the server. You can compile and run it in the same way:

Server console

```
File Edit Window Help I'mTheServer
> gcc ikkp_server.c -o ikkp_server
> ./ikkp_server
Waiting for connection
```

If you open a separate console and start telnet, you can connect, just like you did before:

Client console

```
File Edit Window Help I'mTheClient
> telnet 127.0.0.1 30000
Trying 127.0.0.1...
Connected to localhost.
Escape character is '^]'.
Internet Knock-Knock Protocol Server
Version 1.0
Knock! Knock!
> Who's there?
Oscar
>
```

Everything seems the same, but if you leave the client running with the joke half-told, you should be able to see what's changed:

If you open a third console, you will see that there are now two processes for the server: one for the parent and one for the child:

The ps command shows running processes in Unix and Cygwin.

The parent process

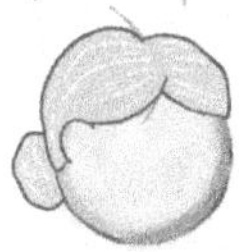

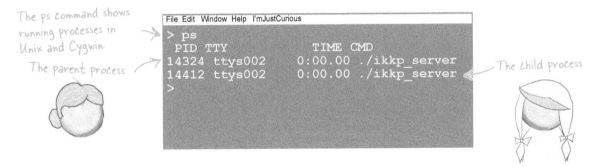

```
File Edit Window Help I'mJustCurious
> ps
 PID TTY           TIME CMD
14324 ttys002    0:00.00 ./ikkp_server
14412 ttys002    0:00.00 ./ikkp_server
>
```

The child process

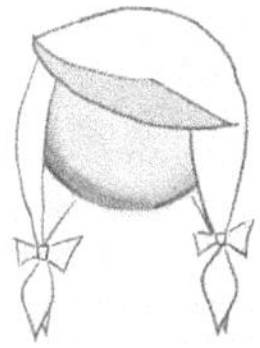

That means you can connect, even while the first client is still talking to the server:

Another client console

```
File Edit Window Help I'mAnotherClient
> telnet 127.0.0.1 30000
Trying 127.0.0.1...
Connected to localhost.
Escape character is '^]'.
Internet Knock-Knock Protocol Server
Version 1.0
Knock! Knock!
>
```

Now that you've built an Internet server, let's go look at what it takes to build a client, by writing something that can read from the Web.

Writing a web client

What if you want to write your own client program? Is it really *that* different from a server? To see the similarities and differences, you're going to write a **web client** for the hypertext transfer protocol (HTTP).

HTTP is a lot like the Internet knock-knock protocol you coded earlier. All protocols are *structured conversations*. Every time a web client and server talk, they say the same kind of things. Open telnet and see how to download *http://en.wikipedia.org/wiki/O'Reilly_Media*.

Do this!

Most web servers run on port 80.

This is the numeric address of Wikipedia. You might get a slightly different address when you try it.

You need to type in these two lines.

And then you need to hit return and leave a blank line.

The server first responds with some extra details about the web page.

File Edit Window Help I'mJustCurious

```
> telnet en.wikipedia.org 80
Trying 91.198.174.225...
Connected to wikipedia-lb.esams.wikimedia.org.
Escape character is '^]'.
GET /wiki/O'Reilly_Media HTTP/1.1
Host: en.wikipedia.org

HTTP/1.0 200 OK
Server: Apache
...
<!DOCTYPE html PUBLIC "-//W3C//DTD XHTML 1.0 Transitional//EN"
"http://www.w3.org/TR/xhtml1/DTD/xhtml1-transitional.dtd">
<html lang=en" dir="ltr" class="client-nojs"
xmlns="http://www.w3.org/1999/xhtml">
<head>
<title>O'Reilly Media - Wikipedia, the free encyclopedia</title>
...
```

This is the path that follows the hostname in the URL.

In HTTP/1.1, you need to say what hostname you are using.

And this is the HTML for the web page.

When your program connects to the web server, it will need to send at least three things:

Most web clients actually send a lot more information, but you'll just send the minimum amount.

- **A GET command**
  `GET /wiki/O'Reilly_Media HTTP/1.1`
- **The hostname**
  `Host: en.wikipedia.org`
- **A blank line**

But before you can send any data at all to the server, you need to make a connection from the client. How do you do that?

Clients are in charge

Clients and servers communicate using sockets, but the way that each gets hold of a socket is a little different. You've already seen that ***servers*** use the BLAB sequence:

1. **Bind a port.**
2. **Listen.**
3. **Accept a conversation.**
4. **Begin talking.**

I was taught never to speak until I'm spoken to.
Server

A server spends most of its life waiting for a fresh connection from a client. Until a client connects, a server really can't do anything. Clients don't have that problem. A client can connect and start talking to a server whenever it likes. This is the sequence for a ***client***:

1. **Connect to a remote port.**
2. **Begin talking.**

Remote ports and IP addresses

When a server connects to the network, it just has to decide which port it's going to use. But clients need to know a little more: they need to know the port of the remote server, but they also need to know its **internet protocol (IP) address**:

```
208.201.239.100
```

← Addresses with four digits are in IP version 4 format. Most will eventually be replaced with longer version 6 addresses.

Internet addresses are kind of hard to remember, which is why most of the time human beings use **domain names**. A domain name is just an easier-to-remember piece of text like:

www.oreilly.com

Even though human beings prefer domain names, the actual packets of information that flow across the network only use the numeric IP address.

Create a socket for an IP address

Once your client knows the address and port number of the server, it can create a **client socket**. Client sockets and server sockets are created the same way:

```
int s = socket(PF_INET, SOCK_STREAM, 0);
```

To save space, the examples won't include the error check here. But in your code, **always** check for errors.

The difference between client and server code is what they do with sockets once they're created. A server will **bind** the socket to a *local* port, but a client will **connect** the socket to a *remote port*:

These lines create a socket address for 208.201.239.100 on port 80.

```
struct sockaddr_in si;
memset(&si, 0, sizeof(si));
si.sin_family = PF_INET;
si.sin_addr.s_addr = inet_addr("208.201.239.100");
si.sin_port = htons(80);
connect(s, (struct sockaddr *) &si, sizeof(si));
```

This line connects the socket to the remote port.

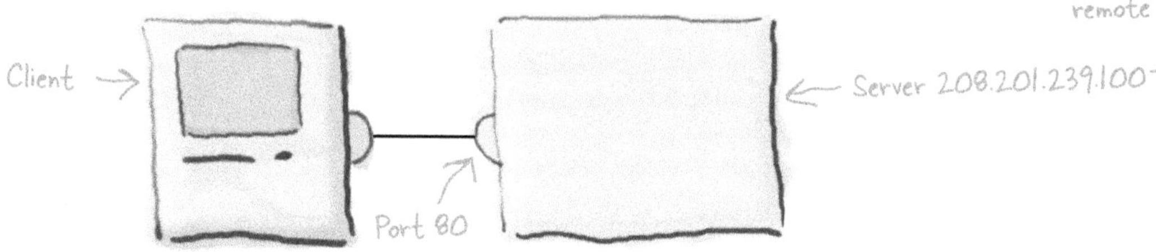
Client
Server 208.201.239.100
Port 80

Hello? I don't want to know how to connect a socket to an IP address. I'm actually **human**...I want to connect to a real domain name.

The above code works only for numeric IP addresses.

To connect a socket to a remote domain name, you'll need a function called `getaddrinfo()`.

getaddrinfo() gets addresses for domains

The *domain name system* is a huge address book. It's a way of converting a domain name like *www.oreilly.com* into the kinds of numeric IP addresses that computers need to address the packets of information they send across the network.

The DNS is a gigantic address book.

Domain name	Address
en.wikipedia.org	91.198.174.225
www.oreilly.com	208.201.239.100
www.oreilly.com	208.201.239.101

Some large sites have several IP addresses.

Computers need IP addresses to create network packets.

Create a socket for a domain name

Most of the time, you'll want your client code to use the DNS system to create sockets. That way, your users won't have to look up the IP addresses themselves. To use DNS, you need to construct your client sockets in a slightly different way:

```
#include <netdb.h>
...
struct addrinfo *res;
struct addrinfo hints;
memset(&hints, 0, sizeof(hints));
hints.ai_family = PF_UNSPEC;
hints.ai_socktype = SOCK_STREAM;
getaddrinfo("www.oreilly.com", "80", &hints, &res);
```

You'll need to include this header for the getaddrinfo() function.

This creates a name resource for port 80 on www.oreilly.com.

getaddrinfo() expects the port to be a **string**.

The `getaddrinfo()` constructs a new data structure on the **heap** called a *naming resource*. The naming resource represents a port on a server with a given domain name. Hidden away inside the naming resource is the IP address that the computer will need. Sometimes very large domains can have several IP addresses, but the code here will simply pick one of them. You can then use the naming resource to create a socket.

Now you can create the socket using the naming resource.

```
int s = socket(res->ai_family, res->ai_socktype,
               res->ai_protocol);
```

Finally, you can connect to the remote socket. Because the naming resource was created on the heap, you'll need to tidy it away with a function called **`freeaddrinfo()`**:

```
connect(s, res->ai_addr, res->ai_addrlen);
freeaddrinfo(res);
```

res->ai_addr is the addr of the remote host and port.

res->ai_addrlen is the size of the address in memory.

This will connect to the remote socket.

When you've connected, you can delete the address data with freeaddrinfo().

Once you've connected a socket to a remote port, you can read and write to it using the same `recv()` and `send()` functions you used for the server. That means you should have enough information now to write a web client…

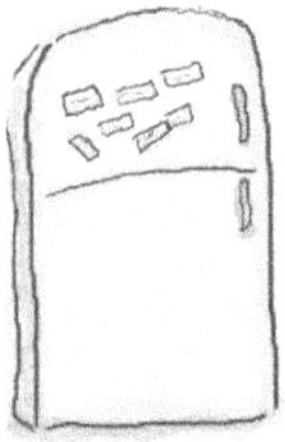

Code Magnets

Here is the code for a web client that will download the contents of a page from Wikipedia and display it on the screen. The web page will be passed as an argument to the program. Think carefully about the data you need to send to a web server running HTTP.

```
#include <stdio.h>
#include <string.h>
#include <errno.h>
#include <stdlib.h>
#include <sys/socket.h>
#include <arpa/inet.h>
#include <unistd.h>
#include <netdb.h>

void error(char *msg)
{
  fprintf(stderr, "%s: %s\n", msg, strerror(errno));
  exit(1);
}

int open_socket(char *host, char *port)
{
  struct addrinfo *res;
  struct addrinfo hints;
  memset(&hints, 0, sizeof(hints));
  hints.ai_family = PF_UNSPEC;
  hints.ai_socktype = SOCK_STREAM;
  if (getaddrinfo(host, port, &hints, &res) == -1)
    error("Can't resolve the address");
  int d_sock = socket(res->ai_family, res->ai_socktype,
                      res->ai_protocol);
  if (d_sock == -1)
    error("Can't open socket");
  int c = connect(d_sock, res->ai_addr, res->ai_addrlen);
  freeaddrinfo(res);
  if (c == -1)
    error("Can't connect to socket");
  return d_sock;
}
```

```
int say(int socket, char *s)
{
  int result = send(socket, s, strlen(s), 0);
  if (result == -1)
    fprintf(stderr, "%s: %s\n", "Error talking to the server",
strerror(errno));
  return result;
}

int main(int argc, char *argv[])
{
  int d_sock;

  d_sock = ..........................................................;
  char buf[255];

  sprintf(buf, .......................................................... , argv[1]);
  say(d_sock, buf);

  say(d_sock, ..........................................................);
  char rec[256];
  int bytesRcvd = recv(d_sock, rec, 255, 0);
  while (bytesRcvd) {
    if (bytesRcvd == -1)
      error("Can't read from server");

    rec[bytesRcvd] = ..........................................................;
    printf("%s", rec);
    bytesRcvd = recv(d_sock, rec, 255, 0);
  }

  ..........................................................;
  return 0;
}
```

```
'\0'
"\r\n"
"Host: en.wikipedia.org\r\n\r\n"
"GET /wiki/%s HTTP/1.1\r\n"
open_socket("en.wikipedia.org", "80")
"Host: en.wikipedia.org\r\n"
close(d_sock)
```

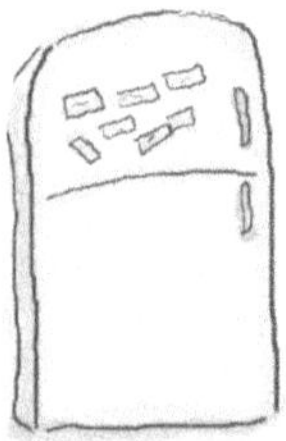

Code Magnets Solution

Here is the code for a web client that will download the contents of a page from Wikipedia and display it on the screen. The web page will be passed as an argument to the program. You were to think carefully about the data you need to send to a web server running HTTP.

```
#include <stdio.h>
#include <string.h>
#include <errno.h>
#include <stdlib.h>
#include <sys/socket.h>
#include <arpa/inet.h>
#include <unistd.h>
#include <netdb.h>

void error(char *msg)
{
  fprintf(stderr, "%s: %s\n", msg, strerror(errno));
  exit(1);
}

int open_socket(char *host, char *port)
{
  struct addrinfo *res;
  struct addrinfo hints;
  memset(&hints, 0, sizeof(hints));
  hints.ai_family = PF_UNSPEC;
  hints.ai_socktype = SOCK_STREAM;
  if (getaddrinfo(host, port, &hints, &res) == -1)
    error("Can't resolve the address");
  int d_sock = socket(res->ai_family, res->ai_socktype,
                      res->ai_protocol);
  if (d_sock == -1)
    error("Can't open socket");
  int c = connect(d_sock, res->ai_addr, res->ai_addrlen);
  freeaddrinfo(res);
  if (c == -1)
    error("Can't connect to socket");
  return d_sock;
}
```

```
int say(int socket, char *s)
{
  int result = send(socket, s, strlen(s), 0);
  if (result == -1)
    fprintf(stderr, "%s: %s\n", "Error talking to the server",
strerror(errno));
  return result;
}

int main(int argc, char *argv[])
{
  int d_sock;

  d_sock = open_socket("en.wikipedia.org", "80");
  char buf[255];

  sprintf(buf, "GET /wiki/%s HTTP/1.1\r\n", argv[1]);
  say(d_sock, buf);

  say(d_sock, "Host: en.wikipedia.org\r\n\r\n");
  char rec[256];
  int bytesRcvd = recv(d_sock, rec, 255, 0);
  while (bytesRcvd) {
    if (bytesRcvd == -1)
      error("Can't read from server");

    rec[bytesRcvd] = '\0';
    printf("%s", rec);
    bytesRcvd = recv(d_sock, rec, 255, 0);
  }
  close(d_sock);
  return 0;
}
```

Create a string for the path to the page you want.

This sends the host data as well as a blank line.

Add a '\0' to the end of the array of characters to make it a proper string.

"\r\n"

"Host: en.wikipedia.org\r\n"

Test Drive

If you compile and run the web client, you make it download a page from Wikipedia like this:

You'll have to replace any spaces with underscore (_) characters.

```
File Edit Window Help I'mTheWebClient
> gcc wiki_client.c -o wiki_client
> ./wiki_client "O'Reilly_Media"
HTTP/1.0 200 OK
Date: Fri, 06 Jan 2012 20:30:15 GMT
Server: Apache
...
Connection: close
<!DOCTYPE html PUBLIC "-//W3C//DTD XHTML 1.0 Transitional//EN"
 "http://www.w3.org/TR/xhtml1/DTD/xhtml1-transitional.dtd">
<html lang="en" dir="ltr" class="client-nojs" xmlns="http://www.w3.org/1999/xhtml">
<head>
<title>O'Reilly Media - Wikipedia, the free encyclopedia</title>
<meta http-equiv="Content-Type" content="text/html; charset=UTF-8" />
...
```

At the beginning, you'll get the response HEADERS. These tell you things about the server and the web page.

Then you get the contents of the web page from Wikipedia.

It works!

The client took the name of the page from the command line and then connected to Wikipedia to download the page. Because it's constructing the *path* to the file, you need to make sure that the you replace any spaces in the page name with underscore (_) characters.

Go Off Piste

Why not update the code to automatically replace characters like spaces for you? For more details on how to replace characters for web addresses, see:

http://www.w3schools.com/tags/ref_urlencode.asp

there are no Dumb Questions

Q: Should I create sockets with IP addresses or domain names?

A: Most of the time, you'll want to use domain names. They're easier to remember, and occasionally some servers will change their numeric addresses but keep the same domain names.

Q: So, do I even need to know how to connect to a numeric address?

A: Yes. If the server you are connecting to is not registered in the domain name system, such as machines on your home network, then you will need to know how to connect by IP.

Q: Can I use `getaddrinfo()` with a numeric address?

A: Yes, you can. But if you *know* that the address you are using is a numeric IP, the first version of the client socket code is simpler.

BULLET POINTS

- A protocol is a structured conversation.
- Servers connect to local ports.
- Clients connect to remote ports.
- Clients and servers both use sockets to communicate.
- You write data to a socket with `send()`.
- You read data from a socket with `recv()`.
- HTTP is the protocol used on the Web.

Your C Toolbox

You've got Chapter 11 under your belt, and now you've added sockets and networking to your toolbox. For a complete list of tooltips in the book, see Appendix ii.

Telnet is a simple network client.

Create sockets with the socket() function.

Servers BLAB:
B = bind()
L = listen()
A = accept()
B = Begin talking

Use fork() to cope with several clients at once.

DNS = Domain name system

getaddrinfo() finds addresses by domain.

12 threads

It's a parallel world

Johnny told me he got his heap variables locked in a mutex.

Programs often need to do several things at the same time.

POSIX threads can make your code more responsive by **spinning off several pieces of code to run in parallel**. But be careful! Threads are powerful tools, but you don't want them crashing into each other. In this chapter, you'll learn how to put up **traffic signs** and **lane markers** that will ***prevent a code pileup***. By the end, you will know how to **create POSIX threads** and how to use **synchronization mechanisms** to ***protect the integrity of sensitive data***.

Tasks are sequential...or not...

Imagine you are writing something complex like a game in C. The code will need to perform several different tasks:

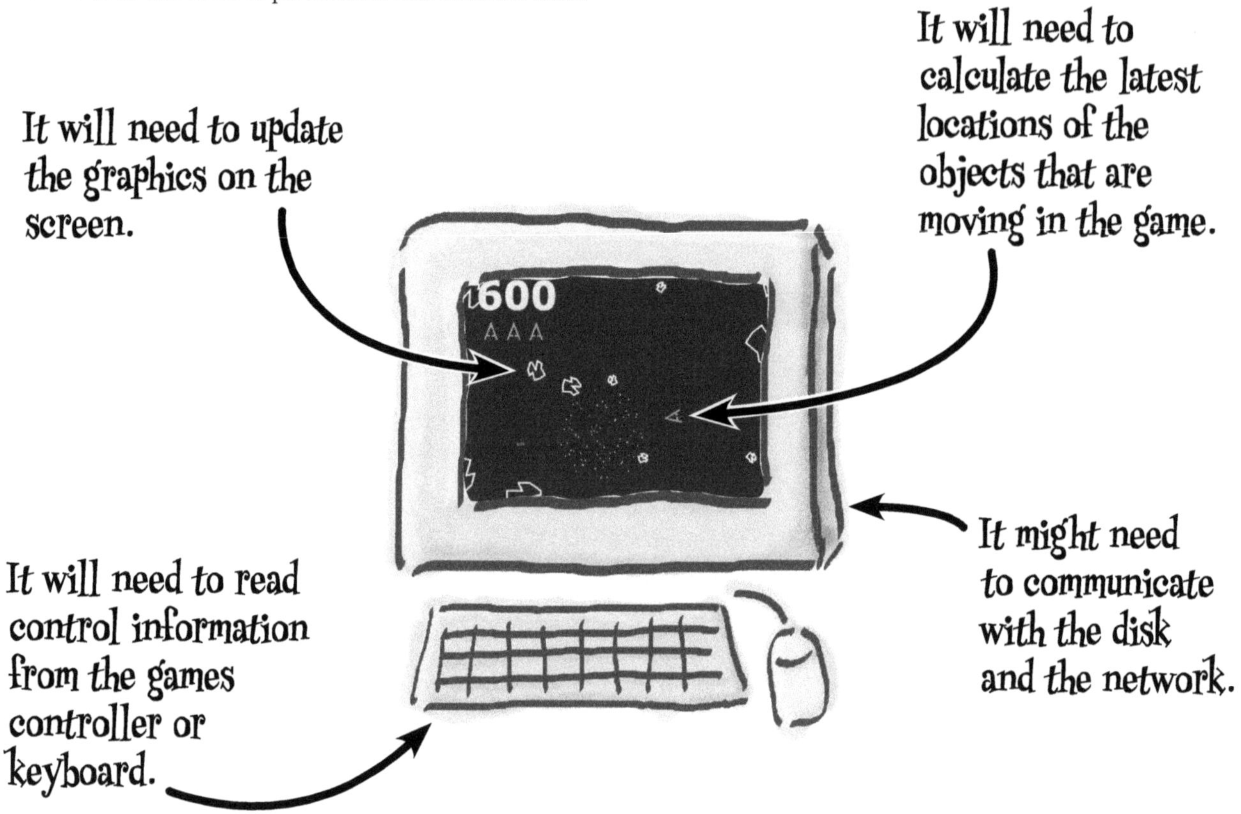
It will need to update the graphics on the screen.
It will need to calculate the latest locations of the objects that are moving in the game.
600
It will need to read control information from the games controller or keyboard.
It might need to communicate with the disk and the network.

Not only will your code need to do all of these things, but it will need to do them ***all at the same time***. That's going to be true for many different programs. Chat programs will need to read text from the network and send data to the network at the same time. Media players will need to stream video to the display as well as watch for input from the user controls.

How can your code perform several different tasks at once?

...and processes are not always the answer

You've already learned how to make the computer do several things at once: with ***processes***. In the last chapter, you built a network server that could deal with several different clients at once. Each time a new user connected, the server created a new process to handle the new session.

Does that mean that whenever you want to do several things at once, you should just create a separate process? Well, not really, and here's why.

Processes take time to create

Some machines take a little while to create new processes. Not much time, but some. If the extra task you want to perform takes just a few hundredths of a second, creating a process each time won't be very efficient.

Processes can't share data easily

When you create a child process, it automatically has a complete copy of all the data from the parent process. But it's a copy of the data. If the child needs to send data back to the parent, then you need something like a pipe to do that for you.

Processes are just plain difficult

You need to create a chunk of code to generate processes, and that can make your programs long and messy.

You need something that starts a separate task quickly, can share all of your current data, and won't need a huge amount of code to build.

You need *threads*.

Simple processes do one thing at a time

Say you have a task list with a set of things that you need to do:

Shop-n-Surf

Run the cash register.
Stock the shop.
Rewax the surfboards.
Answer the phones.
Fix the roof.
Keep the books.

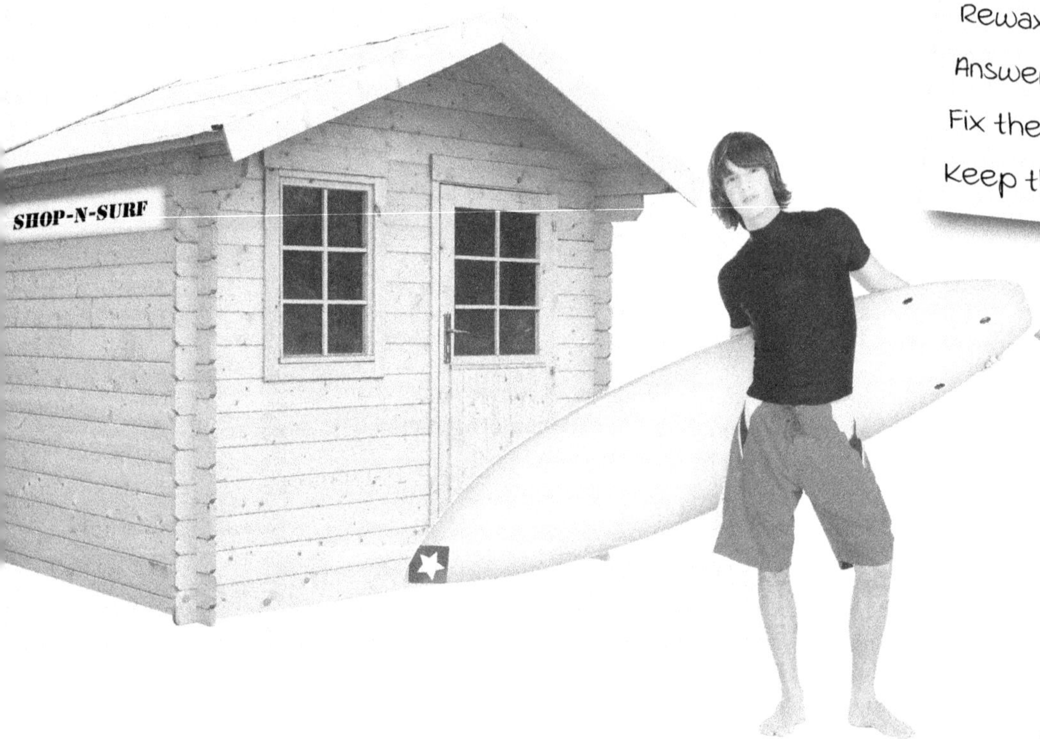
SHOP-N-SURF
Alternatively, just go surfing.

You can't do all of the tasks at the same time, not by yourself. If someone comes into the shop, you'll need to stop stocking the shelves. If it looks like rain, you might stop bookkeeping and get on the roof. If you work in a shop alone, you're like a simple process: you do one thing after another, but always one thing at a time. Sure, you can switch between tasks to keep everything going, but what if there's a **blocking operation**? What if you're serving someone at the checkout and the phone rings?

All of the programs you've written so far have had a **single thread of execution**. It's like there's only been one person working inside the program's process.

Well, I can't do everything all at once. Who do you think I am?
Process.

Employ extra staff: use threads

Shop-n-Surf
Run the cash register.
Stock the shop.
Re-wax the surfboards.
Answer the phones.
Fix the roof.
Keep the books.

A **multithreaded** program is like a shop with several people working in it. If one person is running the checkout, another is filling the shelves, and someone else is waxing the surfboards, then everybody can work without interruptions. If one person answers the phone, it won't stop the other people in the shop.

If you employ more people, more than one thing can be done at once.

In the same way that several people can work in the same shop, you can have several threads living inside the same process. All of the threads will have access to the same piece of heap memory. They will all be able to read and write to the same files and talk on the same network sockets. If one thread changes a global variable, all of the other threads will see the change immediately.

That means you can give each thread a separate task and they'll all be performed at the same time.

You can run each task inside a separate thread.
Read games controller input.
Update screen.
Calculate physics of rocket.
Send text message to network.
If one thread has to wait for something, the other threads can keep running.
All of the threads can run inside a single process.

How do you create threads?

There are a few thread libraries, and you're going to use one of the most popular: the **POSIX thread library**, or **`pthread`**. You can use the `pthread` library on Cygwin, Linux, and the Mac.

Let's say you want to run these two functions in separate threads:

```
void* does_not(void *a)
{
  int i = 0;
  for (i = 0; i < 5; i++) {
    sleep(1);
    puts("Does not!");
  }
  return NULL;
}
```

Thread functions need to have a void* return type.

```
void* does_too(void *a)
{
  int i = 0;
  for (i = 0; i < 5; i++) {
    sleep(1);
    puts("Does too!");
  }
  return NULL;
}
```

Nothing useful to return, so just use NULL.

Did you notice that both functions return a *void pointer*? Remember, a void pointer can be used to point to any piece of data in memory, and you'll need to make sure that your thread functions have a **`void*`** return type.

You're going to run each of these functions inside its own thread.

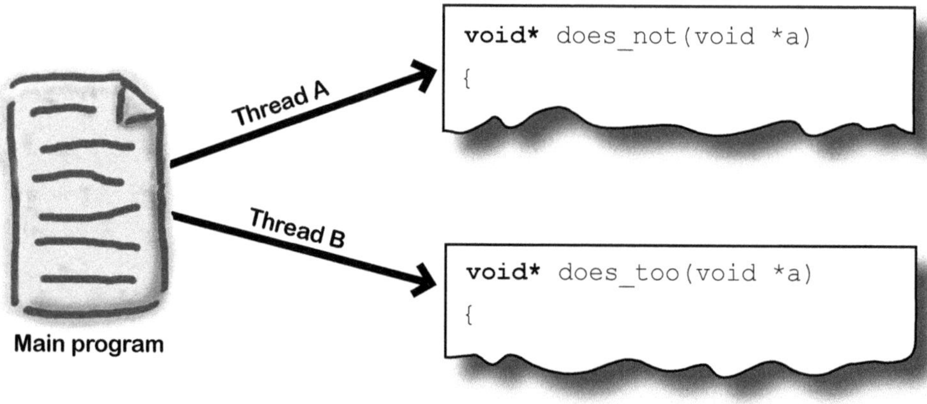
Main program
Thread A
Thread B
void* does_not(void *a)
{
void* does_too(void *a)
{

You'll need to run both of these functions in parallel in separate threads. Let's see how to do that.

Create threads with pthread_create

To run these functions, you'll need a little setup code, like some headers and maybe an `error()` function that you can call if there's a problem.

```
#include <stdio.h>
#include <stdlib.h>
#include <string.h>
#include <unistd.h>
#include <errno.h>
#include <pthread.h>

void error(char *msg)
{
  fprintf(stderr, "%s: %s\n", msg, strerror(errno));
  exit(1);
}
```

These are the headers for the main part of the code.

This is the header for the pthread library.

But then you can start the code for your main function. You're going to create two threads, and each one needs to have its info stored in a **`pthread_t`** data structure. Then you can create and run a thread with **`pthread_create()`**.

```
pthread_t t0;
pthread_t t1;
if (pthread_create(&t0, NULL, does_not, NULL) == -1)
  error("Can't create thread t0");
if (pthread_create(&t1, NULL, does_too, NULL) == -1)
  error("Can't create thread t1");
```

This records all the information about the thread.

does_not is the name of the function the thread will run.

This creates the thread.

Always check for errors.

&t1 is the address of the data structure that will store the thread info.

That code will run your two functions in separate threads. But you've not quite finished yet. If your program just ran this and then finished, the threads would be killed when the program ended. So you need to wait for your threads to finish:

```
void* result;
if (pthread_join(t0, &result) == -1)
  error("Can't join thread t0");
if (pthread_join(t1, &result) == -1)
  error("Can't join thread t1");
```

The void pointer returned from each function will be stored here.

The pthread_join() function waits for a thread to finish.

The `pthread_join()` also receives the return value of your thread function and stores it in a void pointer variable. Once both threads have finished, your program can exit smoothly.

Let's see if it works.

Test Drive

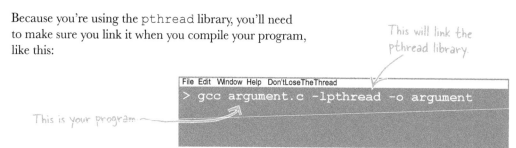

Because you're using the `pthread` library, you'll need to make sure you link it when you compile your program, like this:

This will link the pthread library.

```
File Edit Window Help Don'tLoseTheThread
> gcc argument.c -lpthread -o argument
```

This is your program.

When you run the code, you'll see both functions running at the same time:

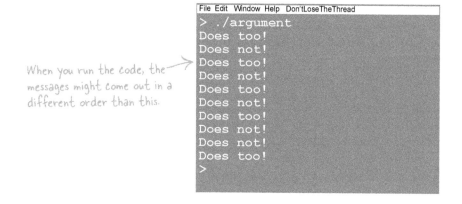

```
File Edit Window Help Don'tLoseTheThread
> ./argument
Does too!
Does not!
Does too!
Does not!
Does too!
Does not!
Does too!
Does not!
Does not!
Does too!
>
```

When you run the code, the messages might come out in a different order than this.

there are no Dumb Questions

Q: If both functions are running at the same time, why don't the letters in the messages get mixed up? Each message is on its own line.

A: That's because of the way the Standard Output works. The text from `puts()` will all get output at once.

Q: I removed the `sleep()` function, and the output showed all the output from one function and then all the output from the other function. Why is that?

A: Most machines will run the code so quickly that without the `sleep()` call, the first function will finish before the second thread starts running.

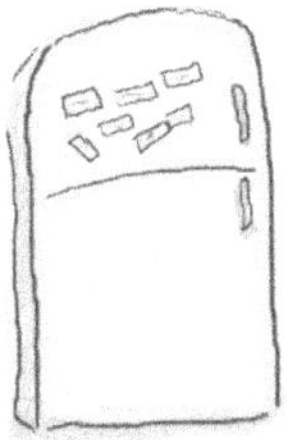

Beer Magnets

It's time for a really BIG party. This code runs 20 threads that count the number of beers down from 2,000,000. See if you can spot the missing code, and if you get the answer right, celebrate by cracking open a couple of cold ones yourself.

```
int beers = 2000000;        <- Begin with 2 million beers.
void* drink_lots(void *a)
{                            <- Each thread will run this function.
  int i;
  for (i = 0; i < 100000; i++) {
    beers = beers - 1;       <- The function will reduce the
  }                             beers variable by 100,000.
  return NULL;
}
int main()
{
  pthread_t threads[20];
  int t;
  printf("%i bottles of beer on the wall\n%i bottles of beer\n", beers, beers);
  for (t = 0; t < 20; t++) {   <- You'll create 20 threads
                                  that run the function.

    ................(................, NULL, ................, NULL);
  }
  void* result;
  for (t = 0; t < 20; t++) {

    ................(threads[t], &result);   <- This code waits for all the
  }                                             extra threads to finish.
  printf("There are now %i bottles of beer on the wall\n", beers);
  return 0;
}
```

To save space, this example skips testing for errors, but don't you do that!

Magnets:

`pthread_join`

`threads`

`threads[t]`

`pthread_create`

`&threads[t]`

`drink_lots`

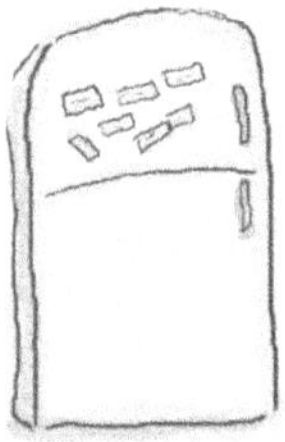

Beer Magnets Solution

It's time for a really BIG party. This code runs 20 threads that count the number of beers down from 2,000,000. You were to spot the missing code.

```
int beers = 2000000;
void* drink_lots(void *a)
{
  int i;
  for (i = 0; i < 100000; i++) {
    beers = beers - 1;
  }
  return NULL;
}
int main()
{
  pthread_t threads[20];
  int t;
  printf("%i bottles of beer on the wall\n%i bottles of beer\n", beers, beers);
  for (t = 0; t < 20; t++) {
    pthread_create(&threads[t], NULL, drink_lots, NULL);
  }
  void* result;
  for (t = 0; t < 20; t++) {
    pthread_join(threads[t], &result);
  }
  printf("There are now %i bottles of beer on the wall\n", beers);
  return 0;
}
```

To save space, we've skipped testing for errors—but don't you do that!

threads

threads[t]

Test Drive

Let's take a closer look at that last program. If you compile and run the code a few times, this happens:

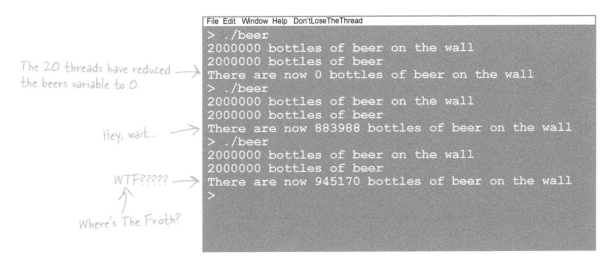

```
File Edit Window Help Don'tLoseTheThread
> ./beer
2000000 bottles of beer on the wall
2000000 bottles of beer
There are now 0 bottles of beer on the wall
> ./beer
2000000 bottles of beer on the wall
2000000 bottles of beer
There are now 883988 bottles of beer on the wall
> ./beer
2000000 bottles of beer on the wall
2000000 bottles of beer
There are now 945170 bottles of beer on the wall
>
```

The 20 threads have reduced the beers variable to 0.

Hey, wait...

WTF?????

Where's The Froth?

The code usually doesn't reduce the beers variable to zero.

That's really odd. The `beers` variable begins with a value of 2 million. Then 20 threads each try to reduce the value by 100,000. Shouldn't that mean that the `beers` variable *always* goes to zero?

Brain Power

Look carefully at the code again, and try to imagine what will happen if several threads are running it at the same time. Why is the result unpredictable? Why doesn't the `beers` variable get set to zero when all the threads have run? Write your answer below.

The code is not thread-safe

The great thing about threads is that lots of different tasks can run at the same time and have access to the same data. The downside is that all those different threads have access to the same data…

Unlike the first program, the threads in the second program are all reading and changing a shared piece of memory: the `beers` variable. To understand what's going on, let's see what happens if two threads try to reduce the value of `beers` using this line of code:

```
beers = beers - 1;
```

Imagine **two** threads are running this line of code **at the same time**.

1 **First of all, both threads will need to read the current value of the beers variable.**

Thread 1
beers = 37
Thread 2
beers = 37

2 **Then, each thread will subtract 1 from the number.**

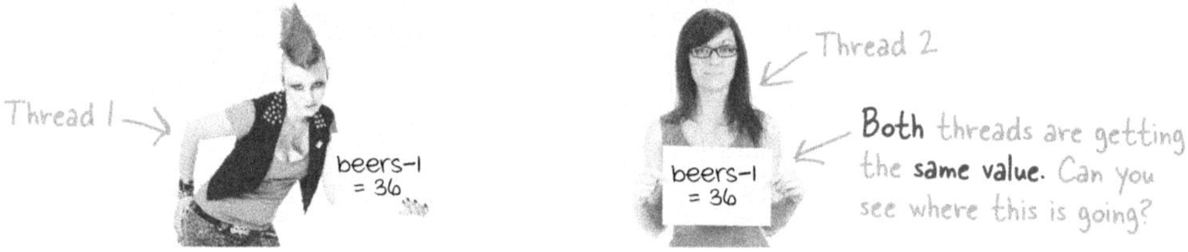
Thread 1
beers-1 = 36
Thread 2
beers-1 = 36
Both threads are getting the same value. Can you see where this is going?

3 **Finally, each thread stores the value for beers-1 back into the beers variable.**

Thread 1
beers = 36
Thread 2
beers = 36

Even though both of the threads were trying to reduce the value of `beers` by 1, they didn't succeed. Instead of reducing the value by 2, they only decreased it by 1. That's why the `beers` variable didn't get reduced to zero—the threads kept getting in the way of each other.

And why was the result so unpredictable? Because the threads didn't always run the line of code at exactly the same time. Sometimes the threads didn't crash into each other, and sometimes they did.

Watch it!

Be careful to look out for code that isn't thread-safe.

How will you know? Usually, if two threads read and write to the same variable, it's not.

You need to add traffic signals

Multithreaded programs can be powerful, but they can also behave in unpredictable ways, unless you put some controls in place.

Imagine two cars want to pass down the same narrow stretch of road. To prevent an accident, you can add traffic signals. Those traffic signals prevent the cars from getting access to a shared resource (the road) at the same time.

It's the same thing when you want two or more threads to access a shared data resource: you need to add traffic signals so that no two threads can read the data and write it back at the same time.

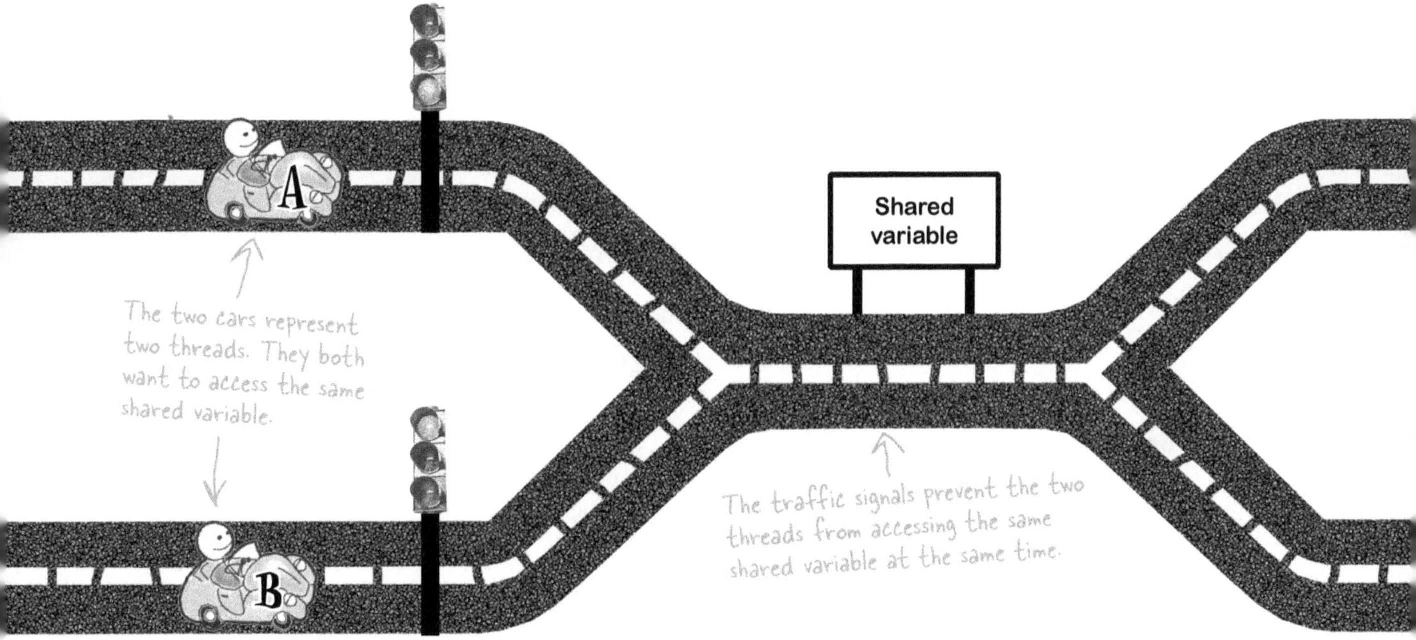
A
B
Shared variable
The two cars represent two threads. They both want to access the same shared variable.
The traffic signals prevent the two threads from accessing the same shared variable at the same time.

The traffic signals that prevent threads from crashing into each other are called **mutexes**, and they are one of the simplest ways of making your code thread-safe.

Mutexes are sometimes just called **locks**.

MUT-EX = MUTually EXclusive.

Use a mutex as a traffic signal

To protect a section of code, you will need to create a mutex lock like this:

```
pthread_mutex_t a_lock = PTHREAD_MUTEX_INITIALIZER;
```

The mutex needs to be visible to all of the threads that might crash into each other, so that means you'll probably want to create it as a **global variable**.

`PTHREAD_MUTEX_INITIALIZER` is actually a macro. When the compiler sees that, it will insert all of the code your program needs to create the mutex lock properly.

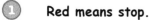

1. **Red means stop.**
   At the beginning of your sensitive code section, you need to place your first traffic signal. The `pthread_mutex_lock()` will let only **one thread** get past. All the other threads will have to wait when they get to it.

A
B
C

```
pthread_mutex_lock(&a_lock);
/* Sensitive code starts here... */
```

Only one thread at a time will get past this.

2. **Green means go.**
   When the thread gets to the end of the sensitive code, it makes a call to `pthread_mutex_unlock()`. That sets the traffic signal back to green, and another thread is allowed onto the sensitive code:

A
B
C

```
/* ...End of sensitive code */
pthread_mutex_unlock(&a_lock);
```

Now that you know how to create locks in your code, you have a lot of control over exactly how your threads will work.

Passing Long Values to Thread Functions Up Close

Thread functions can accept a single void pointer parameter and return a single void pointer value. Quite often, you will want to pass and return integer values to a thread, and one trick is to use **long** values. longs can be stored in void pointers because they are the same size.

```
void* do_stuff(void* param)
{
  long thread_no = (long)param;
  printf("Thread number %ld\n", thread_no);
  return (void*)(thread_no + 1);
}

int main()
{
  pthread_t threads[20];
  long t;
  for (t = 0; t < 3; t++) {
    pthread_create(&threads[t], NULL, do_stuff, (void*)t);
  }
  void* result;
  for (t = 0; t < 3; t++) {
    pthread_join(threads[t], &result);
    printf("Thread %ld returned %ld\n", t, (long)result);
  }
  return 0;
}
```

A thread function can accept a single void pointer parameter. (`void* do_stuff(void* param)`)

Convert it back to a long. (`long thread_no = (long)param;`)

Cast it back to a void pointer when it's returned. (`return (void*)(thread_no + 1);`)

Convert the long t value to a void pointer. (`(void*)t`)

Convert the return value to a long before using it. (`(long)result`)

File Edit Window Help Don'tLoseTheThread

```
> ./param_test
Thread number 0
Thread 0 returned 1
Thread number 1
Thread number 2
Thread 1 returned 2
Thread 2 returned 3
>
```

Each thread receives its thread number.

Each thread returns its thread number + 1.

Long Exercise

There's no simple way to decide where to put the locks in your code. Where you put them will change the way the code performs. Here are two versions of the `drink_lots()` function that lock the code in different ways.

Version A

```
pthread_mutex_t beers_lock = PTHREAD_MUTEX_INITIALIZER;
void* drink_lots(void *a)
{
  int i;
  pthread_mutex_lock(&beers_lock);
  for (i = 0; i < 100000; i++) {
    beers = beers - 1;
  }
  pthread_mutex_unlock(&beers_lock);
  printf("beers = %i\n", beers);
  return NULL;
}
```

Version B

```
pthread_mutex_t beers_lock = PTHREAD_MUTEX_INITIALIZER;
void* drink_lots(void *a)
{
  int i;
  for (i = 0; i < 100000; i++) {
    pthread_mutex_lock(&beers_lock);
    beers = beers - 1;
    pthread_mutex_unlock(&beers_lock);
  }
  printf("beers = %i\n", beers);
  return NULL;
}
```

Both pieces of code use a mutex to protect the `beers` variable, and each now displays the value of `beers` before they exit, but because they are locking the code in different places, they generate different output on the screen.

Can you figure out which version produced each of these two runs?

File Edit Window Help Don'tLoseTheThread

```
> ./beer
2000000 bottles of beer on the wall
2000000 bottles of beer
beers = 1900000
beers = 1800000
beers = 1700000
beers = 1600000
beers = 1500000
beers = 1400000
beers = 1300000
beers = 1200000
beers = 1100000
beers = 1000000
beers = 900000
beers = 800000
beers = 700000
beers = 600000
beers = 500000
beers = 400000
beers = 300000
beers = 200000
beers = 100000
beers = 0
There are now 0 bottles of beer on the wall
>
```

Match the code to the output.

File Edit Window Help Don'tLoseTheThread

```
> ./beer_fixed_strategy_2
2000000 bottles of beer on the wall
2000000 bottles of beer
beers = 63082
beers = 123
beers = 104
beers = 102
beers = 96
beers = 75
beers = 67
beers = 66
beers = 65
beers = 62
beers = 58
beers = 56
beers = 51
beers = 41
beers = 36
beers = 30
beers = 28
beers = 15
beers = 14
beers = 0
There are now 0 bottles of beer on the wall
>
```

Long Exercise Solution

There's no simple way to decide where to put the locks in your code. Where you put them will change the way the code performs. Here are two versions of the `drink_lots()` function that lock the code in different ways.

Version A

```
pthread_mutex_t beers_lock = PTHREAD_MUTEX_INITIALIZER;
void* drink_lots(void *a)
{
  int i;
  pthread_mutex_lock(&beers_lock);
  for (i = 0; i < 100000; i++) {
    beers = beers - 1;
  }
  pthread_mutex_unlock(&beers_lock);
  printf("beers = %i\n", beers);
  return NULL;
}
```

Version B

```
pthread_mutex_t beers_lock = PTHREAD_MUTEX_INITIALIZER;
void* drink_lots(void *a)
{
  int i;
  for (i = 0; i < 100000; i++) {
    pthread_mutex_lock(&beers_lock);
    beers = beers - 1;
    pthread_mutex_unlock(&beers_lock);
  }
  printf("beers = %i\n", beers);
  return NULL;
}
```

Both pieces of code use a mutex to protect the `beers` variable, and each now displays the value of `beers` before they exit, but because they are locking the code in different places, they generate different output on the screen.

You were to figure out which version produced each of these two runs.

File Edit Window Help Don'tLoseTheThread

```
> ./beer
2000000 bottles of beer on the wall
2000000 bottles of beer
beers = 1900000
beers = 1800000
beers = 1700000
beers = 1600000
beers = 1500000
beers = 1400000
beers = 1300000
beers = 1200000
beers = 1100000
beers = 1000000
beers = 900000
beers = 800000
beers = 700000
beers = 600000
beers = 500000
beers = 400000
beers = 300000
beers = 200000
beers = 100000
beers = 0
There are now 0 bottles of beer on the wall
>
```

Match the code to the output.

File Edit Window Help Don'tLoseTheThread

```
> ./beer_fixed_strategy_2
2000000 bottles of beer on the wall
2000000 bottles of beer
beers = 63082
beers = 123
beers = 104
beers = 102
beers = 96
beers = 75
beers = 67
beers = 66
beers = 65
beers = 62
beers = 58
beers = 56
beers = 51
beers = 41
beers = 36
beers = 30
beers = 28
beers = 15
beers = 14
beers = 0
There are now 0 bottles of beer on the wall
>
```

1st

Congratulations! You've (almost) reached the end of the book. Now it's time to crack open one of those 2,000,000 bottles of beer and celebrate!

You're now in a great position to decide what *kind* of C coder you want to be. Do you want to be a **Linux hacker** using pure C? Or a **maker** writing embedded C in small devices like the Arduino? Maybe you want to go on to be a **games developer** in C++? Or a **Mac and iOS programmer** in Objective-C?

Whatever you choose to do, you're now part of the community that uses and loves the language that has created more software than any other. The language behind the Internet and almost every operating system. The language that's used to *write almost all the other languages*. And the language that can write for almost every processor in existence, from watches and phones to planes and satellites.

New C Hacker, we salute you!

there are no Dumb Questions

Q: Does my machine have to have multiple processors to support threads?

A: No. Most machines have processors with multiple **cores**, which means that their CPUs contain miniprocessors that can do several things at once. But even if your code is running on a single core/single processor, you will still be able to run threads.

Q: How?

A: The operating system will switch rapidly between the threads and make it appear that it is running several things at once.

Q: Will threads make my programs faster?

A: Not necessarily. While threads can help you use more of the processors and cores on your machine, you need to be careful about the amount of locking your code needs to do. If your threads are locked too often, your code may run as slowly as single-threaded code.

Q: How can I design my thread code to be fast?

A: Try to reduce the amount of data that threads need to access. If threads don't access a lot of shared data, they won't need to lock each other out so often and will be much more efficient.

Q: Are threads faster than separate processes?

A: They usually are, simply because it takes a little more time to create processes than it does to create extra threads.

Q: I've heard that mutexes can lead to "deadlocks." What are they?

A: Say you have two threads, and they both want to get mutexes A and B. If the first thread already has A, and the second thread already has B, then the threads will be deadlocked. This is because the first thread can't get mutex B and the second thread can't get mutex A. They both come to a standstill.

Your C Toolbox

You've got Chapter 12 under your belt, and now you've added threads to your toolbox. For a complete list of tooltips in the book, see Appendix ii.

Threads allow a process to do more than one thing at the same time.

Simple processes do one thing at a time.

Threads are "lightweight processes."

POSIX threads (pthread) is a threading library.

pthread_create() creates a thread to run a function.

pthread_join() will wait for a thread to finish.

Threads share the same global variables.

If two threads read and update the same variable, your code will be unpredictable.

Mutexes are locks that protect shared data.

pthread_mutex_lock() creates a mutex on code.

pthread_mutex_unlock() releases the mutex.

Name: Date:

C Lab 3

Blasteroids

This lab gives you a spec that describes a program for you to build, using the knowledge you've gained over the last few chapters.

This project is bigger than the ones you've seen so far. So read the whole thing before you get started, and give yourself a little time. And don't worry if you get stuck; there are no new C concepts in here, so you can move on in the book and come back to the lab later.

We've filled in a few design details for you, and we've made sure you've got all the pieces you need to write the code.

It's up to you to finish the job, but we won't give you the code for the answer.

Write the arcade game Blasteroids

Of course, one of the *real* reasons people want to learn C is so they can write **games**. In this lab, you're going to pay tribute to one of the most popular and long-lived video games of them all. **It's time to write *Blasteroids*!**

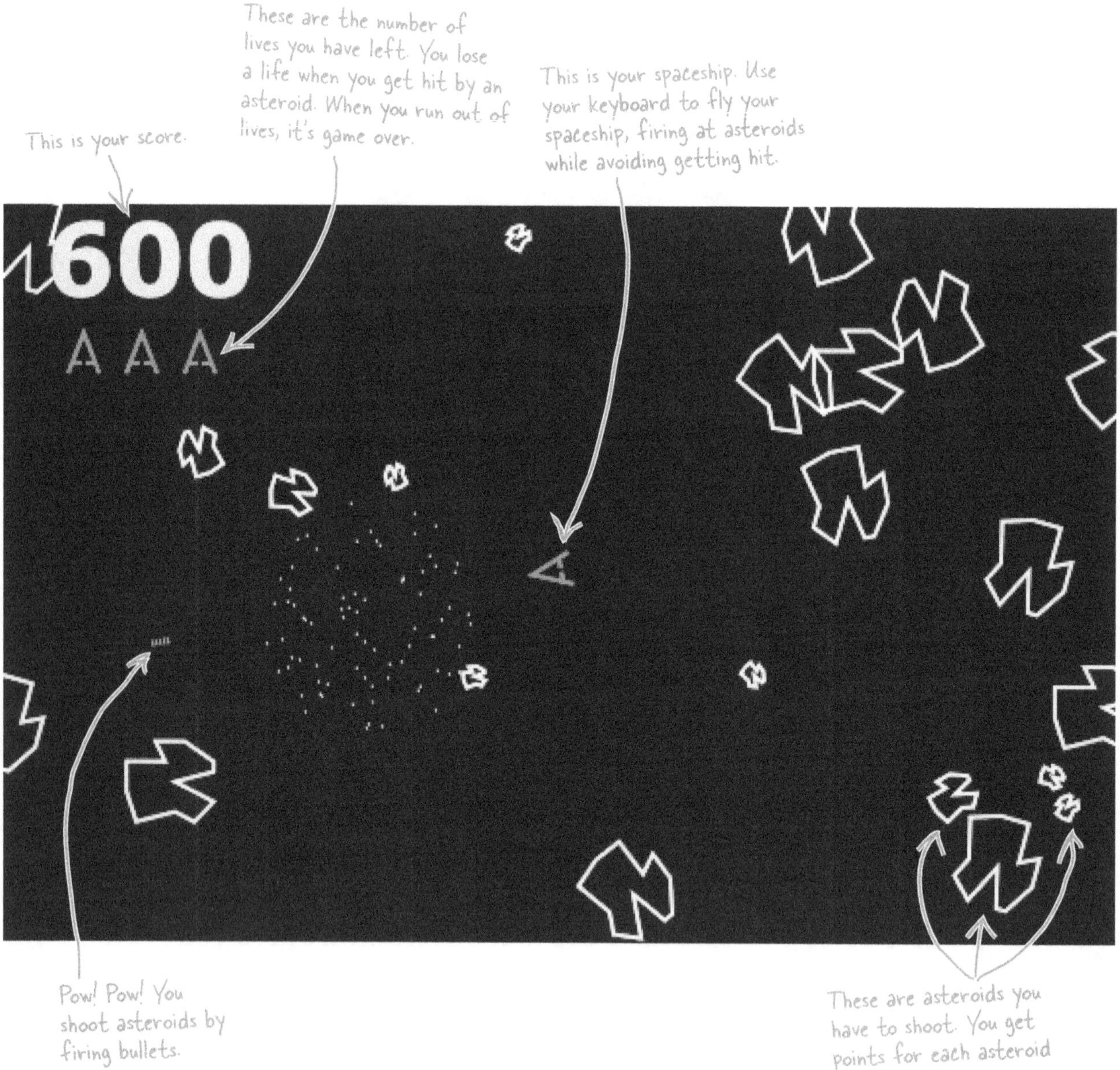
This is your score.
These are the number of lives you have left. You lose a life when you get hit by an asteroid. When you run out of lives, it's game over.
This is your spaceship. Use your keyboard to fly your spaceship, firing at asteroids while avoiding getting hit.
600
Pow! Pow! You shoot asteroids by firing bullets.
These are asteroids you have to shoot. You get points for each asteroid you shoot.

Your mission: blast the asteroids without getting hit

Sinister. Hollow. And all strangely similar. The asteroids are the bad guys in this game. They float and rotate slowly across the screen, promising instant death to any passing space traveler who happens to meet them.

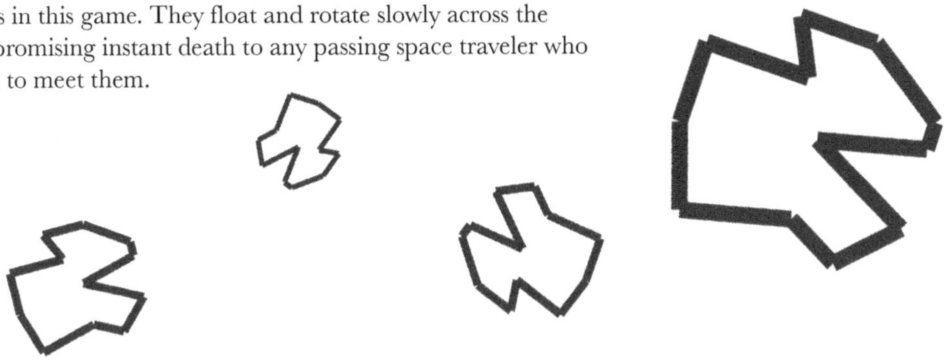

Welcome to the starship *Vectorize*! This is the ship that you will fly around the screen using your keyboard. It's armed with a cannon that can fire at passing asteroids.

If an asteroid is hit by a blast from the spaceship's cannon, it immediately splits into two, and the player's score increases by 100 points. Once an asteroid has been hit a couple of times, it's removed from the screen.

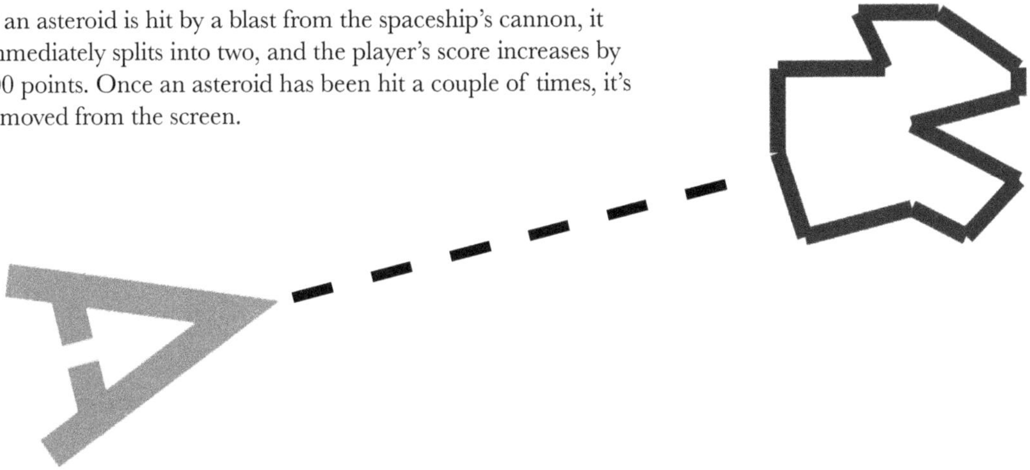

If the ship gets hit by an asteroid, you lose a life. You have three lives, and when you lose the last one, that's the end of the game.

Allegro

Allegro is an open source game development library that allows you to create, compile, and run game code across different operating systems. It works with Windows, Linux, Mac OS, and even phones.

Allegro is pretty straightforward to use, but just because it's a simple library doesn't mean it lacks power. Allegro can deal with sound, graphics, animation, device handling, and even 3D graphics if your machine supports OpenGL.

OpenGL is an open standard for graphics processors. You describe your 3D objects to OpenGL, and it handles (most) of the math for you.

Installing Allegro

You can get the source for Allegro over at the Allegro SourceForge website:

http://alleg.sourceforge.net/

The Web gets updated more often than books, so this URL might be different. Check on your favorite search engine.

You can download, build, and install the latest code from the source repository. There are instructions on the site that will tell you exactly how to do that for your operating system.

You may need CMake

When you build the code, you will probably also need to install an extra tool called **`CMake`**. `CMake` is a build tool that makes it a little easier to build C programs on different operating systems. If you need `CMake`, you will find all you need over at *http://www.cmake.org*.

Watch it!

The code we've supplied in this lab is for version 5 of Allegro.

If you download and install a newer version, you may need to make a few changes.

What does Allegro do for you?

The Allegro library deals with several things:

- **GUIs**
  Allegro will create a simple window to contain your game. This might not seem like a big deal, but different operating systems have *very* different ways of creating windows and then allowing them to interact with the keyboard and the mouse.

- **Events**
  Whenever you hit a key, move a mouse, or click on something, your system generates an **event**. An event is just a piece of data that says what happened. Events are usually put onto queues and then sent to applications. Allegro makes it simple to respond to events so that you can easily, say, write code that will run if a user fires her canyon by hitting the spacebar.

- **Timers**
  You've already looked at timers at the system level. Allegro provides a straightforward way to give your game a **heartbeat**. All games have some sort of heartbeat that runs so many times a second to make sure the game display is continuously updated. Using a timer, you can create a game that, for example, displays a fresh version of the screen at 60 frames per second (FPS).

- **Graphics buffering**
  To make your game run smoothly, Allegro uses **double buffering**. Double buffering is a game-development technique that allows you to draw all of your graphics in an offscreen buffer before displaying it on the screen. Because an entire frame of animation is displayed all at once, your game will run much more smoothly.

- **Graphics and transformations**
  Allegro comes with a set of built-in graphics **primitives** that allow you to draw lines, curves, text, solids, and pictures. If you have an OpenGL driver for your graphics card, you can even do 3D. In addition to all of this, Allegro also supports **transformations**. Transformations allow you to rotate, translate, and scale the graphics on the screen, which makes it easy to create animated spaceships and floating rocks that can move and turn on the screen.

- **Sounds**
  Allegro has a full sound library that will allow you to build sounds into your game.

Building the game

You'll need to decide how you're going to structure your source code. Most C programmers would probably break down the code into separate source files. That way, not only will you be able to recompile your game quicker, but you'll also be dealing with smaller chunks of code at a time. That will make the whole process a lot less confusing.

There are many, many ways of splitting up your code, but one way is to have a separate source file for each element that will be displayed in the game:

asteroid.c

A file containing all of the source code to track and display the latest position of an asteroid.

blast.c

The spaceship will be able to fire its cannon at passing asteroids, so you will need code to draw and move a cannon blast across the screen.

spaceship.c

The hero of your game, the plucky little spaceship. Unlike with the asteroids, you will probably need to manage only one of these at a time.

blasteroids.c

It's always good to have a separate source file to deal with the core of the game. The code in here will need to listen for keypresses, run a timer, and also tell all of the other spaceships, rocks, and blasts to draw themselves on the screen.

The spaceship

When you're controlling lots of objects on a screen, it's useful to create a `struct` for each one. Use this for the spaceship:

```
typedef struct {
  float sx;
  float sy;
  float heading;
  float speed;
  int gone;
  ALLEGRO_COLOR color;
} Spaceship;
```

Where it is on the screen (sx, sy)

The direction it's pointing (heading)

Is it dead? (gone)

What the spaceship looks like

If you set up your code to draw around the **origin** (discussed later), then you could draw the ship using code like this:

The variable `s` is a pointer to a `Spaceship struct`. Make the ship green.

```
al_draw_line(-8, 9, 0, -11, s->color, 3.0f);
al_draw_line(0, -11, 8, 9, s->color, 3.0f);
al_draw_line(-6, 4, -1, 4, s->color, 3.0f);
al_draw_line(6, 4, 1, 4, s->color, 3.0f);
```

Collisions

If your spaceship collides with a rock, it dies immediately and the player loses a life. For the first five seconds after a new ship is created, it doesn't check for collisions. The new ship should appear in the center of the screen.

Spaceship behavior

The spaceship starts the game stationary in the center of the screen. To make it move around the screen, you need to make it respond to keypresses:

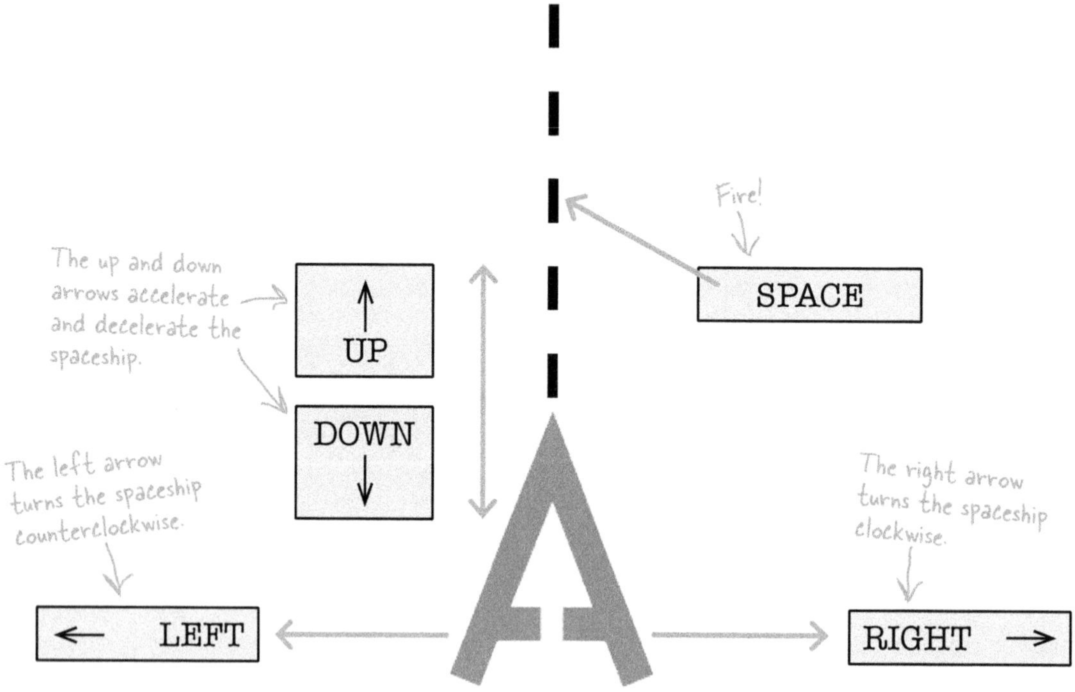
Fire!
SPACE
The up and down arrows accelerate and decelerate the spaceship.
UP
DOWN
The left arrow turns the spaceship counterclockwise.
LEFT
The right arrow turns the spaceship clockwise.
RIGHT

Make sure the ship doesn't accelerate too much. You probably don't want the spaceship to move forward more than a couple hundred pixels per second. The spaceship should never go into reverse.

Reading keypresses

The C language is used to write code for almost every piece of computer hardware in the world. But the strange thing is, there's no standard way to read a keypress using C. All of the standard functions, like `fgets()`, read only the keys once the return key has been pressed. But Allegro *does* allow you to read keypresses. Every event that's sent to an Allegro game comes in via a *queue*. That's just a list of data that describes which keys have been pressed, where the mouse is, and so on. Somewhere, you'll need a loop that waits for an event to appear on the queue.

Even functions such as getchar() tend to buffer any characters you type until you hit return.

```
ALLEGRO_EVENT_QUEUE *queue;
queue = al_create_event_queue();   <- You create an event queue like this.
ALLEGRO_EVENT event;
al_wait_for_event(queue, &event);  <- This waits for an event from the queue.
```

Once you receive an event, you need to decide if it represents a keypress or not. You can do that by reading its type.

```
if (event.type == ALLEGRO_EVENT_KEY_DOWN) {
  switch(event.keyboard.keycode) {
  case ALLEGRO_KEY_LEFT:   <- Turn the ship left.


    break;
  case ALLEGRO_KEY_RIGHT:  <- Turn right.


    break;
  case ALLEGRO_KEY_SPACE:  <- Fire!


    break;
  }
}
```

The blast

Take that, you son of a space pebble! The spaceship's cannon can fire blasts across the screen, and it's your job to make sure they move across the screen. This is the `struct` for a blast:

```
typedef struct {
  float sx;
  float sy;
  float heading;
  float speed;
  int gone;
  ALLEGRO_COLOR color;
} Blast;
```

Blast appearance

The blast is a dashed line. If the user hits the fire key rapidly, the blasts will overlay each other and the line will look more solid. That way, rapid firing will give the impression of increased firepower.

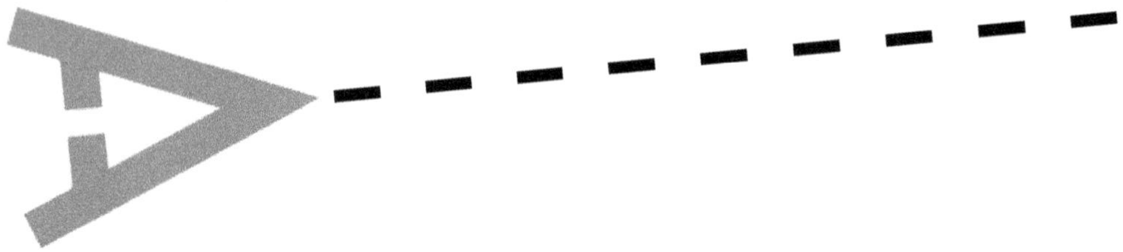

Blast behavior

Unlike the other objects you'll be animating, blasts that disappear off the screen won't reappear. That means you'll need to write code that can easily create and destroy blasts. Blasts are always fired in the direction the ship is heading, and they always travel in a straight line at a constant speed—say, three times the maximum speed of the ship. If a blast collides with an asteroid, the asteroid will divide into two.

The asteroid

Use this `struct` for each asteroid:

```
typedef struct {
  float sx;
  float sy;
  float heading;
  float twist;
  float speed;
  float rot_velocity;
  float scale;
  int gone;
  ALLEGRO_COLOR color;
} Asteroid;
```

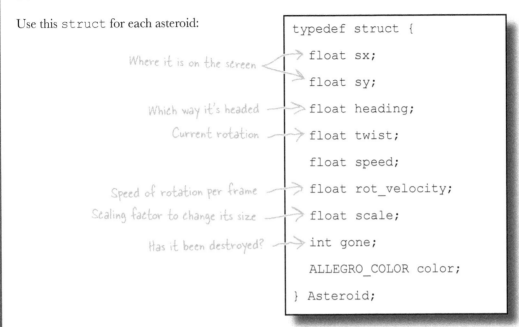

Where it is on the screen (sx, sy)

Which way it's headed (heading)

Current rotation (twist)

Speed of rotation per frame (rot_velocity)

Sealing factor to change its size (scale)

Has it been destroyed? (gone)

Asteroid appearance

This is the code to draw an asteroid around the origin:

```
al_draw_line(-20, 20, -25, 5, a->color, 2.0f);
al_draw_line(-25, 5, -25, -10, a->color, 2.0f);
al_draw_line(-25, -10, -5, -10, a->color, 2.0f);
al_draw_line(-5, -10, -10, -20, a->color, 2.0f);
al_draw_line(-10, -20, 5, -20, a->color, 2.0f);
al_draw_line(5, -20, 20, -10, a->color, 2.0f);
al_draw_line(20, -10, 20, -5, a->color, 2.0f);
al_draw_line(20, -5, 0, 0, a->color, 2.0f);
al_draw_line(0, 0, 20, 10, a->color, 2.0f);
al_draw_line(20, 10, 10, 20, a->color, 2.0f);
al_draw_line(10, 20, 0, 15, a->color, 2.0f);
al_draw_line(0, 15, -20, 20, a->color, 2.0f);
```

How the asteroid moves

Asteroids move in a straight line across the screen. Even though they move in a straight line, they continually rotate about their centers. If an asteroid drifts off one side of the screen, it immediately appears on the other.

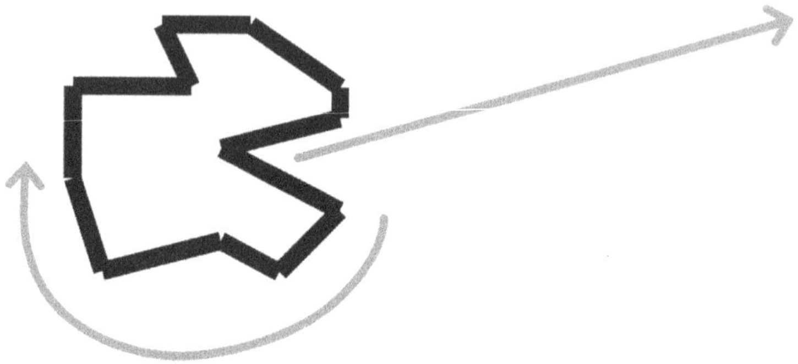

When the asteroid is hit by a blast

If an asteroid is hit by a blast from the spaceship's cannon, it immediately splits into two. Each of these parts will be half the size of the original asteroid. Once an asteroid has been hit/split a couple of times, it is removed from the screen. The player's score increases with each hit by 100 points. You will need to decide how you will record the set of asteroids on the screen. Will you create one huge array? Or will you use a linked list?

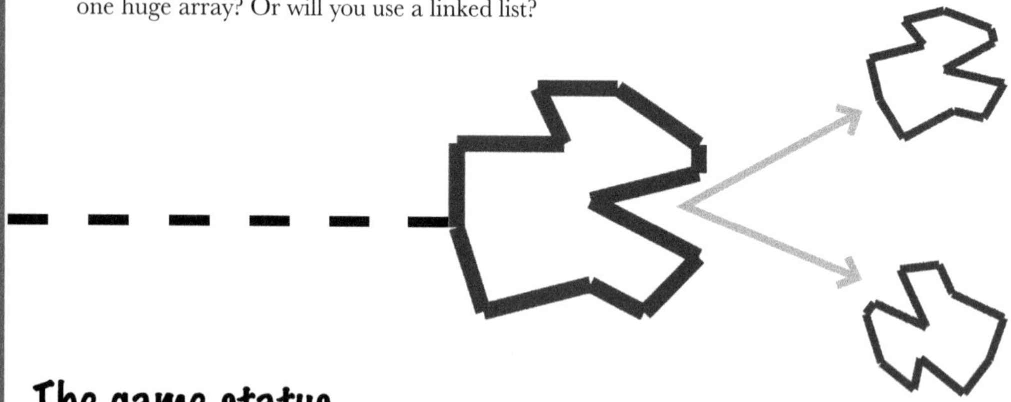

The game status

There are a couple of things you need to display on the screen: the number of lives you have left and the current score. When you've run out of lives, you need to display "Game Over!" in big, friendly letters in the middle of the screen.

Use transformations to move things around

You'll need to animate things around the screen. The spaceship will need to fly, and the asteroids will need to rotate, drift, and even change size. Rotations, translations, and scaling require quite a lot of math to work out. But Allegro comes with a whole bunch of *transformations* built in.

When you're drawing an object, like a spaceship, you should probably just worry about drawing it around the **origin**. The origin is the top-left corner of the screen and has coordinates (0, 0). The x-coordinates go across the screen, and the y-coordinates go down. You can use transformations to move the origin to where the object needs to be on the screen and then rotate it to point the correct way. Once that's all done, all you need to do is draw your object at the origin and everything will be in the right place.

For example, this is one way you might draw the spaceship on the screen:

```
void draw_ship(Spaceship* s)
{
  ALLEGRO_TRANSFORM transform;
  al_identity_transform(&transform);
  al_rotate_transform(&transform, DEGREES(s->heading));
  al_translate_transform(&transform, s->sx, s->sy);
  al_use_transform(&transform);
  al_draw_line(-8, 9, 0, -11, s->color, 3.0f);
  al_draw_line(0, -11, 8, 9, s->color, 3.0f);
  al_draw_line(-6, 4, -1, 4, s->color, 3.0f);
  al_draw_line(6, 4, 1, 4, s->color, 3.0f);
}
```

The finished product

When you're done, it's time to play *Blasteroids*!

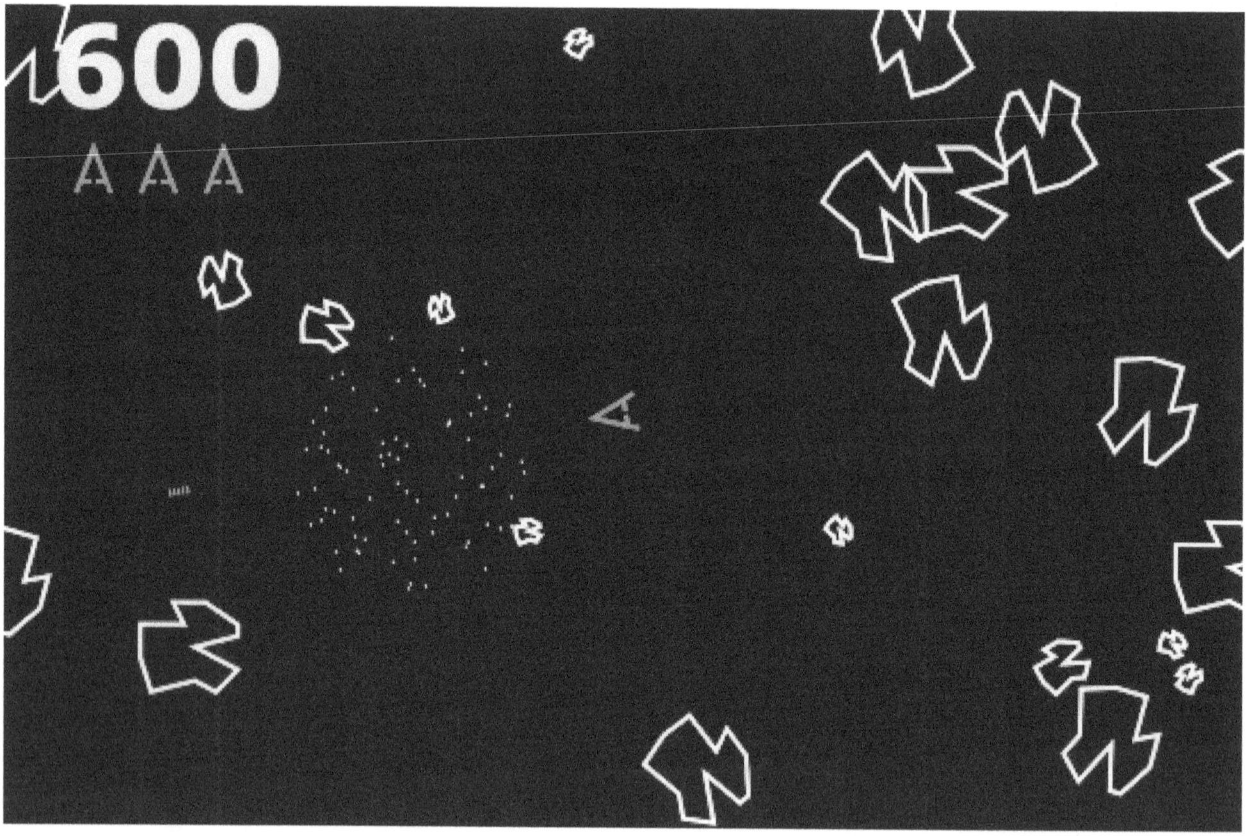
600

There are lots of other things you could do to enhance the game. As an example, why not try to get it working with OpenCV? Let us know how you get on at Head First Labs.

Leaving town...

It's been great having you here in Cville!

We're sad to see you leave, but there's nothing like taking what you've learned and putting it to use. There are still a few more gems for you in the back of the book and an index to read through, and then it's time to take all these new ideas and put them into practice. We're dying to hear how things go, so ***drop us a line*** at the Head First Labs website, ***www.headfirstlabs.com***, and let us know how C is paying off for **YOU**!

The top ten things (we didn't cover)

Oh my, look at all the tasty treats we have left...

Even after all that, there's still a bit more.

There are just a few more things we think you need to know. We wouldn't feel right about ignoring them, even though they need only a brief mention, and we really wanted to give you a book you'd be able to lift without extensive training at the local gym. So before you put the book down, **read through these tidbits**.

#1. Operators

We've used a few operators in this book, like the basic *arithmetic operators* +, -, *, and /, but there are many other operators available in C that can make your life easier.

Increments and decrements

An *increment* and a *decrement* increase and decrease a number by 1. That's a very common operation in C code, particularly if you have a loop that increments a counter. The C language gives you four simple expressions that simplify increments and decrements:

Increase i by 1, then return the **new** value. → `++i`

Increase i by 1, then return the **old** value. → `i++`

Decrease i by 1, then return the **new** value. → `--i`

Decrease i by 1, then return the **old** value. → `i--`

Each of these expressions will change the value of `i`. The position of the ++ and -- say whether or not to return the original value of `i` or its new value. For example:

```
int i = 3;
int j = i++;
```

← After this line, j == 3 and i == 4.

The ternary operator

What if you want one value if some condition is true, and a different value if it's false?

```
if (x == 1)
  return 2;
else
  return 3;
```

C has a *ternary operator* that allows you to compress this code right down to the following:

```
return (x == 1) ? 2 : 3;
```

First, the condition (`(x == 1)`)

Next comes the value if the condition is true (`2`)

Finally, the value if the condition is false (`3`)

Bit twiddling

C can be used for low-level programming, and it has a set of operators that let you calculate a new series of bits:

Operator	Description
`~a`	The value of `a` with all the bits flipped
`a&b`	AND the bits of `a` and `b` together
`a | b`	OR the bits of `a` and `b` together
`a^b`	XOR the bits of `a` and `b` together
`<<`	Shift bits to the left (increase)
`>>`	Shift bits to the right (decrease)

The << operator can be used as a quick way of multiplying an integer by 2. But be careful that numbers don't overflow.

Commas to separate expressions

You've seen `for` loops that perform code at the end of each loop:

```
for (i = 0; i < 10; i++)   <- This increment will happen at the end of each loop.
```

But what if you want to perform more than one operation at the end of a loop? You can use the comma operator:

```
for (i = 0; i < 10; i++, j++)   <- Increment i and j.
```

The comma operator exists because there are times when you don't want to separate expressions with semicolons.

#2. Preprocessor directives

You use a preprocessor directive every time you compile a program that includes a header file:

```
#include <stdio.h>
```
← This is a preprocessor directive.

The preprocessor scans through your C source file and generates a modified version that will be compiled. In the case of the `#include` directive, the preprocessing inserts the contents of the *stdio.h* file. Directives always appear at the start of a line, and they always begin with the hash (#) character. The next most common directive after `#include` is `#define`:

```
#define DAYS_OF_THE_WEEK 7
...
printf("There are %i days of the week\n", DAYS_OF_THE_WEEK);
```

The `#define` directive creates a *macro*. The preprocessor will scan through the C source and replace the macro name with the macro's value. Macros aren't variables because they can never change at runtime. Macros are replaced *before* the program even compiles. You can even create macros that work a little like functions:

x is a parameter to the macro.

```
#define ADD_ONE(x)  ((x) + 1)
...
printf("The answer is %i\n", ADD_ONE(3));
```
← Be careful to use parentheses with macros.

← This is will output "The answer is 4."

The preprocessor will replace `ADD_ONE(3)` with `((3) + 1)` before the program is compiled.

Conditions

You can also use the preprocessor for **conditional compilation**. You can make it switch parts of the source code on or off:

```
#ifdef SPANISH
char *greeting = "Hola";
#else
char *greeting = "Hello";
#endif
```
← If the SPANISH macro exists...

← ...include this code.

← If not, include this code.

This code will be compiled differently if there is (or isn't) a macro called `SPANISH` defined.

#3. The static keyword

Imagine you want to create a function that works like a counter. You could write it like this:

```
int count = 0;        <- Use this to count the calls.
int counter()
{
  return ++count;     <- Increment the count each time.
}
```

What's the problem with this code? It uses a global variable called `count`. Any other function can change the value of `count` because it's in the global scope. If you start to write large programs, you need to be careful that you don't have too many global variables because they can lead to buggy code. Fortunately, C lets you create a *global* variable that is available only inside the *local* scope of a function:

```
int counter()
{
  static int count = 0;
  return ++count;
}
```

count is still a global variable, but it can only be accessed inside this function.

The static keyword means this variable will keep its value between calls to counter().

The `static` keyword will store the variable inside the global area of memory, but the compiler will throw an error if some other function tries to access the `count` variable.

static can also make things private

You can also use the `static` keyword outside of functions. `static` in this case means "only code in this *.c* file can use this." For example:

```
static int days = 365;    <- You can use this variable only inside the current source file.
```

```
static void update_account(int x) {
...
}
```

You can call this function only from inside this source file.

The `static` keyword **controls the scope** of something. It will prevent your data and functions from being accessed in ways that they weren't designed to be.

#4. How big stuff is

You've seen that the `sizeof` operator can tell you how much memory a piece of data will occupy. But what if you want to know what **range of values** it will hold? For example, if you know that an `int` occupies 4 bytes on your machine, what's the largest positive number you can store in it? Or the largest negative number? You could, theoretically, work that out based on the number of bytes it uses, but that can be tricky.

Instead, you can use the macros defined in the ***limits.h*** header. Want to know what the largest `long` value you can use is? It's given by the `LONG_MAX` macro. How about the most negative `short`? Use `SHRT_MIN`. Here's an example program that shows the ranges for `int`s and `short`s:

```
#include <stdio.h>
#include <limits.h>

int main()
{
  printf("On this machine an int takes up %lu bytes\n", sizeof(int));
  printf("And ints can store values from %i to %i\n", INT_MIN, INT_MAX);
  printf("And shorts can store values from %i to %i\n", SHRT_MIN, SHRT_MAX);
  return 0;
}
```

File Edit Window Help HowBigIsBig

```
On this machine an int takes up 4 bytes
And ints can store values from -2147483648 to 2147483647
And shorts can store values from -32768 to 32767
```

The macro names come from the data types: `INT` (`int`), `SHRT` (`short`), `LONG` (`long`), `CHAR` (`char`), `FLT` (`float`), `DBL` (`double`). Then, you either add `_MAX` (most positive) or `_MIN` (most negative). You can optionally add the prefix `U` (`unsigned`), `S` (`signed`), or `L` (`long`) if you are interested in a more specific data type.

#5. Automated testing

It's always important to test your code, and life becomes a lot simpler if you *automate* the tests. Automated tests are now used by virtually all developers, and there are many, many testing frameworks used by C programmers. One that's popular at Head First Labs is called **AceUnit**:

http://aceunit.sourceforge.net/

AceUnit is very similar to the *x*Unit frameworks in other languages (like nUnit and jUnit).

If you're writing a command-line tool and you have a Unix-style command shell, then another great tool is called **`shunit2`**.

http://code.google.com/p/shunit2/

`shunit2` lets you create shell scripts that test scripts and commands.

#6. More on gcc

GCC

You've used the *GNU Compiler Collection* (`gcc`) throughout this book, but you've only scratched the surface of what this compiler can do for you. `gcc` is like a Swiss Army knife. It has an immense number of features that give you a tremendous amount of control over the code it produces.

Optimization

`gcc` can do a huge amount to improve the performance of your code. If it sees that you're assigning the same value to a variable every time a loop runs, it can move that assignment outside the loop. If you have a small function that is used only in a few places, it can convert that function into a piece of *inline code* and insert it into the right places in your program.

It can do lots of optimizations, but most of them are switched off by default. Why? Because optimizations take time for the compiler to perform, and while you're developing code you normally want your compiles to be *fast*. Once your code is ready for release, you might want to switch on more optimization. There are four levels of optimization:

Flag	Description
`-O`	If you add a `-O` (letter O) flag to your `gcc` command, you will get the first level of optimizations.
`-O2`	For even more optimizations and a slower compile, choose `-O2`.
`-O3`	For *yet more* optimizations, choose `-O3`. This will include all of the optimization checks from `-O` and `-O2`, plus a few extras.
`-Ofast`	The maximum amount of optimization is done with `-Ofast`. This is also the slowest one to compile. Be careful with `-Ofast` because the code it produces is less likely to conform to the C standards.

Warnings

Warnings are displayed if the code is technically valid but does something suspicious, like assign a value to a variable of the wrong type. You can increase the number of warning checks with **`-Wall`**:

```
gcc fred.c -Wall -o fred
```

The `-Wall` option means "All warnings," but for historic reasons is *doesn't* actually display *all* of the warnings. For that, you should also include **`-Wextra`**:

```
gcc fred.c -Wall -Wextra -o fred
```

Also, if you want to have *really strict* compilation, you can make the compile fail if there are any warnings at all with **`-Werror`**:

```
gcc fred.c -Werror -o fred
```

← This means "treat warnings as errors."

`-Werror` is useful if several people are working on the same code because it will help maintain code quality.

For more `gcc` options, see:

http://gcc.gnu.org/onlinedocs/gcc

#7. More on make

make is an incredibly powerful tool for building C applications, but you've only had a very simple introduction to it in this book. For more details on the amazing things you can do with make, see Robert Mecklenburg's *Managing Projects with GNU Make*:

http://shop.oreilly.com/product/9780596006105.do

For now, here are just a few of its features.

Variables

Variables are a great way of shortening your makefiles. For example, if you have a standard set of command-line options you want to pass to gcc, you can define them with a variable:

```
CFLAGS = -Wall -Wextra -v

fred: fred.c
  gcc fred.c $(CFLAGS) -o fred
```

You define a variable using the equals sign (=) and then read its value with $(...).

Using %, ^, and @

Most of the time, a lot of your compile commands are going to look pretty similar:

```
fred: fred.c
gcc fred.c -Wall -o fred
```

In which case, you might want to use the % symbol to write a more general target/recipe:

```
%: %.c
gcc $^ -Wall -o $@
```

If you're creating <file>, then look for <file>.c.

$^ is the dependency value (the .c file).

$@ is name of the target.

This looks a little weird because of all the symbols. If you want to make a file called *fred*, this rule tells make to look for a file called *fred.c*. Then, the recipe will run a gcc command to create the target fred (given by the special symbol $@) using the given dependency (given by $@).

Implicit rules

The make tool knows quite a lot about C compilation, and it can use *implicit rules* to build files without you telling it exactly how. For example, if you have a file called *fred.c*, you can compile it **without a makefile** by typing:

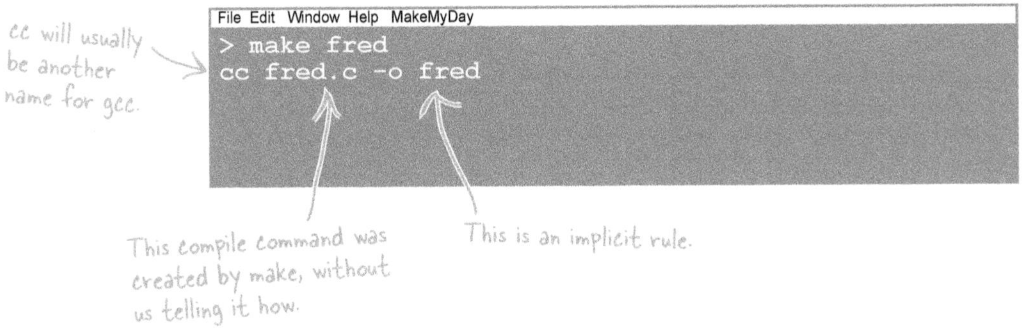
File Edit Window Help MakeMyDay
> make fred
cc fred.c -o fred
cc will usually be another name for gcc.
This compile command was created by make, without us telling it how.
This is an implicit rule.

That's because make comes with a bunch of built-in recipes. For more on make, see:

http://www.gnu.org/software/make/

#8. Development tools

If you're writing C code, you probably care a lot about performance and stability. And if you're using the *GNU Compiler Collection* to compile your code, you'll probably want to take a look at some of the other *GNU* tools that are available.

gdb

The *GNU Project Debugger* (`gdb`) lets you study your compiled program while it's running. This is invaluable if you're trying to chase down some pesky bug. `gdb` can be used from the command line or using an *integrated development environment* like *Xcode* or *Guile.*

http://sourceware.org/gdb/download/onlinedocs/gdb/index.html

gprof

If your code isn't as fast as you'd hoped, it might be worth *profiling* it. The *GNU Profiler* (`gprof`) will tell you which parts of your program are the slowest so that you can tune the code in the most appropriate way. `gprof` lets you compile a modified version of your program that will dump a performance report when it's finished. Then the `gprof` command-line tool will let you analyze the performance report to track down the slow parts of your code.

http://sourceware.org/binutils/docs-2.22/gprof/index.html

gcov

Another profiling tool is *GNU Coverage* (`gcov`). But while `gprof` is normally used to check the performance of your code, `gcov` is used to check which parts of your code did or didn't run. This is important if you're writing automated tests, because you'll want to be sure that your tests are running all of the code you're expecting them to.

http://gcc.gnu.org/onlinedocs/gcc/Gcov.html

#9. Creating GUIs

You haven't created any *graphical user interface* (GUI) programs in any of the main chapters of this book. In the labs, you used the *Allegro* and *OpenCV* libraries to write a couple of programs that were able to display very simple windows. But GUIs are usually written in very different ways on each operating system.

Linux — GTK

Linux has a number of libraries that are used to create GUI applications, and one of the most popular is the *GIMP toolkit* (GTK+):

http://www.gtk.org/

GTK+ is available on Windows and the Mac, as well as Linux, although it's mostly used for Linux apps.

Windows

Windows has very advanced GUI libraries built-in. Windows programming is a really specialized area, and you will probably need to spend some time learning the details of the Windows *application programming interfaces* (APIs) before you can easily build GUI applications. An increasing number of Windows applications are written in languages based on C, such as C# and C++. For an online introduction to Windows programming, see:

http://www.winprog.org/tutorial/

The Mac — Carbon

The Macintosh uses a GUI system called *Aqua*. You can create GUI programs in C on the Mac using a set of libraries called **Carbon**. But the more modern way of programming the Mac is using the Cocoa libraries, which are programmed using another C-derived language called *Objective-C*. Now that you've reached the end of this book, you're in a very good position to learn *Objective-C*. Here at Head First Labs, we *love* the books and courses on Mac programming available at the *Big Nerd Ranch*:

http://www.bignerdranch.com/

#10. Reference material

Here's a list of some popular books and websites on C programming.

Brian W. Kernighan and Dennis M. Ritchie, *The C Programming Language* (Prentice Hall; ISBN 978-0-131-10362-7)

This is the book that *defined* the original C programming language, and almost every C programmer on Earth has a copy.

Samuel P. Harbison and Guy L. Steele Jr., *C: A Reference Manual* (Prentice Hall; ISBN 978-0-130-89592-9)

This is an excellent C reference book that you will want by your side as you code.

Peter van der Linden, *Expert C Programming* (Prentice Hall; ISBN 978-0-131-77429-2)

For more advanced programming, see Peter van der Linden's excellent book.

Steve Oualline, *Practical C Programming* (O'Reilly; ISBN 978-1-565-92306-5)

This book outlines the practical details of C development.

Websites

For standards information, see:
http://pubs.opengroup.org/onlinepubs/9699919799/

For additional C coding tutorials, see:
http://www.cprogramming.com/

For general reference information, see:
http://www.cprogrammingreference.com/

For a general C programming tutorial, see:
http://www.crasseux.com/books/ctutorial/

Revision roundup

abcdefghijklmnopqrstuvwxyz
3X3 = 6
4X4 = 16
22

Ever wished all those great C facts were in one place?

This is a roundup of all the C topics and principles we've covered in the book. Take a look at them, and see if you can remember them all. Each fact has the chapter it came from alongside it, so it's easy for you to refer back if you need a reminder. You might even want to cut these pages out and tape them to your wall.

Basics

CHAPTER 1

Simple statements are commands.

CHAPTER 1

Block statements are surrounded by { and }.

CHAPTER 1

if statements run code if something is true.

CHAPTER 1

switch statements efficiently check for multiple values of a variable.

CHAPTER 1

You can combine conditions together with && and ||.

CHAPTER 1

Every program needs a main function.

CHAPTER 1

#include includes external code for things like input and output.

CHAPTER 1

Your source files should have a name ending in .c.

CHAPTER 1

You need to compile your C program before you run it.

CHAPTER 1

gcc is the most popular C compiler.

CHAPTER 1

You can use the && operator on the command line to only run your program if it compiles.

CHAPTER 1

-o specifies the output file.

CHAPTER 1

count++ means add 1 to count.

CHAPTER 1

count-- means subtract 1 from count.

CHAPTER 1

while repeats code as long as a condition is true.

CHAPTER 1

do-while loops run code at least once.

CHAPTER 1

for loops are a more compact way of writing loops.

Pointers and memory

CHAPTER 2

scanf("%i", &x) will allow a user to enter a number x directly.

CHAPTER 2

Initialize a new array with a string, and it will copy it.

CHAPTER 2

&x returns the address of x.

CHAPTER 2

Read the contents of an address a with *a.

CHAPTER 2

Local variables are stored on the stack.

CHAPTER 2

A char pointer variable x is declared as char *x.

CHAPTER 2

&x is called a pointer to x.

CHAPTER 2

Array variables can be used as pointers.

CHAPTER 2

fgets(buf, size, stdin) is a simpler way to enter text.

Strings

CHAPTER 2

Literal strings are stored in read-only memory.

CHAPTER 2.5

The string.h header contains useful string functions.

CHAPTER 2.5

An array of strings is an array of arrays.

CHAPTER 2.5

You create an array of arrays using char strings [...][...].

CHAPTER 2.5

strstr(a, b) will return the address of string b in string a.

CHAPTER 2.5

strcmp() compares two strings.

CHAPTER 2.5

strcat() concatenates two strings together.

CHAPTER 2.5

strchr() finds the location of a character inside a string.

CHAPTER 2.5

strcpy() copies one string to another.

CHAPTER 2.5

strlen() finds the length of a string.

Data streams

CHAPTER 3

C functions like printf() and scanf() use the Standard Output and Standard Input to communicate.

CHAPTER 3

The Standard Output goes to the display by default.

CHAPTER 3

The Standard Input reads from the keyboard by default.

CHAPTER 3

You can change where the Standard Input, Output, and Error are connected to using redirection.

CHAPTER 3

The Standard Error is a separate output intended for error messages.

CHAPTER 3

You can print to the Standard Error using fprintf(stderr,...).

CHAPTER 3

You can create custom data streams with fopen("filename", mode).

CHAPTER 3

The mode can be "w" to write, "r" to read, or "a" to append.

CHAPTER 3

Command-line arguments are passed to main() as an array of string pointers.

CHAPTER 3

The getopt() function makes it easier to read command-line options.

Data types

CHAPTER 4

chars are numbers.

CHAPTER 4

Use longs for really big whole numbers.

CHAPTER 4

Use shorts for small whole numbers.

CHAPTER 4

Use ints for most whole numbers.

CHAPTER 2

ints are different sizes on different machines.

CHAPTER 4

Use floats for most floating points.

CHAPTER 4

Use doubles for really precise floating points.

Multiple files

CHAPTER 4

Split function declarations from definitions.

CHAPTER 4

Put declarations in a header file.

CHAPTER 4

#include <> for library headers.

CHAPTER 4

#include " " for local headers.

CHAPTER 4

Save object code into files to speed up your builds.

CHAPTER 4

Use make to manage your builds.

Structs

CHAPTER 5

A struct combines data types together.

CHAPTER 5

You can read struct fields with dot notation.

CHAPTER 5

You can intialize structs with {array, like, notation}.

CHAPTER 5

-> notation lets you easily update fields using a struct pointer.

CHAPTER 5

typedef lets you create an alias for a data type.

CHAPTER 5

Designated initializers let you set struct and union fields by name.

Unions and bitfields

CHAPTER 5

unions can hold different data types in one location.

CHAPTER 5

enums let you create a set of symbols.

CHAPTER 5

Bitfields give you control over the exact bits stored in a struct.

Data structures

CHAPTER 6

Dynamic data structures use recursive structs.

CHAPTER 6

Recursive structs contain one or more links to similar data.

CHAPTER 6

A linked list is a dynamic data structure.

CHAPTER 6

Data can be inserted easily into a linked list.

CHAPTER 6

A linked list is more extensible than an array.

Dynamic memory

CHAPTER 6

The stack is used for local variables.

CHAPTER 6

Unlike the stack, heap memory is not automatically released.

CHAPTER 6

malloc() allocates memory on the heap.

CHAPTER 6

free() releases memory on the heap.

CHAPTER 6

strdup() will create a copy of a string on the heap.

CHAPTER 6

A memory leak is allocated memory you can no longer access.

CHAPTER 6

valgrind can help you track down memory leaks.

Advanced functions

CHAPTER 7

Function pointers let you pass functions around as if they were data.

CHAPTER 7

Function pointers are the only pointers that don't need the * and & operators, but you can use them if you want to.

CHAPTER 7

The name of every function is a pointer to the function.

CHAPTER 7

qsort() will sort an array.

CHAPTER 7

Each sort function needs a pointer to a comparator function.

CHAPTER 7

Comparator functions decide how to order two pieces of data.

CHAPTER 7

Arrays of function pointers can help run different functions for different types of data.

CHAPTER 7

Functions with a variable number of arguments are called "variadic."

CHAPTER 7

stdarg.h lets you create variadic functions.

Static and dynamic libraries

CHAPTER 8

#include <> looks in standard directories such as /usr/include.

CHAPTER 8

-L<name> adds a directory to the list of standard library directories.

CHAPTER 8

-l<name> links to a file in standard directories such as /usr/lib.

CHAPTER 8

-I<name> adds a directory to the list of standard include directories.

CHAPTER 8

The ar command creates a library archive of object files.

CHAPTER 8

Library archives have names like libsomething.a.

CHAPTER 8

Library archives are statically linked.

CHAPTER 8

"gcc -shared" converts object files into dynamic libraries.

CHAPTER 8

Dynamic libraries are linked at runtime.

CHAPTER 8

Dynamic libraries have different names on different operating systems.

CHAPTER 8

Dynamic libraries have .so, .dylib, .dll, or .dll.a extensions.

Processes and communication

CHAPTER 9

system() will run a string like a console command.

CHAPTER 9

fork() duplicates the current process.

CHAPTER 9

fork() + exec() creates a child process.

CHAPTER 9

execl() = list of args.

execle() = list of args + environment.

execlp() = list of args + search on path.

execv() = array of args.

execve() = array of args + environment.

execvp() = array of args + search on path.

CHAPTER 10

Processes can communicate using pipes.

CHAPTER 10

pipe() creates a communication pipe.

CHAPTER 10

exit() stops the program immediately.

CHAPTER 10

waitpid() waits for a process to finish.

CHAPTER 10

fileno() finds the descriptor.

CHAPTER 10

dup2() duplicates a data stream.

CHAPTER 10

Signals are messages from the O/S.

CHAPTER 10

sigaction() lets you handle signals.

CHAPTER 10

A program can send signals to itself with raise().

CHAPTER 10

alarm() sends a SIGALRM after a few seconds.

CHAPTER 10

The kill command sends a signal.

CHAPTER 12

Simple processes do one thing at a time.

Sockets and networking

CHAPTER 11

telnet is a simple network client.

CHAPTER 11

Create sockets with the socket() function.

CHAPTER 11

Servers BLAB:

B = bind()

L = listen()

A = accept()

B = Begin talking.

CHAPTER 11

Use fork() to cope with several clients at once.

CHAPTER 11

DNS = Domain name system.

CHAPTER 11

getaddrinfo() finds addresses by domain.

Threads

CHAPTER 12

Threads allow a process to do more than one thing at the same time.

CHAPTER 12

Threads are "lightweight processes."

CHAPTER 12

POSIX threads (pthread) is a threading library.

CHAPTER 12

pthread_create() creates a thread to run a function.

CHAPTER 12

pthread_join() will wait for a thread to finish.

CHAPTER 12

Threads share the same global variables.

CHAPTER 12

If two threads read and update the same variable, your code will be unpredictable.

CHAPTER 12

Mutexes are locks that protect shared data.

CHAPTER 12

pthread_mutex_lock() creates a mutex on code.

CHAPTER 12

pthread_mutex_unlock() releases the mutex.

Index

Symbols & Numbers

$ (dollar sign), $%, $^, and $@ compiler commands for makefiles 548

\0 sentinel character 12

& (ampersand)

  bitwise AND operator 20, 541

  && (logical AND) operator 18, 20

  reference operator 43, 48

< > (angle brackets)

  >> (bitwise shift left) operator 541

  in header files 180, 354

  redirecting Standard Input with < 111

  redirecting Standard Output with > 112, 430

  redirection using > and 2> operators 432

* (asterisk)

  accessing array elements 61

  indirection operator 48

  in variable declarations 74

^ (caret), bitwise XOR operator 541

, (comma)

  separating expressions 541

  separating values in enums 255

{ } (curly braces)

  enclosing function body 6

  enclosing statements 14

. dot notation, setting value of unions 248

. (dot) operator, reading struct fields 222

... (ellipsis) 345

= (equals sign)

  assignment operator 13

  == (equality) operator 13

! (exclamation mark), not operator 18

(hash mark), beginning preprocessor directives 542

- (minus sign)

  -- (decrement) operator 13, 540

  negative numbers and command-line arguments 155

  prefacing command-line options 155

  -= (subtraction and assignment) operator 13

( ) (parentheses), caution with, when using structs 240

% (percent sign)

  %li format string 52

  %p format string 48, 52

| (pipe symbol)

  bitwise OR operator 20, 541

  connecting input and output with a pipe 131

  | | (logical OR) operator 18, 20

+ (plus sign)

  += (addition and assignment) operators 13

  ++ (increment) operator 13, 540

-> pointer notation 241, 245

? (question mark) 540

  ?: (ternary) operator 540

“” (quotation marks, double)

  enclosing strings 13

  in header files 180, 354

‘’ (quotation marks, single) in strings 13

; (semicolon), separating values in structs and unions 255
/ (slash)
  /* and */ surrounding comments 8
  // beginning comments 8
[ ] (square brackets)
  array subindex operator 61
  creating arrays and accessing elements 96
  in variable declarations 74
~ (tilde), bitwise complement operator 541
_ (underscore), replacing spaces in web page name 498
8-bit operating systems 168
32-bit operating systems 168
  size of pointers 54
64-bit operating systems 168
  size of pointers 54

A

accept( ) function 471
AceUnit framework 545
alarm( ) function 458
  calls to, resetting the timer 459
  sleep( ) function and 458
alarm signal, SIGALRM 458
Allegro library 526
  creation of game elements 527
AND operator (&) 20, 541
AND operator (&&) 18, 20
animation, using transformations 535
ANSI C 2
Arduino 207–216
  Arduino board 209
  building the physical device 210
  C code for, what it does 212
  finished product 215
  plant monitor and moisture sensor 208
  useful functions 214
  writing C code in Arduino IDE 209
args parameter 345
arguments, function 32
  fixed argument in variadic functions 345, 346
array functions, execv( ), execvp( ), and execve( ) 406
arrays 11
  array of arrays versus array of pointers 98
  assigned to pointers, pointer decay and 59
  char pointers versus char arrays in data structure 286
  creating array of arrays 85, 96
  fixed length of 268
  of function pointers 338–342
  indexes 13, 61
  length of 13
  linked lists versus 274
  strings as character arrays 12
  structs versus 220, 225
  using to copy string literals 74
  variables declared as 74
array variables
  differences from pointers 59
  use as pointers 54
Assembly language, translation of C code into 184
assignments
  = (assignment) operator 13
  chaining 33
  compound assignment operators 13
  struct assigned to another variable 226
  struct to another struct 238
associated arrays or maps 296
asteroids (Blasteroids game) 533
autoconf tool 202

automated testing 545
automating builds with make tool 198

B

binary literals, not supported in C 261, 265
binary numbers 163
binary trees 296
binary values, converting between hexadecimal and 261
binding to a port 470
bitfields 262, 265, 563
  using to construct customer satisfaction survey (example) 263
bit size of computers 168
bits, operators for manipulation of 541
bitwise AND operator (&) 20, 541
bitwise complement operator (~) 541
bitwise OR operator (|) 20, 541
bitwise shift left operator (<<) 541
bitwise XOR operator (^) 541
BLAB: Bind, Listen, Accept, Begin 470
Blasteroids game. *See* game, Blasteroids project
blasts fired by spaceship (Blasteroids game) 532
block statements 14
body of a function 6
boolean operators 18
boolean values, representation in C 18
bound port, reuse by socket 477
break statements 26, 28, 39
  exiting loops 31
  not breaking out of if statements 31
buffer overflows caused by scanf() function 66
build tools 202
  CMake 526
bus errors 13

C

C
  basics of 554
  how it works 2
  reference materials for programming 552
  similarities to and influence on other languages 39
C++ 39
C11 standard 2
c89 notation for first field of a union 248
C99 standard 2
cameras
  grabbing image from webcam 392
  showing current webcam output 393
  taking input from computer camera 392
Carbon libraries 551
card counting 16
  program for, writing in C 17, 19–21
  modifying program to keep running count of card game 35
  testing program 38
case statements 26, 28
casting floats to whole numbers 164
chaining assignments 33
char** pointer 320, 333
char type 159, 161
  arithmetic with 182
  char pointers versus char arrays in data structure 286
  defined 162
checksum() function 352
child process 420, 450
  clients talking to server 486
  listening to directly 442
  piped commands on command line 443
  redirecting Standard Output to file 435–440
  running with fork() and exec() 421–425

classes, structs versus 225
CMake 526
Cocoa libraries 551
collisions 529
command-line arguments
  avoiding ambiguity by splitting main arguments from options using -- 155
  execl( ), execlp( ), and execle( ) functions 405
  main( ) function with 141
command-line options 148
  questions and answers on 155
  using getopt( ) function for 149
command line, piping commands together on 443
command path 409
commands, types of 14
comma-separated data, reading and displaying in JSON format 105
comma (,), separating expressions 541
comments 5
  formatting 8
comparator functions 327–333
  writing for different sort descriptions 328–333
compilation 2
  automating builds with make tool 198–205
  behind-the-scenes look at 184
  compiling a program using gcc 9
  partial compiles 191–196
  precompilation and 180
  reason for compiling C 39
  speeding up for programs in multiple source files 189
compiled code, saving copies of 190
compilers 9. *See also* gcc
  BE the Compiler exercise 23
  C standard supported by 8
  debug information from 308
  finding standard header file directories 355
  interview with gcc 22
conditional compilation 542
connection, accepting from client 471
constants
  defined 80
  string literals as 73
const char 218, 220
const keyword 76, 79
continue statements 31, 39
control statements 14
convert command 449
count variable 543
create( ) function, using dynamic allocation 282, 284
  fixing with strdup( ) function 286
CreateProcess( ) function (Windows systems) 426
C Standard Library 127
Ctrl-C, stopping programs 451
curl/wget programs 449
cvCalcOpticalFlowFarneback( ) function 393
cvCreateCameraCapture( ) function 392
cvNamedWindow( ) function 393
cvQueryFrame( ) function 392
cvShowImage( ) function 393
Cygwin 449
  fork( ) function and 426
  including PATH variable when passing environment variables on 407
  installing before calling fork( ) on Windows 420
  telnet program 468

D

data entry
  capabilities of scanf( ) versus fgets( ) 68
  fgets( ) as alternative to scanf( ) 67
  using pointers for 65
data streams
  creating your own 138
  duplication with dup2( ) function 433

handling in a typical process 431
opening, checking for problems with 147
printing to 122
replacement by redirection 432
sockets 470
summary of important points 558
typical data streams versus sockets 472

data structures
questions and answers about 274
summary of important points 564
types other than linked lists 295

data types 158
bytes in memory occupied by, getting with sizeof 280
casting floats to whole numbers 164
data not having single type 246
errors caused by conflicting types in example program 170
macros determining size of 544
matching type of value to type of variable it's stored in 163
no function data type in C 319
parameters in variadic functions 349
pointer variables 62
prefixing with unsigned or long keywords 164
process ID 423
quick guide to 162
size of 167
sizes on different operating systems 168
structs 220
summary of 560
unions 249
values stored in unions 254

deadlocks 520
debugger, gdb 550
decay 59
decimal point numbers. *See also* floating-point numbers; float type
computers' representation of 168

declarations
defined 79
function, splitting from definition 173, 561

decrement operator (--) 13, 540
#define directive 542
definitions, function, splitting from declaration 173, 561
dependencies 198
identifying for make tool 199

dereferencing 48, 52
descriptor table
important points about 440
Standard Input, Output, and Error in 432

designated initializers 248, 265
setting initial values of struct fields 249

design tips for small tools 129
/dev/tty program 441
development tools 550
device drivers 403
DNS (domain name system) 493
domain names 491
connecting client socket to remote domain name 492
creation of sockets with IP addresses or domain names 499

double type 159, 161
defined 162

doubly linked lists 296
do-while loops 29, 39
dup2( ) function 433
dynamic libraries 351, 568
dynamic memory 565
dynamic storage 276–280, 294
using the heap 278

E

echo command 401
ellipsis (...) 345
email, sending from command line 449
encrypt( ) function 352
encryption, XOR 182
enums 255, 260
  responses in mail merge program (example) 334
  tracking values stored in structs and unions 256–259
environment variables
  parameters for execv( ), execvp( ), and execve( ) functions 406
  parameters for exel( ), execlp( ), and execle( ) functions 405
  reading and passing to functions 407
equality operator (==) 13
errno variable 408
error handling, avoiding writing duplicate code for system calls 434
error messages
  converting errno into 408
  displaying when Standard Output is redirected 118
  Standard Error 120
/etc/services file 472
.exe files (Windows) 10
exec( ) functions 404, 427
  array functions, execv( ), execvp( ), and execve( ) 406
  failures of calls to 408
  important points about 411
  list functions, execl( ), execlp( ), and execle( ) 405
  many versions of 405
  order-generation program, Starbuzz coffee (example) 412–415
  program searching many RSS feeds at once (example) 418
  program termination after call to 420
  running child process with fork( ) and exec( ) 421–425
  running /sbin/ifconfig or ipconfig (example) 409
execle( ) function 407
  failures of 408
  program searching many RSS feeds at once (example) 418
executables 2, 185
exit( ) function 434
  called by default signal handler for interrupt signal 451
  important points about 441
exit status of child process 439
extern keyword 186

F

Feldman, Stuart 202
fgets( ) function 450, 451
  as alternative to scanf( ) 67
  using for data input, scanf( ) versus 68
file descriptors 431
  descriptor tables 441
fileno( ) function 433
files, making program work with 109
filters 109
find( ) function 313–315
  other types of searches 321
floating-point numbers 159
  handling with floats and doubles 168
float type 159
  casting to whole numbers 164
  defined 162
  finding size of 167
fopen( ) function 138
  problem opening data stream 147
fork( ) function 420, 427
  creating a process for each client 486
  important points about 426
  running child process with fork( ) + exec( ) 421–425
    calling fork( ) 423

for loops 30, 39
format strings, passing to scanf( ) function 65
formatted output, display by printf( ) function 6
fprintf( ) function 122
  updating example mapping program to use 123
freeaddrinfo( ) function 493
free( ) function 279
  call interception by valgrind 308
  releasing memory with 280
  tracking calls to with valgrind 302
fscanf( ) function 122
functions 5, 311–350
  advanced, summary of important points 566
  Arduino 214
  find( ) function 313–315
  macros versus 346
  main( ) function 6
  no function data type in C 319
  operators versus 56
  order in a program 171
  order of running in a program 96
  passing as parameter to another function 317–324
    creating function pointers 320
    identifying function pointers 324
  passing code to 316
  passing pointer to variable as function parameter 47
  passing strings to 53
  passing struct to function that updates struct 238
  sorting data 325–342
    using function pointers to set sort order 326
  splitting declaration from definition 173, 561
  variables declared inside 43
  variadic 343–349
    writing example function 347–349
  void return type 33
  writing 32

G

game, Blasteroids project 523–538
  Allegro library 526
  asteroids 533
  blasting asteroids without being hit 525
  blasts fired by spaceship 532
  building the game 528
  finished product 536
  game status 534
  reading key presses 531
  spaceship 529
  spaceship behavior 530
  using transformations 535
  writing arcade game 524
garbage collection, C and 294
gcc 9
  finding standard header file directories 355
  GNU Compiler Collection 39
  interview with 22
  -I option 356
  optimizations 546
  standards supported 8
  warnings 547
gcov (GNU Coverage) 550
gdb (GNU Project Debugger) 550
getaddrinfo( ) function 493
GET command 490
getenv( ) function 407
getopt( ) function 149, 155
gets( ) function, reasons not to use 67
globals
  defined 80
  variables declared outside of functions 43
global variables 96
  count 543
  errno 408
  storage in memory 47

GNU Compiler Collection. *See* gcc
GNU Coverage (gcov) 550
GNU Profiler (gprof) 550
GNU Project Debugger (gdb) 550
golden rules of failure 408
gprof (GNU Profiler) 550
grep command 443
GTK library 551
GUIs (graphical user interfaces), creating 551

H

hardware, kernel and 403
header files
  angle brackets in 354
  creating 174
  forgetting to include 96
  function declarations in 173
  quotes and angle brackets in 180
  for shared code 186
  sharing between programs 355
heap
  allocating and releasing memory 289
  allocating storage for string copy 285
  defined 80
  differences from the stack 292
  important points about 294
  releasing memory when you're done 279
  using for dynamic storage 278
hexadecimal literals 261
hexadecimals, converting between binary and 261
hex format, memory addresses 48, 52
.h files. *See* header files
hostname 490
HTTP (Hypertext Transfer Protocol) 469, 490

I

IDE, Arduino 209
if statements 14
  break statements and 31
  checking same value repeatedly 25
  replacing sequence of switch statement 27
ignoring signals 459
  interrupt signal 456
images
  converting image formats 449
  grabbing image from webcam 392
#include directive 184, 542
  angle brackets in 354
  header files at different locations 356
  including header file in main program 174
includes section, C programs 5
increment operator (++) 13, 540
indexes, array 13
  starting at 0 61
indirection operator (*) 48
infinite loops 39
integers 159
interprocess communication 429–466
  avoiding duplicate error-handling code for each system call 434
  catching signals and running your own code 452–456
  connecting processes with pipes 443
  death of a process 451
  duplicating data streams with dup2( ) 433
  examining a typical process 431
  finding RSS news stories and opening them in a browser 444–449
  getting descriptor with fileno( ) 433
  listening to child process directly 442
  processes redirecting themselves 432

program saving output of rssgossip.py script to file 435
program testing math skills (example) 460–464
questions and answers about 441
redirecting input and output 430
redirection replacing data streams 432
resetting and ignoring signals 459
sending alarm signal to processes 458
summary of important points 570
using kill command to send signals 457
using raise( ) to send signals 457
waitpid( ) function 438–440
interrupt signal 451
ignoring 456
intruder detector 390
finished product 394
int type 159
compiler assumption as return type for unknown functions 171, 181
defined 162
finding size of 167
I/O (input/output)
connecting input and output with a pipe 131–136
displaying error messages when output is redirected 118
output to more than one file 137
redirecting 430
redirecting output from display to files 109
redirecting Standard Input with < operator 111
redirecting Standard Output with > operator 112
redirection 110
ipconfig 409
IP (Internet Protocol) 469
IP (Internet Protocol) addresses 491
converting domain names to 493
creating socket for an IP address 492
creation of sockets with IP addresses or domain names 499

J

JSON, displaying comma-separated data as 105

K

kernel 403
keypresses, reading 531
kill command, using to send signals 457

L

LED
C code writing to 212
connecting to Arduino board 210
libraries
Allegro game development library 526
GUI (graphical user interface) 551
static and dynamic 568
limits.h header, macros defined in 544
linked lists 269
creating 271
creating and releasing heap memory 287–291
inserting values into 273
linking object code files 185, 191
Linux. *See also* operating systems
GTK GUI library 551
listen( ) function 471
listen queue for clients 471
list functions, execl( ), execlp( ), and execle( ) 405
local variables, storage in stack 47, 278
locks 513
creating a mutex lock 514
deciding where to put locks in code (example) 516–519
long keyword 164

LONG_MAX macro 544
long type 159, 161
  defined 162
  passing long values to thread functions 515
loops
  breaking out of with break statement 31
  continue statement in 31
  running forever, infinite loops 39
  structure of 30

M

Mac computers. *See also* operating systems
  Carbon library for GUIs 551
  script for talking to plants 215
machine code 2, 185
macros 139
  creating 542
  functions versus 346
mail/mutt programs 449
main( ) function 6
  with command-line arguments 141
  ending program with exit( ) instead of 441
makefiles 200
  on different operating systems 202
  generation with autoconf tool 202
make tool 198–205, 225
  additional features 548
  automating builds with 198
  converting Ogg Vorbis music file to Swing version 203
  different name on Windows 199
  how it works 199
  implicit rules to build files 549
  uses other than compiling code 202
malloc( ) function 278
  asking for memory with 280
  call by strdup( ) function 294
  call interception by valgrind 308
  tracking calls to with valgrind 302
memory 41, 565
  addresses 47
  allocating heap memory and releasing it 289
  C toolbox 81
  differences between the stack and the heap 292
  freeing by calling free( ) function 279, 280
  getting with malloc( ) function 278
  kernel control over 403
  order of segments in 79
  overview of computer memory 43
  and pointers 556
  questions and answers about 52
  requesting with malloc( ) function 280
  reuse of space with unions 247
  string literals stored in read-only memory 73
  structs stored in 226
  summary of segments 80
memory leaks 279
  avoding when using data structures 296
  tracking and fixing using valgrind tool 302–308
mingw32-make 199
MinGW, spaces in command-line arguments 405
mkfifo( ) function 450
moisture sensor
  building 210
  C code reading from 212
  connecting to Arduino 211
movement, detecting 393
mutexes 513
  causing deadlocks 520
  creating a mutex lock 514

N

named pipes 450
nested structs 227
network configuration, commands for 409
networking. *See* sockets and networking
NMAKE tool 199
not operator (!) 18
NULL value, following last command-line argument in exec( ) function parameters 405

O

object code 185
  saving copies into files 190
object files, sharing between programs 355
Objective-C 39, 551
object orientation 39
.o files 355. *See also* object code
Ogg Vorbis music file, converting to Swing version 203
OpenCV 389–394
  C code, what it should do 392
  defined 391
  finished product 394
  installing 391
  intruder detector 390
operating systems
  commands to open a URL 446
  controlling programs with signals 451
  different sizes of data types on 167, 168
  GUI libraries for 551
  interview with 127
  kernel 403
  listing processes running on system 404
  makefiles and 202
  network configuration commands 409
  OpenCV 391
  registering new item in file descriptor table 433
  Standard Input and Standard Output 110
  system calls 398
  telnet program 468
operators 540
  functions versus 56
  precedence of 240, 243
optarg variable 149, 155
optimization 546
optind variable 149
OR operator (|) 20, 541
OR operator (||) 18, 20

P

parameters, function 6, 32
  passing by value 238
parent process 420, 450
  piped command on command line 443
  server 486
partial compiles 191–196
PATH variable 406
  including when passing environment variables on Cygwin 407
performance, analyzing with gprof 550
PIDs (Process Identifiers) 404
  pid_status parameter of waitpid( ) function 441
  pid_t in call to fork( ) 423
  waitpid( ) function parameters 439
pipe( ) function 450
  connecting Standard Output of child and Standard Input of parent processes 444

pipes
  connecting input and output 131–136
  connecting output of rssgossip.py to input of program 444–449
  connecting processes with 443
  important points about 450
pointer arithmetic
  and array index starting at 0 61
  and data types of pointer variables 62
  important points about 64
pointer notation with structs 241
pointers 42
  address of variable in memory 43
  array of arrays versus array of pointers 98
  array variables as 54
  char pointers versus char arrays in data structure 286
  conversion to ordinary number 56
  C toolbox 81
  differences of array variables from 59
  file 433
  function 318–324, 324, 566
    arrays of 338–342
    creating 319
    summary of important points 342
    using to set sort order 326
  making it easier for functions to share memory 47
  passing pointer to variable as function parameter 47
  questions and answers about 52
  in recursive structures 271
  set to string literals, avoiding 76
  sizes on different computers 56
  and structs assigned to another variable 226
  to structs 239
  summary of important points 556
  types assigned to pointer variables 62
  using for data entry 65
  using to read and write data 48
  variables declared as function arguments 74
  void 506
port, binding to 470
port number for server application, caution in choosing 472
POSIX libraries 149
POSIX thread library (pthread) 506
  linking 508
precompilation 180
preprocessing 180
  fixing the source 184
preprocessor directives 542
printf( ) function 6
  reading from keyboard and writing to display 110
  variable number of arguments 343
printing to data stream with fprintf( ) function 122
private scope 543
processes. *See also* interprocess communication
  cloning with fork( ) function 420
  communication, summary of important points 570
  control by kernel 403
  examining a typical process 431
  redirecting themselves 432
  replacement of current process using exec( ) functions 404
  running child process with fork( ) + exec( ) 421–425
  server and client, creating processes for clients with fork( ) 486
  simple, doing one thing at a time 504
  speed of, threads versus 520
  using for simultaneous tasks, limitations of 503
Process Identifiers. *See* PIDs
profiling tools 550
programs
  compiling and running 9
  complete C program 5
  exercise, matching candidate block of code with possible output 34, 36

protocols 469, 490
ps -ef command 404
pthread_create( ) function 507
pthread_join( ) function 507
PTHREAD_MUTEX_INITIALIZER macro 514
pthread_mutex_lock( ) function 514
pthread_mutex_unlock( ) function 514
pthread (POSIX thread) library 506
  linking 508
Python
  installing 416
  RSS Gossip script 416

Q

qsort( ) function 326

R

raise( ) command, sending signals with 457
recursive structures 294, 564
  creating 271
recv( ) function 478, 493
redirection 110
  child process output to file 435–440
  descriptor table and 441
  displaying error messages when output is redirected 118
  output from display to files 109
  processes redirecting themselves 432
  programs run from command line 430
  replacement of data streams 432
  several processes connected with pipes 136
  Standard Input, using < operator 111
  Standard Output, using > operator 112
reference operator (&) 43, 48
references, pointers versus 52
reserved words in C 181
return statements in functions 32, 39
return type 6
  compiler assumptions for unknown functions 171
  void return type for thread functions 506
return values, assignments 33
reusing code 182
RSS feeds
  program saving output of rssgossip.py script to file 435
  program searching many feeds at once (example) 417–425
    running rssgossip.py in separate process for each feed 422
  reading news with 416
  reading story links from rssgossip.py script 442
  running rsscossip.py script and opening stories in browser 444
RSS Gossip (Python script) 416
running programs 9

S

ifconfig program 409
/sbin/ifconfig program 409
scanf( ) function 65, 79
  causing buffer overflows 66
  fgets( ) function as alternative to 67
  passing pointer to variable to scanf( ) 239
  using for data input, fgets( ) versus 68
screen, redirecting data to, without using Standard Output 441
security, system calls and 402
send( ) function 472, 493
sentinel character \0 12
serial port, writing to (C code in Arduino) 212
setitimer( ) function 459
sharing code 182–187, 355
  .h header files 356

short type 159, 161
  defined 162
SHRT_MIN macro 544
shunit2 tool, testing scripts and commands 545
sigaction( ) function 453
sigaction structs 452
SIGALRM signal 458
SIGKILL signal 457
signals 451
  catching and running your own code 452–456
  ignoring 459
  matching to cause (example) 455
  order of sending and receiving 465
  program testing math skills (example) 460–464
  resetting to default handler 459
  sending using kill command 457
  sending using raise( ) 457
signed values in binary 163
SIGTERM signal 457
single statement 14
size limits for data types, macros determining 544
sizeof operator 53, 56
  getting bytes in memory occupied by particular data type 280
  use on pointers and array variables 59
  using with fgets( ) function 67
sleep( ) function 508
  alarm( ) function and 458
small tools
  connecting input and output with a pipe 131–136
  converting data from one format to another 104–107
  designing, tips for 129
  different tasks need different tools 130
  flexibility of 128
  output to multiple files 137
sockets and networking 467–500
  clients obtaining a socket and communicating 491
  client sockets, creating socket for a domain name 493
  client sockets, creation and connection to remote port 492
  creation of sockets with IP addresses or domain names 499
  C toolbox 500
  fork( ) a process for each client 486
  how servers talk to the Internet 470
  Internet knock-knock server (example) 468
  other useful server functions 479
  reading from the client 478
  server can only talk to one client at a time 485
  server code changed to fork child process for each client 487–489
  server generating random advice for clients (example) 473
  sockets not your typical data streams 472
  summary of important points 572
  writing a web client 490, 494–498
  writing code for Internet knock-knock server (example) 480–484
sorting 325–342
  using function pointers to set sort order 326
  writing comparator functions for different sorts 328–333
source files 2
  compiling and running 9
  multiple files for code 561
spaceship (Blasteroids game) 529
  behavior of 530
stack 43
  defined 80
  differences from the heap 292
  storage in 278
Standard Error 120, 558
  default output to display 121
  in descriptor table 432
  redirecting with 2> 122, 432
standard header directories 355
standard header files 180

Standard Input 122, 558
- connecting to Standard Output of another process 131
- in descriptor table 432
- redirecting 110
- redirecting with < operator 111

Standard Output 558
- connecting to Standard Input of another process 131
- in descriptor table 432
- redirecting child process output to file 435
- redirecting to file 112, 430

standards 2
- compiler support of 8
- designated initializers 248
- POSIX libraries 149
- return statements in functions 32

statements 14

static keyword 543

static libraries 351, 568

stdarg.h header 345

storage, flexible 268

strcmp( ) function 331, 333

strdup( ) function 285
- calling malloc( ) function 294
- fixing create( ) function that uses dynamic allocation 286

strerror( ) function 408

string.h header file 86
- more information about functions in 95

string literals 13
- char pointer set to, avoiding 76
- important points about 79
- inability to update 72

strings 11, 83–102
- array of arrays versus array of pointers 98
- BE the Compiler exercise, jukebox program (example) 91
- changing, using copy for 74
- as character arrays 12
- code shuffling letters in 69–72
- copying 285
- creating array of arrays 85
- crossword puzzle (example) 99
- C toolbox 101
- displaying string backward on screen 97
- ending with sentinel character \0 12
- passing to functions 53
- searching 84, 86
  - Pool Puzzle example 90
  - review of jukebox program (example) 94
  - testing jukebox program (example) 95
- Standard Library, string.h 86–88
- arrays of, char** pointer to 320
- summary of important points 557
- using strstr( ) function 89

strstr( ) function 89

structs 217–246, 260, 274
- arrays versus 220, 225
- assignment 238
- benefits of using 221
- bitfields collected in 262
- creating aliases for with typedef 232
- designated initializers setting initial value of fields 249
- enums tracking values stored in 256–259
- holding sequence of single bits for yes/no values 261
- in memory 226
- nesting 227
- pointer notation 241
- pointers to 239
- reading fields with . (dot) operator 222
- recursive structures 271, 294
- summary of important points 562
- updating 236
- using bitfields in customer satisfaction survey (example) 264
- using with unions 249
- values separated with semicolon (;) 255
- wrapping parameters in 221

structured data types. *See* structs

switch statements 26

 rewriting code to replace sequence of if statements 27

 summary of important points about 28

symbols, storing in enums 255

system calls 398, 427

 accept( ) function 471

 avoiding writing duplicate code for error handling 434

 checking for errors on 474–477

 exec( ) functions 404–410

  failures of 408

  order-generation program, Starbuzz coffee (example) 412–415

  program searching many RSS feeds at once (example) 418

 fork( ) function, cloning processes with 420

 getenv( ) function, reading environment variables 407

 important points about 411

 listen( ) function 471

 mkfifo( ) function 450

 running child process with fork( ) and exec( ) 421–426

 security breaches 402

system( ) function 398, 426, 427

 exec( ) function versus 411

 opening a web page in a browser 446

T

tab character, beginning recipe lines for makefiles 200, 202

target files 198

 describing in makefiles 200

taskmgr command (Windows) 404

tasks, sequential or parallel 502

telnet program 468

ternary operator (?:) 540

testing, automated 545

threads 501–522

 creating 506

  using pthread_create( ) 507

 C toolbox 521

 deciding where to put locks in code (example) 516–519

 important points about 520

 multithreaded programs 505

 mutexes 513

 passing long values to thread functions 515

 program counting down beers (example) 509–511

 single threads of execution 504

 summary of important points 573

 thread safety in code 512

 using mutex to control execution 514

timers for processes 459

transformations 535

true and false values 19

typedef command

 creasting aliases for structs 232

 recursive structures and 271

U

unions 246, 260, 563

 enums tracking values stored in 256–259

 important points about 265

 reuse of memory space 247

 setting value of 248

 using with structs 249

 values separated with semicolon (;) 255

 values stored in, data types of 254

unistd.h header 149

unsigned keyword, prefixing data types with 164

URLs, opening on various operating systems in web browser 446

Standard Input 122, 558
- connecting to Standard Output of another process 131
- in descriptor table 432
- redirecting 110
- redirecting with < operator 111

Standard Output 558
- connecting to Standard Input of another process 131
- in descriptor table 432
- redirecting child process output to file 435
- redirecting to file 112, 430

standards 2
- compiler support of 8
- designated initializers 248
- POSIX libraries 149
- return statements in functions 32

statements 14

static keyword 543

static libraries 351, 568

stdarg.h header 345

storage, flexible 268

strcmp( ) function 331, 333

strdup( ) function 285
- calling malloc( ) function 294
- fixing create( ) function that uses dynamic allocation 286

strerror( ) function 408

string.h header file 86
- more information about functions in 95

string literals 13
- char pointer set to, avoiding 76
- important points about 79
- inability to update 72

strings 11, 83–102
- array of arrays versus array of pointers 98
- BE the Compiler exercise, jukebox program (example) 91
- changing, using copy for 74
- as character arrays 12
- code shuffling letters in 69–72
- copying 285
- creating array of arrays 85
- crossword puzzle (example) 99
- C toolbox 101
- displaying string backward on screen 97
- ending with sentinel character \0 12
- passing to functions 53
- searching 84, 86
  - Pool Puzzle example 90
  - review of jukebox program (example) 94
  - testing jukebox program (example) 95
- Standard Library, string.h 86–88
- arrays of, char** pointer to 320
- summary of important points 557
- using strstr( ) function 89

strstr( ) function 89

structs 217–246, 260, 274
- arrays versus 220, 225
- assignment 238
- benefits of using 221
- bitfields collected in 262
- creating aliases for with typedef 232
- designated initializers setting initial value of fields 249
- enums tracking values stored in 256–259
- holding sequence of single bits for yes/no values 261
- in memory 226
- nesting 227
- pointer notation 241
- pointers to 239
- reading fields with . (dot) operator 222
- recursive structures 271, 294
- summary of important points 562
- updating 236
- using bitfields in customer satisfaction survey (example) 264
- using with unions 249
- values separated with semicolon (;) 255
- wrapping parameters in 221

structured data types. *See* structs
switch statements 26
  rewriting code to replace sequence of if statements 27
  summary of important points about 28
symbols, storing in enums 255
system calls 398, 427
  accept( ) function 471
  avoiding writing duplicate code for error handling 434
  checking for errors on 474–477
  exec( ) functions 404–410
    failures of 408
    order-generation program, Starbuzz coffee (example) 412–415
    program searching many RSS feeds at once (example) 418
  fork( ) function, cloning processes with 420
  getenv( ) function, reading environment variables 407
  important points about 411
  listen( ) function 471
  mkfifo( ) function 450
  running child process with fork( ) and exec( ) 421–426
  security breaches 402
system( ) function 398, 426, 427
  exec( ) function versus 411
  opening a web page in a browser 446

T

tab character, beginning recipe lines for makefiles 200, 202
target files 198
  describing in makefiles 200
taskmgr command (Windows) 404
tasks, sequential or parallel 502
telnet program 468
ternary operator (?:) 540
testing, automated 545
threads 501–522
  creating 506
    using pthread_create( ) 507
  C toolbox 521
  deciding where to put locks in code (example) 516–519
  important points about 520
  multithreaded programs 505
  mutexes 513
  passing long values to thread functions 515
  program counting down beers (example) 509–511
  single threads of execution 504
  summary of important points 573
  thread safety in code 512
  using mutex to control execution 514
timers for processes 459
transformations 535
true and false values 19
typedef command
  creasting aliases for structs 232
  recursive structures and 271

U

unions 246, 260, 563
  enums tracking values stored in 256–259
  important points about 265
  reuse of memory space 247
  setting value of 248
  using with structs 249
  values separated with semicolon (;) 255
  values stored in, data types of 254
unistd.h header 149
unsigned keyword, prefixing data types with 164
URLs, opening on various operating systems in web browser 446

V

valgrind tool, using to find memory leaks 302–308
values
  copied when assigning structs 238
  matching data type to type of variable it's stored in 163
  parameters passed to functions 238
  storing short-range values in bitfields 262
variables
  matching data type for value stored in 163
  sharing among code files 186
  storage in memory 43
  using to shorten makefiles 548
variadic functions 343–349
  writing example function 347–349
virtual memory size 403
void functions 33, 39
void pointers 327, 506

W

waitpid( ) function 438–440
  important points about 441
  parameters 439
warnings, gcc 547
web browsers, opening a web page in 446
websites for C 552
WEXITSTATUS( ) macro 441
while loops 29
  modifying in card counting program to keep running count 35, 37
  structure of 30
  summary of important points 39
window, creating in OpenCV 393
Windows systems. *See also* operating systems
  CreateProcess( ) function instead of fork( ) 426
  .exe files 10
  fork( ) function and 420, 426
  GUI libraries 551
  ipconfig command 409
  listing processes running on system 404
  make tools 199
  telnet program, built-in versus Cygwin versions 468

X

XOR encryption 182
XOR operator, bitwise XOR (^) 541

Milton Keynes UK
Ingram Content Group UK Ltd.
UKHW012149190924
448528UK00005B/10

9 781449 399917